KU-070-354

JOURNEY
THROUGH BRITAIN

Landscape, People and Books

JOURNEY
THROUGH
BRITAIN

Landscape,
People and Books

DAVID ST JOHN THOMAS

FRANCES LINCOLN

To the memory of Mathew, who was proud to see his granddad's books displayed in shop windows

Frances Lincoln Limited
4 Torriano Mews
Torriano Avenue
London NW5 2RZ
www.franceslincoln.com

Journey Through Britain
Copyright © David St John Thomas 2004

All rights reserved.
No part of this publication may be reproduced, stored in a retrieval system or transmitted, in any form, or by any means, electronic, mechanical, photocopying, recording or otherwise, without prior permission from the publisher or a licence permitting restricted copying. In the United Kingdom, such licences are issued by the Copyright Licensing Agency, 90 Tottenham Court Road, London W1T 4LP.

British Library Cataloguing in Publication data
A catalogue record for this book is available from the British Library

ISBN 0 7112 2369 6

Printed and bound in Singapore

CONTENTS

THE DAVID ST JOHN THOMAS CHARITABLE TRUST
25p of the purchase price of this book is donated to the Trust, which
supports a range of small charities with a 'hands-on' approach to making
the best use of funds, sponsors young people to devote their gap year to
useful work in the developing world, and runs the largest programme
of writing competitions in the English language with many winners
kick-starting their writing career.

Please send a postcard for further details to us at PO Box 6055,
Nairn IV12 4HE

PREFACE

'What is your book about?' is a question I have been asked countless times. Explaining that it describes journeys through Britain isn't enough for most people. They repeat: 'But what is it about?' Or ask: 'Is it like Bill Bryson?' A few who see everything in terms of conflict question: 'What is it for or against?' More understandable, and satisfying to answer is: 'Tell me what you describe.'

I describe real journeys through much of Britain, especially those hilly, moorland and coastal areas where there is still great individuality and the unexpected is easily unearthed. Journeys involve more than just enjoying the ever-changing scene. They include the means of travel (railways, canals, roads, even ships), places to rest and refuel (hotels and restaurants), and meeting people, sometimes off the cuff, sometimes by arrangement.

My journeys have provided opportunities to compare many places today with what they used to be like, and to renew acquaintance with many old friends as well as make new ones. I meet hotel-keepers, artists and craftsmen, gardeners and others; some, such as Patrick Moore, household names, others unknown outside their immediate sphere but nonetheless often colourful. In my pages readers are introduced to those who have played a significant role in organisations that affect our lives.

It is a book I have found great pleasure in researching and writing. My publisher reassuringly said: 'Your text is engaging, entertaining and eminently readable. Even if I disagree (and I do) with quite a lot of what you say, I find it endlessly fascinating and resonant in many ways.'

Not everyone will be equally interested in all the subjects, but the journeys move on into fresh pastures and challenges. Though it is not a practical guide, I hope that some readers will wish to visit or renew their own acquaintance with some of my favourite places, and even try a few of the hotels, restaurants, museums, gardens, early Christian sites and other destinations I have found especially rewarding.

That preconceived ideas are dangerous has been shown by how often I have been proved wrong. Would you not be surprised to discover that Llandudno boasts three of the AA's 'Top 200' hotels while neither Torquay nor Bournemouth has any? But please remember that, except where indicated otherwise, things are as I found them. A hotel at which we were distinctly irritated might have improved as easily as a favourite establishment can disappoint under new ownership.

I set out loving Britain. I end the book loving it more deeply, respecting many innovations, such as the new National Cycleway Network and revitalised canal system, to cite just two examples, and discovering great hope in its fascinating population, especially in areas where man is inevitably conscious of and respects the elements around him.

One of the reasons why I came to know Britain (and love it and understand its ways) better than most is that I am the David of David & Charles, the Devon publishers who for decades produced books on every part of the country, its scenery, communications, crafts, and way of life. The joys and perils of writing and publishing, in past ages as well as today, inevitably sprinkle the pages, adding an extra dimension to my travels. I meet many authors – from the Scottish island taxi driver (who sold me a copy of her latest successfully self-published title handily kept in the glove compartment) to a gallery of individualistic authors whose books I published. I also write about regional novelists and others whose work I've read with delight, and hope that at least a few of my quotations from other writers will make readers want to pursue the books concerned.

At least my mixture is unique. I hope it might perhaps revitalise the reader's own love of our very special country, its landscape, people and often offbeat literary traditions.

Except where it is made clear [in square brackets] that there has been subsequent updating, all references apply to things as I found them at the time of writing. Fitted in with other commitments, the writing has been no more continuous than the journeying on which it is based (both took nearly three years). I am anxious to retain the experiences and feelings as they happened. Several more than I have noted of those met on the journeys have subsequently retired or died. In the days of rapid changes of ownership, some attractions and catering establishments will inevitably have changed. Mention of places visited does not necessarily imply there is a public right of way or permission to visit.

We see Britain in different moods over several seasons. Even the planning was challenging, especially when the railway system was disrupted and foot-and-mouth disease closed much of the countryside. If the book has any merit, I hope it might lie in its variety, for sometimes I am on familiar territory coloured by personal experience, while on other journeys I am more the curious visitor. While the strength of the book should lie in its totality, I would be pleased to hear from readers about any specific errors.

Thanks go to the many interesting people who met me (remarkably every appointment was kept punctually), and to those who organised things along the way. Thanks, too, to those who have helped with the manuscript, especially my wife Sheila and Anne and Lorna. All discovered new skills.

I am also grateful to those who gave permission to quote short sections from their own books. A bibliography seems inappropriate but, to spur further reading, I have included a list of books from which quotations have been taken as well as a detailed table of contents and, to encourage browsing, the index includes thematic headings. There seems little point in including maps that would inevitably be less detailed than the ubiquitous road atlas. The appropriate Ordnance Survey Landranger maps often increased our detailed appreciation of the varied Britain through which we travelled.

David St John Thomas

INTRODUCTION

The Father of Geology

I am in the middle of reading Simon Winchester's *The Map That Changed the World*, about the life and times of William Smith, the father of geology. We are staying in Bath, and I've reached the place in the book where there is a description and illustration of the house where Smith used to live when his geological enthusiasm and knowledge were rapidly increasing. As engineer to the Somersetshire Coal Canal, he was carving through a slice of the countryside where rock structures are particularly complex.

After a soaking wet morning, the sun has come out, and I persuade Sheila to drive Little Car while I follow the map to take a look on the ground. Little Car, quite a character by the way, stays in Bath for our West Country expeditions. Though we have spent most of our lives in the south west, home is now in the North of Scotland. The car takes us through a narrow lane to Tucking Mill, where a plaque recording William Smith's life is said to have been put on the wrong house. I am explaining this when the owner of the house comes on the scene.

'No, it's not a mistake. I live in that house and think that Simon Winchester has it wrong.' He is also reading the book, finding it somewhat challenging.

Smith was the first to understand how to date rocks from the fossils found in them, and to know what rocks would follow upon what. Until his day, and by many for years later, fossils, often called divines, were presumed to have been God-given for the glorification of the earth; but then, when Bibles exactly dated each chapter of the Old Testament, geology was seen as sacrilegious. We will meet curious Smith and his map when later journeying takes us back to Bath.

We go through an inviting gate close by, leading to an intriguing lane. I do my best to push it closed, but it seems to reopen and then close itself. 'You shouldn't push it,' says someone who turns out to be the voluntary bailiff of Tucking Mill reservoir, reserved for disabled anglers. We can see several holding their rods from wheelchairs. 'You're only supposed to come in the gate if you have the code.' I explain why we are here in the first place. 'Yes, William Smith probably lived at Tucking Mill itself, not the house with the sign. But I wouldn't advise you to go there. It's an old-fashioned kind of house; they like it that way.'

Beyond the small reservoir we notice the tall abandoned viaduct that carried the Somerset & Dorset Railway over the valley. The route of the much-loved 'Slow & Dirty' is increasingly traced by enthusiasts, encouraged by a TV series. On the way out, we see that the reservoir was opened in 1981, the Year of the Disabled. On the other side of the narrow road lies the abandoned track of the railway which replaced the Somersetshire Coal Canal. And when I open the map, I gather that Little Car is parked on the Limestone Link. Picked out in red diamonds on the Ordnance Survey map, it heads west through the coalfield and well beyond. We pass several walkers obviously out for a more serious trek than just a Sunday constitutional.

Three Ways through the Hills to Bath

Feeling relaxed, we opt for afternoon tea at the Cliffe Hotel, where the only other couple on the terrace proudly tells us that they had been among the first guests in the early 1960s for their two-day honeymoon. Married in Devizes, they arrived by train without a change at Limpley Stoke. You cannot do that today, but every detail of their itinerary for this trip has been worked out and paid for by their family as a Ruby Wedding treat. The view of the valley and wooded hills from the terrace where we enjoy our tea is compelling.

I recall when, as a boy, I began exploring south of Bath, for example taking a Western train from Bristol to Radstock, returning by the Somerset & Dorset, when at least half-a-dozen mines of the Somerset coalfield remained active. Though I was not hot on geology, it was clear from the superb landscape south from Bath to the Mendips that there had been great disturbances to the earth's crust millions of years ago, eventually resulting in the coalfield and quarries for valuable stone. But it was only in the early days of my developing my publishing house, David & Charles, when pennies were still scarce, that I first experienced the full joys of the Avon Valley between Bath and Bradford on Avon.

A new firm of printers, the Redwood Press, had started in Trowbridge. To bend my ear, they put me up for the night at the Cliffe Hotel at Limpley Stoke. Dinner, at a Bath hotel, had been with the McWhirter brothers, whose fortune was based on the success of *The Guinness Book of Records*. The printer had been given a head start with the guarantee of the gigantic run of this popular annual, yet 'outside' customers were never treated as second rate. One of the McWhirter brothers, Ross, was later murdered by the IRA.

The next morning I was free till around eleven and walked the muddy footpath of the then closed Kennet & Avon Canal, running beside the river Avon and the railway. What magic!

All around were signs of engineering challenges and achievements. Dundas Aqueduct, carrying the Kennet & Avon over river and narrow Limpley Stoke Valley, had clearly been built for posterity. There had certainly been prosperity. For many generations the Kennet & Avon was a vital water artery to Reading, and so by the Thames to London. At this Dundas Aqueduct, it was fed with the coal traffic of the Somersetshire Coal Canal. Later Brunel's Great Western Railway (GWR) cruelly wiped out the canals, and used much of the route of the Coal Canal for its branch line west through the coalfield. The branch line was made immortal by the greatest of all railway films, The Titfield Thunderbolt, but by the time of my visit it had already been abandoned. 'Our little systems have their day; they have their day and cease to be.'

Then a miracle happened. First the Kennet & Avon was rescued; it took many years to bring it all back to life, but once the volunteers got stuck into the task, ultimate success was assured. David & Charles produced the standard history, and also that of the Somersetshire Coal Canal. How far and constructively the wheel has turned! The Kennet & Avon is no longer seen as a cranky project, but warmly supported by all kinds of people and organisations. Its final restoration has been funded by what was at the time the largest-ever Heritage Lottery Fund grant of £25 million. Like many other canals now being restored, it is a major contributor to the economy of the areas through which it passes. Many explore it by narrow boat; even more use the towpath.

So, after our tea, we park and walk to the Dundas Aqueduct, with the Brassknocker Basin and junction with the Somersetshire Coal Canal, a short stub of which, leading to a marina, has also been reopened. A young man on the aqueduct is enthusiastic about the scene.

'There you see three ways by which they used to bring the stone they quarried at Avoncliff down through the hills to Bath,' he says. 'At first it went down the river in flat-bottomed boats. Then the Kennet & Avon captured the traffic, and that was a big improvement. But later the Great Western took it over. Three routes, but no stone traffic today, or coal for that matter.'

The river is undisturbed, even by an angler. Two narrow boats pass at the canal basin while, on a Sunday of engineering work, the railway is exceptionally busy, diverted High Speed Trains mingling with the usual local services.

The Travelling Landscape

Throughout history, Bath has exercised a civilising influence well beyond its size, and it is appropriate that the second impetus that eventually led to my being able to write this book should also come from here.

On a hot summer's evening in 1947, I caught an extremely dirty London Midland & Scottish train from the suburban station of Bristol St Philip's to Bath Green Park. The inside of the wide, five-a-side compartment was no cleaner than the carriage's exterior and the only other two passengers, sitting opposite each other on the left-hand side, routinely brushed their seats before sitting down, in the way that anyone caring about their appearance did automatically on LMS local trains. Though it meant the occasional smut, such was the heat that the other passengers were no doubt pleased I had used the leather strap to pull down the window in the door. With the grime on the windows and the smoke and steam, visibility wasn't great, but soon, through the open window, I saw that we were running on the north bank of the Bristol Avon, and caught a glimpse of a train with a freshly-painted green locomotive racing along the Great Western Railway on the other side of the river.

The GWR, soon to become the Western Region of British Railways, was dominant around here. Trainspotting at the secondary Bath Green Park had revealed persistently light loads, except on summer Saturdays, when the Somerset & Dorset down to Bournemouth, fed by the branch from Mangotsfield, was pushed to capacity. Surely, I concluded, the time would come when Bath would need only one station, and this double-track branch on which I was travelling, along with the mainly single-track Somerset & Dorset, would be closed. Though Dr Beeching was not to wield his famous axe until a decade and a half later, it was already clear that, with increasing road competition and much higher staff wages, the railways would have to cut back, despite nationalisation taking effect at the year's end.

That led to my first-ever thoughts about the rail-way, the so-called permanent way, as a route: a route with gentle gradients and curves involving much greater engineering than roads, and usually offering the traveller a friendlier view – if only steam and smoke didn't get in the way. What would happen to these routes if and when the rails were uplifted? A few lines had already been abandoned: just that, left to the elements, which in practice meant the spread of trees inward from the embankments and cuttings. Wouldn't anyone care about the loss of the view from the Avon's north side? Probably not. Even as an older schoolboy I was regarded as an eccentric, spending pocket money on exploring such parts of our country for which I could afford to buy a ticket.

Most people who lived in towns and cities, though loving their seaside holidays, were uninterested in the countryside. Most rural people instinctively wished to defend the countryside for themselves. Of course, a few people cycled to country picnics, and Sunday school outings were not all beside the sea. The generalisation is nonetheless true. Ramblers were unorganised, seldom encouraged. Farmers regularly ploughed up and barricaded footpaths, the signposting for which was deplorably inadequate.

Bath Green Park did close, and then from Western Region trains you could see the infrastructure of this former LMS branch deteriorate, until only a determined walker would push their way through.

Now a miracle has happened here also. Not only has this section of route been rescued for what is known as the Bristol & Bath Railway Path, but has provided the impetus for the creation of the National Cycle Network. After the failed London Dome, that is the largest of all Millennium projects. Far more people now use the route, cycling or on foot, than in its train days. And all over Britain, sections of yesteryear's travelling landscape have been reopened and made safely inviting. The latest Ordnance Survey maps show the routes clearly, including those along the towpath of the Kennet & Avon and many other restored canals. But there are also many new sections taking cyclists off busy and dangerous roads. You see the route numbers displayed all over the country.

It is a great triumph for common sense. As with so many other achievements, it is essentially a one-man story. That man we will meet when we get to Bath.

Access to the Countryside

Positive influences are at work. As we will frequently find, not merely is there increasing access to the countryside, but full use being made of it, as sales of maps and guides for walkers testify. All kinds of things are being achieved, the downside – if there is one – perhaps being that too much of Britain is being turned into a theme park. Theme Park Britain is an inevitable occasional pet hate, yet what would we really wish for? Traditional industries have largely gone, and our journeys are made while the commercial countryside is under great stress, not helped by the worst postwar outbreak of foot-and-mouth disease.

If there is sometimes a surfeit of museums and scarcity of the genuine country, re-exploring Britain proves that things have not become standardised in the way that experts feared in the early days of television. Today there is often such an abundance of minority pursuits that it is the cynical majority that has been silenced. Record numbers of people cycle, explore, even by train and bus, fish, take photographs, giving country pubs extra purpose, while country houses and ever-lovelier gardens are seen as part of the local landscape. As we will see, even the National Trust has changed its spots. The National Parks have matured and are generally well run while, at many reservoirs that used to be out of bounds, there are sporting and other facilities, even tea rooms. Altogether the countryside is a lot more welcoming.

Not since I first fell in love with the Britain of infinite variety has the future of our marvellous landscape seemed so secure, or a greater proportion of its people fulfilled by their own dreams. Hobbies are increasingly important, since jobs are not now generally for life, nor is the day we have to retire dreaded as it once was by those who loved their work more than their austere living conditions.

Our Own Country

Once the more adventurous, daring to desert the closest traditional resorts, went all the way to Devon and Cornwall for their holidays. Now most of us take our main holidays overseas, and tourism figures at home are steadily declining. Yet more people than ever appreciate our own country, exploring it on short secondary holidays or long weekends. Many have a country weekend retreat, pushing up the price of property and making it hard for young country people to buy their own place.

My own understanding began before I was ten with a three-volume *Our Own Country*, a mid-Victorian work bound in three volumes until, through wear and tear, they fell apart. Rebound in red, they now occupy a treasured place on my shelves. My eyes had been opened when I was eight coming up nine. My parents, free to live anywhere, couldn't decide where, so took a fortnight's trial here and there to test the water. There are vivid, if somewhat unorganised, memories of those pre-war days. Some journeys were by train; others by car, appropriately driven by Mr England, who taught me the secrets of the open road. After a false start in Harpenden, home became Teignmouth, shortly before war was declared a few days after my tenth birthday in 1939. Thereafter, for many a long night during air-raids in the cellar, *Our Own Country* became almost my teddy bear. I read the obvious – about Teignmouth, and how in 1690 the French landed, desecrated the churches and burned the Bibles, while the unfamiliar steadily became familiar. The wood engravings and maps were especial friends. I can almost recite parts of the introduction from memory:

Everywhere, in short, the natural features and boundaries of a district have influenced the course not only of local, but of national history; and historical events, or the growth of institutions and foundations resulting from them, have often modified, and sometimes entirely changed, the condition and the features of large tracts of country. This action and reaction will specially be noted in the descriptions to be given in 'Our Own Country'; and in treating such subjects as are more distinctly historical, the latest lights and the most recent information will be laid under contribution. In this manner the various divisions of the book may suit the purpose of so many 'field lectures', to borrow a term from the geologists, where the features of the country and its connected history may be studied and explained on the spot.

In the dreadful days of the Cold War, I began a more systematic exploration of Britain. It still continues, journeys for this book breaking some new ground as well as returning to places visited just once or many times before. My love of Britain has never wavered. Though enjoying exploring the world mainly on sales trips in the early years of the Jumbo Jet, the moment I was back in Britain was always the choicest. Other countries might have their mountains, canyons and jungles, but it is actually true that, for its size, Britain combines greater variety of scenery than any other. It is true for two main reasons. The first is that Britain is unique in its geology. Virtually all rock types and the landscapes associated with them are found here. We don't have to understand the details of geological complexity to know when landforms and scenery are different. Secondly, perhaps above any other, the British scenery has been positively improved by man. Yes, you can point to monstrosities but, overall, man's influence has been more than benign – from villages in rich Cotswold stone through historic cities to the farmed landscape which many overseas visitors have assumed must be State organised and subsidised.

A third reason can be attributed for the survival of so much that is worthwhile: tighter planning controls than generally found elsewhere. Things are much better than could have been hoped for when the Town & Country Planning Act 1948 was passed. Nor must one forget that even in Our Own Country there are many areas of totally unspoilt natural beauty. Only one per cent of the population may live in the Scottish Highlands and Islands, but the region accounts for sixteen per cent of our land area. Thanks to careful planning, even crowded Southern England benefits (as estate agents put it) from Dartmoor, sometimes described as the Last Wilderness. Each of our National Parks is a treasure-house of outstanding landscape.

Our language and our landscape are perhaps our greatest assets. *The Faber Book of Landscape Poetry* can be warmly recommended for the way in which it uses poetic language to celebrate the physical inheritance. In his introduction to the anthology, Kenneth Baker records how both have changed through the thousand years from which poems have been selected:

The English language, spoken then by fewer than a million people, has developed from its Celtic and Anglo-Saxon roots to become the immensely rich language of today, spoken by over eight hundred million around the world. It was created not by grammarians but from the usage of ordinary people coming into Britain as waves of immigrants – Celts, Angles, Saxons, Romans, Jutes, Germans, Vikings, Normans, Jews, Asians and West Indians. Over the same period the landscape has been changed out of all recognition by the actions of those same people: the great forests have disappeared; moors, meadows, downland, heaths have all shrunk; hamlets have become cities, and estuaries ports. Man has shaped nature and the countryside: the simple assertion of William Cowper that 'God made the country and man made the town' was not true even in the eighteenth century. The landscape is both natural and artificial.

Landscape the Great Stage

For me, the greatest fascination lies in the often stark contrast between continuity and change. The landscape is the great stage, the set changed slightly or hugely, for the ever-varied scenes enacted upon it. Who, for example, can pass Stonehenge without thoughts of how it came to be, or the many happenings in or around it, till today it is fenced securely against further human wear and tear? Many of us never see it without wondering about the skill and dedication of those who brought those great stones and erected them precisely, without the aid of mechanisation; or thoughts of poor Tess of the d'Urbervilles, whose crisis is so dramatically depicted here by Thomas Hardy, the greatest of all our landscape novelists. Often the theme is man versus the elements, and it is perhaps this that makes the starker parts of Britain so attractive to novelists, painters and musicians.

Certainly for the travel writer in love with his own country, the more remote parts inevitably claim special attention. They still provide a sense of adventure and retain strong individual identity. 'More remote' obviously includes the Scottish Highlands and Islands and the West Country, but also substantial parts of mid- and west Wales, and of course the Lake District and the Dales. We should also add the Peak District, since remoteness can be measured vertically as well as in travelling time from the centres of what we call civilisation. One other English county must also qualify: Herefordshire. According to a recent survey it is the only area in England (besides North Devon) still to boast large undeveloped tracts of unspoilt landscape with little light pollution at night. From Hereford, the journey to London by road or rail takes longer than that from places much further away along the main transport arteries to the north and west. Though not immune from light pollution, furthest Norfolk also retains much individuality, and again in practical terms is much more remote than the number of miles from London would suggest. Indeed, a map of Britain redrawn to show distance in time rather than miles from the capital has North Norfolk protruding considerably further into the North Sea (as do both the Cambrian and Cumbrian coasts into the Irish Sea). Another greatly under-rated county is Northumberland, its many contrasting ingredients, including large tracts of unspoilt coastal and inland landscape, still supporting a highly individual though generally more reticent population, little disturbed by the fact that expresses on the East Coast main line bring London artificially close to key places.

Queen Victoria did much to enhance the trend of romanticising our remoter regions, enthusing about her tours of the Highlands and forays into smaller-scale scenic gems elsewhere, such as the Tamar Estuary separating Cornwall from Devon. Good hotels followed. And because certain people feel more at home in the extremities of the country, there are surprisingly strong affinities between them. For example, many West Country folk know the Scottish Highlands better than any other part of Britain beyond their own. This is reflected in fiction, for example Rosamunde Pilcher's novels, often tracing family fortunes in Cornwall and Scotland, between which she has spent most of her time and so writes of with warmth and affection. So I feel I am in good company in having spent nearly all my life in one or other of these extremities, frequently traversing the length of Britain on business and holiday.

Exploration of our varied land and townscapes is this book's driving force, along with looking at people in their geographic setting, people whose lives and wealth (or poverty) have often been shaped for richer or poorer by the soil, rocks and water around them. I have always been fascinated by how people used to and still do earn their living, especially in remote districts, and the way these different parts of Britain are connected, especially by rail and waterway. This book is a personal attempt to show how my Britain hangs together, what makes it such a treasure and, of course, what makes it tick. The aim is to entertain but even more to surprise, to open eyes to unexpected treasures, traditions and values.

How Guide Books and Attitudes have Improved

In this book's literary content, I am in a sense turning the clock back. Favourite travelling companions have long been the mid-nineteenth century Murray *Hand-Books* which, before the late Victorian and Edwardian days when 'trade' ceased to be respectable, described, often colourfully, things as they really were. Then pioneer visitors were as likely to visit a quarry or handmade paper factory as the narrower range of places of interest on which latter guides concentrated. That is not to decry churches and ancient monuments, which will still have their place here, but to give a different emphasis.

Guide books and other works about Britain perhaps reached their nadir in the years before and immediately after World War Two. Thus, in its description of Teignmouth, a book on South Devon devoted two-thirds of its space to visits by Keats. Although Keats's not very happy experiences are part of Teignmouth's story, they are only a small part. The 1949 *Somerset,* in the Robert Hale County Books series, tells us about Westonzoyland's role in the Civil War, but nothing about its unique floodland character in the days when many people living there were marooned in the in-between seasons when the land was flooded but not deeply enough for boating. More extraordinary, it does not even have Weston-super-Mare (larger than all Somerset's other resorts together) in the index. It was against that tradition of concentrating on 'literary' and antiquarian matters that my publishing house of David & Charles rebelled with more down-to-earth titles.

While many earlier books on Cornwall carefully avoided paying attention to Newquay, its leading resort, I find real interest there. Even if it is not quite your cup of tea (though don't be too sure about that for an early or late-season visit), its story is remarkable and certainly belongs in my portrait of Britain, where there is bound to be discussion of the tension between locals and incomers, residents and tourists – Grockles in Devon, Emmets in Cornwall. Did you know, for example, that before 1939, in most of holiday Britain, bad language, excessive bargaining and reneging on agreements were introduced by visitors, whose behaviour frequently shocked hard-working, God-fearing fishermen and the like?

While there are inevitably things to regret, such as more and more acres devoted to roundabouts and wasted areas in industrial 'parks', optimism prevails, and on my journeys I have found much to be grateful for, from the reopening of long-closed routes (railways, canals and footpaths) to the more constructive attitude of the water industry towards access and use of reservoirs; from a return of the National Trust to its core values, to a new common sense approach to co-operation between state and voluntary organisations. Generally there's a greater wish to help and, today, economics do not automatically come first. In today's more positive climate, it is hard to realise that after World War Two a thousand country houses were destroyed.

Take woodlands. Ask people when during the past hundred years the largest proportion of Britain was covered by woodland and most would probably assume the present day or comparatively recently. Not so. There are more trees in Britain today than in 1895, though woods were most denuded after World War One. It was, in fact, that crisis that brought the Forestry Commission into being in 1919, heralding the era of grim plantations of Sitka spruce. The public was routinely denied access. Now, to quote a headline in *The Economist*, forests are for fun rather than cash. Nearly three quarters of trees planted are broad-leaved, such as oak, ash and birch. Today's woodlands are less disease prone and easier on the eye. They attract a greater variety of wildlife, and woodland and tourism now go hand-in-hand. When the Forestry Commission in Scotland held a Tree Fest which it hoped might stretch to 200 locations, 600 were offered.

Ironically the change is partly due to the success of the recycling movement. So much less new soft wood is used, especially in newsprint, that Sitka spruce prices have fallen dramatically. Most of yesteryear's investors who sought to make a packet by combining tax breaks with covering hillsides with Sitkas have not done well. Of course there are problems, one being vandalism of street and park tree plantings, but we shouldn't be downhearted. While global warming threatens much wildlife, especially trees and plants, less able to adapt than birds and animals, there is already an active monitor to ensure full understanding and allow positive action to be taken. Our woods, like our architecture, our appreciation of and access to the countryside, even the way our spa towns are being revived, are infinitely better than when I was a young man and change seemed automatically for the worse. Generally, wonder of wonders, even Government money is mainly being better spent. Developing subsidised broad-leaved woods for example is helping many farmers in their fight for survival.

Come, enjoy my Britain, and do not let criticisms of the failings, unfortunately and yet endearingly part of our culture, deter you. There is so much to see and enjoy, so many people adding colour and vitality to life.

Hotels

Places to sleep and eat are necessary for any traveller, and their quality often colours the experience. Having sometimes to write about them professionally, I find hotels hold a special fascination. I was brought up on a diet of Trust Houses and, when they were taken over by Forte, felt they achieved an uncannily high standard for a large and varied chain. They certainly offered real value. Charles Forte was a genius; standards started slipping, and there were too many management changes, under his son Rocco. The first hotel of his new personal empire, the Balmoral at Waverley Station, Edinburgh, still has a disappointing AA percentage rating, though his new waterside St David's gives Cardiff its first really luxurious hotel. The forced sale of Forte to Granada, who promised much, and then discovered that hotels did 'not fit', and made an overall loss on their disposal, was a disaster. Some of the former Forte hotels remain good; many more are by no means so acceptable.

The other outstanding hotel chain was that of the railway hotels. Outside London, British Transport Hotels were in a class of their own, expensive but first rate, for example with larger and better beds, and profitable until governments deprived them of investment. Maggie Thatcher alas then pronounced that the railway builders such as Brunel had been ridiculous in combining transport with hosting. The way hotels were sold off was a scandal of unbelievable proportions that has never been fully told. At D&C I had to reject the story as told by BTH's last managing director, Peter Land, because it was not clear who would buy the book, yet I am sorry it has not been published. I met Mr Land at the beginning of these journeys, and the ridiculousness of the sale became yet more apparent. A management buyout wasn't even considered. Hotels had to be sold off eight at a time, simply because that is what the civil servants said. Some were resold only days later for twice the price received by the nation. There are honourable exceptions, but most of the hotels have seen standards deteriorate badly – from internal decorations to bedding, from reception to food. The best that can be said is that takeovers are viewed more critically since the Forte/Granada fiasco, and that the politicians and civil servants didn't dare make so bad a mess of subsequent privatisations as they had with BTH.

Today we are less likely to stay in a chain hotel and are more dependent on advice for choice of individual establishments. An outstanding success has been the AA's percentage rating system. David Young, responsible for the AA *Hotel Guide*, told me how they had moved on from their historic star rating (more about facilities than quality) to include a percentage overall rating, with which our own experience usually agrees. A five-star hotel with a low percentage rating can be a wasteful disappointment; two-star hotels with a high percentage rating open a new world of quality stays. 'We have just become the bestselling hotel guide,' Mr Young told me. That means 55,000 to 60,000 copies annually in the UK, and an experienced and well-controlled team of inspectors. Yes, hotels have to pay to belong to the AA, and a few outstanding ones don't, but then all hotel guides seem to demand some kind of payment. Some which profess editorial independence certainly don't have it.

Another useful publication is Johansens *Recommended Hotels*; for some years I distributed it at D&C. Entries are paid for and range from the studious to the eccentric, but – when need be – reading between the lines it is usually possible to make a sensible judgement and enjoy highly individual hotels. There are also some lively regional guides, such as the Scottish *Stevensons Good Hotel and Food Book*. 'It's been uphill work, but worth it. Not a recipe for making money, but certainly to having good friends,' Alan Stevenson told me. While the AA *Hotel Guide* covers the entire spectrum, private publishers like Stevenson both need as well as can afford their personal approach. If you don't like Alan Stevenson, you probably won't get your hotel included, and paying certainly won't get your hotel in if it doesn't click with him. Integrity produces colour, even amusement.

Both Mr Young and Mr Stevenson emphasise they encourage the use of local produce 'left to speak for themselves', one of the catering trade's phrases of the moment. Too ambitious, often inappropriate, combinations of flavours are still the bane of many dining rooms. But then too little is often spent on the basic ingredients. A good piece of meat, simply cooked, always beats a poor one however cleverly presented.

The greater use made of independent hotels brings a few challenges, notably a lack of standardisation of some basics that the chains achieve. For the tall traveller, that includes mirrors placed too low in which to see your face comfortably, and irritations when booking by telephone such as refusal to accept confirmation by credit card, and plugs impossibly placed for the tea-making facilities provided. Worn carpet in bathrooms where a non-porous flooring would be more sensible, lack of face flannels even in expensive hotels catering for Americans, fans that automatically come on with the lights (a separate strip light over the hand basin should be standard) and which continue their murderous groan for up to ten minutes after you switch off, bedside lights that hoteliers have never tried to read by, and piles of clean towels and linen left on grubby corridor floors: these are some of our least favourite things. One piece of advice to the individual hotelier: spend a few nights each year trying out your own rooms!

Generally, though, hotel standards have risen... and are still rising. We have slept in well over a hundred beds on our travels for the book, and still generally look forward to our next hotel, or indeed returning to the same one when we have the occasional luxury of several nights in the same bed. 'Like all hoteliers, I eat too much, drink too much, am too pretentious and don't get enough sleep,' said one hotelier. In our experience, that is not true, though we certainly happened on one or two horribly pretentious and over-opinionated owners. That hotels remain so varied is part of that natural British resistance to standardisation that stems from the very land in which we live.

I

ISLAND BOUND

Our Corner of God's Own Countrry

Though we wake up keen and early this glorious morning at the beginning of May, already the sun has bathed the Moray Firth for hours. The lapping of the waves is scarcely audible. Nairn is our adopted home, and we certainly feel much at home in our corner of what Scots refer to as God's Own Country. Scotland accounts for about 40 per cent of Britain yet has less than 10 per cent of its population, 66 people per square kilometre compared with England's 381. We enjoy the difference.

The cliffs on the opposite shore seven miles away are crystal clear, and walking the length of the promenade I keep pace with a seal progressing at just the same rate fifty yards or so off the beach. The Moray Firth is perhaps best known as home to one of Britain's two schools of blue-nosed dolphins who surely enjoy their acrobatics as much as the visitors watching them leaping and rolling. Only the other day from my bed I gazed as a minkie whale rolled over and over in apparent ecstasy. Yes, there is a lot to see: oil rigs, oil tankers, cargo ships and in summer a couple of dozen cruise ships such as the *QE2*, popping in and out between the cliffs called the Sutors which guard the entrance to the great inland sea of the Cromarty Firth. This was once the base for much of the Royal Navy which, in 1919, when the pay for ratings but not officers was cut, mutinied at Invergordon. Then there are cargo ships and fishing boats, and craft heading for the Caledonian Canal, the entrance of which is at Inverness, further up the Moray Firth.

Sunsets are often dramatic, and both full-orange moon and red summer sun rise majestically over the harbour. Changes of light are a constant joy: rich graduations of blues, greys and creamy whites, patches of sunshine moving rapidly along the cliffs of the Black Isle and Ross & Cromarty opposite, highlighting particular crevices and caves perhaps not seen so sharply for months. Bird life includes huge flocks of migrating geese flying in perfect formation, with their constant honking chorus, oyster catchers, herons, curlews (how we love their cry), turnstones and restless dunlins by the hundred among the ever-changing scavenging visitors on the beach and rocks at low tide. Flocks of redwings (often mistaken for thrushes), red-throated divers, northern wheatears, waxwings: the list of seasonal variations is endless. Locals and visitors freely invite others to watch something special through their binoculars.

At high tide, seen from my desk upstairs, the green of the lawn goes straight into the blue sea. People ask how one can possibly concentrate with such a view. Personally, much more easily than in a noisy urban office. That remains true despite the occasional interruption by an internal telephone call insisting that something should be seen at once: a particularly scarlet sunset against a pale blue sky; a seal sunning on a rock between a pair of cormorants, their outstretched wings barely out of the water; or dolphins exuberantly showing their love of life here.

This seems a perfect time to start a refreshing holiday, called 'Adrift in the Isles', on a converted MacBrayne's car ferry now renamed the *Hebridean Princess*. The cruise begins in Oban, on the other side of Scotland. Oh, may the weather last, but whether it does or not we are grateful for this amazingly warm day. There is regular mention in weather forecasts of the Moray Firth's benign mini-climate. Our rainfall at Nairn is far below that of London, our sunshine hours higher than anywhere along England's south coast. February is often a marvellous month. We are protected by a ring of mountains on either side of the Firth, exposed only to the occasional (but short-lived) fury of a nor'easter. Then you have to raise your voice to be heard. Spring, however, often comes late and only the recent warm spell has finally meant death to most of our daffodils.

At dinner at a local hotel last night, Miriam, who was my personal assistant at David & Charles, the Devon-based publishing house to which I devoted much of my life, tells me of the latest problems with the new owners there and asks how the sale of my retirement business, *Writers' News*, has gone. 'Too early to tell,' I replied. We will see. A local hotel? Yes, just round the corner, but hardly local in the normal sense since the Clifton House Hotel is on the international good food and wine circuit. It is lovingly run by possibly the most individual of all Nairn's characters, Gordon Macintyre, though there are many runners-up. Once seen, Gordon is never forgotten, his clothes often dated, his white beard and clipped enunciation suiting his welcoming enthusiasm. As always, he was the showman at a dazzling presentation (three bowls of flowers on the table), splendid food, excellent wine and conversation, and idiosyncratic decor and pictures combining to make it as unorthodox as it is enjoyable. There is a Clifton House way of doing everything. Many guests, including Americans, come back to be stunned afresh, basking in the heat (even if it's naturally warm) of the log fires and the company of Malibar the over-fed King Charles Spaniel, but wishing that Auberon, the Persian cat with a superiority complex, wouldn't be quite so aloof. There are enough antiques to establish a major dealer, and historic wallpaper which makes those knowledgeable about interior decoration go crazy. The gentle perfume of dozens of bowls of flowers pervades everything. Where better than to start a relaxing break?

Nairn's Characters

Miriam is coming on the first part of our journey this morning. As we load the car, she says she would love to return to the Clifton in winter, when the large dining room is converted into the theatre of Nairn Performing Arts Guild. Classical concerts are by soloists, trios and quartets one regularly hears on Radio Three, while plays are performed by the so-called amateur Clifton Players, though they're more professional than many repertory companies. Although I am, as Gordon's vice-convenor (as we say in Scotland for deputy chairman) on the organising committee, of course I am not biased – not even by the fact that he is a dear friend, especially in the garden, where his cultural knowledge is as valuable as his aesthetic advice. The talent marshalled by Gordon at the Clifton is to say the least out of the ordinary. Two other committee members are musicians of outstanding ability, both authors. One is a solicitor who has retired early to devote more time writing traditional Scottish fiddle music. That he is still a brilliant violin player is due to prompt action when he sawed off a finger: into ice it went so it could be sewn back. Then there's Tim Honnor who, like us, has moved here from Devon. He runs a printing business retaining that rarity, letterpress machines. It is half museum, half high-class business, producing work for royalty and embassies and building up a specialty in wedding invitations for America's discerning brides.

The whole town is a bit like that, with over-the-top social events, and the influence of the nearby castles, and the fertile plain along the coast where crops making British farming records still produce the sort of riches that paid for those castles. Two other authors are seriously into transport history; it was not a bad place for *Writers' News* to grow and flourish.

There are constant surprises, too, like Toby MacArthur, a large distinguished chap with grey hair who, when we responded to the invitation on a sign, happily provided us with traditional afternoon tea, all home made, and then sat at his organ and played *The Old Rugged Cross*. Though I had not heard of him before, it transpires that many in Nairn know Toby. When I asked if he had a card, yes. 'A Taste of the Countryside Bed and Breakfast, Afternoon Teas, Putting Green & Live Music provided by your host.'

A bit like an old-fashioned and very clean New Zealand farmstead, Achavelgin Farmhouse has one of those expansive views of great depth and detail. 'People come to me for peace and relaxation,' he told me. Each year, 450 sheep from Skye come to overwinter on his pastures. 'I'm always busy but never shy, though [as he turns from organ to piano-accordion for *Cwm Rhondda*] I can't read music and only play by ear.' His wife died – 'took a stroke' as they put it in Scotland – seven years ago, but why cease to make people happy? Why indeed? 'Thirty-five are coming for tea tomorrow.' They will be welcome to play miniature golf on an immaculately kept green down a steep slope from the drive and garden with its displays of giant rocks; and surely he will joke. Yesterday, he said, he lost his profit on one breakfast by having to fry four eggs. 'Four or five eggs, this morning?' he asked, to be assured: 'Oh four's ample, thank you.' Back to this morning, Miriam climbs into the back seat of our four-wheel drive from whose extra height we delight in viewing Scotland's far-reaching grandeur.

'Having seen what life's like here,' she says, 'I shan't ever again feel sorry for you living in Scotland.' Nor should others: Nairn offers a great lifestyle in a glorious setting. It came to prominence when a Dr Grigor drew attention to the healthiness of its dry climate.

Most of the large houses in the West End were built at the end of the nineteenth century to accommodate incomers in search of distinctive retirement. Several, however, were occupied by indigenous folk able to support spacious occupation for eleven months of the year by moving out for August, when English families arrived lock, stock, hat boxes and barrel. Ludvic Kennedy spent his childhood holidays next door. Many famous people were attracted.

Doctors still tell of how Charlie Chaplin spent half a guinea daily to be persuaded he was in good health. William Whitelaw was born in our street, and there are many stories about his golf – and about his mother, a somewhat erratic driver. When she drove into the path of a car that had priority at a crossroad and was charged with careless driving, she persuaded the police that the road markings were wrong – and that if they didn't drop the case her son, then Home Secretary, would hear about it. Home Secretaries are not supposed to show favouritism so, when she boasted to her son of her success, he had the case reinstated.

Loch Ness and the Great Glen

Being English, of course, Miriam asks if our route across Scotland will include Loch Ness. It is a lovely, deep loch, its massive quantity of water (more than enough, it is said, to fill every reservoir in the land) filling part of the Great Glen, which continues east to form the Moray Firth.

Geologists describe the great earthquakes of millions of years ago that created the Great Glen.

What Sassenachs mean when they hope to see Loch Ness is that they want to tell their friends they caught a fleeting glimpse (inevitably too brief to focus the camera) of Nessie, the Loch Ness Monster. We take the road south of the Loch, and so at least avoid yet again following the convoys heading for the monster exhibition. The south road is a driver's dream: brilliant prospects open at every turn and hump, with many opportunities to calculate speed so as to 'cross' oncoming vehicles in a passing bay without slowing. For miles the road hugs the loch's shore.

We pause briefly to see the site of Scotland's first aluminium works; it was worth transporting the ore here in order to use cheap hydroelectricity. Nearby, a modern hydroelectric plant cleverly pumps up water to a higher loch during the hours when electricity can be bought from the grid cheaply at night, and sells it back at peak rates when the water comes tumbling down through the turbine. In the Highlands you don't put the lights on but switch on the hydro... one of many linguistic differences. You 'stay' in the house you own, do your messages rather than shop, and talk of the Co-op as the 'coop' or 'cooperator', while a duvet is a downie, drainpipes are rones, and when the council charges for 'removing three bikes' it means you have had a plague of wasps. You ask someone how himself is; and then about herself, meaning his wife. There are endless nuances, and whether you are being taken through to your table in the dining room or saying cheerio, it is always 'just now'.

But these are only the surface differences that are particular to Scotland. In many ways Scottish culture and daily life are as different to their English equivalent as is America, perhaps even more so. Above all there is great friendliness, especially strong in the Highlands. Here you are an incomer or white settler whether you come from Devon or Glasgow. With such scant population, we perhaps need to be kind to each other. Going to a shop is a social event, and everyone knows about you, your home (which you 'have' for your period of occupation rather than own) and who sired so-and-so's dog.

The narrow switchback road continues through a bleak area inland, diving into occasional softer valleys. There, we note, is the turning to a fine country house hotel soon to close and become a private home. Running a quality establishment well off the beaten track is beset with dramatic changes in demand and staffing problems, and over recent years quite a few have given up. Then down to Fort Augustus, where we cross the swing bridge over the Caledonian Canal at the foot of one of its staircases of locks.

Thomas Telford's largest single work, the canal links a number of natural lochs, of which Loch Ness is the greatest. Though occasionally we are held up for a fishing vessel or two taking a short cut from the Atlantic to the North Sea, most delays at swing bridges are for pleasure craft. So much major repair work needs to be done that the canal's closure has long been threatened, but this morning we luxuriate in the knowledge that the waterway has been given a long continuing history (greater involvement of local people has been warmly welcomed), though the thought occurs that for what it is costing a fresh water supply could probably be provided for hundreds of thousands in an undeveloped part of the world. But a good definition of civilisation might be doing things that are not strictly necessary, and the Caledonian Canal is as much part of Scottish history as aspects of its culture are cherished in the subsidised arts.

Fort Augustus, neat if often overwhelmed by traffic, is a canal town, between Loch Ness and Loch Oich. Its outstanding position was confirmed by Benedictine monks – they never chose unwisely – establishing the Abbey which recently closed due to lack of new recruits. Between lochs, we then follow one of General Wade's Military Roads, built to make it easier to shift troops more rapidly to keep the Highlanders under tighter control, and then take the forested shore of Loch Oich before crossing the canal for the last time and running through part of Laggan Forest on the south side of long Loch Lochy. Hundreds of Sassenachs own pieces of forest in the Great Glen, tax-saving propositions pushed hard because prices are generally lower than those nearer to the centres of population, while long spring and autumn daylight hours and high rainfall encourage fast growth.

Loch Lochy's setting is more dramatic, though not nearly so appreciated, as that of Loch Ness. The further west you go, the higher the mountains, better viewed from the water than the road. As on so many Scottish lochs, timetabled steamers are a thing of the past but, if you cannot hire your own vessel, consider taking one of the seasonal cruise ships operating from Inverness to Fort William.

At Spean Bridge the road is joined by that other great piece of transport heritage, the West Highland line, passing the cattle ranch which to those who had previously never been north of Watford once spelt western romance. The awesome majesty of Ben Nevis more usually has to be guessed at than clearly seen, but there is no doubt about its domination. It is frequently in the news if only for climbing accidents and rescues.

Fort William, never a favourite place, hasn't been improved by building the bypass separating the town from the waterfront. Waterside parking space is limited but worth seeking if only for the fine fish restaurant on a small pier. While today's catch is being cooked, there is much to see: a passenger ferry going to and from Loch Linnhe's opposite shore, occasional traffic along its waterside road from which Fort William looks like a neat model, and of course fishing boats, yachts and marine birds. But even if there were only a blank wall to look out at, the meal would be well worth waiting for, especially as north of the Border the variety of fish on offer is generally surprisingly poor... unless, of course, you have one of those Scottish 'arrangements'. Top hoteliers do: Gordon Macintyre at Nairn's Clifton House has developed them with a whole range of suppliers of different kinds of meat, game, fish and other produce.

After lunch we drop Miriam at Fort William's utilitarian modern station, noticing the sleeper is ready for tonight's long trip to London. Nicknamed the Deer Stalkers' Express, it was saved by a technicality after Brit Rail, not for the first time, tried to ride roughshod over the law. Then we are on our way to Oban, the road playing with dramatic geography. It is much shorter than of yore, Ballachulish bridge saving the long detour round Loch Leven, and also far faster. We, however, potter round Loch Leven and pop into mini Port Appin where the panorama of mainland, island and lochs shaped like pieces of a jig-saw puzzle has enriched many a picnic. There is time, too, to linger after crossing the fast-flowing current at the mouth of Loch Etive, another gem, and finally along Oban's seafront to one of the country's best-situated campsites at Ganavan Bay.

Oban's seafront and harbour can scarcely be beaten for situation, and the town also looks inviting, but it has always seemed that many shops are under too much pressure from summer tourists to go out of their way to develop more original stocks. Oban, followed by Fort William, were always the two Scottish places where book sales were most disappointing in publishing days, many remoter bookshops being more rewarding to supplier and customer alike.

The Hebridean Princess

We have had our eye on the clock, and it has just reached the moment we are welcomed aboard. Everyone else seems to have arrived sharply, too. 'Look what they have brought,' says Sheila, pointing to mounds of luggage by way of justifying ours. 'We've learned that you have to be prepared for all contingencies,' says a superior English woman with seven or eight pieces. 'Exactly,' answers Sheila. Yet we all got it wrong: were utterly unprepared for a heatwave at sea. Opportunities to buy sun hats scarcely abound at our ports of call.

One of the most predictable things about British weather is that sometime in May or early June there will be a period of a week or so when the sun shines in the normally damp Western Highlands and Islands. Westerly winds are at their seasonal low, replaced by northerlies from which the Highland massif protects the coast and islands. Hitting it lucky, we enjoy long hours of sunshine, though usually with some cloud around to add visual impact. Meanwhile it has turned dull in Nairn as it often does on the east coast when the west is at its brightest best. The exact timing and duration of the 'heatwave' cannot be guaranteed and occasionally it misses a season. May is the month to come if you possibly can. Then the average sunshine is over half as much again as that in July, with correspondingly lower rainfall. And hotels and roads are quiet. When we return home we read Philip Eden's popular weather piece in *The Daily Telegraph*. In eight days 89 hours of sunshine were recorded at Tiree, compared with a mere fifteen at Cromer.

Converted car ferry and relatively small (2,112 tons) she may be, but the *Hebridean Princess*'s accommodation puts most ocean liners to shame. The advertising is fair: it is a country house at sea. Around forty pampered guests enjoy individually-styled bedrooms. The main lounge is surrounded by picture windows, the living gas fire and hearth providing the centrepiece at night, though it would have been madness to put the fire on at all on this voyage. Most drinks and lunches are on open deck.

Kitchen and waiting staff are drawn from the very best hotels and ships, and food and service are impeccable. Curiously run from Skipton, where the original owners happened to live when they had this dream, it is unique, not cheap but with a high proportion of returning guests. The ship veritably embraces you. Within minutes of boarding you relax, without the tensions of mass processing, people struggling to find their way, and the over-the-top recognition of familiar faces, that epitomise the start of cruises on large ships.

While every detail pleases, the *Hebridean Princess* is ever discreet. From captain to bedroom staff, the crew are Scottish and proud of it in a quiet business-like way. The company avoids much overseas promotion, so most guests are British and conversation is about scenery and birds, not today's shopping. And our country house takes us through some of the world's best scenery. We anchor overnight in sheltered bays, fascinated by repeat panoramas as we swing gently round and back on our anchor. Normally engines are only switched on for a couple of hours three times daily, before and during breakfast, over lunch, and during the evening including dinner, allowing two daily trips ashore. A wee dram in your porridge. Lunch again outside in the sun. Pre-dinner drinks also on balmy deck before descending to the restaurant for another gourmet dinner. It's tough, especially as everyone points out the Paps of Jura in yet another position – it is hard to believe it is we who move – and we join the dash to bring cameras and binoculars on deck when we pass through another 'narrow', and prepare to be welcomed at yet a different island community.

Remote Civilisations: Jura and Colonsay

Our first call is Craighouse, the very mini capital of Jura. Our small boats land us a mile and a half to the north, and a shuttle bus takes guests to and fro, though walking along the placid shore is a delight. No sun hats on sale but we 'live off the land' to the extent of having morning coffee at the hotel, where most of the handful of pub regulars are employed by the small distillery. Thirty miles long and up to seven wide, Jura is a large island but home to barely 250 people. Surprisingly the hotel has eighteen bedrooms and is open all year round. An excellent leaflet tells us that, though Jura is one of the most beautiful islands, it is mysterious and little known. 'Its spectacular mountains, visible from the Argyll mainland some sixteen miles away, tower above a landscape so varied that in a day's walk you may see small woodland, forest and farm, deserted silver sand beaches, rock strewn shoreline with raised beaches and caves to explore, heathland and hills rich in wildlife, and trout-filled lochs.' Moreover, this haven of peace is readily accessible by ferry from cosy Port Askaig on Islay across the narrow Sound of Islay.

George Orwell heads a long list of authors who have stayed here to work in peace. He came in 1946 to finish a novel, staying in a remote farmhouse beyond which the public can drive the single south-to-north road. This, of course, passes through Craighouse, eight miles from the ferry. The Paps, all three between 2407 and 2571 feet high, can easily be ascended on foot.

Lunch is served as we motor through the long sound, between rugged Jura devoid of all habitation beyond that ferry crossing, and larger, more civilised Islay with wooded cliffs as far as its waterside distillery, one of several famous for their peaty malts. Islay has a substantial road network, a fertile plain producing the barley for the distilleries, marvellous bird life, and archaeological interest of international significance. At times you hardly seem to be out of sight of one of those wonderful Celtic crosses; I once heard an American girl boast that the design on her piece of jewellery seemed to have been copied by the builder of one of them.

The irregular coastline has unending interest, though occasionally I still have an uncomfortable dream: as a young man I was running joyously along the cliff edge when a splash from an incoming wave gave just sufficient warning of an abyss ahead. On the west coast of the Rinns of Islay peninsula, the sea penetrates deep through narrow strips of the softer rock interrupting the lush pasture atop the rest.

In the afternoon Colonsay, which I first got to know when approached by its hotelier, Kevin Byrne. He had asked whether, if he purchased several hundred copies, David & Charles would include it in our 'Islands' series. We duly did. I first met him when, after a walk across the island on a previous visit by ship, I called at the hotel, which he said he was hoping to sell to concentrate on his first love: books. The depth of that love was clear when he showed me the bookshop he then ran opposite the hotel. Changing for dinner, I had the idea of selling him the Scottish titles of most of my post-D&C publishing venture, and this duly happened. His House of Lochar operates from what, so far as transport links are concerned, is possibly the most isolated of all today's seriously inhabited Scottish islands.

Remote islands are great for creative ideas. Will I have another today? Yes... the idea for this book! The first notes taken specifically for these pages are written on odd bits of paper as he drives me round the island. Young men of today: get out of your offices, go to distant places and have real thoughts instead of being just busy.

Typical of the enterprising range of jobs held by key people on many islands, Kevin is port supervisor (he tied up the ship this afternoon), has four self-catering chalets and is building a new house for writers taking a sabbatical, is community webmaster concentrating on genealogical matters, JP session clerk, writer, bookseller and publisher. And school bus driver. The lads and lasses we pick up at the primary school are curious about the Englishman sitting next to their driver, the older girls self-consciously blushing.

Over the roar of the engine and grinding gear changes, I hear that while, before the potato famine, in 1841 the population was over a thousand in a land eight miles by three, today it is only 110. It is claimed that over a million people in Canada alone can trace ancestry to Colonsay, a favourite destination for emigrants being Prince Edward Island. No wonder the webmaster is hot on genealogy.

Kevin is a great guide. There is a keen community spirit; the new village hall cost £350,000. A week or two ago, when it became too rough for the ferry to pick up sixty day trippers it had dropped a few hours before, it took just forty-five minutes to arrange beds for all for the night. Since a woman died in childbirth in 1910 before help could be summoned, a full-time doctor has lived here. Smallpox and scarlatina were epidemic until the end of the nineteenth century; Colonsay was the first island to have running water but almost the last to have mains telephone; that tree, a type of alder, is 440 years old; don't miss that marsh marigold; delight, they have just discovered the twenty-fifth type of orchid on the island. So it goes on. Colonsay regularly has minor earthquakes up to 3.4 on the Richter Scale since the fault line of the Great Glen slices through it.

Later the main centre for Vikings, Colonsay was originally settled within a thousand years of the last Ice Age. We stop on a raised beach overlooking a mighty expanse of silver sand with high surf. Even after they have broken, the waves take ages finally to die as they roll gently up the infinitesimal gradient. And here is one of our passengers, Barbara Crawford, author of *Scandinavian Scotland*, bringing archaeology alive for a knot of passengers whose everyday cares have already been blown away.

Colonsay is a friendly, beckoning island with a lush, fertile if small interior. Kevin remembers an urgent mission, and drops me to enjoy the semi-tropical gardens at Colonsay House. In 1904 Lord Strathcona spent some of the money he made building the Canadian Pacific Railway to purchase and improve the house (started in 1722) and begin the gardens. His descendants still own the island.

Next I am deposited at his bookshop-cum-publishing HQ, a utilitarian little building in island fashion in the middle of nowhere. Assistant Jennie, who came to work in the hotel and married on the island, talks of problems of persuading Scottish, never mind English, booksellers to restock titles even if they sell out on the first day. It has always been the case that booksellers aren't keen about the string of people on the road, salesmen, or in the more discreet language of the book trade, 'representatives', calling to 'waste' their time, but when a customer asks about a book out of stock, reply: 'We're waiting for the rep.' And operating on a remote island makes no difference to that other problem suffered by small publishers: slow payment. One chain, says Jennie, is eighteen months behind. She is less interested when I point out that I have been waiting for royalties for longer than that. Authors' royalties are ever the last task to be done, especially by small publishers, short of time and cash. At least the books I buy can be set against mine... or could have been had I thought about it and not automatically brought out my wallet.

Kevin's wife, renowned for her cooking in their hotel days, comes to say he has been held up. The pressures of life tell even here, but we are back at the ship in good time and I walk aboard with another passenger, a former managing director of Curtis Brown the literary agency, with whom D&C never struck real rapport. We grudgingly acknowledge our common background but no more.

The only sad note about this afternoon's memorable visit has been hearing about the recent inevitable closure (as on most islands) of the dairy. EU regulations, don't you know. All farming here is uneconomic, and any that survives will be just as much part of theme-park Britain as tourism. But what a showcase Colonsay is! Alas, another visit and still no chance to see Oronsay – an island only at high tide – with its great ruined fourteenth-century priory and giant stone cross. St Columba was said first to have set foot on British soil here, but moved on to Iona because Ireland is still visible from Oronsay.

Iona: Where Christianity Arrived

During dinner our passage through the Sound of Iona takes us close by the beautiful island of that name, whose importance and fame have always greatly exceeded its size. While looking out for the landing place and then the Abbey, however, my thoughts are mainly about a fairly recent accident in which a group of young men crossing a rough sea after an evening out on Mull were drowned. The loss of four workers badly hurts such a small community and, coupled with the decline in farming's profitability, inevitably means changes in the culture and value system with greater dependence on tourism... not that you would exactly dismiss Iona as a piece of theme-park Britain. Buses and coaches do line up at Fionnphort opposite (only residents may bring motor vehicles), and crowds swarm around the landing place, but Iona is utterly unspoilt.

One can well imagine the feelings aroused in St Columba (or Columcille) when, aged 42, in the company of twelve monks, symbolic of Jesus and the twelve, he first set eyes on it and set about making it the powerhouse of Scottish Christianity. He had set sail from Ireland, as Adammán puts it, 'because he wished to become a pilgrim for Christ's sake'. In AD721, St Bede confirmed: 'There came from Ireland into Britain a famous priest and abbot, a monk by habit and life, whose name was Columba, to preach the Word of God.'

Of this I was reminded a few days ago in John J Ó Ríordáin's *A Pilgrim in Celtic Scotland*. By far his most compelling chapter is 'Iona of My Heart', which everyone might benefit from reading before paying a visit and certainly I will do before next returning.

We are inevitably moved as, between starter and main course, we pass close by the Abbey and recall the sincere ecumenicalism of the Iona Community. Their newsletter, *The Coracle*, is always welcome through our letterbox. Services at the Abbey are often packed, but somehow to arrive here by coach and short ferry crossing, with other coachloads doing the island in a few hours, lacks yesterday's thrill of being more of a pioneer even if arriving by the old tourist steamer *King George V*.

Providing they don't expect luxury, those staying at the Abbey for a week enjoy the best of all worlds. You certainly need at least a couple of days even to begin to appreciate the Abbey; time to explore the marvellous white sandy beaches on the west shore and walk to the far north, where you can hear the tide change while looking at the panorama of islands, Staffa with its famous basalt columns prominent in the foreground. Though the island is never really overcrowded, a deep peace descends when the last of the day trippers departs.

For us tonight, just passing through the Sound is sheer magic.

II

STILL ADRIFT IN THE ISLANDS

Tiree and Coll

Next morning, on our week-long 'Adrift in the Islands' cruise, it is Tiree's turn for us to ask how soon, dear island, can we return to enjoy your special pleasures: workaday, untouristy, with more than a touch of the atmosphere of how things must have been when communities were self-dependent, and those visiting from England might as well have come from another planet. Efforts to rent a car or hire a taxi have failed, so we go on the ship's own bus tour. Ever the journalist, I would have preferred to pursue my own line... and have long been fascinated by this large (eleven by six miles) flat island, the Land Below the Waves, where parts of the coastline boast as sunny and dry a climate as anywhere in Britain.

The bus gives most people what they want: a visit to the museum emphasising Tiree's down-to-earth character, and views of the flat landscape and white beaches beyond the machair's rich grazing with colourful flowers as we go on to the thatched cottage museum, with its collection of domestic memorabilia and farm implements from yesteryear. Next to this is one of the island's sparse catering facilities: we file in for morning coffee. Then there's time to walk toward the white sand and discover it is alive with lapwings (or peewits) with their long crests and poignant cries. When a thick flock takes off, we note the slow beat of their broad, rounded wings. Then a couple of passengers arrive on the ship's bicycles they have borrowed. They cycle at nearly every stop and certainly have done the right thing here, seeing much more of the island than we do by bus. We are allowed two stops at a mini-supermarket. They haven't sorted the papers off the daily plane on our first call; we pillage the stand before the locals came to pick their choice of reading on the second. But the bus doesn't go half far or fast enough for me, and much of my curiosity remains unassuaged on my first visit.

I long for the open road, even to soak up the undoubted sameness of this low-lying land where a population of 800 (just over a hundred years ago it was 4,500) still substantially exists on crofting and fishing. Remember the definition of a croft? A parcel of land surrounded by legislation. Blown sand has enriched much of the soil even on some of the low slopes of the few hills inland. Astonishingly for the Hebrides, little more than a third of the land is too poor for agriculture. Bird-life abounds, corncrakes reviving splendidly, and there are no rabbits to compete with sheep on the grazing.

The history is so utterly complicated and contorted that it is more relaxing to stay with the landscape... except that once a population was imported mainly for military reasons, and crofting and family life somehow flourished alongside the constant warring of past centuries. Later much of the population was cruelly squeezed out despite a valiant effort at kelping, based on burning seaweed. (The remains of the factory is something I should like to have seen.) In the 1939-1945 war life must have been transformed by the squadrons of bombers based here. The flat land has been the stage on which much hardship has been endured, but at least this is no theme park and indeed Gaelic culture is more flourishing now than for decades past.

One specific historical incident is worth recording if only to show that the destructive power of the journalist isn't confined to our own times. In the 1880s there was much agitation in the Highlands for land reform, and when Greenhill Farm on Tiree became vacant the Land League asked the Duke of Argyle to split it into as many different tenancies as possible. However, the secretary of the local branch disloyally stepped in and took the whole farm. Previous grazing rights were cancelled and, to protect the Sheriff's officer delivering the eviction notices, the Duke brought in 25 policemen and forty Glasgow Commissioners. MacBrayne's agent in Oban refused passage, so they had to hire their own boat. When they landed, unassisted, their passage was blocked. The press were outraged at the Duke's behaviour, but a *Scotsman* reporter, who had only reached Tobermory, stirred things up with artistic licence. The police, the paper reported, had been attacked 'from the mountains and hedgerows of Tiree'.

Reading this, the government panicked, and sent three ships with troops and fifty extra police. When they arrived things were surprisingly friendly. Among other common-sense measures, it was agreed that all reporters would despatch their pieces together. Not good enough for the *Scotsman*'s chap, who had belatedly arrived on the scene. He sneakily sent off his despatch by carrier pigeons. But they were attacked by truth-respecting seagulls, and then arrested. Reputedly, the only action the police took was to charge the frightened birds with ungentlemanly behaviour. Fear and farce have ever intermingled in many island crises.

Eight men were later arrested but returned as heroes after concerted campaigning throughout Scotland. Not that even now is there a solution to Scotland's controversial landownership, a different kind of feudalism being exercised by some of the new owners of vast mainland estates.

In the afternoon to the neighbouring but quite different island of Coll. No chance of a taxi or rented car here, nor anything organised. For the first time on this trip we dock (as opposed to using our small boats) but there is no sign of a village. A brisk walk brings us to the beginning of attractive Arinagour. 'Your first visit?' asks an old man cheerfully.

'Cream teas' boasts a notice on the Coll Hotel, but on an early May Saturday afternoon the bar is already heaving with people into serious drinking and is off-putting to Sassenachs. So we go to the adjoining Lighthouse Gallery, where Kip Poulson displays many of his own delicate watercolours together with the work of a variety of local artists. Other passengers take a quick look and disappear. 'The ship doesn't help us much,' says Kip.

He's in Coll because of a career decision to enjoy a better lifestyle. Shortly he's off to Paris for a month or two to mount a one-man exhibition; many of his watercolours are of Paris. He's not short on words. 'I came from Shropshire nine years ago. I love it here, though everything is second rate. There aren't any major archaeological sites; even our standing stones are short. We don't have peat, but do have turbary (peat cutting) rights on Tiree. I haven't had any meat from off the island for six years; the butcher on Tiree will send it, but it's very expensive. But we've got chickens, and in contrast with Tiree, many rabbits – so many that farmers club together to get some control over them.'

It doesn't sound great, until: 'But we've a great community spirit. Everyone listens to everyone and everyone goes to every island happening. Publication of *The Coll Magazine* is always an event, and there's a lively school with nineteen kids. But if you come back on holiday, you'll need a car.'

'But we won't be able to get across the island at all today,' I say, realising just how big Coll is, with roads winding through the hills instead of the dead flat, straight ones of Tiree.

'I'll close up and take you,' he offers. We were not hinting; one doesn't go into an art gallery to fetch out the owner as chauffeur! But, yes, thanks, and we go bumpily off. We pass the remains of early daffodil patches, blooms from here once being sold alongside those from the Scillies. There is a big farm, going cheap at only £70 to £80 an acre, though cottages are keenly in demand. We bump more heavily off the road, to top a hillock: below are miles of sandy beaches stretching south west and north east along the western seaboard. Later we weave a rocky way to one of them, alas with its detritus of oil and garbage. Barra can be spotted above the rollers.

Kip makes a perfect guide. 'We have discovered a Viking dry dock at Eileraig. Ships would have approached it by coming in between two pips on the hilltop. We've not yet told the Royal Commission for Ancient & Historic Monuments.' He is sure he has sold us the idea of a holiday here. 'Book through Scotsell; it's cheaper than CalMac even for their own part,' he advises.

Back on board, while others read the Saturday papers, only we seem to have *The Coll Magazine*, 80 enterprising A5 pages of news, views, ads and community spirit, all for £2.50. Definitely another place for a return visit, with the added attraction of the Project Trust being based at the island's south west. Some of the young people my Charitable Trust sponsors to spend a gap year between school and university usefully in the developing world come here for their briefing. The shock of spending time on Coll provides a useful introduction to the very different lifestyle to which they will have to adapt.

Between Abandoned Islands

Next morning is different: no landing, but an exhilarating sail around the islands south of Barra, with a much-photographed passage through the Sound of Mingulay between that island and Pabbay. Popping out into the unsheltered Atlantic with its heavy swell brings housekeeping to an abrupt halt as most passengers seek the privacy of their rooms. Along with Sandray, astonishingly these islands of great heights and steep cliffs once supported habitation. We feel slightly giddy looking up at the lighthouse atop the northern tip of Mingulay; it comes slowly into view above the sheer cliff as we press on gently westward through a narrow passage. Providing you get your angle right, the bright sunshine makes for perfect snaps.

'An island so remote that it is easier to reach America than get there,' a traveller wrote of Mingulay in 1887, by which time the isolated, close-knit population had already receded from its peak of around 160. The Edinburgh branch of the Free Church Ladies' Association amazingly chose it for a school that usefully gave the island's children a basic education before being closed as a failure because (surprise!) the stoutly Roman Catholic population did not rapidly become Protestant. Evacuation to the island of Vatersay, off Barra, was completed after the final five-year run-down in 1912. We can only guess at the feelings of those saying farewell to the island that was all that most of them had ever known; the little patches painstakingly made cultivable, the cottage looms they had to leave behind (cheap imported cloth had killed the market for laboriously-woven sheep's wool), the coves which provided the fish and the cliffs where men of all ages nimbly went fowling to supplement their diet.

Just south of Mingulay is Berneray (not to be muddled with the larger island of the same name newly linked by causeway to North Uist) whose Barra Head is where the Outer Hebrides strung out over a hundred miles south from Lewis finally peter out. Most visitors prefer the more accessible Inner Hebrides, but the Outer Hebrides have much to offer, including landscapes and cultures utterly un-British. With additional causeways and a direct short ferry between the two groups of Lewis and Harris (always one island) and Berneray-North Uist-Benbecula-South Uist-Eriskay, you can drive through most of them in a day, though you'll not regret a week or longer. Expect the unexpected, especially in the way things are said, and take a good guide book or two for you'll start out by knowing virtually no more about them than when you perhaps first noticed their extraordinary shapes in your school atlas. From the days of the saints, nothing is quite the same here.

This is what the author of *A Pilgrim in Celtic Scotland*, referred to as we passed Iona in my first chapter, has to say about the saints that seem to be attached to so many of the islands:

Mingulay has a Celtic monastic site dating from early mediaeval times. Barra has St Finbarr and the footings of a beehive cell said to have been that of St Brendan the Navigator. Eriskay was the birthplace of Donald-Mac-Iain-Vich-Hamish, a Samson-like warrior who defeated a vastly superior force at the battle of Carinish in AD 1601. It was also where Bonnie Prince Charlie first landed in '45; and the same island saw the sinking of *The Politician* in 1941, freighted with crates of *uisge beatha* – a godsend to the thirsty islanders and the basis for Compton Mackenzie's book *Whisky Galore!* South Uist has a monastic site associated with St Donan, as well as Flora MacDonald's birthplace, a missile-testing site, and probably the tallest statue of the Virgin and Child in the world. On Benbecula – *the island of the small bare hill* – Donald-Allan MacIsaac took me on a tour of a Columban site, and later, pointing to a grassy mound between road and sea, remarked with emphasis: 'That's the spot where St Cormac the Sailor first taught us the Christian Faith.' The little isle of Grimsay boasts the ruins of St Michael's Chapel, the legacy, it is said, of the saintly Lady Amie, heiress of Loarn and estranged wife of John of Islay. North Uist has Trinity College, and Berneray is proud of Donald Macleod, alias '*The Old Trojan*', a veteran of the '45, who married three times and had twenty children by the first wife, none by the second and nine by the third. His third bride was eighteen while he himself was pushing eighty. He died at the age of one hundred and three – the headstone only credits him with ninety – when his youngest child was only nine. St Clement's, at Rodel in Harris, is keeper of his bones. Lewis has the Callanish Standing Stones, and an ancient church site dedicated to St Maelrubha at the Butt of Lewis. And this listing gives only a handful of possible places to which the pilgrim might make tracks.

'I was rather pleased with that paragraph,' Father O'Ríordáin said when giving me permission to quote it. So he should be. 'Yes, writing the book was mainly good fun, but hardship occasionally, especially on a rough sea to the Faroes. I've always been interested in these early Irish saints and wanted to encourage people going to the islands, especially to the Scottish ones, to think in terms of a pilgrimage rather than just tourism... to give them that little extra to reflect on in the context of the extraordinary history and geography.' *A Pilgrim in Celtic Scotland* is published by The Columbus Press at Blackrock, Dublin.

Barra and Self-Publishing

In the afternoon we are supposed to land in Vatersay, but we're pleased the swell is too great and make for our overnight mooring at Castlebay in Barra, the largest of the individual Outer Hebrides and the only one on which we land this cruise. The approach by the castle in the loch, which gives the place its name, is again extraordinarily photogenic, though the castle is a modern rebuild by a later MacNeil since their original mediaeval tribal home was burnt in the eighteenth century. When maintenance became too costly, Historic Scotland took it over for a rent of £1 and a bottle of whisky a year. An improved ferry link to the Western Isles' only mediaeval castle is promised and no doubt tourists will learn of the clan of Irish pirates who first occupied it, of the banquets when it was the seat of Barra's rulers and of the days when hundreds of vessels of the herring fleet filled the harbour and curing done ashore gave much employment. A bit of this and a bit of that, staunchly again Roman Catholic, Barra is as varied as it is compact (eight miles by four), but invariably friendly.

'Excuse me,' I shout to the guy holding our rope on the quay below as we are about to dock. 'I once met a taxi driver who wrote books; think her name was Mary something.' I don't have to add I am hoping to see her, for in this island possibly above all others there is an acceptance of friendships, even relationships, spreading over many visits and absences. 'Guess who's back?' I heard. Then a few minutes later: 'Know who I saw yesterday?'

I'm told I want Mary Hatcher. There is of course no directory in the phone kiosk. 'Nobody by that name in Barra, only in Castlebay,' says the operator, probably in England, though Telecom have pioneered the handling of some directory enquiry calls at private homes in the

Highlands. Mary answers immediately and, though it is Sunday afternoon, is on her way.

First stop the Barra Hotel, one of several built with government money to encourage tourism. One wouldn't want to build in that stark 1960s style today, but the view of bay and cliffs is unbeatable. Mary needs no inviting to present her progress report. 'After success with the three children's books I had written for my grandchildren when you were here last, I broke my leg and was encouraged to self-publish my first novel, *The Marshalls in Hebridean Harmony*. You know I was partially dyslexic at school and given no encouragement. They only told me about my writing defects. I found a printer in *Writers' News*, which I joined after you told me about it last time, and did 500 copies for £1,400, and charged £5.50 per copy. I was terribly anxious to avoid one of those vanity publishers.

'I thought that if jewellery makers could have their own exhibition why not a publisher – I call my imprint Barra Books & Flowers. So the launch was at our Heritage Centre: they sold sixty copies that day, more than many new books sell at an Edinburgh launch I'm told. The local tourist office, shop and hotel sell it. They sell out here [pointing to the reception office] each season. I'm on the Barra website, good for overseas sales. Ten per cent goes to charity; I want to make £1,000 for the Macmillan nurses. It's a hobby that pays a bit but is lots of fun... I sell quite a few for Christmas presents in the taxi.'

After tea, her neat brown hair ruffled in the wind, she poses with her usual smile on a rock overlooking a turbulent bay. 'Oh,' she adds vivaciously, '*The People's Friend* took four extracts. So I'm going to write another novel. It helps, especially as I've given up taxiing after the pubs close.'

Then she says: 'The good thing was that I learned the difference between vanity publishers, who I wanted to keep away from, and being a self-publisher.'

There is indeed the world of difference. Whatever they call themselves, vanity publishers appeal to the ego and, often with false promises, extract substantial sums to 'publish' your book. Nearly everything submitted to some firms is said to be of very publishable standard. A section of a telephone directory broken into lines like verse was once described as an important contribution to the English language. What in fact such publishers do is charge you expensively for printing; what they seldom do is make real sales, so the promise of above-average royalties is meaningless. Though at least one print-to-order publisher honestly explains you won't get your investment back, each year large numbers of authors are hooked by those ads asking if you have a book to publish and pay dearly for very little. Real publishers do not need to advertise for manuscripts.

Self-publishers market their own books. You can employ professional help, as indeed did Mary for things like editing and printing but, like her, you need the ability to push your own wares. It obviously helps to have a 'constituency', which might be your local area, or a specialised subject served by a magazine and society or two – a definite audience you can reach. So while it is hard for an unknown author successfully to launch a self-published novel, an increasing proportion of titles on bookshops' thriving 'local interest' tables come from self-publishers or very small firms, many of which have grown out of self-publishing. Self-publishing is respectable and growing rapidly as fewer commercial houses are interested in titles of limited interest. Probably two-thirds of the titles David & Charles published in the 1960s and 1970s would not now be economic. For one thing, the library demand has withered. Not only did the public library system once absorb around 500 copies of most new books, but they were sales made immediately on publication and helped cashflow. Collectively, libraries now take as few as 25 copies of even medium-priced specialist titles.

So self-publishing steps into the breach. To some extent it is a return to earlier times when most books of local and regional interest came from a bookshop or other institution or were financed by their author or their patron. There is even a return to the tradition of 'subscribers' undertaking to buy a copy or two; once more, lists of them appear in some new titles. Self-publishers can engage in all kind of devices, heavy on time and local contacts and commitment, impossible for the London publisher with high overheads and little local knowledge.

Had Mary Hatcher persuaded a London imprint to take on her novel, there might have been more sales around the country but the local base would not have yielded as much. However, it is said that from now on authors will have to do more of the publisher's job, especially as far as marketing and publicity are concerned. Authors who say they merely want to write and are not interested in sales, and in extreme cases even decline to be interviewed on television, will find it increasingly harder to get published.

Practising what I preach, at this stage of this book's existence it has not yet been mentioned to any publisher. While I hope to find one to exploit general sales in a way that no individual (albeit retired publisher) could manage, I am prepared to do it myself if need be, always thinking of who might buy it, and compiling a mailing list. When I come to present it to a commercial house, this knowledge could be invaluable. I could even buy an edition to sell on myself. The reality is that only a few titles are published in this genre of literary travel. Timing, supply and demand, the state of the national and publishing economies, will decide things. With editors, even ownerships, changing ever more rapidly, there is no point in making enquiries well in advance of completion.

Brought up on the island, Mary went to school in Oban at the age of twelve and at fourteen into service. Her first English husband didn't work out, so with her second husband (recently retired as school janitor) she started the taxi business. She has a keen perception of island strengths and weaknesses. She is proud of the fact that the population is rising; it's now over 1,300. What used to be the smelly fish meal factory is now the supply depot supporting the big housing programme. (There is still a processing plant for edible shellfish.) She loves seeing old homes improved, but we heartily agree that some of the futuristic modern bungalows are ill at ease in the island landscape.

The real problem is arbitrary administrative boundaries. The main ferry goes to Oban, but secondary education and medical care is at Stornoway. As already mentioned, there is a new, shorter ferry link, but the journey still involves extensive land transit – along the road that goes to the sea, across causeways linking South Uist and Benbecula and North Uist, and then along the length of Harris and Lewis. More serious health care, sometimes even an X-ray, means Glasgow, from which there is a daily plane landing on the beach at low tide. This week low tide is in the afternoons. The airport, whose flight controller has won a much-publicised campaign to be paid on a par with those at much busier places, is at the north, where we temporarily leave the round-the-island road to explore the peninsula with its large sand dunes and fields of machair thicker with primroses than we have ever previously seen. Compton Mackenzie's old house is pointed out; *Whisky Galore*, based on Barra, is still a bestseller.

'There's always been heaps of talent on the island – crafts, poetry, ballads. The Barra Live Music Festival really is something. Visitors, especially from overseas, just don't know what goes on. By the way the other day an American lady asked if it was OK that I was driving on the cycle track; she couldn't believe it was a proper road, but we have our own bus service and there's also a volunteer-run bus for pensioners. Don't be sorry for us, I tell visitors. It's them living in crowded cities who should be pitied. Local traditions survive strongly, but I'm afraid table manners have gone the way they have everywhere because kids take their example from the telly.

'Barra is the Western Isles in miniature. We've got high mountains and fertile lowlands, Gaelic culture and up-to-the-minute communications. The only thing it's hard to buy on any of the islands is clothing. We're all dependent on mail order.'

Traditionally it was a happy island, for the McNeils weren't bad. Trouble came when they sold it in 1838. The new owner's idea was to turn it into a penal colony. The government didn't favour that, so instead the owner called in the police to help turn the crofters on a subsistence diet out of their homes. Happily, the McNeils then came back.

We thread down the complicated eastern seaboard, past Mary's home back to Castlebay, and then go across the causeway to Vatersay which has lost its island status and has changed much since the remnants of the population of Mingulay were evacuated here, scattered among several townships so the old community spirit could not be recreated. We pass a monument commemorating those who lost their lives in a wreck in the 1850s, and then the remains of a reconnaissance plane that crashed ninety years later. Then Mary enjoys a tour of the *Hebridean Princess*. When will we come back and actually stay here? And by the way – her last shot – her new novel is 199 pages for £6.95.

Canna and People of Great Faith

Monday is the warmest day yet, 80 degrees Fahrenheit in the shade on the ship's bridge. After smooth passage, we anchor in the delightful horn-shaped harbour of the small Inner Hebridean island of Canna. Having been here before, and enjoying the luxury of a good book, I decide to stay on the sundeck watching our small boats going to and fro, a visiting yacht departing, people walking around the shore to the post office-cum-shop in a hut, and a tractor crossing by bridge to the separate isle of Sanday. The woods protecting Canna House and distant high cliffs complete as delightful a setting as you could imagine.

The house belongs to 96-year-old Margaret Campbell, an American who has lived here for sixty years and still types her correspondence on one of those indestructible black Imperial typewriters that were once the mainstay in newsrooms. It was given to her by Sir Compton Mackenzie. She was sixteen when she first fell in love with the Western Isles, and this resulted in her meeting her husband Dr John Campbell. When they bought the island (just a mile wide and four and a half long) the population was 38; in 1821 it had peaked at 438. Now there are just fourteen, including three attending the tiny school. Because there are no heirs, Dr John gave the island to the National Trust, which runs it as a single farm. Margaret hopes that after she has gone the house might become a study centre.

When a newspaper reporter recently profiled 'Candid Canna', Margaret was quoted as dismissing the recent television series describing the everyday quarrels of castaways marooned by the BBC on the uninhabited island of Taransay as nonsense. 'I'd say it just shows how we human beings have deteriorated,' she declared, adding that it seemed 'nobody could do anything for themselves.' Whatever you think of TV's fictitious presentation of Scotland, or for that matter Ireland's Ballykissangel, for sure seeing real life is much more rewarding. More and more people buy the expanding range of books and pamphlets explaining every conceivable aspect of life here.

For example, religious beliefs are more deeply held among islanders and Highlanders, especially along the west coast, than elsewhere in Britain. In the past, people have often walked many miles of barren countryside and crossed angry waters to take part in services of their particular Christian faith or denomination, the minister waiting to start until everyone he thinks will come has arrived. Impatience has never been a fault here. Roman Catholics have shown especial perseverance in the small islands of the southern Outer Hebrides. In many ways South Uist is more Irish than Ireland.

Most Protestants were left without church or minister when the Church of Scotland divided at 'the disruption' of 1843, when only 470 out of 1,195 ministers were left, and so the vast majority of congregations formed the Free Church. Subsequent divisions and reunions have built into an amazingly complicated yet very human and compelling story told by Douglas Andsell in *The People of Great Faith: The Highland Church 1690–1900*, the book I am buried in for this part of the cruise. 'The disruption' has left a huge mark on society. Only the top brass were left in many Church of Scotland congregations, and the crofting majority had to improvise, using any old building, the open air, and even in one area (where a site for a permanent building was denied) a floating chapel towed around by a steam tug. Up to 700 could worship aboard, the size of the congregation being immediately clear to visiting ministers arriving at the last moment by how low the boat lay in the water.

Buried in the book? Yes, but with breaks to enjoy the vivid, sharp yet gentle, constantly changing prospect of Canna as we drift to on our anchor. It is not surprising that the whole island is a nature reserve and bird sanctuary, the number of species actually breeding being a rich 71.

This is heaven, though my sunglasses aren't meant for sustained reading and my head is becoming steadily redder. I resort to protecting my neck with a handkerchief tucked under a macintosh cap, which Sheila laughs at when she returns from a morning's walk.

Over the Sea to Skye

Over lunch we motor to south-western Skye and anchor in Loch Scavaig for access to Loch Coruisk. I'm hooked on reading, but enjoy the high drama of sea, sky, towering cliffs exhibiting the effects of millennia of wear and tear by the fierce elements, and of course the snow-topped Cuillins. As once more we swing on our anchor, private civilisation, in the form of tea and home-baked fruit cake in an empty lounge, doesn't come amiss either. The rest have gone on their walk round Loch Coruisk and tell me what I missed, silly man. Sheila is exhilarated with the sense of achievement of doing that strenuous walk – chilled champagne served in real cut-glass flutes by the crew en route – and getting close to seals on the way back in one of the small boats.

There are marvellous close-ups of the beetling cliffs and a string of deeply-penetrating sea lochs as we make our way to our overnight mooring in Loch Harport. Sun and shadow, even now occasional mist, offshore islands, traces of past and even present habitation here and there... surely nothing can beat the pleasure of enjoying such a notable piece of our own coastline from a comfortable ship. Cocktails on deck complete perfection.

Tuesday morning is spent circumnavigating the northern half of Skye, past Loch Dunvegan. We have just heard that a new Raven Press, specialising in wood-block prints, is to be established at Skinidin on a side loch of that remote stretch of water. Then calmly through the Little Minch, past Waternish Point, across the entrance to huge Loch Snizort with its port of Uig for the ferry to North Uist and Harris, seeing lots of human activity around Lub Score before rounding Rubha Hunish and soon turning south.

The mainland to the west comes into sight as we keep close to the majestic west-facing cliffs, some with basalt columns reminiscent of Mendelssohn's Staffa, and catch glimpses of my favourite island road. Though you can only walk to the very far north at Rubha Hunish, the clockwise circuit round Skye's northern (or Trotternish) peninsula offers an eye-gripping two- or three-hour drive from Portree. Start out by Loch Leathan, the Storr and his shorter companion the Old Man of Storr enticingly in sight almost from the start, though you only pass them beyond the Loch. Then closer to the coast, and very close indeed past a waterfall before Staffin, where new homes are the order of the day. Near the north, the action increases as you pass one of Britain's most dramatically perched hotels at Flodigarry, then go west for a few miles before turning south, with time for a visit to the monument to Flora Macdonald followed by a cup of tea and a fine piece of home bakery at a cafe-cum-hostel with a breathtaking panorama of sea and islands. The return is via Uig where the ferry (these days a surprisingly large roll-on-roll-off affair) leaves for Tarbet on Harris and Lochmaddy on North Uist to a complicated timetable according to the day of the week. That gives the maximum variety of opportunities for locals as well as visitors to cross the Minch. Finally back to Portree... except that I've almost forgotten we are actually still on the *Hebridean Princess* arriving there by sea. By the standards of the last few days, Portree strikes us as a mega-metropolis.

It is the first time I have arrived by sea since my first visit in 1954. That was by the steamer based there which made a weekday trip via

Raasay and Kyle of Lochalsh to Mallaig and back... a popular duty for the crew since it was almost office hours. In those days one passed only an occasional car or van on the single-track road to Kyleakin, bound for the then small car ferry over to Kyle of Lochalsh. By the last year of that ferry crossing, the summer Saturday queues were as long as they used to be at Torpoint in pre-Tamar Bridge days. Now, it is no longer automatically 'Over the sea to Skye'; just about everyone must have heard of the bridge and its expensive tolls.

Despite the increased crowds, remarkably – in the eyes of the occasional visitor – Portree's centre hasn't changed much, though there is massive new housing and industry on the outskirts. Certainly people no longer wait discreetly in a back street for the Sunday papers to arrive in mid-evening, smuggled in by a special small boat since all public transport halted for the Sabbath. Portree's centre somehow manages to combine saying 'Here is a civilised place' along with making sure you realise just how far away you are from the real centres of Britain. Real? What could be more real than Portree or the large, complicated island it serves as capital?

Quality has been maintained, since nobody goes to Skye for beach holidays and getting tanned. Just how big climbing and walking have become is demonstrated by the number of shops that will kit you out for the Cuillins, and sell you books about them. Except possibly at Hay-on-Wye, nowhere in Britain are books sold at a greater proportion of retail outlets than in Portree, but, apart from one well-balanced proper bookshop, they nearly all concentrate on walking, climbing and exploring the islands. Buy your book and boots in the same transaction.

The weather has started to deteriorate and it is a bit late for sun hats but, deprived of even window shopping for nearly a week, Sheila persuades me that here is a once-in-a-lifetime opportunity to acquire perfect footwear, which I have to admit proves useful.

There is much new building on Skye, and many incomers practise old or new skills in their craft workshops, producing articles such as Batik with Celtic designs, soaps, silverware, paintings, cloth and clothes. Many others work at their computers and word-processors doing jobs which were once town based. The range of hotels and restaurants has greatly increased, amazingly Skye now boasting more red rosettes than many resorts with a far larger number of hotel beds such as Torquay.

If you have just one fine day for a drive when in Skye, devote at least part of it to the road from Broadford to Elgol. Stop at the ruined chapel and its graveyard only a few miles out from Broadford to experience a touch of Skye's sad past and to learn about how Britain's highest mountains (deeply eroded roots of old volcanoes) were once under the ground... and how for a few years from 1907 another marble company ran a 3ft-gauge railway to take the stone to Broadford quay. First heading this way and then that, up and down and around a loch, the road, itself substantially improved, is no longer the hunting ground of an occasional lonely charabanc with grinding gears, but on busy days carries substantial traffic. The needs of motorists and climbers are served by three cafes, the last of them with a view of many of Scotland's inhabited islands as well as the beach at Elgol beneath. Be careful before you boast of naming the islands, for even experienced island-hoppers are confused when viewing from a new angle. What struck me on my last drive was how young are most of the visitors, Continentals and Brits, enthusiastic but patient, cycling and provisioned for hours of climbing. For the older or less adventurous who seldom explore beyond their cars, this is as close to the awesome Cuillins as you will get. Here as elsewhere in Skye there are new houses and community spirit, but don't think of settling here till you have experienced a whole winter of battering winds and soggy mists. The population decline that started with the Clearances, the cruel removal of people to make way for more profitable, less demanding, and more law-abiding sheep, went on remorselessly for the best part of two centuries but is happily reversed now in a modest kind of way. Expansion is in the air.

There is still some older industry, too, including Skye Marble at Torrin on the road from Broadford winding among the hills and rocks to Elgol. The quarry employs a dozen folk but, though some lumps of white marble are used as garden ornaments, it doesn't slice well and so is mainly crushed on site for use in exposed aggregate and roughcasting. When first visiting Elgol in the early 1950s, I was overwhelmed by the scenery. My patronage had been canvassed over breakfast in a boarding house by the owner-driver of a charabanc who made one of those happy island understatements. Most people found the trip, including a connecting boat for a walk round Loch Coruisk 'not too disappointing'.

Skye's beauty and variety are breathtaking as we get into our small boat at the landing stage at Portree to rejoin the *Hebridean Princess* for dinner. We determine that we must come back soon. Not doing so is inexcusable since improved roads and the new bridge mean we can now have a leisurely breakfast in Nairn and an early lunch in Portree.

Through the Islands back to Oban

Next through the Sound of Raasay, past Scalpay, and under the new bridge to the Kyle of Lochalsh, where we tie up. Let's go to the bar on the railway station where everything happens, I suggest. No longer is that true; it has become a fish restaurant. The high-class touring train, the *Royal Scotsman*, is also here overnight, and some of its crew and ours show off each other's brand of luxury. Only a dozen or so have sat down for a sumptuous dinner in the renowned restaurant car but I am assured the train is full; the others have gone by road to Skye for dinner. Our drink? We decide on an old favourite haunt, the former railway-owned Lochalsh Hotel, long and narrow, all rooms having a view across to Skye. One cannot help missing the sound of the ferry – the ramps are already industrial archaeology – and I also miss the gracious style that was once the hallmark of railway hotels.

Next day we continue on our route south, through the Sound of Sleat, a delightful stretch of water between Skye and the mainland, where there are now few opportunities to travel by larger boat, though discerning motorists in no hurry use the seasonal Glenelg-Kylerhea private ferry. Says its timetable leaflet: 'When you leave the A87 you will enter a different world, steeped in history and abundant with wildlife, travel through the spectacular scenery and discover a hidden sanctuary off the beaten track, and the home of the original ferry to Skye.' It is a remarkable way to reach Skye, but the simple ferry and its ramps are without any facilities. This morning, as we motor down the seaway that makes Skye an island, we delay a ferry carrying two cars and a van.

Further on, we pass the less frequent but much larger CalMac ferry on the run from Mallaig to Armadale. Visitors who use maps and timetables for their planning often don't realise that the usual public transport route from Kyle of Lochalsh to Mallaig (connecting the two separate railway systems in the Highlands) means bridge to Skye, bus through the Garden of Skye (or Sleat) and ferry back to the mainland. Those who do delight in it, for this gentler part of the island has many of its own attractions, such as the opportunity to travel through the colourful grounds of Armadale Castle in a traditional caravan behind a West Highland heavy horse.

If you plan well, you can even spend a night at one of Sleat's many hotels and guest houses. Top of the range is Kinloch Lodge run by Lady Claire Macdonald of Macdonald, a lively, bubbly host who somehow has time to write articles, books, give cookery demonstrations and cook at the hotel, relish life and her extensive family, and make any guest she greets seem uniquely welcome.

Later, when we visited Sleat, we had to choose Kinloch Lodge. So the Achiltibuie cold smoked and South Uist hot-smoked salmon terrine served with cucumber and dill vinaigrette, the lightly curried cream celery and apple soup, roast saddle of Highland venison with port, ginger and green peppercorn sauce, pear almond tart, Scottish cheeses with Hebridean oatcakes, and the home-made fudge with coffee around the fire in the small drawing room were (as I'm sure readers will readily appreciate) only consumed by me in the interest of reportage. Sheila, and my son Gareth and his Australian wife Benny, who happened to be with us, tired from New York a few days after September 11, were of course free to enjoy it enthusiastically. All four of us agreed that it was one of the very best meals we have ever had. Five courses plus coffee, guests served in unison at a sensible pace by friendly staff, the chef excelling in every detail.

Why so many (fourteen to date) books? 'I'm greedy; I like to eat,' replied Lady Claire, just back from a busy day at a packed Broadford and Lochalsh festival of Skye food. Her authorship began accidentally when she was told an article she had written for the *Scottish Field* had won the Glenfiddich Cookery Writer's Award and a publisher asked her for a book. She is a person who knows her way around anything in which she becomes involved; her comments on a string of publishers and their houses are all spot on, or at any rate uncannily correspond to my own assessment. She must be a model author, willing to listen and learn, keen to promote her own books which dominate in the hotel's small shop, where we complete an order form for her soon-to-be-published latest book.

The hotel was 'once a doss house' under previous ownership, and Lady Claire has turned it round. It is the life she loves, though occasionally 'when people wish each other a lovely weekend, I ask myself what weekend'. With an excellent annexe (open fire in its lobby and its own bar), the operation is big enough to allow real delegation and make holidays possible. Staff training obviously comes naturally, making that vital difference from one of the chain hotels where you might either be well looked after, or suffer from an inexperienced waiter having a bad night.

Lady Claire says she 'fell into' being an hotelier, but born ones don't come better, and there is more to come, for beside the hotel second daughter Isabella and her husband are about to open Kinloch Cafe with 'real afternoon teas'... not that the fruit cake ('sorry it's so untidy but it should taste all right') and shortbread left anything to be desired. Lady Claire's parting shot: 'Skye provides such splendid ingredients that providing you take time to find them and cook them imaginatively without spoiling them, you really are on to a winner.'

Gareth, who used to be with me at David & Charles, has just given up the rat race. His farewell party on September 11 didn't happen, because his last task had to be to order his New York staff home. He tells us of his and Benny's plans for expanding their own publishing operations in New Zealand and Australia. Happily, this book's Australian and New Zealand edition is published by their imprint. But these are diversionary reflections as the *Hebridean Princess* passes Mallaig.

Just how little publicity is given to the connection between Kyle of Lochalsh and Mallaig was brought home when questioning people for *The Highland Railway Survey* I undertook for Highlands & Islands Enterprise. Many complained they could not go by train up one coast and back down the other. An Italian told me: 'I wasn't surprised my local station didn't know, but a bit upset when even Brit Rail in Rome couldn't help me. I was cross when nobody in London could help either, and flabbergasted when even in Inverness they didn't know if it were possible.' At least at busy times, Inverness station seems rigorously to restrict advice to train services, giving answers like 'We don't go there' when people try to book to places off the railway even if there is a connecting Post Bus.

The bus link between Inverness and Fort William is not in the railway timetable. 'Nothing to do with us.' How can we, decade by decade, admire the Swiss for doing it properly and insist on getting it wrong ourselves? British transport history is littered with examples of different operators preferring to maintain their independence rather than exercising common sense. One still hears of trains and ferries moving off just as connecting passengers approach them. Co-ordination seldom happens voluntarily and the mechanism to enforce it isn't there, though some local authorities including the Highland Regional Council do sometimes try to help before retreating dispiritedly.

Our last cruise call is at an oddity not listed in many guide books: Inverie, a cosy green enclave with lovingly cared-for gardens in mountainous Knoydart. Though it can be reached only by sea, it has its own local road system: when we were there, a fair trickle of traffic. And still the sun shines.

Finally we pass Mallaig, terminus of the wondrous West Highland Railway, celebrating its centenary. Most days in the summer there is a steam train from Fort William and, though it is lamentable that most trains are only Sprinter units with poor visibility from many seats, one can still feel a sense of adventure. At the very moment this paragraph was being written, Scotrail faxes a press release headed 'I'll have a black coffee, tuna sandwich and a guide book please!' *Iron Road to the Isles* is excellent value at £5.95 (Wayzgoose) and is being sold on the catering trolley. The House of Lochar now publish what was one of D&C's bestsellers, John Thomas's *The West Highland Railway*.

John tells the fascinating detail of how the Mallaig Extension (from Fort William) was forged through the inhospitable country. Robert McAlpine & Sons of Glasgow were the contractors, Robert, known as 'Concrete Bob', for concrete was used to an unprecedented extent and, curiously, concrete bridges and viaducts fit better into the landscape than masonry ones would have done. The local stone was anyway unworkable. There were other innovations, too, including the first water-driven turbine tunnelling. Robert's son, Malcolm, suffered serious internal injuries supervising the blasting of a tunnel, and one of the epic stories of railway buildings in remote areas is how, on hearing by telegraph that he was unlikely to survive, the father persuaded a distinguished Glasgow surgeon to come with him on a mad dash to Lochailort, first by special train along a route where the signal boxes had been closed for the night, to Fort William, and then by coach over the terrible Road to the Isles. They reached Lochailort in the early afternoon, and the surgeon performed a major operation with unsophisticated equipment. Four days and nights later, with the patient's condition still critical, the father and surgeon determined the only thing was to get him back to Glasgow. To prevent injurious jolting, relays of navvies carried him by stretcher (with breaks for two nights) most of the way to the railhead.

On his own luxurious special train to mark the line's centenary, the present Sir William McAlpine, a railway enthusiast, lovingly recalled the extraordinary exertions of the navvies. Thanks to them, the patient lived to the ripe old age of ninety, and of course McAlpines flourished as contractors. Sir William also used the opportunity to confirm a legend, that a horse and cart had plunged into the void of a tall pillar during concrete pouring in 1899. State-of-the-art technology clearly shows the cart with the skeleton of the horse still sitting vertically on top. The animal's neck was broken in the fall. The site was Loch nan Uamh, not as legend had it the famous Glenfinnan viaduct, for a long time the world's largest concrete structure.

So, still heading south, the distinctive shapes of Eigg, Rhum, Muck and more distant Barra, and then of Coll playing hide-and-seek with each other, show up before we enter the Sound of Mull and catch a rewarding glimpse of Tobermory. So into The Sound, another of those long narrows so many more people once appreciated from the water. Our last night is spent swinging around our anchor just off the mainland looking across to Mull.

The engines come to life early, we pass the southern tip of treeless Lismore, and return to the berth within a bustling Oban. We have a five-minute journey to the ferry for Mull. We have decided we need to let ourselves down gently from being Adrift in the Isles. One thing is certain: tonight's hotel room and dinner will not match these of the *Hebridean Princess*. Book your cabin early, especially for May or early June – before the midges arrive! But allow a little time for Oban, too. It looks most welcoming this sunny morning – but even in west wind is well protected by the island of Kerrera. The ferries large and small always add interest, while McCaig's folly sits over the townscape as it has since horse-and-carriage days. Oban's chief landmark is actually an unfinished building since McCaig, a kindly banker, ran out of money, though it is easy to tell his granite rotunda was based on Rome's Colosseum.

Perfection in Mull

One of the pleasures of journeying in different ways is the interest in the mode of the moment itself. In its own way, the modern, sizeable (two car-deck) CalMac ferry is as welcoming and as interesting as the *Hebridean Princess,* which before its transformation earned a living here in the days of lighter traffic. One fascinating thing about the forty-minute crossing (smooth this morning, but where the tides meet it is often rough) to Craignure is that passengers divide sharply between those for whom it is a regular happening and who know each other and of course the ferry staff, and those visiting at most half a dozen times in their lives. Several coachloads of those going on a day trip to Iona usually dominate in the morning.

Caledonian MacBrayne, universally referred to as CalMac, is a merger of the rival Clyde and Hebridean services of the LNER and LMS. Once competition was stiff, three pre-grouping railways luring business in a manner that today's supporters of privatisation can only imagine. Successive generations of families often remained loyal to their chosen line. This morning's paper worries the staff with its report of government intentions for CalMac. Will privatisation mean breaking up the company route by route? Will the managers be able to make their own bid? To what extent will the 'social' element of serving minority communities be honoured? But soon after our attention is concentrated on the panorama of mainland and islands of different size and character. This was the route of my first Scottish boat trip half a century ago and is as exciting as ever.

At Craignure, a fleet of buses wait for those crossing Mull's 38 miles on a day trip to Iona, and only a few of us take the short walk to a connecting 'boat train'. The first passenger-carrying railway ever built in the Hebrides, the Mull & West Highland Railway takes us in steam-hauled (though diesels are often used) miniature splendour to Torosay Castle, one of those Scottish baronial creations which, like its amazing gardens, is open to the public on a seasonal basis. Don't confuse Torosay with Duart Castle, seen clearly from the ferry. For centuries Duart has been the base for the MacLean clan, and was destroyed after the 1745 rebellion, but now restored. The railway, 10¼-inch gauge, one and a half miles long, and with three steam engines, two diesels and a sixth locomotive powered by the engine of a Mini-Minor, opened in 1983, and is the child of Graham Ellis. What a lovely life he must lead! Yes, in that he's a true enthusiast. 'Nearly all our services are boat trains'; and have I heard of the rally of steam cars being organised by the Alford Transport Museum (an excellent place)? But it's a 'very tight operation', traffic declining slightly, in line with the number of visitors to the island, and 'everyone has to be paid other than directors'. His big regret is that the planners wouldn't allow any development, not even the occasional appearance of a miniature train to meet the ferry more closely, on the sea side of the road. He reverts to steam road vehicles, recalling how steam lorries such as Fodens and Sentinels, once clustered around ponds at lunchtime – to take on water and let their drivers enjoy their pieces (baggin in Cheshire where he lived when young, or perhaps plain lunch in English).

The wettest of all the islands, Mull is gentler than most but still varied, with soft valleys, clusters of fertile farms, and endless variations of green even on some of the high, ribbed cliffs facing south west into the Firth of Lorn. Mull also boasts several attractive villages, and Tobermory is by far the nicest of all island capitals. It is undoubtedly where I would live if I had to move to an island. Much of Mull is civilised, with good hotels and restaurants, many cultural activities, entrepreneurial craftsmen and small industries. If you are a youngster fancying an island stay, visit in May when you will find nearly every one anxious to give you a summer job. The pity is that many visitors underestimate its size and worth, dashing off the ferry briefly to 'do' Tobermory and then taking the tortuous coastal road to Fionnphort for the Iona Ferry. From Tobermory to Fionnphort it is quicker to go back via Craignure, though you miss Mull's best scenery. Mull deserves at least a few days and I promise you'll not regret spending at least one night on Iona. You can then comfortably take the direct route to the Iona short ferry crossing and return by Tobermory.

Tobermory: The Entrepreneurial Island Capital

With the luxury of many previous visits, today's route starts along the main Tobermory road to Salen, then inland along the single-track road through Glen Aros and on, with mountains first on one side, then the other, but also woodland and farms, to Dervaig. It gives another opportunity to visit David Pitman who has run the village's bookshop-cum-cafe-cum-grocer, seller of coal, plants, petrol and almost every other conceivable thing for the past thirty years. Publication day of the *Oban Times* always brings increased activity, but customers also collect their daily papers, buy petrol, a tray of pansies, pork chops on special offer, while regulars wait patiently for their coffee. There is also a steady trickle of postcard sales, pamphlets and, of course, books. I first met David when he became a major customer for the *Mull* volume in the D&C 'Islands' series and many other titles of both local and general interest. Nowhere will you find a more fascinating range of books, or a bookseller with greater appreciation of their content. When at Oxford he co-edited *Isis* with Richard Ingrams, 'who didn't believe in doing the hard work'. I'm asked for my views on the new *Oxford Dictionary of Words of the Twentieth Century*, but handle it with care, for he has selected it as a birthday present for his sister. When a visitor buys a bottle of the local malt, one of the regulars mutters 'cauterised Dettol'. I'm asked will I have time to go to the nearby Mull Theatre? What am I writing? Why has D&C gone off the boil?

Tobermory also has an enterprising and formerly wonderful supportive bookseller, where as 'rep' I used to wait for people to select their fishing tackle before being 'seen'. Duncan Swinbanks has just expanded so that, though they are connected, he now has separate book and tackle shops. Books and tackle is just one combination of local trades. Browns of Tobermory, for example, advertise themselves as wine merchants and ironmonger. It has always been a joy to walk round the harbour with Main Street's colourful buildings and individual shops. The baker buys in little from the mainland. Four staff on the premises are supported by another four plus seasonal extras working in the bakery toward Dervaig. The fish shop has for decades supplied my businesses' Christmas 'thank yous' in the form of smoked trout, gently cured and, when tested blindfolded, preferred by most to smoked salmon. Also try the whisky cure, Tobermory trout, gravalax and the mixed hampers: spoil yourself and support an island economy. Smoking started in 1973, the shop following later, employing another eight people. There is a large craft shop in a disused church, a laundry in a shop building complete with ironing board for all to see, a jeweller making pieces of Celtic design on the premises and, up a stairway just off the street, the Tobermory Chocolate Factory.

Like the Tobermory Fish Company, it runs an excellent mail-order service. Fancy dark chocolate squares flavoured with Tobermory malt whisky (the distillery is at the end of the street), or maybe the Island Selection, all chocolate 70 per cent cocoa solids? Children under twelve are offered a half-hour chocolate workshop to make their own for mums and dads. Thanks to the Internet as well as tourism, business thrives and expansion into a purpose-built factory will mean Keith and Rhoda Drake employing two people besides their busy selves. They typify the spirit of Tobermory.

Schools not yet having broken up, our only disappointment is that none of the tea shops is open. So we walk breathlessly to Uppertown following a signpost to An Tobar Arts Centre, Gallery and Cafe.

Someone looking just like the retired farmer he turns out to be studies me surreptitiously and asks Sheila where we live. 'Nairn, I thought so, I've joined *Writers' News* and am taking a home study course... Tried to get in touch with you about a friend's railway heritage... Farming was great, especially until the 1960s. I used to take my bullocks over to Oban market, into which the railway ran. The stationmaster came round taking orders for trucks: there were two trainloads on tap... I've wanted to write all my life and have the time now... there are so many wonderful people about!'

His name is Kenneth Way, obviously a man of many interests. I thought he said he used to grow and graft fruit, but Sheila has to point out that he was talking about playing and teaching the flute – and the cello and clarinet. So we are into classical music with a railway touch: did I know that Rubbra started life looking after horses on the Great Western Railway? 'Do listen to his Mediaeval Latin Lyrics... I like the way he's sometimes described as having his back-to-Elizabethan style in a modern idiom. You know, there's still a great antagonism to classical music in the Highlands and Islands, but I've a wonderful pair of students, brother and sister, right now.'

Then back to railways: 'As a boy I went round those great locomotive works in Springburn.' And to writing: 'Can you teach writing?'

'Yes,' I say, adding, 'Of course, you must have some innate talent, but *Writers' News* home study courses have given enormous help and satisfaction to many.'

Kenneth is not so sure. 'Actually I've stopped my course; I don't like not being allowed to know my tutor personally.'

For obvious reasons, we have to protect tutors working from home. (On return to Nairn, I study his student-progress card, and the director of studies persuades him to get started again.)

Someone remembers that what we had come for was a cup of tea, and that is hastily organised while we pop into an exhibition of children's papier maché work. Plates, mugs, and other seemingly enamel, metal or porcelain objects, are almost unbelievably all paper. Perspective broadens to learn that the former school, of 1876, then in near ruin, was converted partly with money from the National Lottery, by a group led by an American into the present obviously thriving arts centre. An Tobar is Gaelic for The Well.

Mull once supported a population of over 10,000 nearly all living on a potato subsistence diet. Potato blight and the Clearances hurt especially hard here. Conditions for the starving in and around Tobermory, in what was in reality a squalid refugee camp, were shocking. All was made worse by the even crueller and more complete expulsion of the population of the adjoining island of Ulva, where 'Starvation row' and whole decayed villages remind the curious of harrowing times. Now there is little activity in Ulva beyond sheep rearing.

Yet there is a brighter side. The British Society for Extending the Fishing & Improving the Sea Coasts of the Kingdom, founded in 1786, sent a committee to Mull the following year, when Tobermory was little more than a 'change house' or inn, though already famous for its oysters. Land was bought and work started on a planned village only a year later again. The population of the island capital rose to 1,500 by 1821 and, if only to a small extent, offset the forced decline elsewhere a few decades later. The museum tells a very special story.

It is perhaps a strange place for a planned town, and the Society's only real achievement. Always popular with yachtsmen, and an important naval base in the 1939-45 war, Tobermory has worked well through the generations, developing and maintaining its own small but distinctive lifestyle in one of Britain's most picturesque settings. Not even Cornwall can better the scene: colour-washed houses front the middle of the bay with salt water lapping woods at one end and wooded cliffs the other.

Just how beautiful and favoured it is strikes home as we walk along the footpath beyond the Western Isles Hotel to the north west. They are removing scallops from their shells at the harbour, and below the path is the headquarters of an oyster farm. Out in the bay, fishing boats meld with yachts and other pleasure craft, some perhaps carrying divers, for ever since the wreck of a Spanish galleon escaping from Drake the long way home, this has been base for one of the nation's popular attractions for underwater exploration and hoped-for discovery of treasure. The peace is temporarily broken as the ferry on a third route to the mainland re-established only in recent times arrives with a couple of cars and three or four pedestrians, probably on a shopping foray from Ardnamurchan, a treasured peninsula we have no time to visit on this journey. A CalMac ship from the Outer Hebrides is following the last part of our route yesterday toward Oban, disappearing briefly beyond Calve Island, which helps protect Tobermory. For centuries many ships from eastern Europe came this way to the Mediterranean; it was safer than the pirate-ridden English Channel. I wonder if their captains had an eye for the scenery?

Along the path, well used by visitors to Tobermory who are naturally of the enquiringkind, we note there are more species of trees, shrubs and plants than we have seen on any English cliff top: a new species a yard it seems, for a considerable distance.

We are staying at the Western Isles Hotel, which throughout my youth was the subject of grumbles by adult relatives either unable to book when they wanted to, or not well looked after if they did. The largest hotel in the islands, it commands a fine situation, but its sheer size and shortage of local staff must make it hard to run. Our room is fine, but lunch suggests that meals are probably better elsewhere. So one evening we take the long, windy single track by Dervaig to the Calgary Farmhouse Hotel near Calgary's super sandy beach. It is still light after dinner and we go further along the road toward Ulva Ferry, squeezing past an over-sized lorry in one of the larger passing bays before turning back and catching a red sunset over Calgary Bay. The next night we go for dinner in Tobermory itself to Highland Cottage, living up to its claim of being a 'small hotel of quality'. A pleasing ambiance and good, uncomplicated local food at sensible prices, it's just right for the visitors Mull attracts. The current *Taste of Scotland* includes nine places for good food on the island, a far cry from the old days. It should be added the Western Isles Hotel is one of them, though predictably its entry begins by extolling the position. Putting setting ahead of food is often a warning sign. Anyway, ringing the changes is pleasant.

Next morning we start our complicated route home by catching the small vehicle ferry across the Sound of Mull from Fishnish to Lochaline, bisecting the route taken by the *Hebridean Princess* two days ago. Then along the northern side of Loch Linnhe looking across to Fort William opposite where, at the start of the trip, we had lunch watching the traffic on the level road we are now using. Then all around the right-angle extension of Loch Linnhe which is Loch Eil. Those peculiarly West Highland long, mainly level journeys at only a few feet above the high tide line, with views of lochs and ever-changing hills and mountains, sparse traffic and interesting one-off large houses, have been a part of my holiday scene for most of my life. They have no English equivalent since their very character depends on their sheer length and sparse population. You would pass through a dozen Kent or Cotswold villages in the distance between the very minor settlements here. No wonder drivers wave cheerfully to each other at the passing places: such driving has the excitement denied on wide, modern roads. The roads themselves are an endearing feature of the landscape, and they sure have tales to tell if you stop to find out. Almost everywhere suffered great hardship as people were forced out to make room for the sheep. Today it is hard to see the mothers and their frisky lambs as an evil consequence of man's greed. As usual in the late spring we have to watch out for youngsters suddenly bolting from the pasture on the other side of the road back to their mums for a comforting feed.

As though we have not had enough of surprisingly good though not expensive restaurants, for lunch we happen on an outstanding one on Spean Bridge railway station, the next station to Fort William on the West Highland line. Like several others which have taken over part of old railway station buildings in the Highlands (Dingwall and Plockton are other good examples), it celebrates past railway glories but seriously looks after its customers since it mainly relies on local repeat business. Unfair it may be, but so ingrained is the feeling against railway catering (back to the days when sandwiches were said to be moved from the first class to the third class refreshment room after they've been displayed for a week) that few passing through Spean Bridge would think of it as a natural place to eat. We are glad we did, as we relax and look around the railway exhibits, as interesting socially as technically, before pressing on along the busy main road back along the north side of Loch Ness to Inverness and Nairn.

THE SLEEPER FROM INVERNESS TO LONDON

But First to Elgin

Going east we almost immediately cross the border between the Highlands and Moray. Since the area around Nairn is flat, mountains only beginning a few miles inland, it is more a cultural than a geographical border. When travelling in the opposite direction, Dr Johnson and Boswell quickly noticed the difference, with poorer Highland housing and food starting in Nairn. The coastal country right from this border has always been more entrepreneurial than is the case in the Highlands.

Though much has of course progressed since Johnson's day, and housing for instance has been revolutionised, even now finding staff willing to take responsibility is far harder in the Highlands. Only in relatively recent times has an up-to-date selection of fresh fruit and vegetables been freely available here. Pineapples are even today too exotic for some substantial greengrocers to stock.

From Moray on the other hand, come an amazing proportion of the British goods you find in duty-free shops around the world: whisky, of course, followed by the best smoked salmon, Walker's shortbread and Baxter's luxury lines, and Johnston's fine cashmere and other top-of-the-market cloths, enterprisingly made into a whole range of finished garments and accessories. Chairman of Johnstons of Elgin is John Harrison, neighbour and friend (we have looked after each other's dogs, meet on the promenade and give each other impromptu invitations for drinks). John has often remarked on Dr Johnson's accuracy about the cultural divide. 'It's a bit like living in one country and going to work in another,' he once joked. Having a free day before taking tonight's sleeper south, I am visiting him at 'the mill'.

On my way I marvel at the many different Scotlands that wait to be richly experienced, and regret that time cannot be spared for these present journeys to stretch along the coast. There is a string of still-active fishing ports, notably Buckie with its large fish market and Buckie Drifter maritime heritage centre, as well as dying and almost dead ones such as Sandend near Portsoy, and also little resorts all the way to Fraserburgh ('the Brock') and then south, fringing the granary of Scotland as one approaches the Granite City, Aberdeen. Or for the return via the lush Dee Valley, with Ballater and Balmoral, and through the castle distillery country toward the massif of the Grampians. There are marvellously individual places developed and still substantially occupied by another race of Scots, with a finely-tuned value system (mocked as the meanness of Aberdonians), driving fairness, and fascination with their neighbours, and a well-above-average but no-nonsense lifestyle.

It is territory that years ago I first explored by steam train, noting that the Great North of Scotland Railway, nicknamed 'Little and Good', developed its monopoly with determined attention to detail, the timetablers skilfully arranging connections between the sparse trains. The old Great North of Scotland was however very much self-contained, relations with the Highland Railway strained. It is interesting to note that when the first railway in the Highlands was opened, from Inverness to Nairn, there wasn't even a once-a-week carrier service eastward from Nairn. And when peace returned in 1946, the demand for through travel was still met by a single service from Aberdeen to Inverness not involving a change at Elgin, where the Great North had an extensive station and a shunting engine was kept busy. Once Ramsay Macdonald, the first Labour Prime Minister, patronised a through sleeping car from King's Cross to his home town of Lossiemouth, served by one of the Great North's many branch lines subject to huge seasonal variations in fishing, agriculture and tourist traffic. But, back to the present...

Cashmere King

Johnstons of Elgin is an economic marvel. Like Baxters, who it is said are about to get into *The Guinness Book of Records* as the family business that has rejected the largest number of take-over offers, since its start in 1797 Johnstons has always been privately owned. John Harrison's picture hangs along with portraits of previous chairmen for visitors to see, for beside today's mill stands an extensive visitors' centre, with tempting displays of garments, accessories and carefully-chosen gifts over two floors, a restaurant, an imaginative small cinema, and displays telling us about the firm, with photographs of illustrious customers giving a real sense of long and continuing history.

As you might expect, John is a cautious man, but running the business hasn't always been easy, and behind his benign gentleness and touch of schoolboy naivety with ever so innocent a smile, there lies not merely great experience but typical Scottish determination and acumen. Though he now only works part-time, his enthusiastic appreciation of every detail of what is happening around the mill is as natural as it is deep. It is no small operation either. Some 450 are regularly employed here, plus 200 at a separate but closely-associated business at Hawick; with seasonal summer undergraduates preparing for the Christmas trade, the total swells to 700.

The original family of 1797 survived until 1920; two brothers had been killed in the Great War. Then there was a management (partnership) buyout. Times were difficult. Most of the once-dominant West Country cloth trade (based around Trowbridge) disappeared. Though he makes no claim to personal success, things seem to have changed when John came into the accessory end of the business. The emphasis changed to making 'fringe' goods, not dependent on processing bulk raw materials – what we would now term 'value-added' products – with customers steadily influencing what they would like made. Margins improved, but the real turning point came in the 1960s when, instead of selling to wholesalers, Johnstons became their own wholesaler selling direct and starting up new products. It was a bold (many people thought risky) step, involving bigger stocks and many more customers and inevitable debt. The strategy paid off, not least because lines of communication were shorter and the firm's own salesmen were better able to report back what lines were more in demand and what might do well next. A knitwear machine was added in the 1970s... again not an easy time since labour became increasingly hard to retain, especially with the oil rig platform yard at Ardersier near Nairn handsomely paying its labour force of thousands. That was when the Hawick factory was started up in the Borders with their higher unemployment.

Cashmere (the combed out undercoat of the Kashmir goat) and vicuna (the finest of fibres, banned for a long time as the animal had to be killed to obtain its hair) first became well known when shown at the 1851 Great Exhibition, but imports from the Andes, the obvious source, were prohibited, so from the middle of the nineteenth century cashmere started to be imported from the central Asian plateau – Afghanistan, Mongolia and parts of China. John recalls that even in his young days there were always supply problems, but it converted nicely into more expensive lines to sell to the retail trade: wraps, scarves, gloves and other accessories. John, a tall man, takes me to the bulk store and stoops slightly as he delightedly picks out small samples of things like mohair, from the outer coat of the Angora goat, and fine camel hair... and tells me in just which parts of the central Asian plateau they still have camels freely wandering about. The cost of each bale, even its airfreighting, is breathtaking. I'm then shown it being woven into cloth, and have each process explained down to the finishing of individual garments, many created by Johnstons to market themselves, others – such as the waistcoats in the familiar Burberry tweed – under contract to major trade customers.

Johnstons do their own research and development including the engineering side. Modern machinery, working alongside the older British machinery, however, has to be imported. They have their own team of ten graduate designers, while computers are relied on heavily, especially in tracing order codes, including size and colour. But the humble teasle still plays a key role in producing a sheen-like finish. 'We've tried everything, but there's a water marking you still can't get any other way,' John says almost apologetically; but he then shares that he, too, loves the survival of a traditional technique along with the new.

The business has had many crises, not least a fire in 1979, the year John became chairman, and a furious flood in the 1990s which ruined many machines and resulted in the restaurant having to be totally recreated. A trick not to be missed, red boards marking the flood line in white are displayed to fascinate visitors, along with full-sized models of cashmere goats where factory tours pass. But what of the daily nightmare of producing, often for long stock periods, such an enormous range of goods in different colours, many in size ranges?

'Every business has its own problems,' says John. He has discovered that through a portfolio of non-executive directorships, some of which we discuss over lunch in the restaurant in the company of tourists and locals.

John guesses who are the customers most likely to make a purchase, and continues doing so as I go to my car and two parties of quite extraordinarily-dressed women get out of theirs and converge on the entrance. 'I'm just glad it's not our garments they're showing off,' says John. 'They can only be Italians in such exaggerated outfits.'

As I drive out of the car park it is hard not to feel a touch of pride at our nearest city [Inverness was awarded its city status shortly after] being home to such an enterprise. [A few months later John Harrison died suddenly. Walks along the Firth don't seem quite the same without the possibility of meeting him with Lucy, the Labrador wagging her tail, or catching a glimpse of him busy in his prized library.]

Elgin has always struck me as special. Civilisation came here early, and its continuance is told in examining its remarkable architectural legacy, though wedged-in modern buildings do not fit sympathetically. It was always a good book place but, for individuality in the age of grocery standardisation, go to Gordon & McPhail in the secondary shopping street parallel to the main pedestrianised one. In Johnstons I noticed a display including an old description of the ruins of Elgin's thirteenth-century Gothic cathedral (rivalling Tintern in sheer scale): make one want to return: 'It remains a display of regularity in the plan, a richness in design, and an elegance in the execution that calls forth to this day the unequalled admiration of the Architects, Artists, and Persons of Taste.'

The Brodie of Brodie

So back through Forres, Nairn's neighbour but still across the border in Moray. Like Elgin, it has extensive, beautifully kept parks and gardens. Both are civilised places but lack the key draw of Nairn: the sea. Then to Brodie Castle to meet another character, the Brodie of Brodie, or for short just 'the Brodie'. I'm taken through the National Trust procedures to his private quarters, and shown into what was the dining room when the castle was the family home.

To all who know him, the Brodie is a loveable elderly man with a slightly sorrowful streak. He is a natural supporter of Nairn Performing Arts Guild at Nairn's Clifton House Hotel, only slightly put out when a cat sought to steal the show while he was reading poetry at a members' evening. At worst you could describe him as a failed actor, for he was in weekly repertory, 'something that's utterly gone'. He found it increasingly hard to learn his volume of weekly-changing lines. But he will go down in history as a colourful local benefactor.

To go back a generation in his family history, his father was one of many who returned from the Boer War by hospital ship, and never fully recovered. A keen woodman, he was a first-class estate manager but after the 1914–18 war it was thought that the best thing for the loyal tenant farmers would be to let them buy their own holdings, something then quite unusual. Needing another interest beyond forestry, for a reason not recalled, he became passionate about daffodils. It is said that he sometimes exchanged a farm's entire year's rent for a single rare bulb. The Brodie tells me: 'One of the first things I remember is all the talk with our visitors about daffodils over meals in this room... sometimes even in the ballroom next door.' Now encouraged by the National Trust, daffodils are still a Brodie Castle speciality; a booklet about the Brodies' achievements including creating new varieties ('mine has been modest compared with my father's though I did a few crossings') is on sale in the shop, and each spring there are daffodil walks and a bulb sale. Whatever the time of year, the one thing certain to bring out a smile on his face is a question about daffodils.

When the Brodie's much-loved wife Helen died in 1972, the castle was offered to the National Trust, but rejected without an impossibly large endowment. However, his wife had already played a part in encouraging the formation of the Land Fund, and later in the 1970s that made feasible the sale to the nation of the castle's pictures for £500,000. The money was used for endowment, and the castle became National Trust, with the Brodie retaining a few rooms for personal use. For years he was a regular guide and still occasionally does lunch relief, answering questions wearing his National Trust Brodie of Brodie label.

Sorrow is caused by his son periodically being reported as saying he's been denied his inheritance with talk of suing to get the castle back. 'It annoys me, but I shan't be dismayed,' says the Brodie. 'Anyway, he couldn't stay here without me.'

Like most people of his age, he enjoys reminiscing; being in weekly rep both before and after the 1939-45 war was 'jolly tough; it's no wonder weekly rep has disappeared from the face of Britain'. And he finds it harder to get around. 'Walks' are now by buggie, but you can't go too far in that, and he is thankful for the development of the nearby Brodie Country Fair shopping and restaurant complex. So, for quite different reasons, are most local people. It is a good place for young and old to meet and to buy or simply drool over a huge range of clothing, gifts, books and food.

The return from Brodie Castle is by the back way, alongside Culbin Woods planted on sand hills to stop rapid sea erosion, though once there was an estate of 3,600 acres and sixteen farms here, steadily destroyed when over-run by sand incursions culminating in a great storm in 1695. Buried under the trees and sand are said to be many a ruined building. So, drinking up the majestic view of snow-capped peaks across a blue Moray Firth, back home to complete urgent tasks before tonight's departure.

Dave the Taxi Reports

There is a well-oiled routine preparing for a journey on the sleeper, *The Royal Highlander*, from Inverness to Euston. Once the luggage is closed and other tasks performed, there is always a little sadness as we wait for our friendly taxi driver to fetch us from our home beside the Moray Firth. Why indeed would we want to go away? Yet the night journey south still retains a touch of romance, and there is Dave's car ready for us in the drive.

You cannot really know Britain without its taxi drivers' view. Ours has hardly opened his door before he bursts forth about the idiosyncrasies of some English visitors attending a series of house parties in a lodge near Loch Ness, rented at an astonishingly high price which includes limited fishing and shooting rights. This makes for complicated transport arrangements as different people go fishing and shooting on different days and return with their own agendas for the evenings. Every one of them seems a caricature of the successful youngsters of the Thatcher era. That era always had cautious Highland people with a deep-rooted value system look aghast at Yuppies, and at the house prices 'doon soouth'. Gazumping is not possible in Scotland with its different legal system.

Night after night Dave is engaged to pick up various members of the changing parties, sometimes only to take them to a nearby pub. After he has made a considerable journey and is just about to arrive at the lodge, they call on their mobile to say they have changed their mind and don't need him. And when they do need him, to drive them perhaps only a few miles, it may be two or more hours later than arranged before his fares take their seats. The young ladies in particular think nothing of keeping him waiting for their changing whims. But, says Dave, the last of them have returned south, expressing gratitude for his service and tipping generously on top of his bill inclusive of fruitless journeys and waiting.

Construction work makes it difficult to get close to Inverness railway station. Without station parking for well over a year, many business people who might have welcomed the improved service to Edinburgh will surely drive there. The faster train means an earlier start, but at least one can now reach Edinburgh at the same time as the businessmen's train from Newton Abbot arrives in London. Time-wise we are further from the Scottish capital than Newton Abbot and Torquay are from London, and making the station's access and parking difficult substantially increases the time one has to allow. A friend, R J Arden, has just published a letter in a local newspaper outlining how awful the permanent arrangements are going to be after the prolonged period of disruption is over. 'It seems that in the Highlands, the convenience of rail passengers comes last and commercial developers call the tune.'

Taxi drivers happily park where lesser mortals fear to pause and Dave comes with us on to the platform. He is the first to spot the blackboard apologising that tonight's sleeper will lack a lounge car. Usually a light supper at home is followed by friendly if erratic service in this 'bistro on rails' as the sleeper sets off on its lengthy journey. At least they have warned us so where, Dave, can we buy at least a drink? The station refreshment room and bookstall have just closed. The adjoining hotel cannot help either. Established as the pride of the then independent Highland Railway, the Station Hotel was once four-star perfection, the true centre of Highland social life. There I enjoyed my first-ever lobster thermador as the fish course in a table d'hôte meal. The other week, however, we had to be content looking at the marvellous cast-iron staircase, with its banisters resting on miniature wheels, since all on offer for afternoon tea was three stale doughnuts and two ill-treated scones. Used dishes and soiled cloths had not been cleared from most tables. 'This place is a pigsty. I can't keep on top of it,' complained an Australian waitress not even trying. In fairness most antipodean staff that Highland hotels seem to attract are enthusiastic and good.

Not surprisingly the hotel is aghast at tonight's request for takeaway sandwiches or wine. So Dave takes a tour of the town, trying to track down at least a touch of alcohol. The only nearby wine shop still open only has whole bottles and, though they will gladly open one, cannot provide glasses or plastic mugs. A pub likewise, but the barman happens to know of a place across the river selling miniatures – too small to be much in demand hereabouts! Dave and I have left getting back so late that Sheila has fantasised she'll be travelling to England alone, but departure is still a minute or so away. We take my purchases to the staffless lounge car. Among those travelling to London, Prince Michael is not amused that there is no food or wine to help start the journey and wistfully watches a pair of lads who each tuck into an oversize pizza they have somehow acquired.

Capital of the Highlands and Gaelic Broadcasting

For decades, Inverness station, with a fascinating range of trains, and the adjoining hotel were for many English people the gateway to the Highlands. My visits for pleasure and business always included a few days at the hotel, steadily getting to know Inverness, capital of the Highlands. Though only small (60,000 population), for some time it has been the fastest-growing place in Britain. There are several reasons for this, the least attractive of which is that it steadily sucks in retail and administrative business from the rest of the Highlands. It has the region's only Marks & Spencer and various other chain stores, while the Highland Regional Council serves the whole vast area and, though there are many small hospitals elsewhere, it's Raigmore that attends to the needs of an incredibly extensive territory including Skye and other islands. Indeed, many who come to hospital take the opportunity to shop at M&S. More positively, unemployment is low here, and it attracts retired people with a love of the Highlands but who don't want to be too remote.

The town is beautifully situated on the famous, if short, fast-flowing River Ness, though whether sufficient use is made of the river front is a moot point. Many visitors seem unaware of the riverside's attractions, and of the delightful circular walk up to the wooded Islands. The traffic system is poor, roundabouts among the most awkward you will find anywhere and, as we will see in a moment, the postwar architectural record unenviable. The new out-of-town centre on the Nairn road is of a particularly disappointing quality, and on prime agricultural land to boot. Nor is there much that is exciting about the in-town shopping malls and, as in so many parts of Britain, the sheer volume of extra retail space threatens many old-established businesses.

Against this, Inverness has many special qualities. Friendliness, especially in the many traditional businesses still holding on, is exceptional even by Scottish standards, and service is generally good, certainly better than on the west coast. Because of the distance from the nearest larger places – Perth and Aberdeen – Inverness is unusually self-sufficient for its size. Everyone is helpful when it comes to tracking down any special need. Restaurants have improved out of all recognition. There are still many fine older buildings, on both sides of the river. Across the river from the pseudo-castle used for local government offices stands a successful theatre pulling audiences from a huge area to all manner of shows. Other leisure and sporting facilities are excellent, as are floral displays year round. The late daffodils on the river bank have enlivened my late spring walks to the Islands over many years. Such walks usually involve crossing one of the endearing pedestrian suspension bridges, which can sometimes bounce sickeningly, spanning the river. Another great point about Inverness is that many residents live close to the centre.

The countryside is seldom out of sight, in winter the hills often covered by snow even when it feels quite warm in the centre and along the river. If you are visiting, go to the eastern end of the Caledonian Canal and its basin and first flight of locks, and in summer catch one of the public trips out to Loch Ness.

Even visitors who arrive by public transport generally rent a car locally, though all four of the very different railway routes out of Inverness offer fine scenery. One of my funniest memories of early visits is going to the tiny Budget office, facing down a road off one of the main streets, to pick up a car. The assistant on duty invited a room full of other renters to put me right. Because of an article I had written about rental cars, the worldwide president of Budget had sent me a personal letter and voucher which, when booking, I had mentioned to the Inverness office.

'Remember, I've a voucher for a free rental,' I mentioned as the paperwork was being started.

'Of course, we always let out cars free.'

'No, I really have.'

'Folks, just what do you do with an Englishman who comes expecting a free car? Maybe you'd all like one? That's how we make our money. Now, come on, your credit card please.'

'Look, here's the letter and voucher.' He looked at the voucher reluctantly, and his face froze. 'He means it. I'm done for. Goodness, he's got a letter from our president, folks. Look at it! How can I live this down?'

Next time I called, he'd moved on, though I hope not on this account. Certainly getting behind the wheel after a night on the sleeper, the major part of the journey over, makes one far more enthusiastic about driving around the Highlands, though it was the same when you could bring your car as you slept. There used to be several daily car-carrying trains in summer. Once it was thought worthwhile running one just from Perth, so atrocious was the A96. That is much improved, though still mainly single lane and with those frustrating miles of gentle curves restricting vision that someone in the Department of Transport insisted was what we needed. Buying picnics from the Victorian Market opposite the station for the continuing journey by road was once also a regular routine. Now there are reasonable and often good eating places almost everywhere in the Highlands, but it was not always so.

Raigmore Hospital deserves special mention. Medical attention is of a high calibre with an interesting mix of enthusiastic local and in-coming staff. Residents and visitors speak equally well of it, and it compares favourably with National Health Service hospitals even in spa towns. Many patients travel long distances, emergency cases by helicopter. But even in friendly Inverness, they cannot conquer bureaucracy, especially at the emergency department's reception. Go with a letter from a doctor saying you need an urgent X-ray, and by the way he has alerted the radiographer, and you will still be kept waiting for your turn. The receptionist makes it clear she sticks to the system and is the sole judge of urgency... with the background of an electronic message flickering along saying that while you will be seen as soon as possible, be prepared for a long wait... hardly appropriate when so many people will have come so far. And when my grandson had been referred to Raigmore from the local hospital since 'his injuries could be serious', it took best part of 45 minutes for me to be told he wasn't there. And where had I been, they wanted to know. The police had been looking for me ever since, in my absence, the ambulance driver had taken him to his own home.

Raigmore, of course, is not alone in needing to revamp its casualty arrangements. Once when I wrote a report about a horrendous Saturday night carry-on at Torbay Hospital, the response was warm thanks from the administrator. The 'evidence' of my report had helped persuade the next day's meeting of the regional health authority to cough up the money for a new department. It was almost as astonishing as the reply by the head of a large regional branch of one of the major accounting companies who I had told that, because of their cock-up on a major transaction, I wouldn't pay a penny of their £30,000 bill: 'That is very generous of you.' My statement must have implied I wouldn't sue, as no doubt had been feared.

As they say, it is a funny old world, and nowhere does laughter ring louder than in Inverness, the only problem at the theatre being that (by English standards) people break too readily into giggles and sustained applause.

While visiting that common denominator, Marks & Spencer, recently, it was my turn to share laughter with one of the area's real characters, the architect Hector MacDonald, not to be confused with a former CalMac and British Rail steward and leading light on the Harbour Board by the same name. The Highland telephone directory may be Britain's thinnest, but there are more than enough people of similar MacThises and McThats to confuse.

Highly creative, never in a hurry, genial Hector is good fun and has optimistically done his best for the architectural scene almost all over the Highlands, admitting that Inverness itself has caused him most grief over the years. It has put in a bid to become the European Cultural City later in the decade, as Glasgow was with all-round benefit in 1990. Yet what should have been a centrepiece of local culture, Balnain House, has had to close because nobody would provide regular funding. All they could get was bits and pieces for individual exhibitions and events. 'It makes you despair,' says Hector.

On the river bank, Balnain House is a distinguished Georgian mansion which has itself at least been saved thanks to the plan to establish a unique centre for Highland music. Before agreeing to advance any money for the building's immaculate restoration, Highland & Island Enterprise commissioned three reports, each estimating annual visitors. The lowest figure of the three was 50,000 a year. Though Balnain House, described as one of Scotland's most novel museums, was a wonderful tribute to Highland music, it achieved less than half that number of paid visitors. The National Trust, which bought the building and leased it to the Balnain company trust, has bought back the lease from the receiver and now intends using it as Highland HQ. Balnain House is not the only property to which Hector MacDonald has given new lease of life only to see its intended purpose abandoned. Another was the Highland Club, once a social institution, now popular as a backpackers' hostel.

Hector is highly critical of the council and its planners: 'They just don't set their architectural targets anything like high enough. And they need to make a lot, lot more of the river and give it proper signposting.'

He is also critical that the Scottish Executive is helping fund the development of the bus station separately from the railway station's back entrance. But he assures me that things will get better. He is even optimistic about the two much-criticised postwar huge, box-like buildings on the riverfront: 'It wouldn't take that much to give a lift to the Caledonian Hotel if it were done sympathetically,' while next door the hideous headquarters of Highlands & Islands Enterprise (the quango doling out government funds to attract new employment) 'is bound to be rebuilt sometime for other plans are impracticable'.

Happily, he says, there is a new, caring generation of fine Highland architects being encouraged by the lead taken by the Scottish Executive, which has published a valuable paper to inspire better things: 'significant green shoots of a renaissance'. [Later, a competition for architects to redesign a crucial section of the river front was announced.]

One of the grand old houses of yesteryear houses the BBC, the intimate studios reminiscent of how most provincial broadcasting stations used to be. With stories of fairytale weddings, shipwrecks, people struggling against the elements, the Highlands & Islands naturally contribute rather more than their share to the national news and the Gaelic service is housed here. Another friend, also one-time chairman of Balnain House, Fred Macaulay devoted thirty years, of which he was in charge for twenty, to developing it. A native of once very Gaelic North Uist, he came to Inverness as a schoolboy of fifteen with little English, to make his way at an English-speaking school. 'You should have heard me struggling with the English in those days,' he laughs looking like a benevolent warrior with his beard and hair continually around his face. He was known to hold his chin up when encountering official obstacles.

'When I joined the BBC, there were one and a half hours of Gaelic radio programmes. By the time I left in 1983, there were thirty hours. Now it is forty-five, plus bits and pieces on television. It is still not enough. People who don't understand sometimes question the cost, but Gaelic speakers won't listen to that. It's our language, an entity, an important part of Scottish culture, and it was systematically beaten down for 500 years, the defeat at the Battle of Culloden just being the last straw. Even in my early days old people were said to be "cured" if they gave up speaking their native language. You can't undo the damage of five centuries overnight. Unfortunately those who speak the Gaelic as their main language are still declining, but many others are learning it and they now form a significant proportion of the BBC's listeners.'

Fred still talks the Gaelic to his friends 'who have it', but his Edinburgh-born wife is a lost cause, and he has to admit that today, when searching for a word or a phrase with an exact meaning, he himself might as easily think in English. It depends on the nuance. The Gaelic tradition runs deep. It is a lovely language, and he writes poetry in it, though he calls it 'a high degree of prose'. He has also written a book and edited others – certainly done his bit to make the fight for Gaelic much more than rearguard action.

[Some months later, Fred – who had twice earlier overcome cancer – passed away. Obituary notices paid tribute to the way he fought those masters at the BBC not so keen on funding the burgeoning Gaelic programmes. Once, when his mileage claim was challenged, he pointed out that of course he'd charged twice for some of the same route: Highland and Island roads were single track, and he had to do a lot of backing up.]

The Royal Highlander

As we finish our miniatures in the sleeper's lounge car, though it is dark, we realise we are passing Culloden Moor, with the battlefield on which, after the last Jacobite Rising of 1745, Bonnie Prince Charlie was beaten. With its National Trust centre, it is one of the region's chief tourist attractions, but tourists also usually see it in somewhat romantic, certainly over-simplified terms. While the battle's outcome was perhaps inevitable, few English realise the extent to which it spelt doom to Scottish traditions and culture. The forbidding of the wearing of kilts was just one minor detail of the vicious campaign to extinguish the individuality of the old value system and way of life. Many would argue that Highland pride has never fully recovered, and Gaelic is not the only traditional ingredient to be served and preserved somewhat self-consciously. Kilts and bagpipes are still naturally used for social occasions, as well as attracting the tourists.

Just beyond Culloden Moor, I am recognised by Frank Spaven, a rail enthusiast who comes across to our table and flatteringly starts by apologising for hitherto mistaking me for my son, since I seem too young to have been the David of David & Charles the publishers 'all those years ago'. He is especially concerned about the future of the Far North line to Wick and Thurso. Then, after pleasant conversation (Frank also shares a common political and religious background) comfortably to bed.

Sheila always drops off on the sleeper long before I can switch off my mind, one problem being I always know exactly where the train is and what there would be to see if it were daylight. Anyway I like the blind up and so am able to look out at every stop until Perth, which must now be the most-oversized, ugliest and down-at-heel station in Britain. It was once an exciting place where the different-liveried carriages brought this far by rival companies were formed into those famously-long 'caravan' trains for the north as the Glorious Twelfth, the start of the grouse season, approached. It has just been announced that £2 million is to be spent on the station's refurbishment. It would be interesting to know how much less that might have been had it been properly maintained in the first place. New traffic patterns make nonsense of the layout. The busiest platforms are the least protected, while the huge train shed stands astride those much less used since the Caledonian Railway's route through Forfar was closed.

We are wakened at Edinburgh, already into the next day, when the Inverness, Aberdeen and Fort William sections are joined to make the nation's longest passenger train, for the electrified part of the route south. How much banging we endure depends on who drives the shunting engine, and how much he cares about our comfort. Sadly, not very much tonight. How the skill and temperament of the drivers vary.

After Edinburgh I am firmly off, missing even our stops at Carlisle station made famous by Trollope's *The Eustace Diamonds* and at Preston and Crewe. Sleeper berths are more than adequately long even for over-sized men, the 'cabin' (as they call it) well-equipped if small, especially if there are two sharing. First class means a cabin to oneself or two inter-connecting ones if with a companion. Using it so often, we have almost come to regard it as our second home.

The *Royal Highlander* sleeper is a great institution which in its time has carried most of the famous and great of their day. Some touches inevitably belong to the past, such as lists of passengers and their carriage allocation exhibited at principal stations, but the sleeper is still well used, often completely filled, and would be sadly missed. Missed indeed are the cross-country Edinburgh-Plymouth sleeper and the ability to take a car while you sleep between England and Scotland. Other losses since I moved to Nairn ten years ago include a second night and a day train both of which went via Birmingham with useful West Country connections. Added to that, British Airways have switched Inverness flights from Heathrow to Gatwick, also less convenient for the West Country.

Though I am delighted to have taken root in the Highlands, had these changes happened before I decided to move, I doubt I would have taken the plunge. An increasing number of people realise it is nonsensical to pour government money into attracting new business to the Highlands while making it harder to reach, and hopefully one day better co-ordination will be achieved. [A few days after this journey, following the Hatfield accident, the backlog of maintenance work it revealed, and the implementation of numerous speed restrictions, resulted in the sleeper being withdrawn for months. Then we really felt cut off.]

After a good night's sleep our mini-breakfast, much edited by accountants, arrives with *The Glasgow Herald* as we switch from fast to slow track. That is something Richard Branson, owner of Virgin Trains, and Railtrack plan to make impossible by segregating the two pairs of lines into quite different railways. The West Coast Main Line, Britain's busiest, has been subjected to more than its fair share of crazy ideas, and not just in the recent past. For example, when the

London Midland & Scottish Railway was formed in 1923, Midland Railway men held sway, especially in the locomotive department. The Midland had always favoured fly-weight trains, and officials insisted that the much heavier trains out of Euston on the London & North Western's West Coast route needed two engines. Some North Western men, who had a great tradition of punctuality with one powerful machine, were brought to tears by this political waste. Remember the first – British – attempt at a tilting train? Essentially a good idea, it was ruined by packing in too much unnecessary new technology having nothing to do with the tilt or speed. While welcoming innovation, a letter to *The Times* headed 'Concord of the Rails' made a personal plea not to depend on this new, totally untried technology in immediate 'squadron' service. British Rail predictably replied there was no risk – there never is until it is too late – and sixty something trains would soon be providing the backbone of service. The prototype utterly failed, and the whole concept was abandoned, leaving no replacement for this essential national artery, while other countries went on to develop tilting trains, one version of which we are going to import to run on this very route.

Not long before today's journey, another revolutionary concept was abandoned: the moving block with in-cab signalling. Traditionally only one train is allowed in a 'block section' between say A and B, fixed points with signals. As its name implies, moving block keeps a predetermined distance between trains, but not between fixed points. It is undoubtedly tomorrow's technology, but to depend on its reliability being proven in great haste is the latest piece of stupidity. When it became clear that the new system wasn't going to be proved in time, the government expensively bailed out Railtrack from its misjudgement. So we will all be contributing to the massive cost of delay and having hastily to renew the fixed signalling.

Switching to the slow line means we are late, crawling through London's northern suburbs obviously behind a stopping train. In fairness most sleeper journeys are excellent. And so a long walk along the platform, and across the busy concourse at Euston, surely one of the least characterful pieces of postwar rebuilding. What excitement it was in the past when a taxi drove one through the Doric Arch to the old station with its Great Hall where they sang carols at Christmas. Finding your platform was however a bit more difficult. But then the new station, functional to the core, doesn't even function well, certainly not for those of us arriving with loads of luggage. It has to be carried down several flights of steep steps to the taxi. A curse on it as we struggle this morning. Yet even at Euston, with the station announcer apologising for yet another late Virgin Train arrival, there is reason for optimism. While car-carrying trains and newspaper trains may be things of the past, passenger business has increased beyond the wildest dreams of the planners of the 1950s.

Our time in London, a quick trip to another station, almost seems to treat the capital with the contempt many provincials feel. We recognise it as our largest and greatest city with its wondrous old buildings, unique theatreland and so much to offer. We do not, however, see it as Britain, certainly not synonymous with civilisation, good food and culture. Thrilled though we are to be privileged to share the rich excitement of London, nonetheless we despise those who believe all good things end at Hadrian's Wall, if they know where that is, if not at the Watford Gap. As usual, the taxi driver is amazed that we have already been travelling for twelve hours. He has never been north of Manchester.

· I V ·

SOUTHERN
ENGLAND

Pretty But Too Civilised

Kent, the Garden of England. Surrey, regarded by many as England's prettiest county. Sussex, with its Downs and ninety miles of coastline. South East England! Home to a large proportion of those who run and work for UK plc.

Therein lies my difficulty: people. Too many of them. Yes, there are many delightful areas, odd corners of real countryside – and of course great cliffs, brilliant hill walking, and a general state of woodedness not now found in much of the rest of England. Usually alas, behind the woods are houses. Good houses, many of them, with their own trees, but still where people live, keep cars and clog the roads each Monday to Friday morning as many of them make their daily pilgrimage to London.

In a sense, the Garden of England is a good description for much of the Southeast, for it is like a garden which is beautiful but the owner has over-developed, as are many of even its finest individual gardens, themselves without a hint of wildness.

While making our journeys, I have turned to many works on parts and aspects of Britain (though not tours through it). For variety, I tend to pick out different guides and general books, many of them written a long time ago. For this trip, I took down from the shelves a 1948 Oldhams' compendium, won as a school prize. *The English Counties*, edited by Dr CEM Joad, who older readers may recall from the BBC's radio Brains Trust, has chapters on each county by a broad range of yesteryear's top writers.

How things have changed! Much of Kent was then still beyond the daily reach of London, reported Richard Church. He complained that the problem for those interested in the arts was not just that most people were still born and bred in Kent, but revelled in their rural ignorance. Yet throughout the Southeast tourism was much stronger than today.

Ramsgate, Folkestone and Hythe were among Kent's fully-fledged holiday resorts. It was while visiting Folkestone for a conference on rural transport in the early 1960s that I first realised that the notion of people coming for a fortnight's family holiday had become faintly ridiculous. Steadily that has applied to much of the southeast, also visited by many fewer day trippers in the motor age than in the days of excursion trains and steamers. As surely as yesteryear's luxuries have steadily become today's necessities, so going on holiday has demanded a greater change of scene (if not also climate). Southeast England may be beautiful, much of it thoroughly worthy of exploration, but for those needing 'to get away from things' today it is altogether too tame, too congested... added to which it has never been well served by roads and railways.

I don't record it being said, but it's likely that someone has: if God had intended the south east to be filled with commuters, he would surely have given us the East and West instead of the North and South Downs which block easy access from London. The transport corridors, taking advantage of the few natural gaps where the chalk has been worn away, have been seriously over-developed, while Dr Beeching's railway closures viciously mopped up rural routes that didn't fight the unnatural grain of the country on the way from the capital. Mind you, 'gaps' didn't mean that the main routes from London could be exactly level. Gradients abound... and tunnels on the railways.

How badly the Kent coast is served by trains was emphasised by a recent train trip to Dover. Once, leaving from platform six at Charing Cross station was thoroughly civilised. Civilised is not a word you would apply to our train, still in the livery of Connex South East which deservedly lost the franchise. One seat was ripped out of our so-called first-class compartment, and the others were distinctly down at heel. Though electrification in Kent was heralded as a great (postwar) improvement, the ride was jerky, so bumpy as occasionally to descend from uncomfortable to plain alarming.

I longingly recall the journeys by steam train before and after World War Two. True, by standards elsewhere, the engine was often under-powered, and ran better down than up hill; occasionally there would be a pause, perhaps outside a tunnel, while more steam was raised before the final gradient could be conquered. But once well away from London, the journey was through a rich kaleidoscope of the Garden of England: fruit and other farms, hop fields, oast houses, quaint villages where houses sold for a few hundred pounds. (Even close to the cathedral, well into the 1970s you could still buy a small terraced house in Canterbury for £2,000.)

Now it is hard to get a decent view from the train even of housing estates, for the windows are grimy and/or scratched while, for long stretches, trees grow alongside the line almost continuously. Since the abolition of steam and the mowing of embankments and cuttings, trees have spread more rapidly on railway land than in any other environment. No wonder there are problems with leaves on the line. Behind the trees, the hop gardens have gone, and surviving oast houses have mainly become upmarket homes. Apart from stoppages caused by leaves and snow on the line apart, there was once a much richer seasonal variation. Passengers were aware of how the crops were growing, while the migration of cockneys by the hop-pickers' specials is just one colourful seasonal episode consigned to history.

For the observant boy, there was once huge railway interest, too... lines of old engines outside Ashford's locomotive works, for example, and branch lines to Hawkhurst (terminus of many of the hop-pickers' specials) and Hythe. Alas, we never changed at Sandling Junction for Hythe, but were met by taxi at Folkestone Junction. Then that station was a smart affair; on our recent trip to Dover it was disgusting almost to the point of being comic with abandoned tracks, broken windows and general dilapidation. For today's sleek and modern, we have the new link between the Channel Tunnel and London, with international trains that leave ours standing and provide an extra clue to why Kent is so over-developed. As well as the expresses from London to Paris and Brussels, some stopping at Ashford, every few minutes there are the shuttle trains each absorbing a queue of cars, lorries and coaches at the terminal near Folkestone. And still the ferries are far busier than when I was a lad.

Beyond Folkestone, the Dover train of course took us beside the white cliffs... where the northern flank of the great horseshoe of the Downs, encompassing much of the centre of the south east's three counties, hits the sea. To emphasise the influence of geology, we were delayed by a cliff fall. The chalk cliffs are crumbling at such a rate that there is talk of this east-west section having to be abandoned.

Hythe

Yet, I am probably biased and exaggerate, for there are places in this crowded region where geology has made it easy to commune with nature. When the wind blows on the seafront at Whitstable, you can still enjoy the feeling that man hasn't yet conquered and spoilt all. And at Hythe, one of the Cinque Ports, and westward across Romney Marsh. My first summer holidays were at Hythe, where my mother's family lived, close to the promenade, more visited then than today, though the same weather conditions are necessary to see across to France and the Martello towers still stretch east and west. The Royal Military Canal was also built as a defence measure against Napoleon, and still gives peaceful pleasure to those hiring boats, while the Lady's Walk and gardens rapidly help soothe the troubled mind. There is the fine Imperial Hotel in its own garden.... and, of course, the High Street, without rows of multiple shops, a civilised remnant of what once one took for granted in quality England.

Never was I happier than staying with Mum's parents in their modest semi-detached on the edge of the shingle with its military range just before the start of the marshes. Grandfather was a military man, a gentle person who in his small greenhouse at the bottom of the garden overlooking the shingle indoctrinated me with the mysteries of growing tomatoes. Actually, he was also the family's first journalist, for he wrote a column, 'Did You Know' for the town's weekly newspaper. Each item started THAT. The editor used over-matter as column fillers, where out of context THAT looked distinctly odd.

I've always put my dislike of bathing down to Hythe's waves crashing on the steep shingle. Conversely, my love of railways was encouraged by another of the town's features. The miniature (15-inch gauge) Romney, Hythe & Dymchurch Railway, was controversially built across marsh and shingle in 1926 and soon extended to Dungeness. It was still very much in its original state when I first travelled on it in the mid-1930s. Then it carried both shingle and fish into Hythe, but largely lived on, as well as helped develop, holiday camps along the coast. There was a wartime interlude when pleasure trains were exchanged for military ones including an armoured one with aircraft gun. Advertising itself as the world's smallest railway, the RH&D was built as a double-track 'main line', with frequent trains in and out of the four-platform terminus at Hythe. On a recent visit, the same steam engines of my boyhood, displaying the same names and smelling and sounding exactly as I first remember, were hauling long rakes of newer passenger coaches, one bringing children back from school. Thanks largely to a long innings by author John Snell as general manager, the railway survived difficult times, when holiday camps closed and there were many fewer visitors. It is scarcely where one would build such a thing today. Once Dungeness was a lonely place. A new lighthouse had to be built when the original became well inland as the shingle headland was steadily built up by the sea which of course sometimes creates land as well as eroding it. Dungeness is dominated by an ugly atomic power station.

Beyond is still lonely country though, with the continuing line of Martello towers along the coast, and ports – notably Rye – now well inland because here again the shingle advances. It is only when approaching Hastings, of which the less said the better (well, there go sales of this book in one town), that the coast becomes almost continuously built up to the Dorset border. In the marshes, man is still an individual, tradition strong, and keeping land free of water an everlastingly demanding business. But everywhere there are commercial pressures and silly house prices that undermine the old community life. If you're in search of individuality, visit Romney Marsh and its villages sooner rather than later.

Lacking time to make a special visit to Kent for these travels, these comments come from earlier visits. Off the sleeper from Inverness, still only half awake, we cross London by taxi to Victoria.

Sad Exit from London

Departure from Victoria is only a couple of minutes late despite the packed incoming train arriving just three minutes before our departure time. Though our journey to Horsham is supposed to take only 54 minutes for the 38 miles, it is slow getting into its stride. We pass several stationary crowded trains waiting for signals to clear.

'This is awful,' says Sheila, looking out on a scene of abandonment and graffiti in which hundreds of people are living happily; well, living at any rate. 'Any chance of a coffee?' No.

Nobody smiles. Most have vacant to grim faces, though a few are deep into reading their paper, one man stuck on a tabloid page three before he sneezes over the nude. Maybe it is a regular part of his morning ritual.

'How late are we?' asks Sheila half an hour later. Astonishingly, we are on time. She adds: 'All I can say is that I am glad we don't often have to travel south of the Thames.'

Though there had been some earlier electrification, it was the Southern Railway taking over the ramshackle kits of the old companies that made sense of this area – by adding a third rail for electrification without grandiose modernisation schemes. Signals, and even the carriages (steam-hauled sets simply placed on electric bogies) remained the same, but the 'product', the miles run, increased dramatically. The Southern used to be like a good family business, pragmatically on the ball with good *esprit de corps*. The driver of a late incoming service at Victoria would run the whole length of his train to save a precious minute or so. Then came nationalisation: bags of money, remote and ever-changing management, one unpopular supremo spending his retirement saying that tracks into London should be torn up and replaced by bus lanes.

Yet many individual railwaymen perform nobly. Our driver has done his best. When we alight at Horsham and question the porter, he is enthusiastically polite. But then perhaps we are today's first passengers – beg your pardon, customers – to treat him as a fellow human being. It is not the done thing to talk or smile, and Sheila's sister Barbara seems positively to be breaking the rules in greeting us as though we were at her front door. Nobly getting out of bed even earlier than we did on our sleeper, she has come to take us on our journey along the coast.

Polly Samson's Writing Hideaway

Finding our way around Horsham is difficult, cars appearing to be as aimless dashing round the bypass as drunken wasps. I do however catch a glimpse of the High Street, or rather West Walk, which looks inviting, and at the second attempt we stop in a beguiling Causeway. At its top are attractive individual shops including a coffee shop and a listening service run by local churches and staffed by volunteers. Then idyllic old cottages stretch down to the church with its perpendicular-style windows and shingle spire. The winter sun has come out to give a hint of things to come. In late spring the fragrance of chestnut and lilac will surely add a magic touch.

The Causeway is where the extraordinary daughter of extraordinary parents is meeting me. She doesn't live here but on a farm where being mother has priority. This cottage, dating from 1430, with original panelling, and a flying freehold room over the front door belonging to next door, was bought last year. Says Polly Samson: 'It's strictly where I work. I didn't look for it; it found me. It has certainly made writing a lot easier. Isn't it terribly inconvenient when one is driven to write? Mind you, friends do other things just as obsessive. When I come here I can put the children on a shelf, though I bring them as an occasional treat.' She has three children, a fourth on the way, and four stepchildren. 'They have a little room with bunk beds here. Normally, this is where I concentrate and am very disciplined.'

I first knew of Polly's existence as daughter of her parents; later she and my son were at the local grammar school together. Her father, Lance, was editor of the weekly *Mid-Devon Advertiser*, Newton Abbot's informative weekly newspaper.

A dedicated Communist, once diplomatic correspondent of the *Daily Worker*, Lance remained loyal to Moscow during the invasion of Hungary but deflected, heartbroken, when it was Czechoslovakia's turn. He had edited a students' newspaper in Prague. But this I am only discovering this morning for, a real professional, he was politically neutral in charge of a market town's much-read weekly rag. When he and his wife came to dinner, however, I did discover something of the earlier life of Polly's half-Chinese mother, Ester. She hadn't always been a Devon village schoolmistress – for a time she was in the Red Army. I must find a copy of her memoirs, *From Black Country to Red China*.

Polly, as bright and breezy as young mums come, talks of her husband 'in a band called Pink Floyd: I wrote a song for them'. And of her brain disorder, 'not dyslexia but I can't find the way to London or give directions'. With that background, she's naturally been driven to success. She was made a director of Johnathan Cape when only 24, and has had a brilliant career as a journalist, doing a regular column for *The Sunday Times* and contributing to many of the other quality papers, while her short stories have been much broadcast as well as published.

She presents me with copies of two books published by Virago: *Lying in Bed*, a collection of short stories, and her first novel, *Out of the Picture*. This is no ordinary writing. She has a penetrating power of sharp description, an almost cruel incisiveness. The quest for sexual fulfilment is as elusive to her characters as the short route to the Pearly Gates was to Bunyon's Pilgrim. Cressida Connolly's comment, 'Rueful and Witty', is hard to beat. Fay Weldon's 'When I give up she can take over', is another of the quotes used by the publisher that any author would find rewarding. Polly Samson is undoubtedly a writer with a future and one who seems to have her life well balanced. With her long dark hair, quick movements and sallow face giving a hint of Asian genes, she's a real one-off.

People's comments are obviously important to her. 'When I started I feared I might be writing Cosmo fluffy fiction. But I had something to say; when I worked at *The Sunday Times* they said you were only a real writer when you knew what you wanted to say. It's a hard lesson, but trying to write without a message must be awful.'

When I say goodbye at the door and comment on the lush surroundings, she says: 'It is much lusher where we live. Did you know we breed show-event horses?' Then she extols Horsham. 'Elegant and modern,' says the official guide. Yes, I unfairly do down much of the south of England yet, pretty as it may be, I don't really feel at home in it. It is too digested: white bread when I prefer brown.

Yet many country, nature and garden lovers have chosen to live in Sussex. One was Arthur Hellyer, possibly the greatest gardening author of all time, who developed the splendid patch which gave him much of his practical authority nearby at Rowfant. For many years he and Robin Lane Fox shared the *Financial Times*'s unique gardening coverage with a pact suggested by Hellyer that while they were working together they never visit each other's garden. Arthur Hellyer died some years ago, so it is too late to accept the invitation he extended to me. I'll probably now never see the garden. But before leaving Horsham I pause for a moment's homage to a great gardener whose books inspired me. I never had the good fortune to publish him, but admired the campaign he waged (and usually won) to be allowed to appraise new gardening books in his columns rather than let them be sent to the literary editor, who would surely find too highfaluting a reviewer.

Brighton

We have to go east before turning on to the Brighton Road of many roundabouts down to the resort made famous by Royal 'dirty weekends'. This morning, interest along the way is enhanced by a felled speed camera poised drunkenly in the central reservation, and a fair already attracting a crowd at Preston Park. It is always a fascinating route. There's that marvellous railway viaduct, the huge St Peter's church ahead, dominating a large area, and the Royal Pavilion. A reminder that the 'dirty weekend' was invented here by the decadent Prince Regent, later George IV. His visits with his mistress gave impetus to rapid tourist expansion. We forget that Queen Victoria, not approving of her predecessor's behaviour, had the Pavilion stripped of valuables which were carted off to Buckingham and Kensington palaces. She established her sedate seaside presence on the Isle of Wight. Then the Pavilion was relegated to concert hall, hospital, radar station and other humbler roles. There was even an arson attack. It is a wonder it has survived. But it's good: so splendidly over the top, inside and out.

Much of Brighton thrives on being over the top; and in two ways, often cheek by jowl. There is truly great dignified splendour, and utter tack. They cheerfully mix even on the seafront, especially to the east where ugly arcades are overlooked by great buildings on the higher layer.

It is stormy; the beach deserted except for a trio systematically covering the shingle with metal detectors. That's Brighton for you; elsewhere metal detectors usually work in lonesome isolation, but here they beaver away as a team under the shadow of the much-neglected West Pier. [Later part of this fell on to the beach and when discussions began about restoration, there was a bad fire, allegedly the work of arsonists.] Brighton, said SPB Mais, is 'unalike any other town in the world'. Still true? Certainly not his next sentence: 'It is always gay, always clean, always happy, a quite miraculous blend of all that is best in the cosmopolitan and all that is best in the countryman.'

Commenting on the different states and fortunes of the piers, we go west and turn round to the really Grand Hotel, leaving the car with an ever-so-posh doorman. Previously I've always used lesser establishments, so I want to look around the place where in 1984 a bomb came near to decimating the Conservative cabinet. The Grand has been perfectly restored. They are obviously security conscious so, when an official eyes me, I make directly for the Gents, already crowded with delegates from a conference session just broken up. I eavesdrop.

'Lovely to see you again, Mr Goodman.'

'Was I ever such a person?'

'So sorry, how are you, Mr Wellow?'

'Fine.'

Pause.

'A man of few words.'

'Very well, then. Really fine.'

'That's better.'

People pay real money to have such conversations in Brighton! Then I follow a wave of the delegates into 'the sumptuous King's Restaurant', where a brochure I've just picked up says lunch is served, to find it laid out self-service for the delegates. When I don't go to pile up a plate, a waiter asks me what I'm doing and tells me I'll have to order a bar lunch in the conservatory. We just squeeze in, for many delegates have brought their heaped plates. No complaints about our lighter lunch, however. None of the delegates says a word about the conference or the session they've presumably sat through. The talk is about house prices, cars, lawnmowers, and babies, usually in that order.

Then a brief visit to the Lanes. Now this is different. You could spend days sifting through antique shops and eating and drinking in this enclave which was the original fishing village, or fishertown as we would say north of the border. But the cost of chests of drawers! I recall that, in a slump, on the spur of the moment sometime in the 1980s, I bought a couple of chests for a tenth of what one of lesser quality would cost now. The following week I returned with a small van to collect them. I quickly learned that by mentioning 'my van', I gave the impression I was in the trade elsewhere. The universal message was: 'Wouldn't want my colleagues to know, but if you're going straight out of town and are paying cash...' Many prices were cut by well over half. Antique dealers often struggle.

The Lanes was the birthplace of the Body Shop. Earlier another retail revolution was driven by the Brighton Co-operative Society, whose journal *The Co-operator*, first published in 1828, became that movement's principal mouthpiece. Brighton has always been a trend setter, and not least as a resort that first flourished when doctors ordered their patients to 'inhale the sea air at the village of Brighthelmstone'.

Not that the booksellers of my day were exactly innovative. When publishing a title with considerable local interest, I travelled down in style by the old *Brighton Belle* and was met by our regional rep to make a presentation. After five minutes of hearing rather than listening to our enthusiasm, the town's then principal bookseller interrupted: 'Hold it. Save your breath. You've obviously put a lot into it. All right, we will buy a copy.' Today Brighton's booksellers are more adventurous.

Even now, Brighton is about exuberance. 'Let's come for a weekend,' says Sheila. 'Even though you're married?' queries Barbara. Then we think about the characters in fiction whose lives were affected by weekends here, and about the many writers who made their home in or around here. Such as Kipling, who wrote:

> God gives all men all earth to love
> But, since man's heart is small,
> Ordains for each one spot shall prove
> Beloved over all.
> Each to his choice, and I rejoice
> The lot has fallen to me
> In a fair ground – in a fair ground –
> Yea Sussex by the sea!

Kipling actually chose Rottingdean, brought closer by the curious, short-lived 'Daddy Long Legs' (or Brighton & Rottingdean Seashore) Railway 'on spindly steel girders rising twenty-four feet above rails set in concrete piers on the seabed'. And he travelled around in what must have been one of Brighton's earliest cars. *The Oxford Book of Literary Anecdotes* says that he told Henry James that the motor car was 'calculated to make the English man think'. But frequent breakdowns made the conservative James retort that the vehicle was 'calculated to make Mr Kipling think'.

Concrete Jungle

The locals comment that Brighton ends and Hove begins where the seafront lights are off, but after crossing the border we still see some of those hotels (Graham Greene wrote *Brighton Rock* in one) that periodically look irretrievably set for decay, and then just about bring themselves back to life with a semblance of refurbishment on the crest of an economic cycle... before the process of lingering death again takes hold. Anyone who has used such hotels will have personal memories of how hope and fear meet in the decor – and sometimes in the staff. Especially vivid is the image of a gaunt waiter whose expression was stuck in a forced smile exposing his molars, ninety per cent gold, ten per cent tooth. He moved stiffly as though the effort of serving had become too much when old age set in years ago, but droned automatically: 'It's my job to give you satisfaction. If there's anything I can do, don't hesitate to shout.'

My son Gareth, then studying at Sussex University, was with me; we dared not glance at each other lest we (he at least) dissolved into uncontrollable giggles. There are also memories of bargain dinners with those running a new book club based here who needed my help to break the monopolistic hold of the largest book club group. They failed, and then sold themselves to us... resulting in the most embarrassing but effective short speech of my life. We'll come back to that in the chapter A Provincial Publisher's London.

Heading west, we are soon running alongside the long harbour, miles long, noting a Shoreham pilot boat tossing as it reaches the sea going out through the mouth of the River Adur. Worthing, Littlehampton, retirement land by the sea. One of the few Butlins remaining in business at least makes a change at Bognor Regis, though it's closed for the winter. I would not want to live here either. The whole coast is a concrete jungle, and much of it not very good concrete. Times must be hard, for an hotel advertises 'Snacks for £2.50' and, what at a distance looks like a bookshop, turns out to be a paperback exchange service. Can't be much profit in that, unless of course non-stop reading is all they do to prevent boredom in Bognor. In fairness, I've only ever been to Bognor in winter and know people who swear by it for a summer visit.

Though the number of huts and stalls offering seafood has steadily declined, a plus for the coast all the way from Whitstable is the quality and variety of fish on offer. Enjoy the full fresh flavour in Bognor. Yet this strikes me as one of the few parts of coastal Britain where going inland gives one better air and outlook.

We backtrack, through villages that almost run into each other, before striking the dreaded A27 – I have never decided if the railway or the road journey is the less desirable along the coast across the north-south grain of most traffic – and go east until hilltop Arundel's gorgeous skyline comes into view. What a contrast from the grotty coast.

We're in a hurry today, so no time to visit the castle (not as old as it looks for, destroyed in the Civil War, it was only restored just over a century ago) or the cathedral (again relatively modern), a formidable Roman Catholic beacon in these parts. We 'need' afternoon tea: Barbara because, having been up so early this morning, is again hungry, I because I love the ritual, Sheila to 'support' us. It's good that I never have to worry about the sisters' appetites. Alas, our favourite Tudor Rose cafe – 'no one is permitted without sleeved shirt' – is closed. That means we have to walk further, at least giving an opportunity to soak in more of the atmosphere, enjoy looking into the windows of several antique shops and see the landing stage for summer river trips. There is a lot to see and do in Arundel. I love the lake and trout feeding pond, and admiring the old buildings that escaped destruction in Cromwell's day. It is a wonderful place for music, too. But the alternative busy café has all the charm, though not efficiency, of a motorway service station. On the way back to the car I dive into a bookshop.

'I do wish we had time to go to Midhurst; you'd love it,' says Sheila, when I come out with a purchase. Our schedule doesn't allow, and anyway I'm lukewarm about the idea.

Foolishly Not to Midhurst

By one of life's surprisingly frequent coincidences, I've just written the above when two visitors arrive at home: Allan Garraway, who I first got to know when he was general manager of the steam, narrow-gauge Ffestiniog Railway in North Wales and now lives in Speyside, and Vic Mitchell, founder and owner of the Middleton Press specialising in mile-by-mile railway history. Our conversation can hardly not be included. It starts by Vic seeing a map of West Sussex open on my desk, and I tell him I'm writing about a visit.

'Did you get to Midhurst? No? Great mistake. It's a jewel in the best part of West Sussex. For goodness sake, come and see us there.' Then he asks if I recall his submitting *Branch Lines to Midhurst* to David & Charles. Afraid not.

'Well, I'm glad you and everyone turned it down. You all said there weren't enough pictures of trains, too many of stations.'

Allan: 'I didn't think it would work either.'

Vic: 'But I knew it would.'

He says that he self-published it; 3,000 copies for £5,000, in 1981. 'We thought it would take us three years to get our money back, but we had it in three months.'

From there he's gone on to build a list of several hundred titles, mainly about branch lines and sections of main-line. Paddington to Penzance, for example, is covered in ten separate volumes. There's even a national index of stations directing you to the right volume. Introduction and pictures and captions, it is pretty predictable stuff, well researched, pictures being drawn in from many sources including readers of earlier titles.

Once a dental surgeon, Vic then spent a period experimenting in a laboratory. The stock is housed in 'the lab with several mezzanine floors'. He writes the books, often with a colleague; his wife, Barbara, does typesetting; his daughter, Deborah, the design; his son-in-law, Ray, much of the commercial side. Hey presto! A not-so-cottage self-sustaining industry.

'We never set out to make a lot of money, but it's been lots of fun, and we do it in a marvellous place: Easebourne on the A272 just outside Midhurst.' And how right he was to self-publish, though on this scale you can hardly call it self-publishing but a fully-fledged professional operation. He knows what his customers want. Almost certainly changing circumstances, not to mention staff, would at some point have upset the applecart had he effectively worked full time for a publisher. Prices would probably be higher, too.

'We keep things very simple; almost all titles, papercased, are £13.95. I do the footwork round the bookshops, but specialist railway shops, including those at the steam railways are important, and perhaps a third of sales are retail direct to the customer. Two nice things: we get marvellous reviews like "another gem in the Middleton Press series", and we've opened up the local-interest market as more people want to know about their area's past and realise how important the station once was.'

Returning to the A272, he adds: 'But nobody gets it right all the time. You didn't recognise that *Branch Lines to Midhurst* would have the potential eventually to sell 8,500 copies, and when a Dutchman offered me a book on our local road, booksellers joined me in saying it wouldn't work. But it has been a rip-roaring success, including in Holland. Sometimes authors see potential that others don't.'

Sheepishly, I'm glad that Sheila isn't in my study to crow about Midhurst. I look at the A272's somewhat zigzag route from Petworth to Petersfield. 'It's so much nicer than the A27 running nearer the coast,' says Vic. 'And I'll show you why. Of course, it's back to geology. At home we've windows looking out north and south; the views are equally good; well-wooded limestone hills. We're in the bowl of Wealden clay toward the east of the great horseshoe of the chalk downs with the limestone ridge within it. There were three branch railways to Midhurst, forming a T-junction, coming from the east, south and west. They couldn't economically get across the limestone to the north; they had enough trouble getting the Portsmouth Direct over. So this has never developed as commuter land. I wouldn't want to live in that to the north, or along the concrete jungle of the south coast.

'Here we have more woodland than anywhere else in southern Britain, delightfully unspoilt villages, Roman roads, the South Downs and the Monarch's Way, farming country, Lord Cowdray country, so close yet so far from London. When the lines were open, I never saw a really busy train at Midhurst.'

And not too many visitors today, either; Midhurst isn't even in the index of some contemporary guide books.

'So when the book is done, we can go to Midhurst?' asks Sheila.

Meanwhile I place an order for Middleton Press titles, including Allan Garraway's *Father & Son*, about his father's railway career, mainly on the Great Eastern, and his own – he helped develop automatic train control or ATC after the terrible Harrow & Wealdstone accident of 1952 – before becoming general manager of the Ffestiniog Railway.

Back to our present journey, it was time to backtrack again, across the meadowland of the unspoilt Arun Valley and across the bridge at Ford to Barnham to meet an old friend and author. Crafts are our theme for much of the next 24 hours.

The Chairmaker

Not every author co-operates with a publisher's publicity department and few do so as enthusiastically as Jack Hill, the craftsman and especially chairmaker. He co-operated so brilliantly with Fran, in charge of our publicity operation, that he took her off and married her. Though they had met several times in the office, it was what happened while they were presenting his book at the Edinburgh Book Festival that led to our having to find a replacement. Allowing staff out of the office is always risky!

Fran has since died – 'We had eleven terrific years, the best of my life,' says Jack – and now he's in the early stages of Parkinson's disease. We haven't met for many years, but retain warm memories of pioneering days with craft books; especially of the occasion I persuaded him to make a rocking chair as an heirloom for a friend. He was ingenious in the excuses he made for taking her measurements, and later luring her into the room where the finished chair was waiting and making her try it, without giving the least hint of what it was all about. The chair, featured in his *Making Family Heirlooms*, was made of three woods: elm for the seat, ash for the framework and beach for the combe (or top rail) in which her initials were deeply carved.

The first thing I notice going into his home in a pleasant residential street in Barnham is Fran's painting of their cottage... blow me, near Midhurst. Quickly we are into how Jack became a craftsman. The son of Lancashire cotton workers who wanted him to break into new pastures, he began work with a company making wooden car bodies. Then he became an RAF radio operator, going to the Antarctic for two years where he was injured. So back to the motor trade... but next he took a three-year course to become a secondary school teacher. His subject: rural studies and rural craft.

'I was interested in the subject because of the general lack of awareness. They were the days of modernisation, when plastic was much hyped, and the pressure on to mass produce. The people doing the old crafts were dying out. Books about them, like James Arnold's *All Made by Hand*, had an air of finality about them. So I made it my job to track down some of the older people still practising the traditional skills: a drystone waller in the Yorkshire Dales, hedgelayer in the Lake District, blacksmiths, basketmakers, potters... and chairmakers such as Fred Lambert, who was living in Worcester when I fell in love with the country style of chair. I left general teaching just ahead of a nervous breakdown and, when Fred retired, got his job as tutor, demonstrating at country shows and writing articles for *The Woodworker*.

'Do you remember, you asked me to write *The Complete Practical Book of Country Crafts*? I gave you twice as many words as the contract stipulated and you published them all, along with a huge number of pictures. I enjoyed that. Perhaps we helped turn the tide? Next weekend I'm at the Weald & Downland Open Air Museum for "Out of the Wood". There'll be 25 craftspeople all making things in wood.

'I've always seen myself as an educationalist whether standing up in front of students or writing books and articles or actually making furniture.' His grip has deteriorated, so he can't do the latter anymore – 'the last chair I made was for Fran' – but is full of hope and praise for those following in his footsteps, and for West Dean College, ten miles away where we go tomorrow. He says that, started by an eccentric rich Englishman who filled his house with crafts, arts and music, it has gone through a 'toffee-nosed phase appealing to the educated middle class', but is now broadly based. 'I've been lucky to be associated with it. You'll love what it's doing.'

Before we part, we talk about his other books. Back to an earlier interest, Jack is now researching Arctic and Antarctic exploration ships. Anyone interested?

It has been a long day, so we're pleased when we reach our hotel at Crouchers Bottom, close to one of the many arms of Chichester Harbour. This is where the geography of the south coast begins to get really interesting with large areas of tidal water.

Crafts College in the Countryside

Next morning, we negotiate the rush-hour traffic through boring residential areas of Chichester, but enjoy the hills on both sides of the road through real countryside heading a few miles north to West Dean, just beyond where the Monarch's Way crosses the road. There is more visual evidence, though, of the abandoned railway, one of the branches to Midhurst. Over a dozen of my authors of craft books have worked at West Dean College, mainly as part-time lecturers.

'Don't underestimate the value of short residential courses,' Jack Hill said last evening. 'You can teach and learn more in a few days than months of evening classes.'

Everyone has described West Dean as a rural idyll inspiring respect for traditional crafts, especially country-based ones. On this crisp winter morning, the gardens alone are worth fighting the traffic for. Sheila and Barbara have the best of the deal, since they'll be able to spend all their time exploring them and there's plenty to see: walled garden, acres of glass, sunken garden, water garden, arboretum, and many more separate areas that the grand country houses of yesteryear like West Dean needed as part of their support system. Unless, of course, Barbara succumbs to the café in the visitors' centre since she only had a light cooked breakfast!

Armed with an informative leaflet, blending history and horticulture, I only have time for a quick dash around before presenting myself at reception. Today the college is being validated, a reminder that it is part of the wider-education system, so it is the head of continuing education, an enthusiastic and talkative Caroline Pearce-Higgins, who gives me a quick tour. Nearly all the courses are residential, two to nine days. Again, 'being resident you learn as much in five days as you would in a couple of terms of evening classes. There's something happening all except two weeks a year. Five hundred short courses a year, attended by 5,000 students. It's pretty intense.'

Access is open to all, though you need a grade to get into some courses. There's a nice mixture of near-beginners with those honing their specialist skill and between young and mature students... not that with trendy (and in some cases startlingly simple) clothing it is easy for me to tell the difference. As I move from ceramic to silversmithing and jewellery, pottery, book binding and other classes, and pass students in the corridors, accents suggest this is no longer the exclusive province of the educated middle class, but that you do indeed have to be pretty committed. There is a single-mindedness of attention. If you're into making a crumhorn or other musical instrument, nothing else must matter.

With such motivated students, teaching here must be a doddle. I just hope that the students don't see their crafts as too isolated from life, art forms with little practical purpose other than perhaps to produce an income. Probably not, for there is certainly good coverage of how things came to be as they are, and today's trends and uses. There is an outright professional element, too, such as courses for career gardeners, building conservation masterclasses, and 'professional conservation in practice'.

No wonder, I reflect, that the staff have the skill to write craft books, though – like publishers – they must find it ever harder to be original. Unless one is into some especially esoteric craft, pioneering days are over.

Most of the tutors, over 200 of them, are on short-term contracts. 'Every week there are more offers from would-be tutors. I suppose you could say we are part of the new life-style portfolio especially appealing to those – tutors as well as students – who take early retirement to change direction but not give up.'

Caroline talks about how things have changed, and of her own earlier involvement, notably the organisation of an international conference for blacksmiths and iron forgers in Hereford in 1980. It was the second of two events the Crafts Council ran focusing on specific crafts. 'People then were totally skills orientated... a lot of very skilled men but isolated, totally divorced from anything to do with architecture, and in the outside world artists and craftsmen were being ignored. We inspired many young blacksmiths from around the world to become more part of life.' We chat about the role of the Rural Industries Bureau which became the Council for Small Industries in Rural Areas before changing again – and about pioneers such as Bernard Leach in potting, and Ethel Marriet in weaving, Robert Welsh in silversmithing, and of those who had grasped the nettle to alert public opinion and create the environment in which rural craft councils and other organisations took root, and teaching crafts could be accepted into the main stream of education. She recalls how Lord Eccles had helped set up the Craft Advisory Committee in 1971 (the same year that West Dean College was tentatively founded). The Committee became the Craft Council later in the decade.

Yes, it's a bit intense, self-conscious, but it's great. In the immediate postwar years, one couldn't possibly have imagined anything like it, and we mustn't take it for granted today. When I find Sheila and Barbara – yes, in the café – we all say what courses we'd like to take. I fancy 'Your SLR camera', and of course some of the gardening courses.

Patrick Moore and his Jeannie

Then to that curiously separate if not exactly isolated world of Selsey. Shopping is nicely old fashioned; so is courtesy. The sea must however be an acquired taste for those who love it here. It strikes me as threatening without any special quality, but many swear by it. Selsey is certainly not over-populated like so much of Southern England. At the end of the road down at Selsey Bill, we walk along what seems a makeshift path past a refreshment stand that probably has already been blown over or away several times and certainly doesn't look a sound insurance proposition. A reminder that Selsey has had more than its fair share of storms and hurricanes, several huge machines are close to where the waves peter out on the steep shingle. They are moving it around – silently it seems, because the noise of the breaking waves drowns even a low-flying plane – and building up a great protective bank. The large ferries popping in and out of Portsmouth and other shipping are more interesting than the immediate beach.

The home of astronomer Patrick Moore is suitably called Far Places, a cottage looking a bit like a gingerbread home from Hansel and Gretel, and with an intriguing notice about the greased-lightning speed of his white ball of fluff, Jeannie, the cat:

Caution: Patrick's cat is a fiendishly clever master of escape, a veritable Papillon of the feline world.
Please observe the airlock procedures:
Shut the external door before opening the inner... and vice versa.
Before opening the outer door check the little blighter is not lurking in the airlock, disguised as a coat or potted plant.

I've heard much about Jeannie. Letters and phone calls have told how she likes waking him up in the morning by nibbling his toes under the duvet. And she has a range of purrs the likes of which no other cat has equalled!

So this is where Patrick lives, and until surprisingly recent times with his mum, Gertrude Moore, who wrote and illustrated *Mrs Moore in Space* and was still a force to reckon with well into her mid-eighties. 'Tell me what it's about and I'll decide whether it's urgent my boy calls you tonight or if it can wait till morning. He's very busy you know. Oh yes, that's very urgent, he'll phone you before I give him his supper but keep it short. He's a hungry lad.'

An arch-bachelor? Not really. 'My girl Lorna – we were engaged – was killed in the blitz. It was the end of me.'

Speaker at our staff dinner, author, protégé of several of my staff, and good friend, Patrick was a model author, though decidedly not run of the mill. When I hinted that his agent was excessively greedy he took a half-finished memo out of my typewriter and wrote a letter sacking the guy. Our business involved listening to each other, as happened especially with his last book, before I sold D&C, *A Passion For Astronomy*.

'Tea or coffee?' I go to the kitchen to help, and see Jeannie. Patrick has just lost the use of a wrist, a spinal problem, so things have suddenly become harder. He can't do his buttons up, for example. Youth through to old age is very much our theme this morning. Back in his work room he goes into his history.

'When I was a boy of six, I well remember sitting in the armchair in the dining room in our old house at East Grinstead feeling thoroughly bored. It was raining and there was nothing to do. So I went across to the bookcase and picked out a book which I saw was called *The Story of the Solar System*, by GF Chambers.'

Purposefully, his head giving one of those characteristic slight shakes, he goes and picks the volume from its special place on today's shelves. It changed his life, led to his writing a hundred books ('I always wanted to be a writer'); having an observatory in his garden ('Selsey is good for that'), frequent TV and radio appearances, including the world's longest-running series The Sky at Night ('But the BBC's budget is absurdly low'). And of course many awards including honorary Fellow of the Royal Society: 'I was totally unprepared for that.' He passes me a letter from a twelve-year-old boy. 'Thank you for your phone call. I'm sorry if I sounded shy and confused, but it is not everyday you get a phone call from a TV personality and a Sir as well. I was stunned to think you had taken time from a busy schedule to help a schoolboy with his science project... PS congratulations on your BAFTA award last night.'

Sheila looks round to see where she can park her coffee. 'No you can't put your glass down on the xylophone,' shouts a notice. There are other musical instruments including the beloved piano Patrick has only just had to give up playing because of his wrist. He is an accomplished musician. I sometimes listen to his CDs, sold at lectures still given all over the country. When a friend asked him to play at his wedding he wrote a wedding march: that was for Chris Lintott, his next guest on The Sky at Night, and another reminder that he's always been a greater supporter of the young. He'd always find time to show any youngster round his observatory. And all around are reminders of other things, especially old typewriters. Once he typed accurately at ninety words a minute, but is down to twenty: 'Never been good at dictating.' But he's still what a former Astronomer Royal described as the 'master in the art of synthesis and simplification, yet without compromising on accuracy'.

When you check the map, Selsey is alarmingly close to Bognor Regis, but it feels light years away. It is the largest of the peninsulas along this part of the coast. At Bosham, we take the road that floods at every tide. Thorney Island also sticks out into Chichester's extended harbour which ends at Hayling Island, much more of this world, curious yes, but beautiful, definitely not. Then comes the peninsula dominated by Portsmouth which we miss this morning. There are happy holiday memories of Southsea and of ferry trips. Every time we catch sight of the sea there are the enormous ferries of today's rival operators who have brought new prosperity to Pompey, where the urban overspill with dense housing and ugly barracks would be a serious contender for Britain's motorway least-attractive view. We are soon off the M27 – certainly a blessing to those who struggle along the south coast on mainly poor and over-roundabouted roads – to slip into Fareham, the home of Johnathon Clifford.

Enemy of Vanity Publishers

While I have not always found him easy – sometimes his campaign of almost religious intensity has seemed to make him his own worst enemy – the case against Vanity Publishing owes much to Johnathon. Many of the abuses he's documented are hair-raising. Vanity publishers prey on would-be author's vanity and naivety (a potent mix) and often lack the least intention of doing what they promise. Lies, threats, and the same people moving on to operate from a different address when things get too hot, have long been characteristics of this seedy business. Often addresses are only PO boxes. Authors who have fallen for flattery, and paid over their hard-earned savings, have no recourse. Officers of Fair Trading have seen it all, made possible by unbelievable gullibility. Even firms that do abide by their one-sided agreements offer poor value, usually acting as expensive printers' agents. Most titles are genuinely unsaleable, at least in the scantily-edited, badly printed way in which they are offered to booksellers. Of course an odd exception can be found to break any rule, but in the vast majority of cases only the author and a few local bookshops are genuine customers. An unusually high royalty rate is offered, but it only amounts to the author receiving a few pounds of their own money back – if the firm hasn't moved on, operating under a new name so that even that minor expense is saved.

Johnathon's regular reports are invaluable in saying who is who, describing for example how it's not unique for a 'clean' new guy to attack his predecessor's iniquities when he is one and the same person. Many poetry anthologies are also a form of vanity publishing. Whatever nice things might be said about their quality and 'contribution to English literature', poems are only included if copies of the anthologies are ordered, at a high price for something cheaply produced.

Johnathon has been awarded an MBE for his services. He has only been able to push the boat out so valiantly because he's without money. Threats of legal proceedings and damages thus mean nothing. *Writers' News*, though slightly more careful than Johnathon, was never actually taken to court though threatened several times by solicitors possibly as ignorant about publishing as the victims of their clients. One suggested huge damages for calling his client a vanity publisher, unaware of the term's common usage.

But, in all walks of life, doesn't the buyer have to beware? There are many antique dealers who pressurise old ladies, for example.

'The comparison doesn't stand up,' says Johnathon. 'Of course there are bad people in all kinds of business, but here is a multi-million pound trade making itself look respectable by advertising without hindrance in all but a handful of publications. The Department of Trade & Industry look on with horror, while the crackdown by the Advertising Standards Authority could only ensure that approved ads were honest, not that the practices of the firms placing them were. Even where there have been multi-court orders against publishers, they still get their ads published. Added to that, most authors who realise they have been duped feel too foolish to complain to the paper whose ad got them into trouble. Indeed, to begin with I felt a fool when I realised I was the only person understanding the scale of abuse. There are some "real nice people" in the business, like a couple who met in prison. To their like I'm just a nuisance. If only they could get rid of me.'

Since a car accident, he has dedicated his whole life to the campaign, with a huge dossier covering up to sixty firms. Bulletins available from Johnathon Clifford, 27 Mill Road, Fareham, Hants PO16 OTH, johnathonclifford@compuserve.com.

Southampton

Southampton: city of antiquity, poor and atrociously expensive hotels (look at the prices and the AA's percentage rating, starting at the time of writing with 5 stars = 57 per cent) and great shopping. The first time I came here was from Cheltenham by what – until the GWR got its hands on it in 1923 – had been a marvellously independent and enterprising Midland & South Western Junction Railway. After an all-stations tour of a surprisingly empty slice of the south of England, I alighted at the old Terminus station with one other passenger. En route there had been a maximum of eight of us. Just outside the station was the enormous but closed luxury railway hotel that had become impossibly expensive to maintain. The next time I visited Southampton was to broadcast from the BBC's base established within renamed South Western House. On later visits, it was possible to park between the station's platforms where the tracks had been torn up. Then, as I built an association with Cunard, there were visits to its offices also within what was a pretty decrepit building.

Southampton was the gateway to (and especially from) the world, particularly North America. Cunard's fleet brought in the famous and the great: the view of the gangway was an animated *Who's Who?* In April 1970, I first left Europe on the *QE2* to develop the American market for D&C's books. Now, in preparation for writing this book, I have carefully avoided reading accounts of any previous writer's tours of Britain, but in Arundel happened on a copy of HV Morton's *In Search of England*, which I have always intended reading. Though studiously trying to avoid doing so just yet, I did however open it – and found a page headed *An Atlantic Liner*, which summed up many of my own feelings. What a puzzle, wrote Morton, it is to write a few words about a town in which every stone tells a story:

> So I went down, and towards the docks, still wondering, thinking about the giant Ascupart whose painted figure rests in the Bar Gate with that of Sir Bevis, and about God's House (or the Hospice of St Julian) which holds another different story. Then on the quayside at Southampton I came upon a live drama: the thing at the very heart of this town.
>
> An Atlantic liner lay at the dockside. Over the gangways swarmed porters carrying luggage. Men shouted and cleared a

space as the huge cranes swung round lifting piles of cabin trunks. There was the throb of imminent departure. Men looked at watches. Each second had its value. Smoke came from the funnels of the monster whose bulk was lifted above me, deck piled on deck. The sides of this ship were like the side of a cliff. From the high portholes gazed here and there a face like the face of a caveman looking down into a valley.

Someone shouted my name from the top of the mountain. Looking up, I saw a rich man known to me.

'Get a pass and come aboard!' he shouted.

In a few minutes I was sitting in a dove-grey boudoir like the reception-room of an exceptionally famous actress (only tidier), which this man called his cabin. He had an oxidised bed. A door led to a marble bathroom of the latest design full of oxidised taps and gadgets, cold showers and hot showers. He had paid £200 for all this.

'A sailor's life is a hard one,' I suggested.

'Pity you can't come over,' he said, with an idiot disregard of time and duty which is characteristic of those unhappy people with too much money.

His account of the monstrous inequality between his easily-bored rich friend, and those with humbler bags crying and laughing in the melee on the lower decks as they left to forge a new life in the New World, ends with a telegraph boy arriving with a fist full of envelopes. Just too late. The liner had set off. The boy watched the widening gap between quay and ship 'full of injury and resentment', as 'ridiculous as a frog feeling annoyed about a volcano', before taking his bundle of pink farewells back 'into the grey Town of Good-bye which men call Southampton'.

I vividly remember my first QE2's departure. We were delayed by one of those stoppages for which Southampton was then famous, and when we did leave it was a muted farewell. Only 500 people were on the great liner, barely a year old. Jets had stolen the Atlantic business far more quickly and thoroughly than anyone had calculated. Cunard was facing extinction. My second Atlantic crossing was by the *France* which was withdrawn only weeks later; my third by the *Empress of Canada*, pride of Canadian Pacific, that made only one further voyage before she was also sold off to new owners for Caribbean cruising. The *United States* was already just a legend, going to the breakers as did many other fine vessels before their time.

The *QE2* voyage was characterised by emptiness and union meetings; but the food was of an entirely new and different order, starting with a magnificent lunch between long periods of walking round the deck while we were still tied up. I learned the geography that became so familiar over the years as there were repeated voyages as lecturer and publisher of Cunard titles including one of my own – and occasionally just as passenger, luxuriating in sea, space and often solitude after busy periods.

When we did get started on that first voyage, I gave full attention to the passage down the Solent past Fawley, the views of the coast east to Southsea and Selsey Bill, and of the east and south coasts of the Isle of Wight, whose resorts were surprisingly inconspicuous, ending with the white cliffs petering out in the Needles. That things didn't always go well on the *QE2* was brought home by an incident off the Needles. A helicopter was to land on the Helicopter Deck. 'As a precaution, would all women on deck please ensure they are wearing a scarf or other loose item of clothing.' It was corrected, to the amusement of the newer union-prone staff and the irritation of the old timers who came from the *Queen Mary* and *Queen Elizabeth* and tried valiantly to preserve the old standards. In the moonlight the Needles assume a dream-like quality or once, in a pattern of light and cloud shadow, a nightmarish ferocity.

Times always change. Miraculously the *QE2* continued its lonesome life, but often weeks – sometimes months – passed between its bringing the postwar terminal to life for a few frantic hours. Suddenly sea travel has regained popularity, with many new ships. One of them is at the *QE2*'s berth this very morning, the 109,000 ton *Golden Princess* starting her maiden voyage. Curiosity makes me take a look. The chatty taxi driver began his working life in the shipping business and is a mine of information. South Western House is to be converted to luxury flats; I'll hate the *Golden Princess*, 'an ugly duckling'; Southampton has at last woken up to the importance of the cruise business, 'but hotels are terrible and on busy days like today taxis and coaches can't cope'; and what will be worth coming to see is the *Queen Mary 2*, recently commissioned by Cunard's new American owners, 'with its Yacht Club 150ft above the waves'.

He's right. I have quickly seen enough of the *Golden Princess*, longer than the *QE2*, with almost twice as many passengers, but infinitely less distinguished. 'The largest one we've had so far, but there are bigger and uglier to come. They're holiday camps at sea, except they don't even go far. This one won't come back. It's short fly-cruise business, in and out of the same Mediterranean or Caribbean ports. Plenty of booze, though.' She is certainly intrusive at the *QE2*'s berth, where I recall I once had a clothing dilemma. In picking up a piece of luggage, my trousers ripped top to bottom. Already wearing a pyjama jacket as my shirts had been accidentally packed, I now had to wear a buttoned-up raincoat on one of the year's hottest nights. It was almost as good as the time I dressed so hastily on arriving at Heathrow after a long flight that the chief steward remarked: 'Sir, never let it be said of British Airways that they allow an eccentric old gentleman to leave the plane with his anorak on upside down.'

There is only one *QE2*, the world's most famous, fastest ship, a unique institution, always *the* ship. Shore-side's organisation has often remained chaotic, but the ship's embrace invariably welcoming, soothing away anxiety and enhancing the celebration of life – and the respect for the great maritime tradition which for two decades Cunard alone seriously upheld.

So much for memories. Now back at the hotel I am joined by AGK Leonard who I first knew by his initials as we alternated writing the short leader page feature in the West Country's Sunday *Independent*. 'Remember the day Walter Taylor [the editor] put the fee up from a guinea to 25 shillings without our asking?' Indeed I do; riches. I was then working for *The Western Morning News* to which AGKL was also a frequent contributor. Ironically we first met when I was covering the Plympton inquest of his father who had been knocked down in a road accident.

Though AGKL had an early spell in Fleet Street, he was administrative assistant to the great Dr Scott who directed Plymouth's postwar education and came to Southampton for promotion a long time before retiring. We talk about newspapers' love of local history, 'though today some groups feel their staff can write about any subject'. He adds: 'My first leader-page article for the *Morning News* was on 13 April 1951 about the visits to the Theatre Royal of Wm Macready. It mainly came from his 1875 diaries I'd bought for six shillings, enough to make me really interested. I was paid two guineas for it. That went up to three guineas in 1953 and four the following year.'

'I can beat that! My first *Morning News* leader-page article was in 1949,' I say sadly telling how my parents, alternately proud and jealous, had said publishing the article showed what a bad paper it was. 'What decent paper would have such a subheading 'NO SNOOPERS' in the piece about our model railway?'

> Though stopping at Taunton, Exeter and Plymouth, and bearing destination boards labelled Penzance, our trains invariably finish their journey at Seagood – the perfect holiday resort, in which hotels still charge pre-war prices, and where no Ministry of Food snooper has yet dared to venture.

'We knew our market,' says Alan. 'Lucid prose that's read has always struck me as better than wonderful writing nobody wants.'

After ordering our sandwiches in the bar, we turn to books and Alan tells me of his dozen local titles, starting with *Stories of Southampton*

Streets. He regrets he's not had the advantage of a subject like railways. 'Good for sales, but many people don't think railway books are real ones,' I mutter. So we go on good humouredly over our chicken sandwiches.

'I'm still reading old newspapers for material,' he says. 'I remember you doing that in the library when they let you have real papers, bound volumes. Now it's microfilm. Gives you a crick in the neck after an hour. But you can get printouts. And censuses. People don't use them like we used to – great sources.' I pass him an August 1867 cutting about how the South Western got even with fare dodgers – by leaving their carriage behind in the station and letting them be laughed at.

GEORGIAN GEM

Bath Here We Come

Our thoughts are beginning to turn to Bath where, to retain a foothold in England, we have a 'wee pad' and keep Little Car. She is a cheaper alternative to renting with its collision waivers and other expensive complications. Not to mention that sometimes we used to have to wait for a vehicle to be ready. Or that, despite pleas about needing a compact to fit into our tiny garage, 'you'll be pleased to know you've been upgraded'. Once with a vehicle so large that, having a struggle to squeeze out of the door once it was in the garage, we didn't dare turn a wheel for the several days before it was time to return the beast. We were nervous about leaving it on the street since, outraged by the cost of all the extras, which make nonsense of the headline price, it was the one occasion we had declined part of the optional insurance. But we've still one night of travel before our chance to relax in Bath. First call is just outside Romsey.

Ice Cream Parlour

Sheila tells how, as a young child in the war who had only just experienced the joy of ice cream when it was abolished, she periodically persuaded her mum to allow her to visit Mrs Bishop's, the corner shop in Stafford in the forlorn hope they might have some. In her sixties, occasionally she demands the stuff with a passion that only comes from someone seriously denied in childhood. Alas, she and Barbara say they are stuffed from lunch. 'Fools,' I say. 'You can't not have *and enjoy* ice cream this afternoon.' I repeat it as we drive up to Carlo's Ice Cream Parlour.

We have previously met Tony and Barbara in the *QE2*'s Queen's Grill where our assistant restaurant manager of many years (earlier he and I worked our way up the ship's restaurant hierarchy in tandem) is Tony's cousin, Colin. They share the same surname – Donnarumma. This is a long-anticipated social occasion. As we park, Colin rushes to help Sheila and our Barbara. Then we smile that rare, totally natural full-face smile that denotes familiarity and deep respect and pleasure. Colin has long been part of my support system. On the ship, he cossets, surprises, teases – and in ports around the world we've enjoyed a range of experiences that can't be bought. He's excellent at changing tyres by the way. He has a wicked sense of humour, doesn't accept silly rules easily and has been revered by 'his' passengers since the old *Queen Mary* days.

He is a source of memories and current news, too. For example, he describes how one evening a waiter, thinking he had the dining room to himself, and anxious to get off duty, gathered everything from a table into the table cloth and tossed it out through one of the chutes that directed in fresh air in those pre-air condition days. The china and cutlery lie at the bottom of the Atlantic somewhere. He has often told us of the foibles of the famous and not always so great. And of the poverty in Southern Italy that made his dad and his uncle Carlo, Tony's dad, come to Hampshire for a better life. That was in 1894.

When Carlo died in 1990, Tony was already deeply into ice cream, but today's Carlo's has a number of new features, including an extensive tea room and a pets' corner. It is famous for miles around. Good wholesome fare at bargain prices prepares the way for splurging on an ice cream sundae (six varieties) or just a large plain or mixed ice cream, all made on the premises. 'In some ways we're upmarket of the *QE2*,' says Tony. 'You'll not find a sundae at sea to match ours,' adds Barbara. After greeting us, daughter Beverley who makes the cakes, shyly returns to busy herself in the kitchen.

Our conversation ranges from reminiscences with Colin through plans for the new *Queen Mary* ('I was on the old *Queen Mary* with Colin's dad,' says Tony) to the state of the world and Barbara's marvellous collection of teddy bears ('they're not teddies, they're beanies,' she tells Sheila), punctuated by comments on ice cream. That is clearly more a way of life than a business.

'Tony won't put our prices up,' is interrupted by Tony himself saying that there are 25 different flavours. 'We make vanilla every day, pineapple Monday, strawberry Tuesday, cherry Wednesday... look at the expression on that little lad's face. That ice has put him in heaven.'

'This is where children come into their own. They are their own characters here,' says Barbara.

'£2,000 worth of cornets, a hundred gallons of ice cream a day,' shouts Tony.

'Tony dreams ice cream.'

'Barbara often can't sleep at all.' So she makes dolls and dresses them. She designed the tea room and the miniature fairground carousels which go round with festive music at Christmas.

Then the two Donnarummas become slightly maudlin regretting the disappearance of the graceful ships of yesteryear. There's obviously a close bond between them, one, having missed life's opportunities to set out on his own, struggling to retain high standards of individual service on the *QE2*, the other enjoying turning down offers for the business, content to charge 50p for a large ice-cream filled cone because his property costs are minimal, while £1.50 might not be enough were he renting space at Southampton's Ocean Village.

'What a set-up,' says our Barbara, as we get into her car and think the emotional farewells have finished. But Colin opens my door: 'Tell me when I'll see you again.'

'And what ice cream at what prices. You can see why they are so popular,' Barbara continues when we're finally under way.

'And why they need such an enormous car park,' adds Sheila.

Hilliers Nurseries

We make our way down lanes to what, just north of Romsey, will surely be a more welcoming hotel than last night's. We pass Keats Restaurant, where I thought we had booked. Near to the headquarters of Hilliers Nurseries, that is where in the past I've enjoyed many fine meals with Robert Hillier. It seems it is not a hotel at all. I'd forgotten the name and after talking to Robert's secretary fell into the trap of reserving our room plus dinner at Potter's Heron Hotel instead. The Hilliers have remained good friends and we still meet on special occasions round the country, sometimes in Bath, but it is ten years since I was last here.

Business connection with Hilliers started when I noted that a relative keen on her garden spent hours poring over *Hillier's Manual of Trees & Shrubs*, a trade catalogue with descriptions of various lengths. The pages were hard to hold open and easily frayed. For a hundred pounds, Robert's father, who became Sir Harold Hillier, gave me permission to use the typography. D&C reprinted the manual as a fat hardback, with a quality paperback for Hilliers to use as their catalogue. Never was a bestseller more easily established. Immediately, Hilliers was a brand name respected throughout the book trade. The *Manual* was extended, improved with more consistent entries and reset. Other titles followed. Just mutter 'Hilliers at our sales conferences and you had instant attention.

'The only trouble is that we didn't know if we were nurserymen or authors,' says Robert jokingly. Then I explain the mistake over the booking.

'So where do you want to feed us?'

'Us' is himself and his partner Jean Savage, also a good friend. She suggests he rings Daverio at Keats. He returns quickly, smiling success.

The hotel good-naturedly accepts why they are losing five diners. We jump in the car and minutes later are enthusiastically greeted by Daverio. 'Guess ten years is a long time.'

To miss returning to this choice of fish and pasta would have been a crime. Daverio, owner and maître d', assures everyone they've made the perfect choice. Our conversation returns to the thriving horticultural business. Started in 1864 and now in its fourth generation, Hilliers is still a family business, turning over £24 million and employing 400 people.

'We have twelve garden centres, which have been consistently profitable, so can concentrate on the supply side. We supply several hundred garden centres, and the contracting side is also important.' Though Robert has no children, there are family working in the business. We discuss the tough times we both suffered. Sharing problems certainly helped when things were difficult.

'It's different now. Today we have managers with targets and we delegate. Dad tried to manage everything himself, a real autocrat. But a great plantsman. Grandfather was interested in conifers, father fanatical. He made great finds around the world, brought specimens of hundreds of trees back home and grew them. We all owe a lot to that. But the catalogue had 10,000 lines and nobody knew a thing about many of them. Now we're down to about 1,000 lines, and that's complicated enough to manage.'

In his later days, Sir Harold was especially devoted to the Arboretum, now run by the County Council. There you can still appreciate his contribution to horticulture. I recall wondering if the personal tour he once gave me would ever come to an end. Such fanaticism began when he started his notes, aged six, as determined to be an exceptional plantsman as Patrick Moore was to be an astronomer. But, well after my involvement, Hilliers were in danger of turning sour. 'Dad's ambition was beyond the means of a then not very profitable nursery, heavily into one-off mail-order customers. My brother, more the plantsman than I am, was especially pleased when the Arboretum's future was assured. It's unique. Then, when he was 78, Dad was persuaded to accept a knighthood, performed by the Queen Mother. He'd known her and her garden in Glamis in 1926. He had a struggle to kneel and couldn't get up afterwards, but he was justifiably proud. We all were.'

So back to our hotel ready for a bath and Bath tomorrow.

Bath and the Pump Room

In the morning, Barbara puts us on a train at Romsey. Apart from the view of Salisbury with its cathedral spire, the later part of the journey is the most interesting. We follow the gently winding Avon through

Bradford-on-Avon, a beautiful place of mellow Cotswold stone. The graceful stone bridge over the river still retains the lock-up in the middle. What a spot in which to be left to cool off for the night! There is a fine architectural legacy from the days Bradford prospered as an important centre of the wool trade, while in recent years, with some of Bath's dealers moving in, the town has become a mecca for antique collectors. Bradford is a place well worth visiting for at least a few hours, and has an excellent train service and a generous car park.

Still beside the Avon, we soon pass under the aqueduct mentioned at the beginning of this book, and then join Brunel's route from Paddington for the only level access there is into Bath. Though the river plays a vital role in its life, Bath, like Rome, is built on seven hills. The city is in a vast bowl, which makes for marvellous views but an oppressive climate. Avoid Bath when a thunderstorm gets trapped in the bowl and rolls around the hills for hours.

Not a cloud in the sky for our arrival this morning. The midday winter sun lights up south-facing buildings in the city, and up the northern slopes. Since there is no food in the flat, having discarded our luggage and turned on the heating, we walk briskly along broad Great Pulteney Street – an old picture shows it appearing even wider when tree-lined in pre-motor days – across Pulteney Bridge with its shops on either side, around the corner into Grand Parade overlooking the weir, racing fast after recent heavy rain, past the magnificent Abbey (gleaming from its recent cleaning), across the paved area known as Abbey Churchyard and into the Pump Room where, over the generations, so much of Bath's social life has taken place. The restaurant is relatively quiet just before lunch and we are in time to see the long-serving trio of musicians reach a crescendo and pack up.

I love eating here. After a long spell in Nairn, there is something delightfully civilised about a buttered Bath bun with morning coffee to the accompaniment of the trio. The restaurant is comfortable, spacious. You get to know the friendly staff, and there's always something to look at, such as the flunkey dressed in Georgian costume serving doses of the horrible-tasting Spa water to visitors who have been round the Roman Baths (the busiest fee-charging venue outside London), and feel they need to sample the stuff to complete the experience. Another good thing about the Pump Room is that visitors and locals alike feel special, mingling as happily as anywhere in tourist Britain.

Bath is a wonderful antidote to Nairn although, however much we enjoy the architecture, the centuries of history all around us, our friends, restaurants and entertainments, it is not long before we begin to miss the sea. Though few West Country folk believe it possible, we also miss the greater sunshine and lower rainfall of the Moray Firth, especially in the winter half of the year.

As often happens at the Pump Room, a friend at a distant table waves and then comes across for a coffee. Like many others in Bath's society, her husband's military career brought them here. The Admiralty's headquarters used to be here, with jokes about matelots learning seamanship on the Kennet & Avon Canal; and the Ministry of Defence has long been a major employer, though most of today's staff work out of the city at Abbey Wood.

'But we knew Bath well before that,' says the friend. 'In fact my dad once drove us through the centre before the war. We were on our way to Bristol with its small tramcars around that part of the harbour that has been filled in.' To which I say that I stayed at Bath's Francis Hotel in pre-war days and clearly remember its layout, the lift, the bedroom... and the food. And the first occasion I was disillusioned by a doctor. Mum called in the hotel doctor when I had a stomach upset.

'What do you think is wrong?' he asked, to which Mum questioned if the rich food and cream might be to blame.

'Yes, it's the cream.' Followed half a moment later by 'Half a guinea, please.'

Decades later, an American visitor to a nearby resort, not Bath itself, suffered from a giddy fit, or labyrinthitis. 'Just take it gently,' advised the hotel doctor. 'Don't fly and of course avoid the sea. Best take a train home.' Followed by how much the charge would be for the consultation.

When the Roman Baths Ran Dry

After lunch, we decide to take a rare visit to the Roman Baths, paying for the undoubted privilege of descending the stairs to the uneven slabs around the colonnades, the baths steaming gently in the middle. This is where it all began. Several visitors have their cameras out for what must be one of Britain's most-photographed scenes: the Baths in the foreground with the Abbey and its tower beyond.

We try to imagine what it must have been like in Roman days. Civilisation personified, no doubt. And the consternation and agitation of the city fathers in 1810 when the hot springs suddenly dried up. Bath's very raison d'être was at stake.

At which point thoughts return to William Smith, the Father of Geology, mentioned at the beginning of this book. Well known in the area, Smith was the natural expert to consult. He happened to be in London, and came racing down to save Bath's fortunes. He wasn't at all popular when he suggested digging deep down to see if the cause of the failure could be found. As the only alternative would have been to close a new coal mine three miles away which some blamed for causing the problem, he was allowed to dig into the hallowed ground. With temperatures up to 119 degrees Fahrenheit, burrowing down through the limestone and clay must have been miserable work for him and his team of navvies. Candles melted before they gave adequate light. But, success. 'Some large ruminant' was discovered, a large crystallised oxbone that had somehow rolled into the path of the spring, causing the water to find another route to the Avon. The bone removed, all was well.

All, however, was not well for William Smith. He became one of the least happy of the gallery of famous people who spent part of their career in Bath. It may be recalled that he was the first to realise what rocks would follow each other in the strata, aided by the discovery that each kind of fossil was unique to its own rock bed of successive geological eras. Finding a fossil anywhere in the country therefore told its geological age, and what would be the strata above and underneath.

Smith's career was not unlike some of the strata he pursued, with occasional uplifts, numerous folds and ultimate disappearance under the weight above. While he was still young, his experience and knowledge were greatly helped by his appointment as chief surveyor to the Somersetshire Coal Canal. That meant cutting through a part of the country with dramatic terrain. As the canal pushed forward, increasingly his expectations of what would be found next were confirmed. He realised that, generally speaking, younger rocks are found to the east, older to the west, so that a journey along the south coast from Dorset to Kent steadily takes one to more recent geological times.

This kind of knowledge was obviously of interest to land (and especially coal mine) owners. He built a reasonably profitable consulting business, but relied heavily on his core appointment as surveyor to the canal, no doubt for the secretarial support and kudos it offered as well as the salary. He was shattered when he was suddenly sacked. It seems that the canal's shareholders were not amused by a few extra acres for his home at Tucking Mill being added to the land acquired for the waterway. Moreover, when he was awarded a medal by the Society of Arts for a monograph describing how he had rescued what had given Bath its very name, it was an unfortunate reminder that delivery of his long-planned geological map of Britain, which the Society had encouraged, was long overdue.

Back in 1799, Smith had produced what was possibly the world's first geological map, covering five miles around Bath. But it showed only limited rock distribution. The larger map promised far greater significance. Like many breaking new ground, at first Smith was afraid to publish his broader findings lest others might benefit. But he was also held back by lack of discipline and purpose. Often he lurched from crisis to crisis, seemingly constitutionally unable to make the best of opportunities that presented themselves. And though, when not paid for by clients, his perpetual travelling through England was necessarily costly, his finances were ruined by maintaining too expensive a lifestyle, with homes above his station successively at Tucking Mill, central Bath and London. His station in life was to trouble him greatly. Of Oxfordshire yeoman stock, even when his genius shone through he was not readily accepted into the higher echelons of society. Certainly not by the Geological Society: 'The theory of geology is in the possession of one class of men, the practice in another.' Added to all that, his own Somerset quarry failed, and he married a woman about to become mad. Ironically, his fortunes were at their nadir when his large map was finally published. He went to debtors' prison.

His one-man achievement can be gauged from the remarkable similarity between his map and a modern geological map of England and Southern Scotland. They appear side by side on the end papers of Simon Winchester's *The Map That Changed the World*. Partly because it is so complicated a story, and partly because it is hard to warm to Smith, who was so frequently his own worst enemy, perhaps this book is not such a good read as the author's *The Surgeon of Crowthorne* with its combination of real-life drama and the telling of a tale of genuine historical significance. (It is about the doctor who contributed the greatest single number of entries to the *Oxford Dictionary* while in a lunatic asylum.)

Smith's map didn't even sell particularly well, for the passage of time had allowed the competition to steal data and catch up. A rival version sold more cheaply, with an even cheaper offer to members of the Geological Society. But Smith's huge map still hangs behind drapes above one of the marble staircases at Burlington House, on Piccadilly's north side. And eventually his brilliance was recognised and, to relieve his debt, the British Museum bought his unique fossil collection. Then, in 1831, the Geological Society selected him as the first of a long line of prestigious people to receive the Woolstan Medal.

Smith's work obviously did much to hasten the realisation of geology's importance... always, of course, opposed by those who thought it sacrilegious to question the literal interpretation of the Bible's telling of how the world was created. More people came to be aware, for example, of why Wells and Lincoln have Jurassic cathedrals, made of limestone of the same age, while around Britain may be seen some of Smith's physical works, such as improvements to the little Welsh port of Kidwelly, of Dylan Thomas fame, and the building of the embankment at Laugharne, where the poet is buried. One of Dylan Thomas's early poems was called *The Map of Love*.

And here in Bath, though no doubt the hot spring would have been saved anyway, Smith's rescue was effected quickly, before much damage had been done to the Spa's reputation. Before climbing back up the stairs, we think of the excitements and disappointments his career must have brought. Possibly his mistake was in expecting to be welcomed among better-educated people. The genius, of say, George Stephenson, was the more notable because, self-educated, he unashamedly remained a rough diamond. We wonder if Smith would agree with today's council's brochure on the Spa water:

> Bath spa water fell as rain up to 10,000 years ago on the nearby Mendip hills. Driven down through carboniferous limestone cave systems by pressure from the high water table on the Mendips, the water has reached depths of two to three kilometres.
>
> The water penetrates overlying strata of impermeable Lias clay through fissures and a fault to rise at three points in Bath. The greatest source is the King's Spring. Here the flow is thirteen litres per second or 1,106,400 litres (about 250,000 gallons) per day. The temperature is 46°C (115°F) ... In mediaeval times a cure for conditions such as paralysis, colic, palsy and gout was sought from bathing in spa water. Lead poisoning was a cause of many of these afflictions. Many occupations involved exposure to lead. Alcohol, especially port, was adulterated with lead as a sweetener and fungicide. Eighteenth century records from Bath Mineral Water Hospital show that patients benefited from the cure. Today it is fashionable to be sceptical about the curative properties of spa water although spas in Europe remain popular.

The fashion for drinking spa water arose from new medical ideas in the later seventeenth century. The Pump Room was opened in 1706 to provide a place to drink the waters, but was rebuilt in 1795. There were severe criticisms about its lack of facilities for visitors at the point 'when the waters begin to operate'... not surprising since the amount prescribed could be up to a gallon in a morning. Very few of today's visitors take more than a sip from their glass. For most of us, the experience is not one to repeat, but it is fun watching the expressions of visitors trying their fifty pence worth, many giving up when they have sipped tuppence worth.

Going out into Abbey Churchyard, we have gently to push our way through a crowd enjoying a juggler pedalling away on his oversized cycle while tossing flaming torches into the air and catching them with meticulous precision. When he takes a well-earned break, the crowd cheers, and no doubt his takings will be fatter than those of most performers. The council organises a rota, so the scene and sounds change constantly.

It is only a few steps to the Abbey's entrance. A large family are busy pointing out the details of the carved Jacob's ladder on either side, angels ascending and descending, those coming down carved head first since in mediaeval days they didn't know how better to show them returning to earth. We follow the family inside and, as we look down the long nave, are once more struck by the lightness, for it used to seem so dark and gloomy. The transformation happened in the mid-1990s. Even those organising it were amazed at the difference made by removing the grease and grime of generations of candlelight. The greatest joy was the revelation of the richly-coloured bosses at the top of the fan vaulting and the rainbow above the choir's east end. Nobody expected such treasure to shine forth. Along with other visitors, we gaze at the great east window telling the life of Christ in its 56 stained-glass panels.

History is all around us. It was here that the first King of all England, Edgar, was crowned in 973. There are numerous monuments, though mainly from the nineteenth and twentieth centuries. The fan vaulting in the nave is Victorian from the 1860s, a faithful copy of the original that has survived in the choir. The Abbey was Britain's very last major perpendicular-style building to be started, just forty years before it was suppressed with so many other monastic houses under Henry VIII. Part of it was roofless for many years, and it was a miracle that more was not destroyed. It played a negligible role in Bath's life when the city attracted the greatest number of people seeking cures and the famous terraces were built. Today it is as busy as a church as it is as tourist attraction, and a fine venue for concerts. This morning's feeling of well-being is enhanced by ethereal organ music. Especially since the restoration of the great instrument, also in the 1990s, organ recitals and CDs, including those of the resident organist, have achieved international acclaim.

It is time to buy food for our stay. As soon as I have a full load, I set off 'home' on my own while Sheila takes time to visit old haunts and friends. She cannot go anywhere near the Abbey without being stopped; she made her mark there as its first woman churchwarden.

All-of-a-piece Bath and its Visitors

Even in winter, Bath is being 'done' by many visitors, including Americans. They give just sufficient support to sustain the rival bus companies offering open-top tours with commentary. To prevent the opposition stealing an advantage, the rivals leave at such frequent intervals that even in summer there are often mere handfuls of sightseers on board. Today one couple, huddling downstairs rather than on the open top, have a whole tour to themselves. With their intrusive glib commentaries, the buses are much hated by residents: they clog the already congested roads, slow down at narrow spots, and generally give the impression that the whole city is a glass-case survival. Which in many ways it is. Though even here a few architectural monstrosities were permitted before Bath's heritage was universally recognised and so better protected.

Despite Hitler's bombs, Bath is the only provincial English city which can be said to be all of a piece. York, Chester and Canterbury have their gems, but not unified top-quality buildings en masse as does Bath, where the functional things like superstores and railway bridges as well as most houses are of Bath stone – well at least faced with it in the case of more recent buildings. Architecturally, in Britain only Edinburgh is a serious contender. And many transatlantic visitors 'doing' Britain in a few days concentrate on these two before hopping around Continental cities.

Taking a moment's rest above Pulteney Weir, where in summer tourists catch boats, too, I'm approached by an overweight woman probably from somewhere in middle America holding out a map.

'Xcuse me, where's Princes Street?'

'Honey, that's tomorrow in Edingberg,' says her embarrassed husband, scarcely half her size and with less than a quarter of her confidence.

'Yes. But I'm chilly. I need a sweater now.'

'She shops every day,' puts in her husband.

'Of course.'

I explain that there's so much to do in Bath that if she's going to Edinburgh tomorrow, she should stick to sightseeing and, on the map, point out the Roman Baths, Abbey, and Pulteney Bridge right in front of us.

She can't wait till Edingberg, so reluctantly I direct her to the Edinburgh Woollen Mill but suggests she 'does' the Roman Baths on the way.

'We've picked off the Baths and the Abbey,' she announces. Intrigued, I ask her how they're going to Edinburgh.

'Edingberg. By train tonight. We've a Britrail pass to save money. We transfer stations this evening, 'cause there won't be enough time to shop on a day trip.' I say we often use the sleeper.

'Neat. Say, what's the bathroom like?' She's not too sure about it being at the end of the corridor. 'You need your bathroom handy. Can't we upgrade?'

Afraid not. She then waddles off, followed by her husband, to the Edinburgh Woollen Mill who have no doubt served plenty like her.

An American friend came to Bath years ago when hotels had fewer private facilities. Not merely could he not have his own en suite, but he had to collect the key to 'the bathroom' from reception. He held out as long as he could and, when bursting to pee, had to stand in line at reception to pick up the key. He dashed into the bathroom undoing his flies... to find it only had a tub bath. It was a British, not American, bathroom. Toilets were, of course, readily available all the time.

Many Americans and other visitors from far away come to Bath within days of first arriving in Britain, lots of them making it their first provincial stop and so using hotels and restaurants where they are puzzled by things being different from back home.

'Why can't they call it macaroni and cheese like we do?' asked one when told that macaroni cheese on the menu is the same thing... well, almost, anyway. Apart from the lingo, turbot shockingly being pronounced as turbot instead of turbo, they can't get used to the fact that Brits order rapidly and our waiters aren't used to lengthy discussions and look blank when someone asks for a bowl of soup for themselves but a cup for their partner. The behaviour of some doesn't go down well. 'When I ask for melon, I expect just that: melon,' grumbled one woman about pineapple also being on the plate. She ate the pineapple and left the melon!

The trouble is that these days many Americans are from inward-looking mid-America, genuinely amazed that things aren't the same everywhere. It is to be welcomed that they are venturing forth, but there are bound to be teething problems. I recall, admittedly in an airport, a girl of about fifteen stamping her feet in anger, bawling out 'that's ridiculous', when someone explained to her that the stamps on the card she had prepared before setting off on her first overseas trip would not be acceptable to the non-American post office. In Bath, I've seen Americans post American cards home. It is part of the 'it's all the same' syndrome, which has Americans ever likening the most individually British of landscapes to something with which they are comfortably familiar. 'It reminds me of...' How I dislike that phrase.

Not that it is right to dwell too long on the downside of Americans. Many are deeply respectful of Bath's history. On the whole they get pretty well integrated, along with visitors from all parts of the world, including Brits enjoying one of their own natural treasures. The probability is that far more readers of this book will have been to Bath than any other place outside London. Bath has much going for it. The legacy left by the Romans. Many outstanding individual buildings (besides the obvious trio of Abbey, Pump Room and Assembly Rooms), and the city as a whole is crammed with architectural and historic interest. It is compact enough to explore on foot, even to walk up to the Circus and turn left, through a civilised shopping enclave with several of the city's excellent art galleries, to the Royal Crescent. It boasts probably the best range of restaurants in Britain outside London, and excellent hotels as well as a few grottier ones. Its people are friendly with an acceptance that visitors will wish to share their treasure, for local pride is intense. And, though far nearer to Bristol than Inverness is to Nairn, it enjoys a totally different political, cultural and every other kind of set-up, down to a very different evening newspaper.

What was it Dr Johnson said about it being a dull man who couldn't appreciate London? Bath is more accessible, easier to understand and analyse. It is a place you can appreciate in a day, as with the help of tour guides do many visitors coming off the *Orient Express* on its regular visits. Yet those who have lived here all their lives still unravel new joy, perhaps in one of the public buildings, the walk along the river or canal, the corner of a park, gallery or the Abbey. Culture is an essential essence. The Theatre Royal is a gem with an enterprisingly varied programme. Concerts of the highest quality are held in many venues, including again the Abbey and the Assembly Rooms.

Museums abound: American, costume, photographic, postal, and a particularly fascinating Bath at Work, or Bowler Museum. Even the Bath Abbey Cemetery on Ralph Allen Drive has become something of a theme park with a trail past the graves of many famous and extraordinary characters. And there are many other surprises such as Sainsbury's, built on the yard of Green Park station, incorporating the preserved terminus where the Midland Railway met the idiosyncratic Somerset & Dorset, or Slow & Dirty. The navigable Avon and the restored Kennet & Avon Canal add great possibilities. We are steadily walking the canal with its many historic structures and unspoilt setting.

All-of-a-piece Bath is never dull. And it grows out of the landscape. I love those old prints showing what the great crescents, including the Royal Crescent, Lansdown Crescent and the Circus, looked like before the land between them had been in-filled (though generous parkland remains part of the scene), and the tales of how architects and contractors rose to new challenges. They were helped by what for its day was a unique degree of standardisation. For example, nearly all Georgian townhouses, in top and secondary locations, are three windows wide: two for the main rooms, front and back, on each floor, and one for the lesser rooms, including the hall on the ground floor where the front door takes the place of a window. There was a degree of standardisation in making the great Palladian buildings, too – standardisation which along with the universal Bath stone gives unique unity. A wonderful heritage was created (and fortunes made) in a surprisingly short building burst in the early eighteenth century.

As well as establishing the rules of etiquette, Bath's dictator or Master of Ceremonies, Richard or Beau Nash, played a key role in the layout and building design. In many ways he was ahead of his time. Health conscious, he banned smoking in public buildings, and taxed the public gambling he encouraged. That didn't prevent him becoming poor later in life, and nor could he have foreseen the motor vehicle and the trouble it would bring. The traffic is one of Bath's negative points, though much has recently been achieved to calm it... rightly at the cost of inconvenience to many motorists. But just try explaining to a harassed American, daringly driving on 'the wrong side' of the road for the first time in their life, how to take the inevitably long way round between adjoining zones!

Old-fashioned Bookbindery

There are so many museums, that when I approach the bookbindery and shop of George Bayntun, not far from the main railway station, I am not much surprised when someone asks for the exact whereabouts of 'the book museum'.

'It happens sometimes,' says Mr Edward Bayntun-Coward, today's owner. 'I suppose we ask for, it since any hint of a machine, and it is thrown out. It's all handwork here, old-fashioned if you like, but great craftsmanship, art, and still very much a business.'

There are sixteen staff, not all in the bindery, and computers are freely used for normal business purposes. The shop displays a magnificent array of the bookbindery's offerings. Prices are not for the faint-hearted. Many rare works in their rebound form are priced in thousands of pounds.

'Anyway, do you want to see what your friend called the museum?' asks Mr Bayntun-Coward. Behind the scenes is a magic land of the skills and tools discarded by most binders decades if not generations ago. The collection of individual brass engraved hand tools exceeds 10,000. There is a huge collection of hand-set type and decorative features (or brasses) so that the style of almost any old binding can be copied faithfully. For one who has had to publish books with ever fewer individual features, this is most refreshing. Even in the thirty years I ran David & Charles, details like hand tipped-in frontispieces and folded maps, coloured tops and ribbons became impossibly expensive, while the range of real cloths commercially available shrank. Many other aspects, such as ensuring words are split the correct way, the avoidance of breaking words at page ends, always having at least three lines of text in a paragraph ending at the top of a new page, have also disappeared with computer typesetting. Handwork is impossibly expensive... hence this handbindery's prices well out of the range of ordinary book buyers and readers.

I am taken through the various processes involved in rebinding an old title. Incidentally, at auction a skilfully rebound book, certainly one from here, frequently fetches a higher price than one in an original binding. Over a hundred hand processes are involved in rebinding to a high standard.

A particularly delicate process is removing the original covers and unpicking the pages, of course getting rid of threads. Each section is then sewn into lined cords dangling from an old wooden sewing frame. The strength of leather bindings depends on the covers being hinged on to these cords until the whole thing becomes a single unit. The bulk of the sewn sections, collected together, is reduced under the nipping press, which expels the air. The choice of end papers is as great as that of binding materials. A matching design and/or colour will normally be chosen. Some of the marbled end pages have designs popular since the days of Charles II.

To explain some of the processes individually, the ends of the cords are frayed across a tin sheet, and a film of glue brushed between each section, after which the book is clamped in what is described as a mangle lookalike, or backing machine, while the spine is rounded with a hammer and heavy roller. Two sheets of heavy millboard form the guts of the cover, into which the dangling cords are laced. The boards are nicked with a Stanley knife, and holes produced with a bodkin greased lightly with a slick of (surprise, here) Brylcreem. I have often wondered who buys that stuff these days.

The frayed cord ends are pointed off and slipped through the holes and hammered flat into their niche. A large pile of books is now stacked under a massive standing press, where they will be left overnight to squeeze out further air. And so, as described in an excellent leaflet *Glory Bound*, it goes on: of course much more fascinating to watch as the scarcely-slim craftsmen binders move from one process to the next with great dexterity, sometimes using brute force, others delicate fingers, with the silence of a library reading room suddenly interrupted by hammering or the squeaky motion of an old press. All around are distractions in the form of hundreds and hundreds of pieces of hand-type, blocking brasses and rolls of cloth.

'It would certainly make a great museum,' I comment.

'I suppose in the end, generations ahead, it could come to that,' comments Mr Bayntun-Coward, 'but our job is to maintain tradition. As you can see, we have the craftsmen. There's a keen desire for us to excel at one-offs, serving the world market for rare books with fine binding.'

Much of the stock of books bound for sale (classic and already-scarce books given a new lease of life) will eventually be sold to overseas customers. Local people have the privilege of looking at them before a famous overseas bookshop takes away dozens of titles. But the other side of the business is bespoke, individuals and institutions sending their precious volumes to be rebound. 'The trouble is that sometimes people send us too many at once,' says Mr Bayntun-Coward. 'As you can see, this is the exact opposite of a mass-production factory. Every book is individual, and there's a natural limit to what we can handle. But it's good that the demand is there.' Handbound books here make the handsome titles of the Folio Society look cheaply mass-produced.

[After this visit, I opened an old book on Bath and discovered a bookmark advertising 'The Book Museum: Bookbinding & Jane Austen,

Charles Dickens and other authors adjoining the Bookshop and Bindery of George Bayntun Established 1894'. It is therefore not surprising people still ask for the museum. The management is perhaps coy about a side enterprise which closed down.]

One of the titles I've had to have rebound due to excessive use is that mid-Victorian in-depth guide to *Our Own Country*. Its Bath chapter begins: "'Go to Bath!' is a well-known formula in the English language to express desires uncomplimentary to the person addressed.' The writer couldn't understand why the name of such a beautiful place should be so abused. Nobody at the bindery nor, later in the day, friends at a party can help, or indeed has ever heard the expression used. It must have died out years ago. Was it, perhaps, that the person addressed was obviously in need of a cure, the equivalent to telling today's youngster to go and sort out their brain?

Book Bath

For centuries books have played an important role in Bath. An early (1751) title few of us are likely to read but which had much influence was the *Practical Essay on the Use and Abuse of Warm Bathing in Gouty Cases*. One of a number of books by William Oliver, it helped swell the ranks of people coming to Bath for a cure. Their business was fundamental to the prosperity of Regency Bath. An enterprising fellow, Oliver founded the Bath General Hospital so that even the poor could be cured, but is now better remembered as the inventor of the Bath Oliver biscuit.

There are these two curiously related strands that ever since have run through Bath's life. First is the medical one. Even today there is the Mineral Water Hospital, or to give it its full name the Royal National Hospital for Rheumatic Diseases. And biscuits and cakes have always been prominent in local fare. Bath Olivers, and their indulgent chocolate cousin, are useful minor exports and may be found in many parts of the world where upmarket British goods are sold. But the Bath bun, with its sticky sugar-covered top, doesn't travel well and has to be made daily even for local consumption. In a narrow street behind the Abbey, in the oldest house in Bath, is the quintessential English tea house, where the stouter Sally Lunn bun was invented and still overwhelms visitors keen to try out local delicacies. There's even a museum element in the basement at Sally Lunn's, recently voted Britain's best teashop by an American travel magazine. Another Bath specialty, chocolate Mikados, sometimes mispronounced mik-a-doos, a gooey confection finished off with a seductive arrangement of chocolate drainpipes, sadly disappeared when their home at Fortes in Milsom Street was unsympathetically modernised – 'we're a coffee house so how can you expect tea?'. The oblong plain bun coated with pink icing still has a strong following; you see business people buying half a dozen or more for a meeting. Once it was de rigueur at the Abbey's staff meetings.

Where there are wealthy people, fine architecture and good buns and food, there are bound to be authors. Bath is one of those places where you are not in the least surprised to come across them. For a start, nowhere else of the same size has anything like so extensive a literature. However, I wasn't persuaded to add to it when someone offered me for publishing, a lengthy history of pre- and post-Roman Bath. 'I'm leaving out the middle bit because it's been done to death,' said the accompanying letter. You could of course legitimately produce a history of early or modern Bath, but not the two together with a hole in it. Not, I suppose, that that would be so extraordinary, since Bath is the place where every rule of etiquette has been as freely broken as made.

'Proper behaviour' remains important. My earliest memory of an argument beyond the family confines was over tea at the next table in the lounge of the Francis Hotel in 1938. It was on some aspect of what was and what wasn't polite. Opinions differed so sharply that I half expected a fight to break out. I didn't know that Beau Nash had banned the wearing of swords (along with white aprons) in public places, and set a civilised tone which by and large has held ever since.

Another early memory is of the receptionist at The Francis continually turning people away because the house was full. The shortage of accommodation became much worse after Bath was targeted in those senseless Baedeker raids. The Francis had a direct hit and lost many rooms. Yet, in the 1960s, when it was my turn to bring a young family to Bath, often as a stopping point on a long pre-motorway journey, I would be shocked if it were not possible to park round Queen Square, or at least within a ninety-second walk of the hotel. Since then Bath has seen the opening of numerous hotels. The Francis is still an honourable establishment, though no longer anything like top of the tree.

That distinction now belongs to the Royal Crescent Hotel, a superb establishment discreetly looking as though it is just another part of the long, gently curved residential row. The restaurant is in the Dower House, across the garden from which there is an excellent view of the Royal Crescent's less elegant rear. Over the years, the crescent itself has had natural appeal for authors. The first time I was shown round an interior was by the doyen of railway photographers, Ivo Peters, who lived in splendid style on two floors at the far west end.

On this visit, we have been invited to morning coffee by Sheila McCullagh, one of the most successful children's authors of her day. Shared with a friend, her large flat incorporates the first floor of two houses. The rooms are spaciously grand, furnished with quality understatement.

'I never really needed an agent,' she begins when the conversation turns to writing. Not, at least, until complications such as TV rights arose. Educational publishers such as Rupert Hart Davis, EJ Arnold and Granada approached her, and long series of titles – called Platform Readers – were developed. You might possibly recall being handed out copies of successive 'readers' in your school days. Many were short one-lesson books, though jolly good stories encouraging reading and the stretching of vocabulary – such as those in the Pirates series. Some were longer works, while others again were written specially to help those with reading difficulties. It all began when she was a young teacher herself.

'What was available was pretty limited, and my colleagues pointed out that the kids in the stories we used in class weren't very real... not a bit like the friends they'd make out of school. "If only Janet would hit John," said a letter from another teacher complaining how goody-goody the characters were. It spurred me on to write about real children, like some with only one parent, against the background of the imperfect world. I was just fortunate in my knowledge and my timing.'

She talks about changing times. The publisher of one series told her not to include any black children. Her travels, paid for by royalties, helped provide the background especially for the Buccaneer series of 150-page books. The Pirates series was translated into many languages, including Icelandic in the middle of the Cod War.

'When my teacher's salary was £35 a month, I was able to earn more from writing. It was so much fun, working closely with illustrators, seeing the different series steadily grow, and getting letters from children everywhere. There were lots of contacts with teachers, too, though if you answered every letter properly it would take you all week. I always answered every child's letter, though.'

In those days books lasted longer than they do today, and sets were used for a lesson or two by successive classes every year. The Pirates were in print for forty years. Altogether, nearer 400 than 300 titles were produced. Even keeping pace with the royalty statements must have been a time-consuming business. She quickly learned that not all publishers were trustworthy, and after one bad experience – an almost non-existent royalty on bulk overseas sales – she joined the Society of Authors and had them check out each contract.

'It's all in the past now,' she says as we prepare to leave. Maybe, but the legacy in the education of hundreds of thousands of children must be far greater than the comfortable lifestyle yesterday's royalties still support.

Jane Austen's 'Charming Place'

Jane Austen may not have done so well with royalties in her lifetime, but she is in a class of her own among authors who have lived in Bath and written about it. Bath and Austen go hand-in-hand. 'People who appreciate the elegant prose and incisive wit of the one, generally admire the harmony and proportion of the Georgian architecture of the other.' The quote is from *A Charming Place: Bath in the Life and Novels of Jane Austen*, a delightful pocket book by Maggie Lane.

Jane Austen's parents were married here, and John Wood, the architect and builder, was one of her ancestors. She paid leisurely visits in the 1790s and lived here for the five years between 1801 and 1806. But it is wrong to think that Bath was an instant love affair. She was never unhappier than when her parson father decided to bring his family here after early retirement from his Hampshire parish. Bath, she declared, was all smoke, vapour and confusion, while social occasions were spoilt by being too crowded. For three years she gave up writing... not yet having had a novel published. Her own love life already prematurely ended when she was dropped for a better 'prospect', she could only secretly enjoy her success when *Sense and Sensibility* was eventually published. The author was 'A Lady', though one reviewer denied that possibility, for such a brilliant work had to come from a man. Things of course improved, and her growing love of Bath paid handsome dividends:

> In two of the six novels, Bath provides a specific setting which not only assists the progress of the plot – gives her characters something to do, in other words – but helps reveal where they stand on a scale of moral values. Jane Austen could depend upon Bath, its customs and topography, being familiar to her readers. Second only to London, the importance of Bath to the national culture during her lifetime is evident from the fact that none of her novels is without reference to the city, whether the story takes us there or not.

In her private writings, after her initial unhappiness Jane comes across as an energetic young lady full of fun. A new portrait, done by a forensic artist, whose subjects are normally murder victims, shows her as an attractive woman in her thirties matching a friend's description of her 'appearance expressive of health and animation'. Despite the impression given in the novels, she was even interested in technical innovation. A proposed walk to 'the Cassoon' would be a three-mile hilly trek to Combe Hay. The caisson was a lift on our old friend the Somersetshire Coal Canal. Boats floated in and out of it. By her day, it was already abandoned in favour of an inclined plane (and later expensively replaced again by a flight of locks).

Having bought a copy of *A Charming Place* from Whiteman's Bookshop, close to the Abbey, I was curious to know who was behind its publisher, Millstream Books. When I track him down, it is Tim Graham, former owner of Whiteman's, who I remember as a special friend of publishers of books on transport and industrial and local history. With several well-run individually-owned shops, Bath was a wonderful place in which to sell books... better than much larger Bristol whose flagship George's couldn't always get round to unpacking a new title in time to benefit from television publicity on publication day. Whiteman's Bookshop is still among my favourites.

Tim's kind of publishing must be a pleasant retirement business: a tight-knit list of several dozen titles of local interest, including a history of Bath in nine volumes (some out of print) and quite a few on canals and railways, prices ranging from £3.95 to £25. 'I'm a one-man band,' he says, 'but a rep from whom I used to buy books does much of the selling to bookshops, though mail-order is also important.'

Sales total about 7,000 books a year spread across the list. No prize for guessing the bestseller: *A Charming Place.* Perennial interest in Jane Austen's Bath means a steady 1,000 sales a year, not enough to set London publishers on fire but respectable. No prize, either, for guessing a recent disappointment. *One Man's Bath* was published just as Canon Richard Askew completed a long and productive stint as Rector at the Abbey. The book is full of interesting detail, but he was warned that the title was too personal, especially as he was leaving the city. 'I told him too,' says Tim, 'but he wouldn't listen. Sales stopped after the first 600.'

Captain of the *QE2* and Nunney Castle

Though highly dependent on his job for his book's sales, our next author is different again: Ron Warwick, captain of the *QE2*. A friend who we usually see in grandeur, he has invited us to lunch at his cottage across the stream from Nunney Castle, eight miles south of Bath. The food provided by his Hawaiian wife, the beautiful Kim, is superb but, in a building site, we eat on garden chairs in a bleak conservatory mostly devoted to storage.

Ron is a do-it-yourself freak. He's transforming the centuries-old cottage inch by inch... and, yes, part of it already looks quite different, indeed of stunning quality. But if I were captain of the *QE2*, doing this painstakingly slow manual work in crowded conditions (since the place has to be furnished and functioning at least to a degree since it is home) is not how I'd want to spend my leave. 'But I love it,' he protests. 'He really does,' adds Kim, though whether it's blind love or understanding conviction we're not quite sure.

Ironically, when we were first told on the ship about where its captain lived, it was 'in a castle'. Visions of more grandeur. Though still dominating the little village, the moated castle is however a ruin. A smaller version of Harlech and Beaumaris in North Wales, it is still impressively tall and, as an empty shell, looks gaunt especially when seen emerging from a morning mist. It was 'slighted' in the Civil War. Its last private owner handed it over to English Heritage. This morning the brook looks threateningly lively. Ron confirms this is a Grade Three flood area.

First, however, to talk about the book, simply called *The QE2*. Published in New York, it sells thousands a year, largely to a surprisingly small audience – passengers on the ship. Those queuing for the captain's cocktail parties have to stand by displays (including open pages) in the window of the library and bookshop, and then pass the table where once a voyage there is a well-announced signing party. All very sensible, almost holistic, for Ron has done more to encourage people to travel by the ship than any other single person. A copy of the substantial book on the shelves in innumerable well-heeled homes must prompt many thoughts of return trips, while having an autographed copy to give to friends is a nice piece of one-upmanship.

There will only ever be one *QE2*, a unique survival from the time when crossing the Atlantic was the norm for the great and the mighty, into the days when millions take cruising holidays. Says Ron: 'Yes, we are totally unique, the last of the transatlantic liners, the fastest ship afloat, a great heritage whose origins go back to the first Cunard Atlantic crossing on 4 July 1840. And the quality. The ship embraces its passengers. There's huge emotion, especially when flotillas of small boats come out to meet us and crowds are everywhere when we go to unusual or distant places. It all adds to the joy.'

He goes on: 'One of the things that is special about the ship is the way it has adapted to the happenings of the last thirty years. It was designed with good intent in the mid-1950s, but they were times of rapid change such as the jets, and when she was launched in 1969 she was already out of date. At the beginning there were Turkish baths; the jacuzzi hadn't been invented. You couldn't imagine the computer power of today's Learning Centre.'

A glance at the original plans shows how much has changed. She has been given new decks of luxury cabins, new restaurants, arcades of shops and much more. The Radio Room outside which one queued to hand in a telex, and later a fax, became redundant and has been transformed into another luxury cabin. Yet so many things, even the slight irregularity in the fine deck planking laid down on Clydeside, where the *QE2* was one of the last ships to be built, remain exactly the same. And how different are today's passengers from the originals, and the thoughts of those of us who record their miles round the deck, each mile being five rounds. Food fads change, but in the top restaurants at lunch the well-heeled still place their special dinner orders. No ship has ever had a greater fan club, among staff as well as passengers. It was quite an event when the linen keeper retired after thirty proud years in the job.

Ron's father was the *QE2*'s first master, 'but retired long ago, when pensions were different'. Everyone has a problem. Ron's has been providing for his parents, concerned that as he reached his own minimum retirement age he'd have to leave before his own finances were in order. The book's royalties have certainly helped. Another worry has been about the ship's own survival. A lively management book could be written about the brilliance or ineptitude of successive managements under different owners. Ron admits it has sometimes been tough enthusiastically peddling the changing policies, but is genuinely delighted by the recent sale to the American giant Carnival, exploiters of mass tourism at sea but also respecters of traditions such as Cunard's... and with deep pockets.

What will that mean to his retirement? 'Too early to say, but at the end of the day retirement is an attitude of mind. I always remember my father taking me, just with a few things, to the station to catch a train on my way to make my first voyage when I was seventeen. Never get bored, he said. Good advice. I've always had more things to do than there's time for. Yes, I'd miss the ship, but I'd love to get on with the renovation of our home. It needs real time, not just leave. My great grandfather was a builder, and I remember my grandfather saying that to achieve something as you want it, you should do it yourself. And Kim's passion is cooking. She'll soon have a proper kitchen and space for her cook books.'

Then he tells me that Carnival are about to commission another ship, the *Queen Mary* (or will it be *Queen Mary 2*?) accommodating 2,885 passengers on the transatlantic run. 'They promise a grand classic ship, with plenty of space for passengers.' [Ron need not have worried about his pension prospects, for not merely has he continued as master of the *QE2* but has been appointed first Master of the *Queen Mary 2* ... a family tradition indeed.]

GLOUCESTERSHIRE AND CANALS

South Cerney and Charles Hadfield

Living by the sea gives life an extra dimension. It does, however, restrict the directions in which you can travel. The joy of spending time in Bath is that there is interesting territory round 360 degrees. This morning we decide to head north especially to celebrate the canal age and to honour the memory of the greatest canal historian, the Pevsner of waterways. Charles Hadfield was also once my publishing partner.

As one climbs out of Bath on to the plateau, there's the most spectacular view of the city. To avoid starting by the London Road we go up Lansdown Hill, past the cemetery belonging to Christ Church, never a parish church itself but set up for the servants of rich people who attended one. That's Bath for you. And, bang in the middle of its cemetery, two more miles uphill is a folly, the Beckford Tower. What a splendid panorama that must command. Beckford is a name that crops up later today. After the racecourse, we thread through lanes full of other cars also taking what is today called the rat race to the A46 and across the M5.

At the crossroads at Old Sodbury we record the date, 13 December 1981, when the pub, the Cross Hands, gave refuge to a snow-bound Queen; and passing the Petty France Hotel just before Dunkirk we think of the cancer patients who will have been treated by drugs made from clippings from the hotel's great yew hedge. Passing Westonbirt, now on the A433, the Arboretum is always a pleasure, and what gardener would not like to be shown round Prince Charles's garden at Highgrove a couple of miles further on. A constable discreetly guards the entrance. Surprise, he doesn't beckon us in.

I often wonder why this curvy route was developed in preference to the parallel Foss Way to the south east which runs across the country as straight as a ruler but is largely abandoned and in places no longer exists even as a lane. At least we have the pleasure of passing through delightful Tetbury, once the terminus of one of those Great Western branch lines that fitted so perfectly into their countryside. We pass the junction station, Kemble, still with trains to London, and near to the source of the Thames. The Thames & Severn Canal crossing the watershed, never a commercial success, is being lovingly restored. Then across country to the village of South Cerney, a few miles south of Cirencester.

South Cerney is Gloucestershire's largest village and has changed more than most. There's been an influx of light industry, while the quarries which once gave most employment have become pleasure lakes. There are a hundred of them, many dedicated to a specific purpose: canoeing, jet skiing, water skiing, fishing and so on. This has placed South Cerney firmly on the tourist map, with two holiday home villages and a new eighteen-hole golf course. South Cerney itself has much less of a village feel, certainly many fewer shops, than when I first spent time here in the early 1960s. What had been one of the cross-country railway glories of southern England, the Midland & South Western Junction, with amazing traffic developed by its general manager, Sam Fey, one of the Victorian era's greatest railwaymen, was on its last legs. British Railways hadn't yet completed the legal process of closure. There was only one daily service. However, the line was busy with training trips for Swindon drivers on the new diesel multiple units.

I used to stay with Charles Hadfield and his wife Alice Mary in the substantial Cotswold stone Silver Street House. Today's owner happens to belong to *Writers' News*, and out of the blue invited me to visit it once more. It is going to be emotional, for I can hardly look at a photograph of Charles without being mesmerised, and I had to deal with him through successive crises. More of that in a moment.

Susan Gibbs gives us the warmest of welcomes... only beaten by Fuffino Pussion's. Fuffino, the Siamese, instantly grasps that I'm a willing cat servant; dogs have owners, cats staff. The border collie would love attention, too, but Fuffino cunningly dominates. Coffee is with talk about how the village has developed, writing, and of course Charles and Alice Mary. And how the house has changed since their time. The industrial boiler, and the nearby loo I retreated to when things became too tense, are both happily still working; the Little Room is much tidier. When they moved in, they invited Charles and Alice Mary and learned much about the house's earlier history.

Because there had been no mains water, Charles connected taps to a couple of wells behind today's sofa. Recently the Gibbs have discovered a collection of old press cuttings from South Africa left behind by Charles, who was born and spent his early life there. The Gibbs themselves spent much of their life near Bulawayo. 'My husband was born there and so were our four children. We loved it. Africa really enters your soul. We left when there were only ten per cent whites in our area and eleven had been murdered on a farm. We came here with no job, but we've taken root here and the house suits us well.' It is a fine property conveniently placed with a pleasant courtyard garden. 'But this is one of the coldest places in England.' I remember it, especially as Charles rationed heat.

David & Charles, a combination of my and Charles's first names, possibly sounding like a pair of avant-garde hairdressers operating furtively under the stairs, was founded on April Fool's Day 1960. Neither of us was anxious to advertise to our employers that, however tentatively, we were in business on our own. I was a railway author and Charles had already built a reputation as leading canal historian. Since we both edited series for Phoenix House, a branch of Dent, our first connection was exchanging material we unearthed on each other's subject. The idea of setting up a publishing house to supplement what our London publisher was prepared to take was happily developed by both of us, though from the start it seemed to me that, being considerably older and more experienced, Charles inevitably thought he was right on pretty well everything. He had indeed benefited from a pre-war spell in bookselling, been an Oxford University Press editor, and was now newly-appointed overseas controller (or did they call him comptroller?) of the Central Office of Information.

That Charles knew and loved his canals was never in doubt. Even in his early years in South Africa, he had taken an interest in the local waterways, while at school at Blundells, near Tiverton, he explored the land-locked Grand Western Canal, conceived to save the lives of mariners from going round Land's End, though what was built first, and all that was left by Charles's boyhood, was the landlocked Tiverton branch.

Being in business together was altogether different. While one difficulty was Charles's belief in his superiority, another was his official position and the respect it carried. Not only the rank, but the way he was insulated. Getting through the protective secretaries was time consuming, and I was frantically busy broadcasting, writing and running a fruit farm as well as doing the donkey work for D&C. Inevitably there came a time when, as the down-to-earth practical half of the partnership, I failed to consult. The catalogue of disagreements disclosed in Joseph Boughey's *Charles Hadfield: canal man and more* makes depressing reading but is somewhat one-sided. For example, Charles *was* consulted on a book about floods, but the decision hastily to reprint (it needed reprinting again three days later) was taken when it was difficult to reach him and when, with one wholesaler taking 500 copies daily, delay might have destroyed impetus. But I had to admit that, even though he was incommunicado overseas, Charles should have been consulted about one major hardback. That was our final undoing. 'Any profit goes to the company and you make up any loss,' was scarcely fair, but the writing was anyway on the wall. It seldom works to have two equal owners of a business.

Another strain had been John Baker of Phoenix House admitting he had never obtained Martin Dent's permission to distribute some of the books we were publishing to supplement those we had written for the Phoenix House imprint. Martin would neither allow the distribution of our set or let us buy the other. Unable to persuade Martin to change his mind, Charles scoffed when I asked if I might have a go. If an experienced negotiator such as he failed, what chance would there be for me? But I did persuade Dent of the fairness of our case, for the two sets of books obviously belonged together. That, as it happens, was as Charles offered me his D&C shares and withdrew as director. He failed to persuade Dent to change his mind again so that his own titles could stay with them. As Charles quit D&C, his major canal books were taken over by it.

Since we both had much to lose if things went wrong, thereafter we treated each other with mutual respect and care. Charles was given considerable authority as canal editor, while I politely declined his insistent demand that he be given a wider role in D&C, especially on the public relations side. There were a few other isolated incidents that demanded careful handling. Notably his book on sex, which he wanted published anonymously. Uniquely among his friends, I read about his sex life with Alice Mary. It was a second marriage and very physical. 'Get yourself a bigger bed,' was his regular advice to me. Written as a personal handbook of guidance for the less fortunate, it was actually very good, and I would have loved to publish it... under his name. I couldn't, however, see how so personal a work could flourish with a non-existent author or at any rate one unable to sign copies or appear on radio or TV. The book never saw the light of day.

So here I am sitting in the room, in the very place that so many arguments took place. I still shudder when I remember being mesmerised under Charles's intense glare which always seemed to imply 'if only I'd listen to common sense'. Yet there were light-hearted times, too. In this room is where I first enjoyed classical 78s. We made occasional excursions together by train. One was on a Sunday from Swindon Junction to Andover and back; another to Tetbury; and there were exhilarating non-stop journeys from Kemble to London in steam days.

After the dinner at one of our Victorian weekends, the final dance, the Lambeth Walk, had just finished when Charles confided it was the first dance he and Alice Mary had ever had together. I jumped on to the platform, persuaded the orchestra to start playing again and, explaining why, had the two of them perform solo in front of 400 people. Yes, there was occasional warmth, certainly mutual professional respect.

If Charles kept me on edge, I was in fear of my sanity with Alice Mary, whose erratic moods were punctuated with everlasting references to and quotations from Charles Williams, and a gentle superior sneer that suggested that of course the likes of me wouldn't appreciate that genius. She wrote a biography of Williams, but mercifully D&C were obviously not a suitable publisher. As I shudder typing this, the machine goes berserk (Alice V||£? +||? – ? ?Z_/ Z£/X_||£ ?)

'Sounds as though you had quite difficult times,' says Susan. An understatement. The army of canal lovers who bought his books couldn't begin to realise... though early on there was a telling falling-out with the Inland Waterways Association, and Charles was always miffed that he was allowed only one term on the Waterways Board, and that his ideas for the regeneration of commercial canal and river traffic were not taken seriously. Yet without him, it is unlikely I would have started publishing, so in a sense I owe him everything, and it is perhaps fair to say that without me his books would not have been so well exploited. And how thrilled he would be by today's mass restoration of canals, if only for pleasure.

Never really happy in the country, Charles took Alice Mary back to London for a period. When they returned it was to a much smaller, modern house on an estate. 'I wonder how they coped with that,' Susan reflects. 'Mind you, there was something peculiar about this house. When we redecorated a room that had been a teenage boy's, we found an inverted black cross with black writing "Worship Satan in all his glory". The vicar came with a sprig of yew and we held a communion service in the room, but still funny things happened, so later the diocesan exorcist was called in.'

After the death of his beloved Alice Mary, I visited Charles at his modern home on one of South Cerney's estates. On the last occasion, with a part-time secretary, he was trying to put his papers in order. He died before finishing that, leaving Joseph Boughey a formidable task in producing the biography.

Our mood lightens as Susan shows how Fuffino loves to be swung by his tail. As we prepare to leave and the Siamese does a sulk, Susan hands me a sample of her writing, which I much enjoy later in the day. It is a true tale about uncanny happenings in Zimbabwe. Over the years, but it becomes rarer now, I've met many who felt they had to come to Britain but left part of their heart behind in Africa. Charles himself probably did, and might well have over-compensated in his adjustment to becoming British.

Stroud: HQ of the West Country Woollen Trade

We head next for Cirencester, or rather its frighteningly busy bypass. Then through Chalford and down narrow, steep-sided Golden Valley, past much of industrial archaeological interest, river, road, railway and canal packed closely together in the style of the South Wales valleys, to Stroud. First to lunch in a wine bar. The Retreat is a great venue suggested by an author who is as practical and easy to get on with as they come: Anthony Burton. He was the obvious author for *The Great Days of the Canals*, skilfully combining human interest with engineering, social history and a constant reminder that canals were built by commercial companies to maximize their traffic potential and profit. Before the railways spoilt the party, the top canals were among the most profitable businesses of their day, though (as with later railway building) ambition and greed often outstripped prudence, and some routes – such as the Thames & Severn – were born losers.

The Retreat offers a wide choice of wine by the glass and there's a substantial daily blackboard menu. It is busy, too, but we find a quietish table. I remember Anthony as an author able to tackle a wide range of subjects and come up with lively work of depth and accuracy, something rarely achieved by those willing to take on varied commissions. His *Shell Book of Curious Britain*, for example, didn't look as though it was written to order and went down a treat. But who exactly is Anthony Burton? I have never discussed his background.

He's a big man, enthusiastic and good-hearted. Over lunch he explains his background and then – with his outward-going personality – his professionalism makes sense. Trained as an industrial chemist, he went into the printed word via scientific papers. In the 1960s he became editor at Weidenfeld & Nicolson. His last 'proper job' was at Penguin where he directed publicity and ran the promotional *Penguin News*. I first knew him when he lived in Bristol. He came to Stroud, moving into a disused synagogue, because prices were cheaper and he loved the compact town and its industrial background, especially its old woollen mills and the houses of the master clothiers. In the days when the West Country produced more cloth than Yorkshire, there were around 150 mills in Gloucestershire with a special concentration round Stroud. Some of them were huge, planned and run almost like estates of the gentry. A few of the magnificent buildings have found other uses such as conversion to flats, and the elegant stone-built Ebley council offices, while others were left empty too long after the industry's collapse at the end of the nineteenth century and fell to pieces or had to be demolished. Most were substantial, unique pieces of architecture, though the largest one on its way to ruination today, the Hill Paul clothing factory of later vintage than most, is by no means the best.

Anthony thinks it's worth rescuing, though, saying it would make a wonderful working museum celebrating Stroud's unique legacy as headquarters of the West Country woollen industry. However, it seems as though a developer has bought it cheap for conversion into flats; certainly better than leaving it empty. Stroud was once so busy a place that virtually all women were in full-time employment and Sunday was accepted as the normal washing day, with laden clothes lines flapping in the breeze as they would virtually everywhere else on Monday. Some cloth is still made in Stroud, notably at Lodgemore Mills, now American-owned, where they make baize. But it is a far cry from the days when 'one person with great stock and large credit buys the wool, pays for the spinning, weaving, milling, dyeing, shearing, dressing etc ... master of the whole manufacture from first to last and probably employs a thousand people under him'.

Back to books, Anthony says: 'Earning a living from book writing is hard work, and you have to balance what you want to do with bread and butter. My agent has helped, though I won't be doing what one author famously did... sending him ten per cent of my ashes. If you're a writer don't throw up a regular job lightly. It may not be quite what you would choose but allows you to write what you want.' Certainly not many have his skill in working on such a broad spectrum of subjects such as, currently, some of the official guides to long-distance walks.

One of the delights of the earlier Stroud I knew was its bookshop by the station run by Alan and Joan Tucker. It consumed large consignments of titles on industrial archaeology, canals, railways, local history and the like, and was always good for a launching party. 'Er, you might just possibly know the name, Awdry, railway books, but not serious ones, just tales for children,' said the tall parson softly, the last person in the queue for an autographed copy of a book on the Great Western. How Awdry would hate today's high-pressure selling of everything to do with Thomas the Tank Engine and Friends. Do I need a franchise even to say that?

Though closed as an all-round bookshop, the Tuckers still have the shop packed with antiquarian titles, many now sold on the Internet. And new ones are still obtained specially for their loyal customers. Joan points out a copy of *Gloucestershire Woollen Mills*, a pioneer work by Jennifer Tann. Many people thought we were mad publishing something so specialist, but it sold out, and fetches a high price second-hand.

'Jennifer is still active in the area,' says Joan, but she herself is author of *Stroud* in Phillimore's local-history series showing that the town was not just about wool and cloth, for there were large quarries, brewing, brickmaking and even – on a considerable scale – boat building. Though the Thames & Severn Canal was a lost cause almost from the start, the Stroudwater Canal that it met in Stroud was a lively concern, putting the town on the international trading map. At one time, just one of the owners of the sizeable barges that plied it, ran a twice-weekly service to Bristol, where connections were made with all kinds of ships. Joan is on the committee guiding the canal's restoration. The railways of course killed the canals, and during their era were extremely busy, with keen competition between Great Western and Midland.

'David,' says Joan suddenly changing the subject, 'do you remember when you found our tiny shop on a backstreet and persuaded me to try selling a few of your books? Until then we were second-hand only. One of those life-changing moments for which we are extremely grateful. But these days we're only here when we want to be.' Which is the cue for them locking up and taking us home with them for tea. It doesn't mean the end of books and book talk, though, for shelves everywhere are burgeoning. The room in which we have tea is obviously devoted to their personal selected treasures collected over the years. I take down *The Pleasure of Ruins* by Rose Macaulay, and read that castles, like temples and churches, are always reproductive, generating newer castles. So, wherever there is a castle, there will be an older one buried under it, 'probably prehistoric, a pile of stones and earth without form.' There you go.

Book chat is fascinating. 'There was this Mormon who called trying to convert us. Instead we sold him a Mormon bible.'

And then about Beckford again, the author of *Vathek* and eccentric millionaire whose life Alan is busily researching. Beckford's follies include both the tower that bears his name that we passed on the outskirts of Bath this morning and Fonthill Abbey in Wiltshire where the tower fell down. The Bath folly actually began life in Bristol and we learn that it has just been acquired by the Landmark Trust who will rent a flat with that amazing view, though in the middle of the cemetery. Then it is back to canals. Alan and Joan are equally thrilled that the Trust arm of British Waterways has agreed to take over both the Thames & Severn and the Stroudwater Canals, so not all the industrial heritage is lost. 'Very important to keep it alive,' says Joan. 'It shaped the landscape and created the traditions that are part of Stroud today.'

That's our last call today. Though it is quite a distance, we drive to The Elms at Abberley, near Worcester, for a first-class dinner we didn't really need after that wine bar lunch, a restful night – and to position ourselves for tomorrow's first call.

Eckington and a Walk to a Weir

First stop next morning is at the village of Eckington, on the Warwickshire Avon, near Pershore, the plum capital. Starting in the early 1950s, for decades I stayed here with relatives several times a year. It was quite different from any other village I knew personally. Slightly dour and often cold, it used to be pretty down-to-earth, strongly farming oriented, with few larger houses. There were more shops than you'll find today, but they catered for pretty basic tastes. The few incomers to the village who cared about good living went to Cheltenham for their clothes, lunches and groceries. Most people seldom left the village so, when they still ran along the Midland's main line to Bristol, few used the stopping trains. There were hardly any buses. There used to be a level crossing by the station. That has been replaced by a pedestrian-only bridge because today's expresses roar through at far greater speed, making much greater noise. Today however the railway is as irrelevant to local life as RAF planes practising overhead.

It is the handiness of the M5, and of course the high price of property nearer to Birmingham and Cheltenham, that has rendered Eckington sought-after commuter territory. So a much smaller proportion of the population is now local born and bred. Today just about everyone has a car and does at least part of their shopping elsewhere. Even those who fish the Avon are more upmarket than their predecessors the pubs catered for half a century ago. 'Life's changed out of all recognition,' says an elderly gentleman I get in conversation with outside the post office. 'Mind, I'm not sure people's any happier – not according to my paper.' He's holding this morning's *Daily Express*, a reminder that so down-to-earth was Eckington years ago that, despite labour being freely available, newspapers weren't delivered. There wasn't sufficient demand.

As we park the car near the war memorial and walk up the road going east to the Combertons (Great and Little), I wonder whether the change of the last half-century has been anything like as rapid as it was in each of the three previous such periods. When I return home and look at my shelves burdened with the outpourings of authors desperate to record the changes they had witnessed in the village, I realise that that genre of publishing has almost ceased. Archaeology, on the ground, and from the air in the case of at least one village near to Eckington, tells us about how the Romans and other earlier people lived and worked, but it's not about the people and things, habits and superstitions that we *knew*, or at least had verbally handed down to us. The days when villages really were self-contained centres, each with its own flavour, have passed out of nostalgia.

The walk is interesting as it is familiar. Gently climbing, first we pass through what is now a prime residential area, and past the house where I used to stay at a time when there was an abundance of staff happy to work for one of the few better-off families. Then past the former home of one of the leading lights of the campaign to restore navigation up the Avon to Stratford-upon-Avon, to which I used to deliver parcels of books the society sold for fund raising. The books would always have included copies of Charles Hadfield's *Waterways to Stratford*. Then through farming land, apart from a field obviously 'set aside', more intensively cultivated today, down a dip and up another hill until between the passage of cars (now of course far more frequent) we can hear the distant roar of water pouring over the river's weir.

It is a bit muddy but, following a fisherman who has arrived by BMW, we walk down the field overlooking the weir and the lock which had to be rebuilt to enable boats to bypass it. In summer, pleasure boats frequently make their way up to Stratford-upon-Avon and beyond. It is good to see the river back in use as a highway. However, there are no boats this morning. The river is in flood and there's not enough clearance under the humped bridge.

The only time I've seen an otter in the wild was just here. Other river wildlife abounds. You just have to sit still and be patient. It is a spot I've come to love over the years.

Yesterday's Countryside

On our walk back, we see the river's flat flood plain – most of Eckington itself is as flat as it's cold – with very distinctive hills on either side. Bredon Hill, where the crops farmers grew, the stock they reared, and the methods they used, changed as you went up the contours, is relatively close and now attracts record numbers of walkers. To the west, further away, but with a familiar profile, lies the long line of the Malverns. That is marvellously individual country, under increasing pressure since it is now within convenient reach of a large population.

Even fifty years ago, a Sunday school outing from Eckington to the Malverns would have seemed fairly adventurous. Before the motor age, though it could be done by changing trains at Ashchurch and taking one of the few a day that crossed the Severn near Tewksbury, a compelling reason would have been needed to make the journey. Before the railway age, it would have been by horse, or – if you had the time and money – horse-drawn conveyance.

Nothing perhaps emphasises how time has moved on during my lifetime than a visit to a museum specialising in horse-drawn vehicles. When in the 1970s I published James Arnold's *All Drawn by Horses*, portraying in pictures and words vehicles grand and everyday, it was as though we were simply prolonging human memory. Today's younger readers might glance at it in the same way they would look at a book on how the Romans got about. Yet what interest we have lost! Few books have I enjoyed recently more than George Stuart's *The Wheelwright's Shop*, for which in 2002 I have to pay £30. Emphasising the point I'm making about reliving country memories, it was first published in 1923 at 7s 6d (37½p) by the Cambridge University Press. It was listed in a range of country titles that certainly wouldn't justify their place in a prestigious publisher's programme now. It might sound an especially esoteric title, but it quickly ran through several editions.

It describes the era when every village had its own bakery (where most people's Christmas lunches were cooked), and its own blacksmith and wheelwright's shop which often worked together in the making of wheels. Until the spread of iron components, which generally didn't happen until well into the second half of the nineteenth century, every wheelwright's shop was dependent on local timber of the right kind, workable, bendable, durable or whatever, and what the blacksmith could make. There was a tangled web of country prejudices, every curve even in the basic farm cart reflecting experience and ingenuity. The sawyers, a hard-drinking lot who generally worked outside, were as different from those who made wheels as cheese is from chalk.

The wheels, incidentally, were dished, that is to say leant outwards, so that as they revolved the top cleared the side of the wagon which was wider at the top than bottom. Calculating the exact amount of dish seems to have been as much art as science. Its need stemmed not merely from the greater width of the top, so that when the cart was tipped backward its load would more easily slide out, but from the fact that horses always exerted a slight sideways movement or jiggle and carts had to negotiate deeply-rutted roads. Especially in a hard frost, the ruts accommodating this slight sideways movement, were almost as restrictive as a railway line. So it wasn't an enormous jump when vehicles were first put on rails, our standard 4ft 8½in gauge, which Britain gave to much of the civilised world, reflecting the distance between ruts on the main horse-and-cart routes serving Northumberland's colliery districts. However, the distance between ruts, and therefore of the cart wheels, varied sharply according to area. It could by no means be assumed that a cart from one district would be afforded an acceptable ride in another, especially when frost had set in and there was no give in the mud.

I have always found fascination in the story of how tightly self-contained villages of pre-railway times gradually came to fit into a more standard pattern. Politics and the church were the first unifying influences imposed, though for the most part passively accepted. They didn't much affect everyday details such as hygiene, clothing, food, furnishing, cottage architecture or indeed farming methods. Though loyal to the crown and to their church, most villagers would rarely have seen, let alone got to know intimately, someone from a village twenty miles away. But farm workers' Sunday afternoon relaxation often took the form of a family walk to the next village where the crops and growing methods would be critically reviewed. Most innovation spread slowly, village to village, as improved methods were noted. Only dramatic events, such as the arrival of the turnip and, increasingly from the Napoleonic Wars, the abandonment of the traditional open-field system in favour of enclosure, achieved by local Acts of Parliament, had any national unifying influence. With enclosure, of course, arose a sharper division between employer and employed. Steam ploughing, which perhaps initiated rural depopulation, spread fast. It was red-hot news exploited by the early manufacturers of the equipment. Seven men, with steam engines at either end of a field alternately pulling the plough, could achieve in one day what twenty had taken a fortnight to do. It naturally favoured larger farming units.

Taking man quicker than the speed of an animal, the steam engine on rails also made enormous impact. Almost everywhere, its arrival in the neighbourhood was the most important event ever in village life. Not many might have actually travelled by train but, along with the electric telegraph and daily papers, came a steady stream of mass-produced goods and new attitudes. It was attitude that put old England to death: above all, the need to economise, to earn to survive. While writers might still hark on about the colourful differences between neighbouring communities, harsh economics – especially after the farming crisis of the tough 1870s – forced the abandonment of time-honoured methods of construction and decorating of carts and much more. It could be said that the adaptation to harsh realities, the priority that survival demanded, was precursor to Thatcherism a century later.

Farmers, for example, could no longer afford carts built to last beyond their lifetime. So when they arrived, people were ready for motor vehicles that obviously had to be factory mass-produced and wouldn't become family heirlooms. Farm gates had to be made more cheaply. Clothes and much more didn't last as long. The expendable society was born.

So this morning we look at many distant villages and hamlets, in the valley, up Bredon Hill, and in the distance toward the Malverns, and think about all the good and bad things that happened as living standards slowly rose but the quality of many artefacts fell and individuality mattered less. I think about how the river and the railway served the community, how for example the village station came to life in taking the cream of manhood to fight in two world wars, and how after the first of them roads were steadily sealed and widened, though hereabouts many minor ones still have sharp bends following the field pattern of centuries. The countryside has always presented a mixture of old and new.

Then I recall a telling sentence in Fred Archer's *A Lad of Evesham Vale*, as good a read as you'll find about village life immediately after World War One: 'Then there was the news which came from Tewkesbury market on Wednesday when the landlord could not sell cider because he made more profit on beer.'

It is the small things that emphasise the pressure to hold on. And it usually was that rather than 'making good'. On our way back to the car, I again recall that while World War One exercised a great levelling of society, extreme poverty was suffered by most people in all those villages and hamlets in our view until World War Two. So endemic was that poverty that many country people encouraged their children to move to towns for a better life; coupled with that, farms and market gardens had to become progressively less labour intensive to survive. Though people are no longer united in caring passionately about the success of each season's crops, at least this countryside is alive and kicking, if not in quite the timeless way that depopulation has preserved many French villages. One final thought. Within our view we will have seen places once administered by scores of different local authorities. Though many parish councils have been given new life for their limited role, the process of amalgamation and standardisation has been remorseless.

Gloucester and its Canal Museum

It would have been pleasant to renew acquaintance with civilised Cheltenham for lunch and shopping, but we take the M5 between the Tewkesbury and Gloucester junctions to pay a long-planned visit to the Waterways Museum at Gloucester Docks. I have only been there once before, for a special occasion involving Charles Hadfield, but it was then new and incomplete. That so much that is positive has happened in the waterways world since then seems amazing. Maybe Charles would have preferred more priority given to carting heavy goods by water, as they still do in much of Europe, but in his wildest dreams he couldn't have imagined the change in attitude heralded by the 1999 establishment of the Waterways Trust 'to promote greater public enjoyment and awareness of the UK's waterways; to develop partnerships to secure funding for the conservation and restoration of waterways; and to help realise the social, environmental, educational and economic potential of living waterways.' Says one brochure: 'Historically inland waterways have shaped our landscapes, communities and economic life. Today, as a focus for regeneration, they once again bring major benefits to the communities they connect.'

There is certainly an enormous programme of restoration. While the old Waterways Board inevitably functioned like a government department, the Trust has developed close relations with many groups of enthusiasts and raises money for its projects from all manner of quarters, including the National Lottery. It is a great exercise in common sense; belated, perhaps, but thoroughly worthwhile and honourable, though in the last few years there's been a decline in the number of people renting boats for canal holidays. A pity, for so many new routes are opening up, such as 'the impossible restoration' (£30 million) of the twenty-mile Huddersfield Narrow Canal, the highest in Britain, and a link between the Grand Union at Fenny Stratford and the Ouse at Bedford. Over half the population lives within five miles of a waterway, so opportunities abound. Water taxis and commuter boats are being considered by local authorities. The demand for new personally owned boats is high, as is that for overnight canal-side accommodation and meals. Maybe the need is for more luxurious hire fleets.

Canal archives were once regarded as almost secret, dangerous documents. Now: 'The activities of our museums and archives broaden understanding of the value of our waterways to society, past and present.' It is a bit like hearing the enthusiastic pragmatic doctrine of Dubcek, the Czechoslovakian leader, when he led the short-lived revolution, or Prague Spring, that cost him his life but ultimately helped free Eastern Europe from the tyranny of Communist empire. Good will and common sense which had been singularly lacking for decades.

Gloucester is a lovely place, once you have got rid of your car. But most of this morning's blockage seems to be beyond the point where we turn down to the docks. We are greeted by a fantastic scene of tall red buildings, some still revealing the names of their original owners, such as the warehouse of Fellows, Morton & Clayton, carriers supreme of the canal age, who employed only the best men and maintained meticulous schedules.

With a nip in the out-of-season air, and most of the human movement being of classes of children who have arrived by bus, we're spoilt for parking choice. History is everywhere including, for instance, the old boats and railway adding their own distinct touches. Yet when we go to pay for our admission and are handed a rather poor leaflet, I ask if there isn't a guide book.

'No,' says the cashier. But I see one.

'Oh, that's only about history,' she says. Who'd want anything to do with history in a museum?

'You want it anyway?' She's quite put out when we buy it. History indeed. Yet *Gloucester Docks: Living in History* describes itself as the official guide, and is just what we needed.

A look at a map quickly shows why Gloucester was so important. It was the gateway to the West Midland's busy waterways system. That includes the Severn itself, still navigable in Coalbrookdale, with its famous Iron Bridge where the industrial revolution began, the Warwickshire Avon, and canals to Birmingham, Wolverhampton and many other places. Though Gloucester was given port status by Elizabeth I, it was the 1793 decision to build a canal bypassing a dangerous part of the river that led to prosperity. The Gloucester & Sharpness Canal suffered many vicissitudes, but was the widest and deepest canal of the realm, and linked with the Stroudwater Navigation. Ocean-going vessels of up to 800 tons came from many parts of the world to unload their goods for distribution inland, and few returned empty. Business really boomed with the repeal of the Corn Laws in 1846; the tonnage entering or clearing the docks quadrupled. One of the exhibitions shows how wheat, oats, barley and maize were handled and stored with ingenious hoists and chutes; the trade dense in prodigious quantities for the growing population of Midland industrial towns and cities. To ensure that trade wasn't lost elsewhere, in 1849 the Canal Company opened the inner Victoria Basin, reached through a swing bridge, to supplement the main basin and quays.

Eventually, the railways stole much of the inland business, and sea-going ships grew beyond the canal's 800-ton limit. Things were in sharp decline in the 1870s but final death didn't happen until the coming of containerisation.

The canal age made a few wealthy. In the main museum, however, Sheila quickly learns how fickle investing in canals could be. At the first of several computer terminals dotted around, she 'buys' her starting shares. The programme skilfully lulls players into believing they have the midas touch. By the third or fourth terminal, she has of course lost the lot. Good fun, which is echoed around the complex. That cashier should be made to realise that history doesn't have to be dull. She avoids comment when later we return to buy some more detailed history, while I note that many canal titles I launched are on sale second-hand at gratifyingly high prices. But then there has always been greater certainty in collecting transport literature, and certainly railway and canal artefacts, than in buying shares in transport, as recent experience with Railtrack demonstrates. Bungled management decisions and actions have always made it dangerous to invest in canals and railways, and indeed, in more recent times, airlines. And there's the inescapable point that you cannot sell yesterday's surplus seats, however cheaply, today.

Museums, mercifully, are not run for profit. The cost of maintaining this great complex, with many identical red-brick warehouses, must be enormous but, as do so many places today, Gloucester depends on tourism. The only sour note is that the Robert Opie Museum of

Advertising & Packaging, in one of the warehouses, has closed for good. We don't quite know why, but detect a 'not part of us' attitude. A shame.

The quays and the boats, even a large, ugly concrete boat, are all worth studying, while back in the main museum the short video and the panels describing the exhibits are first class. Though only offering soup and sandwiches, the tea room isn't bad for lunch, either. Yet if only one could relive, even for a few minutes, the activity when the port was at its busiest. Videos can't really do that, and today we are surely in danger of spending too much time reliving the more recent happenings that have been recorded on film.

Which brings us back to having to have earlier history in written form. The cashier isn't the only person against that. While a forest of little hands pop up every time a teacher asks their class about something they've seen, one woman asks her husband: 'Why on earth didn't they send it by road in the first place?'

When he tries to explain that then roads weren't fit for heavy transport, and anyway horses and carts moved slowly, she snaps back: 'Well, if they built roads properly to begin with we'd have avoided canals and railways and other stupid things.'

She'll no doubt be glad when her husband has had his fill of waterway exhibits and she can exit in her little metal box.

The Mysterious Lower Severn

Unlike the Thames, on which much of London's history has taken place and which, above the city, soon becomes a pleasant, intimate affair, the Severn is sinister, if not positively unfriendly – until its higher reaches above Worcester. With the second highest tide range in the world, and its famous bore or tidal wave that churns up everything in its path, the lower Severn has to be contained within flood banks that restrict visibility by both land and water. Though at places the main channel is narrow with tricky bends – there are nasty reefs, too – the river's sheer width also destroys any intimacy. Some places, such as Slimbridge, seem positively to disown the river. At least for the first twenty miles north of the Severn Bridges, the river banks are not yet great territory for the developers of luxury flats, so the countryside remains less spoilt and more individual. Few people along this stretch mess about in small boats.

Catching salmon is not what it once was, either. It certainly doesn't involve the historic range of methods and equipment. At one extreme, fishermen used actually to chase and catch individual fish with collapsible nets; at the other extreme were great fishing stations with dozens of basket cages through which the tidal water flowed. Where the river makes a horseshoe bend at Upper Framilode, they say the tide comes in for one hour and ebbs for eleven. Around here the bore gets interesting. Excitement builds up when a major one is due. Though the best bores seem to be at unsocial times, the banks are lined with spectators waiting for the swoosh and the sight of one or two people riding the crest of the wave. The onlookers jump back as water spreads wide of the river and turbulence reigns for a minute or so till all that seems to have happened is that the tide is higher.

Even when it is not foggy, the river is a confusing place, and successive generations of fishermen tied their sons, being introduced to it for the first time, to their boats, for fear they might lose perspective and balance. There is still interest where the Gloucester & Sharpness Canal enters the river in the once-thriving inland port complex at Sharpness, but I much regret I didn't visit it in busier times, and especially that I failed to take the train from Berkeley Road station through Sharpness and over the river to Lydney. Though Dr Beeching would certainly have claimed it later, the railway ceased when on a foggy night a barge hit one of the piers and felled the superstructure.

At the museum (incidentally only one of three operated by the Waterways Trust), we noted that in season there are various kinds of boat trips. You can take a scheduled boat to Tewkesbury, or go by river or canal to Sharpness, enjoy a light supper or even a disco on a sunset cruise, take your children to Santa's grotto, and hire a different boat on which to get married. Generally, however, the Severn is now an empty river in the middle of a highly-populated country. Navigating it has never been easy.

The Severn? What does it mean to you? To older motorists, perhaps long waits for the Aust car ferry or a long drive round via Gloucester. To railway travellers, the Severn Tunnel, a truly pioneer achievement pre-dating the Channel Tunnel by a century. To today's motorists, the choice of bridges, but both disappointing in their views. To those interested in rivers, it probably denotes the complete system, including the picturesque Wye, the Somerset Avon which helped Bristol become Britain's second city and, also, that other major tributary, the Warwickshire Avon. Few people have ever intimately known all of the great system that drains into the Severn Channel and some, such as workers at Berkeley's atomic power station whose site was chosen for its isolation, don't care much for their part of it. What a contrast there is between the atomic station's setting and that of Tintern Abbey on the Wye, less than ten miles away as the crow flies.

The most visited spot near the river is undoubtedly the Wildfowl Trust's base beyond Slimbridge and across the Gloucester & Sharpness Canal. This is where Peter Scott, son of the Antarctic explorer, artist and compère of the BBC's first wildlife TV series Look, built his study with large picture windows, enjoying and sharing the enjoyment of his thousands of honking geese but making it plain to book publishers that he was interested in the greatest reward for the least effort. But back in 1964, he did write, without question of charge, a foreword to *The Severn Bore*:

My home lies opposite that indefinable part of the estuary which is not quite river, not quite sea. From the house, at the times of Spring tide, we can hear the flood as it rushes in over the sand on its way into the funnel-mouth of the river which will turn it into a bore. Over our sands the little wave is only a foot high at most, but up in the narrows round the great bend it will gradually build up into a breaking roller more than six feet high, a strange and fascinating sight which draws hundreds of spectators on those special days of equinox when it is expected to be at its highest and best. Why and how does it happen? This I have wanted to know in detail ever since the first day I saw it, but no such details had I been able to discover until I saw the manuscript of Fred Rowbotham's book. Now I find that the anatomy and origins of a bore are no less fascinating than its appearance, and that they are most lucidly described in this book – the first ever to be devoted to this particular kind of bore. It has given me a new insight into the Severn Estuary which has been the centre-piece of my special interests during the last fifteen years – the noble expanse of brown sand and grey mud, blue water and green salting beside which I have made my home.

Much though I would have liked to revisit Framilode, the isolated village of Arlingham with the river on three sides, Slimbridge and the old quays and warehouses at the port of Sharpness, they will have to wait for another day, for this afternoon we have to hasten down the dull M5 to Bristol to talk about another form of transport that has been remarkably revived: cycling.

First, though, for the sake of perspective it should perhaps be added that much of the upper Severn is delightfully intimate, especially when it runs between high hills and in a gorge as at the famous Iron Bridge. You can still see a lovely part of it from a traditional steam train on the preserved Severn Valley Railway. But my fondest memory goes back to Great Western days, when an aunt and uncle with whom I was staying in the Black Country brought me by their new motor car for an evening picnic high above the river at Arley, one of the stations on today's line. The setting, the evening, was idyllic, though utter perfection began with a shrill locomotive whistle echoing in the hills. A train of three carriages hauled by a 2-6-0 Mogul tender engine was brought almost to a standstill before the signal lowered. Being allowed cautiously into the station meant it was going to 'cross' a similar train in the other direction at the loop on the single-track route. Soon the other engine also whistled, the second train drew in alongside the first, the signalman madly collected the tokens, put them through the machine in his box and changed points and signals. The single porter dashed about helping with luggage and collecting tickets from the handful of alighting passengers. As the sun fell below the hills, he followed them out of the station yard on his bicycle at the end of his duty. It was then I discovered it might be better to record the scene in one's mind than to take photographs.

Bristol and the National Cycle Network

Our route into Bristol takes us under Brunel's Clifton Suspension Bridge. The piers, always thought to have been solid stone, have just been discovered to be hollow. No doubt on the back of an envelope, the great engineer concluded it was safe to economise on stone, and it is a bit late to say he was wrong: the bridge of course carries far greater weight than could have been imagined. It is low tide and the Avon a dull ditch. I recall the fun of coming up here on the full tide aboard an empty *Waverley*, the paddle steamer, moving from the restored pier at Clevedon to the heart of Bristol Docks – an extremely tight fit and only possible on occasional tides – for its next cruise. More extraordinary to realise it was down this highly-tidal, twisting estuary that Brunel intended that passengers on his Great Western Railway from Paddington could continue on to New York. The restored *Great Britain* tied up in the docks over there is part of the evidence. It is just one of the special tourist attractions Bristol offers its visitors, not to mention the cathedral and other fine churches and, among the dross, some impressive new buildings as well as historic streets that somehow survived the blitz.

For a time it looked as though planners, and especially traffic engineers, would do more damage than Hitler. The late Sir Arthur Elton, who gave Clevedon Court to the National Trust and, as outstanding producer of industrial films, had a keen interest in things past, chaired a committee desperately trying to prevent Brunel's original terminus of 1838 being swept away for development. Even Brunel didn't think people would wish to travel further than from London to Bristol in one go, so the railway that extended the line west, the Bristol & Exeter, also ran from a terminus. This, too, has a remarkable frontage, clearly seen from the station car park. Today's station is on the loop that linked the two separate systems.

Not only were the historic termini threatened but, as you joined the main road into the city, you were confronted first by a Meccano-like footbridge and then by what looked like a temporary military flyover by a roundabout enclosing a decaying hotel. My worst-ever hotel night, unbelievably awful with a lumpy bed and cars rattling the loose boards of the flyover for music, was spent here. Things began going wrong when twice I was allocated and given a key to a room with a woman already in bed. It transpired that reception hadn't kept a record of who was where, and there were spare keys to most rooms. They said they would send up a glass of free wine. It went to one of the ladies, a Muslim forbidden alcohol, and was as warm as the stifling night when it eventually reached me. It was charged on the bill next morning, but of course I was given one of the women's bills. Now the whole area is Shipshape and Bristol Fashion.

Soon we join the route along which each Monday I used to walk from Bristol Temple Meads to the BBC; a stiff twenty minutes saving, there and back, 6d which I invested in a second-hand book at George's the booksellers at the top of Park Street. Many of the purchases were Murray's *Hand-Books* to various counties, especially the mid-nineteenth century editions which have become serious collectors' pieces and given great enjoyment. As mentioned in the introduction, they were more rounded and honest than later guides concentrating on what was prudishly fashionable.

Around what is generally regarded as Bristol's centre, and which used to be water alive with shipping, we slip into Queens Square and head for King Street. Even in mid-winter, Nairn often feels warmer than Bristol does on this autumnal day. However, the welcome at the offices of the National Cycle Network, or Sustrans, that name a play on sustainable transport, couldn't be warmer, with a cuppa rapidly rustled up. John Grimshaw describes himself as chief executive and engineer. The offices are probably the same he and a small band of enthusiasts used when extending cycleways to old railway routes and canal towpaths seemed a worthy but amateur calling. Amateur is a word that quickly disappears from today's thoughts.

Here is a small, informal but obviously highly effective powerhouse of one of the most ambitious transport schemes ever: the creation of a truly national cycle network, involving the purchase of hundreds of miles of route, building new bridges as well as buying and maintaining hundreds more, having routes signposted on a national basis and their numbers clearly indicated on Ordnance Survey maps. After the London Dome, it was the largest of the Millennium schemes, with a £43.5 million grant. The EU has chipped in handsomely, and there have been many other grants, often for a specific section, as well as solid financial and practical help from supporters.

'Supporters, not members,' John emphasises. 'We run a very tight ship.' Timewasters not welcome. Nor staff requiring high salaries. 'What we do isn't really work at all,' he says. 'When we got started, our finances were appalling. Now we've got money for the job, I don't have to worry, but we still need to get real value out of what we've been given.'

There are twenty headquarters staff, and 120 around the country plus many part-timers and volunteers. What they do here is plan and negotiate. That means building good relations with scores of local authorities, the National Parks, highway people, and those involved in railway and canal land. Skilled negotiators and in-house solicitors steadily buy missing sections of route, take over bridges, viaducts, and so on. For example, when the owner of a house decided it had become too small for him after he had acquired a piano, but refused to sell a narrow strip at the bottom of the garden, they bought the property outright, fenced off the few feet at the bottom and sold it on without loss. A routine piece of action by Mark Tucker, 'the land wheeler-dealer'. Often considerable tact, patience and persuasion are needed, especially when the last owner of a section of route holds out thinking he is on to a good thing.

Though Sustrans commission more outside sculptures and other art than anyone else, and small decorative details are not forgotten, there is a wonderfully practical, hands-on approach, exactly what our railways have been especially lacking since they fired most of the engineers. Give finance priority, and what happens: impossibly expensive engineering. Who seriously believes that relaying the Windermere branch, ten miles of single track, with complete closure so it could be done economically, need have cost £3milllion, never mind the £6 million actually paid, or that redoubling just 9½ miles of the Chiltern Line from Aynho to Bicester should cost anything like the ridiculous £50 million it has.

Not a fair comparison? Actually it probably is. John detests the culture of frequently moving staff around and reorganising so that the best people leave. He has not only produced outstanding value for money but achieved high credibility in keeping to budget and schedule. The map of the current state of the cycleways shows activity throughout the United Kingdom. (To request a catalogue including a wide range of maps, books and leaflets, tel: 01179 290888.) He rapidly gives me up-to-the-moment comments on any section I refer to.

So, I learn, the longest single completed new line of cycleway is between Lincoln and Boston, on former railway land raised above flood level. The Minehead to Torquay route will incorporate the whole of the old Holsworthy-Hatherleigh line. When visiting mid-Wales, I should make a point of seeing the new bridge on the route of Bailey's Tramroad, around the hill and so avoiding the tunnel near Clydach Gorge, on the old Heads of the Valley Abergavenny-Brynmawr route. He marks the spot on my OS map. When I get to North Wales, I'm to look out too for the new bridge over the Dovey at the end of the Cob at Porthmadog in Cambria. The new cycleway beside the A9 through the Pass of Drumochter, on the way to Inverness, might seem extravagant for the amount it is currently used, but every year or two a cyclist on the main road used to lose their life. The Eden Project in Cornwall, where the engineer is another Grimshaw, his cousin, is soon to be put on the cycleway map. The Waterways Trust's takeover of the Thames & Severn Canal and Stroudwater Navigation will enable people to cycle all the way between England's two main river systems. And so on. His knowledge is as encyclopaedic as his enthusiasm is catching.

As told in the introduction, it began with the Bristol & Bath cycleway, and early achievements were tentative. The time most people heard about Sustrans was when the millennium award was announced. Then one soon noticed things happening in different parts of the country. Much of the success is due to transparent openness and lack of politics. Railway managers have always been too proud and driven by the latest fashion or dogma to behave like this. When the old Britrail tried to sell off the Settle & Carlisle, for example, the brochure inviting interest was full of legal nonsense and restrictions placing quite pointless strain on would-be purchasers. Other organisations speak well of relations with Sustrans. Things work especially well with the Waterways Trust, with the satisfaction of knowing that expensive restoration schemes mean that walkers and cyclists as well as boaters will be welcome.

Is it the right use of money, or another inverse piece of Robin Hoodism, the gambling poor paying for rich folks' toy things? Unlike say opera, canals, cycling and walking appeal to all kinds of people. John admits that only two per cent of Britons cycle, with ten per cent in flat regions, notably East Anglia. Yet the original Bristol & Bath route attracts 1½ million journeys, far more than went by train in the railway's last days. The nonsense is that railways cannot be reopened (as revived railways or cycle/walkways) until they've been closed, depriving people of what in most cases is still a vital service; and that, while canals and cycleways are seen as worthy of charitable support, even the remotest part of the national railway is subject to the complicated nationwide rules of privatisation. What many individuals feel is badly needed (but there is no chance of happening in the present climate) is selecting a dozen or so sections of the network to be run more for tourism than transport. Involve 'amateur' operators on the professional railway? What next? So, and pitiful it is to see, lines that would be major tourist attractions in Europe, and used to be here, are now served by standard diesel units with their sardine-like seating and poor visibility. Yet, who expected so many waterways and old railway routes to be brought back to life? One day common sense may yet strike the railways, but don't put your money on it.

On our way back to Bath we follow John's instruction to visit the Bristol to Bath cycleway at two points. The first is Warmley where, in the declining light of evening rush hour, there is a steady trickle of cyclists plus a few walkers. By pressing a plunger, they stop road traffic over the level crossing. There are curious though not very memorable sculptural figures (still a nice touch, though) on the platforms between which the cycleway passes on the old track bed. Then, at Bitton, we see rakes of old carriages lined up in the sidings of the short Avon Valley steam railway. This is one of several locations where an old railway route is shared by a steam railway. 'There's no problem,' says John. 'Why be restrictive? All we need is room for cyclists and walkers.'

John nicknames his baby The Travelling Landscape, a title I've appropriated with his blessing for part of my introduction. [Shortly after our meeting in Bristol, John and his bubbly partner Sue, who has just won her first grant for a scheme for midwives, came to Bath to have dinner with us. A unique excuse for arriving somewhat late: their boat to Bristol Temple Meads missed their train connection. We didn't even know there was a service of commuter boats in Bristol, though are scarcely surprised for much is happening there including a new tramway serving the old dock area. From Bath station they of course walked. You can't say John doesn't practise what he preaches. Such is his belief in sustainable transport that, even as chief executive of what by any standard has become a substantial operation, he doesn't own a car.]

THE GREAT WAY WEST TO DEVON

Brunel's Paddington and God's Wonderful Railway

Having been back in Nairn, we have just arrived in London by overnight sleeper and transferred stations by taxi. Brunel's Paddington is still London's most glorious and practical station. The only problem is that, for all his foresight, Brunel did not allow for the Heathrow Express and the extra passengers it would disgorge needing taxis. Never have we been more ashamed to be British than on this wet morning. Arriving taxis make their passengers leave well short of the station entrance, and we and many Americans have to push, literally shove our way pulling luggage between the solid double-backed (because otherwise it would be out in the rain) queue of hundreds waiting for taxis. 'Kennedy and La Guardia, yes, but is this mess really Britain?' asks one American.

The scrum makes Sheila miss her train to travel the route which was the world's best-engineered railway, until the building of Japan's Bullet Train. She is going to Bath to collect our small car; I have appointments in my old hunting-ground. Sheila is however still on her way long before my direct train to Devon is ready.

In the belief that many will miss their trains, even if they don't have to hang around because of cancellations, Railtrack have let one franchise to the Caviar House, so you can perch on a stool and choose between Beluga or Seruga with your champagne. It is part of Paddington's special status. After a wander, admiring the roof of this cathedral of steam (Brunel's office naturally looked out across the transept), I make do with the more modest first-class lounge and its free tea. But no first-class trolley on the 9.33; 'staff shortage'. Soon we are up to 125mph; over two miles a minute, trains passing at a combined speed of 250mph on Maidenhead bridge across the Thames. Brunel's critics said its arches were far too flat and predicted the bridge would collapse into the river. How those early railway engineers got it right. Their calculations might have been back-of-envelope, but they always *thought*, and had ample time to do so as they galloped up and down the country they were destined to shrink. It should be added that, buoyed by his success here, Brunel built a bridge across the Parret in Somerset designed with an even flatter arch which did fail. Conveniently critics did not hear about that.

Quarter-mile posts flash by faster than eight a minute. Isambard Kingdom Brunel, who my father nicknamed the 'poet engineer', built no ordinary railway. To some the Great Western Railway might be the Great Way Round, but God's Wonderful Railway is perhaps truer. Built to a much wider gauge than other lines, it went straight through obstacles rather than around them, and was soon and for many decades the route of the world's fastest and also longest non-stop trains.

At first it was a Tory concern favouring the well-off: a coroner's verdict of 'died travelling third class on the GW' needing no explanation since the proletariat were relegated to open trucks. Its safety record was as unique as the love and respect in which it was soon held by its staff and customers alike – a respect that ultimately was held by almost everyone. Indeed, across the total history of mankind, no form of transport, even by horse or ship, has ever equalled the safety record of the GWR between the wars. Good morale born of great continuity (the Great Western was Britain's only major line not to lose its identity in the 1923 shake-up called the Grouping) and the world's most advance signalling system (called Automatic Train Control) were the chief reasons. The legacy of extra space once the GWR had to narrow its gauge to conform to the British standard also helped – and still does.

That makes it the more poignant that two of our most recent major railway disasters have been just outside Paddington. This morning everything is at its normal best, 125mph much of the way to Reading, and then 110mph maximum on the Berks & Hants route.

The attraction of the 'new' (1906) direct route to the Southwest lies in its delightful rural nature. It is a series of former secondary lines and later links, pieced together. For well over a hundred miles, the largest place we pass is Newbury; yet this is overcrowded Southern England. We bowl along for many miles alongside the restored Kennet & Avon Canal. We note its great pumping station at Crofton, the war-time pillboxes guarding what was once an important junction – and now wait for the canal to disappear into a tunnel, coming out on the north side of the railway. The sun has emerged, and the Vale of Pewsey sparkles, as does that most visible of all Wiltshire landmarks, the chimney of Westbury cement factory, seen from the train for over thirty miles, though less enjoyable than the more fleeting glimpse of the Westbury White Horse. The White Horse is in today's news, locals appalled that it should have been remade in concrete with less delicate features than when the turf was simply removed revealing the chalk beneath and frequently edged afresh.

I have come this way regularly since 1938, almost weekly for thirty years, as well as writing about the route (*The Great Way West*). So if you want useless information, I am your man: mileage posts beyond Westbury are from London via Chippenham, which was the junction for the long branch to Weymouth – the route we are now using. Just beyond Bruton look out on the north side for an embankment to take a connection demanded by Parliament but never once used. It was with the dear old cross-country Somerset & Dorset (Slow and Dirty or Sweet and Dear) which used to bisect our route here. The rival railways might be ordered to make the link, but co-operation was out of the question.

Once more I am pointing out the local landmarks, for the only other passengers in the first-class coach have told the ticket collector (interested in their free pass) that they live fifteen miles from Inverness which turns out to be Nairn. It emerges that Gill Challis is in charge of Inverness station for one shift on most days, a Sassenach who prefers the way she is treated with a smile as an individual in the North of Scotland, and one of the new breed of enthusiastic railway workers passionate to make things go smoothly for the customer if sometimes against great odds. 'Just where do you put Americans' oversize luggage in sprinter trains?' Husband John is into breeding maggots in a big way, naturally for fishermen, but has recently also trained as a chimney sweep. Beyond Castle Cary we are on a 1906 link; the workmen were paid 6d an hour; we arrange to have our chimney swept as we sweep across the Somerset Levels where the expresses have always been as irrelevant to local life as the aeroplanes above.

At Langport we join the former Taunton to Yeovil branch, and are now passing through fields of withies or willows enjoying the damp soil, though the popular belief that they needed regular flooding has been disproved by better flood control. Glastonbury Tor is in the distance of this magic land where time seems to have stood still. We look out to the left at the row of houses strung out along a river bank. They were said to have been built in a day to gain squatters' rights. We bypass Lyng to the north of the line as we take another 1906 cut off to Cogload Junction where trains from Bristol, South Wales, the Midlands and the North – and also a few by the original Great Way Round from Paddington via Swindon – join the route.

What memories of crowded trains when in pre-package days adventurous holidays for Midlanders and Northerners, even really go-ahead Glaswegians, usually meant Devon and Cornwall. Speed was usually fine until the quadrupled track that used to run from Cogload Junction through Taunton petered out at Norton Fitzwarren. 'Then we crawled all the way, stopping at every signal,' was frequently no exaggeration. On the busiest summer Saturdays in the 1950s trains queued from Paignton on the Torbay branch line all the way back to Norton Fitzwarren at the foot of the steep Wellington Bank. The route's capacity depended on how quickly steam engines handled their heavy loads up to Wellington and then further up and through Whiteball Tunnel. Often it took over three hours, signal to signal, to Paignton; sometimes four or even five. Today we sweep up the bank (man is said first to have travelled at a hundred miles an hour coming down it in the opposite direction), dash into the tunnel and emerge in a brilliant Devon. There to the right is the Grand Western Canal, part of a grand design to save the lives of mariners who would otherwise have to sail round Land's End. A particularly gentle piece of Theme Park Britain, it is now used by craft of the Grand Western Horse Boat Company of Tiverton that glide at a few miles an hour through what is to all intents and purposes a nature reserve.

In the sparkling sunshine, every hedge and stream, cottage and church, looks as though it has been carefully arranged by an artist. This is a splendid downhill ride, enjoyment increased by seeing a fox walk steadily beside a hedge, the train no more an enemy than it is to the heron stalking the bank of the River Culm. It has long been a family tradition to note Cullompton's bowling green, which you can now do from the M5 as well as the railway. We dash on, overtaking even the fastest cars on the motorway round sweeping curves [soon to be subject to a 20mph limit as a result of tomorrow's Hatfield disaster, and then along track which will be left suspended in mid-air after a flood a few days after that]. All too soon we are into Exeter St David's. Who in their right mind would have wanted to drive?

Dawlish and Jim Holman's Dawlish Gazette

Because time is short and connections loose, it is into a taxi. I comment on the Mercedes. 'Quite frankly, this is the only decent taxi in Exeter,' the driver assures me, soon pitching into the City Council for not making more of the Maritime Museum. This is now substantially reduced and without the adjunct of the ferry across the basin once served by ships coming up the canal. 'The last ferryman was killed when he was pulling his way across and a block got detached that hit his head. But that's Exeter these days, a sad city. What's there for visitors beside the Cathedral?'

I don't argue but remember recent visits with pleasure. As we take the Exminster bypass overlooking the marshes where there used to be a pillbox useful for courting in the good old days, he is obsessed with safety and critical of other drivers. 'But the police weren't interested,' he says, when describing how he killed several people on a road so crowded with refugees on the Rwanda-Zaire border that it was impossible to get through safely with the truck he was driving as a volunteer relief worker.

Living in Scotland is wonderful but, yes, one does miss the more gentle grandeur of South Devon, whose cliffs never looked more lovely than on this crystal-clear day between rainstorms. And there are so many different bays and headlands to enjoy at a single visual sweep. 'God's in his heaven – all's right with the world,' I find myself saying over and over. Starcross and the river ports across the Exe, including Topsham and Exmouth, and then even downmarket Dawlish Warren, are as visitors might hope to see them but so seldom do. The only jarring note is that a particularly bad attack of Theme Park Britain seems to have attracted yet more entrepreneurs preying on passing tourists to this area once dominated by farmers and growers and their honest pursuit of growing anemones, violets, strawberries and cauliflowers. Each season's problems and yields used to make good journalistic copy.

Dawlish, about the same size as Nairn, is also on the sea, and has an independently-owned local newspaper. There the similarity ends. It is emotional visiting it today. Once it was a vital part of life, but then things went wrong, and much water has poured down The Stream through the gardens in the town's centre (newer Bournemouth took part of its inspiration from here), and many generations of the famous black swans have been hatched and died, since I last dared return. The café, where as a boy I was once teased for ordering an almond maroon, has like most other shops changed trades as well as hands. That embarrassment happened when I proudly edited Teignmouth Grammar School's magazine, and found frequent excuses to visit the printers, Holmans at 39 The Strand.

When David & Charles the publishers was founded on April Fool's Day 1960, here were the natural printers. At least I could understand what went on and wouldn't be blinded by science. The first title, *The Hay Railway*, happened to coincide with Holman's losing the printing of Exeter university's weekly paper on the *Dawlish Gazette* machines. Steadily D&C took over much of the capacity, which dramatically increased, with linotype machines, and automatic printing machines superseding those wound up by hand. Soon 21,000 copies in five weekly editions of *Devon Flood Story 1960* gave the fledgling D&C valuable practice and confidence. Jim Holman became colleague rather than supplier.

His father had reported (and hand-typeset two long columns) the Urban Council's meeting for the *Dawlish Gazette*'s first issue in 1897, and went on reporting for it while working for a rival Dawlish paper: for a time there were three papers in the town. He rescued the *Gazette* when it went bust and then bought it and its printing works, in which

Jim caught printer's ink, a contagious devil he later passed on to me. He was still under 21 when he completed a three-year paid-for apprenticeship at a Newton Abbot printers with a newspaper. Saying he wanted to be a printer rather than go to university, he was handed the works to run while his dad concentrated on writing.

With his soft, almost flat, Dawlish accent, unassuming air but natural authority, Jim got the best out of his men from the start, and when he became organist at the parish church was much respected by the choirboys, though in those days a cuff on the ear was par for the course. On a choir outing to Plymouth, a café owner was so impressed by their behaviour that all 35 (from eight to sixteen) were given a free ice cream. With newspaper, general printing, organ and choir, Jim worked all hours. When proofs needed passing to adhere to schedules others, customers included, were also expected to be eager for deadlines to be met.

Ever anxious not to outstay his welcome, he gave up as choirmaster and organist at the date he had decided upon when he started and also planned to quit the *Dawlish Gazette* before normal retirement age. In the days of scarce printing capacity, D&C depended on 'the works', so when Jim phoned to say he had an offer of purchase, we immediately matched it, making up and proofing the newspaper's front page announcing the new ownership so we could take it along the street to show the manager of Lloyds Bank, where we both had our accounts. By then the works had crossed the street from an adjunct of Jim's home to the former cinema where once on Sunday afternoons 'The Pleasant Sunday Hour', an interdenominational service with a small orchestra was held.

Our first take-over started brilliantly, but things then suddenly fell apart. Experts say that only one in three take-overs succeeds long term. One member of the staff had always leant to the extreme Left and, with a new like-minded colleague, it became the goal to make such losses that (since the unions would not allow closure) the whole of D&C would be brought down to help the working class. Mercifully that is yesterday's peril. The cost of introducing litho printing was not properly budgeted while, when Jim finally retired, the new manager rejected a new book to set, only to run short of work the following week. The place became ungovernable, men drifting to the beach on evening shift, the good ones being as worried as we were. At a tough meeting, the regional organiser of the principal union agreed we had no alternative but to close. The ringleader was thrown out of union membership. Nonetheless, closure was a horrid Christmas present to give Dawlish, and I have stayed away since, hardly daring even to enjoy the glimpse of the town from the train.

Though Jim's wife Ida died several years ago (we admire her favourite plumbago blooming away for all Dawlish to enjoy), and Jim himself is just turning ninety and now blind, it is not too late for renewed friendship. We assure each other that we haven't changed a bit. He talks of the excitement of building up the works; the Sunday afternoon a railway porter was seen pushing a truck up the street piled high with art paper (for *Devon Flood Story*); of how his mum had preached that hard work never killed anyone and Ida always had his breakfast on the table the exact moment he arrived home for a brief break, having been 'first in' in the way that employers living on the premises used to do.

Jim says that my 1970s D&C financial director, who had special responsibility for the works, 'had too big a laugh'. He adds: 'During my time there was never a moment a man lacked a job to do, and they always worked better if they knew the next task was waiting, but after I retired, one evening there wasn't a soul in the place.'

What about Jim's role in the town? 'What about it?' he asks, playing for time. Though blind, he still seems to have a glint in his eyes as he says: 'I never thought about it till I retired and everybody told me how useful I'd been. I didn't realise till later how unusual it was for the council to invite me to committee meetings providing we didn't report anything secret. They seem to have been as grateful for us as we were for them, though that didn't stop me banging away at them on certain development matters, like one that's come up just now right in front of us here.' And when I recall the Town Talk column of gossip bits and pieces – a valuable common denominator in any paper – he shows all his old enthusiasm. 'I needed readers to make it work. It was all the local news.' The paper is still independently owned, but no Town Talk and 'too much news from outside Dawlish'.

Today, once more, I can pause peaceably by the stream as I did when a lanky schoolboy. And now, walking upstream on the opposite bank where the swans build their nests, I look forward to lunch with the editor of the *Journal of the Railway & Canal Historical Society*, Dr Joan Cutler. Not merely as a Society member am I fascinated by the magazine's content, but Holmans used to print it here in Dawlish.

Joan's specialised interest in transport developed from running the industrial archaeology courses at Sheffield Polytechnic's archaeology centre. Like many who move West to be close to relatives, she has come to be near her mother but, also like many others, is not entirely happy. Integrating into a small town like Dawlish always takes time. 'I feel isolated.' She took over the editorship on the death of an author friend, Professor Pat White, but is threatening to give it up following a number of recent controversies. The whole committee has to decide on format and even typeface, and she is not on the committee. There are the usual complaints from readers about wasted space if a quarter page is left blank and, dreadful sin, she included something flippant. She recently asked for help to bring the *Journal*'s housestyle up-to-date. It is still the basic slightly *avant-garde*, unfussy one we introduced at the sapling

D&C in the early 1960s and certainly seems at home in Dawlish. Once more I too feel at home in Dawlish.

Sea Wall to Teignmouth

To the station where the platform has occasionally been washed away by the sea, and into a local train for Newton Abbot. It is not hard to concentrate on looking out of the window, so avoiding the eye of an offshore worker celebrating the beginning of leave with an armful of cans of beer he is anxious to share. But the sharpness of the majestic red sandstone cliffs is almost too much. Were the English seaside always this welcoming! In and out of the five short tunnels, and we are on the Sea Wall proper, a ledge Brunel daringly built between the foot of the red cliffs and the sea – always an expensive piece of line to maintain. It was along here in the post-war years I used to share the delight of up-country kids taking in their first sight of breaking waves. On busy Saturdays most trains slowed down to walking pace (part of the signal-to-signal queue mentioned earlier) and amusing was the banter through the open windows between passengers and walkers. An old gent preaching the end of the world to thin audiences would turn round showing his banner and gesticulating to larger on-board audiences as trains slowed. And this is where my mother taught me my nine times table. I invariably see the scene when working out seven nines.

Almost everywhere except the Lake District, the railway was welcomed by the authorities and populace, if not by owners of stately homes whose privacy was threatened. So when Brunel announced he would like to take his line to the west this way, Teignmouth had no difficulty... but wisely demanded that a walkway or narrow promenade be included. Generations of railway watchers (including Joan's grandfather explaining happenings with her on his lap) have enjoyed the rare combination of a busy main line under towering red cliffs on one side and the open sea with magnificent distant views on the other. The only regret is that today's expresses pass too rapidly to see the passengers inside, and the passengers have much less time to savour the scene, though for a few days early and late winter you can still enjoy the sun rising out of the sea while having porridge in the dining car. When trains had windows that opened, I once had a splash of seawater in my Great Western porridge.

Imagine how it must have felt on the first trains when the line was opened for Whit weekend 1846. This is how that great nineteenth-century source of knowledge on regional life, *The Exeter Flying Post*, summed it up:

> Things have been effected and works done, that even within the life of man would savour of romance, and such have been the

monster trains that have as it were flown from here to Teignmouth, and returned from thence to this city ... On Sunday the officers of the Company did their best for the accommodation of every one, though the number of passengers was such as they could not possibly have anticipated. All, however, was surpassed on Monday. At the station at Exeter, from the hour of seven in the morning, it was a most animated scene, the numbers continually increasing in order to [join] the trip down. Indeed, such was the amount that twenty-one carriages were required to contain them, and it was computed that upwards of 1,500 persons went down by the morning train: while about an equal number came up! Language would fail adequately to describe the scene. At Dawlish and Teignmouth bands of music were stationed, flags floated from every tower and eminence, while from the bosom of old ocean came the echo of the joy and hilarity that reigned on land.

We slow down rounding the curve (catching a glimpse of the main promenade) to stop at Teignmouth, where much of my upbringing took place. Though not intending to, I cannot resist getting off. Even if I met those I was at school with, I would not recognise them, though some of us have kept in touch and nearly a dozen masters and mistresses came to my 65th birthday celebrations. Teignmouth Grammar School may not have been Eton or Harrow, but (though the school has long been replaced by a comprehensive) the old pupils' organisation still thrives and many of us count ourselves lucky that we had an education we could respect and remember with fondness. 'I wouldn't want my teachers to come to my birthday party,' comment those less fortunate. The well-run grammar schools achieved much. A lot depended on the headmaster or mistress and, also, on the nature of the towns and villages served. To this day we recall how we looked down on the much rougher one at Newton Abbot.

As you can judge from the best of the Georgian architecture along the Den, the green between the town and promenade, also from the building housing Smiths in the triangle, Teignmouth was once a civilised, cultured place, with its famous club welcoming the cream of those retiring here from other parts of the country. The promenade, including the railway Sea Wall and the large Point car park, is probably the longest level walk beside the sea in the West of England. Beyond the Point at the western end is the narrow entrance to the Teign estuary with one of Britain's fastest tide races. Opposite is picturesque Shaldon ending in the landward sloping red sandstone mass of the Ness, clothed in trees planted for Victoria's Jubilee.

To our right where the estuary opens out are the busy harbour, Shaldon's passenger ferry and, beyond what was once England's longest bridge, a fine view to Hay Tor on Dartmoor. Middle-class visitors especially revelled in Teignmouth's individuality for it has always been more than a resort. For centuries, shipping, including the export of much ball clay from the Newton Abbot area, has been on a considerable scale. Fishing has a long tradition. Women used to congregate on the Den when it was time for their menfolk to return from the Newfoundland banks; beyond the Ness is a bay called Labrador. Netting salmon still attracts a considerable audience. You could never mistake Teignmouth for anywhere else. Always you are aware of the state of the tide and sea.

That it is just as well, for like so many others, its tourism has gone downmarket. The broad swath of the post-war road that greets you as you emerge from the station doesn't help. Most hotels have become flats, and many seafront properties have obviously had better days. In its effort to cater for the masses, the Den's spaciousness has been compromised with all kinds of bits and pieces of 'attractions'. But in all weathers I enjoy the broad promenade, with its flower beds sunken out of the east winds, the pier (cut back and no longer served by steamers), the Ness, views to Babbacombe with Berry Head beyond Brixham sticking out in the distance. Today, as one of those increasingly rare pure Devonians enthusiastically assures me: 'It's proper,' only it sounds more like 'praper'.

Things that were right, from weather to locks on doors, were always 'proper'. Equipment that failed was 'not man enough for his job'. Most articles have a gender, the more despicable ones being female. In the days when those living in the larger houses were upset if the taxi employed for shopping could not instantly park bang outside Woolworths, Teignmouth was a great place in which to grow up. The war changed things. Teignmouth was the most-bombed town – its whole centre was taken out – and suffered the greatest casualties for its size in the whole of Britain. We, like many others, were evacuated for part of it, though not until most of the night and daylight tip-and-run raids had happened.

Wartime fears were deeply ingrained. For the next twenty years, it was hard to resist the instinctive reaction to dive under the bed when a plane flew low. Long nights spent in the cellar with the double drone of German planes overhead were character-forming. We were in little danger during the first night raids on midland and northern cities but, when the RAF had become strong enough to send up fighters to intercept the raiders, some Germans dumped their bombs over the nearest town, which often happened to be Teignmouth, rather than return to base with them still on board.

The town never really got back on its feet after the war. The manager of Smiths who had earlier told me I was unfair in snapping up part of his meagre allocation of Everyman's Library before customers had time to enjoy thumbing them on the shelf, summed it up on a wet morning in the peak season: 'If these blasted people got out of my shop, I might sell something.' The industrial workers who took over the resort from mid-July till the end of August were not the kind to buy books but they needed shelter on wet days. That might mean gossiping in shops or lingering in a cafe, possibly over a single plate plus coffee between three or four. For other food it was snacking. Hundreds slept rough in shelters or their cars, and hotel owners resorted to shouting 'Fire! Fire!' to get people surreptitiously doing their washing out of the bathrooms. Of course it was right that more of the population should take holidays, but the postwar masses had absorbed no traditions to guide them, were usually skint (just being here was joy enough) and anyway greatly outnumbered the number of decent beds available. And the locals overcharged and cheated. Cakes and portions, for example, were smaller in the peak weeks than at other times.

Even before the more adventurous went overseas, the middle classes stayed away... and those who would have enjoyed an early or late break found hotels, especially guesthouses, closed since they made their packet in the short main season when you had to book up months ahead. Bookings had to be from Saturday to Saturday. However poor the service or food, there was no point in complaining, since you had partly paid upfront and there was nowhere else to go. Added to that, at peak times, especially when it rained, it was difficult even to ride a bicycle and impossible to drive or park. Birmingham motor workers were the worst of drivers. As I walk back past what used to be the theatre I recall how, in about 1952, I had to stop sharply to avoid colliding with a green Morris Minor whose driver had jumped in the parked vehicle, stuck out his indicator and driven straight out. Angrily he got out and in Brum bad language said I should read the *Highway Code*. Everybody knew that sticking out your indicator meant others had instantly to stop.

It was natural to criticise that flood of new holidaymakers who had no holiday precedent. Once I appeared on Midland TV saying that many of them didn't wash except in the sea. Yet their eyes were opened, and many of them were so gobsmacked by the scenery and different culture that they decided to move down at the first opportunity. Local people's promotion hopes were often dashed by the incomers taking jobs. Many more came to retire, peopling the new estates way above New Road which during the war effectively marked the built-up limits. Dreams often crumbled as they found it hard to integrate and frequently were unable to continue driving (widows rarely did in those estate's early days) or walk up the steep hill. Local newspaper ditors took perverse delight in reporting such human misery by the sea.

'Home' to Newton Abbot

So, now by taxi, out on the Newton Road, past the old gasworks whose staff enjoyed one marvellously important and busy weekend just after it should have closed, because Torquay's larger works had failed. Along the road skirting Bishopsteignton, we pass the former home of our family doctor, Rosalind Cooper, sister of Robert Graves, the poet. I used to come to her children's parties. Then Mum 'sacked' her for being a dirty doctor who didn't wash her hands. Many years later I was sent to her home with the BBC Radio Car to interview her on the old Light Programme's Radio Newsreel about the imprisonment of her son in Bulgaria, allegedly for spying. The next time she turned up in my life was as D&C author of an excellent *Games of an Edwardian Childhood*. Then we went to tea with her in her nineties, when her sight was failing but she was still doctor to some old ladies, who she found benefited from being put on dexedrine.

This section of road skirting Bishopsteignton was also where there was folly in the transport world. For generations the family firm of Gourds had served Bishopsteignton's transport needs and, probably from horse-drawn bus days, had charged a halfpenny less than the much larger Devon General on its route to Newton Abbot. Someone in the Devon General then discovered that their own 'territorial rights' stretched back even further than those of Gourds, who they took to the Traffic Commissioners. 'Wouldn't you like to earn more money?' was the substance of the enquiry, 'justice' forcing Gourds to put up their fares against their wishes. The family protested by hanging banners from their buses telling everyone that they didn't want to charge more. It was not in the culture of the Devon General, part of the huge and monopolistic British Electric Traction group, to take ridicule, so an over-generous offer was made to buy Gourds out. 'Cashing up after the runs on the final Saturday night was the saddest time of our lives,' said a member of the family.

Now across the upper Teign estuary, round the roundabout at the edge of Newton Abbot and into a bus bay, where I ask to be let out. When I gaze up at what is probably the nation's largest remaining signal gantry, a bald-headed, sharp-nosed gentleman kind of half-knows me, and I him. 'I look at 'em every day,' he says reassuringly. The signals are a much-admired icon of the steam age. I couldn't resist saving them when railway modernisation came to Newton Abbot. They are seen by many more than those who gaze across the grass to the historic Forde House, where Charles I was lavishly entertained, but William of Orange made less welcome when he chose it as his first stopping-point after his 1688 landing at Brixham. The house is now part of Teignbridge Council's headquarters and often used for celebrity entertainment.

I walk past David & Charles's offices which I have not entered since leaving in 1990 when, though even directors were instructed by the new owners to use a side door, I made my last exit out through the front. And across the bridge, looking at a scene much-changed since I first came here train-spotting in 1941, the day before Railway Cottages across the track and an off-duty steam engine received a direct hit from a German bomber. In the steam age, not merely were dozens of locomotives being prepared 'for the road' or having their fires dropped, still belching their impurities, but the railway's two repair works, a large electric power station and a variety of private companies contributed to the soot. When I lived five miles away at Ipplepen it was often sunny there while Newton shivered in its local smog. Many still remember the railway factory hooter, which when I lived in Teignmouth, Kingskerswell and then Ipplepen told you the direction of the wind as well as the time. Nicknamed the Swindon of the West, Newton Abbot had a vitality and dirtiness few up-country folk associate with Devon.

Moving David & Charles into the railway station was a revelation. Rubbish was sent to Swindon every Tuesday. Electric outlet points were to a patent Crabtree GWR standard and would not take ordinary plugs. Even the gas meter was a GWR design; as collecting railwayana became more prevalent, I feared some buff might try and steal it. The few radiators were served by a boiler in the basement running on coal shovelled from a truck that had to be specially shunted. Often the fuel ran out and we were cold. But the station was great for meetings. Seeing the signal drop told us when to leave the office to arrive at the foot of the platform steps exactly as visitors' trains stopped. Many books were sold from the showroom, where the Dartmoor-loving Archbishop of Canterbury waited for his trains. We made tea for the ticket collector and of course knew the staff, who were as friendly as could be though not exactly sophisticated. One plumber said British Railways could not afford the length of pipe needed to go round the gent's loo, and thought it perfectly acceptable for chaps to have to duck under its direct route five feet high in front of the urinals.

Another worker seemed to be having a heart attack slouched near some Midland Railway fire buckets I had bought in an auction, on the basis that, if you lived in a railway station and occasional members of the public said they were 'just looking round the museum', you might as well go the whole hog.

'So it's come to this. I never thought I'd live to see this.' I ultimately discovered he was muttering. 'In God's name, what's wrong with our own Great Western buckets?' When I explained I had purchased these 'foreign' intruders, all he could say was: 'Who gave you the right to pollute things?'

Courtenay Park is as brilliant as ever. I reach it across the pedestrian crossing opposite the station – past the gents' toilets where once, within a few days, the best part of a hundred men were caught importuning by a policeman lying on the roof trusses. He pulled a cord to raise a flag which alerted a colleague who then rushed inside. Most were brought to court together same day but, perhaps because D&C were well known, the police chose to crucify one of our managers by prosecuting him ahead of the rest and so let him suffer most from the publicity.

And there is the pillar box. There used to be two, one for late letters collected by a postman from the Up Great Western Travelling Post Office, which alas no longer stops here. Finally to the Queen's Hotel. It also figured large in our history, for once our warehouse was in the ballroom and our stock and records nearly burned with the rest of the premises, and in more recent days, after his premature retirement due to ill health, my right-hand man used to prop up the bar. The last time I saw him before his recent death was indeed here; I could do with his company since tonight is one of those rare times I am on my own. A quiet dinner and to bed. It has been quite a day.

IN AND AROUND
NEWTON ABBOT

Railway Junction, Market Town and Publishing Base

There are bound to be memories as I wake up opposite the station where so much of my life has been lived out: from boyhood engine-spotting to making television films; from starting and ending significant journeys to building a publishing empire. Perspective is always easier in places of great individuality. You understand your place in the universe and see yourself as minor player on a fascinating stage, privileged to be part of such a scene, even if you are critical of some of it. For all its warts, Newton Abbot was a love affair for me.

In many ways Newton has always been a poor town. It was not only in regard to its Grammar School that Teignmothians looked down on it, but also its general lack of sophistication and its utilitarian shops. My mother was shocked when told at the market that bananas were only stocked for Christmas. Described by guide books as railway junction and market town, most of its residents were indigenous, the salt of the earth but with few aspirations. It was perhaps a silly place in which to start a publishing company (after a period of using Holman's of Dawlish as an accommodation address and a very short spell in a hut on my fruit farm).

Newton Abbot's librarian told of occasional cases of kids being forced to return a book they had dared to borrow. 'Your mum and I haven't needed books; why do you put on airs?' Some dads were furious on finding out that their daughters had started working for a publisher, and abusively instructed us to send them home.

Staff came to 'help out' rather than work. It was impossible to imbue most women members with proper respect for our customers. Few could be persuaded to go on training courses and, even when they were prepared to do so, their partners sometimes phoned to ask who, then, was going to get their tea... not an isolated incident. The bank manager, used to farmers selling their two-toothed ewes, laughed when seeing a cheque for £3,000 being paid in. 'What people spend that kind of money on books?'

Our address was perhaps slightly odd: The Railway Station, Newton Abbot. Yet it seemed the most natural thing in the world to go to work in the station at which I had done my boyhood train-spotting. It was fortuitous that, when a generation later the time came to sell D&C, the tax inspector arguing capital gains tax admitted he had also done his train-spotting here too. Later we moved to a purpose-built building where Railway Cottages had stood before the 1941 direct hit.

David & Charles could not have survived and flourished as a conventional publisher with the high literary content then found in the lists of London imprints. As well as that, the fact that I was a provincial, and the son of a literary journalist and poet, forced me to be different. My interest in nostalgic and practical subjects happened to coincide with the public's increasing appetite. In our early years books on railways and canals, industrial archaeology and local history, specialist collecting, cookery, gardening and needlecraft not only met with little competition but enjoyed a strong public library demand.

So good were our sales that D&C quickly became a national and then international institution. The particular joy was that our books even sold well locally, many a Devonian becoming a keen reader after being indoctrinated by one of our titles on their favourite down-to-earth subject. We were loved for employing up to 300 people, and keeping busy many local freelances, hotels and cafés. I could tell how good the day's takings would be from the number of trolleys ('Brutes') loaded with our books lined up on the platform for evening trains with through vans to many destinations.

There were continual visitors. Whereas it had been hard to attract any staff, since at first publishing was assumed to be suspect, or at least dangerous in opening new horizons, now seventy folk applied for a new warehouse post. And so Newton Abbot became a great place to be in, and the ugliness of sloping terraces of narrow tightly-packed yellow-brick houses seemed a natural part of the scene.

Most of the large publishing houses had been long established, though immediately after the war a new breed represented by Weidenfeld, André Deutsch and Maxwell imported their tough, mainly European, skills flourishing where virtually no indigenous Britons did. Virtually all the start-ups after the immediate period were small and under-capitalised, though a few of them, such as Peter Owen, were editorially outstanding and have lasted long. David & Charles was a one-off. It was the only major new imprint or 'brand' led by an Englishman and, apart from Maxwell's Oxford-based Pergamon, the only major English house operating outside London.

The extent to which we were arriving, if we had not actually quite 'arrived', was brought home when for the first of many occasions I was invited to lunch with Lloyds Bank's regional board at Exeter. One bank manager or senior official after another furtively approached. 'I don't know who buys your books,' was how they nearly all started, and indeed concluded. In between they whispered: 'I wouldn't want my colleagues to know, but I keep a ferret [...have a steam organ... or whatever...] and have your book.' In most cases it was the only one on the subject. Majorities are always built of minorities was something I learned at that lunch. Niche marketing and its techniques were not popularised until decades later.

Our great growth coincided with British Rail's retreat. Where 1,950 railway workers had been employed well into the 1950s, the 1960s and 1970s saw dramatic decline and by 1990 fewer than fifty reported for duty here. Except of course on the closed branch lines, the train service is probably still the best ever, though lost forever is the sense of occasion there used to be when an express had its Torbay coaches added or removed in complicated manoeuvres taking advantage of scissor crossovers. (The *Torbay Express* was the only daily complete train from London to the resorts.) The layout has been much simplified. The carriage and wagon repair shop became our warehouse. The locomotive repair works, where the finest maintenance work was achieved (and once broad gauge locomotives were built from scratch), is surrounded by desolation and an attempt to have it listed and turned into a major tourist attraction is faltering. The library's specialist railway collection (I am president of the Friends), and artefacts at the Town Hall may however be brought together. Newton Abbot does not want or need to forget its great railway past. My life's most popular single act was to rescue that big gantry I've already mentioned – fourteen lower-quadrant arms – and erect it outside D&C. Literally hundreds stopped to say well done, though the police were not so happy, saying that at first motorists taking their attention off the road were continually bumping into each other.

Newton Abbot was always a touch individual. Going up the street, I pass the dental practice where the police once grabbed me outside the front door and held my arms in the middle of the night and held my arms until the dentist came out and explained that I had just had to have emergency stitches. Later, after a short 8am appointment on a First of March, the dentist brought me a glass of champagne to celebrate St David's Day in the dental chair.

So let us walk up Queen's Street, where many of the shops, though not luxurious, were highly individual. Two amazing ironmongers, both on several floors opposite each other, worked closely together, staff regularly searching the stock rooms of the rival as freely as their own.

Madge Mellor's cake shop and restaurant was a world within world, imperiously ruled by its owner cherishing tradition. Everything was done exactly in the Madge Mellor way, the girls' uniforms which had seemed a touch antiquated even in the early days looking increasingly ridiculous as time went on. Newton girls were however taught to wear what their bosses liked. One day it suddenly occurred to me that none of mine wore 'slacks'. I commented on this to one of our few women managers, who replied that it was thought I wouldn't like them. It happened to be payday and, learning there was no rule at all, the entire female staff went from shop to shop till Newton's stock of slacks of all sizes was exhausted.

Then there is the fish shop, possibly the best in Devon, where John Arlott of cricket reporting fame always bought plaice on his visits to D&C, including latterly by plane (once we chartered one specially) from Alderney. John was always good fun – if a demanding author.

At the top of Queen Street is the bank where once the manager (actually friendly and efficient) announced that his boss, the regional director, had suggested he needed a psychiatric examination (presumably for being argumentative). Later this Newton chap stormed into the regional HQ at Exeter insisting on a change of decision, which he claimed he instantly won. Respectable facades successfully hid strange goings on.

And now, emotionally, into the Market Hall, where as part-time though serious fruit grower I used to take my produce first thing every Wednesday and Saturday morning.

'How are you doing, Dave?' A bent old man sees me. He pauses a moment but is reluctant to stop and I'm not confident enough to call him. Having so long been 'one of them', I have been set apart partly by moving to Scotland ('Why on earth did you want to do that?') but mainly by the newspaper and television coverage dubbing me 'a millionaire' when ultimately the firm was sold. It was only at Newton market I was Dave. Today it is easy to confirm I was right in moving away. Not merely did the new owners quickly 'let go' or otherwise quickly lose the best part of 150 of my staff, but the town seems to have lost its impetus and direction. The short-term prosperity of the late seventies and eighties has evaporated. Many shops are closing down or on short lease to charities. The House of Fraser bought one department store, then took over and soon closed the rival, only to withdraw totally. Under the terms of their sale, neither premises can ever again be a department store. Newton Abbot has the good fortune that one of Britain's few family-owned department stores happens to have taken root here, steadily growing in size and stature. The Charlie Austin of my time knew every detail and square inch of his expanding empire, and still came in to check on things well into his nineties. Without it, the town centre would be even more desolate. There has been hideous over-expansion of out-of-town shopping. Teignbridge Council sold its soul - to be precise a park and open-air swimming pool given to the townspeople for their enjoyment in perpetuity for gold – to the Co-op, who despite promising otherwise immediately closed its town centre store.

Such grasping, it has to be said, is much out of character with that of Newton Abbot generally. Few traders actually seem to have enjoyed the act of taking money, and over the years many extraordinary obstacles have been placed in the way of your handing it to them. Service has always been slow; even this afternoon, more important for assistants first to assure themselves that their hairstyle is sufficiently impressive than to serve. On the spur of the moment I go into a wine shop where years ago I was told I could not have a dozen of this, that or the other wine. No, no, no, I couldn't. When asked if there was any wine they could sell by the dozen, the answer was: 'No. Come back some other day. Now I'm on my own and if I serve you, someone might come in for his box of matches and I wouldn't be free to give him help.' Today I pick out a quality bottle for a present for my daughter. When the assistant finds it convenient to serve, she tells me I didn't have to choose so expensively.

'There he goes throwing his money around,' once said an ironmonger's assistant to his colleagues. 'Wants to buy a new one; never thinks of having it mended.' It was a padlock, which several assistants, after fetching screwdrivers and an oil can, proceeded to dismantle and determine how it could be made functional again. Meanwhile, a market-day queue of customers stretched out well into the street.

I once asked if I could buy three trays of pansies. 'Not going to let you set up in opposition,' was the speedy retort without enquiring what I was going to do with them. They were wheeled away to the store for the night.

'Where do you live?' demanded the assistant in a kitchen shop of a new member of our staff. Only when she cited her superior address was she told 'All right, you can go on looking'.

If assistants show you a range of prices for something you want, they usually suggest that a cheaper one is perfectly adequate. And several times I have had the classic: 'I'm always telling people there's no demand for it.'

Mind you, extraordinary though visitors (and especially Americans) find this in post-Thatcher England, how much nicer it is than the pushiness that characterises so much business elsewhere. Devonians still seem to dominate Newton Abbot, or at any rate set the tone not exactly of contentment, more as they put it 'belonging to be', fitting in where they are and disliking the natural order of things being overthrown. Ask a young hairdresser where she will spend her holiday:

'Well, here of course. If you live here there's no point in going away, is there?' It is accepted that incomers are different, respected even if lacking the good fortune to have been born here. If the locals are not easily content with 'the powers that be', they are distinctly not troublemakers either.

Local dialects and habits occasionally provide amusement. A sophisticated American visitor had to guarantee he would not laugh when I took him to a greengrocer. 'Eat me, my lovely,' was all I asked, and was handed a box of dates of the Eat Me brand with 'there you are, mi beauty.'

The only serious personnel problem we experienced at D&C was that some staff refused to work the agreed overtime at the Christmas peak. Why give up a day's fishing to speed up customers getting what they want? Why the rush? And what need to say sorry? Misunderstandings were invariably the customer's fault. When asked to send a voucher by way of tangible regret to appease customers who were upset, my 'helpers' would cringe and object it was quite wrong to reward mistakes. The dislike of spending a penny unnecessarily, or recklessly as the staff no doubt saw it, was instinctive. 'That parcel you asked me to get off urgently yesterday by airmail to New York; it was too expensive, Mr Thomas, so I've sent it by sea.' My normally reticent receptionists accused me of spending too much on phoning our customers in New York. Earning money was seen as almost as bad as spending it. 'You're going to be the richest man in the churchyard,' a taxi driver on the station rank echoed almost daily for years.

'What's the rush?' is perhaps the favourite Devonian question. The proprietor of a taxi business looked hurt when pressed for a bill for journeys made during the previous twelve months. 'I'll send it presently,' was seen not to put the customer's mind at peace, so the proprietor added: 'It will only get spent if you pay it. You'll look after it better.' No doubt it would have been demanded in an emergency, but never was... and what today would be the equivalent of hundreds of pounds remained unpaid. The proprietor, however, was a happy man. Many a Devon builder has preferred drinking his cider unhurriedly with his mates to pushing out the paperwork and remaining solvent... and one suspects that capital is more tied up here by the disorganised and leisurely completion of building and decorating jobs even than elsewhere, builders' delays being one of the talking points of our time.

This may be placing too much emphasis on one side of what might be termed Newton's non-businesslike or shall we say laid-back character, but then I think not. Only recently have some shop owners and professional people realised they can no longer afford the time to take morning coffee in a café. The bank balance matters less than the kind of person you are. How much colour you can extract from life remains important. This is undoubtedly one of the places where you are still better respected if you inherit a fortune than make it. Flatteringly, I am more or less exempt from criticism, because 'you've been good for Newton Abbot,' which, of course, includes the railway signals. Certainly D&C was never run with a view to cashing in, any more than you would sell your kids, and today, reluctantly, I admit there has been a heavy price to pay for selling – for, if not actually criticised for what I did, I'm no longer 'one of us'. And how I miss that cause and effect, the seasonal, weekly and daily rhythm, knowing who, and what, many cars and lorries are carrying and why. Yes, it was a sad day I ceased to belong to be, and there is a strange feeling returning almost as a ghost. They were good years here.

Good years? Yes, in the sense that David & Charles gave purpose in the community, enjoyed frequent publishing successes, and was an unusually happy company. And, yes, also in the sense that we survived. Our competitors and detractors, and even a few of our far more numerous supporters, thought we would be bound to fail, and there were occasional rumours of our having called in a receiver. I often likened guiding the company to paddling a canoe in mid-Atlantic. Somehow we not merely weathered storms but used them to grow stronger. When times were tough, top colleagues pulled together, looked for guidance, and – for example – believed me when I said we could improve our cash-flow by a million pounds in a month if only the chasing of debt could be done quickly, imaginatively and in sufficient detail.

It was when times were better that conflict developed. While shop-floor staff from production, computers and finance to post-opening, sorting, packing and despatching, were ever loyal and proud of D&C, we could only home-grow part of our management. When the pressure was off, imported managers drifted into giving too much priority to their own agendas. Sales people thought of the books they liked selling, rather than what was intrinsically more saleable. Editorial kept their favourite titles on schedule at the expense of those they would have preferred to be without, but which would probably have sold better. When asked personally to consider an important, and confidential, idea, one manager, who disliked anything not invented by himself, came back only hours later to say he had called a departmental meeting and everyone was not merely against it but thought it unworkable, so that was that. Self-fulfilment of prophecies was often a danger. Since publishing is an art rather than a science, it is easy to make the unwanted fail. Once we discovered book-club sales forecasts were amended after sales had happened. The perpetrator had built a reputation for uncanny accuracy but provided a smokescreen by getting a title or two grossly wrong and apologising.

As I walk back past the station across to the offices, less happy memories crowd in – especially recollections about the pathological need of some managers to boost their own images. 'I've ordered a bigger quantity because otherwise we won't be taken seriously,' was said several times. 'Why can't we show people how important we've become?' was a recurrent, dangerous line of thinking. Surely we should all be staying in the best hotels and show those we are entertaining our splendid new set of wheels!

At one time company cars accounted for at least a third of the discussion at successive board meetings. What the directors wanted was a car policy that firstly they could challenge to make it more generous and then secondly show off their masculinity by breaking it. Good salaries, generous bonuses, pensions and health arrangements paled into insignificance compared with wheels. I look across to what used to be the boardroom in which I once thought there would be bloodshed. Irritated by the time devoted to discussing cars, I announced to astonished colleagues that in future I would personally authorise each individual purchase *on its merit*. A year later my own company Jag was seven years old, going perfectly, certainly more reliably than the average brand-new ones. Replacing it would mean everyone else would expect a new vehicle. The restless among the directors chose a spokesman to point out bits of rust on the Jag and declare how embarrassing it was that the corporate image was being let down, implying I needed a new car. OK, I said, I'll take action. A week later, he sheepishly thanked me for taking notice. The Jag had been re-sprayed. 'Why don't you get yours re-sprayed too?' I suggested.

Now crossing the bridge over the railway I need to breathe deeply as I relive some of the physical stress and recall the exact pains caused by such time-wasting diversions, and the everlasting need for personal aggrandisement among the contingent brought in from London publishing houses. In some departments the effective leadership came from a more junior member of staff we had trained ourselves, yet was not quite of the calibre (or smooth enough) to represent the company elsewhere. Despite gruelling interviews, and warnings that we were not for the faint-hearted, many who came from London thought they had bought a ticket for a gentler life. So staff turnover at the top was high. As I look up to the old signal gantry, I still feel guilty about that. Yet the ever-popular advice to delegate more could only have blurred our publishing policy and resulted in the directors spending yet more time competing with each other to have the best-equipped office and smartest car. All along I felt that I should have been routinely more autocratic and not only when crises demanded. Two chief lieutenants agreed and later we formed the real government, perpetually correcting the worst excesses of others.

What degree of democracy is desirable in a publishing business? Anyway, our chosen kind of publishing could only be made profitable with productivity and efficiency far above that achieved by most London houses.

But now Sheila has arrived. We start by going from the station via Coach Road, the way I went to and from work for many years. It takes us longer than expected to reach Coach Road, and is even more nerve-wracking along there than it used to be. Newton's traffic has never been well organised and inevitably gets heavier. Apart from the usual growth in the number of journeys made per person, there are so many more people. Every ten years, Devon's population goes up by roughly the present total population of the Highlands and Islands, and increase has been disproportionate in this popular part. It hurts. It feels especially shocking when you have known the area well for many decades and return after an absence. All the time you notice development where hereabouts there were fields of the highest class of agricultural land.

Along a familiar Totnes road with new pieces of theme parkery, such as a golf course and club, and right into Ipplepen at a junction 'they' suddenly over-lit, strings of bright lights robbing the village down in the valley of its vision of the stars on clear, moonless nights.

Ipplepen and Fruit Growing

When I moved there in 1958, Ipplepen was a poor, almost exclusively farming and working-class village with appalling shops, none having a freezer, so you could buy ice-cream only from the van sounding its chimes twice a week. The first Devon County Development Plan forecast the need for twenty new homes in twenty years, overlooking the fact staring them in the eye: that as the Torbay resorts, and even the first villages inland, such as Marldon, were reaching saturation point, the pressure from continuing population increase would inevitably move inland to the likes of Ipplepen. Soon more than twenty new homes were built each year, whole new estates of them.

New blood helped raise the tone and pace; soon the school had running water and then a new school was built. Shops acquired freezers, and about anything (including pharmaceuticals) could be bought in the village. Then a new kind of poverty struck. Shops closed as it became harder to compete with increased car ownership and the out-of-town superstores. Though there is a good school and health centre, and enthusiasm is still poured into several social organisations and events, today's residents are far less likely to meet each other than they used to do shopping locally or on a bus. The appointment system at the health centre means only one or two are usually waiting while in the old days thirty might cough and sneeze in a minute waiting room. Without such natural meetings, integration is harder. The pubs lack their old local support, too, though you can still be amused by the up-country coach parties on evening 'tours': straight from steps to bar without a glance at the surroundings.

Then through the lane between high hedges that used to be marked 'Unfit for Motors' to my old farm. The situation is perfection: a lush valley in the foreground, an immense patchwork of hundreds of fields and several church towers in the middle ground, the busy undulating plateau with Dartmoor's occasional granite outcrops as a backdrop. I see it in my mind's eye almost daily wherever I am and shall do for the rest of my life. Though nature has healed many of the wounds, you can still trace where a North Sea gas pipe cut through the fields, close to the farm. Living through that upheaval gave some of the flavour of what it must have been like when the navvies descended on the countryside to build the railways.

You need to have earned part of your livelihood from the land to know how low in esteem those who do it full-time are held. A neighbour, a gaunt retired colonel with yappy dogs he was always shouting commands at, scarcely nodded when passing me in the lane, till suddenly the cat was out of the bag: 'Thomas, you never told me you wrote and aren't just a grower. We must get to know each other.' No doubt in a mac too shabby for further use even to climb steam locomotives, I was riding my 1948 Ferguson petrol tractor (the petrol ones lasted much longer than the vaporising oil version that followed) when a smartly-dressed man walked into our main orchard. 'You'll be pleased to hear I've got the paperwork, so you'll be getting your money soon,' he started.

'What money's that?'

'Oh, you know, for the new pylons through there. All been agreed now, so sign there and I'll make sure you get your money soon.'

Encouraged by questions from a poor young man who appeared only able to run a small fruit farm, he divulged details... all totally unknown by anyone.

'I'm the local government correspondent of *The Western Morning News* and we're always interested in how planning applications are handled,' had him shooting off as though he had been caught in an indecent act, which indeed he had. Nothing more was ever heard, apart from a small paragraph at the foot of a column in the local weekly a few months later; it stated that, the Central Electricity Generating Board had decided on a different route. So part of the view was protected by my mixing farming with journalism. The distant view up to Dartmoor is hopefully timeless. But our sixteen acres are now divided between half a dozen ownerships with many buildings.

The farm workers were lovely people, but they could also be frustrating if not maddening. At first they thought hand-picked apples meant those you did not shovel up for cider. Fingernail cuts in high-class Cox's Orange Pippins 'shouldn't upset' the customers. Excessive cider drinking led to male absenteeism; the Queen on afternoon television meant no women 'helping out'. This was hard in the days before pick-your-own strawberries, our second most important crop, half a ton of them daily, 36 pickers, at the season's peak. Not that we would ever have sunk to growing the variety most popular with growers today: Favourite, which travels and keeps (and even freezes) well but at the expense of flavour. For the record, Vigour is still hard to beat. Now, if out-of-season imported strawberries often seem better than high summer British ones, it is not because they have had more sunlight but are better varieties.

When we started the fruit farm the message was that the local market was so poor that you had to send crops to London, at huge cost in boxes, transport and commission. By skilful marketing of our Bittons Farm brand, not an apple, strawberry, raspberry or anything else was ever sold further than ten miles from Ipplepen. On business trips to London, I could easily have bought strawberries retail from London street sellers and sold them wholesale locally at an acceptable margin. There had not been a tradition of fruit buying (most Devon homes had a productive garden and at least the odd apple tree), but this was the great period of expanding horizons across the social spectrum. We were more or less free to set our own prices, though still sold better quality fruit at a cheaper price than Marks & Spencer. Before the Common Market there were few Continental or American imports. Apples came from New Zealand and Canada (we used their strong shipping boxes for storage of our crop in our 500-year-old barn where the temperature was hardly affected by the seasons) but the strawberry market was totally British-supplied. That meant 10s (50p) a pound, but in two-ounce punnets, for they were a real luxury, at the season's start. Adjusted for inflation that might be around £10 a pound, or £1.25 for two ounces – about 35p per prime berry today. These early berries were grown under lengthy rows of cloches.

Growing the crops was interesting and seldom a problem. It meant taking and editing often contradictory advice, and conducting our own experiments. On heavy red clay, premature sowing or planting produced crops both later and smaller than those started when the soil had warmed up and did not set like concrete when compressed underfoot. Traditional deep digging was out. The frosts that were said to improve the soil were seldom sharp enough anyway. In fact. we pioneered not disturbing the soil at all, getting it clean and then keeping it weedless with use of the new herbicides. All good stuff for the monthly column in *The Grower*.

Another relative novelty, indeed total revelation hereabouts, was that you get better crops of better-quality strawberries, and also earlier, if you replace plants annually, or grow maidens as the experts put it. You do, however, need to get your maidens planted early. In South Devon delaying seven days from 25 August reduces the yield next summer by up to half. We discovered that this was one of the very few things that 'had' to be done so precisely by timetable. We all know of the nonsense about having to put your potatoes in on Good Friday, whether it be in March or mid-April, and equally nonsensical was the belief that if you grow mustard as a 'green crop' to turn into the soil for humus, it is only the little yellow flowers that work magic. Great was the upset when I ploughed in a crop scarcely showing a flower, for the growth was good, we had time on our hands but a heap of tasks were forthcoming with a bad weather outlook. 'Tis your money, maister, but I hates wasting mi time.'

But dear old Emmanuel Blatchford never could understand that though he was then three times my age, if he didn't kill himself with cider meantime the day would come when he would be only twice as old as me. 'Logic be damned. Us all knows that if I be three times as old as 'ee now, us'll always be three times as old.' His own farming days were indeed brought to an end by the cider devil for, however ingenious his wife's efforts to keep him on the straight and narrow, he showed yet greater genius for selling off something or other for cash and travelling by horse and cart a roundabout route to reach the boozer (even Devonian's creativeness has not come up with an equivalent word for cider house) undetected, passers-by being sworn to secrecy.

Growing and selling were fun; getting supplies delivered promptly and educating staff were much harder. We suffered in the same way as, slightly later in history, high-class restaurants did setting up in gastronomic wildernesses. No traditions were on our side; everything had to be learned afresh. So many of the traditional skills have been lost that it is vital to teach new ones, and eventually they take root.

We struck a lucky period. Growers as well as farmers now face tough, suicide-inducing conditions. I found great joy in growing, being in the open air, especially with a view of such depth and detail. Some farmers regret the loneliness, and everywhere the old babble of planters, hoers and harvesters, with kids playing noisily on the field's edge, belongs to yesteryear. But the days I really miss are those when there was nobody else on the farm. I can still see successive bouts of rough weather approaching across Dartmoor, the wind soon drowning the murmur of distant traffic. Then it was easy to 'belong to be'.

Pausing briefly in Ipplepen's square we remark that, like the surrounding fields, villages themselves are devoid of pedestrians and that those going to the post office nearly all drive even though they live close by.

KK and the Clash of Cultures

Then through a familiar network of sunken Devon lanes to the village of Kingskerswell, or KK as it is called locally, whose main shopping street crosses by bridge over the trunk (still single-carriageway) route to Torquay. There has always been an interesting clash of cultures here. Though outnumbered by incomers occupying most of the acres of surrounding bungalows, native Devonians cling on. Some have moved to new homes here from Newton Abbot and Torquay, which begin only about a mile away on either side of the village. The unifying factor is that locals and incomers treasure the village character equally. Building on the few fields between KK and the places on either side has only been prevented by strict planning. Relax that and KK would just become an area within a united conurbation. As it is, it remains its own place, the church, for example, still very much a village church. There are still local shops and services, and, though there have been some amusing misunderstandings between people of Devon stock and up-country incomers, the use of local phrases and emphases is increasing rather than disappearing so that when someone says something will be done 'presently' it implies it is not seen as at all urgent.

A particularly colourful episode in KK's post-war history was when the growth of tourism was most rapid in the early 1950s. The overflow from Torbay, especially acute in the peak fortnight – the last week in July and first of August – gave the village its own 'season'. There was scarcely a cottage in Yon Street, running up from the long bridge across the railway, not taking in visitors. Many of the locals then on holiday themselves relished doing something different and profitable. They did not have to be shy about welcoming strangers, for hordes of those without anywhere to stay swooped through the village, begging for accommodation. While many were given beds, often vacated by the locals for the duration, others were content to sleep in an easy chair or put a tent up in the garden. The season only lasted a few weeks, mainly the peak fortnight, and those encouraged to set up in tourism in a regular way were bitterly disappointed. Though a few visitors were so delighted by the village's hospitality that they returned for years afterwards, naturally most holidaymakers wanted to be closer to the sea. While it lasted it was great fun. The village baker once woke up to find a queue of thirty people wanting breakfast in his cafe. Crowds using 'Runabout' tickets to go off to different beaches every day descended on the normally quiet village railway station soon after breakfast. The garage was so full of disabled vehicles waiting repair (spare parts ran out everywhere) that its proprietor had to park elsewhere. From the doctor's waiting room to the queue at the post office, every aspect of life was changed.

By using the bridge, we join the Torquay road on the correct side, but still have to wait several minutes for a gap in the traffic.

Queen of the English Riviera and its Famous Hoteliers

It is the usual stop-start entry to Torquay. Traffic lights are a particularly successful crop here. Then, when you think you really must be about there, there is a convoluted one-way system. Eventually, at the third green showing of the last lights before the sea, we pass Torre Abbey and its refreshing gardens tastefully floodlit at night. On to the seafront for a quick diversion to the harbour and back.

The English Riviera, the Queen of Resorts, or an over-rated difficult place to reach and impossible to park in at busy times: you either like Torquay or you don't. Hundreds of thousands do. Despite economic and political vicissitudes, Torquay retains a positive place in the scheme of things. The bay is stunning and, if the main beach between station and town is covered at high tide, there are many others within easy reach. Torquay has the one thing that cannot be found at any other resort west of Bournemouth: critical mass. There have always been councillors and officials with foresight, though they sometimes complained that under County Council rule they had to struggle to prevent Torquay being relegated back to the fishing village it once was. After a big fight in the 1950s, Torbay (basically Torquay, Paignton and Brixham) won county borough status, only to lose it in the early 1980s. Independence has been regained (as a unitary authority) more recently. Three rapid changes in status cost hugely in all kinds of ways, but enthusiasm prevails.

Critical mass perhaps applies particularly to the parks and gardens offering never-ending variety, enhanced by contrasts of alkaline and acid soil (as between Torquay and Paignton), and even climate according to the degree of exposure to the cruel spring east winds. Once, each park superintendent of the separate resorts sat in his own office pontificating on the following season's flower displays; that yielded good January journalistic copy. Now the process is more democratic.

Andy Philips, who works on the procurement side (those who do the actual planting, grass-cutting and so on are in a different stream) tells me how strong the sense of co-operation has become. Four town action groups across the Bay first talk among themselves and then put forward their ideas on things like colour schemes at a joint meeting with the parks people, while the staff are 'sympathetic about the need to cut costs and maximise results'. Once the parks departments were a world of their own; now an in-house contractor happily works alongside two commercial ones. Overall staff numbers are down from a hundred to sixty in recent years, but economy has not always had a negative result. For example, many grass areas which used to be mowed weekly are now treated as hay meadows, cut only twice a year, encouraging colourful wildflowers.

Andy is not untypical of local people. He went to local horticultural college and then moved away to gain practical experience, delighting in 'being able to bring my experience back to the Bay'. The future is never dull: new trees and shrubs are being selected to ring the changes along the floodlit strip opposite the theatre to the harbour, while the three resorts develop their individual colour schemes, Torquay's based on blue, yellow and red.

Another respect in which Torquay is helped by its sheer size is in the number and range of hotels. It can accommodate all but a few of the very largest conferences. In the *AA Hotel Guide*, at the time of writing there are one five-star, two four-star, ten three-star and 24 two-star hotels, though between them they muster only six red rosettes for good food, four of them in the three-star category. Originally a winter resort which first expanded seriously when the Continent was closed during the Napoleonic Wars, Torquay's peak of summer popularity was in the late 1950s and early 1960s, before the number of Britons going overseas exceeded the number taking holidays for the first time. Much pre-war quality gave way to post-war quantity. Though the season has lengthened considerably, most hoteliers now have a tough time. Many are effectively on the payroll of the banks.

In my time in Devon one hotel, the best, stood out against the tide, the five-star Imperial, with a commanding view as good as that across the bay of Naples. It was seldom full at the peak of the season when Rolls Royces looked as out of place as in Greenland, but did solid business with its unique clientele during most of the rest of this year... and positively thrived with a rich calendar of special events including the famous Gastronomic Weekends. My first Imperial 'meal' must have been in about 1956, when the pressure of journalism resulted in late arrival at a lunch celebrating Torquay's 'first' air service. Not actually first, however, since before the war, planes in Great Western chocolate-and-cream connected with tiny dark red Devon General buses for Torquay, landing at Haldon aerodrome above Teignmouth, much nearer to Torquay than Exeter's airport which later services used. Despite the civic pomp of the occasion heralding this 'inaugural' flight, the plane only ran for a couple of weeks before the new venture went under. But my meal! They were already on dessert; I had not expected anything. The waitress brought successively generous helpings of the three alternative puds, each a gastronomic coup.

I was then introduced to that great hotelier, Michael Chapman, whose father, a Yugoslavian Jewish refugee had been manager at London's Savoy. Michael Chapman undoubtedly made the Imperial the best British hotel outside London – a triumph for Torquay. Leading the industry's enthusiasm, Chapman helped make the Technical College's catering course possibly the best. Years later when I was writing *The Breakfast Book*, he agreed I could go behind the scenes in the kitchen. There I met a rising star of the catering world, Harry Murray, who shared his enthusiasm and explained less obvious points. Later again David & Charles published the hotel's history and held many events there including the annual dinner for 500 staff and spouses.

The ultimate triumph was that never once in many dozens of family, public and company occasions was there the least possibility of saying a meal was indifferent, never mind poor. Such perfection is only attained by painstaking attention to detail. Chapman, and after his retirement Murray, knew their business, read the guest list early each evening, checked how the head waiter had arranged the seating, and toured every restaurant table making note of special requests or problems. Now running Lucknam Park near Bath, Harry Murray is still proud of how the Imperial became Trust House Forte's provincial flagship and played a role in group management.

After Charles Forte's retirement it became harder for this unique hotel to be different, even in the matter of supplies. So off Harry went to South Africa for a time. Predictably, later managing directors changed frequently, never got to know their customers, and key staff who held the place together retired or disappeared. After Granada's notorious take-over of the Forte empire the 'property', as it was now unlovingly referred to, was sold off: a classic example of how a group ruins value for its shareholders and satisfaction for its customers. Among others who respected the great tradition and continuity, I dare not risk spoiling the memory and shall not return.

There are, of course, plenty of other good hotels. The Palace, a former Bishop of Exeter's home, secluded in its spacious grounds but with access to the sea, is a particularly reliable four-star establishment run for decades by Paul Uphill and also often used by D&C for events such as a Victorian weekend. Paul was trained by Chapman as trainee manager at the Imperial at 25s a week. He tells me: 'Our business is summed up in four letters: CARE. It's only possible when you retain a loyal key staff over many years.' Whether there will be such characters in Torquay hereafter is a moot point, but thanks partly to the Technical College (where catering students provide splendid meals at knock-down prices) there is a greater pool of expertise and enthusiasm, especially in kitchens, now than formerly. It will always be hard to attract the right staff to hotels which close during the winter. Fewer of Torquay's now do, but for many staying open is a struggle.

Torquay is not alone in sometimes having been too ambitious. The new postwar theatre may be larger and more functional, but the intimate older Pavilion Theatre was much loved. Many of my BBC broadcasts were from the self-operated studio in one of the decorative little pavilions on its roof. When demand proved inadequate to support both theatres, the Pavilion was converted, not too sympathetically, into an ice rink, and for a while it looked as though its days might be numbered. Though generally there has been too much retail development, the Pavilion now flourishes as a discreet mini-shopping centre and a piece of history has been saved – a reminder of the days when Torquay was primarily a winter resort and weekly repertory was still the rage. As late as the mid-1950s, performances were introduced by a twelve-piece orchestra who invariably concluded with a chorus from *The King and I*.

So to Paignton, which had a meteoric boom after the war. On a routine Sunday morning call for coverage of the tourist scene, I was able to inform the brilliant publicity officer, Sydney Lovegrove (he later took the job for the whole of unified Torbay), that it had attracted more railway passengers from beyond Bristol than had Torquay the previous day. Between the two resorts, almost 30,000 long-distance passengers had arrived, putting the railways, taxis, hotels and cafes under enormous strain, but also bringing prosperity. Many visitors came on overnight trains, residents waking to hear spontaneously-formed choirs passing away the time until the first cafés opened. One Paignton café served 300 eggs within an hour or so that particular Saturday morning. Paignton has its own neat harbour and two great sandy beaches which attracted up to 10,000 day trippers by train in the 1950s, but is perhaps now best known for its enormous 'retirement' estates climbing up the hills, with wonderful views of the bay but (because there are few local meeting points) thin in community spirit.

For centuries Devon's chief fishing port, Brixham is different again. The harbour and the *Golden Hind* can be looked at endlessly, but how did the rest of the town come to vie with Ilfracombe in North Devon to be the west's most downmarket tourist trap by the sea? We move rapidly to Berry Head, and a walk around the fortifications built to keep Napoleon out. Someone must surely have been a complete idiot to think that it was worth spending a fortune to fire on Bonaparte's navy at this particular point. A quarry once ate remorselessly into the headland itself, limestone being loaded straight into ships tied up below. Brixham was good for stories about the valiant deeds of the lifeboat crew, the building and launching in the most thunderous of thunderstorms of the replica *Mayflower*, and the fight to prevent the quarry company consuming ever more of Berry Head. Its closure marked one successful journalistic campaign.

· IX ·

FROM THE DART'S MOUTH TO HIGH MOOR

Dartmouth and a Call from the BBC

Another media furore surrounded the post-war plan to demolish Dartmouth's famous war-damaged Butterwalk. Several councillors waxed lyrical about what could be built in its place. Mercifully, others, prodded by public opinion aroused by the Press, respected history.

Spirits are always high on a visit to Dartmouth. Tucked just inside the Dart's mouth, where there is deep water at all tides, it is reached from Kingswear on the Torbay side by two car ferries and a third ferry for foot passengers. Their continual crossings are part of the ceaseless waterborne activity. In summer, several times daily, long steam trains in Great Western livery gently descend through the wooded bank opposite to run beside the river into their Kingswear terminus. Dartmouth itself also used to have a fully-fledged Great Western station, though passengers had to take the railway ferry to catch their train.

Talking of railways, while we are filling up with petrol the mobile phone rings: BBC Scotland want my reactions to today's railway accident. What accident? At Hatfield; they will fax details to the hotel and then phone for a live interview at five. A Great North & Eastern train has mysteriously come off the track at Hatfield. It has, I say, to be something wrong with the train or the track. It is decades since people were killed by a train simply falling off the rails, but I opt for track, for there is already a hint of broken rails. Four people were killed. Though there have been accidents with a much higher number of fatalities, Hatfield will surely go down in the annals of Britain's railway history as a turning point, when Railtrack's stinting on spending in order to make fat profits finally came home to roost.

Even a railway accident must not spoil our enjoyment of Dartmouth. Three things go to mould its character: the Royal Naval College; retired people who enjoy watching the river, if not sailing on it; and tourism. All these were good for copy, a particularly useful contact being the friendly director (always a mine of information and anecdotes) of the River Dart Steamship Company, which ran the seasonal trips up to Totnes. The most appreciated of the West Country's navigable rivers (still used by passenger ships and freighters carrying timber to Totnes), the Dart is also the hardest to view as a whole. Its magic is in the way it appears to open up as a series of unconnected lakes. Villages on and near the river have a special charm. Dittisham, famous for its plums, winds down a steep hill to another small car ferry. Tuckenhay is where they used to make hand-laid paper in the most charming of country factories, with a clock proudly astride a gabled entrance. Stoke Gabriel, on the Torbay side, made much of its estuary setting and was for many years home to Agatha Christie.

Dartmouth itself is a place visitors once left as quickly as possible, for its main business (when so many towns had their own speciality) was coal bunkering. Because of its deep, sheltered water, it was an ideal place for steamships to replenish stocks. Cranes on a great hulk moored midstream dropped the steam coal into their fuel holds, sending filthy clouds into the air, and spreading a layer of dust everywhere.

For decades after that the town was renowned for its bookshop, enterprisingly run by Christopher Milne, AA Milne's son, unwillingly immortalised as Christopher Robin 'who was saying his prayers'. Between more ordinary trading sessions, tourists – especially Japanese – only interested in meeting the son of a famous writer descended on the shop whose owner couldn't hide his embarrassment at having to pose. It was almost cruel.

So to the modern Dart Marina opposite the ferry by which we have just crossed. Then a short snooze and my daughter Alyss arrives for dinner. We walk to one of Devon's most famous restaurants, the Carved Angel, for delicious fish charged to the hilt but worth every penny. Much was the pleasure when a member of D&C, now married to a wealthy husband in North America, invited former colleagues here to lunch – the kind of place they had always hoped to go but perhaps couldn't afford. The note just before the event suggesting everyone go Dutch produced strong reaction and disappointment. No one went.

While we relish the food, the delight this evening is in relaxed family conversation... what life is surely about. Not having seen her for some months, Alyss is coming to dinner again tomorrow night, on

Dartmoor. Hesitatingly, she asks if she might bring a friend? Yes. Um, he's a man. Excitement.

We are on a high as we walk back beside the river to the hotel.

A Restless Night

A rich meal at the end of a long day with the emotion of being back in the part of the country I know and love best, worry about the railway accident (already seeming a horrid further demonstration of the privatised railway system being on a disaster course bound to hurt the cause of public transport), excitement and maybe anxiety about my daughter's new romance: it adds up to a recipe for a restless night. What should have proved a soothing setting, itself seems to cause tossing and turning.

I wake from early broken sleep thinking I hear a steam train descending the Dart's opposite bank. It must have been the wind, but it led to thoughts about the crack *Torbay Express,* which for many years left Paddington for Kingswear, and Torquay for Paddington (meaning an earlier departure from Kingswear), at exactly noon. Exeter was the only stop between London and Torquay, the Castle Class locomotive achieving good speed with its light load (seven coaches in winter, eight in summer, including full restaurant car). Even well after nationalisation, except on those over-busy summer Saturdays, you could set your watch by it, and revel in the fact that the engine was still in Great Western green, the coaches in traditional chocolate-and-cream.

Stimulated by yesterday's splendid trip down, I'm led to memories of many other long-distance train journeys and the reasons behind them. I drop off peacefully for an hour or so, just as used to be the case in the early 1940s, when many nights were spent in the cellar while we listened to the German planes overhead and, as the whistle of a falling bomb steadily changed its note, looked at each other wondering if it might be our turn to be hit. We returned to our beds when the all clear rang out over Teignmouth, often as the first birds began to sing.

Despite falling asleep so late, we are up keen and early, for a light breakfast after last night's feast, and start by driving to the end of the road overlooking the river's mouth. The castles on opposite sides now look laughably ineffective, yet once guarded this entrance to safe anchorage much-used by mariners since before Norman times.

It is not a happy sea this morning. Already there is a thick drizzle, the beginning of a really rainy day, and the wind is stiff. But it is important to get going, our journey roughly following the river's course back from its mouth here to the High Moor.

The Dart is one of Devon's most important rivers, both in its navigable lower and fast-running higher portions; it begins with two separate streams, the East and West, which, after their tortuous descent from their remote sources, join at Dartmeet. I always think of the Dart being Devon in miniature, capturing so many of the large county's moods and landscapes.

We drive slowly back along the narrow road, to the town centre, having to back several times when cars coming the opposite way are entitled to priority or their drivers assume they have it. Everywhere there are personal reminders: the home where one of my best-loved late directors lived, and the steps from which he once threw half a dozen cream teas into the Dart to dramatic effect. D&C ran many Sunday trips as part of the annual conference of the Booksellers Association, but this one, to take several hundred booksellers and publishers up the river, almost didn't happen. The ship allocated had broken down, and in those days captains stuck to their own vessels. The captain of a ship was just returning from an earlier trip and not unreasonably wanted to get home to his wife. No, he wouldn't work any longer, not for 'all the tea in China'.

However, good men have always hated wasting food and, when my director said OK, he might as well start throwing the teas into the river since they were now worthless, the hoped for reaction was 'Hang on a moment'. I could see the teas being thrown in. It was the classic occasion when one needed a mobile phone before they were invented.

Then there is the hotel where I once spent the year's hottest night suffocating in a four-poster in an airless inside room. On this visit, however, our Dartmouth hotel has been a delight, with a grandstand view of the busy river. It might have been standard Forte but was warmly welcoming and efficient, in great contrast to a hoity-toity, not to mention expensive, place where we had first planned to stay – but not after the previous visit. Carry your own luggage; What, you both want champagne? (when brought, the second glass came unchilled); and an endless wait to pay the bill while they talk to their other hotels – they are doing so well, don't you know. But what does the future hold for the Forte hotels. Having said it would be the perfect owner as it forcibly took over the Forte chains, Granada, it has just been announced, has changed its mind. Forte 'doesn't fit'. So it is being sold off, hotel brand by hotel brand.

Even if you do not start with the advantage of your own personal memories, Dartmouth is a town to be savoured – for its position, its architecture, its historic points, restaurants and shops and its gardens. I proudly show Sheila the Butterwalk that my press campaign helped save from demolition after its wartime damage. Then we pause briefly on the promenade to take a final glance at the three ferries crossing to and fro, and the railway coaches in Great Western chocolate-and-cream at Kingswear on the opposite shore.

The road takes us well inland and we catch only brief glimpses of the river's isolated lake-like reaches, but note the steep road down to Dittisham. At Halwell we pass the house of the man who told me 'if God had intended people to use gas, we would be born with masks'. That was in the early 1950s, when an electricity supply was not even vaguely planned but new-fangled gas lighting was being fitted.

Halwell is where we join the Kingsbridge road, leading to the South Hams and its showpiece Salcombe. A short time ago we branched off this road, just before Kingsbridge, to reach the remote village of Buckland-tout-Saints, approached by long stretches of narrow sunken lanes without passing places. Apart from being an attractive little village with a well-known hotel, Buckland-tout-Saints is remarkable for one of the best of the crop of Millennium Books. 'To celebrate the end of the twentieth century, here is a house-by-house account of Buckland-tout-Saints, Goverton, Ledstone and outlying farms.' Of the 303 people recorded in the 1851 census, it tells us, about eighty were in agriculture, and many others in vanished village trades like shoemakers, blacksmiths, washerwomen, millers and even a retail cider seller as well as innkeeper. By 2000, of the total of 130 homes only thirteen 'are occupied by those in any way concerned with agriculture'. The owners of the handful of second homes and many long-term incomers, and all 'those who have discovered this favoured corner of South Hams... are united in feeling responsible for keeping it as a rural idyll and the envy of many not so privileged'.

We drove round the parish with the book, looking up the changing fate of many individual homes, including those that have fallen into disrepair. Some, like 1940s council houses with concrete cancer, have been demolished. We see new barn conversions, and cottages that were once shops or lived in by tradesmen working at home. Nothing is better than examining a village in such detail to gauge the change to which the countryside has been subjected, yet only the huge reduction in hedges as fields have been amalgamated has changed the physical appeal of this rolling land that our ancestors also no doubt enjoyed.

Curiously, I first drove into this remote area to meet a would-be author who in Berlin in the 1930s had been a friend of Hitler. I well recall a colleague, whose disbelief in the book led to us not publishing it, grabbing my arm on an internal American flight where a news magazine featured the author, the influence he might have had over Hitler, and the success of his title. Ah well, you can't win them all.

Often we would take the Kingsbridge road to visit an author with whom we had great success, the naturalist Tony Soper, living in a farmhouse on a creek of the Kingsbridge estuary. It started with his *Bird Table Book*, dreamed up after we had chatted on a television programme, which went to umpteen editions in Britain and around the world, and more to the point persuaded thousands to encourage wild birds to their gardens. Decades ago, I recall a commissionaire at BBC Bristol pointing out Tony as one of the 'rising young stars'. Alas, the faces of few celebrities remain popular as they age and, though considerably younger than me, Tony has that weatherbeaten face that younger producers tend to regard as old hat, quite apart from the fact that 'not invented here' means they like clean sweeps and a chance to introduce their own people. Now we're lucky to catch Tony at home, since he earns his living lecturing on board ships, including a small one that each Antarctic summer penetrates deep into the land of penguins... about which he wrote one of his other successful books. He is a great friend.

North then from Halwell. This was never a quick road; now it is bumper-to-bumper. At Harbertonford, where my daughter who is coming to dinner tonight with her new friend lives, I notice the Hungry Horse. This is where Brian MacArthur, short-term editor extraordinaire of *The Western Morning News*, told me he was going to work for Eddie Shah as launch editor of *Today*, and over coffee produced the preliminary highly-imaginative budget. [A few months after today's visit we had to return to Harbertonford for the funeral of my nineteen-year-old grandson to whose memory this book is dedicated.]

Totnes and the South Devon Railway

Skirting Totnes, like most head-of-estuary ports full of character and hot on alternative lifestyles, books, and culture, we take the circuit via Dartington Hall. Dorothy Elmhirst, one of the founders of the modern estate, was always ready to pontificate about the successes of their social and economic experiment. There were classic failures, notably fruit production, but the estate, the Great Hall with its superb music and the gardens with their fine trees, and the Cider Press with bookshop, craft centre and restaurant, are honourable members of Devon's tourist attractions, while Staverton Contractors have kept large numbers of building employees busy for generations. Most property in Staverton was church owned – just how appalling the Ecclesiastical Commissioners were as landlords provided compelling human copy.

We delay briefly once more to absorb a touch of the remarkable creation that is Buckfast Abbey, and again to admire the modern stained glass window and to buy books. Then to Buckfastleigh station, today's terminus of the South Devon Railway, of which I am patron.

It is hard to imagine the economic activity in the Dart valley in the railway's heyday. Buckfastleigh was the busiest station for despatching goods traffic on the original South Devon Railway after which we have named our little line. Traffic was much heavier than at places like Newton Abbot, Torquay and even Plymouth. Mineral ores and woollen goods were the main staples, employing a small army of shunters and porters. Reading the files of *The Exeter Flying Post* provided an especially abundant harvest of Ashburton and Buckfastleigh titbits for A Hundred Years Ago features throughout the 1950s, for great were the riches in good times, deep the despair in bad.

Passenger trains, on the other hand, have always been of only minority interest, since even before motor vehicles it was usually quicker to get from Ashburton (the terminus) to Newton Abbot by road than take the long detour via Totnes. Being a backwater is what made the branch so endearing in real railway days.

Much though we try to recapture realism (and we do achieve it to a remarkable extent), we have to acknowledge that today's South Devon Railway is only there for enthusiasts and tourists. There are, of course, many more of them in summer than there used to be ordinary passengers, whose numbers only swelled for things like Sunday School outings and race specials, sometimes non-stop from Plymouth. (Buckfastleigh racecourse has long been closed.) But preservation is an attractive thing, enabling older people to relive the once familiar, and teaching the young what they would never understand just from a book.

There is another aspect, too: the saving of the route itself, so beautifully levelled out along the river's bank in the way that the Victorian builders preferred: the longest possible straight sections between curves. Engines whistle as they would have done in the nineteenth century and, if many trains are busy, it is still possible early and late season to find yourself again enjoying that solitary state that was such a feature of travel on many rural branch lines. In my time trains used to be auto-cars, the GWR name for locomotive and coach that could be driven from either end, the engine's controls repeated in the carriage. Once again we have auto-car trains. As a publicity stunt for the railway, I once hired one especially for Sheila and myself so we could again enjoy the privacy that was especially attractive to the courting young. That was when as patron I formally opened the bridge over the Dart at Totnes, and named it Bulliver, after the nickname of the branch's usual engine.

With the bridge, we thus regain pedestrian access to our out-of-town Totnes station. When Bill (now Lord) Bradshaw was general manager of the Western Region, he encouraged our running trains into Totnes BR, but such common sense was not the flavour of the day. Three times daily we had to pay for a BR driver to come by taxi from Plymouth to reconfirm our engine was up to the job of popping on to the nationalised system. Of course it was too expensive, and later BR management was relieved when we gave up: 'One less complication.' (Lord Bradshaw we will meet in a later chapter.)

Naturally I believe the South Devon is the best of all the West Country steam lines; it is certainly the happiest and most intimate, playing hide-and-seek by the freshwater Dart with cherished reaches like Nursery Pool. Thankful that he'd swapped banking for becoming railway general manager, Richard Elliott takes us to an office intriguingly cluttered with yesterday's artefacts, to give a snappy progress report on plans to get the track back to Ashburton, but tears his hair out over the years of delay in reaching agreement to buy our line, currently only leased from the larger Torbay & Dartmouth Railway between Paignton and Kingswear. Railway politics were always dominated by intrigue.

'Are you coming?' asks the guard, David Potter, author of *The Talyllyn Railway* and husband of a girl in Sheila's year at school, looking at his watch and clutching his green guard's flag. Alas not today. Allan Lovegrove might be along shortly: one of the leading lights on the South Devon Railway, he is son of Sydney Lovegrove the Torbay publicity manager, and the only youngster I ever employed on his dad's say-so... successfully, since he rose to be manager of our forty-strong warehouse staff. But Allan is either late or giving the railway a miss today.

Everybody knows everybody in these parts, but much depends on exactly where you were born. A fierce argument in danger of degenerating into a punch-up took place between two Buckfast chaps, one who dismissed the relevance of the other's argument because 'you're not one of us'. He had the misfortune to be born in Ashburton – only three miles away. There would be great joy if we could restore trains to Ashburton. Having opposed the line's closure, the County Council then opposed its reopening, preferring to snatch the land for widening the A38.

We are always pleased to be in Ashburton, where many touches of bygone wealth have been preserved since it was bypassed in the 1930s, when traffic was less threatening. Turning into North Street we make sure we don't miss the Dartmoor Bookshop, one of the best in the West. Continue straight on into New Road and you will find examples of the famous woollen mills where in good times they milled money.

In pouring rain, however, we take the bridge at the top of North Street, and soon thread through that much-photographed of all Devon villages, Buckland-in-the-Moor, whose thatched cottages appear in umpteen calendars, and go through the first of several gates which Sheila has to open to allow us to pass. Descending rapidly through dripping trees, shrouded in mist, and by a series of bends down the Webburn Valley to Spitchwick, and there's the Dart. We follow it until we can park. Many a family picnic was spent on the rocks on the reach we named Favourite River where the Dart temporarily slows round a graceful bend. Attractions included having the place to ourselves, seeing salmon jump for flies, a mini-beach from which the kids could paddle, with plenty of twigs around to make a small fire. Except possibly at a few busy weekends, parking was not difficult in those days. Only the privileged few yet owned a car. Inevitably motorists' rights have been reduced by the sheer popularity of today's Dartmoor, but the neatly hidden car park is not that far away (on fine days).

Dartmoor: England's Last Wilderness

Despite the rain, we linger before joining what used to be an A road but has now been designated the B3357 and remember there is now a 40mph restriction on all Dartmoor roads except the trunk A30 cutting through the northern edge. Keeping the A30's dual carriageway out of the National Park was a battle lost. The railway was there first, they argued, but whereas its narrow piece of land intimately twists and turns as part of the landscape, the dual carriageway, much of it elevated, is wide, straight, ugly, utterly alien. 'At least it makes use of pretty worthless ground,' was another argument. Having been attracted by the wilderness, man ever seeks to destroy it. 'It saves good farmland to the north.' But farmers produce more than is needed, and north of Okehampton there are in fact hundreds of square miles of not-so-good land, while Southern England's Last Wilderness is minute. Before the 40mph restriction and when traffic was light, a fast car might cross the moor on the Ashburton-Tavistock route we have just joined in half an hour. Dartmoor is that small: small, unique, irreplaceable.

It has to be admitted that thousands more people enjoy views of Dartmoor from the A30 than would ever explore the area in detail; yet there are fine views to be had from many major roads, and the character of this special moorland edge, with dramatic contours and intimate valleys has been killed. Dartmoor is too small to suffer such loss. On the other hand, being only human, I recall the irritation felt when first discovering it was no longer possible to drive round Burrator Reservoir. Herein lies human inconsistency. On balance the setting up of the Dartmoor National Park has been a great success, and one dreads to think what more would have been ruined without its special planning powers. Sensible development has not been stultified, but benefits from the positive advice from the planners about house building and extensions. The essential high moor has been well preserved, the rich heritage of ancient monuments protected, even car parking increased discreetly and access by public transport skilfully encouraged. At Dartmeet we pass a bus (presumably from Tavistock) marked Newton Abbot, on a route only opened a few years ago.

That no organisation is immune from embarrassing mistakes has been humorously brought home to the National Park. It has just had hurriedly to withdraw the advice that, to save the appearance of the moor, people should dig their own latrine. The Ministry of Defence stepped in to warn that this could lead to them blowing themselves up, for at one time most of the wilderness was used for military training. Unexploded shells, some a legacy of practice for D-day, might be detonated through digging just about anywhere. There are still three live firing ranges on the northern moor, angering the preservationists who demand that they be closed and that the army tidy up like everyone else.

We note Pixies Holt with its Little People display so excessive that it has become acceptable. Pixies and pixie lore are now big business, the lore seriously considered even in *The Transactions of the Devonshire Association*. Temporarily abandoning its usual academic tone, it even reported happenings at a Totnes police station. The duty constable had been plagued with phone calls reporting the activities of a pixie thief. Tired at the end of his duty, the constable walked out to find his car surrounded by the 'Little People'. Dartmoor should be fun as well as foreboding as it is this morning. However, we relish the mist swirling across the top of the undulating moor, visibility changing from moment to moment.

The prison appears out of nowhere. Mention Dartmoor and most people think you are talking about the prison. At an elevation of 1,400ft, exposed to east and north winds, it is in an abominable situation. The town, Princetown, which serves it, is England's least cosy. Most homes house the warders, hating the location as much as do the prisoners, but the morbid interest of visitors grows. Even the former post office now serves cream teas. Once refreshed, grockles are ready for more gawking and go to the museum to savour not the scenery, nor even history, but the nastier side of human nature. Former prisoners come back for their own gawking. A taxi driver who jokingly asked, 'So what was your number, sir?' quickly learned not to repeat the mistake.

Princetown owes its existence to Thomas Tyrwhitt, later knighted for loyalty to the Prince of Wales, though driven by his obsession to tame and cultivate Dartmoor. The horse-drawn Plymouth & Dartmoor Railway was one of a number of pre-railway age railways penetrating deep on to the moor. It never paid, but made possible the building of the prison for French prisoners from the Napoleonic Wars, who kept sane in the cold and damp by recreating a slice of Parisian social life with the poor at the beck and call of the rich. Many drew funds freely from their London agents. Every conceivable kind of trade was carried on. Prisoners made things and sold them to each other and locals. Personal services such as hairdressing and entertainment, could be bought for a price. Top of the pecking order were 'Les Lordes', followed by 'Les Labourers', 'Les Indifferents', 'Les Minables' (the gamblers) and 'Les Romains' (who had lost everything in gambling and practised communism and nudity). Imagine it, and the markets held inside the prison where Dartmoor folk were allowed to trade with the prisoners. Only later, after a period of accommodating American prisoners from the War of 1812, did Dartmoor become a regular prison, as expensive to maintain as it is unpopular. It should be torn down and replaced more sensibly elsewhere, but don't tell that to those who serve the cream teas.

Two Visitors with Romance in the Air

Then back a few miles to our hotel, Prince Hall (AA 78 per cent), a new discovery. A home has stood here since 1443, the present mansion dating from 1787, built for Mr Justice Buller, who allowed Sunday worship in his sitting room until Princetown took shape and had a church of its own in 1810. Historic notes thoughtfully left in our bedroom say Sir Francis Buller, as he became, was the first judge to send convicts to Australia. In the twentieth century the building alternated between private home and hotel. Don't expect modern plumbing, but accommodation, food and service are matter-of-fact superb. So two nights are not really enough, especially as we have dinner guests on both. The first is my daughter Alyss with Stephen, who I discover I already know, so introductions are easy and we quickly relax in a way a really good hotel with fine but unpretentious food encourages. Romance is definitely in the air, and maybe this time her choice of man is on cue.

Next day is off-duty, savouring the position of the hotel down a tree-lined drive and overlooking a hump bridge now partly obscured by drifting mist, now in sharp sun, now disappearing totally in fog. We explore locally in a desultory way, enjoying favourite haunts, glimpses of the sea when the mist finally lifts, memories of the Princetown branch railway and of celebrations and stories lost almost as much in the mist of time as the bridge had earlier been in actual mist. The bridge is, we are told, used by Prince Charles for visits to a farm. This is Duchy of Cornwall land. Publishers often enjoy learning from the books they handle, and my knowledge was enhanced by *The Duchy of Cornwall*, explaining the extent and complexity of ownership, which includes our hotel building.

For dinner, we welcome an old personal friend, and a great friend to Dartmoor, Brian Le Messurier. Most of our talk is naturally about the moor, which he has always worshipped. He says his whole life changed when in 1965 I invited him to write an introduction to a new edition of *Crossing's Guide to Dartmoor* which had long been out of print, its two previous publishers having lost their records in air raids.

Reprinting *Crossing's Guide* was a catalyst. Our trade distributors, Macdonalds (part of the British Printing Corporation) failed to release any copies on 'publication'. So scarce was *Crossing's Guide*, and so great the publicity, that booksellers were frantic. Eventually the binder sent 500 copies by passenger train to Newton Abbot. The one and only time I have ever seen booksellers come to fisticuffs was when the copies arrived and evaporated in a trice. We had been worried about the risk involved in the reprint and at the last moment increased the price from two to three guineas so we could manage if we sold fewer copies. It was the first lesson that, within reason, price is far less important than natural demand. So the infant D&C had a profitable injection of much-needed funds, and from that moment enjoyed a higher local profile. Because no copyright owner could be traced, royalties were salted away in a fund that eventually sponsored publication of other Dartmoor titles, including *Dartmoor: A New Study*, which became the first in a regional series. Other Crossing's titles were steadily reprinted under Brian's guidance, including a 'new book', a collection of newspaper pieces about the colourful way in which Dartmoor folk earned their living, which we titled *Crossing's Dartmoor Worker*. After I sold D&C, *Crossing's Dartmoor*, like many other backlist staples, was dropped. It is now published by Forest Publishing of Tiverton whose Mike Lang is solicitor's clerk in the morning and publisher in the afternoon.

Many more people started walking on Dartmoor, using the guide which went through many editions. As for Brian, his life was taken over by Dartmoor and writing about it. Even his introduction to the *Guide* turned out to be a formidable contribution to understanding the moor. He was lucky to enjoy his last sixteen years in banking on the NatWest payroll seconded to Dartmoor, where he was a full-time warden and served on the National Park Committee. At first the National Park was administered by the County Council Planning Department, the focus sharpening when it was given independence in the early 1970s.

Dartmoor is so compelling that it is not surprising it has been fortunate in having a sizeable band of distinguished and colourful allies. Brian, whose appetite hasn't diminished with the years, is of course one. Over dinner at Prince Hall, he tells us that his mother was born in a lighthouse; his grandfather and great grandfather were both keepers, the former the last keeper of the original Lundy light. Hardly an ordinary background. Living and breathing the moor, Brian has encyclopaedic knowledge and driving enthusiasm which shows in the number of letters he fires off. Also sound judgement. Ian Mercer, the first chief executive of the independent Dartmoor, was 'a splendid chap', and if any one person was responsible for putting the moor 'in safe hands' it had to be him. Nick Atkinson was 'trained in his mould'. Lady Sayer 'gave spine to protests and that was perhaps more significant than the way she put people's backs up'. I remember how her Admiral husband bellowed down the telephone at *The Western*

Morning News. Everyone was supposed to be unfair to Lady Sayer; but 'without her Dartmoor would be very different today'. Beatrice Chase's novels, though perhaps not top literature, had heightened the West Country public's awareness of the uniqueness of the moor. An earlier evocation of the moor by Eden Phillpotts's eighteen novels has remained under-rated. They do not quite achieve what Thomas Hardy did for Wessex but are still to be treasured. *Eden Phillpotts on Dartmoor* tells the background.

Brian says that the official walk guide, and author of *High Dartmoor*, Eric Hemery, might have been a quarrelsome codger but 'defined values', while a vital role was also played by Crispin Gill – assistant editor of *The Western Morning News* before going to *The Countryman* – author, and editor of *Dartmoor: A New Study*, and also an early member of the National Park Committee. Brian talks about more recent books commissioned by the National Park. His own scrapbooks are going into a new visitors' centre at the former Duchy Hotel in Princetown as part of a mammoth bibliographic effort by Peter Hamilton-Leggett.

No part of Britain is better documented, more discussed or raises more violent feelings. Things to rejoice over include keeping conifers, such as the plantations around the Fernworthy reservoirs, off the high moor, the increased access enjoyed through marking new paths across the moor, the prevention of major road works or development on the moor's core, and sustaining a lively economy in many of the towns and villages, while discouraging much of the kind of development happening elsewhere. The downside? The A30, the continuing military presence, and the china clay industry's rights (dating back to the 1950s) to expand on the moor's southwest margins that would be too expensive to be bought out.

Over coffee, conversation becomes more relaxed: the pity that the Logan Stone was toppled over by vandals; how the trees at Wistman's Wood are now growing more normally than their former stunted survival in the clutter of boulders that protected them from sheep; and the accuracy of Dartmoor's age-old saying 'scratch my back and I'll break your purse' (since most mining and quarrying ventures have failed). We talk about how few industrial efforts, apart from clay in the south west corner, have done material damage, some remains now being historic monuments in their own right. One is the Haytor Granite Tramway, built out of the material it carried on the first part of its journey for important works such as London Bridge. We could talk all night.

Where are we staying next? The Nare Hotel in Roseland. 'That's where June " the lady of my affection" will be staying.' We congratulate Adam Southwell of the Prince Hall hotel on our dinner. 'All saints can do miracles but few can run a hotel,' he cheerfully replies. [Shortly after, they were closed for four agonising months because of foot-and-mouth, but business quickly returned to normal – 'or better, thanks to loyal support'.]

As we go to bed, thinking of romance (Alyss and Stephen, and Brian and the lady of his affection), Sheila wants to know how soon we can come back. 'Exactly,' is her comment when, just before we switch off the lights, I read her an extract from Arthur Conan Doyle's *The Hound of the Baskervilles*:

> The longer one stays here the more does the spirit of the moor sink into one's soul, its vastness, and also its grim charm. When you are once out upon its bosom you have left all traces of modern England behind you, but on the other hand you are conscious everywhere of the homes and the work of the prehistoric people ... If you were to see a skin-clad, hairy man crawl out from the low door, fitting a flint-tipped arrow on to the string of his bow, you would feel that his presence there was more natural than your own.

ACROSS THE TAMAR INTO CORNWALL

Of Ufflets, Mini Trains and Artists

Little is more exciting than setting off to drive round Cornwall, or the Royal Duchy. Inland Cornwall certainly has its fascinations: Bodmin Moor made famous by Daphne du Maurier's *Jamaica Inn*; the nearby mysterious but shallow Dozmary Pool; and the mining region around Redruth and Camborne, where even within living memory the night sky shone with fire and steam. But for us 'round' Cornwall usually means just that – keeping close to its coasts. It always seems better to do it clockwise, enjoying the rich mellowness of the south and finishing with the Wagnerian drama of the North. (Some style sheets may say it should be north, but somehow the very thought of the drama of the Atlantic coast has me using the capital N.) And, yes, this part of Britain deserves more than its share of pages: it deserves it for its rich individuality of active and retired people and of scenery, as well as the fact it has been one of my chief hunting grounds.

Our start is from Prince Hall Hotel at Two Bridges, near Princetown, where we pause to note the High Moorland Visitors' Centre mentioned by Brian Le Messurier last night. We also enjoy the swirling mist as we take the Tavistock road, passing the Dartmoor Granite Company's erstwhile works. That was the last of Dartmoor's granite quarries, closed only a few years ago, and bringing to an end a once prosperous and colourful industry, though the granite used in many famous buildings will be appreciated for centuries.

Sunshine is breaking through the mist as we descend to the Tamar, crossing it by what for centuries was its lowest bridge. It is really sunny as we climb steeply through Gunnislake's street; extraordinary to recall that once Cunard maintained a full office here for the emigration business following the collapse of the Tamar Valley mining industry and featured in Chapter 12. The railway no longer crosses the road high above the village for the line has been cut back to a new halt, well signed and displaying good information. The Tamar Valley line, with its high viaduct across the river at Calstock has, like other surviving West Country branches, been given a new lease of life with imaginative publicity.

Next we take the high road to Hingston Down, a diversion of not much more than a mile, but a steep one, to Kit Hill, midway between Dartmoor and Bodmin Moor and about as far inland as this trip will take us. Though we are little more than 1,000ft high, beneath us to the south east we trace the circuitous Tamar estuary, pick out many tors, ancient monuments and old mine stacks, and see a shimmering English Channel. A mill, destroyed by the wind that powered it, once worked a nearby mine, and here every few years Cornish miners met their Devon counterparts to discuss mutual problems and plan what they could do to hold their own. Here, too, battles were fought, notably when the Cornish Egbert beat the Danes and British in 835.

I used to think Callington the plainest and most cut-off town in the county. Thanks to the Tamar Bridge, it is now effectively a Plymouth suburb. We do not bother to pass through its square but (first time for me) take its bypass. We however have to negotiate Liskeard before descending to join the A38. Cornwall's prettiest branch line runs from its own platform at right angles to the main station at Liskeard, taking a spiral down to a reversing point, where it joins a long-abandoned route from a miscellany of former granite quarries and mines to the north. That moorland line was never approved for passengers so, with Cornish ingenuity, they were carried free. A toll was levied on an umbrella each passenger was forced to carry. The early passenger trains from Liskeard brought few visitors to Looe, and even fewer lingered, for the bustling granite and ore quay was dusty and the whole place smelt of fish, both fresh and rotting. Looe's delight owes much to its workaday origins; it is amazing how often that goes with quality today, such as award-winning toilets and the bridge connecting East and West Looe, doubled in width in a way which isn't apparent.

We note the clay dries (literally where clay is dried) at Moorswater, and soon reach Dobwalls, turning right to visit the Forest Railway. That is what it is called once more having for years been the Dobwalls Adventure Park. 'We're returning to our roots.' The familiar words we hear from those running all kinds of enterprises are uttered by the owner John Southern, a man with an extraordinary story. He found his feet, though often in danger of losing his footing, while carrying a dog with bleeding paws, as a shepherd on Snowdonia... a life seldom removed from the elements, sustained by love of landscape, sheep and his dogs. He then became a farmer. 'This building was once full of cows and, even if we were ill, we still had to get the milk churns out for the lorry,' he tells me. Then it became the biggest pig farm in Cornwall. 'Trouble with pigs is that however efficient we'd been, we'd have gone under if nobody wanted them.' Whether the railway was born out of a desire to have trains or because it seemed a better crop commercially is not obvious. Whatever, as the trains grew, the pigs withdrew.

Based on US practice, with steep grades, tunnel and bridges, the first circuit was opened in 1970; the second in 1979. The system is intensively signalled so that eight trains can carry passengers simultaneously, though this means lots of halts at red signals. The most intensively-signalled line in the world, for a time it attracted BR officials who were replacing the traditional semaphores. The gauge is only 7¼ins, yet a Big Boy locomotive with tender weighs two tons and stretches 21ft: hardly a toy. Nearly six million passengers have been carried.

John had another love, Thorburn, the artist of often bloody hunting and shooting subjects. A gallery of originals encouraged me to commission *Thorburn's Birds & Mammals*. Later, insurance problems led to the paintings being sold, for £2.6million, which paid off borrowings and financed a big play area for children... a godsend he says impishly, to the business and to the (mainly) dads entertaining kids at winter weekends. Cornwall's declining visitor numbers hurt. Seldom is the intensity of the railway's signalling now justified. 'When we started, only a handful of Brits went overseas; now the competition is intense. It rained nearly every day this summer. Who can blame them?' What he does blame is Cornwall's poor publicity, a topic echoed almost wherever we go. 'Groups and associations come and go, ideas fall by the wayside. They charge the earth and give us things like 'Caradon' Country which no one's heard of. Cornwall just can't get it together.

'We had to analyse what was bringing people here. The trains. Ten locomotives. Unique.' We enjoy another ride around the steeply-graded circuits, the steam train naturally being busier than the diesel. Operators (including John's two sons) and adult passengers dream their dreams; kids are quickly absorbed. The art gallery is still devoted to nature. Next door is a replica of a Victorian arcade of shop frontages, including one called David & Charles; John twisted our arm to sponsor that more years ago than we care to remember. He too has completed his three score years and ten.

Then by the narrow A38 down into the Glyn or Fowey Valley, the last stronghold of that little Cornish animal, the ufflet, hunted so close to extinction, before Charles Wesley tamed Cornish miners, that it never properly recovered. That at any rate was a BBC April Fool's broadcast, one of many. While most who heard it laughed, there are always those angry to have been made fools of, like the guy who thought he had shot everything in the west and took a taxi to the public library to look up the ufflet. The librarian who had heard the broadcast played along and solemnly handed him a selection of natural history books.

The Fowey, both freshwater and salt, is my favourite Cornish river, and this delightful valley has been little spoilt by that pioneer of out-of-town stores, the original Trago Mills, a West Country institution. Charles Robertson, attracted to the site by his love of fishing, was one of a group of entrepreneurs of the late 1950s and early 1960s included in *The Sunday Times*'s Prufrock feature. Philip Clarke's *Small Businesses: How They Survive and Succeed* was developed out of the series and is very much of its age. Robertson and I are among a small minority of those featured who didn't ultimately go bust. Then by a back route giving a tantalising glimpse of a full Fowey estuary, long out of sight on our journey (though very near) to our next destination, Trenython Manor, hotel and timeshare.

The building was designed by an Italian architect commissioned by Garabaldi as thanks for the part played in his famous campaign by an English contingent. A later owner, the third Bishop of Truro, added a private chapel. Then in the early 1920s the Great Western Railway spent £25,000 reconditioning and turning it into a convalescent home, mainly for railwaymen suffering from heart conditions. For half a century, up to seventy slept in dormitories, but were turned out into the public rooms from first to last thing each day so as not to feel sorry for themselves in isolation. Visiting wives and families staying in the Three Villages (Tywardreath, Par and St Blazey) boosted the local economy.

A supporter of my *Writers' News*, Eve Parsons, who dabbles in one-act plays and short stories and chairs the Lanner Writers' Group, near Redruth, has suggested I visit today's hotel and timeshare, and has also come along to meet us. Her husband said he once found me under great pressure at David & Charles in its railway station days when he was window cleaning. The jolly Irish manager of this and several other timeshares shows us round the galleried landing, then outside to enjoy the panoramic view across St Austell Bay with its clay works and Par harbour, an outlook the railway invalids must have soaked up for hours at a time. There are new self-catering bungalows. 'We've bags of energy to make it work,' she enthuses.

Next to Lostwithiel, down the town's narrow and very Cornish main street to the level crossing and up Bridge Street to meet an old friend, Don Breckon. I first heard of Don when a colleague persuaded me to visit the Barbican Gallery in Plymouth to see his painting of GWR *King Henry V* splashed by a rough sea between a pair of tunnels on the sea wall at Dawlish. £120 seemed a lot of money in 1971, yet Don was just being discovered and two years later the gallery offered to buy it back for £1,200. It adorns my study looking out across the Moray Firth, appropriately for me having the views of the sea at these two places so distant from each other. By 1982 the market was ready for *The Railway Paintings of Don Breckon*; others followed.

Abhorring anything as public as going on TV or speaking to an audience, it is not surprising that Don was unhappy in his first job as art teacher. A turning point was visiting a London gallery. 'People came in and spoke loudly, not really looking at the paintings, but drawn like a magnet to a defect, real or imaginary. I asked myself if this is what is required to be successful, so I began wanting to paint the things that interested me.' His wife, Meg, cuts in: 'The older I get the more remarkable it seems that Don could support his family through his art.'

All three of their lads are into creative things, Ian the oldest trying his hand at a novel. I interrupt to ask where we are going to lunch, having asked Don to make a reservation. 'We'll be happier here, won't we?' asks Meg, which indeed we were.

'My pleasure is in thinking of people enjoying a picture over their fireplace,' says Don tentatively. 'Galleries are not really for me. Mind you, I never expected to be welcomed into the fold.' Possibly he still isn't, although he is certainly one of Cornwall's most successful artists. But success comes at a price, and it's no surprise that he is not quite sure what to do with the rest of his life.

'His style has been honed over the years,' Meg interjects: 'There's no further to go. He's driven by commission. It's time for him to break out.' Everyone wants their favourite train at their favourite spot. He is stuck over one of trams in Edinburgh's Princes Street and, for the first time, has actually turned down a commission.

Don explains: 'People want this image they have in their mind but, the more they define the detail they want, the more they hedge you in – the precise angle, include this and that, and in a small picture, please.'

It is Meg's turn again: 'He's experimenting with abstract. He doesn't have to follow others. He just needs to be himself, loosening up, so he's not so frustrated.' I feel guilty thinking about the precise details I've requested in past commissions, though he accepted them gladly.

Don talks about the greater creativity of Italian art. 'Half the things the great Italians did wouldn't have been possible here.' There's a glint in his eye; a future is opening up.

Over cheese, he changes the subject. TV may be out for him, but he's proud when Meg's on it, as one of Cornwall County Council's nine executive councillors, with the portfolio for lifelong learning, including education, libraries and the arts. She is one of Cornwall's majority independents. 'I couldn't do it for a party.' Individualism always counts in Cornwall. The Council's 'opposition' is from the scrutinising councillors who look at the executive's proposals.

Don and Meg, what a match. When he became disenchanted with life as an art tutor and said he'd just like to give up and travel around, Meg replied: 'Why don't we – *now*?' They uprooted, came to Cornwall and took a winter break in Lostwithiel less than a mile from their present home. Sheila is delighted to have an unpretentious lunch of quiche, cheese and salad and enjoys the company. She wants to come back here, too.

The Magic of Q Town

You can no longer reach Fowey by train down the tree-lined estuary, arriving in style and without the embarrassment of a car. The road is longer and less intimate, and parking usually a nightmare, but today we risk taking Little Car into the narrow streets and triumphantly leave her on a quay, able to enjoy the hidden-away world of Fowey without anxiety or the prospect of a long climb back to an inland car park.

Ocean-going ships pass up the estuary to reach the deep-water quays, served both by rail from Lostwithiel and a private road through what was Cornwall's longest railway tunnel from St Blazey. The ferries go to and fro and yachts are always on the move. Fowey is a real river town. The higgledy-piggledy mixture of mainly ancient buildings lining its main street now accommodate what might well be the country's greatest single concentration of quality shops – fish shop, butcher, baker, as well as art and gift shops with imaginative ranges – and eating houses specialising in local fare, especially fish, and pubs with nautical names. Every now and then there is a charming river vista though, when seen in a gap between two quaint buildings, a modern bulk carrier bound for the USA is breathtakingly surprising.

Fowey is often fondly referred to as Troy Town, so named in the stories of its most famous resident, (Sir) Arthur Quiller-Couch, or 'Q'. When I read it as a young man, his account of the last meal a destitute couple had in their cottage before they moved into the workhouse with its separate male and female quarters, couples only allowed to meet on Christmas Day, spoke more to me about poverty than *Oliver Twist*. Opposite the Daphne du Maurier Centre, the town's main bookshop, Bookends, gratifyingly filled some of the Q gaps on my shelves. Though it doesn't look much, it is a real antiquarian bookshop with many treasures on its packed shelves on two floors, along with a smattering of new (mainly local) titles, and classical music as peaceful background. Its story is typical of Fowey. Its owner, Christine Alexander, and her husband Howard, sailed back from South Africa, limping into the estuary with their mainsail blown out.

'People were so kind, and we immediately wanted to settle here but had to find jobs in London where we stuffed all the money we could into the bank. Two years later we bought a small cottage here, and then saw the shop, which had been a cheap paperback exchange, on the market. "Let's run an antiquarian bookshop," we said, without knowing anything about it. We learned on the job but had incredible luck... wonderful advice from that real Cornish publisher Len Truiran, and a visit from Ron Parry of Exeter Rare Books who'd picked up a marvellous selection of Cornish titles he didn't want which gave us a perfect foundation, though in those days you could go to an auction, bid for a few mixed boxes of books and make out. You couldn't do that now.

'Of course, the out-of-print books of Daphne du Maurier and Quiller-Couch have helped. One American came saying she lived in the same New York apartment block as Helene Hanff, whose correspondence about books made the famous *84 Charing Cross Road*. "Helene says I must read a C-o-o-c-h," she said, and that resulted in my exchanging letters with Helene Hanff too, though alas only a few before she died. And it went on from there. *Troy Town*, or as it was first called, *The Astonishing History of Troy Town*, was much in demand. I told Howard I could sell dozens of copies if only I could find them. To which he replied: "If only I could buy a laser printer," which he did, and reprinted that and Q's wonderful *The Art of Writing* to get his publishing business started. He'd had to stay on in London for a time after I had started the bookshop, but now he's a Fowey publisher and I'm a Fowey bookseller.'

She persuades me to buy the expensive but, as it turns out, very worthwhile new *Cornwall*, written by Philip Payton, 'doyen of the new generation of Cornish scholars,' but published by her husband's imprint, Alexander Associates.

'We don't make a lot of money but it's enough and we're very happy. Fowey's a wonderful place, and the people have been so welcoming. Because there's not much beach, and perhaps because it's an industrial port, it's never attracted family visitors, but lots of people who seek it out fall in love and come back. And we get between 5,000 and 7,000 visiting yachts a year, though today's sailors are a bit like luxury car drivers. Today's yachts are easy to sail, and the maritime library on board is a thing of the past. But they're interested in Cornwall, of course – good customers for us and for the shops and restaurants.'

Finally, at the end of another long day to Carlyon Bay on the coastal fringe of St Austell. Now a member of the family-run Brend hotels based in Barnstaple, the Carlyon Bay is steadily regaining its dignity having fallen into that awful state that is the lot of large hotels when annual maintenance is not kept up to scratch. I reflect on Sir Arthur Quiller-Couch's Cornishness. While he was, like many other famous people, persuaded to join what might be called the Cornish Revivalists, he was too realistic to over-romanticise. He also understood the Cornish dilemma. While criticising the Great Western Railway's 'Cornish

Riviera' as an 'inexactitude', his own *Delectable Duchy* also pandered to visitors. But then, reluctantly he agreed that the future lay not in mining and fishing, but tourism, with the appeal: 'Since we must cater for the stranger, let us do it well and honestly. Let us respect him and our native land as well.'

To the Nare

Next morning, through Tywardreath, St Blazey, Par and St Austell, to the little man-made port of Charlestown. This is the part of Cornwall that lives and breathes the extracting (or 'winning' as the Cornish term it) and transport of china clay, the only raw product Britain now exports in volume. Expanding just as the bottom fell out of copper in the 1870s, and so preventing even greater hardship, china clay itself has an eventful history, and has had an enormous impact on the landscape for many miles north of St Austell. I made journalistic calls for many profiles of the industry and its ports over the years, but personal memories are mainly of work and pleasure trips on its unusual, often dramatic, railways – in guard's vans of ordinary clay trains and on enthusiasts' specials exploring the oddities. The clay lines were pioneered by a local landlord, Thomas Treffry, who built 'for posterity' a viaduct of ten magnificently-proportioned arches across the Luxulyn Valley. Today's Newquay-bound trains struggle up the steeply-inclined valley underneath it.

Much of Charlestown's little dock was literally dug out. Height meant designing a unique chute for lorries to tip their clay into waiting ships. Alas, the last coaster called earlier in the year. Only 600-ton ships can get in here. Today's standard ones start at 1,000 tons, and go to Par instead. Now Charlestown's dock, owned by Square Sail Ltd, is filled with tall ships including a fleet of three square-riggers for films like The Three Musketeers. Charlestown is changing, the Shipwreck & Heritage Centre recently sold. The owners and curators for 22 years, Richard and Bridget Larne are, as they put it, raising the drawbridge, thinning their assets and moving to the Scillies.

Over tea in their lounge, Richard recalls the early days of writing for D&C, with a series of books on West Country shipwrecks, the one on the Scillies especially popular, and *The Commercial Diving Manual*, often reprinted. More recently he has completed the first five of seven volumes of the *Shipwreck Index of the British Isles* for Lloyds Register of Shipping. From D&C experience, he learned how to publish on his own, including an instant book. Nearly 20,000 copies were sold of *The Cita*, whose Polish crew were fast asleep when it ran straight into the Scillies in the dark. Unable to cope when the £10 million cargo spewed out, Customs & Excise turned a blind eye. Much Marks & Spencer children's clothing went to Romania once the locals and their mainland friends could take no more.

The list of Scilly wrecks seems endless, dating back to the 1600s when 80 tons was a big ship, wrecks reaching their peak in the 1800s. Richard and Bridget were both keen divers, realising that few sunken ships are ever uplifted, no wreck completely removed, the rocky shores concealing as much treasure as they have so far yielded. Few people have built so successful a business around their hobby as happily or successfully as the Larnes. His first dive was with adapted escape gear from a German submarine which he used to explore a sunken Salter's steamer in the Thames. Love of underwater exploration and nautical archaeology is balanced by a sensitive appreciation of the human tragedy behind wrecks, and commercial expertise in extracting money from visitors through admission fees and the sales of books. Only when you delve into the detail do you realise the enormous impact of wrecks, rescue and wrecking. Once over a hundred ships were lost annually rounding the South West peninsula.

The drawbridge is being raised because Charlestown is changing: more traffic, drunkenness, crime. 'We've now more friends on the Scillies than the mainland. It's different there. The Scillies never have a bad season. They're friendly, and everything's in its place. I'm going back to model making and will be able to see everything from the window.' No doubt including more wrecks.

And so we go quickly through Veryan to The Nare at the beginning of the Roseland Peninsula, unwinding for a short time walking on the huge expanse of low-tide sands with only one other human being and his dog – but a nasty high-tide line of the detritus of modern life.

At dinner we ask the waitress to point out June. Between courses, the standard of choice, food and service excellent as ever, I walk to the table she is sharing with the retired parson. 'I bring you fond greetings from Brian.'

'Good gracious. How did you track me down? Has he really sent you?' We arrange a pre dinner drink tomorrow.

Truro and the Challenge of Planning for a Better Cornwall

We enjoy early morning tea in our dressing gowns looking down on the great sandy expanse of Pendower Beach. The Nare is probably Cornwall's best hotel, delightfully civilised and well-placed for real escape from worldly cares. It is not so convenient if you have to dash off hither and thither. First Veryan, one of coastal England's most attractive villages, largely a legacy of a vicar who enjoyed a 47-year stint in his Georgian house overlooking the green. He built the five round houses (four thatched), said to have been one for each of his daughters. But there were only three daughters. One theory is that the lack of corners would keep the devil away. We are on more certain ground saying he came to own much of the village and landscaped it with trees now in their adult glory. Veryan looks particularly neat, desirable in this morning's sunshine and the sense of community is demonstrated by inviting notices and a group of nine ladies, each with wicker basket, waiting outside the village hall for the Women's Institute market to open. Yet well into the twentieth century this was working men's country.

The next village of Tregony, with its long street of traditional cottages, some of which were once shops and pubs, more obviously displays its down-to-earth origins. When the Fal was navigable this far to 800-ton ships, Tregony was a major port and fully-fledged town, returning two MPs until the Reform Act. It once boasted three dozen ale houses, the beer made from local hops.

The road's every turn opens up further evidence of the difference that is Cornwall, the approach to Truro being as familiar from journalist days as successive passages of Beethoven's Fifth. Cornwall's capital is compact, individual, with good private shops, and traditional architecture not wholly overshadowed by monstrously ugly replacement buildings. First call is at the railway station, still with its traditional semaphore signals. Mercifully there is still a Gents.

Alas, the *Cornish Riviera Express*, whose reliable punctuality was the pride of the Great Western, arrives 49 minutes late from Penzance. It is worth reflecting a moment on this most famous of trains for, even those of us who know, have to remind ourselves of the lengths to which the authorities promoting Cornwall's tourism went to avoid visitors having to see how most people earned their living. The main line's value is that it serves (or is within taxi distance reach) of nearly all Cornwall's trading centres. But even in the 1950s, the year-round prime holiday express, and one of only three daytime services from London, passed non-stop through the key industrial places like St Austell, Redruth and Camborne. Today's visitors enjoy paintings of traditional fishing scenes, but yesterday's tourists were kept well away from the sight and smell of trawlers, mines and clay works.

Such reflections continue as we descend from the car park to the Truro Bookshop, started many years ago by Bradford Barton, who wrote and also published other people's titles on Cornwall's railways, mines, quarries and fisheries. We are not alone in picking out books about yesterday's real Cornwall, including the novels by EV Thompson vividly portraying the hardship suffered by fishermen and miners in the nineteenth century. There is a marvellous stock of regional titles... also of national bestsellers and reference. I wonder what the thousands who delve deeply into Cornwall's workaday past would say if, for example,

Looe again became a thriving port with a fishing fleet and stone dumped dustily into the holds of ships, or if again the night sky around Redruth and Camborne were lit up with flames and smoke from the mines – lit up, yet obscuring any view of the stars. The downside of industry is emphasised in a volume I buy on the granite trade, which used 'moorstones', including many important prehistoric dolmens that could be gathered from the surface to avoid expensive quarrying.

My old favoured Truro eating places have long gone. The Red Lion, where market-day lunches included the tallest heap of root vegetables imaginable, was damaged beyond repair when a lorry carrying stone came down the hill opposite, out of control. When we eventually choose an upstairs cafe, we find a long queue. So we buy sandwiches and eat them on a seat outside the cathedral, quickly enough to allow us to go inside to listen to part of a lunch-time concert by the new assistant organist. Part of Stanford's Six Preludes and Postludes is specially enjoyable.

Truro Cathedral, first seen from a train crossing the viaduct high above the city, has always attracted me. Not completed until well into the twentieth century, it was the first English Anglican cathedral since Christopher Wren rebuilt Saint Paul's following London's Great Fire. In fact, the Diocese of Truro was only separated from Exeter after the main collapse of mining in the 1870s. But then the Church of England, like today's Episcopal Church in Scotland, was always a minority institution in the far west. That did not prevent the stained glass being particularly fine, probably the very best of the Victorian era. The enjoyment of organ music and stained glass go curiously in parallel. *Truro Cathedral News* reports on an enterprising range of local and outreach activities that now make this as bright a beacon of Christianity as any in England. Though the welcome is warm, the cathedral's real purpose is not so compromised by mass tourism as at many others. Not that things were always sweet. At first, Truro Cathedral was unpopular for its Anglo-Catholicism implying that the county's predominant Methodism was irrelevant as a means of reaching God. After an Anglo-Catholic church had been attacked, a Low Churchman, who had formerly been a Methodist, was appointed bishop in the cause of harmony.

Back to Saturday 22 March 1955. I had a bad cough and my sister helped me read the first of many reports about Cornwall's first Development Plan over the phone from a kiosk to the West Country's Sunday paper, where it was taken down in shorthand. My sister had difficulty with my writing, and I spluttered to explain. An impatient group outside summoned a passing policeman to remove us. 'This isn't the place for necking,' was answered by my showing the copy, in which the policeman, true Cornish, became so interested that those outside thought he had joined us in some improper act. Of such trivia are memories formed.

Earlier that day, I had interviewed the first Cornwall County planning officer about the twenty-year Development Plan which, running to hundreds of pages, was almost a post-war local *Doomsday Book*. HWJ Heck was of the old-fashioned, outspoken, opinionated, doesn't-matter-who-you-upset breed that were then at the top of many aspects of local government. Agriculture, he pontificated, was all important, and in twenty years only 0.5 per cent of agricultural land would be allowed to be taken for housing, and only an additional 0.1 per cent for other purposes including roads, industry and entertainment. Hands off, Plymouth, hoping to spread westwards across the Tamar: 'There is no case for spoiling or altering the present shape of life in Torpoint and Saltash.'

Talking about the country's precarious economic balance, he declared: 'Misguided development for Cornwall would not just be detrimental; it would be catastrophic.' There was almost a personal 'depend on me' element from the county planning officers of the 1950s. There was also much common sense: Falmouth was too dependent on ship repairing, employing 2,840. Then, 2,400 working in mine engineering was also putting too many eggs in one basket. Cornwall's problems included too short a holiday season, over four times the national average of roads per square mile, and an unusual, often pepper-potted population distribution, largely dictated by sources of employment, especially mining. But then Heck felt that mining would be bound to revive one day. While by 1952 car ownership was up by 59 per cent since pre-war, only a few roads would need improving, the top priority being the protection of scenery and again farming land. It was anticipated that Cornwall's coastline would be given National Park status.

The science of hindsight is always tempting, but at least Cornwall's Heck understood the problems well... especially the fact that whatever the county did to boost its own economy was nothing compared to national influences. Industry moved in when capacity was tight elsewhere, and could not be attracted when sites and labour were available closer to the nation's core.

Over the years, reporting for newspapers and the BBC, I was constantly in touch with Mr Heck and grew to admire him. So, nearly half a century later, I have an appointment with today's county planning officer, David Pollard. The new County Hall is on the bypass, a pleasant, functional building where everything feels Cornish. Meg Breckon, happening to pass through reception on her way to a committee meeting, gives a cheerful greeting.

HWJ Heck has, until now, been but a name to David, and he is as interested in hearing a first-hand report about how it all began as I am in his views on today's and tomorrow's Cornwall. 'The rural slums have gone, but the rest hasn't changed that much, though inevitably they got their sums wrong,' he says. 'Only four other areas of Britain have such deep-rooted problems as Cornwall. The big issue is still employment.'

'Sums wrong' include population forecasts, though in fairness the big increase happened well beyond the twenty years covered by the first County Plan. In 1951 the population was 345,000. At the time of our meeting it was 490,000, up a staggering 41 per cent.

David optimistically refers to Objective I Status the county has just achieved, and expounds his philosophy: 'We haven't been giving sufficient importance to trade and industry. Above all, we must add value here in Cornwall. It's not enough to sell raw materials. We need to make better use of our attributes, inventiveness, quality of life, and much-improved communications, to compete on equal footing in the "just-in-time" world for low bulk, high-quality goods and services. But you can't have your cake and eat it: you can't restrict housing and promote the economy. In the 1980s there were more new jobs in Cornwall than in any other southern county, but things got out of sync. Finding that wonderful state of balance between the economy, housing and services is especially hard when you're out on a limb. For instance, there's a deep need for more health facilities.'

The Peninsula Medical School (Exeter, Plymouth, Truro), and hopefully a University of Cornwall, would provide welcome help. Back to employment. More Cornish branding was needed, especially in tourism with higher-quality facilities which would attract surfers to Newquay, yachtsmen to Falmouth, golfers everywhere, even gig rowers in the Scillies. The 'Stein effect' (Rick Stein's seafood at Padstow) was typical of what could be achieved. 'Cornwall is distinctly different and should exploit it.' But, yes, there were many problems. I mention the TV programme 'Cream Teas and Concrete' in which North Cornwall district councillors glowingly described bungalows – 'we love them' – as the most useful crop. 'Everyone in the planning business teases us about that one, saying that but for the grace of God they'd be mocked on TV too. We keep hearing about the need for cheap housing for working people, but maybe too much is left to the planners. Is it right for the planning system to be responsible for low-cost housing? But people in villages, such as Rock, Betjeman country, react violently against rowdy night-time parties. Forty-seven per cent of the homes in St Minver, which includes Rock, are second homes.'

The county's scattered population distribution is still a problem. To prevent settlements joining up, the policy has long been to encourage development in towns and villages with good facilities, but those moving in to enjoy the Cornishness of Cornwall don't like 'in-fill' sites.

If I were alive 47 years hence, what I wonder would be the agenda with the then planning chief. Solutions, someone once said, equal uniformity. David reflects that already the differences between southeast and southwest Britain have narrowed... and, though at the time of meeting we can only guess, clearly the 2001 census will show a far smaller proportion of the county's population being born within it than the 67 per cent when a question about place of birth was last asked in 1951. Solutions? We agree that the one thing unlikely to change is that in Cornwall, if you have ten people, there will be five different opinions. Walking back to the car, it occurs to me that the aforementioned 47 years represents a whole quarter of history since censuses began in 1801.

Through the city and round the roundabout beside the tidal Truro River, where 2,000 tons of Cornish barley has just left from a brand-new quay for France, I head for the BBC. During a twenty-minute discussion on Radio Cornwall's afternoon programme, its presenter Chris Blount and I talk about the tremendous changes we have seen in Cornwall, especially in its transport and holiday trade... a topic to be picked up when I talk to him privately near Newquay (in the North Cornwall chapter). In the last decade, I remind Radio Cornwall's listeners, every year an average of 18,000 people have moved in and 14,500 out. How many of those leaving have been here only a short time, we wonder, and hark back to the great emigrations of former days when mining and fishing were declining. Cornwall has gone through successive changes faster than most counties. Resorts bursting at the seams and fifty trainloads of broccoli a day in winter, along with abundant pilchard harvests and working tin mines, are now only memories.

Immediately we are off the air, I am propelled to the other studio. Radio Scotland has unexpectedly arranged another interview on the Hatfield accident. It is satisfying broadcasting live to the two extremities of Britain within a few minutes of each other, though I don't altogether like the nickname Mr Angry at Radio Scotland. Railtrack's arrogant behaviour and general culture, however, I have always seriously hated. Already it seems that Hatfield was an accident waiting to happen and which could destroy Railtrack and general confidence in the railways.

Roseland and Mevagissey

Sheila, who has listened to me in reception, is furious: 'How could you use such rude language on the air? Arses, indeed.' I haven't the foggiest idea what she's on about, and it's not until the next broadcast, when my interviewer said I had complained about the dangerous way in which Railtrack 'sweated their assets', that the penny drops.

So back by the complicated route to The Nare. In the hall we pass Bettye Gray, head of the family owning the hotel, but miss the opportunity to say hello. Only as we prepare to leave a couple of days later do we find that the first advance copies of her life story are on sale. Since she and most of the family have devoted much of their careers to Newquay, that is where we will come across her again. Now it is time for that pre-dinner drink with June and her parson friend, Canon Michael Hocking. He is yet another author – one sometimes feels there are more people writing books than reading them. His three titles are about pastoral and parish work. His experience is typical. The first publisher he approached only commissioned books, refusing unsolicited manuscripts. Whatever the policy, no publisher returns a book without taking at least a secret glimpse. So his was 'commissioned' in a slightly revised form, immediately to be followed by a second. You only have to see the size of the 'slush heap' of unsolicited manuscripts, and their appalling average quality, to understand why publishers need to protect themselves.

Michael is a Canon of Guildford Cathedral, but just one memory from his early post-war days as vicar of Penzance's mother church. Passed down orally in several families were colourful details of how the first intimation of the French defeat and Nelson's death at the Battle of Trafalgar reached England, at Penzance, by a fishing vessel intercepted by a warship. A ball was being held at the Assembly Rooms in Chapel Street, so the mayor stopped the dancing and relayed the tidings from the balcony. The ball was instantly transformed into a memorial service. At a naval happening in 1946, Canon Hocking instituted what has become a regular memorial tribute.

The following day is a much-needed day messing about. The tone is set by the first person we meet: 'When the sun's out, everyone has a smile on their face.' None of us knew that shortly the South West would experience almost three months with at least some rain every day, and that nationwide floods would add to transport disruption.

When I was last at The Nare, I read a romantic novel with a fishing background set in the village of Portscatho. Then, without a car, I could not investigate and, though I've visited every Cornish coastal village several times, couldn't identify Portscatho in my memory. So we take the surprisingly flat road, but find the village has become disappointingly upmarket: commercial fishing is out, catering for English society is in. Restaurants, two galleries, a good shoe shop, a well-stocked general store where offerings include videos and bank cash machine, tell of a new prosperity, as do improved cottages. This isn't the Cornwall I first fell in love with. Though physically it is possibly more attractive than ever, and the main street still runs straight down a ramp into the sea, it doesn't feel at all like it did when those born here occupied the cottages and were always conscious of tide and sky and never spent a penny carelessly (even if they did so unwisely at the pub).

'Had a good season?' we ask a shopkeeper in St Mawes. 'Not too bad, thank you.' Catching visitors' money is much like fishing.

As lovely as ever, with its Castle and fine views over Carrick Roads to Falmouth, St Mawes perhaps first came into prominence in the days *The Times* carried ads on its front page and two local hotels guaranteed that, if snow fell during your winter visit, your stay would be free. In this morning's paper we see that one of them, the Idle Rocks, is the subject of a long-drawn-out controversy over the current owner's plan for extra bedrooms. There is still a foot ferry to Falmouth, but these days Natives and Emmets alike look for excuses to take the car, and it is forty years since an early D&C book on *Music Making in Cornwall* described taking a piano as personal luggage on the foot ferry as routine.

Thirst strikes, and on the return we stop for coffee at Melinsey working mill with an active water wheel by a pond as three car loads of happy mums and kids emerge from their café treat and pheasants stalk noisily around. The mill (its original equipment in its basement 'museum'), is in a narrow valley, the road's deep banks on either side, thickly covered with moss. The owners deserve to succeed, but we hope they don't do so well that they want to expand... the everlasting theme in a county which needs to retain the small and intimate and already has too much of the large and ugly, yet also urgently requires greater prosperity.

I often think of Britain as one of the world's few countries whose appearance has generally been improved by man. That can hardly include Cornwall where industry, caravans and bungalows have compromised many areas of fine landscape, and where developers and their architects of the last two centuries have left little of lasting value. Yet, if expanding towns are generally disappointing, there is much natural beauty left... and still much hidden Cornwall to be savoured far from crowds. Though coastal Cornwall was never declared a fully-fledged National Park, the coast itself has been well protected, and is now in safe hands. Yet, while we toy with the idea that it is the very permanence of the coast that thrills, we find the footpath out of the garden at The Nare has been rerouted because a section of cliff has fallen. Our presence on earth may be transient, but not even the best-preserved landscape is forever.

With which thought, it being such a lovely day, we drive rapidly back to St Austell to return with leisurely diversions at points along what, excepting popular Mevagissey, is probably the least-visited part of Cornwall's coastline. Pentewan with its abandoned harbour, Gorran Haven and a magnificent walk to Dodman Point, the lush valley leading to Porthluney Cove, and Portloe all deserve far longer than we can give them today. In the days of deep, rutted lanes, each port and many a beach saw goods coming in by boat for its little hinterland. In some cases, such as Gorran Haven, despite periodic rebuilding of a pier, only lighters could be accommodated. Their cargos were transhipped in smooth water at Fowey. The cliffs demonstrate that great height is not necessary for impact. Especially when lit by sunshine, sections look as though they were sliced off and shaped by a sharp cake knife, the white sand in bays being powdered icing sugar.

Of Mevagissey I am uncertain. Murray's 1859 *Hand-Book* tells us it is noted for dirt and pilchards, while the Cornish historian Polwhele said its fishwives were 'boisterous females, ruder by far than those who toil at Billingsgate'. As at Looe and St Ives, that kept most tourists away, but – despite a notice welcoming you to the 'working' fishing port – visitors dominate the summer streets today. Downmarket souvenir shop windows make that abundantly plain. There is active local social life, led by incomers attracted by good-value housing and the wonderful setting. I used to spend long happy days here in the 1950s and 1960s marvelling at the place's sheer size, long history and utter Cornishness. Though pilchards have long gone, at least locals are proud that fishing survives.

Among Mevagissey's visitors are many who, having seen it on TV, come to enjoy the Lost Gardens of Heligan. My 65p 1974 OS map duly names Heligan two miles inland from Mevagissey and shows a bit of garden layout, but that cannot have been surveyed post-war. In World War One, the house ceased to be home to the Treymayne family, and the gardens went into a long sleep. In the mild, damp climate, hedges became steadily higher and thicker and trees and shrubs rampant over lawns, paths, vegetable and fruit areas alike. We missed the TV series but when we return to the Nare, looking forward to another of its excellent dinners, we spot a notice inviting guests to take advantage of an exclusive arrangement they have with the gardens for a private tour led by one of the leading figures. Yes, they'll arrange it, for quite a modest fee.

· X I ·

A LAND
OF GARDENS

The Lost Gardens of Heligan

It is not surprising that those of us who have lived in the West Country for half a century and think we know it well are suspicious of new tourist attractions, yet here at Heligan cynicism is utterly laid to rest. The only thing that might possibly eclipse its uniqueness is another horticultural inspiration: the Eden Project, near St Austell, of which more in a moment.

Our guide is Colin Howlett, director of marketing. He quickly demonstrates that he is one of those incomers from England that Cornwall needs. In quick succession, he expresses delight at having such a worthwhile job in such a setting; shows respect for his boss, the inspirer of Heligan, Tim Smit; and enthusiasm for the loyalty of the local staff who have helped make it all possible. This is the most fascinating garden tour of our lives, through park-like gardens, highly productive fruit and vegetable gardens, a New Zealand and Italian garden, jungle, swamp and lost valley. Colin deftly brings past and present together, points out perfectly-sited trees, admires the gently-curved wall designed to catch the maximum daily sunshine, describes how olive oil has been used to enable the Victorian handwriting to be read on 234 metal plant labels, and introduces us to the cultivation of pineapples using heat carefully created by constantly changing dung (300 tons of it a year), together with the right amount of water. Before the days that ships were fast enough to bring in imported pineapples, serving them at one's own table was the hallmark of the gentry; having your own oranges and lemons was child's play in comparison.

Here are the fastest-growing trees in Cornwall, delectable vistas, peaceful surroundings, fruit and vegetables chosen for their flavour, and not because supermarkets favour a variety for the way it grows and ripens evenly and never disappoints the public in its appearance, even if it seldom excites the palate either. Here also is a true Paxton greenhouse; he sold them to the wealthy as a profitable sideline. Whatever your interest in gardens, allow ample time here. Bamboos? There are sixty varieties. Fancy a Chinese handkerchief tree (*devidia*)? Allow four years for the seed to germinate, fifteen for the first flowers to appear. Cabbages and runner beans. Substantial use is made of seed banks of old, rare varieties. It all hangs together remarkably well.

The gardens flourish again. Though already visitor numbers are creeping up to quarter of a million annually, it is on such a scale (2½ miles of footpaths in the North Garden alone) that you feel you have much of it to yourself. It is distinctly not National Trust; they turned it down because they could not afford to support it. Notices are few, litter bins absent, but hardly any rubbish ever has to be picked up, for even non-gardeners look in awe and behave with respect. It is good for Cornwall, employing eighty, of whom fifteen are gardeners. No machinery is used, things being done as they would have been before the gardens went into that long sleep. In 1914, there had been 22 gardeners, working long hours, the headman controlling his own empire with only occasional guidance from on high.

Visit at any time, for camellias flower in January, rhododendrons start displaying in February. Especially look out for a huge red one towering high, beneath which the gardens steadily disappeared in a mass of vegetation and which now seems to supervise the lesser species around it. Even the shop is different, with much of the produce expensively grown for sale. Well, when did you last eat a home-grown pineapple? The second grown in the new era was sent to the Queen after the first had been home-tested to ensure it didn't taste of the dung in which it had been grown.

Over a cup of tea in the restaurant Colin relives the excitement of cutting through the hedges that had been unchecked for two generations, the uncovering of paths, discovery of the tools of gardeners who had gone to the front in World War One. The boiler and pipe system for the hothouses was of 1886 vintage, 'modern times in this garden'. Bee bales date back to the 1820s. Colin again expresses pleasure at being in Cornwall. His earlier mixed career included marketing in the Thames Valley; his wife is a botanical artist. But yet again we are asked: 'Why does Cornwall find it so difficult to get things together? You have to do things for yourself to get anywhere. Some of the gardens, including National Trust ones, have co-operated to market themselves as the Great Gardens of Cornwall, but already visitors, especially Americans, complain of the shortage of good hotels. They are keen to come but won't tolerate the standards of most local hotels. Things are going to get very difficult when Eden is fully opened.' He hands us a brochure on the budding Eden:

A late summer sun turned the giant Goonbarrow china clay waste tip above St Austell an ochrous red, an Ayers Rock in a minor key inspiring images of Ziggurats and Arthur Conan Doyle's Victorian Lost World fantasies; of ancient forgotten civilisations nestling in volcanic craters, of fabulous plants and ... an idea was born.

One of the world's largest enclosed areas fills a huge disused china clay quarry excavated down to solid granite, explains Colin. The cost: £73 million, of which £36 million comes from the Millennium Commission. Such is the scale that Truro Cathedral would fit into a side dome. Divided into climatic zones, Eden will represent the world's vegetation, from rainforest trees growing at ten to twelve feet a year to two-inch Alpines. The plan is Tim Smit's, and initially, when funding was next to zero, was supported by Heligan. Already planting has started; they've bought a nursery to help things along. Even now, thousands a day are being given a ride round to view progress from a miniature railway. What is more, the enormous enterprise seems to be taking shape without the disasters associated with the likes of the London Dome. As though Heligan isn't enough, Tim Smit apparently needs the challenge of Eden. It will surely rank as one of southern England's top attractions, though the main purpose will always be research. I recall earlier false tourist promises around St Austell, still the china clay capital. This is going to succeed, but we decide to wait to see it until it has more fully taken shape. Then it will surely be a real treat, demanding a full day.

On the way out we buy Tim Smit's book linked to Channel Four's TV series: *The Lost Gardens of Heligan.* The tale of just how lost the gardens were, of the work of rediscovery and the financial hazards along the way, makes compelling reading. Smit had once been a county archivist, and then spent ten years as record producer and composer. He is clearly a persuasive chap with a purpose, as these brief extracts show:

Hundreds of sycamores and ash trees had obliterated the shape of the landscape so totally that it was difficult to get our bearings. There were no obvious paths and the famous lakes seemed to have disappeared. The only indication that this had once been a garden was the large number of bamboos and tropical-looking tree ferns that were growing in magnificent clumps despite the shade of the trees. The productive area was the engine room of the garden. It was Peter Thoday who pointed out the irony that none of the great gardens in Britain celebrated the tradition of the working garden, preferring to emphasise the pleasure grounds and their associations with lords and ladies at leisure. However, from the supposedly humble walled gardens, those pleasure grounds were stocked with marvellous plants from around the world, propagated and nurtured, developed and hybridised to a perfection rarely seen in the wild. In the glasshouses, fruits and decorative plants were being produced in defiance of natural conditions and were admired by all who saw them. A majority of the garden staff worked here, yet their story was never told.

And finally, having discovered the signatures of the gardeners by their loo, a few days later he examined the parish war memorial only to find many of those same names:

Our bitter-sweet musings on lost innocence now seemed dangerously sentimental. The truth was nasty, vivid and full of pain, and only the passing of seventy years or more would dull it back to sepia... It sounds odd, but we had the impression that everyone had left the garden in the middle of a working day, fully intending to come back. For seventy years Heligan had waited, with the garden in mourning like a naval widow forever looking out to sea for a husband who never returns.

It was eighteen months later that we returned to visit Eden, staying again at the Carlyon Bay Hotel which had by then gained four-star status (along with five others in the West Country's own Brend group), a high percentage AA score and rosette. Outstanding for a large hotel, both benefiting, and benefiting from, Eden only a few minutes away. I overheard a management group led by a family member discussing quality points down to the biscuits left with tea/coffee-making facilities in the bedrooms. If you care, it surely shows. During our stay, everything worked, with marvellous attention to detail and friendly service.

When first seen from the top of the vast former clay pit, Eden's biomes looked disappointingly small, but by the time we descended they towered over us, and inside the humid tropical one we had to crane our necks to see the top of a gigantic waterfall. Again, Truro Cathedral would fit in here, and it is high enough for trees to reach their full potential.

Most visitors may think first of the sheer scale, but rapidly we were drawn into the detail. In the main gents' there were already 25 urinals, yet I quickly observed a notice on the wall published by the Eden Project and South West Water 'working together for a better environment'. In 1976, it said, on average everyone used 110 litres of water a day. By 2021, 'if we do nothing about it', it could be 190 litres and that would mean many more reservoirs where there is no room for them.

Tim Smit introduces the guide by welcoming people to Eden and talking briefly of the initial challenge. He continues with a message which makes a perfect quotation.

But if this place becomes no more than an upmarket theme park it will all have been the most gigantic waste of money. We have intended to create something that not only encourages us to understand and to celebrate the world we live in, but also inspires us to action. Eden isn't so much a destination as a place in the heart. It is not just a marvellous piece of science-related architecture; it is also a statement of our passionate belief in an optimistic future for mankind. Yes, we hope you will feel moved at the scale of the ambition; yes, we hope that you will be awestruck by the beauty of our living theatre; and yes, of course, we hope you will be entertained by the highly individual approach we have taken to telling our stories. But more than that we want you to leave here feeling that we all could make a very real difference to the world we live in if we could work together. In a world of -isms and -ologies, of expertise so refined that only experts understand it, we have brought together scientists, artists and technologists to create a distinctive culture, one that makes the possibilities of the future come to life in a way that we can all comprehend.

Throughout, the notices were splendid; entertaining, informative, provocative, and suggesting what we could do about things. In the warm temperate biome, a huge display of colourful, cut *fynbos* (including *proteas*) invited us to buy them from shops to help sustain their production in South Africa's 'Flower Valley', where the Eden Project's intervention helped stop the ploughing up of one field of them for vines. Interested adults couldn't help being drawn into the details and problems of olive production.

'This is much more interesting than the tropical side,' said a superior woman being personally shown round by Tim Smit.

'A lot of people say that,' he replied. True, if you are only interested in what you've seen on your travels. We found the larger humid tropical biome more interesting for several reasons. 'That's the first time I've seen anthuriums growing,' from Sheila, was echoed by youngsters seeing their first pineapples and bananas. On a dull winter's day, it was also nicely warm, and it was made clear that many plants of greatest food and medical value, and also many of the most urgent environmental problems, were found in the tropics. And plants extraordinaire, such as that with the world's largest seed and the bamboo that grows up to 47.6 inches skyward *a day* in its native habitat. We learned that bamboo was used daily for one purpose or another by half the world's population. Many of the uses were displayed.

'Look – ginger,' said someone who had never before seen it, while simultaneously a New Zealander swore: 'That's the weed I just can't get rid of, nuisance that it is.' The former grunted disapprovingly.

'That sounds like the song of a robin,' said Sheila. 'And that looks like one,' I echoed. That night's regional TV news reported that in a storm, when doors were blown open, two robins slipped in, enjoying the life of Riley with shelter, food constantly on tap and virtually no predators. Exactly how they will be caught and ejected when the weather is warmer will be much discussed.

The Eden Project was still very new: plenty to see, but also ample space for plants to fill out. At this stage, much of it remained a building site with hugely ambitious developments under way. Its success was however assured and it had already exceeded projected visitor numbers and given Cornwall's economy a great shot in the arm. It surely requires more than a single visit. Locals, who enjoy cheap out-of-season tickets, commented that much had changed even after three months.

When I sat in the guard's van of a clay train trundling up the short industrial branch, the idea of a corner of this scarred landscape being home to an enterprise of such size and positive influence would have seemed ridiculous. Remember, the Eden Project is just that, an ongoing attempt to help us understand and improve our world. There are powerful links with many environmental agencies around the world.

Over the Fal

Back to our main trip round Cornwall, next morning we first make a brief stop close by the joining of the Fal and Truro River estuaries, at the Smugglers restaurant at Tolverne, where there is still considerable evidence of preparations for the D-Day landings. A French minesweeper was bombed and sank here. There is a pictorial display of the D-Day despatch activities and the cruise ships (including two Cunarders) once laid up in this reach. It is provided for the curious by Peter Newman who came here in a very different era in 1934, catering for river steamers, running his own boats and serving the laid-up ships. At the time of writing, he still runs the restaurant.

Then across the Fal by Cornwall's most romantic ferry, the King Harry, just put up for sale. It is a short but deep crossing, ships laid up above and below. Trees come down to high-water mark reflected in the calm but gently flowing water, as is a gull taking a slow ride on a floating log. The ferry, with steep hills either side of the ferry, used to take the mail to and from Falmouth when as a packet port it was one of the main entrances to Britain. We hope the King Harry will find a good new owner who will enjoy running it. It is certainly busy this morning.

On the opposite side, we quickly climb past the National Trust's Trellisick Gardens, one of several famous ones long open to the public. This whole land is one of gardens. The further west we go, the lusher the vegetation. Council-owned public gardens are of a high standard, and many private houses have showy ones, but what we especially delight in is the way so many species thrive in the wild. Where there is protection from the southwest wind, trees grow tall, ferns flourish, and all the way to the Lizard Peninsula and Mount's Bay the hedgerows are resplendent with the richest variety of wild flowers you'll find anywhere in Britain. Those who consider Cornwall to be bleak have never sojourned in the valleys hereabouts.

We turn left to go through Feock down to Restronguet Point, where the creek of that name meets the Fal. Sheila recalls a holiday here fifty years ago, long before most of today's posh houses had been built. Taking a road marked 'Unsuitable for motors', we then follow the creek to Point, where a notice tells us that trains of packhorses brought copper ore from the Gwennap district for export to South Wales, while coal and timber for the mines, and limestone for the nearby kiln, were imported. And that later on, in 1827, the Redruth & Chasewater Railway was extended here from Devoran further up the creek, where there were problems with silt. Point Quay, closed since 1915, is now a Grade II listed structure managed by the Point Quay Association on behalf of Feock parish council. The continuing Old Tram Road follows the course of the railway, one of Cornwall's many independent industrial lines which only carried passengers on local holidays, when old and young crowded into mineral wagons. Carriages could not be borrowed from the main line railway since the gauge was different.

Lunch at the Old Quay Inn is tasty, and we like the way it celebrates the industrial past with displays of pictures and cuttings. Then through Devoran, another village that has moved sharply upmarket, to join the busy Truro-Falmouth road.

Falmouth and the Helford River

Falmouth is unusually free of traffic this Sunday morning. Though hotels continue rising and falling in standard, it generally looks more prosperous than when I was last here. That was to do a broadcast on a steam locomotive whose sole purpose seemed to be carrying rubbish round the dockyard, the link with the main railway already having been severed. It was a colourful example of how traditional industries were locked into extravagant practices. It reminds me of a visit to an ice-cream factory when I had the temerity to suggest new marketing methods. 'But we don't believe in marketing. If people don't want our ice cream, they can do without it.' They went out of business. Quite why, when Cornwall had been so commercially adventurous in the mining and pilchard-fishing age, attitudes became so entrenched it is hard to say. Maybe the Cornish didn't approve of anything English, like pushing your goods? Happily, ship repairing is now accompanied by luxury yacht building. Falmouth is said to be the world's second-largest natural harbour and in this morning's sun looks as though it could accommodate every ship afloat.

Living on the town's outskirts, and recovering from a replacement hip operation, is Sir Alan Dalton, who tells the not untypical story of how he came to be in Cornwall and found a job. 'I was on the beach at Mylor one day, dreaming of living here, and jokingly asked the harbour owner if he had anyone to run it. He pointed out a yacht run by someone connected with English China Clays and suggested I approach him. "They're all mad, the directors," this chap replied, but gave me the name of the one he thought least mad.' The result was a job. He worked his way up to chairman of ECC, and became a leading Cornish light – other appointments included director and then chairman of the British Rail Western Region Board.

I first met him in his railway capacity though I persuaded him to commission a history of ECC. Sir Alan proudly boasts that those initials, ECC, once were almost Cornwall's 'industrial theme song'. The industry went from strength to strength, a major employer and exporter, setting high standards such as courteous lorry drivers, and in increased dividends giving shareholders annual magic. On this trip I have repeatedly been told that things fell to pieces after Sir Alan's retirement in 1989. The business is now French owned and renamed but the Cornish refuse to call it other than the ordained ECC. Of BR, Sir Alan is not very kind. 'They couldn't get it together. For example, I kept saying we were pricing ourselves out of the market, but even when we demonstrated higher traffic and better profits when fares were slashed on suburban trains out of Paddington, the main Board never came back to us.'

Then by minor road to the north of Helford River to the privately owned Trebah Gardens beside the National Trust's Glendurgan which we have enjoyed on previous occasions. This really is gardeners' country, several of the hotels catering for visiting enthusiasts having their own plant paradises. Trebah, partly overlooked by a private house, is intimate enough to give you the feeling it might be you giving the head gardener his guidelines. The family cat accompanies us on part of our walk. The short publicity description is accurate: 'Dramatic, uniquely-beautiful sub-tropical 26-acre ravine garden running down to private beach on Helford River with water gardens, koi pool, waterfalls, colour all year.' A world apart in one of Britain's most beautiful corners, blessed – even compared with Truro – with mild weather, though defences against spring southeasterlies are very necessary. It is a garden which, if you take the high and low paths, has you constantly looking up and down, always satisfies but never overwhelms. Had I been born aristocratically rich, Heligan marvellous though it is, would have been too much, but Trebah I fancy, though where would I put a fruit cage? Our squirrel instincts are satisfied by picking up a few chestnuts.

One or two divine glimpses of the upper reaches of the Helford and next we approach Loe Pool by road. Though Tennyson's influence belongs to Tintagel, Loe Bar always reminds me of *Morte D'Arthur*:

> A broken chancel with a broken cross,
> That stood on a dark strait of barren land.
> On one side lay the Ocean, and on one
> Lay a great water, and the moon was full.

But vertigo prevents me from walking up the steep uneven steps on the way to the bar from Porthleven, though many take it in their stride and when I stumble there are instant offers of help. The wind is getting up; the baulks are firmly in place in Porthleven harbour's lock gate. We drive along the harbour's edge where a decade or two ago two policemen lost their lives when a powerful wave spilt over and washed their car into the outer harbour. There are memories everywhere: in Helston, through which we just passed, of the murder of the landlord a couple of nights after I had stayed at his inn; of the last night of the railway when, despite management assurances to the contrary, the last train left empty after a harassed guard provided next morning's headline 'It is advertised to run empty, and if you travel on it it won't be empty, will it?'; and of reporting sundry events at Culdrose airfield.

Porthleven in a Storm

Porthleven is one of those happy villages small enough to be intimate, large enough for hotel, shops, bus service and an active social life. The Harbour Inn is a predictable comedown after three nights at The Nare, but we didn't expect to be unable to close our bedroom door because the lock had stuck when it was opened. The visiting Norwegian airmen in the rooms opposite are, the owner says, 'a safe bet', meaning don't pose a risk. We can hear and see the steadily roughening sea and waves of infinite power crashing at the harbour entrance. Anyway we are out to dinner, our journey providing the excuse to renew another longstanding acquaintance. Tonight's homely meal without menu and waiter is most welcome.

Andrew Bell first wrote many years ago agreeing enthusiastically with one of my newspaper pieces. He is one of that declining race of great writers of supportive letters. He has had his clifftop house, which seems to rock in tonight's wind, since the days that the main road across Goss Moor was a dirt track. Then it was a holiday home, but he soon came to live here, having put everything he had into buying a ship whose first cargo was 600 tons of china clay. Though well removed from the centre of today's clay industry, Porthleven was the original china clay port; William Cookworthy's historic (c1746) discovery of the first large reserve was close by at Tregonning Hill.

Then Andrew founded Curnow Shipping, for a long time based in Porthleven, and ran the last remaining UK mail ship, serving the 5,000 people of St Helena 4,500 miles away, and once a year Tristan da Cunha, even more isolated. Both are still without airport. The current *St Helena* was the last ship ever to be built in Aberdeen. The five-year contract is nearly up, but Andrew has anyway been thrown out of his own company in a coup. Only yesterday, he says, settlement was reached, ahead of an Industrial Tribunal hearing. [Later it was announced that the government had preferred to contribute £26 million to an airport instead of subsidising a replacement for the Royal Mail ship *St Helena* in 2010.]

Harveys of Hayle bought and improved Porthleven harbour by building the long breakwater but, as we can tell from tonight's Southwester, it can never have been a particularly reliable refuge. It is twenty years since the last cargo of bulk fertiliser arrived, so it is now just fishing and sailing, while shipbuilding has declined to ship assembling. But the seafaring tradition continues through Andrew Bell's work, mainly consultation over the carrying of passengers by sea. It was curious to find him in Gavine Young's *Small Boat from China* which I recently read. We thank him and his wife for an evening to remember, and for his purchase of all those D&C books on ships, trains and industries packed into his clifftop library. So out into the storm to the Harbour Inn where the noise of rattling windows is drowned by that of the raging sea. We are grateful that the baulks at the entrance now prevent huge waves washing over the harbour walls.

THE FAR WEST

Mining and Methodism

This morning, first to the small village of Ashton, to see the bungalow rented for family holidays in the 1960s and once more briefly to enjoy the view: intricate fields, honeysuckle in full flower astride many lush hedgerows, and abandoned mines in the foreground, with the huge expanse of Mount's Bay as backdrop. Then by lanes as familiar as they are narrow, winding through Godolphin Cross to Leedstown, and along a B road from Leedstown to Hayle on the opposite side of the peninsula, with only about four miles of land between salt water at the narrowest point.

Often described as handmaiden to the Cornish industrial revolution, Hayle, with its famous Harvey's foundry, had the technology to make most mines practical and economic. The first piece of the Paddington to Penzance truck railway route to be built was from Redruth to the port of Hayle. Hayle was proud and important, servicing a vast hinterland.

The story of Cornish mining is long and complicated, but one cannot understand the county without a few of its basic facts. Even by 1801, 16,000 people were employed in 75 mines; by 1862 the labour force was over 50,000, working in 340 mines, the largest concentration being in the Redruth-Camborne area, though there were few parts without some underground activity. Three things made this rapid expansion possible: higher world copper prices; steam pumps, mainly provided by Hayle, to enable deeper lodes to be worked; and better transport, usually in the form of mineral tramways or railways to the nearest port. Most mines were small, family businesses or partnerships, working conditions and life expectancy awful. The other great traditional employment, seafaring, was of course scarcely safer.

Then came Methodism, whose great power produced the most unexpected of changes. One generation of heavy-drinking, vulgar and often unruly miners was replaced by the next of tea-drinking, chapel-building men whose most shocking attribute was a love of gaudy clothing and decoration.

Happy Camborne, happy Camborne.
Where the railway is so near
And the engine shows how water
Can accomplish more than beer

was what they sang in 1852 on the first of many teetotal excursions to Hayle, 79 mineral truckloads of happy Methodists pulled by three engines. Charles Wesley's influence was greater (certainly more astonishing) here than anywhere else. Not surprisingly, he loved the Cornish. Even when he was 86, some 25,000 people came to hear him preach at Gwennap Pit, an auditorium formed out of collapsed mines and terraced by his supporters.

Most famous among later Methodist leaders was Billy Bray. The story is told of how, when a preacher made the point that the joys of religion were not confined to heaven, Billy who was in the congregation responded 'Praise the Lord, I've felt them at 250,' meaning 250 fathoms down. One mine was even described as a Well of Salvation, the pious miners enjoying 'times of refreshing from the presence of the Lord'. If they did not die in accidents, men were rapidly worn out; at one time the life expectancy of those who went underground in their youth being only half the Biblical three score years and ten. But chapel was not just an escape, and neither was Cornish Methodism dour. Fun and the joy of life came shining through in a way not normally associated with Methodism, and certainly not enjoyed by Cornwall's small but 'superior' ruling class.

Not merely did the latter do everything it could to discourage the love of finery, condemning the waste of money or coquetry encouraged by packmen (travelling salesmen), but unfortunately any pastimes different or even uniquely local – and especially wrestling for which miners were noted – were seen as a bad influence and strongly criticised and often manipulatively stopped. Football, increasing in popularity, was the one recreation which was accepted as old boisterous pastimes were edged out. The love of finery actually developed because there was so much time to display oneself at chapel and at its frequent social gatherings, especially teas. Ministers, however, had to be plainly clad, certainly not wearing collars or gowns to give themselves airs. Things were ever different in Cornwall. Nowhere were Methodists happier, their dignified confidence perhaps epitomised by the line of walking mourners on their way to chapel paying their last respect to the departed with the 'burying tune':

'Sing from the chamber to the grave,'
I hear the dying miner say:
'A sound of melody I crave
upon my burial day.'

Then came catastrophe, especially in the mid-1800s. Firstly, the railway from England 'exported' cheap Cornish meat and fish to London, increasing the cost of living. There were food riots when the first trains crossed the Tamar in 1859. Next was the most serious of several mining crises, brought on by a sudden drop in the price of copper. That resulted in production being roughly halved in the 1860s. Later, even the pilchard shoals disappeared. They were grim days. The 'English railway' came into its own, carrying away thousands of miners to start a new life elsewhere.

As the price of copper dropped, the cost of working it rose. What was not realised was that, in the deepest lodes at about 1,000 feet, as copper became harder to find, there was tin underneath. When Cornish mining is mentioned today, people usually think of tin, but it was generally mined later than copper and, even where there might have been continuity of production, the opportunity was usually lost.

Though the old system of 'adventurers', local part-owners of mines, had worked well when conditions were reasonably stable – there had of course always been bumpy ups and downs – it could not cope with deep crisis. Under it, profits were split regularly on a cash basis, so any new development had to be financed afresh on a share basis, impossible for most to afford. The larger companies that steadily took over the remaining mines were able to marshal resources with banking aid, but the opposite side of that coin was that management became more distant and often less caring. That was to hurt in later troubled times. For example, having enjoyed high prices free from much overseas competition during World War One, the industry – now mainly tin – collapsed violently a few years after peace returned. In 1920 tin was at a then astonishing £400 a ton; two years later it was £141 a ton, or less than before the war, though coal had gone up more than threefold meanwhile. Within three years a flourishing Camborne was turned into an impoverished place where they had to turn off the street lighting since so few could afford their rates. It was only the Cornish togetherness of people helping each other, and earlier emigrants sending money home, that prevented suffering possibly worse than anywhere else in twentieth century Britain.

As the service centre, Hayle experienced fully the highs and the lows... especially at its eastern suburb of Copperhouse, at the end of Copperhouse Creek, partly turned into a canal. Ultimately even Hayle welcomed the railway's chief import, tourists, who enjoyed camping in various degrees of comfort on the vast Hayle Towans, and understood little, and probably cared less, about the industrial past. In my early days as a reporter, only a handful of historians took serious interest in mining and fishing. But many a lonely widow, outliving her husband by a generation or more, passed down some of the history and traditions, orally. Without those, Cornwall would be less colourful today.

As earlier in Ireland after its potato blight and famine, emigration divided many families. Though Cornish traditions might have been kept alive in mining settlements around the world, thousands of parents and children said their last farewells as the train came in to their local station and departing miners, hoping to fare better elsewhere, climbed on board. Especially was this true at Camborne and Redruth. From the late 1860s, many of those who went off to make their fortune (or more likely just to survive) sent occasional gifts home, but could spare neither time nor money for long voyages. Only in the age of air travel did return visits become practical. Yet as late as the 1970s and 1980s Britain, and especially Cornwall, was still lovingly called 'home' by those of the next generations.

The full poignancy was brought home to me when, in the late 1960s, I picked up two hitchhikers, New Zealand lasses, whose families had saved long and hard for their trip 'home'. In the Camborne district, I was privileged to be fly on the wall (so far as Cornish hospitality ever allowed that!) as the youngsters visited their respective uncles and aunts of their parents' generation and pieced together bits of their common heritage. There was familiarity with some of the names, and even a few personal idiosyncrasies or achievements of former relatives were well known. Yet generally they were scarcely more knowledgeable about each other's families and lives than total strangers happening to stand beside each other outside Buckingham Palace. What had endured was a feeling for the comradeship, the excitement but harshness, of copper and tin mining, obviously passed down orally 12,000 miles apart. And there was Methodism and teetotalism on both sides of the world.

It used to be said that wherever there is a hole in the ground, there will be Cornishmen or 'Cousin Jacks', the legacy of the great emigrations surviving, for example, in Minnesota, where at least one community of expatriates maintains a Cornish male voice choir, while in South Australia local customs are preserved in a 'Cornish triangle' of three towns. The skills of the Cornish miner have led to competitive head-hunting as the last handful of mines closed in recent years, and there is a world-wide respect for the School of Mines at Camborne, which has just won extra funding and is now a wing of Exeter University. There is excitement that one of the last mines to close, South Crofty, is scheduled to reopen, giving opportunity for some Cousin Jacks to return and for better hands-on practical experience for students at the School of Mines, close by. However, not even a single mine re-opening is universally welcome, and any major revival would be fought by environmentalists... and incomers who have escaped from industry on their doorstep elsewhere.

Cornwall's Cornwall

The man at the Engine Inn said: 'You're not really Cornish unless you're from west of Hayle River.'

> Seeing that the Engine Inn is at Cripplesease, about halfway between Splattenridden and Skillywadden and a good four miles west of Hayle, everyone present agreed. Folk from Camborne might just squeeze in, but people from Liskeard and Launceston, Falmouth and Truro, could as well be from Devon. Here in this final toe-joint of Britain, roughly fifteen miles long by five miles wide, was concentrated the real essence of Cornishness, perhaps the last drops of it. It was Cornwall's Cornwall, the very end of the very end. There are softer, more comfortable corners further east before you reach the Tamar, but west of Hayle River we like to think only the fittest have survived, people who greet each other on deserted January mornings with a special nod that means: 'We know.'

The quotation is from Gerald Priestland's introduction to a book he wrote, and his wife Sylvia illustrated, called *West of Hayle*. Priestland may be remembered by some as a former BBC religious affairs correspondent. He points out that should the sea rise, as when he wrote it was forecast to do by fifty feet, the Land's End peninsula or Penwith would become an island. To which one might respond that for centuries it has acted as though it is! I have often said that Penzance feels more like an island capital than the end of the railway from London. The rocky land to the west has always been rich in traditions and folklore. Mines were run differently here from the rest of Cornwall. The very value system is still more Cornish than Cornish. Had the peninsula been self-governing, there was a time in which its economy would have healthily balanced the books for, though the far west has always been poor, and beyond Penzance, architecture even more strictly functional than most of Cornwall's, mining prospered and fishing supported thousands of people on both its coasts. Land is mainly rocky but, especially from around Penzance, much of the early Cornish produce was grown, blessed by England's mildest climate. Even more, the climate has always been a special gift to the Scilly Isles, which in many ways feel part of the 'Island Kingdom' of Penwith.

Cornwall's Cornwall has an extraordinarily dense network of winding lanes but only two roads, the A30 which peters out at Land's End, and the direct route to St Just, give pretence of wishing to encourage those going from A to B. Visitors seeking to hug the coast find that, even in quiet times, it takes twice as long as they expect. On the way, however, they will enjoy dozens of granite crosses (neither truly Celtic nor as good quality as found in other parts, though if you know where to look there is a rich legacy of evidence of ancient days), see a profusion of wild flowers not even hinted at thirty miles to the east, and possibly notice a score or so of Methodist chapels, mainly closed and many ingeniously converted for other use. And that ignores the main attraction, the sea, in its many guises. Mind you, to enjoy the rich variety of cliffs, you need to sail round Land's End. No sizeable vessel does that to schedule, and landlubbers are wary of the stretch from Land's End to St Ives in a small boat.

The south shore, however, can be comfortably enjoyed from the *Scillonian* on its way from Penzance to St Mary's. From the ship, you can happily view the fishing fleet at Newlyn, the intimacy of Mousehole beyond St Clement's Isle, and the open-air theatre with its stage and tiers of seats cut out of solid rock at Minack near Porthcurno. Porthcurno is where the first Atlantic telegraph reached Britain, and where telegraph operators were first trained for overseas stations. It is now home to the Secret Wartime Telegraph Museum.

Once you are beyond Gwennap Head, look north to the west-facing cliffs and Land's End with the Longships and their lighthouse well offshore. The rocky Longships have claimed many ships, the most notorious wreck being that of the *Torrey Canyon* whose spilt cargo of oil caused widespread havoc to wildlife along the Cornish coasts. Those of us who have smelt beaches covered in oil with dead and dying birds will forever recall that, when hearing of an oil tanker in trouble anywhere in the world. As always, a wreck proved profitable to some, the *Torrey Canyon*'s propeller blades being seen on a quay at Penzance on their way to market. There is an assumed right to help yourself to artefacts from abandoned wrecks.

The Friendly Isles: The Scillies

Would that we were on the *Scillonian* this calm, sunny morning. Nowhere else in the world is as restorative as the Scillies, or 'The Friendly Isles' as they are affectionately nicknamed. Whenever I've had the good fortune to visit them, for work or pleasure, it has been so much easier to slip into their pace, leisured though gently purposeful, than to adjust to being back on the mainland. St Mary's, the main island, is wonderful for walking. Distances are just great enough to support tour bus and taxi, though most people are concentrated in the capital, Hugh

Town, with its surprising range of quality hotels. Hundreds of mainland people choose to live in today's Scillies, very different from the more utilitarian days when evening entertainment included listening to the bands of Atlantic liners on their way to New York. There is much friendship and social life, boating and golf; interest in wildlife and the islands' past being common denominators.

Good hotels are also to be found on St Martin's and on Tresco with its famous tropical gardens. In the early 1950s I was lovingly shown favourite trees and shrubs by the gardens' owner, Arthur Dorien-Smith, near the end of his life, who sorrowfully regretted that the twelve gardeners had had to be reduced to six, more than I am sure there are today. But my favourite island has always been Bryher, only separated by a narrow channel from Tresco, but totally different. In the 1950s, with an indigenous population of less than a hundred and tight development constraints, it was seen as the world's last surviving piece of relatively undisturbed Neolithic culture. Though more recently development has been delicately controlled, even Bryher is now of this world, and I suppose I should admit to playing part in popularising it with our books on the Scillies. On getting off the little boat from Tresco one March morning, I was told 'Café's open, up north end'. What a delight to find the owner busy unpacking a large consignment of our books ordered for the coming season. The boxes contained the first copies of John Arlott's *An Island Camera*, using the marvellous photographic legacy of three generations of the Gibson family. A publisher's dream to colonise so remote a spot, yet scarcely Neolithic.

Reporting planning matters in the Scillies was a special pleasure and for a period I was adviser to the Isle of Scilly Steamship Company. My recommendation that they should not commission a second ship went unheeded. The ship soon had to be sold at a loss. It is the nature of transport that, unless you are prepared to turn down excess traffic at peak times, you will lose money much of the year. Yet the local company's desire to support the economy, with extra capacity for daffodils when in their flush and another summer Saturday crossing for visitors, was admirable. However in the slack midweek time even in high summer, the second ship of shallow draught was not really needed and so did occasional cruises that were not well-supported. One, having no cargo and only half a dozen passengers, from St Ives to Penzance was memorable for close-ups of huge waves fiercely crashing against the northern shore. Alas, for most people the desire to explore the coast by sea is less than the fear of feeling sick; and it has to be admitted that even the Penzance-St Mary's trip, though much quicker than formerly, is often bumpy. One used only to be able to fly from Land's End airport to St Mary's, but now a single helicopter based in Penzance includes occasional flights direct to Tresco as well as frequent ones to St Mary's, while there are summer plane flights from several places like Exeter to St Mary's. Within the islands, everything is by small boats and those journeys can also be distinctly exhilarating.

Penzance

Penzance is undoubtedly my favourite English town. It is a place of substance, the end of the railway, starting point for the *Scillonian* and the Scillies' helicopter. The capital of the far west, it is very Cornish and a true working town, too busy ever to have been totally dedicated to tourists. Maybe it is the scale and business of its harbour that gives it that feel of capital of an island kingdom. The lush vegetation certainly stresses the difference from the 'mainland'. Even from before the days that more adventurous visitors began basing themselves here, daily to explore by bicycle, it has attracted those interested in vegetation, rocks, scenery, history and the arts. Distinguished people born here include Sir Humphrey Davy, inventor of the miners' safety lamp, while authors such as WH Hudson have enjoyed fruitful sojourns.

It is most famous for its artists, though they mainly drew their inspiration from adjoining Newlyn and Mousehole. Mainly, but not totally, for two of my favourite pictures are of Penzance itself. The first, by Norman Garstin, shows the broad promenade with a few walkers bent into the wind, battling with their umbrellas, the sea splashing in the distance. It is called *The Rain It Raineth*. The other, by Stanhope A Forbes, is of people boarding an express shortly to depart for 'England' from the railway station with its ugly overall roof. These passengers are totally different from today's matter-of-fact travellers, while the station we pass on our way into the town today is little changed from the picture. Both prints were bought from the Morrab Studio at the top of Morrab Road, one of many good individual shops.

The Spaniards invaded briefly in 1595 and burned the town, so there is little ancient architecture. But even before the Napoleonic Wars Penzance was attracting the cultured, and some of those who were then forced to switch their allegiance from Baden Baden or Florence chose regularly to return to Penzance after peace was reached. That gave culture a critical mass, with art, theatre, assembly rooms, and beautifully-kept gardens. That in turn encouraged many visitors to become permanent residents who built quality villas and exploited the mild climate with exotic gardens.

When I first came here at the end of the 1940s, the contrast between workaday but largely unemployed Redruth-Camborne and cultured Penzance made you feel you were in another world. There seemed to be continual business at station, harbour, the Trinity House base, and across the bay at Newlyn, while in the other direction it has always been hard to take your eyes off the view of St Michael's Mount. Despite the view, the wide and long promenade is perhaps Penzance's least-impressive feature. The lack of sandy beaches, as well as its occupation with more workaday pursuits, still keeps tourism in check.

The gardens always repay study, and so does much of the town's Georgian and Regency heritage. Look, for example, at the scale of the Town Hall, and at Lloyds Bank and the market place with its great columns at the head of the main street, Market Jew. That is now one-way, but for many years was a two-way bottleneck. The only time I was cheered by a large street crowd was when a Western National bus caught the back bumper of my Morris Eight and dragged it down the street. It stopped. I stopped. The whole of Penzance stopped. A policeman arrived to take details, while the bus driver worried about his career.

'Can't we just forget it?' I asked.

'Not if you want to claim on insurance,' said the bobby. When I replied that it didn't seem worth holding up Penzance any longer, the bus driver shouted that I was a gentleman and shook my hand vigorously. Hundreds cheered, and continued to do so as the driver arranged the bumper inside my ageing car. Somehow it was so different than had it happened say in Newquay. As I walked round the town later, people (mainly local, but some visitors) who recognised me still smiled. Penzance has always been warmhearted.

Much of the warmth is (or at any rate used to be) drawn from Methodism. Wonderful Chapel Street takes its name from the pretentious Italianate Wesleyan Chapel of 1864, the cathedral of Methodism in the far west. As with the Church of Scotland, it has long attracted the heart of society though not the top establishment. To preach in Chapel Street has always been an honour for any Methodist bigwig, as well as for local preachers normally allocated more humble chapels. And in times past, theatrical indeed were many of their twenty-minute-plus sermons and their extempory prayers. The comparison with the Church of Scotland is perhaps unfair, for there was nothing so sombre here, but a joyous faith, congregations ever ready to respond with Hallelujahs. For all that, the chapel breaks the continuity of what is generally a street to be savoured, with both Georgian and Regency buildings. Treasures include the National Trust's mock-Egyptian House, next to the excellent bookshop which has often engaged in local publishing, fine antique shops, restaurants, the Union Hotel, Admirable Benbow pub, and zesty maritime museum – its colourful founder, Rowland Morris, long ago presented me with a Piece of Eight brought up from a wreck. A particularly enjoyable TV slot was about Chapel Street's delights. I have always enjoyed sleeping, eating and shopping in it as well as marvelling at its rich mix of buildings.

There is quite a lot of Penzance, including the pedestrianised main shopping street. And it is a wonderful centre, especially if you have a car. The alternative hilly minor road to St Ives through Nancledra is another joy. St Michael's Mount is approached by causeway at low tide, ferry at high. Eight double-decker buses were needed to take the 500 day excursionists from London we attracted on several occasions in a David & Charles/National Trust joint venture. Such was the organisation that four parties each of 125 caught no glimpse of each other while on the Mount exploring and enjoying their cream teas. An early seat of Christianity, it bears a notable likeness to Mont-Saint-Michel off the coast of Brittany.

Fishing Exploits and Today's Pilchard Works

While in Penzance, nobody should (or judging by the amount of traffic ever does) forget Newlyn and Mousehole. Despite its art galleries, Newlyn is still a great fishing port, and it has to be said that visitors and large-scale fishing don't mix happily. That is certainly the experience of Nick Howell who, though at the time of writing is chairman of the Cornish Association of Tourist Attractions ('We apply a stringent quality test with 34 [locations] attracting 2.7 million visitors annually: on average each goes to 1.8 attractions'), is so far only achieving 14,000 to 18,000 of the 30,000 budgeted at his Pilchard Works.

A pity, for many who do visit the joint factory and museum start eating the oily fish supposed to be excellent for health. 'The difficulty is people can't park. Even if there's room, they have to give way to a forklift truck and feel unwelcome, as though they're in an industrial environment. Many just move on.'

He adds: 'Newlyn is England's largest port for English fishing boats, landing many kinds of fish, roughly 11,000 tons, or £21,000,000 a year. But fishing isn't quite what it was. The attitude of the industry is "go out and take it", fishermen and merchants viewing each other as the "plunder machine". Its all too high-pressured, and few of today's fishermen have the skills of yesteryear.'

At least this morning's sunshine makes the harbour look romantic. True, examining the boats emphasises that fishing has become high-tech, and there isn't a commercial sailing vessel in sight. Neither for that matter is there a large boat loading granite from Penlee quarry to the west, over which there used to hang a constant mist of dust, a feature captured in many old photographs. For decades one of the busiest, though narrow-gauge, railways in Britain ran between the quarry and the ship currently loading stone. Every two or three minutes a train of full wagons passed one of empties at a loop. Even the enclosed conveyor belt that replaced the trains has gone – along with laden lorries that used to thunder along the seafront waking visitors in early morning. The quarry was closed when its remaining stone was said to be too hard for road building.

Pilchards were once *the* Cornish fish, huge shoals darkening the water and conveniently splitting at Land's End to give fishermen on both coasts a share of the bounty at every cove or beach from which it was safe to launch a boat. It was a seasonal business, the shoals arriving around the end of June and staying for about four months. The chasing, catching, salting, packing and despatching of the small oily pilchards (adult sardines) provided employment for thousands of folk. It needed heavy investment and was as uncertain as mining, profits yo-yo-ing The most profitable month was October 1862 when just one seine, *St Ives's Good Intent*, made what would then have been a monumental profit of £13,125 after expenses (including £1,300 worth of salt). But a few years later another landing which promised to be another bumper profit was lost along with many boats in an unexpected storm. Such uncertainty suited the Cornish temperament. Occasional drownings, and deaths through rock falls in mines, have always been viewed as part of the natural order of things. Anyway, what other work was there, especially in the far west with its generally unfertile land?

It was easier to spot the fish and their direction of travel from land, so a key player was the huer who, on a vantage point and distinctly clad, gave hand signals (or at a few locations operated a semaphore) to guide the seiners. 'Heeva!' shouted the huer. 'Heeva, heeva!' rang in the air as men, women and children excitedly emerged from their cottages to join in the action and relief that the pilchards were back, especially at the season's start. Said a St Ives eye-witness in the 1870s:

> The fishermen in their heavy boots, lumbered past at top speed: question and answer were shouted across the road; but, over all nearer sounds, we heard, from half-a-mile away, the boom-boom of the speaking trumpets as huers shouted their hoarse commands. The welcome alarm had come at last.

A shoal of half a million fish might be caught in a day, but to ensure freshness only as many fish as could be processed immediately would be landed, the others kept netted in the water. The seines, with traditional names like *Poor Man's Adventure*, consisted of three boats, two nets and cellars on land. The leading vessel of each seine needed seven or eight men to shoot the primary net round the shoal, the second one carrying the tuck net to lift the fish out of the water. Things were directed by the master seiner from the third, faster boat who, when necessary, looked to the huer for guidance.

On land, in the curing cellars (sometimes called palaces) 'bulking' was usually women's work. Fish were laid tails inward, in salt that was imported in prodigious quantities. Some fish were consumed locally, but most was sold as a 'cash crop' to Mediterranean countries, where the demand was heaviest especially for their Lenten fasts. By 1871, the peak year, when 16,000 tons were exported (that was just before the collapse of copper mining), there were nearly 400 seines, Mounts Bay/Newlyn and St Ives having the largest number on their respective coasts. St Ives was a much more important fishing port in seining days, Newlyn gaining ascendancy when drift fishing (for pilchards further from shore, and deep-water fish) became the norm. The pilchard shoals then arrived less reliably, and early in the twentieth century the industry was in sharp decline.

Though not in such huge shoals, pilchards are still in the sea waiting to be caught – and there is no quota. The Newlyn Pilchard Works absorbs about 300 tons annually, and surprises visitors because essentially it is a working place. 'That doesn't go down well with the authorities these days,' regrets Nick. 'We had a real struggle to get going, and were constantly told it would be easier to get grants if we closed down and formed a trust for a museum. Some pilchards are exported in the time-honoured way, in fact some to the same Italian family customer as started buying them four generations ago. But steadily we are exploiting the heritage and the health value of the pilchard and the multiples are taking more fish, in jars of olive oil. It is going well. We have a mail-order business too for those who want to stay healthy, especially if they have a heart problem. You just need to forget the standard pilchard in tomato sauce we had as kids. It's a marvellous fish that can be used in all sorts of ways. I think more boats should fish for pilchards but they concentrate on more expensive fish. The value might be greater, but so are the costs and I'm not sure it's always more profitable.'

Then on to picture postcard Mousehole (listen to how the locals pronounce it, something like Mouzzel), a more typically cosy Cornish harbour. This morning we cannot find a resting point, not even a Micra space for Little Car, and so only briefly enjoy its narrow streets. A group of retired fishermen are basking in the sun, no doubt mulling over happier times when the harvest from the sea was more plentiful and quotas unheard of. Penzance looks splendidly inviting across the blue sea, and that is where we briefly return, before regretfully abandoning the coast for a quicker inland trip to the furthest west.

The Most Westerly Town

When people were less blasé about travel, roads used to be the subject of many articles and books, the story of the A30 being specially popular. We are unfashionable in recounting our memories of the 'up country'

A30 as we enjoy the rural wanderings toward its termination at Land's End. Land's End itself is now too commercialised to be savoured, so we turn down to archetypal Cornish Sennen Cove, once thriving on pilchards, before briefly retracing our steps to take the B road past Land's End miniature aerodrome and head north to St Just.

St Just in Penwith: the most westerly town in England and traditionally one of the poorest, with for many years the lowest proportion of homes with running water and indoor sanitation in all England – a one-industry (mining) town that until recently most guide books suggested tourists ignore. Most did drive through as quickly as possible, amazed, if not downright annoyed, to find such a place spoiling their preconceived idea of the far west. Yet for the minority prepared to invest time in getting to know it, it is one of the friendliest and most fascinating places. Like the very different St Just in Roseland with which its mail is often confused, it is named after Justus (not the Archbishop of Canterbury Justus) thought to have been a twelfth-century martyr. While such places seem remote today, they were more accessible to the early Christians and traders centuries ago when the sea was the only highway.

Of course, when I first came, only half a century ago, it was by land – for a BBC West Region programme called Faith in the West, to investigate local Methodism. There were then nineteen chapels in three rival circuits: the Wesleyan Methodists, the Bible Christian Methodists and the Primitives. There wasn't much animosity, just deeply-held beliefs and traditions. Then I was asked for newspaper pieces about why St Just was so poor, what was different about it, how its pioneer comprehensive school was performing, and the life and times of local mining, right to the final local mine closure, Geevor, following another crash in tin prices in 1986. Impossible competition, coming from South America's virtually opencast mines, put the last 300 West Cornwall miners out of work.

Everything has always been different in St Just and district. During most of my journalistic career, it had its own Urban District Council, where, in a spartan upstairs office in a back street, the clerk ran things in the time-honoured way of dealing with most callers himself and taking instant action, such as ensuring a blocked culvert was rapidly freed. An anachronism with just 5,000 population it might have been, and with so much poor and desolate property the rate yield was meagre, but the council served the needs of a town completely different from the surrounding countryside.

Even the mines were run on their own different management and technical lines, while geography certainly added to distinctiveness. Alone among the major mining districts, St Just lacked railway or port, so everything had to be taken by road to Penzance, first by packhorses, then carts, next by 'trains' of wagons drawn by traction engines and, finally, lorries. The mines were deep, and several stretched well out under the sea, the sound of stones rolling on the seabed clearly heard by miners when the Atlantic was angry. Pictures of desolate engine houses and other buildings on the cliff's edge appear in thousands of books and postcards but that was mainly after the miners had left and industry ceased to be threatening. Botallack's two engine houses (now restored), crouching on a ledge close to the sea, are especially famous, and it's worth going out from St Just to Cape Cornwall, which offers more spectacular cliff views than those at Land's End, and the remains of the most westerly of English mines.

Another famous mine of the string, with parallel territory including a sloping hinterland down to the cliffs and undersea workings, was Levant. It suffered one of Cornwall's worst disasters when the 'man-engine' collapsed and 31 miners were killed at a change of shift. The man-engine was devised to take miners to ever deeper levels. A large notched framework was attached to a cylinder moving up and down one level at each stroke of the engine, men lowering themselves or coming back to the surface by repeatedly stepping on and off. Levant's misfortunes also included the sea coming in through a fissure. The underwater hole was valiantly plugged in the 1960s, when the mine became part of the expanding Geevor whose own reserves were becoming exhausted.

Changing times are immediately obvious as we enter St Just. Bank Square has only one bank left. More basic shops have closed (there's a free bus to Tesco), but galleries and other tourist attractions opened. There is even a St Just 'art and craft' leaflet listing nearly a dozen galleries. B&B notices, once conspicuous by their absence in this corner of Cornwall, have sprouted and, whereas I remember only one café with limited hours, you are now spoilt for cream-tea choice. Above all, there are fewer people abroad, no old men gently chatting on the benches outside Plan-an-Gwarry, the amphitheatre enclosed by earth and stone banks where mediaeval miracle plays were performed in the Cornish language until the end of the seventeenth century.

St Just has always been good for a perspective on history and the shortness of human life. The retired miners I made friends with sitting on those benches (occasionally one was taken up by old women with their separate agenda) in the 1950s and 1960s must long have passed away and probably many of the next generation too. Shy at first, but warming when you showed you cared about their traditions, they lived and breathed the underground life and were never at a loss for another recollection of individual exploit and eccentricity. Yet many would have died earlier of accident, disease or sheer wear and tear had more mines remained open. Though hardly anyone seems to be venturing abroad this morning, and so the pavements seem an unnecessary luxury, you can tell from the planned street layout, especially round a second square, that St Just really was a town deserving its own administrative status.

Lunch at Geevor Mine and Rural Slums

As one means of gauging how things have changed, we have invited the Methodist minister, Katherine Smith, to lunch. After picking her up outside her modern manse, we get talking about rural slums, though today indoor sanitation is standard, and about the drop in population. The comprehensive school's number of pupils is forecast to drop from 620 to 400. 'These aren't easy days. You could say there is unhealthy nostalgia. Geevor closed ten years ago, but things haven't moved on much. There are still many people around St Just adjusting. But in some ways it's a lively little place – a lot goes on. A theatre group put on a mystery play, performed in the old amphitheatre, and the St Just Festival is going strong. We put on a feast and bazaar and people still have a special meal at home on St Just's Day. Perhaps nowadays that is more a dress-rehearsal for Christmas, but it used to be the holiday when families sat down together, and miners who'd gone overseas to earn their living did their best to come home and still be part of things.'

Methodism, she confirms, has suffered continual decline. Her circuit now has nine buildings between Pendeen and St Buryan in which services are still held at least occasionally, though in St Just there is also one chapel still not recognising the Methodist Union of the 1930s. 'They use our hymn book but not our theological college.' Even the usual congregation at the circuit's key St Just chapel is now only in the upper twenties, nearly all retired folk. She talks of a wave of apathy, and today is obviously downhearted, yet the circuit newsletter, *Crossroads*, is full of depth, enterprise and fun, events listed for young and old. It is a far cry from her youth in Truro, when 150 attended ordinary Sunday School and the annual 'Praisemakers' outing needed fourteen buses. So many ministers are now trained for inner-city work that it is good to see someone happy to tackle rural deprivation. It surely needs to be seen as a separate discipline. But then St Just was always a one-off, and Katherine, vivacious but obviously mercurial, suits it well.

These thoughts are shared after we arrive at our lunch venue, the coffee shop at the Geevor mine, a few miles to the north and now a lively tourist attraction with the advantage of the atmosphere, staff and smells of productive days. 'The Geevor Experience' is skilfully done by the Trevithick Trust. You can go well underground, and in a range of buildings can learn much about mining hereabouts, its complexity and how it changed over its long history. There are lots of ore samples, and it is explained how stamping noisily extracted the ore with equipment from Holman's of Hayle. It is a real experience rather than a museum, and the enthusiasm of the retired miners to explain their trade really helps. So do the many photographs, including those of royal visitors venturing underground and demonstrating how important mining once was. Lunch is a large Cornish pasty supplied to cafés and shops over a large part of Cornwall by Warren's Bakery, the largest remaining employer in St Just.

After a brilliant morning following last night's storm, the wind has come back and we return to St Just where we hardly meet a soul as we explore. Nor are there customers in any of the craft and art shops lining narrow Fore Street, about the last place in the world one would once have expected to find such shops. When a picture in the window of The Turn of the Tide Studio grabs our attention, we are almost surprised to find someone ready to welcome us. Gabrielle Hawkes shows us some of her own work (we buy a couple of postcards of one of her paintings) but the picture we are interested in is that of her partner, Tom Henderson-Smith: a dramatic view north toward a mizzly Atlantic with promontories and a distant mine chimney looking as though they are only transitorily there, with a true Atlantic Cornish green mixture of intricate fields in the foreground. He's out painting on what's become another afternoon of driving drizzle, but telephones later to offer a discounted price if he can retain the picture for his one-man exhibition in St Ives two-thirds of a year hence. We have a reduced-size print to savour meanwhile. It is good to support someone who delights in 'coastal forms and the endless drama of skies over the Atlantic'. For those born and bred here, it must be hard not to look back; new life and vitality inevitably means incomers and not altogether welcome change.

The Romantic Coast to St Ives

Back through the once-populous mining field through Botallack and Pendeen, we are on our way to St Ives. Many lovers of coastal Cornwall would say this was their favourite section, the path passing a succession of such outstanding headlands as Pendeen Watch, Gurnard's Head and Zennor Head, with a rich selection of historic and more recent ruins and points of geological interest, including granite veins penetrating slate at Porthmeor Cove just beyond Zennor Head. The twisting road often opens up fine vistas, but this afternoon clouds of ever thicker mizzle roll in from the Atlantic and at each bend in the road we look forward to reaching St Ives and enjoying a cream tea.

For old time's sake we have booked (not without trepidation since the new regime isn't customer friendly on the phone) at the former Great Western and British Transport Hotel, Tregenna Castle, once the only four-star hotel in Cornwall. Its core is of 1774 vintage, a private house. Ribbentrop was said to fancy it as his English country home when Germany 'won the war'. Apparently he enjoyed a pre-war stay. It used to be marvellous. This afternoon all is not well. A caricature of a receptionist is more interested in her nails than attending to us or answering the phone. There is no sign of a cream tea or indeed any kind of tea. 'You make your own in your room.' Our bedroom has been requested because of its fabulous outlook, but there is a new raised area forcing you to sit without being able to look out. A previous guest has obviously lost his temper with the door, while a GWR tap – the GWR went out of existence in 1947 – comes off in my hand. It is not today's obvious quality choice.

Looking around the hotel makes me want to cry, for disappointment and nostalgia for how it used to be are intense. In some places what seems to be old BTH carpet is threadbare, while everywhere the fittings and furniture strike one as inappropriate. The long line of the hall, which the BTH interior designers turned into a pleasant feature, has been broken up by a couple of pot plants. The ageing, subtle pastel colour scheme has to compete with a gaudy cart spewing tourist literature, hard to reach under its awning. The phone goes on ringing.

Dinner does nothing to improve first impressions. Our room number is demanded four times. The music is ear-achingly distorted, reducing the family at the next table to helpless giggles. The fish promised at the buffet isn't there. The telephone rings endlessly, unanswered. There are no spoons for coffee in the lounge. At breakfast the only fruit is prunes, and coffee cups are not replenished. At dinner on our second night the same music is still distorted, and again no spoons laid out for coffee... and I daren't ask (there is nobody to ask anyway) for tea instead. The privatisation of the railway hotels was mentioned in the Introduction. I just wish Mrs Thatcher had been here in Tregenna Castle's heyday and was forced to stay again now. However half-term family parties seem happy enough, the children positively bubbly, and patronage is certainly better than in BTH days and things might have improved since our visit.

I first came to St Ives by the long-abandoned row-boat ferry from Hayle, where the harbour was still thriving, to Lelant, and on by train hugging the cliffs overlooking the Atlantic with that famous deep blue turning to azure as the waves gently broke over the white sand of successive beaches. The stationmaster who opened the carriage door said 'Welcome to Great Western on Sea'. A picture in my small gallery of transport art shows the

Cornish Riviera Express, diverted here on summer Saturdays, disgorging holidaymakers, some of whom would no doubt spend much of the next fortnight on the beach beside the station.

Fish, Art and Lifeboat Call

Murray's *Hand-Book* describes how those arriving by horse-drawn vehicle would react:

> By road St Ives is brought suddenly to view, when the stranger will probably draw the rein and rest awhile in admiration. Its old rickety houses lie nestling on the very skirt of the sea, and with the blue of sky and ocean, the green tints of the shallows, and the sparkle of the bright yellow sandy shore, altogether form a very pleasing picture. The traveller may gaze at this gem of western scenery with yet greater interest when he learns that it has been compared, as seen from this point, with a Greek village; and it must be admitted that 'the charm of blended and intermingled land and sea, the breaking waves and changing brightness of the resounding ocean, amidst picturesque cliffs richly tinged with aërial hues,' which have been said to characterise Grecian scenery, here lend their aid to complete the resemblance. A descent into the streets, or rather lanes, will, however, somewhat qualify his admiration, although in this respect there is no want of resemblance to the Greek type. The town is the headquarters of the pilchard fishermen and therefore tainted with the effluvia of the cellars.

Added to that, one of Cornwall's richest mines was close by, and so the harbour was a busy place. Tourism initially grew mainly with railway families, since Great Western workers could travel free anywhere on the company's system and St Ives gave the longest journey. It was especially popular with those at 'the works' in Swindon.

From the Tregenna Castle we enjoy looking down to the Island with its chapel, floodlit at night. In the morning our walk down the garden, past the bus station, down the steps and along the footpath beside the beaches to the harbour, and finally through the narrow streets of tightly-packed and now much-upmarketed fishermen's cottages to the Island, is as enjoyable as ever and shows the town in good fettle. Half-term holiday has brought out the crowds. It has become one of the year's busiest weeks since, increasingly, those who go abroad for their main holiday come to Cornwall for a second one. Incredible to think that, had an idea of the 1950s been adopted, many of the visitors might be in caravans on the Island, happily still an open, green area (where in former times fishermen laid out their nets).

Local outrage didn't however prevent the War Office pulling down the chapel at the seaward tip in 1904. The original was built in 1434, and in 1538 a traveller recorded: 'There is now at the point of Pendinas a chapel of St Nicholas and a pharos for lighte for shippes sailing by night in these quarters.' The chapel was rebuilt by a local ship owner to commemorate George V's Coronation. Local churches co-operate to take responsibility for spiritual care, while the physical side has been taken over by the recently-formed National Coastwatch Institution. Local volunteers have moved into the former Coastguard's station, one of dozens closed around our coasts. Explains one of the volunteers: 'There are still 85 registered fishing vessels in St Ives and (mainly) Hayle, and it's easy to get into trouble over Hayle Bar or out at sea when the weather suddenly changes. We don't have a statutory role, but keep an eye open and work with the Coastguard Service in Falmouth, who co-ordinate any rescue.'

Back in the chapel, we note several recent improvements and the many overseas visitors' signatures in the visitors' book. 'It's sure windy,' writes one from Florida. Back between the fishermen's cottages, we see that this is a no-alcohol zone. A tabby cat begs to be stroked; seconds later one of the few people we hear with a Cornish voice says: 'You've made a friend.' Out on the pier, there is an octagonal lookout with cupola, part of the eighteenth century original by Smeaton (best known as builder of the Eddystone Lighthouse). Suddenly – Bang! Bang! We watch the smoke of two rising rockets. The lifeboat has been called out. The crew start arriving it seems within seconds, though the vessel is already nearing the water when the last two run to clamber aboard. Practice or real alarm? We see her disappear at speed round Godrevy Point up the coast toward Newquay, but two hours later watch her return, be picked up by an amphibian trailer drawn by tractor at the Smeaton's Pier end of the beach and come back along it and up the slip for a thorough washing down with military precision. One of the crew explains they have been off Hell's Mouth to see if they could retrieve a body reported floating under those gruesome cliffs, 'but it's too dangerous to get close enough'.

Many of the best books on all kinds of aspects of Cornish life were written by Cyril Noall, a retiring person whose poor sight sometimes made him seem standoffish though he was the warmest and least assuming of men. His sight prevented academic life but, from middle age until his death aged 65, he produced a stream of studies of many aspects of Cornish life, handling complicated material with rare clarity and vision. A Bard of the Cornish Gorsedd, he was one of the founders of St Ives Museum, and I have happy memories of meeting and interviewing him on the radio. Cornwall has been lucky in such historians, most of whom were local people (Noall was a product of Penzance Grammar School) though relying heavily for support from incomers.

And so to the museum which is opposite Smeaton's Pier. The story of the building itself is remarkable. Originally stone was dug out for the pier, making the site ideal for a pair of limekilns. Later a pilchard palace was added, and later again this was extended with a pressing ledge: pilchard oil was standard for railway lamps including those in carriages in pre-dynamo days. Then the pilchard cellar successively became a Bible Christian chapel, a laundry, and a cinema, the upstairs finally accommodating a British Sailors' Society mission, where fishermen played billiards when it was too rough to go to sea. When the Sailors' Mission pulled out in 1969, the museum was founded, and now lovingly tells the story of the town's ever-changing times. See the pilchard pressing stones and how oil was channelled, glance at the stocks in which in 1864 three boys were incarcerated for daring to play marbles on the Sabbath – there was once a fight at the harbour to prevent 'up country' fishermen landing their catch on the day of rest – and admire the Victorian engineering of the clockwork mechanism that kept the 2,000,000 candle power of Pendeen lighthouse shining without failure for seventy years. A cut above most museums, it is run devotedly by Brian Stevens and his wife – 'we tick with one heart' – and pays loyal homage to Cyril Noall: no 'not invented here' syndrome. Brian is as Cornish as they come, but regrets it is mainly incomers who have 'more zeal for the old days than local people'.

Though acknowledging it is an interesting building in a super situation, the St Ives Tate remains controversial. Since I've found little of interest in the past it is easy to miss it today. Sheila cannot, but when we meet later is – surprise – unenthusiastic about the pictures, though likes the row of television sets simulating waves breaking on a beach (useful I suppose if you haven't time to enjoy the real thing) and admires the ceramics. But then she finds much more of interest in the windows of other galleries and tourist shops – better quality than a decade or more ago – of the main shopping street. There is of course far more art outside the Tate than in it, though nothing matches the picture we bought in St Just yesterday! Despite our experience at Tregenna Castle, many hotels have obviously improved their quality, St Ives carving itself an individual role in tourism. Once it was overwhelmed with Newquay's day trippers just coming to gawk. Now conversation on the park-and-ride train from Lelant represents the new English middle class who have gained the confidence to know what they like and make sophisticated comparisons.

As a crowd alights from the single carriage at the much-reduced station, someone I shall always remember seeing play tennis as a supple young woman, a new recruit to my staff, stops to confirm I'm not my double. She and her architect husband have come back by train having walked to Lelant. There is much to catch up on over a cream tea though predictably she avoids the cream. One of three staff who between them served D&C for the best part of a century, she has suddenly been made redundant. 'Old faces no longer fit. It's a sad place now.' But I recall that even in happier days there was opposition to my taking her back when, soon after marriage, her husband was based for a spell away from Devon. With maternity breaks, in all she served five separate terms as in-house trained production assistant, and if I were still running things I'd have her start again tomorrow. But she is more shocked at the sacking of our equestrian editor than at her own.

As we turn out the lights at bedtime, we look at the harbour and imagine what it must have been like when it was lit by dozens of boats in their quest for pilchards. With or without boats, and whatever the current craze in human endeavour, St Ives will always be a very special place.

· X I I I ·

THE NORTH
CORNISH COAST

Along the Atlantic

Two themes are ever present on the journey from St Ives to Newquay, Padstow and Bude: the Atlantic's constant influence, and changes wrought on the scenery by man. These range from the burial mounds and fortifications of Bronze Age settlers on the headlands, through ruins great and small in varying states of decay (a few artificially preserved) of Cornish mines, to the sometimes hideous bungalows and caravan and chalet estates of today.

First we have to go around the Hayle Estuary. That is always a pleasurable combination with occasional glimpses of sea, cliff and estuary, and recollection's of Hayle's former industrial greatness. Copperhouse! What evocations of good and bad mining days. Then past the Towans and back to the coast.

Our road passes close by Hell's Mouth with its frightening chasm; the sea boiling over rugged rocks. A stop has become *sine qua non*, but today we don't want to risk seeing the body they failed to retrieve yesterday. Fine views of the coast, blue sea and white waves and foam dashing against the cliffs, can be savoured even from the car at one of the informal lay-bys on Reskajeage Downs. We are now only a few miles from the heart of Cornish mining. The steep descent into Portreath with its neat, manmade harbour basin used to be something to look forward to visiting. There was often a boat loading and the harbour master always ready with a tale of the old days. Cornwall's very first railway descended here as early as 1810. Modern housing now surrounds the harbour, long abandoned by commercial traffic, but there is a steady pilgrimage of industrial archaeologists.

Next comes Perranporth, again with vast sands and campsites and a neat shopping street that has improved since my first visits. At the northern end of the sands is Holywell, home to Chris Blount, now of

Radio Cornwall, but earlier with Plymouth-based regional radio, and before that a Spotlight South West TV cameraman. The first time we spoke was many decades ago when he stepped shyly from behind his camera to tell me that he, too, was a railway lover. In the 1970s and early 1980s, we treated ourselves, and the West Country public, to a series of roving transport reporter pieces, discovering oddities such as a steam locomotive hauling waste paper around Falmouth Docks, and supplies taken to the top of St Michael's Mount by an underground, narrow-gauge inclined tramway. Gentle and truly Cornish, Chris now rarely crosses the Tamar but is much loved by an exceptionally loyal radio audience. Once he extolled the joys of Newquay but, as we will discover in a moment, concluded it was no longer a safe place to live.

Newquay: Capital of Surfing

The approach to Newquay is gently deceptive. Crantock is a delightfully unspoilt village with a sandy beach sandwiched between Pentire Points West and East. Near the East flows out (or in at rising tide) the Gannel, possibly the least known of Cornish estuaries even though just round the corner from the county's chief resort. On the Newquay side, new housing overlooks it, as does a whole suburb stretching toward Pentire Point East. The Gannel is not the real attraction to visitors. What makes Newquay special are the great surfing beaches. Today it is the European capital of surfing, its contests attracting participants worldwide.

However well you think you know the resort, nothing quite prepares you for its sheer size, and the magnificence of the beaches only yards away from hotels. The resort has been unique for a long time, though in differing ways. In my days of reporting the holiday trade, it attracted the more adventurous and younger visitor no longer content with traditional Blackpool or Skegness. Its rapid growth resulted from happy understanding between the Great Western Railway (later BR Western Region) and the council and tourist association. Things were done with foresight. The railway relished carrying armies of holidaymakers so far west, even though the mainly single-line branch with its sharply curved incline up Luxulyan Valley under Treffry's viaduct meant full-length through trains required three locomotives, two in front and one at the rear. Their noise echoing up through the valley was unforgettable. Before World War Two, the platforms of the usually quiet station were lengthened to take fifteen coach trains, and bridges along the branch line strengthened so that the route could be used by the powerful Castle-class locomotives. Workers' rights to holidays with pay date back to the end of the 1930s, but were only generally implemented after the war. With military precision the railways somehow coped with the ever-increasing crowds, 6,000 from beyond Bristol on many Saturdays.

Peak weeks at the best hotels and holiday camps sold out in early January, and by March enquirers were sent printed cards saying they were fully booked until the end of September. Undeterred, visitors without accommodation queued at the information bureau near the railway station from the early hours of Saturday morning. By the time the bureau opened, hundreds of people and their luggage sometimes stretched down the street. Locals gave up their own beds to make substantial pin money. Surrounding villages, like Bugle deep in the china clay country, became holiday resorts in their own right, attracting loyal regulars through the boom years. It was still not enough. On peak Saturdays at the end of July and beginning of August, my regular journalist call to the bureau was answered with requests to broadcast the message that anyone with a vacant bed anywhere in Cornwall – yes, anywhere in the whole county – should phone in to make their contribution to dealing with the overflow. Visitors who wanted to stay in Newquay were sent as far as Saltash and St Just in Penwith. Penzance, which somehow did not have its own publicity well organised, received the largest single contingent.

It all made good copy, regular readers even being interested in the length of the often mighty queue for the weighing machine with its excellent view of the Atlantic on the road into the town. Never did anywhere else in Britain enjoy such a boom. George White at the tourist bureau, and 'Trem' the esteemed publicity manager, organised lunches at which my role in putting the town on the map was recognised. One house agent reckoned the reporting had added ten percent to the value of Newquay's property, for many wanted to move in to participate in the prosperity. Other resorts naturally accused me of favouritism, but the facts spoke for themselves. It was routinely impossible for taxis to take 400 passengers from, say, a London express to their hotels and camps before getting people from the next North Country train. Added to the mêlée, kitchen and waiting staff frequently had to be persuaded to serve latecomers long beyond normal hours. Doctors' waiting rooms were crowded with hoteliers and their lieutenants needing Valium as they strove to cope with the pressure, especially when chefs stormed out. Shops ran out of even basic foodstuffs. Pavements were no more able to cope with the press of pedestrians than the street system with the vehicular traffic. The police regularly helped to find cars for people who had forgotten where, at long last, they had found somewhere to park.

Why Newquay? There were several reasons going back in history. The outstanding collection of the, albeit separated, beaches within easy reach of the town centre, plus the railway – with some of the earliest corridor trains – from London, attracted the first hotels. To this day there is not a major well-balanced holiday resort that did not first develop around the skeleton of major hotels. We see them today: great lumps of them, the likes of which nobody could possibly have afforded to build at any time since the outbreak of World War One. The Headland Hotel we are planning to visit for lunch is the most prominent... so prominent that when building began the townspeople (abetted by the rival Atlantic Hotel) tore down foundations, destroyed the scaffolding and threw the foreman's hut into the sea. The 'Newquay riots' left a deep impression, especially as local workers feared for their families if they took part in the building, which was mainly done by 200 unemployed miners from Redruth. The Headland opened in 1902, its local promoters achieving their ambition of creating the largest and most palatial hotel in the West Country, with electric light and lifts, together with sea views from every window. King Edward VII and Queen Alexandra stayed there on several occasions. Between the wars the Headland was for the stylish who danced on the sprung floor to the tunes of famous London orchestras. The BBC's Sunday evening Palm Court concert was often broadcast live.

If not quite in the Headland league, there were other fine hotels, too, again supported by a go-ahead council, and amenities including beach cafes and the enterprisingly laid-out gardens in Trenance Valley. All the ingredients needed for the post-war boom were in place. The new visitors were not welcomed by the old clientele, many of whom would within a few seasons say they would no longer be seen dead in Newquay. In turn, the younger and more adventurous family people were largely of a kind who wouldn't wish to be seen there today. Newquay has changed again. As Chris Blount puts it: 'Newquay is the Ibiza of the twenty-first century. The young and noisy have frightened away the families. I remember ten years ago coming out of the Camelot cinema – it's closed now. My wife and I were really frightened, the young crowd were so boisterous and noisy. It was about then that we began thinking we didn't want to live in the town anymore.'

Surfing is today's thing, kite surfing growing in popularity alongside the traditional. The youngsters surf in the day and drink heavily at night. It doesn't mix with catering for families, says Chris. Even though many fewer beds are on offer, Newquay is now never full. But he adds that some of the remaining hotels have smartened up their act. 'The Headland is an anachronism hanging on in there.' The very day I talk to him he has interviewed on Radio Cornwall Bettye Gray, the hotelier whose new book I bought an advance copy of at The Nare, about her family's life and work.

Having seen but not spoken to her at The Nare, I call her, having read much of the book meanwhile. *Oh My Dear Life: A Cornish Family Saga* has been privately published. 'I didn't think of sending it to a publisher, just spent £10,000 on 1,000 copies. I think I'm going to have to reprint it.' Pity, for it deserved commercial publication, albeit with a touch of editing, the family story not always mixing elegantly with that of their hotels, though in the end I did find it worthwhile getting to know who ran which hotel and when. She and her family were particularly successful in Newquay tourism until times changed, when they were glad to sell their last hotel here (other than the Headland of which more in a moment) as discriminating people moved 'up the coast'. The Watergate Bay and Bedruthan Steps, a few miles out of Newquay, are still run by the family.

Of The Nare, on the opposite coast, she says: 'It wasn't ever meant to be commercial, just a labour of love; but if you know what you're doing somehow you seem to succeed. Horses for courses. Every one of the family hotels has always set out for a definite style and market, knowing its particular trade. Too many people think you can run a hotel for every kind of person. It doesn't work.'

She recalls Newquay's stylish days when, for example, visitors at the Tolcarne Hotel enjoyed full afternoon tea on the beach and dressed for dinner. 'My son at the Headland still has a dress code, but most of Newquay's not like that now. Today's trade is quite different.' It is not long before she joins in the litany of criticism of the needless damage inflicted by the district council, Newquay having lost its own.

'They haven't a clue. What's Newquay about? Beaches and surfing, of course. So in the town guide, paid for by the local hotels, there are no pictures of the great surfing beaches identified with captions, or any pictures of Trenance Gardens or the Gannel – but whole pages of other different resorts such as Fowey, miles away on the other coast. It puts another nail in the coffin. It's dreadful the way Newquay's always been ignored by people outside it. Writers have always avoided it like the plague, yet it has given more people great holidays than anywhere else in Cornwall. Perhaps it's been just too successful.'

We reflect that wherever we go in Cornwall the resorts are severely critical of the publicity efforts of the larger councils uneasily serving huge tracts of country areas, market towns and coastal stretches. Surely Newquay would never have developed as part of Restormal, but only as a place in its own right understanding its particular business. Further east, the slogan Carrick Country means nothing to most visitors, who choose a specific resort, not an administrative area, for their holiday.

It is time for lunch and we're on our way to the Headland, a huge Victorian building, basically in pale brick, though from a distance what stands out are the terra-cotta features including around and between the long tiers of white windows. Its architect certainly did not seek to make it inconspicuous in its controversial position. Though it is perhaps hard to believe that royalty and gentry once took suites here, today's atmosphere is one of bustling warmth. You have to go to the gents' loo in the basement to experience the true period piece. When the coast is clear, men routinely take their wives to admire the decorated china ware and Victorian tiling. Outside the gents' is one of those magnificent contour maps of the Great Western that used to adorn many stations. On the ground floor you can learn about the hotel's origins and the Newquay riots from old framed photographs and newspaper cuttings. Views are stunning on three sides. And the lunch is excellent, the staff busy and efficient.

Is Chris right that it is an anachronism? Yes and no, for Bettye Gray's son John Armstrong and his wife Carol have made it their life work – 'to push back the tide'. They were young and with very limited means when they bought it in poor condition twenty years ago. Through hard work and imagination, above all knowing what they wanted to achieve, the Headland is back on the quality map. John's mother hopes they will soon regain the fourth star. It has a high AA percentage score. Her book has an especially interesting chapter on some of their early escapades.

'We're still here, an elegant, modern hotel perched on the cliff top,' says John, admitting that in the 1890s he might have supported the rioters tearing the foundations apart. But he is proud of his new holiday village replacing old buildings around the hotel. And, yes: 'The rest of Cornwall has a difficult relationship with Newquay.'

The Headland is the largest hotel in a county ignored by most of the hotel groups. If John has a problem, it is mixing functional business with tourism but, worldwide, such hotels struggle with that. It is perhaps politic to be less critical of Newquay: 'There's not as much rowdiness as in the 1980s. Things have calmed down a bit... a lot of drinking, certainly, but more controlled. Many parents bring their teenagers to the shrine of water-skiing. Think of us as the equivalent of popular snow ski hotels.'

He adds a touch defensively: 'Anyway, you can get to and from the Headland without going through Newquay.' That is certainly an advantage from the traffic point of view, and the hotel offers so much, the Atlantic grabbing attention whatever the weather, and Fistral beach beginning only fifty yards from the steps, so that many guests are probably happy to stay put for much of their stay.

We opt to leave by the town. Some sizeable hotels have obviously shut shop or will do so soon. Others, such as the Victoria, with its unique lift through the cliffs to the beach, have been tastefully restored – which is more than can be said of the railway station. A single track leads to a buffer by an ugly kiosk, though summer Saturday expresses from London and the North still reach here and are busy. You wouldn't come here for quality shopping, but all those stepping off the coaches parked nose to tail during a surprisingly long season must be impressed by the surroundings. There is no cinema or large hall, but Trenance Valley with its extensive gardens now includes a large indoor swimming pool.

As we leave the town, I note the traditional weighing machine has gone, probably long ago, and if it were still there it would hardly attract a crowd. Weighing ourselves is no longer a public amusement.

We will be back again to stay at the Headland. Newquay is always best early and late season anyway, perhaps especially in early June when thrift flowers all along the clifftops.

Newquay to Padstow

Newquay to Padstow offers another rich range of North Cornwall's exposed cliffs and sheltered coves and beaches: Watergate Bay, Bedruthan Steps, Mawgan Porth, Trenance Head, Trevone among others, each with its unique seasonal magic and, for us, personal memories of holidays and business past. But let us skip the next part of the coast until we approach its largest estuary, the Camel, through a series of narrow lanes to Hawker's Cove, overlooking the Doom Bar, where many a sailor has met his watery end at the river's stormy mouth. Then into Padstow, checking in at the Metropole, at the time of visiting surprisingly still a Forte, jolly if a touch tired, celebrating its centenary. The railway reached here much later than it did Newquay, and the Metropole was the only large hotel ever built. Padstow was the furthest point that could be reached by the *Atlantic Coast Express* from Waterloo. The station building still stands, but today probably more people walk the old line, now known as the Camel Trail, than were using the trains when they ceased in the 1960s.

Padstow, always a favourite, has changed dramatically since I was last here, yet somehow retains its old essence. It is no longer quaint in the best old sense, and certainly eating options are not as limited as they used to be, but here are bookish, interested people crowding into the cramped bookshop, watching the ferry go to and from Rock, and the dredger fetching up another load of sand to be grabbed out by the lorry load. Small boats, seagulls and even a semi-tame seal give an impression of non-stop activity. Yet it is all peaceful, even if the enormous car park on the old fish quays built with government money to relieve unemployment between the wars is constantly full.

The Camel sets the tone. It is an enormous estuary, horribly exposed to the north wind, but generally quiet inland from Padstow, with a touch of the mysterious. Perhaps it was Claude Berry's *Cornwall* in Hale's immediate post-war County series that helped give me a love of Padstow, his 'home–along'. A journalist of distinction, he wrote with passion and authority on the social differences between up-along and down-along, the early arrival of Christianity, the excessive number of wet days, and the Rock ferry whose passengers were once drowned. I remember Claude Berry's book for another reason; the original manuscript was lost in a fire, any author's nightmare in the days before photocopiers and word-processors, and he had to rewrite it. He did so brilliantly and, had the work stood on its own instead of being in a series of mixed quality, it would surely remain a classic.

Home-along, he says may conjure up different pictures but all these fall beautifully into place on one large canvas:

> Home-along to me means this little place on the Camel estuary, this friendly town, which – I know, for I have looked at it long and with the eye of a lover from every point of the compass – is best seen as you sit in a boat in midstream between the quay-heads and St Minver Sands. There, scores of times, I have shipped the paddles, thrown the gripper overboard, and squatted on the stern-sheets. From somewhere forward comes soon one of the loveliest sounds I know: the urgent, excited ripple of the tide in ebb or flood. Sometimes a butterfly passes low over the boat, and the eye follows anxiously its adventurous flight towards the soft, warm dunes. Or suddenly a shag will break surface a few yards away, and, with some little distress, you watch the head-shakings and neck-stretchings as this diving-bird deals vigorously with a tiny plaice.

A few paragraphs later, CB as he was affectionately known on the *West Briton*, echoes what I have always found delightfully true: 'Cornish independence, which here and there is apt to be angular and thrusting, is solid enough at Padstow but not aggressive.' Its soul has not been lost through what the county planning officer described as 'the Stein effect'. Rick Stein's Seafood School on the quay, his Seafood and other restaurants, and many imitators, are the visual manifestations of this effect. Stein's disciples or patrons may not be the genuine Cornish who still seem to predominate around here, but at least they are people with a touch of taste searching for the real local thing, not a souped-up commercialism.

Rick Stein

When I arrive for our appointment at his original Seafood, Rick Stein is still tied up at a meeting about making a further property purchase. Right-hand-man Sam Harrison tells me Rick is unassuming, passionate, doing his best to work with local people even if some seem to find his success hard to take. A total of 140 staff are now employed and on a big day 300 to 350 meals might be served, including 150 on a busy night at the Seafood alone. So far there are also 29 bedrooms. Accommodation: a commodity of which Padstow has always been short.

'How did it start?' I ask Rick when he arrives. He is obviously stressed. His wife has just told him so. He came down in 1965 with his retired parents, and started a nightclub in what is now the Seafood. The law closed him down.

'I didn't know what to do. I had no training, but had enjoyed cooking fish so I converted to that just to pay the bills. Cooking fish just began to catch on. I've always loved fish, yet wherever I went found it difficult to find simply cooked fish... and especially hard by the sea, partly because, from so many places, it all goes to Spain. It doesn't speak kindly about us as a nation, does it? Newlyn, Looe, Plymouth, or for that matter Scrabster and Peterhead, everywhere the middle men think, if not about sales abroad, then certainly not locally. Yet our fish, with such variety, is so good, especially if you let it speak for itself and don't drown it in artificial flavours.'

Ironic, isn't it? Just as Rick's books and television are encouraging armies of us to let our local fish speak for itself, fishermen are fighting for survival with reduced quotas and other restrictions. Adds Rick: 'It's worse than that. I sometimes wonder whether someone out there is organising an extraordinary nightmare. It's very, very bad for fishermen.'

So where's Padstow now?

'It's irksome to admit it, but it's down to tourism. We do our best. I teach cooking fish, the appreciation of our inheritance, so vital now that South Crofty (the last Cornish mine to close) has gone the way of the rest, and fishing employs only a fraction of what it did in pilchard days. I like to think I'm someone they trust to champion the Cornish fishing industry, and in their way tourists make that possible. But what do you do?'

More immediately, when does Rick stop expanding? Will this most genuine of TV personalities expand to his own level of incompetence? Can he help himself? If in his shoes, would you have turned down the latest television series? Stacks of signed copies of the book that go with the series are waiting for buyers. As in all businesses, no doubt budgets have to be met.

So to the table to join Sheila, my daughter Alyss and her new friend. We all seem in harmony. So we should be, over whole crabs and perfect sea bass, but life teaches that harmony is not automatic and can't be bought, not even with the best fish. Our mutual enjoyment stretches to a walk around the harbour lapped by high tide, noting a couple of fishing craft ready to sail in the early hours. As we return to our hotel, I go back in memory. It was here that after the war I first enjoyed fish as a separate course. From the bedroom window you could then see the steam of the engine, perhaps one of those grand T9s (or 'Greyhounds') built by Dougal Drummond in Queen Victoria's day, and trace its progress along the banks of the estuary and over the bridge by Sea Mills. If I close my eyes I can still see a Greyhound being turned on the turntable in a sunset. I was on the last train of all, a sad occasion. John Betjeman said 'the five and a half miles beside the broadening Camel to Padstow is the most beautiful train journey I know'. But at least one can walk the old line, and popular it is under the name of the Camel Trail. I especially love crossing the bridge by Sea Mills where latterly the weight of locomotives was causing serious wear but pedestrians and cyclists aren't a strain. The waterwheel worked by the tide has, alas, long gone.

John Betjeman Country

Next day, after breakfast with the realisation that the younger couple are already 'an item' as we say these days, we wish them well and move on again. After we return home a wonderful bouquet of flowers arrives with their thanks for a lovely time.

First we take the road's more roundabout route to Wadebridge, another of North Cornwall's gems. Like many estuary towns, when ships were smaller and the main channel dredged, Wadebridge was once an active port, the largest trade being in the sand that is landed at Padstow today. Much of the sand went inland on the pioneer (1834) Bodmin & Wadebridge Railway, the first in Cornwall to have locomotives and carry passengers. Researching its old records produced fascinating insights which make running today's railways seem a doddle. In his Day Book, the superintendent, who constantly gave out vouchers for free pints of cocoa to reward staff making special effort, catalogues mishaps. 'Broke off Chimney of the Engine.' 'Stopped the Engine in consequence of the wheels being of different sizes.' 'Unprofitable to work' [in bad weather].

The B&W was a small, independent concern with business acumen. Crowded trains were parked on the embankment overlooking Bodmin jail for passengers to observe public executions. The system played a major role in the territorial battle waged between the conservative Great Western and the radical London & South Western, for in 1846 it was illegally bought by the latter. Though the LSWR's western terminal was then still 200 miles away, the purchase (never challenged by Parliament) gave the impetus to press on ever westward. It took the LSWR 48 years to link up with the B&W. It built a chain of gable-end station houses stretching across the countryside as it did so. The prize was keeping the GWR off the Atlantic seaboard between Minehead and Newquay. The picturesque branch up to Wenford Bridge, mainly used for clay and De Lank granite, and providing colourful journalist and broadcasting fodder, has also become part of the Camel Way, and at the time of writing there is great controversy over the scheme to re-lay the rails for clay trains.

After Wadebridge, the weather becomes the Atlantic's least charming. Drizzle-laden mist whirls inland, clearly demonstrating the wind's usual direction, at each blast trees seeming to stoop at yet more evasive angles. One moment their gaunt outlines clearly tell the trouble life has given them; the next only disconnected bent limbs peer mockingly through the murk. We had planned to keep close to the estuary through Rock. That would have enabled us once more to visit the church of St Enodoc on Daymer Bay which for generations had been buried by the sand overlooking Doom Bar from the east. John Betjeman is buried here, a place from which he drew much inspiration.

> What faith was his, that dim, that Cornish saint,
> Small rushlight of a long-forgotten church,
> Who lived with God on this unfriendly shore,
> Who knew He made the Atlantic and the stones
> And destined seamen here to end their lives
> Dashed on a rock, rolled over in the surf,
> And not one hair forgotten. Now they lie
> In centuries of sand beside the church.

The swirling mist made such a diversion pointless, and even that we do take off the B3314 to Port Isaac proves more nuisance than pleasure. Cars and vans are interminably locked in the impossibly-narrow mist-filled streets. Nothing looks half interesting. Yet what joy these streets offered in the days of few cars. We gave up on Portgaverne of happy memory, promising ourselves an overnight stop on a sunny pre-season day if we should ever strike lucky.

Old Delabole the Deep

Determined that this now treeless land of the South West wind would yield something of interest as it has done so richly in the past, on reaching Delabole, on the spur of the moment, we turn off to the slate quarry, Old Delabole, not knowing what to expect. Worked for hundreds of years, indeed already famous for its quality when Drake scattered the Spanish Armada, its 500ft deep hole is a mile in circumference. A number of formerly separate quarries have over the years been merged into one. This great hole has given countless Cornishmen from these grim parts an honest if sometimes dangerous living. The last time I was here men seemed like ants beavering away. In 1886, there were 1,500 of them. Women once laboured up the steep slopes bearing the newly-won rock on the first and most difficult part of its journey, to the top of the hole. In those days thirty wagons and a hundred horses were needed to load a 60-ton vessel lying on the beach at low tide at Portgaverne, women mainly stowing the piles of slates between hay. Other slate went out through several ports, notably Boscastle. The steam age arrived at Delabole in 1834 when rubble started being pulled out mechanically, but the railway did not come till almost the century's end. Then, from the occasional train twisting its way along the follow-the-contour North Cornwall line, you could look down into the hole and the numerous inclines with trucks being pulled up filled with slate that would roof buildings in many countries. Old Delabole has a rich history, its own folklore and literature, including Eden Phillpotts' *Old Delabole*, still worth reading if you're into rustic romance set against a grim background.

Though we are not expected, Howard Pankhurst, the financial director of today's Old Delabole, immediately shares his delight in being able to move to North Cornwall and be part of a traditional industry kept alive through technical and marketing innovation.

'It's fun because we're one of a kind: unique. But things have changed. Of our 35 workers, only four are now actually in the quarry, sawing into the slate with wires with diamond teeth. It's a bit like a cheese knife; there's little waste.'

Today the pit's bottom cannot be seen, for the three lowest 'benches' are drowned. The active benches are pushed back two metres a year, so the hole still grows. Whole fields and cottages have been consumed by it in the past. Eighteen months were spent removing old waste from the top of the seam now being worked. The end is not nigh, since at the present rate a further 600 years of slate-winning are possible. It has not all been plain sailing for, back in 1869, fifteen workers were killed by a huge rock fall.

Slate is labour intensive, too expensive for all but the most prestigious flooring (though some is still used for high-class roofing). So the modern showroom of the private company (annual turnover exceeds a million pounds) inevitably appeals to the tourist, interested in house names, window sills, fireplaces, table and work tops, coasters and other small goods. The slates can be crafted to accommodate practically any design. We wonder if we can find practical use for a large slab, not daring to calculate the cost of transport to the other end of Britain, though what is that distance when one learns that centuries ago Delabole slate was the fashionable roofing material in the West Indies? Pristine, natural in wonderful shades of blue and bluey grey, long may Delabole slate find adequate demand. None that is quarried is now wasted, some gift items being made of reconstituted dust.

In a brief lull in the storm, we venture out and peer down into the hole, one of the world's largest. Uncannily little seems to be happening, yet production is as great as when hundreds of men descended. Tourists are offered tours and you will not be surprised to hear that the next development planned is for a tourist centre. Adding one to an active industry is certainly more rewarding than a pure museum piece.

'Arthurian' Tintagel

Little Car, much buffeted, heads into the wind to Tintagel, on a day like this looking almost as if visitors had left it forever. Tintagel is at once one of the most magical and detestable of Cornish places. My worst-ever night was spent in the vast King Arthur's Castle Hotel. It had been a quality Trust House before the 1939-45 war, which treated it badly. After the war, it was tentatively reopened by someone with inadequate backing who obviously could not pay the bills. Even the main phone seemed to be ripped out. So it appeared that the half-dozen or so rooms they had managed inadequately to furnish were to be let only to those who turned up on chance. Supplies to the kitchen were so strictly rationed that the entire dinner would have made a skimpy starter, and in those immediate post-war days it was hard to find anything else to eat in Tintagel late in the evening. Bed sheets were left hanging over bushes in the garden soaked by the last shower while waiting to dry. The experience set the tone for Tintagel for me: grand, but slightly tainted. The hotel with its Arthurian Style Bar, is now 'Camelot Castle Hotel – The Home of King Arthur and Camelot', charging too little to have a presence in most good hotel guides.

It is all Tennyson's fault for popularising Arthur and his Round Table. There are of course people interested in the castle's real history but, without their sales of cheap Arthurian mementos, the shops in the plain village would die. The tourist guide is ingenious in attempting to claim Arthurian credibility:

> Tintagel castle by the Cornish sea ... It was here, said Tennyson, that the infant Arthur was swept by the waves into Merlin's Cave. Today those legends come alive through storytelling amongst the ruined battlements of Earl Richard's thirteenth-century stronghold ... the discovery of a sixth-century slate inscribed ARTOGNOV (the Latin version of the ancient British ARTHNOU) has fuelled the belief that this was Arthur's palace. The new visitors' centre ... helps put some flesh on those ancient Celtic bones.

In fairness, the ruins could not be more dramatically placed in a piece of vertical landscape and, when you descend the steep steps and explore out on the island (building began when it was an isthmus, but the sea has worn away the connection), you invite romanticism. That anyone chose this spot to build is surely remarkable enough, but the fun is in exploring what was created in successive centuries, beginning with the twelfth when it must have seemed the end of the earth. It was indeed in the twelfth century that the legend of Arthur being here was founded, and all historians know that legends are often more enduring than hard fact. What we do know is that the site has been both a monastery and fortification with periods of desertion. Man's first building here was 1,500 years ago, though there is nothing that old to see. But that is the stuff of the official guide.

For me the remarkable thing is the quality of life monks once enjoyed, their earlier building being constructed to a higher standard than the later. An abundance of South Gaulish pottery was found in the earliest strata, so perhaps it didn't seem so cut off after all. Things became tough economically, even if the monks were still allowed to pursue a peaceful existence, when the Saxons reached this far west. When I first came, you rang someone's doorbell and paid what recollection says was three old pence and walked down in splendid isolation. Now summer visitors queue to buy their tickets and descend and ascend the steps, though across the connection to the island there is ample space to spread out. And if some can only use their imagination in Arthurian terms it is surely better than having no imagination at all.

Boscastle and on to Bude

If Tintagel is like a beautiful woman who has lost her principles, neighbouring Boscastle is as pure as Cornish coves and ports come. Nor is it without drama. The narrow harbour entrance is reputedly the most dangerous in Cornwall. It leads into a sheet of water with an S-bend beneath high cliffs on either side. A hole in the eastern cliff noisily spouts forth at a certain state of the tide. A rocky island outside, and neat cottages landward add to the drama. Here is the National Trust at its best. Many an hour have I sat on the slate cliff to the west. Don't tell anyone, but as a young man, I enjoyed peeling off thin layers of slate with a pen knife, and still have a sample. Vandal!

Boscastle's drama heightened when a wartime mine floated in, blowing up part of the breakwater and damaging much property. More damage followed when waves piled up, driven in by the force of the sea through the unprotected narrowing harbour. Seldom has praise been heaped on workmen more than on those who fought continual storms to gather together the scattered boulders of the old breakwater and feed in new material by a miniature railway to restore protection in 1962. Shops and catering are more individual than Tintagel's, but then there is no great legend to commercialise here.

Boscastle always produces another poignant memory – from Thomas Hardy's *A Pair of Blue Eyes*, the first novel to be published under his own name, drawing much from the most significant journey of his life, to Cornwall in 1870. He was then 29. His story reaches its climax as the rival suitors for Elfride's love are uneasy companions when meeting on the train from Paddington while delayed at Chippenham because 'a singular carriage' at the rear is mistakenly unhooked and has to be reconnected. Later during the journey this vehicle must have been transferred to their South Western train at Exeter since on reaching Camelton (Camelford), they see it greeted by an undertaker's party. The coffin is put on a cart for the long miles to Endlestow, actually based on a village near Boscastle but with Boscastle's cliffs, where an earlier life-and-death scene takes place. Of course, the coffin is Elfride's. The two long-standing rivals each react to the discovery of her death by blaming themselves for breaking her heart, but a few weeks before, unknown to them, she was married to someone else, with more class and wealth.

The pathos is piled on in a way that the public were eventually to dislike so much that Hardy, finding the bitter criticism more than he could take, abandoned fiction, though not until the best of the Wessex novels had been written. If you read *A Pair of Blue Eyes* at an impressionable age yourself, you will always associate it with the grim landscape and the long descent to Boscastle which I first made in a thunderstorm. The early Hardy's landscape is perhaps more real than his characters, and few realise that one of his main purposes was to expose the relationship between rich employers and their struggling farm workers. His own escape, enjoying his independence from the village system, is replicated in the desires of the youngsters. Poor Elfride, pitiful lovers, great setting.

Down, down and down, now into Crackington Haven with one of the least-used beaches for its size in Southern England. I first walked out across the sands to look up at the roaring Atlantic rollers in 1951 as part of a survey of the North Cornwall coast for *The Western Morning News*. My returning to work, pale from the effects of 'flu, coincided with the news editor, Frank Booker, having been impressed by another piece of my writing. He had come across a Press release about the plan to create the first section (from St Ives to the Devon border near Hartland Point) of the now-continuous coastal path round the South West, he said: 'Take three days and see what you can make of it.' A wonderful brief.

Many Cornish people told me they thought the path might be good for business but bad for Cornwall itself. Further west, one local inhabitant hoped that at least they would now remove those melancholy reminders of Cornwall's industrial past, the mine stacks and their chimneys that now romantically appear in tourist publicity. Some pieces of path were already in existence, but poorly signposted and maintained. Climbing the steeps cliff either side of Crackington Haven was impossible... and is still not for the faint-hearted. Overall, the footpath has been a great success. There are sections where you have miles to yourself, and then spot someone coming the other way who you will pass in, say ten minutes, clutching the same map and guide as yourself.

Then up, up, up from Crackington Haven illuminated for a few seconds by a flash of sun, crossing at about forty miles an hour, the harbinger of better weather to come. Two or three such flashes light up Widemouth Bay on the approach to Bude. But Bude itself remains dull, melancholy. It still retains a feeling of a frontier town since its early ambitions, demonstrated by the tightly-packed clifftop terraces, were not fulfilled.

'Why do we have to come here?' demands Sheila, whose memories of visits years ago were not good. Today's first impressions are no better.

'What are those people doing?' asked an American cresting a sand dune and seeing before her a sea of human beings crouched behind colourful windbreaks. Why, obviously, sunning themselves. What here, in this wind, and anyway where's the sun? They must be mad. Many such people now sun themselves beside overcrowded pools at Spanish hotels which the builders may not have quite finished. Progress? But wait, Sheila, after lunch I'll show you the magic of my Bude of which I never tire.

· X I V ·

BACK TO
NEWTON ABBOT
VIA TAMAR VALLEY
AND PLYMOUTH

Bude and its Curious Canal

I've not seen this part of Bude,' says Sheila as we walk from the wharf, and cross the canal by a gate of its great sea lock toward the breakwater. It is a huge breakwater, built to withstand the southwest wind's worst efforts, and to protect the sea lock. Long before we are anywhere near it, the Atlantic's roar makes conversation impossible. Already beginning to be encrusted by salt, we retreat. Even at low tide on a fine day, the Atlantic is fortissimo.

Years ago the council planned to brick up the sea lock, killing Bude as a port. I tell Sheila about the fun it was publicising their plan and stirring up opposition until the council faced Bude's angriest and best-attended protest meeting ever. Who says a journalist's work cannot be positive? Today only occasional pleasure craft may lock into the canal basin at high tide, but accessibility from the sea remains an essential part of Bude's character. Time has moved on – so much so that the lock gates have needed replacement again. A public notice lists the participants in 'Bude Sea Lock 2000', ranging from the Inland Waterways Association's £3,000 through contributions of the now Town Council and the North Cornwall District Council to £200,000 from English Heritage and £222,150 from the European Regional Development Fund. A lot of money, but worth it.

In pre-railway days, sloops, barques and other sailing ships brought coal from South Wales, the canal basin often being full of vessels as tall as they were long. Together with building materials, and early manufactures of the industrial revolution, part of the cargoes were

259

transferred to tub boats for transport inland, the canal's main branches serving Holsworthy and Launceston. The chief cargo was sand. The rusting narrow-gauge rails, on which trucks were hauled up from the beach to tip the sand into the canal's craft, are still part of the scene.

So vital was the sea sand doing the job of lime in the sour hinterland that, after the canal's opening, land prices along its length shot up and the depots or wharves were important trading stations. The landscape is the least suitable you could imagine for a waterway. The canal was only economically possible by building it at several self-contained levels, linked by incline planes into which all the climbing and descending was gathered. The tub boats, each carrying four tons when sand was the cargo, ran in horse-drawn trains of six or eight on the water, but as single trucks (for they were all fitted with wheels) on the rails of the inclined planes. Murray's *Hand-Book* tells us:

> The inclined plane is an ingenious substitute for a chain of locks, and consists of a steep roadway, about 900 feet in length, which is furnished with two lines of rails dipping at each end into the canal, and traversed by an endless chain. Barges... are raised or lowered on the roadway by being attached to the chain, which is set in motion by two enormous buckets, each of eight feet diameter, alternately filled with water and working in wells 225 feet in depth. As soon as the descending bucket has reached the bottom of the well, it strikes upon a stake, which raises a plug, when the water runs out in a minute and finds its way back to the canal below. This bucket is then in readiness to be raised by the other.

This was in the 1820s in what the promoters called 'the fag end of the kingdom'. Thirty miles of canal had been built by 1826. The particular incline described by Murray was the Great Plane at Hobbacott Down, two miles from Stratton. We can still enjoy its great westward view, though without boots today we cannot search out the well's cover and throw a stone down to hear it crash at the bottom. There were six inclined planes, only this one on the essential main trunk before the route split at Red Post having a standby steam engine – yet another thing to go wrong. While in 1829 the final touches were being put to the world's first inter-city railway, the Liverpool & Manchester, the canal's superintendent and resident engineer, John Honey, was dashing hither and thither on horseback effecting emergency repairs. If the chains did not break or the plug fly right out of its bucket, or wheels come off a boat halfway down one of the inclines, then the banks slipped or a hinge of a sea lock gate became warped. The management committee, meeting far away at Exeter, seemed neither to listen nor give support; the traders were careless, or the farmers ungrateful. With high tolls, farmers resorted to collecting the essential sand themselves, so the independent traders who plied the canal suffered, and money ran out for the nucleus of the canal's own employees. When times were good, the traders encouraged horses to trot too quickly and the rear boats in the train damaged the canal's sides.

One of the joys of researching the canal's history in the 1950s was to discover many records in an attic beside the Bude basin. They included John Honey's letterbooks, bound volumes of tracing paper for an early form of carbon copying. He poured out his troubles and sometimes bared his soul. There were good times, too, when everything worked, and traffic increased after the farmers had won a reduction in tolls.

Partly financed by the government to bring relief to the poor area, the canal once carried nearly 60,000 tons annually inland, enabling the interest to be paid on the exchequer loan. For a few years, it even declared a dividend. Yet, difficult a time though Railtrack is experiencing as we explore this corner of England where trains came late and were withdrawn early, spare a thought for poor Honey. His pain comes vividly through the years in his diary or 'Daybook' accounts of the problems he encountered: chains broke, sending boats crashing down an incline and tearing up track; while the buckets damaged themselves dropping like stones to the bottom of the shaft. In what in today's language might be called special pleading as he struggled at the cutting edge of technology, he pontificates that were the whole system his own he could not do more for its betterment. Nobody, direct employees, the rival traders who often seem to have had trouble paying their bills, or the farmers for whom the whole thing was designed, ever seemed to think of the common good.

These records were used extensively by Charles Hadfield, the Charles of David & Charles, in *The Canals of South West England* and by Helen Harris in *The Bude Canal*. I spent many a day filling in the history, perplexing people through whose land the canal had once run. In the 1950s and 1960s, it was thought curious that anyone could possibly be interested in such a thing. Bude yielded magnificent memories and photographs. Many of the maritime trades created in the canal era continued to flourish, serving sea-going cargo ships that still visited in the first half of the twentieth century. By my day, coal was unloaded from railway trucks shunted to the quayside for Pethericks the merchants, whose history went back to the canal's early times.

It is exciting being back here today, exploring and recalling, realising that the canal's heyday is so much further in the past than it was in 1950.

From Bude out on to the high road through Kilkhampton for the traditional side trip to Morwenstow to pay homage to RS Hawker. His *Footprints of Former Men in Far Cornwall* remains a classic of local literature on the characters of yesteryear. What eccentrics this remote area bred. Not that Hawker was ordinary himself. Like many other clerical thinkers, he was all too aware of the paucity of parish life, and naturally realised what bonus the occasional shipwreck brought his flock. The tombstones around the church tell their grim story of wrecks. This coastline of 'watery grave by day and night' was dangerous enough in the days of sail, without our needing to believe the legend that Hawker's followers lured ships to the rocks by exhibiting a lamp on the clifftop. It's a muddy but always joyous walk from the church, sheltered in its little cleft, down the field's edge to the sheer cliff where Hawker built his famous and still much-visited hut in which to contemplate.

Joan Rendell: Parish Clerk 53 Years Not Out

Now we start cutting across the peninsula, going south on the Launceston road, up and down hills demonstrating what an impossible countryside this was for a canal. We stop just short of the village of Yeolmbridge, to visit Joan Rendell, whose many claims to fame include a 53-year stint (not yet over) as clerk to the parish council. It was through a newspaper contact in 1950 that she and I agreed to share the cost of a farm van to explore the canal. Our research on the ground yielded much, there still being a few around who remembered the canal's last days. Fertility of the fields increased wondrously as greater quantities of sand became affordable, as tolls dropped in the final (and, for the canal, fatal) competition with the railway. In 1950 most of the inclined planes were intact, the canal retained its original appearance for some miles out of Tamar Lake, its own reservoir later absorbed into the Bude water supply and today a nature reserve especially rich in migrating water birds.

I ask Joan if she recalls the evening before our exploration. 'Yes, I'd walked into Launceston to check on things and there was a man – I think he said he worked for the Ministry of Agriculture – who quickly suggested he drove me home.' That, I explain, was Sheila's father, who had driven me to Launceston for the night and had plans other than spending the evening with this diminutive young lady (though several years older than me) with brightly-painted toenails.

Joan's fiancé had been killed in the war: 'Nobody could possibly measure up to him.' So her life has been one of extraordinary dedication to a long list of causes. While she was a Landgirl, she raised the then enormous sum of £100,000 in sixpenny and later half-a-crown National Savings stamps. All were purchased from the village's post office and general store, now long closed. She went on to be the national chairman of the National Savings Committee (until the government abolished it in 1977) and earned herself an OBE. For over fifty years she has been an active journalist and broadcaster. We mourn last week's passing of a familiar regional radio personality, Peggy Archer, studio manager and reporter in radio and television. We all enjoyed the mixture before demarcation became tighter. We talk of other West Country broadcasters. Angela Rippon 'kept getting her introductory lines wrong'. Hugh Scully had to work harder for Spotlight South West before he also went national. Sheila Tracey, so nervous when she conducted her first-ever TV interview that I had needed to wave my arms around and ask as well as answer the questions, was another 'brought up well' by BBC Plymouth.

It was actually Joan's father I knew well for many years. A senior staff officer at the Admiralty, he had a great store of memories. 'You're paid to do things, not think. I do the thinking,' snapped Winston Churchill, to whom he was secretary in the early days at Devonport Dockyard. On one visit I discovered that, among Joan's collections stretching the tolerance of her house-proud mother, was one of matchbox labels. Her first of many D&C books, *Matchbox Labels* was an instant success, for there were sufficient mad collectors and no rival title. *Flower Arrangements with a Marine Theme* (it was to have been 'Seaside Flower Arrangements', but Praeger of New York would only take an edition if we avoided 'seaside' unfamiliar to Americans), *Collecting Natural Objects*, and *The Match, the Box and the Label*, and a highly-successful *Corn Dollies,* eagerly snapped up by another publisher when management dissent was destroying D&C's soul, give more than a clue to Joan's character. Suddenly she looks depressed: 'My last book was delayed because a new publisher broke their promise. But then, though there's now a Bude Canal society, which is a good thing, so much of what we found fifty years ago has been lost since, both the physical canal, and many documents that have gone walkabout.' Suggest that things aren't what they were, however, and she's full of enthusiasm for today's world. 'So many more people have special interests.' Good for specialist book sales.

'Can I spend a penny?' I ask. Only with embarrassment and manoeuvring of much hay, for the downstairs toilet has become a store room.

'I've never been house-proud like my mother,' is true enough, but Joan's achievements are endless. She is Bard of the Cornish Gorseth. Of course. And until recently secretary of the Federation of Old Cornwall societies. Blow me, she is bringing a group from the Launceston branch, to stay at a hotel in our very street in Nairn in a few weeks' time. So we arrange to meet again and for me to give a talk.

Launceston and the Liberal Chief Whip

Tourists now dash down the A30 to the seaside so, with its muddle of narrow streets where local accents prevail, Launceston is as unspoilt as

Cornish towns come and still has many individual shops. Though trains disappeared decades ago, they still talk of Railway Weather after a sousing opening day in the 1860s: just one example of how little things adding to a town's individuality and sense of history are handed down orally. We tend to forget this simply because there is so much written history. Of necessity the written word is selective.

Our visit this afternoon is primarily to meet Paul Tyler, North Cornwall's Liberal MP.

We talk of our mothers who used to be friends. His is celebrating her 99th birthday; mine died when she was 81. And about journalism and political ambitions. Paul first went to Westminster representing the old Bodmin constituency with a majority of nine in February 1974, the Three Day Week election which cost Edward Heath his government. In October Paul lost by 600 votes, and so earned his living as a journalist, specialising in rural and transport matters.

'Being in the real world is what made me a better MP today', he says. 'Too many MPs are wholly dependent on their political careers. They've been political advisers, research assistants, councillors, but don't have marketable skills, so they daren't quarrel with their party.' So speaks the Liberal Chief Whip – yes, different from those of the other parties. He adds that he also had the joy of seeing his family grow up. 'Whatever MPs say, bringing up a family, especially if you've a big, remote constituency is fraught with difficulties.'

In 1989 Paul was persuaded to stand for Cornwall & Plymouth in the European elections. 'Tyler's back.' So he was invited to stand in North Cornwall (a constituency I once had thoughts about) and won with the biggest swing in the country. In 1997 he secured the largest Liberal Democrat vote and a majority of 13,847. 'But I always treat North Cornwall as a marginal.' I tell Paul that, much though I liked him, I used to dismiss him as a lightweight. Thanks to experience and confidence, he is certainly not now. Ah, it was that long time out of Parliament!

North Cornwall takes its politics seriously. As we sit down in his tiny, tucked-away office, he switches on the answerphone. Caller after caller leaves a message. When will he get back to them? 'This afternoon, of course', and he means it. Constituency work takes up two thirds of his time. Back in 1974 the postbag produced a daily dozen local letters and the same again (mainly hobbyhorse lobbying) from further afield. Now there are forty letters, nearly all local, and countless phone calls. Coping is only possible by keeping on top of it and with keen staff. The biggest number of cries for help – most after other avenues have been fruitless – concern housing and benefit and medical problems, the latter especially because the main hospitals serving the constituency are situated well outside it. The University of Plymouth recently conducted research, sponsored by the Joseph Rowntree Reform Trust, under the title 'MP=Mr Phixit?' Of those responding, 95 per cent who had been in touch with Paul thought he was easy to contact, 92 per cent were happy with the speed of the response, and even more impressive nearly 80 per cent were happy with the help they received. It is possible. But you think you were busy?

Paul knows and relishes his constituency, walking on its beaches in rare leisure moments. Then he talks on a range of local topics: how some traditional industries such as Delabole slate and De Lank granite hold their own; a new company has over thirty PhDs among its eighty employees in Bude; and of the 500 people who turned up for a Launceston interdenominational service expressing heartfelt feelings for the pressures under which farmers now labour. 'It's the non-metropolitan approach.' Happily, under the heaving surface, the economy of much of the constituency is 'rock solid'. He is naturally an enthusiast for IT, seeing it as turning the clock back. The Phoenicians, he explains, hadn't found Cornwall inaccessible. It was Brunel and Macadam who opened up some parts of Britain at the expense of others. Perhaps it is all a build up to hearing that he is directly descended from the great Trelawny, famous for making the Cornish heard. We talk of Cornwall's value system. 'You find the same kind of thinking in the Highlands, rural Wales and even West Ireland.' True enough.

As I stand up to leave, the Chief Whip hands me a paper *Time to curb the party power,* in which he cites how Ken Livingstone confessed he would have liked to vote for a Liberal Democrat amendment to the London Government Bill because he happened to agree with it. He couldn't, because, despite Labour's large majority, he 'speculated about de-selection'. (This was before he had ambition to become Mayor of London.) And 'while public respect for Parliament as an institution has steadily declined, electors generally reckon that their own local MP (of whatever party) works hard and does a good job.'

Tamar Valley and the Horn of Plenty

We leave Cornwall, crossing the freshwater Tamar at Greystone Bridge. Through Milton Abbot and by a short cut to the restaurant with rooms, the Horn of Plenty, with a broad view over the Tamar Valley where the mines were once among the world's richest. There is a sterile patch of land, testimony to the long-lasting affects of the arsenic found here. A short lake-like glimpse of the Tamar estuary belies the river's importance. All valleys and routes, however minor, on the Devon and Cornwall sides descend to its mainly-hidden course, though it was once a vital route to the outside world and made possible the development of the mines. There is never-ending detail in the view, and great poignancy when you reflect on the economic, social and human dramas enacted over the centuries. As a young journalist in the early 1950s, I attended various functions in villages all round here, and that produces reflections, too.

Tonight we have invited the original owners of the Horn of Plenty restaurant as dinner guests. Sonia and Patrick Stevenson are a remarkable pair. She is visiting her old kitchen, he already drinking beer when I come down from our bedroom. As a lad he was what today we would call a railway nut, so his doctor father wrote to the general manager of the Southern suggesting he be 'taken on'. After cramming to pass the obligatory matric, he became one of four privileged cadets, sent here and there to learn the ropes through practical experience, starting unglamorously at Portsmouth Goods. Though not supposed to ride engines, drivers heard of his extraordinary ability to drive them. 'I was terribly proud to be involved with the Southern.' But music beckoned him when, after the war, he made good progress as singer and composer. Good progress but not enough in a highly-competitive field. So how could a congenial living be earned bringing up a family? Sonia was also a musician but had greatly enjoyed cooking for a hungry husband. So, untried, they went into the restaurant business. That was in 1966. Theirs was probably the first of the Devon restaurants of today's good food guides to get started. The only dress rehearsal was cooking Sonia's specialities for a few friends. Patrick dropped a plate of soup the first night.

The restaurant began with three dishes. Fillet of lamb en croute was the winner. A fish and cream dish was dismissed by many as disgusting. Peppers and aubergines had not been heard of. 'We intended to serve exquisite meals, and the five tables we started with were always sold. But we hadn't reckoned on all the people who came to sneer,' says Patrick. 'It was awful. I was outspoken, unpopular. People knew how terrible I could be, but it didn't have any effect.'

Sonia's cooking became world renowned. Though she was usually confined to the kitchen, in 1984 her photograph went on the jacket of *The Master Chefs of Great Britain*. That meant rich Americans buying a dozen copies to stow in their baggage, and hasty calls to D&C: bring copies and there'll be dinner for two, a nice perk for the sales department. Eventually there were 55 covers, AA rosettes for cooking, and rooms to let. Sonia's own first book, *Magic of Saucery*, was just beaten by Rick Stein's *A Fresh Look at Fish*. The West Country's gastronomic revolution was under way.

'Whatever else has changed at the Horn of Plenty, you clearly haven't,' swore one guest 'reading the bones' on her plate, endlessly waiting for service. 'And you're still a bitch,' was the alleged reply. Patrick was never wholly at ease, though always respected Sonia's creativity and ability to deliver, even if the kitchen was in 'a state'. Though Devon and Cornish people were slow to enjoy as opposed to gawk, steadily those appreciative of exquisite cooking predominated. A candle and then a bright light of excellence in what had been a dark culinary desert, the Horn of Plenty became a legend long before the Stevensons completed their 25-year stint.

Our attractive bedroom is enormous. Carpet might not have been so stylish but would have been more comfortable as the bare boards groan. Perhaps this is a one-off experience? The bill is frightening, drinks offered by the new owners enjoying the Stevensons's company are charged to us. Poor Patrick only nibbles one course of the set dinner, but of course the whole works are charged. Is it greed or lack of imagination that results in lost return business because guests think they are being taken for a ride?

'Would you like to have a drink with me?' is the routine question at one hotel, many miles from this one. Glasses for the owner and wife appear along with yours. You've guessed it. When the bill comes, all the drinks are on it. Few complain, but probably many stay away. It has little to do with money (I would willingly have entertained the Stevensons back at their old haunt whatever the price), everything to do with style, trust, and again imagination.

Next morning we descend to sea level (a few feet above high tide, anyway) to the Tamar at Morwellham Quay. With its replica elevated railway leading to the quays, the restored quays themselves lined with their neat rows of bollards, a train ride deep into a mine, museums and much more, it deservedly attracts large crowds who hopefully soak up some of the extraordinary facts. Here, deep inland, in Victoria's heyday ships queued for a berth before they could tie up at one of those bollards. This was perhaps the Empire's busiest inland port, exporting prodigious quantities of ore, especially copper. It came by private railway from Great Consols of incredible riches, from the Tavistock Canal down an inclined plane, and from local mines, into one of which pops today's tourist train.

Though I admire and have enjoyed today's Morwellham, I shall always remember it as I found it one sunny day in January 1951. The morning had begun by my taking a 1s 5d Workmen's ticket from Teignmouth to Plymouth, and enjoying the ride up the Tavistock branch, where closure in a snow storm (the last three trains had to be abandoned) provided a journalistic coup decades later.

Without much help from the locals who didn't seem to know where it was, I found the canal running through the public gardens. Joyfully stepping out along the muddy tree-lined towpath where nobody else was to be seen, I eventually rang the doorbell of a house near the entrance to what was, in its day, one of the world's great engineering works, certainly at 1¾ miles the longest tunnel anywhere. Permission was freely granted – industrial archaeology hadn't yet been invented and requests for access were rare – to go through the garden to climb down the steel ladder to a concrete platform at the dank entrance. Here, not only did the construction workers enter the tunnel, but miners were boated in to do their twelve-hour days, for rich ore was discovered during the building. And here in 1817 (construction began in 1803 and took fourteen years), members of the opening party had their last opportunity to disembark before their nine lamp-lit, iron boats floated down the current, deep under the downs, celebrating 'the completion of that arduous of laborious undertakings'. In the canal's heyday, the current which had been deliberately created, was used to turn innumerable wheels to provide power. I, of course, had to walk above the canal, eventually descending the remains of the inclined plane used to transport the ore from the canal's terminus high above the river to the ships at the quay.

The scene was unforgettable. Marooned in what had become a vast rush-filled swamp, trees sprouting from the edges, were acres of weed-free tile paving surrounded by rows of bollards. Above the estuary's channel, a notice drunkenly about to fall into the water stated that the proprietors of the Tamar Manure Navigation thereby gave notice that the navigation was no longer fit for navigation. With difficulty I found my way to that undertaking's one and only engineering work, a huge lock (now protected as an ancient monument) which allowed ships to bypass the fresh-water river's lowest weir and so reach Gunnislake. An article for *The Western Morning News* helped secure my first job; more importantly, it inspired its news editor, Frank Booker, to delve more deeply into the valley's history, which later resulted in one of the best books D&C ever published, *The Industrial Archaeology of the Tamar Valley*.

Between those times Frank and I explored the ruins together, noting how the quay's tiles were steadily being removed (they contained arsenic which would always prevent weeds popping up between them), and people were even helping themselves to mileposts 'To the Quay' with a finger pointing the direction. We paid homage to the sailors, especially those travelling to or from California via Cape Horn, who must have enjoyed the respite from the elements tied up at this extraordinary port. Although, in 1951, a hydro-electric station, taking advantage of the water flowing down the canal, was the only thing active at Morwellham, round a couple of the deep bends in the gorge which impressed Queen Victoria almost as much as the Scottish Highlands, there was still a ferryman willing to take you to Calstock. There you could find more abandoned quays, including one that used to serve Cothele House, a different monument to another kind of Cornish wealth and civilisation.

Frank's book captured the excitements and tragedies of the mining industry and the quays that serviced it, and also the colourful competition between river steamers for the market traffic. The Tamar Valley then supported a much larger population and served the whole Plymouth area with strawberries and other produce. D&C celebrated publication by hiring two pleasure boats going all the way up to the lock of the Tamar Manure Navigation, several coaches and a train all connecting with each other at Calstock. The book's TV publicity helped restore the Tamar Valley to the tourist map. Calstock's regatta was revived. Dartington Hall Trustees were inspired to turn Morwellham into a heritage centre. Frank played a leading role, as he did in Devon's history generally, not least as the county's first industrial archaeological adviser.

Today's Morwellham has been revitalised with enthusiasm and good taste. Yet my memory will always be of it caught between its two eras of prosperity, for real and for pleasure. Then you could commune with those who during the Napoleonic Wars had put their all into developing the mines, their railways and waterways, and who enjoyed heady success until the bottom fell out of the copper market.

Latimer Trend: The Printing Revolution

Next morning, we return via Tavistock, noting that the canal wharf is now prominently signposted, and through Yelverton where the shops are still minus their upper storey, removed for planes using the wartime aerodrome. Then across Roborough Downs, close to all kinds of monuments, including the ancient leats which gave Plymouth and Devonport their first reliable water supplies – and a spur-of-the-moment diversion down to Clearbrook, which lost nine-tenths of its small population by emigration to America when its local mine closed. So down the charming wooded Plym Valley and by ancient Plym Bridge to the outskirts of Plymouth.

After the inevitable taking of wrong turns, for Plymouth is as complicated as it is spread out over many hills and valleys, first call is Latimer Trend, printers, on an industrial estate. It was on our way back from Plymouth Hoe, having experienced the complete eclipse of the sun a couple of years ago, that I noticed the old works near the city centre that still displayed the company's name, but had obviously long been abandoned. Gone were the sounds and smells of monotype, and cars parked three deep in the crowded site next to a school. A local resident commented on the move to bigger premises. 'They are doing well.'

D&C acquired Latimer Trend when Faber & Faber had poured too much into stock in a new upmarket paperback series and were desperate for cash. Latimer Trend had one great virtue. Such had been the training of their typesetters and compositors that, however untidy a manuscript, the page proofs (we pioneered abolishing galleys) would be perfect. They cared. When it was pointed out to the publishers Gollancz that different house styles were used in the first and last parts of one of their manuscripts, and asked which they preferred, there were loud moans when the reply came 'Follow copy', ie print the inconsistencies. Not the right kind of customer. Almost monthly for my first year or so as boss, I visited the works on a Friday evening to present a gold watch to someone retiring on their 65th birthday who had joined on their fifteenth. Craftsmanship flowered with continuity.

One of those business turning points that happen just occasionally, though much less frequently than most people realise, was when as chairman I was brought in supposedly to rubber stamp the chosen candidate for Latimer Trend's new managing director. He was a Scot. Now, the Scots are either very good (they indeed command much of English commerce) or have a defect, which in many cases is excessive whisky. There was something odd about this character, though not his drinking. In exploratory questioning, he dropped a hint that someone else had been credited with success that was really his. 'Is that the first time it's happened?' I asked. He went off like a cannon, my colleagues who had chosen him looking more sheepish by the moment as he exclaimed how unfairly he had been treated – scandalously – many times over.

The only other possible candidate was John Turner, a rough diamond, with plenty of go and opinion – probably too much for anybody's peace of mind, but then the business demanded energy, especially on the sales side. He got the job, pulled the place up while still retaining the ability to make excellence out of any kind of manuscript, foreign language, mathematics, plays, whatever. Later he persuaded us to invest in film setting. Then, of course, he demanded we sell him the business, or he'd be off. The printing world was changing rapidly, and it no longer made sense for publishers to own their own works. John won. We helped guide him through a couple of transitional years, and then contact ceased. Here am I, best part of two decades later, going to find out just how well 'doing well' means.

Last week John apologised for the fact he would be away... still his old self, worrying that trade was getting tougher. But worrying can get you everywhere. The factory, I find, is enormous. There are nice historical touches, the old checking-in clock and The Gem Press No 1, in the entrance hall. Otherwise all I recognise are a couple of staff, including Bill Buglar, still second-in-command, who takes me round.

In our time staff numbers fell from sixty to forty. Now even in this industry of constantly increasing labour efficiency, there are 100. 'Caxton would have recognised what we were doing when you were boss,' says Bill. 'He mightn't make much sense of it today.' A clinically-clean litho machine stands in what seems acres of space. 'It hasn't been easy, 24 hours a day literally sometimes, but we've extended our customer base, done well with land and buildings. John's been a right hard taskmaster... an autocratic domineering bastard who is never wrong. But then, nice though you seem, David, I'm sure you didn't get where you are without upsetting a few.'

It transpires that this isn't their first new building after leaving the old site; and that they seem to have taken over almost all of the other Plymouth printers of my day. Bill smiles as he recalls how very old fashioned most of them were, sitting targets when recessions came.

'"Young Mr Frank" at Underhills, where I started myself, was over seventy.' At another printers, automatics meant machines you didn't have to wind up by hand. The pick of the labour force and customers came with each takeover. What he didn't say, but was obvious from rapid conversations with customers and staff, is that worrying is the basic culture, today's price for success. Yet I feel a touch of pride as I see all this complicated typesetting and printing from 'up country' entrusted to a Plymouth firm, turning over £4 million annually, specialising in medical and other journals, still printing Samuel French's plays, proof copies of which I enjoyed in my day.

I ask Bill if the firm is holding its own on typesetting. 'Most companies think they can do their own cheaper, and so they can; but knowledge and expertise produce quality, and there are those who have learned that, even if they've had to learn it the hard way.'

Plymouth and its Newspaper Life

Plymouth: large, especially in geographical area, the only city in which I have lived and gained a taxi driver's knowledge. By any standard, it is a stunning city, inevitably impressing first-time visitors, especially those taken on an organised tour. A bit like Sydney in Australia, it wears its heart on its sleeve and it is not easy to get under its skin and understand its subtleties. It was always the West Country's hardest place to sum up in newspaper and television pieces.

So I take refuge in personal minutiae, possibly boring Sheila – as anyone I have driven around it in the past – by saying that a guy living in that house took his daughter away from her mum and disappeared across the Channel; that three sailors said that all they were doing was helping a struggling woman relieve herself just over there (it used to be a bombsite) and that in the theatre, when I rose from my box where I had eaten sandwiches sitting on the floor while reporting a revivalist meeting, I was mistaken for a convert on his way down to the mercy seat. And that to this day, whenever I eat Christmas cake, I recall sympathising on Boxing Day with the mum who used to live in the house we are just passing, about the death of her son in the Korean war. Alas, she had not been told and so realised the worst from my comment. Her automatic reaction: 'Have a piece of Christmas cake.'

When I joined *The Western Morning News*, Plymouth was a city of fading traditional life, bombsites and temporary shops, including Tin Pan Alley as entertaining as any fairground – and great expectations, forged by the new centre laid out afresh. There was continuing great dependence on the Navy and dockyard. The latter seemed as timeless as the Hoe commanding possibly the finest city view in Britain. Culture was thin, self-satisfaction considerable. There was universal belief that Plymouth was the hardest done by place in the war, and yet the greatest. Tales were repeatedly told of how people were rescued from buildings largely demolished by bombs. The *WMN* headquarters, Leicester Harmsworth House, now at an angle from the new street grid, was the sole pre-war central survivor, bravely saved when incendiary bombs were thrown out by staff on night watch. Plymouth was also a city of social systems in which 'high-ups' took themselves seriously: the Navy – dare to titter at a court martial and you might be court martialled yourself – the council, the railway, above all the dockyard. There was also a substantial commercial dock, and substantial fishing. Always a young reporter was made to feel as though he could not possibly adequately be in the know.

That feeling was fostered by the chief reporter, a tall, soft-spoken Scot said to owe his position to having saved one of the Harmsworths in a swimming accident. Had he been in the building trade, he would have stepped straight out of *The Ragged Trousered Philanthropist*. Working conditions were Victorian: three days a fortnight off, never two together; the diary (of reporters' duties) made up much earlier but never released until mid-evening. You were not allowed to ascertain your next day's programme by telephoning from a job or until you had filed your report on return. Girlfriend and her family would be in bed before you were free. Sundays were often triple duty, spread out from 9.30am to 10pm, after the last bus had left.

'Look you, mister, there's no point in your sitting there,' the chief reporter might say at 9.45, just in time to get the last bus. 'On your way home go and see what this poor woman who has just lost her husband has to say.' A far longer walk home for me but, as the chief well knew, such visits seldom made publishable copy. It was the penalty for daring to do something positive, like read, when on duty. Alternative punishment was to write a report on something useless fished out of the paper basket in front of you.

Life became more tolerable when I bought my 1936 Morris Eight. It needed repairs rather than petrol, but took me out into the countryside, free of the chief reporter's eye. Mind you, it led to scrapes, too. 'This young lady who's selling the wedding gown she's only tried on in the shop – she's obviously upset. Go and see what she has to say, mister.' Armed with the proof of the woman's small ad to appear in the next day's paper, I eventually tracked down her remote caravan. Sure, she was delighted to see me, anything in trousers no doubt, and off came her clothes so I could see the wonderful dress. It has to be admitted her figure was better in it than without it, but it was hard preventing her blocking the exit.

At first, the car was expensive to run on a salary of five guineas a week, leaving about 14s after deductions and lodgings. But it proved a great investment, both for ordinary jobs and also for such things as the county shows in the days when they were held in different towns each year. If a team of us went to North Devon or West Cornwall, you might persuade three car-less reporters to be your passengers and charge 6½d per head a mile... riches, especially if a more senior member also driving his car insisted that the best way wasn't the shortest.

The car was essential for 'Specials'. Partly because of my knowledge of the railway, tourist and economic scenes, but also because somehow I could make sense of complicated issues and charm an audience, increasingly my duties were Special, which meant being off the diary and working in one's own way. The important thing was to give value, writing material that was widely read and which influenced key people... as well as provoking letters to the editor, which railway matters always do.

The editor was an elusive socialite who, despite the evening being the busy time for journalists putting a morning paper to bed, only appeared in the office for a short morning. My luck was having the support of the next two in line: assistant editor Crispin Gill (with whom we are having lunch today) and news editor Frank Booker (of Tamar Valley fame). Though they were not especial friends with each other, both liked my work and encouraged more, the former often concerned by the level of expenses that went along with it, the latter enjoying seeing the chief reporter's irritation at more Specials coming my way. Both became close friends and valued authors.

When I was back on the diary, the chief reporter's revenge came in the form of truly down-to-earth duties: fish market, Conservative women's coffee circles, jobs involving endless queuing (one week over forty hours of it) for the Torpoint Ferry. 'Don't be above your station, mister.' And that was the message when he reported, as though it had come from the Kremlin, that the 'high ups' in Plymouth railway management were increasingly upset by my criticism of their slack regime. 'You're getting yourself into trouble, mister.'

Luck would have it that that very morning, out of the blue, KWC Grand, august general manager of the Western Region, had written thanking me for doing part of his job, since the local timekeeping was awful, mainly because of slack station work. 'Keep up the good work.' He invited me to go and see him at Paddington. 'That's awkward,' I replied to the chief reporter, 'for I've just got this.' His relations and friends on the railway were implicated in the letter I handed to him. For once the man was speechless. Not even a 'mister'.

Fortune lay in having made myself indispensable, and so able to take my railway, tourist and other reporting into a new freelance life. Frank Booker was frequently on the telephone with a request, often at around ten in the evening for the paper's lead story; the start had to be phoned within twenty minutes.

It would be too easy to be sidetracked here especially by recalling railway matters. Suffice it to say that when the rival Western and Southern routes were rolled into a single Plymouth Division, the new superintendent's first job was to call on me saying I was obviously better informed than he (stationmasters and others from all over the region regularly enjoyed a listening ear) and so could I work with him to bring about a better railway? We went up on the inaugural businessmen's *Golden Hind* to have lunch with Jeremy Thorpe, then holding Liberal dominance in North Devon, and to see one of Winston Churchill's last appearances in the Commons. It was the beginning of a close relationship with much railway top brass which, however, did not blunt criticism where deserved. On the holiday side, in season, daily reports from around the resorts commanded a large audience, those telling of the peak summer Saturday treks of visitors and their delays positively increasing sales of the Monday paper.

So, after the personal reminiscences, let's get down to understanding the real Plymouth. By far the most remote large city in England, it has always been very much its own place, with a tendency to judge others by its standards. Call it inward looking or civic pride, but nowhere are local dignitaries more admired than their national counterparts. The South West's commercial centre, it is not Devon's capital and instinctively it serves a region rather than its own county.

The sea has always played a key role, and even today you cannot help but be conscious of salt water, the two great rivers of Tamar and Plym with their many tributaries and creeks flowing into the vast Sound, under the showpiece Hoe where Drake is reputed to have finished his game of bowls before routing the Spanish Armada. The Hoe is unique in scale and outlook, a place where for centuries Plymothians have gathered for great occasions. And there is always activity out in the Sound.

This morning, as often, a naval ship is slowly weaving its complicated passage into the Sound in readiness to head west up the Tamar to Devonport Dockyard – following the route of so many ships through the ages bringing back the spoils of victory, or escaping the enemy and leaving less fortunate colleagues behind. Several fishing vessels and a cargo ship are making to or from Sutton Harbour to the east, while a pleasure craft reaches Drake's Island in mid-Sound, well beyond which is the lengthy just-above-sea-level breakwater built a couple of centuries ago to ensure storms did not ravage the shore.

The Three Towns of Plymouth, Devonport and Stonehouse (each once had its independent tram system) were not merged until relatively modern times, and it took Hitler to complete Plymouth's supremacy, since all the rebuilding, after the incessant blitzes that took the heart out, was concentrated here, though much of Devonport was equally shattered. It began with a far-sighted plan in the war's darkest days, and by the time I arrived as a journalist in 1950 the new road system was already taking shape, though only the broad, dual-carriageway Royal Parade, on a gentle uniform slope, had been completed and only one of the huge white, rectangular stores of the new era, Dingles, was about to open its doors. For up to a decade, department stores – each the pride and joy of its owning family, such as the Yeos, Spooners and upmarket Pophams – operated from a series of smaller premises, many in Plymouth's (as opposed to Devonport's) secondary shopping area of Mutley Plain.

Royal Parade and the rest of the new central grid system may seem excessively post-war in style but it has worn well, the only major changes being in traffic management, which for a city of this size works well. But then Plymouth has never been short of land; some of the post-war industrial estates were indeed at an epoch-making distance from the centre, as were the new factories, Bush and Berketex being examples, employing thousands of women whose husbands were mainly 'inside' at the dockyard. At the top of Royal Parade, St Andrew's, Plymouth's mother church, was restored, Charles Church in the middle of a roundabout further to the east being left in its ruined state as a memorial to those who lost their lives in the blitz. Starting by St Andrew's, I have to refind my way to the historic Barbican, for again the traffic system has changed. The Barbican's narrow streets, some still cobbled, are as cosy as ever, for bombing was surprisingly concentrated in the centre and many of the tightly-packed ancient buildings have been sympathetically restored. Plymouth Gin still has its presence, though most traditional traders have made way for art galleries, antique shops and restaurants, and down at the bottom the fish market has become a jolly shopping centre with the emphasis on high-quality local crafts.

We are making for an Italian restaurant specialising in excellent fish: Bella Napoli, where Crispin Gill, increasingly dapper as he ages, is already waiting, drink in hand. I say we have been walking along the waterfront reviving memories. 'The point of sending new reporters to the fish market was to see if they came back with any stories beyond fish prices. Anyone who was going to get anywhere would surely do so.'

In our day *The Western Morning News*, or 'the paper', was broad-sheet. Its front page was probably the best in the history of regional daily papers. The lead could be international, national, or local if strong enough, such as Dr Beeching's railway axing. It would be balanced by other medium-length pieces from different spheres. A total of thirty or forty stories, including the briefs in the first column, gave a fair view of the world from the South West. Many Cornish folk took it as their only daily paper. Top historians contributed features, large numbers of which were cut out and kept by readers.

Especially in the days before local television, the paper was a vital opinion former. Its strength was always out in the deep countryside, what we called 'the shires'. In the evening the resident reporters from all over the South West phoned in their pieces: they were a colourful collection of individualists if not eccentrics, many of whom I got to know on my journeys around the region in later days. Even in Plymouth it was the establishment paper, taken by everyone in high-class Mannamead, if not lower down in the city.

Crispin regrets there is now no Plymouth edition, but then he seldom 'bothers' with today's tabloid, and dislikes the fact you can't walk into the editor's office without making an appointment. We say we have also just been across the hydraulically-controlled lock (beside the splendid new Marine Aquarium) which keeps Sutton Harbour at permanent high tide. 'At least I can still see fishing vessels from my window... and a lot more. Plymouth is still a busy port.'

But where are our fish? One of the brothers running Bella Napoli is putting his coat on. 'We love each other but this is one of the days we can't get on,' he explains. 'It will be OK tomorrow, but I'm leaving him to it today.' So that is why he has been quietly reading his paper for the last half hour. Eventually the other brother, also clearly upset, brings three enormous, large and whole pan-fried sea bass. No nouveau cuisine here. On or off the bone? We opt for 'off'. Our sea bass is superbly fresh, its delicate flavour to be savoured in temporary silence.

Crispin and I often say we could write a book about each other. I regard him as my first boss. He wrote books for D&C including a history of Plymouth, an excellent *The Scilly Isles* and several on Dartmoor. Then he went to edit *The Countryman*, taking its circulation from 53,000 to 98,000 in a decade beginning in 1971, and we published many *Countryman* books. Warm, professional, good fun.

Today's tabloid *WMN* adopts the fashion of allocating a large space to whatever it chooses as its lead. 'The champion of the West,' it loves pursuing favourite causes. It has however long given up any pretence of well-balanced coverage of matters elsewhere, and contributions by outside experts are no longer welcome. West Country affairs are well covered and, whenever I come back to the region, I am impressed by just how much there is worthy of reporting.

Today's issue includes a supplement with the chief constable's very accessible annual report. We are told that patronage of rural bus services has doubled over the last two years, that fishermen have been cleared of illegally taking pebbles from Budleigh Salterton beach, and how another historic Cornish garden might be restored. Details are given of the plan to extend china clay quarrying on Dartmoor. Wind farms are playing an increasing role, and here's how one village post office has survived. Braunton's Great Field, where strip farming has been practised for centuries, is to be saved by a new government deal. Fascinating stuff.

After lunch, along a much-declined Union Street to Stonehouse and across what is still called Halfpenny Bridge, though the toll ceased a century ago, to Devonport, where faded touches of architectural glory demonstrate the pride of this once independent town. Down to the Torpoint Ferry, the busiest in Britain, still with queues – and a glimpse across the Hamoaze, as the lower Tamar estuary is called, to Mount Edgecumbe's Country Park, the only real parkland in all Cornwall.

It is coming-out time at the now-privatised dockyard, but the crowds are not what they used to be, the long queues of buses now disappeared into history. When we stop at some shops north of the ferry, deprivation is the word that comes to mind. Parts of Plymouth are as awful as ever, and we hardly suppose that many people round here derive much compensation from the view of the river. The pull of the city centre has reduced the feeling of local community at St Budeaux. To another great view: overlooking the Tamar Bridges, Brunel's 1859 masterpiece dwarfed by the road bridge of over a century later. A High Speed Train on its way to London crawls across the bridge at more than right angles to its approach. The Cornish said the bridge would let in the Devil. In practice it took away tens of thousands to new worlds after the collapse of mining, and up to fifty trainloads a day of spring broccoli, Scilly Isles daffodils, West Cornwall early potatoes. Perhaps the Devil came in the form of visitors to whom so much of Cornwall ultimately sold its soul.

Early journalistic duties involved frequent trips across the bridge, at peak times Saltash was often on the journalistic patch. At peak times that usually involved a ride on an all-stations-and-halts suburban train, with an 0-6-0 pannier tank sandwiched between two pairs of crowded auto-cars. The magistrate's court at Saltash was usually a dull affair, but after a couple of people were remanded on a sexual offence one week, the charge sheet grew and grew. 'Can you handle the heat, mister?' The list was beginning to include well-known people. Interest intensified till, when there were several pages of accused, the police withdrew charges. Sexual perversion was not unusual in the local river communities.

Back to Newton Abbot

Then up the A38 dual carriageway through the city's northern outskirts to the flyover at Marsh Mills Roundabout, and up the continuing A38, now dual carriageway but once part of the longest lane in England. Every mile of the A38 has its story. So cut off did Plymouth feel from 'up country', even from Exeter, that for years every scheme to improve a section was front-page news. It took twenty post-war years to complete the dual carriageway from Exeter to Plymouth, still far below motorway standards but with good Dartmoor scenery, and a close-up of Dean Prior where the poet Herrick struggled with his soul in the cultureless countryside.

Back to Newton Abbot. Every few days I have continued broadcasts to Scotland about the railway situation. The Hatfield accident was indeed bad news, floods since contributing to widespread chaos, the greatest ever apart from times of strike. Wartime bombing was a trivial inconvenience compared to this. Railtrack is paying the price for sweating its assets beyond their proper replacement date, and for its dictatorial attitude. There are still no through trains between England and Scotland. A poor time to have started our travels? In reality we have to return to duties in Nairn for a time anyway, but it is going to mean flying.

THE HIGHLAND CHIEFTAIN

Express (3½ hours) to Edinburgh

It is seven o'clock again and Dave the taxi is at the door. But this time it is 7am, still pitch dark. At his earliest ever, the postie dashes down the drive in his van and we are able to extract our personal letters while leaving the office's for the staff to deal with. The postie races off: maybe he hopes to finish early. Dave drives more sedately but, even at this early hour, is full of accounts of previous fares and the silly goings-on of some of the drivers of the firm who have bid for the sole right to pick up passengers from Inverness airport. Providing there is extra cash in it for the airport, passengers' convenience seems to be a low priority. So even if there is a queue of waiting people, other taxis, having dropped off their incoming passengers, cannot pick up. 'It's ridiculous, some of them don't know their basic geography,' says Dave.

He himself seems to be doing well with work from both BA and the rail companies taking fares who have missed connections 'doon south' on trips of up to 100 miles. 'ScotRail were paying, but this woman said she wanted to do shopping on the way,' says Dave. 'I asked: "How long?"'

'She replied: "I never tie myself down. It might be twenty minutes or an hour."'

'"In that case, you'll have to pay," I said. That upset her. I'm surprised she didn't expect the railway people to pick up the tab for her groceries as well.'

Inverness station has always been a magical place. For one thing, nearly all trains are starting or finishing journeys that will take longer than those, say, from King's Cross to York. The layout is fascinating, platforms on two sides of a triangle. Some trains take the third side and back in for their continuing journeys. In the days of steam most trains used to do that in order to be alongside the connecting service for the north or south.

The coat of arms of the Inverness & Nairn Railway, the first isolated section to be built in the Highlands, is among the interesting things to see. Founded by local people who had everything to learn about land acquisition and engineering, not to mention how to treat passengers, the I&NR was taken over by the Highland Railway and later formed part of the original route from the south. It was the way I first came to the Highlands by a train which seemed to sniff at every telegraph post all the way from Perth.

Today's unit or Sprinter trains shrink the distance though, as already hinted, are not ideal for passengers wanting to revel in the landscape. No longer is there an observation car to Kyle of Lochalsh, where patronage has dropped sharply. But costs have probably dropped more, and that's all that anyone seems to care about. This is not Switzerland! The only true tourist train up here is the *Royal Scotsman* we met in Kyle of Lochalsh: delightful but far too expensive for most holidaymakers, and anyway can only be joined further south.

The emphasis on economy, and constant paring, leaves *The Highland Chieftain* as the sole remaining daytime train to England. Though an ordinary High Speed Train set, the Great North & East Railway provides a stunning level of service, especially in first class, so that the journey itself is a great introduction to a visit south. Sadly patronage of breakfast in the dining car is disappointingly thin. Except possibly going along the Sea Wall at Teignmouth, nowhere does a traditional British breakfast taste so good as when climbing the first of the route's two great gradients, on the 'new' direct route to Aviemore, though it is now over 100 years old.

An American couple sitting opposite are delighted to have things pointed out to them as a faint sun comes out playing hide-and-seek, emphasising how much we twist and turn on this part of the journey. Daylight reveals a particularly heavy frost, which for several hours remains on the ground shadowed by buildings and even our bridges and viaducts which, as the sun gains strength, are seen with exaggerated broad piers.

Every journey is different and it is the intimacy of the familiar pattern that is most endearing, a fox seen here on our last journey, a stag on that hilltop years ago, snow in profusion on the higher slopes of this showpiece landscape today. All the rivers and streams are full. We miss seeing the sleeper waiting in a loop for us to pass twenty or so minutes out from Inverness: with all the disruption after the Hatfield accident, it still hasn't been restored. Beyond Culloden Moor, where Bonnie Prince Charlie was roundly defeated in April 1746, and Scotland lost its nationhood (even the wearing of kilts became illegal) we cross the great 600-yard long Nairn viaduct of 28 ordinary and one longer central arch over the valley of the bubbling River Nairn, itself surprisingly narrow.

Past Loch Insh on one side and then alongside one of General Wade's military roads on the other and, as usual, we hold up a small queue of school buses waiting for us to clear the level crossing at Kingussie. The modern school vies with Nairn's to be the ugliest in all Britain. Ruthven Barracks on the hilltop overlooking Kingussie must also have looked pretty ugly when new but, now in ruins and bathed in the faint morning sunshine, look as though someone has positioned them to enhance the view. They were built to hold down the Highlanders after the earlier rebellion of 1715, but were taken by the Jacobites in 1744. After Culloden they were blown up to prevent that happening again.

Half a dozen passengers join here, one bound for a short day out in Edinburgh, coming to the restaurant car. Kingussie is one of a pair of small resorts with a string of rather grand Victorian villas under the western mountains, and old-fashioned shops. It is home to the pleasing Highland Folk Museum and also doubles as the Glenbogle of TV's Monarch of the Glen, which has proved as useful for the business of catering for the film crews and actors as the extra tourists it has brought. Its station is beautifully maintained, while that of the other resort, Newtonmore, has been reduced to a single platform with a bus-shelter type waiting room. *The Highland Chieftain* ignores it, but Newtonmore is well worth a visit. Attractions include Waltzing Waters, illuminated fountains only feet away from theatre-style seating, truly stealing the thunder as audiences are as attentive as though the performers were human. The fountains and music beat time together.

Don't miss the Wildcat Centre for details of the Wildcat Walk, a 6.5 mile trail around the village 'taking in native woodland, moorland, shelter belts, magnificent views of the Monadhliath and Cairngorm Mountains and the banks of the River Spey, Calder, and Allt Laraidh'. The trail links some forty hectares of woodland managed by the Newtonmore Community Woodland Trust, while the centre houses Newtonmore's Millennium Book. There is great community spirit involving our friends, James and Janet Davidson. They routinely enjoy the marvellous walking country. Their energetic Labrador, Sheila, once racing to high ground sent a loose stone tumbling hundreds of feet to land just ahead of us as we walked beside the Calder in the pass leading to Glen Banchor.

James is a self-published author of a book supporting his Flower of Scotland campaign to encourage Scottish youngsters to eat and live more healthily; Highland diet and habits are not compatible with long life. When James farmed in West Aberdeen, he was persuaded to stand as Liberal candidate and surprisingly found himself at Westminster. He never really enjoyed that. What he especially disliked was the occasion when the nation's eyes were on him, since he was the last of the then handful of Liberal MPs to vote for Jeremy Thorpe's successor as leader.

The others had split their votes equally, and it was James's vote that ultimately gave the leadership to David Steel. Now he is thinking of writing a history of Scotland's associations with the sea.

Over the point leading to the double-track section from Dalwhinnie beside the picturesque distillery with its cooper-top pagodas. Its fifteen-year-old malts are a favourite of Sheila's (my wife, not the Labrador), but since modernisation it employs only a few staff.

Our engines are at full power. Up another 700 feet to Drumochter Summit (1,484ft, the highest point reached by a railway in Britain) beside the increasingly busy A9. And down, down and still down, from a gloomy pass twisting and turning to a less harsh landscape where people farm and live. Be ready to look out, I tell the Americans, as we approach the Pass of Killiecrankie. With trees bare of leaves, they get the best possible view of the gorge. One of the things that made me first want to travel this way was Murray's *Hand-Book*'s splendid description of the journey in the opposite direction:

> At the N. end, the rly. is conveyed over a small burn on a noble Viaduct of 10 arches, bending l. before a tunnel is entered, and from this viaduct the whole Pass can be seen by looking back... Leaving Struan, the rly. begins to ascend, more slowly at first, rapidly afterwards, more than 800ft being ascended in 12m. The first 2m are through a birch plantation - Clunes rt.; then the country becomes much wilder and more desolate, and trees are not seen again until Glen Truim and Strathspey... The Garry is crossed; snow posts and strong palisade screens for the rly. against snow drifts testify to the severity of the winter in these parts, and well-marked moraines are seen... At 53m. 'the summit, 1484ft.' is passed and the train hastens down the Pass of Drumochter, 'by far the wildest scene through which any rly. passes in this country' (Geikie).

'Great view,' say our Americans who have not spared their necks to study the Pass but, alas for me, their enthusiasm is spoilt by them telling us it reminds them of somewhere back home. Unique though Scottish scenery is, nothing is spared from such comparisons.

As I wrote in *Double Headed*, a railway book written jointly with my father, Murray had the skill not only to tell the Victorians what they wanted to know, but to give them pride in personally having traversed the trail with him. Queen Victoria no doubt had her train stop so that she might enjoy the Pass, but suggestions that an occasional tourist train might do that today are regarded as faintly ridiculous. One day, perhaps, enlightenment will shine through. Part of the trouble is that the Scots are pretty blasé about their own landscape, and – excited though they are when key features are pointed out – the English no longer arrive as though they were in an exotic foreign country. Things have changed since Murray stated: 'At all the important points good hotels, sometimes rising to the magnitude of palaces, have been erected, while, where possible, railways and steamers convey travellers into the very heart of the mountains.' Anyway, Richard Branson has just decreed that his travellers don't want to look out of the window but watch a film as though they were on a plane. Happily that is not yet generally true, but it shows the trend.

When we come this way by car, going south, we like the diversion by the House of Bruar, its range of clothes, garments, food and gifts and the size of its car park and café as surprising as its remote position, and then through Blair Athol with its castle and only private army in Britain, staying on General Wade's road through Killicrankie rather than the modern A96. Here there is a stylish hotel, enterprising visitor centre and nature trail beside the Garry at the foot of the pass we look down on from the train. Inevitably you will learn that the pass was the scene of another of those bloody Scottish battles. A notice tells us:

> The pass of Killiecrankie was the main route North in the seventeenth century and it was here, in 1689, that an army of men, drawn from the western Highland clans and loyal to James VII, was led by Graham of Claverhouse, Viscount Dundee, into battle against Government troops under the command of General Hugh MacKay. MacKay led his army into Scotland to quell the Highland uprising against the offering of the Scottish crown to the Protestant William of Orange. MacKay's army was defeated at Killiecrankie where Bonnie Dundee also died of gunshot wounds.

By car, at the southern end of the pass you can cross the Garry by the lonely road to Rannoch station on the West Highland Railway. Occasionally walkers and cyclists transfer here between the East and West Coast train systems; in Murray's horse-drawn coach days there was a well-advertised daily service. Our hardy forefathers enjoying Loch Tummel's famous scenery on the way.

We continue descending to Pitlochry, where several dozen people are waiting to join and our carriage stops alongside the decorative water fountain on the platform. We talk of happy memories of staff outings and other visits for plays at the Festival Theatre at this more substantial Victorian resort, delightfully set in the Tummel Valley. Beginning as a tent erected for a few summer weeks, the theatre has steadily increased in status and now has a fine building suitable for year-round use. Don't miss one of the better-known salmon leaps beside it. Still down, over the Tay near which the newest millionaire to secure a Highland home has her hideaway (J K Rowling of Harry Potter fame), through a sample of Perthshire's park-like landscape, and again we arrive at ugly Perth station.

Next stop is Gleneagles station, built primarily to serve the great hotel, but providing only two London-bound guests this morning. Building an exceptionally grand hotel here was the idea of the Caledonian Railway. World War One delayed it and it was still only a shell in 1918. An attempt to sell it to Americans failed, so it was the later London Midland & Scottish Railway that fulfilled the luxurious expectations, capitalising on the name of the nearby estate whose owner remained infuriated till the end of his life. The hotel's service (summer only) was impeccable, and such was the scale of operations that it had a private siding. It was a prestigious place to work. The LMS chief bandleader, Henry Hall, who spent his summers here, took a fifty per cent cut in salary when he went to the BBC. Things may have changed since then but at least Gleneagles, where golfers have always been significant among the guests, is thoroughly alive and kicking, and now provides year-round luxury and of course employment.

On the opposite, southern, side I notice the road over the hill once regularly taken to visit that doyen of Scottish historians, ARB Haldane, a solicitor with a human touch. His *Drove Roads* and *New Ways Through the Glens* were two of the finest Scottish titles to grace the David & Charles list in the days when virtually no publisher north or south of the border cared about Scottish books.

After a rapid run, we see the hilltop castle as we approach Stirling. My namesake author, John Thomas, never tired of telling me how the Scots poured molten metal down on the English trying to climb the cliffs on which it is perched.

Ten days or so ago, when our schedule was impossibly tight, Dave the taxi brought us to Stirling, regaling us with the story of how the group of VIPs who had flown into Inverness for a stay at the exclusive Skibo Castle found they had arrived sans fishing rods. The private plane's captain was called out to search and, sure enough, he found them still on board. Dave duly collected them, but making delivery through Skibo's tight security net was a time-consuming business full of misunderstandings. 'Cost no object at Skibo,' he said, adding kindly: 'You'd be quite out of place there.'

Trying to find our hotel, formerly a girls' school, he edged into what might be the right street; a police car instantly dashed round the corner with comical coincidence. 'Think it might be one-way,' said the constable, obligingly getting out to check, though he must have known. It was the right street, but we had to find the lower entrance.

After breakfast there was time for a quick visit to Stirling Castle, on far greater scale and more interesting than I'd expected. There are just too many castles in Scotland to take them all seriously. Stirling, with high walls on its precipitous bluff, shouldn't be missed. 'The mighty Royal castle of Stirling towers above some of the most important battlefields in Scotland's history including the site of Stirling Bridge, William Wallace's victory over the English in 1297 and Bannockburn where Robert the Bruce defeated the same foe in 1314,' begins one of the publicity pieces. The Scots weren't always so lucky, and of course we learned about Mary Queen of Scots, who spent her childhood here but came to a sticky end. The glorious view of the Forth meandering in its broad valley, the vast Great Hall and the reconstructed mediaeval kitchen, all warrant that over-used adjective unique.

We came to Stirling for my annual lecture to the postgraduate course in publishing studies, first lunching with one of the staff lecturers, Andrew Wheatcroft, a formidable academic author of books such as *The Ottomans* and *The World Atlas of Revolutions*, publishing consultant to Routledge & Kegan Paul and then after its take-over to Weidenfeld, and, with his wife, having an interesting diversion in horticulture. We talked of the possibility of launching a specialist quarterly for self-publishers, even forming The Institute of Authorship & Small-scale Publishing.

As always here, the lecture audience was attentive, many studiously making notes. Taking the one-year course is expensive. The serious tone is underlined by those, almost half, from overseas, mainly (like the Chinese) paid for by their bosses who expect results. The nature of questions changes over the years. This time they were fascinated by publishing on a small scale, asking if one can make a decent living publishing from home, or combine publishing with running a bookshop. It is not a new thought that in future innovative publishing will not be done by the conglomerates or medium-sized firms (the latter have anyway nearly all been swallowed by the former), but by individuals or at most three or four-people bands able to spot trends and talent and act swiftly. 'If you take the risk in launching a new author, make sure they cannot leave you in the lurch with no reward when wooed by one of the big boys who's seen your success,' I told them. The students wrote it down.

Returning to today, next stop is Falkirk, where for some time a station notice has recorded the interchange with the Forth & Clyde Canal towpath. Though once one of Scotland's chief trade highways, the canal had been closed for so long that it seemed that only the ridiculously optimistic could hope it might ever be reopened. With a large Millennium grant, it soon will be. At Falkirk itself there is a wheel more remarkable than the London Eye which picks up boats and turns to allow them to float off at a different level. It is the world's first rotating boat lift, funded through a co-operative effort, the largest grant coming from the Heritage Lottery fund. Day trippers are being offered a ride on the wheel up to the Union Canal and will then be able to sail along a twenty-metre high aqueduct before passing through a tunnel under the Antonine Wall, the Roman defence dyke that traverses Scotland between the Firths of Clyde and Forth.

With thoughts of anticipation of that experience, we nod off until we slow for Edinburgh, passing the Murrayfield stadium and soon enjoy a fine view of the castle and the Royal Mile as we trundle through Princes Street Gardens, the Old Town to the right, New Town to the left. So we stop at Waverley station, which completely fills the valley between the two. So eagerly were railways welcomed that protests were muted when this prime site was seized. After the first three and a half hours of the journey (far longer than the best journeys from Plymouth to London) we arrive a few minutes early.

That gives time to stretch our legs and have a touch of retail therapy, the station announcer monotonously droning 'ScotRail's railway [such and such] train calling at Haymarket...' Traditionally Sheila is encouraged to visit the delicatessen on the platform to survey the shelf of miniatures, leisurely deciding which malt she will take for today's nightcap. Today it is a Dalwhinnie. On our way back to platform 19 we catch a glimpse of what is undoubtedly the draughtiest spot in Britain: the long Waverley Steps up to Princes Street which act as a funnel attracting cold air from Siberia. If you don't have a heart attack climbing them, you are in the middle of one of the finest shopping centres anywhere, the smell of processed hops helping to stamp Edinburgh's character on one's mind. How exhilarating generations of southerners paying their first visit to Scotland's capital found their breathless emergence into the invigorating air and businesses of Princes Street after a night's broken sleep on the train.

A new restaurant crew welcome us. The Inverness gang have asked them to reserve our table for lunch. Away we go, with many fewer passengers than normal. No wonder the estimated cost of the recent disruptions continually increases. Though the Hatfield accident is now several months ago, south of Edinburgh *The Highland Chieftain* is still scheduled to take nearly an hour longer than usual, which means we cannot relax with the normal pattern of punctual northbound trains passing us. We are now 'under the wires' as railwaymen say of electrification but, like services from Aberdeen, *The Highland Chieftain* is diesel all the way. Once it was assumed that when electrification started on a particular route, it would steadily be extended but, since privatisation, under Railtrack it has virtually ceased. Even new trains for the fifteen-minute interval service between Edinburgh and Glasgow are diesel. Continental railway operators find it extraordinary. However, we have long since left the last piece of single track behind and, with a higher line limit, our speed is quickly up to 125mph as we head east with fine views of the Firth of Forth before turning south, the first major speed restrictions coming later.

Along the Coast to Newcastle-upon-Tyne

Beyond Dunbar, we see a variety of shipping as we race along the clifftops, and count the fishing vessels making their way to and from Eyemouth, a busy, picturesque, if not cosy in the Cornish style, port which anywhere in England would attract and cater for visitors but is on few people's itineraries here. It is not visible from the train but, as we return to the cliffs after a short diversion inland, if you catch exactly the right angle, there is a tantalising glimpse of nearby, much smaller Burnmouth, a smaller fishing port.

Aboard those fishing vessels there may well be descendents of the 189 fishermen who perished in a single storm in October 1888. In those days Eyemouth could only be entered safely at high tide, and the fleet, out fishing, was caught by the ferocity of the storm. As they made a desperate dash into the harbour, bubbling with white water, many perished within yards of safety with their loved ones lining the shore. Others stayed out to ride the storm but were swamped, or lost making for other ports. *Children of the Sea: the story of the Eyemouth disaster* is as telling a piece of Scottish local history as you will find on any place or subject.

Peter Aitchison knows his Eyemouth intimately, indeed turns out to be related to one of the unfortunate fishermen, and skilfully puts the disaster into context. For decades there had been talk about the need for an all-tide refuge, but most energy – and much bitterness – had been expended in a lengthy feud with successive ministers of the Church of Scotland over their monstrous fish tithe. The unique local life and architecture, the close-packed streets and cholera, the precipitous decline in fish yields coinciding with the struggle to put Eyemouth on its feet again, and the tentative start of tourism, also come into the story. It is a long read. Fishermen still complain there's not enough space but, with a deepened entrance and extended harbour, today Eyemouth is back in the top league of Scottish fishing ports. The sheer scale of operations so far from other major ports takes first-time visitors by surprise.

Having done the journey many times, we are hot on spotting each bay, cove and headland. Again, the sheer familiarity, even of a hotel closed after a bad fire, is part of the joy. We also know exactly where to look out for the railway's cut-out notice marking the border, seen by many fewer passengers as speeds have risen dramatically on this route. And we never fail to enjoy slowing to cross the Tweed by the Royal Border Bridge, in fact several miles within England.

From the north, you get a good view of much of the bridge from the train itself, for part of Robert Stephenson's monumental work of 1850 is gracefully curved. At its south end, it is high above Tweedmouth. There is time to take in much of the detail of Berwick-upon-Tweed, with its tightly-packed streets, two contrasting road bridges and the Town Hall's proud steeple. Berwick, as we will discover when we come back tomorrow, is possibly England's least-typical town, with a fascinating story to tell. That Berwick has remained little changed is because of the constricted site which forced the railway to favour development in Tweedmouth, where today's commerce and industry are concentrated, but there is also a fully-fledged if short promenade quickly noted from the train.

Speed rapidly rebuilds as we pass two electric 225 trains followed by a Virgin 125 diesel set; there has obviously been delay further south. Again, we are close to the sea, though without high cliffs, along a sparsely-populated coastline, noting the position of long-closed local stations which can never have been busy.

The gem of this East Coast Main Line comes next: Holy Island, or Lindisfarne, low lying, simmering in the late winter sun. Detail is clearly discernable: the great sands crossed by a causeway covered at high tide with a platform people can climb to take refuge. And there are the Priory ruins, the castle, and the two towers to guide seamen opposite the harbour at the northern tip of the next sandy peninsula toward Bamburgh with its castle. Unlike the West Coast Main Line which gives you only a very half-hearted view of the Irish Sea, the East Coast route lives up to its name. Those coming from Aberdeen enjoy a further marvellous section of clifftop riding, the sea being closely in view for much of the two and a half hours it takes to Edinburgh.

Though the West Coast has delightful intimacy with the western edge of the Lake District, and fine scenery north of Carlisle, the East Coast certainly wins in another way: it is far better engineered. King's Cross has always competed with Paddington for the highest sustained speeds out of London. There has been rapid growth in passenger business and, when things are normal, there are fast trains all the way to Edinburgh every half hour during much of the day. We race as straight as a dart across flat country mainly just out of sight of the sea, but there is another coastal treat as we cross the wandering Aln and savour the sun-drenched small resort of Alnmouth and its harbour, set out like a well-lit model town you would cheerily pay to walk around with camera.

Unspoilt Northumberland has much to offer, coast and inland. Over our generous Cumberland sausage in the restaurant car, I tell an interested young man at the next table about how I spent part of the hot summer of 1959 in the county undertaking research for a report on the rural transport problem. To this day, the people are as individual as the rolling, unspoilt, always welcoming, accessible landscape. Even in 1959, the demand for the few surviving rural railways and country bus services was fast declining. Visitors were few, though there was much to admire at villages like Warkworth on the River Coquet which we pass next. Inland, summer was only busier because of harvesting and the extensive programme of village shows and fairs, not because of tourists. It was unheard of for southerners to buy cottages for holiday homes, but housing was limited, and traditionally the eldest son didn't marry and take his new wife into the family home until Dad had died or become seriously ill.

One country bus operator, I tell the lad, as Sheila has a pudding and I take the cheese, ran half-a-dozen vehicles when his dad became ill, but apart from collecting the fares still wasn't allowed to have anything to do with money or see the accounts. When the old man died, the son couldn't wait to get his hands on some cash, marry and take his bride off to Paris on honeymoon. Since my report was nearly complete and my time in Northumberland coming to an end, I needed to see him immediately on his return. He handed me the accounts before he had opened them himself, and continued talking about the way they drove in Paris. Sure, it would be different from the empty local roads of rural Northumberland!

Alas, alas, while he was still regaling me with tales of Parisian near misses, a quick analysis showed he was bankrupt. No wonder Dad had withheld everything. When I dared to explain, he coolly replied: 'That's a bit of a humdinger, isn't it! Still, we enjoyed our honeymoon... if I hadn't been there I'd never have believed how they drive buses in Paris. But don't tell the wife yet, please!'

Coffee is served as we go slow through Morpeth, scene of two frightful accidents when the drivers failed to apply the brakes. Coffee with chocolate, is free, as is the pud, if you pay £9.95 for one of the specials such as our Cumberland sausage. Great North & East certainly know how to please passengers. Many in first class are being served light dishes and sandwiches at their seats, but a break in the restaurant car is always welcome. Soon we are in industrial country, with a view of a series of bridges over the Tyne as we round the curve into Newcastle.

The Kingdom of England, Scotland and Berwick-upon-Tweed

We are on our way to Peterborough, but break our journey at Newcastle to make a long-promised visit to Holy Island, which of course means driving back part of the way we have just come. The Inverness catering crew, who have ridden passenger since Edinburgh, alight here with their trolley and have only a short time to wait for the northbound *Highland Chieftain*. Somehow they always manage to remain cheerful throughout the long day, with the compensation that they rarely do more than three trips a week. 'Why don't you come back with us?' they joke. We doubt if we would remain as boisterous. 'See you soon.'

The station announcer is droning an apology for a late running Virgin train. We are punctual but northbound services aren't. Later we heard that a missed connection gave Dave another excellent fare at Virgin's expense that evening. Meanwhile we rent a car for our mainly magic miles – once we are clear of Newcastle.

Most of us know just a few things about Newcastle. Traditional industry, especially shipbuilding and coal mining, is only a shadow of what it was; the accent is one of the hardest for visitors to understand (an American hearing a Geordie on television asked what language he was speaking, not recognising a word he was saying); the crime rate is high, ram-raiding of premises once being a speciality; and the Metro Centre is one of the world's largest shopping complexes. Graceful and now sparkling clean city-centre buildings tell of past success and civic pride, and to the casual motorist trying to exit rapidly, the central area looks brilliant. Our priority is still getting out, which means passing through rundown outer districts and past numerous abandoned industrial sites and railways.

We miss the seaside strip with Whitley Bay once served by speedy trains on a route British Rail de-electrified, but admire the natty trains of Tyne & Wear Metro which use re-electrified sections as well as a variety of other routes. Some would say the urban system is Britain's best, appropriate since much of Britain's early railway technology was developed here. Coal was everything, leading to the invention of railways and its steam engines. I always marvel at how the father of railways, George Stephenson (father of Robert), obtained the basic knowledge he needed for his vocation, from study at the library, free reading being available a generation before free medicine and several more before free contraception. Priorities may have been right! Certainly the lead we had in the industrial revolution wouldn't have been possible had not our inventive geniuses been able to educate themselves.

There isn't time to go by Blyth on the coast north of Newcastle, to see how much it has changed since visiting it by train in the 1950s when it really was the dusty black-of-beyond, single-minded with coal and its despatch by ship, and usage in power stations. They were the days you routinely saw heaps of the stuff dumped outside people's front door, especially those of miners with their generous free supply. I recall that half a century ago even my apples I carried in a paper bag were soon coated with grime, and there was nowhere decent to wash them. You needed to be pretty pressed to visit the gents. Geordie speech might be thick, but the Blyth dialect was totally incomprehensible – even when it came to familiar details such as when did the next train leave. Passenger trains disappeared decades ago, as also at Newbiggin, which shares Weston-super-Mare's insecurity in having to call itself Newbiggin-by-the-Sea. But it is here that we catch today's first out-in-the-open breath of the North Sea.

Though built round a crescent-shaped bay and once attracting many day trippers, Newbiggin won't be our choice for a summer holiday. Industry and its scars continue north till we join the A1068. Then it is real though boringly level countryside, midway between sea and railway till we get near to the treasure of Amble-by-the-Sea by Warkworth Harbour with Coquet Island, where Benedictine monks once paid their homage to God. Coal was king here, too, but gentrification seems a better bet today. You *could* imagine spending at least a lazy weekend here.

After running beside it a mile or so, we cross the Coquet River lower down than did this morning's train, and enjoy the picture-postcard ruins of Warkworth Castle, unusual in being both a fortification and a true work of architecture. Then beside the railway where trains overtake us as though we were standing still until we again see Alnmouth, and go round the harbour into its neat main street. For the first time, we are in today's real holiday country with a few early tourists enjoying a fairly ordinary meal before turning in for an early night.

Next morning we wish we had allowed more time for Alnwick. You could spend at least a week here delving into historic buildings and ruins. A local garden makes challenging use of hedges and upright features (this was before the Duchess of Northumberland's controversial water garden was open, which we plan to visit one day). And there are vast tracts of undeveloped countryside to explore. You can breathe easily here. While the Cheviot Hills are sometimes called bleak, they aren't really. They have their own character if not exactly charm, with lots of empty miles away from Theme Park Britain, though you don't have to go far without finding something of gentle interest. The real threat to inland Northumberland's character is expanding forestry, useful though that may be.

We press on north, to Bamburgh Castle, somewhere we have always wanted to visit, a huge pile on a natural, uneven pedestal on the coast's very edge. Out of the car in a stiff bracing breeze, all the different aspects of the Britain we know seem light years away as perhaps for the first time we experience how very different is this part of the country.

We ponder about the former glories of the kingdom of Northumbria (this was one of the king's strongholds), look inland across to the Cheviots, and especially along the little-developed coast and out to sea to the Farne Islands, edged with the white spray of breaking waves. The Islands must have their attraction, for once the Benedictines were active here, too. On fair summer days, services are held in a chapel, but there is no regular population. Then we gaze northward over a couple of bays where the sands are steadily being covered by the incoming tide, to Holy Island where we will be tomorrow.

The website claims that Bamburgh 'is probably the finest castle in England', while its guide book talks of the 'extraordinary continuity which has been from first to last the keynote of Bamburgh's history', again so different from that of those parts of Britain with which we are more familiar. The history is as complex as it is long. Much of it can be told from the extraordinary height, thickness and variety of walls, though you have to rely on written evidence and excavation for details of how it started, as early as 547. We are not surprised to discover that, much later in history, the height of the main walls was increased to keep out marauding Scots. Earlier the castle had withstood several sieges: the guide book sets it out with admirable clarity. Among its tales there is this. 'Its [the Castle's] most crowded hour came in the War of the Roses at the end of the Middle Ages when, after Henry VI had briefly revived it as a royal capital over the little kingdom he ruled round about – a strange and little-known episode in English history – it finally fell to the artillery of Edward IV. It was the first castle in England to succumb to gunfire.'

With such a bloody history, the marvel is that successive ages enjoyed all the trimmings of civilisation to the hilt, and that so many artefacts have survived in the extensive range of rooms and lofty halls. Yet, whatever the attractions inside, the first marvel is the setting. Rushing away seems a shame, but the car's heater is a lifesaver once we have explored the massive exterior from every angle, other than of course the sea, from which it must look its best when floodlit.

The rising tide means it is too late to get to Holy Island tonight, so we check in at a hotel in Berwick-upon-Tweed, that very individual town with ample evidence of it moving back and forth between England and Scotland. It finally became English in 1482 though in 1551 the English and Scots agreed that it and a small surrounding area should be neutral, hence the kingdom was of England, Scotland and Berwick-upon-Tweed. It was another 300 years before Berwick was absorbed into Northumberland. We spend an hour or so looking round the walls and forts with their own complicated stories, and marvel at the narrowness of the first bridge with massive cutwaters not built till the danger of warfare had seemed to recede. Until 1928 it was the only road crossing, a ridiculous bottleneck. I watch the progress of each train on Robert Stephenson's Royal Border Bridge of 1850. Berwick would be a perfect centre for exploration, and its guide book assumes you will use it as stepping-off point, even for a day trip to Edinburgh.

Across the Sands to Holy Island

After another indifferent dinner, sleep is difficult, for the hotel's floorboards creak as people constantly pass our room, and everyone seems to have a megaphone. Outside, the screams of youngsters sound as though a raiding party of Scots have met stiff resistance. We're not sorry to leave and are expectant as we pause briefly for a goods train crossing the level crossing a mile before the start of the causeway to Lindisfarne, or Holy Island as it has been called in more recent centuries following the loss of Christian blood. The receding tide has already exposed large areas of sand where thousands of birds are filling themselves, tidal sand being richer in nutrients than the best pastures.

Excitement is hard to suppress, since everything about Holy Island seems of exceptional interest. For a start, though in total it is only just over 1,000 acres, a walk around it encompasses a great variety of rock types, and there is the famous dolerite dyke. The high dolerite intrusion, with its commanding outlook echoing Bamburgh, is naturally where the castle was built. Sand dunes – linear, crescent and irregular – reaching considerable height dominate, and the neat farming fields are of course also on sand. Yet limestone has been quarried, and iron ore and even coal mined.

There is a reminder that climatic changes of our day might not all be caused by global warming, for once Holy Island was joined to the mainland and then became completely separated. During its long and varied human history, it has been accessible at low tide. After 1860, that was across the direct Pilgrim's Way, where in later times horse-drawn carts and even early motor vehicles had specially-raised chassis so that crossings could still be made even when the route was not totally clear of water. Marker posts ensured that walkers and riders kept to the path, though there were occasional drownings. The present causeway dates only from 1954: it was improved in the 1960s when the road skirting the sandbanks at the south of the island was raised. Now you can cross safely except for two hours before high tide and three and a half after. However, the tides come in quickly, especially when driven by a storm and, when taken by surprise, people occasionally still climb the refuge box halfway across.

The sheltered estuary – and there aren't many of those on the Northumberland coast – once had great strategic importance, the markers on the mainland shore opposite the harbour being of life-and-death importance. But there have also been shipwrecks, the crews of the lifeboat once stationed here occasionally gaining national awards for bravery. The sands provide a valuable support system for a rich range of waders, wigeon and other ducks, geese, swans and other species, with huge counts – for example over 50,000 waders, 25,000 wigeons. Vegetation on the rich salt marshes is just as varied, though somewhat under threat (as are some of the dunes) from human activity, and also from nature not always perfectly controlling itself. With reliable farming, wildfowling and fishing, it is not surprising that Lindisfarne attracted man as far back as c8000BC.

But that doesn't yet touch the real magic of Holy Island – its spiritual significance and remains. My favourite guide book is a small self-published Holy Island by Scott Weightman, which has been through many editions and is concise, imaginative, and for us said exactly what we wanted to know without being overwhelmed. This is how he starts out:

> In 634, Oswald, a Christian convert, following years of exile in Scotland, defeated Cadwallon, King of North Wales, and reunited the Kingdoms of Bernicia and Deira. From his capital at Bebbanburgh (Bamburgh) Oswald established Northumbrian supremacy from the Humber to the Forth. It was Oswald who sent to Iona for a missionary. Corman, the first missionary, found the Northumbrians 'uncivilised people of obstinate and barbarous temperament' and he returned to Scotland. Soon after, in 635, Aidan arrived in Northumbria. Aidan chose Lindisfarne, close to the royal residence at Bamburgh, and secure in its island position, as the site for his church and monastery. From this base, Aidan preached the gospel throughout Northumbria, King Oswald sometimes acting as his interpreter... The presence of Aidan's mission on Lindisfarne changed the Northumbrian people. According to Bede 'many Northumbrians, both noble and simple, laid aside their weapons, preferring to take monastic vows rather than study the art of war'. Missionaries trained by Aidan travelled throughout Britain, some even journeying to the Netherlands.

A huge statue of the seventh century St Aidan standing against an oversize Celtic cross first catches our attention as it does that of many others, and we have to wait our turn to get the best angle for a snap. In the company of the same visitors, we are drawn into the remains of the priory, and photograph the single rib at the crossing at the church's centre that miraculously survived when the twelfth-century tower collapsed at the end of the eighteenth century. We follow the plan and substantial remaining outline of what was obviously a fine complex, and hear of various spiritual and other exploits and the centuries of peace with prosperity. And especially about Cuthbert, who in 685, was the sixth bishop to succeed Aidan. The history is convoluted, but basically there were three long periods of prosperity. The See created by Aidan lasted 250 years.

The first disruption was caused by 'the heathen' Vikings raiding in 793. The monks left and took Cuthbert's body. This was later moved several times, including returning for another sojourn on the island, until it finally came to rest in Durham Cathedral. It was after the completion of that Norman masterpiece that monks and masons came from Durham to create the priory, the ruins of which we enjoy today.

The second disruption was caused by the Borders becoming a dangerous frontier zone after Edward I's invasion of Scotland. Though the marauding Scots didn't attack the island, they repeatedly stole crops and damaged the mainland farms from which the monks drew much of their income. Soon the church was fortified and, despite being on the front line, a reduced number of monks continued to enjoy their accustomed standard of living.

Until the third disruption. The Reformation. Then, largely neglected, and used as a quarry for building materials, the complex slowly disintegrated though, as already said, the central tower only collapsed at the end of the eighteenth century. Since then the remains have been protected which, in practice, has meant regular restoration.

On a sunny day on the island, where everything seems so peaceful and the ruins are such a prominent feature, it is somehow easy to imagine the hope and fears, not only of the monks but of the local population dependent on their business – poverty was rife after all three disruptions – and to wonder at the beauty created in homage to God. That includes the Lindisfarne Gospels which have also amazingly survived, inspiring many quality gifts now offered by the shops catering for tourists, still evident even at this time of year. The ruins, in their dark red stone, weathered in different ways, are overpoweringly impressive in the late winter sun, against the background of fields of various colours and a pale blue sea.

Yet it is easy to lose oneself in Holy Island's other joys. We enjoy a gentle walk looking at the rich soil of level fields, the very ordinariness of the village and the inns, with the locals' conversation over a pint. After a quick bite in a café busy with day visitors, we check into our modest hotel and, with the sun barely above the horizon, walk down to the harbour with its upturned boats acting as fishermen's huts. There is a gentle ripple of distant waves as the tide has started to come in, mixed with a mellow chit-chat of busy birds making the most of the offerings of the sand nearest the tide line. An electric train purrs gently as it races along the unseen East Coast main line. It is quite a walk to the castle but, the National Trust not yet having wakened it from its winter slumber, we hardly meet anyone. The castle, too, has a complex history, but is best known as a stylish conversion of a decayed mediaeval fortress into a country home by Edwin Lutyens. Bleak vaulted chambers became delightful rooms for Edward Hudson, owner of *Country Life,* who bought it in 1902. There are echoes of Lutyens's much larger Castle Drogo in Devon.

Thank God for the Tide

After buying a Celtic CD and plate – real imaginative quality on offer, together with a fine selection of books – we go to Said Evensong at St Mary's, with its long chancel and history going back to the thirteenth century, close by the priory ruins.

Since the last day-visitors had to leave a few minutes ago to catch the tide, there are only seven of us; the others probably locals. Like the village, it seems delightfully matter of fact for such an unusual setting. However, naively we are not quite sure how it fits into the scheme of affairs, or who is the person leading the service... a monk possibly? Shaking hands afterwards, we ask. 'I'm the vicar of Holy Island,' comes the reply.

'Oh, David Adam?'

'Yes, that's right.'

Someone I had often wished to meet. I had only just read his *Flame in My Heart: St Aidan for Today* with these introductory passages:

Before the great saint of Assisi taught us a love for the world, saints like Aidan showed us a love for all about him. Aidan wrestling with demons but at one with much of nature. Aidan who gave his horse away to a beggar. Aidan who refused to ride because it placed him above others. He walked the lanes and taught people to meditate. Aidan who bought slaves to give them their freedom, and then housed and educated them if they so required. Lindisfarne had a school where royalty and slaves were educated together... Lindisfarne is a small island but its influence on the history of England and Europe is all out of proportion to its size. Here were a great school and monastery that would influence the minds of the English for generations. From here men went out to convert the English and parts of the continent of Europe.

Sheila says she has a collection of his books. He has written 22 books, and is still writing, as part of his ministry treading in the steps of the Celts. 'There are still definite traces of Celtic thought and practice in the Northern church,' he says. He sounds so down-to-earth that it isn't surprising to learn that he began life as a coal miner.

After the rest of the congregation have gone, he shares that being here and writing are both part 'of a joy and obsession. There are more people sharing what it's all about than is generally realised. People come here, relax and are not afraid. Celtic prayer really touches them. It is very simple, no extra words, very natural. It takes God as natural and everything else is superimposed – the reverse of what usually happens in our world. Probably it helps that we're just an ordinary parish church.'

But is it? 'Yes; we're just a country church... happening to be visited by 150,000 people a year. That's a bit of a strain. Apart from me, everyone is unpaid, and handling that number of course has its problems, but we meet many delightful people... it's so worthwhile. We have a minimum of three services a day, over 1,000 a year. How many attend varies dramatically from a crowd down to four or five. Peace comes when the tide comes in. Thank God for the tide. The tide comes in and most people go out.'

Two of his own prayers in a book called *The Edge of Glory: Prayers in the Celtic Tradition* are thoughts on Holy Island and begin with the line 'There are times I need to be an island' and 'I must be part of the mainland'. This is the former:

Lord,
There are times when I need to be an island,
Set in an infinite sea
Cut off from all that comes to me
But surrounded still by thee.
Times of quiet and peace
When traffic and turmoil cease
When I can be still and worship thee
Lord of the land and sea.
Full tide and ebb tide
Let life rhythms flow
Ebb tide, full tide
How life's beat must go.

Then back to our hotel for a simple dinner with just one other couple and a lone gent; like us, the couple have at last realised their ambition to come here. The lone man is a regular visitor who tells us all the things we have missed and must come back to enjoy another time. Sheila readily agrees we have to come back soon, forgetting how much more of Britain we have yet to visit.

BERWICK-UPON-TWEED TO LONDON VIA THE MIDLANDS

On to Peterborough

Breakfast is down to earth in the extreme. You don't come to Holy Island for fine dining, and anyway we haven't time to linger. As soon as the tide has sufficiently retreated we must be on our way.

The morning mist is thick, and it is eerie as we drive across the still-wet causeway strewn with seaweed and even a few stones deposited by the tide. How much of Holy Island's character would be lost if you could drive at any state of tide, not that we have heard that such a daft idea has been suggested. Soon we are in Tweedmouth's substantial industrial estate looking for the garage where we must return our car, and be given a lift back over the Tweed to catch our train south, repeating the section between Berwick-upon-Tweed and Newcastle that we did on *The Highland Chieftain* from Inverness two days ago.

That was on a diesel High Speed Train. We are now on a faster (140mph when track and signalling allow) electric 225 set but, because of extra stops, this is actually a slower journey south. The first stop is at Alnmouth, of which we catch another glimpse in a break in the mist. We are again taking advantage of the Cumberland sausage offer in the little-used restaurant car, where our seats have been allocated. The newer 225's seats are narrower, making one feel more trapped. In the old days, first-class seats were said to be designed for the railway managers, nearly all over-size men. You had to be big to rise in the railway hierarchy, it seemed. Shorter women complained the seats were too deep for them to be able to lean back comfortably. In the age when more of us are substantially taller and we are more conscious of our posture, it is harder for anyone much over six foot to be really comfortable on longer journeys.

After Alnmouth, we leave the coast for good, and much of the remaining countryside, the hundreds of miles still left to London is England's dullest. It is now the cities that provide diversions.

However often you travel, you'd have to be blasé not to look out of the window at Newcastle's marvellously mixed bridges placed at various heights and even angles across the tidal Tyne deep in its narrow valley as in a superior model railway. We see the river before the huge station and, after squealing round a sharp curve, cross it afterwards. We identify the famous transporter bridge, and make a mental note that later in the year an elegant rotating bridge, suspended from a giant arch, will be floated into position (watched by crowds on both shores expressing total delight). Tyneside's sheer scale never ceases to surprise; nor does the fact that the loss of the staple of coal provided a challenge that has been more than met. Newcastle is now thriving in a new, and much cleaner, way, though exactly how everyone earns a living or pays their bills isn't clear to those from far away.

Who are the new workers? It occurs to me that, substantial a repertoire as I enjoy of former authors and other work-related friends and colleagues, I don't really know a single person from Tyneside. In fact there is only one acquaintance I can name, Ian Bone, who has occasionally come to Nairn as visiting tailor, first when Burberrys made what seemed an extraordinarily generous *Financial Times* offer to have yourself measured and fitted in your home anywhere on the mainland for a bargain suit. The day he came, all he achieved was measuring me; an appointment on the way in Edinburgh couldn't be kept because of parking problems. It wasn't surprising that Burberrys soon dropped this service, indeed abandoning their traditional business, including manufacture, reinventing themselves as a fashion-conscious marketing company.

When most youngsters were set on following their dad into coal mining or shipbuilding, Ian learned tailoring, beginning with a Saturday morning job as a lad when duties included going up a ladder to whisk-dust shoulders of jackets displayed high. He recalls gloomy years of poor business managing a secondary high street chainstore shop, and was later delighted to become a visiting tailor for Burberrys.

'That used my real skill at measuring, fitting and relating to customers. When Burberrys gave up, Austin Reed wanted me but I decided to go independent, like lots of other people have had to do. I am only making two-thirds of what I did, but I'm my own boss, a lot happier and less stressed.' Solicitors, accountants and retired doctors, especially those with awkward shapes, are prominent among his customers, scattered all over northern England and Scotland.

'Mind you,' he added, toying with his tape measure on his last visit to Nairn, 'though many of us work for ourselves these days, they're taking

2,000 on at Swan Hunter to build the first ship in eleven years.' During the week Ian, now using his own beloved BMW daily, doesn't see much of Tyneside – and, having to pay his own bills, stays in more modest accommodation.

Because of one of those increasingly frequent bridge strikes by lorries, the last time I went south my train had to be rerouted. That meant crossing the river and going along the coast via Sunderland, still wearing the scars of coal mining and the transporting of coal, and through less than delectable places such as Hartlepool and Stockton, where the iron road was developed to give Britain that vital lead in the industrial revolution. If I had to nominate the gloomiest spot around Britain's generally invigorating coastline, it would be where North Cemetery Junction Signalbox once stood north of Hartlepool. The signalbox, too, has joined the abandoned.

I recall once I asked a taxi driver to take me around Hartlepool on a whistle-stop tour. He told me nobody ever had or ever would do that just for interest, and insisted that I must be a spy for a Japanese car company. He wouldn't tell anyone that he had shown me the housing estates and places of entertainment, but the Japs would be bound to want to know they were good. Maybe he puts Nissan's concentration in Sunderland down as his personal failure. Mind you, there are plenty of other places around here a country-loving person wouldn't want to live in... even Saltburn, at the end of England's possibly most dreary branch line, despite the fact it has by no means given up the pretence of being attractive to visitors. By comparison with some hideous spots where largely derelict mountainous industrial structures dominate the housing, Saltburn no doubt is heaven by the sea for an afternoon with the kids.

Next stop, Durham. Here is the best of the views of the cathedrals we look out for journeying south; this used also to be nicknamed the Cathedrals Route. There it is, Durham's great cathedral beside the castle in the horseshoe of the wooded River Wear, reminding us of the lunchtime we became separated by a bomb scare in Market Square before walking down the narrow North and then South Bailey, with dozens of old buildings housing two of the university colleges on the way to the bridge over the river near the horseshoe's tip.

Darlington, junction for an under-used but joyous branch to Whitby. Then York, where the sight of the Minster standing proud above the plain gives ample opportunity to pack your belongings should you be alighting under the station's gracefully-curved trainshed; there is however little else to see from the train. And Doncaster, which still has the feel of a railway town, though nowhere is engine building what it was when Nigel Gresley, probably the world's most famous locomotive engineer after Stephenson, had his power base here. Among his intuitive acts, he asked the French racing-car firm of Bugatti to help fashion the streamlined front-end of the A4s. That class included *Mallard*, still holder of the record for the world's fastest steam locomotive and now in York Railway Museum. For decades before the diesel era these engines rushed up and down the East Coast main line. They could be said to be the world's first high-speed trains. Come to think of it, with today's speed restrictions, because of Railtrack's cracks in rails around curves, we are scarcely making as good time as did the A4s in the 1930s.

You aren't at Peterborough station long before realising there is a level of service unthinkable in the 'good old days', when express services were so infrequent that any railway-loving person worth his salt could cite them from memory. Peterborough is a well-run if over-used station with audible announcements offering brilliant connections as well as great frequency to main destinations. Based on the service from London, 'The Peterborough Effect' the town once advertised has brought unparalleled prosperity to a wide surrounding area.

Stamford with Cousins

Now on my own, for Sheila has remained on the London-bound train on her way to spend a few days with her sister, I go to Stamford, where my cousin Anne is already ensconced at The George, a real old coaching inn with much coming and going, maintaining what must always have been a busy atmosphere. The George also offers considerable comfort and excellent food.

A limestone town of seventeenth- and eighteenth-century buildings lining the narrow streets leading up from the River Welland, Stamford is always pleasant to explore. The Romans forded the river, while later the Danes made it their regional centre. Then it settled down to long mediaeval prosperity based on the wool trade. Stamford cloth was noted for its fine quality. Later again, the Welland was made navigable and the town retained its prosperity by becoming a busy port. *The Rough Guide to England*, possibly the best of today's pretty enterprising bunch, so much more lively than the guides even of the 1980s, points out that Stamford escaped the three main threats to old English towns: the Industrial Revolution, wartime bombing and postwar development. In 1967 it became Britain's first Conservation Area.

After some fun shopping, Anne and I enjoy a quiet dinner, talking about our parents and other memories and planning her next visit to Scotland. A decade older than me, Anne, who with her vivacious smile can't help frequently dissolving into giggles, has played an important part in my life. I recall playing with her in her parents' garden (her mother was Dad's sister) at Gidea Park, her struggling with medical studies at Exeter and falling off her bicycle on St David's Hill, and the family pride when, qualified as a doctor, she was sent as Methodist missionary in charge of a hospital serving a large area of South India. Her circular Christmas letters about her work, and her feelings when suddenly forced to do a life-saving operation, which at home would have been undertaken by an experienced specialist, were a memorable feature of my childhood. One detail I especially recall. During a drought, the poor workers pumping water continued to be paid. After the monsoon, they demanded that, since they had been paid for doing nothing during the drought, they should receive more now there was again work to be done. Come to think of it, there's a well-known parallel parable here. And that there is always the opposite side to the coin was brought home when Anne sent a copy of a report from Indian Railways: a 'gratifying increase in complaints' showed that the publicity given to the complaints service had been well heeded. Of such minutiae in childhood are characters formed.

We share much fun, including a love of music. Anne was in the choir at Bart's Hospital, where for some years after coming back from India she was GP to the nurses. The choir's annual Handel's *Messiah* at the Royal Albert Hall was always a red-letter occasion. We retire early for the challenge of tomorrow, when we are hosting another cousin, Jack, for lunch.

Oh dear. Poor old Jack. Poor us. Always an odd one out, while he had good sight, Jack was an inveterate traveller, turning up unexpectedly – how to persuade my parents he really was at the door when I'd just goofed about his being there? – and not turning up when he was meant to. Nobody more reliably missed trains and buses, went more frequently to sleep when he should be alighting (lacking money for the return fare), or missed more turnings when forced to take unexpectedly long walks. Almost always he arrived soaked to the skin, for if it were sunny he'd stay out – once overnight on a mountain top – till it poured.

He refused to see a doctor or dentist and, when suffering from glaucoma, went blind unnecessarily. He was discovered in his native Leicester lost in the street having run out of food at home. Jack is not a person to accept help, and it was with difficulty friends manoeuvred him into an excellent home for the blind. The staff there love him. They accept his need for privacy, and for much food even well into his eighties. However, he refuses to try Braille, listen to the radio or tapes or attend social functions or services – and complains he feels cut off.

Few people visit him, his chief support system being Ena, to whom he was briefly engaged over half a century ago. He broke it off saying the world wasn't a fit place in which to establish a family. Ena, so supportive, has been ordered by her doctor to go less frequently because visits stress her. I cringe at the thought of another trip to the home.

Whatever our disability, we should surely make the best of what life remains. Jack won't buy that. Visits usually end with his telling me: 'You fail to appreciate the tragedy that I am. You don't realise I'm blind.'

To ring the changes, as an experiment, this morning the home has agreed to put him in a taxi. When it arrives, Anne and I can't get it right. At each stage, Jack needs more or less help/interference. Don't we know he can't see? But when eventually, having attracted the attention of dozens of guests, we sit him down, he relishes the thought of food. We read and reread the menu; he repeats each item, though usually several behind what we have read in a slow but very audible drawl.

'Like a menu?' the waiter asks several others.

'No need; we're ready to order,' they say almost knowing what's on offer by heart now and anxious to get going.

The portions are generous to huge. Jack munches slowly away until all has gone. He then goes back on the conversation we've meanwhile been having. He comments on each topic, in the right order and with great intelligence. There's still so much he could do to make his life worthwhile, but when we're foolish enough again to suggest exchanging occasional tapes to keep in touch, the silence is angry. Recording machines, radio and TV, the telephone: they are all abominations.

Cross Country through Leicester

Eventually Jack is put back in his taxi and I phone the home to tell them he's on the way. Anne and I also leave by taxi. At the station I join a busy train bound for Leicester and Birmingham. The start is through gently rolling countryside, though I note where there used to be junctions for two lines to Corby and its former steel works a few miles to the south. Then, after a short tunnel, a tantalisingly brief glimpse of a small part of one of England's most intriguing lakes, Rutland Water, a reservoir. Horseshoe-shaped and with a long peninsula jutting into it, it has over twenty miles of shoreline, today supporting a variety of leisure activities. Rutland Water is pleasingly relaxing without being scenically exciting.

Our first stop is Oakham, once again county capital since Rutland has won back its status as smallest English county. Then – hardly in a direct line – Melton Mowbray, which *The Rough Guide* (with an American readership in mind) says is 'famous for pork pies, an unaccountably popular English snack made of compressed balls of meat and gristle encased in wobbly jelly and thick pastry'. After that Leicester, its two island platforms with their yellowish-brick buildings thronged with Pakistanis who make up a large percentage of the city's population. *The Rough Guide* describes it as 'a resolutely modern city'. In truth, I've never liked it – despite our family connections.

303

My grandfather ran a chain of gentlemen's outfitters from Leicester and was deeply disappointed when my father – but not until he had learned to pack the most perfect parcels, which stood him in good stead mailing over 500 review copies a year to a bookseller – decided business was not for him and became a writer instead. Seen as a great non-conformist Liberal in his day, my grandfather thought nothing of selling the home they had only recently moved into on their 'way up' (already having ceased to live over the shop) without consulting his wife. The whole family would benefit; why need to consult? How different were those days was emphasised by my father's account of a train journey. Note the reference only to his father on what was the family's main holiday. However, my grandmother, a forceful figure in my childhood, determined the family luggage arrangement:

As children, my sisters and I were taken annually by my father from our home in Leicester to visit his parents at Redbrook-on-Wye. Getting from Leicester to Redbrook was, in those days, at the turn of the century, an exciting if leisurely affair. That journey, occupying less than four hours, is now made as far as Chepstow in a through express linking Newcastle-upon-Tyne with South Wales. Forty years ago it filled the day and necessitated six changes. It began in a Midland train that stopped at all stations to Birmingham, excluding those owned by a 'foreign' company over whose metals part of this route lay. I could tell when our mere running-powers ended and we rejoined our own Midland line by the change back from one type of signal-arm to another.

New Street station at Birmingham, shared by London & North Western and Midland trains, seemed so vast and noisy that pleasure was temporarily turned to dread. It had for me, perhaps because of tunnels by which it was approached and left, a slightly sinister atmosphere, emphasised by the excessively shrill locomotive blasts from the North Western platforms and by the weird blowing of horns that here formed part of that company's signalling arrangements. I was glad that we kept safely to the Midland side, and was relieved when we were seated in the North of England to Bristol express, which, with its spacious clerestory coaches, took us on our next lap.

At the top of Lickey incline there was a moment's compulsory stop, and the descent to Bromsgrove made me hold my breath, save when, peering through the window, I was diverted from thought of danger by the spectacle of a train climbing in the opposite direction, with the special banking engine puffing energetically in the rear. At Worcester (Shrub Hill) we alighted; and though, in its chocolate-and-cream livery, the Great Western train was already standing, engineless, in the bay, we had an hour to wait for its departure...

The rest of the journey lay over Great Western territory; and while for other reasons my affection for the GWR is still so lively that it gives me immense satisfaction to be living now on its main line to Cornwall, my love for it was born of those travels to Monmouthshire. The romantic scenery through which it passed added to its own spell; the romance of the railway in turn invested the landscape with greater charm. So far from spoiling the country, except at certain points, a railway for me gives it the final perfection. The fact that the Great Western track ran sheer alongside the sinuous Wye, and that the quiet single line crossed from the far to the near bank of the river within sight of my grandparents' window, completed my happiness in the estate.

My own memories of Leicester in the late 1930s are dominated by tramcars and their track and overhead wires. From the Bell Hotel, there was a commanding view of what was claimed to be Britain's greatest tramway junction, with intersections, curves and loops. In the 1960s, when everywhere but Blackpool had scrapped its trams, *Modern Tramway* spoke of the iniquity of the 'victory' of imported rubber for tyres and oil over our own steel and electricity. It eagerly looked forward to the day when modern, clean Light Railways would whisk people along reserved tracks where possible, and through the streets of the city centres. It seemed a forlorn hope. The firm which had built Leicester's tramway junction decades earlier seemed mildly ridiculous spending money on an advertisement with a large picture of it, years after it had been destroyed. Yet the message took root. We now have a growing number of cities served by modern trams. One unfortunate factor in the 1950s and 1960s was that, in the age that worshipped newness, the remaining tram fleets looked more and more old-fashioned simply because they had lasted so well.

Birmingham and its Characters

So to Birmingham New Street where, within two minutes of arriving, I used to be in Hudson's, the largest bookshop in the Midlands, only yards from the station entrance. Family run, it welcomed publishers and their representatives with a warmth you'll be hard pressed to find in today's large, almost all multiple, bookshops. Hudson's was a treat to supply. After it was bought by an entrepreneur, who preached that publishers should give extended credit to finance the stocking of their books, alas we frequently had to put the shop on the stop list. Most of the 'pedigree' bookshops of yesteryear have gone: Willshaws in

Manchester, John Smith in Glasgow, Thin's in Edinburgh. Some that continue, such as Blackwells of Oxford, have been the subject of a bitter family dispute. Books are readily available, often at cut prices, and can quickly be obtained on special order at many more locations today, but it is no longer a business for gentlemen.

The Birmingham I knew in the 1960s-1980s was still a busy city with influential families such as the chocolate Cadburys and metal-bashing Kendricks. It wore a slightly inferior provincial air (the centre was small, no rival to Manchester), with leafy western suburbs where, as in most cities, the better-off lived so that the prevailing wind didn't blow factory fumes and smoke their way. Partner in the writing and illustration of some railway books, Patrick Whitehouse, epitomised the well-heeled wheeler-dealer establishment who ate solid lunches in solid clubs and restaurants and lived in detached houses with well-kept gardens.

Wherever he went, Patrick was recognised as a powerful individual, and his love of steam locomotives, which had everyone turning to see their passing, was well matched to his personality. Though he was co-presenter of the BBC *Railway Roundabout*, the only serious television series there has ever been for enthusiasts, he disliked being interviewed when our books came out, and preferred I took that heat even on *Pebble Mill at One* in Birmingham and at the National Exhibition Centre close by. At the Car Show with a live audience, closed-circuit TV and also live on BBC 1, some lord-of-the-moment young interviewer, enthralled by a pop singer whose spot preceded mine, could scarcely summon politeness let alone enthusiasm to ask me about 'those engines':

'They're sexy,' says I.

'Sexy? What do you mean?'

'Put girls with as few clothes as you like beside you on the stage, let me run one of those green GWR Star, Castle or King, at full throttle, with its sexy tapering boiler, at the back of the hall, and everyone will turn to look at the engine.' That woke him up and we were in business.

Pat approved. In his private coach immediately behind one of his preserved Castles, he enjoyed seeing heads turn as his specials took enthusiasts up and down the former GWR territory.

His power-base was the Tyseley's steam centre, formerly a GWR running-shed. 'We still turn heads,' says his son Michael, partner in Birmingham's solicitors who have served the establishment for generations. I mention a partner of a previous age, Ag Norton, with whom I happened to have family dealings as a young man. 'He's still much talked about, the life and soul of the Birmingham mafia. One or two senior partners still quake at the mention of his name.'

Turning to railways, he says: 'Steam locomotives still exercise a powerful influence. You can feel them go by, awe-inspiring, historical, beautiful mobile power-houses.' Pat died a decade ago, 'but he'd love what we're doing. For a start, every Sunday in July and August we run the *Shakespeare Express* from Birmingham to Stratford-upon-Avon, eight coaches in chocolate and cream, full restaurant car service. Real business, not a toy thing. We won't run a train out of Tyseley unless it pays, but we have the locomotives and rolling stock, the workshop base and engineering experience. Pat would really respect it, now run as a Trust. I still miss him, for he was my best friend. We took many railway holidays together.' In the next chapter we meet his sister, Maggie.

Over afternoon tea at the Midland Hotel, I meet my favourite cartoonist, Larry, alias Terence Parkes. His to-the-point humour has decorated many D&C books, *Writers' News* and now even the back page of my Charitable Trust's newsletter *Aspire*. There were also several successful Larry books.

'I always wanted to be a cartoonist and went freelance 45 years ago. It wouldn't be possible now. Only a few cartoonists, like Matt, are at the cutting edge. To get anywhere, you'd have to be on the staff today.'

So why are cartoonists now out of the mainstream? '*Punch* went off the rails and in doing so killed itself, the freelance cartoonist and people's expectations. They suddenly changed to strip cartoons: far too much to look at and read. The joy of the one-off cartoon is that the message is instantaneous. You mightn't find them all funny, but you didn't waste time having to study complicated messages. Often the penny dropped, people roared their heads off and told their friends. Some cartoons were talked about for years. It was Brockbank who hired me. I submitted two roughs. He quickly used them as they were and got me started. People who bought *Punch*, perhaps at the railway station, wanted amusement. Humorous column fillers such as a quote from a local paper putting their foot in it, were like the cartoons: the source of instant pleasure. That's why people bought *Punch*, not for long articles and double-page strip cartoons.'

To Warwick and Leamington Spa

The Great Western's Snow Hill, bright and airy where trains raced in, was rationalised out of existence and years ago I thought I had taken my last walk to it. But it has been rebuilt, first as a terminus just for suburban trains, but now as a busy through station with a generous Chiltern Line service from London Marylebone. At rush hour, it is extremely busy, with both trains and people.

Running south, my commuters' train to Leamington Spa soon stops at villages rather than suburbs. Immediately beyond Lapworth, there are canals delightfully on either side. The Grand Union, which we follow for a time, was once one of England's principal trade arteries, and is used by many of today's narrow boat explorers. There are several narrow boats in the succession of locks at the approach to Warwick, where I am one of several dozen alighting. There's just time for a meeting at the Lord Leycester Hotel before reporting to my sister who lives near the Castle.

The hotel is often used by the Guild of Railway Artists, whose administrator, Frank Hodges, tells me that railway art is 'very much human life in microcosm with landscape, urbanscapes, people, engineering, architecture and often an intense feeling of the moment. The artist sees a subject in a different way, recreates it with artistic interpretation and skill – like Monet did in the early days of French trains.'

The Guild started in 1977 with a Midland group of artists based at Leamington Spa and has steadily snowballed to become a powerful force commanding respect and many sales. In addition to its popular exhibitions, the Guild has produced books with several publishers. For D&C it was *The Seaside Railway*, stuffed with evocative pictures of the days when, at least for young males, the journey was the best part of the holiday.

It is then a short walk through Warwick's main street with its antique shops and, beside the castle walls, the noise of the traffic steadily replaced by the echo of peacocks. Ruth and her husband Walter are waiting. Blood being thicker than water, there's immediate familiarity. Brother and sister know each other warts and all, and something of our parents' hopes, fears, and of course tastes, live on in the pictures, rugs and other artefacts chosen and displayed with flair at their successive family homes and, in the next generation, still today. I remember, for instance, catching a glimpse of that soothing sketch of the mouth of an Essex estuary as we raced to the cellar in a tip-and-run air raid. And there is a chocolate-and-cream coach from Dad's model railway. I used to hook it up to the front portion of a train from Paddington bound for Seagood (an imaginary resort where landladies never disappointed) when it 'divided' into two at the Junction.

Ruth and I share a common background, having gone to the same school (Sheila and Ruth were in the same class). We both worked for *The Western Morning News* – and were both unorthodox, if not rebellious. Moreover, in her ripening years, she's taken up publishing. So much in common, yet so different. While the countryside and landscape is everything to me, and my whole career was based around avoiding having to live in a city, she comes to life in the inner-city.

We talk about her background and how it has affected her. When evacuated to South Molton (described in detail in later chapters) in North Devon with the family, Ruth didn't go to school for two years. She learned the statutory three Rs at home with the help of our mother, a former primary school teacher. She roamed the market town, the cattle market and the countryside, and helped two elderly women run their haberdashery shop (corset bones and liberty-bodice buttons) and, later, found formal schooling 'less than satisfactory as a learning process'. While still a girl at Teignmouth, she spent time on the tramp cargo boats taking out china clay and bringing in wood or coal. She would cook in the galleys and post letters home for sailors. Curiosity about life later led her to explore London Dockland, and to drink tea in Pyrex cups with Ideal milk in workers' cafés – and then into journalism.

As her children's needs developed, she became a founder member of the National Pre-school Playgroups Association and, in 1965, started a pioneer housing association in Nottingham for homeless young people, many of them lone mothers. Sometimes living and often working in inner-city areas, she has since contributed to a portfolio of practical projects.

'As National Director of the Action Resource Centre from 1976, I found that there are very few in high positions who understand that people are no less accomplished, and certainly no less trustworthy, simply because they are "different". The way that inner city areas are used and abused by policy-makers denies the truth that many people choose to live in inner city areas, are life-skilled, and have sturdy networks of family and friends. Yes, they are probably on a low income. But is that a character defect? I call it patronising. And we get these endless stories of crime as if it all began and ended in the inner city.'

While home is in leafy Warwick, where the main problem is peacocks levering off the occasional roof tile, she has chosen to spend part of most weeks in the St Ann's inner-city area of Nottingham. She has written a large, lavishly illustrated book about St Ann's. The story is mainly told in the words of its own people. 'Reading it,' Ruth says, 'would be a much cheaper way of trying to find out what goes on in an inner-city environment than asking a firm of consultants to do yet another expensive report on "what needs to be done". Inner-city people could teach most consultants a great deal.'

St Ann's Nottingham: Inner-city voices is published by her own Plowright Press and includes the history of how the district was bulldozed and 30,000 people were compulsorily uprooted and scattered in the late 1960s and early 1970s. Many different people moved in to the 'new' St Ann's, though a lot of the elderly stayed, desperately missing their role in three-generation families.

It is indeed a terrible story. Without any real consultation with the local population, notice was given that everything in a vast area just beyond the old Nottingham Victoria station, of which only the clock tower survives in today's Victoria Centre, was to be flattened. The more enterprising soon started moving out. Landlords naturally did the minimum of repairs. And the improvement to housing that would naturally have taken place as living standards improved was stopped.

That enabled councillors to point out that things were worse in St Ann's than surrounding areas: it is known as planning blight. The developer naturally wanted to knock everything down – it's simpler and more profitable – and sung the praises of what was to come. But much good property, including churches, schools, shops and pubs, was unnecessarily condemned. And, surprise, the new wasn't much liked, let alone loved. A lot of time and money have had to be devoted to improving it since. Yet, as Ruth shows, much of the old community spirit has somehow revived.

I love Ruth and her driving sincerity but such is her unbridled enthusiasm that, even at home, sometimes feel I'm being addressed at a public meeting. Walter, whose mother got him and herself out of Nazi Germany just in time in 1939, is mellowness personified. They are obviously good for each other.

Soon we're off for dinner at Leamington Spa. Royal Leamington Spa is so close to Warwick yet so different. It is less matter-of-fact about its history because it isn't as illustrious, but still has ambitions behind its slightly faded Spa. It is a pleasant place, but you won't find Bath's or Stratford-upon-Avon's American visitors here. It was among the towns where, as children, we spent a fortnight while our parents sought the perfect home. Since it is far as you get from the sea in England, I don't know why, for Mum felt hard done by if she wasn't frequently able to enjoy the sight and sound of breaking waves.

The hotel was, like most we stayed at, incredibly cheap out of season, and with extraordinary year-round residents. An elderly woman, who didn't seem to like young lads, devoted her energy to trying to find fault with me and another boy while lavishing gifts on Ruth. The mood of a gentleman who had 'retired from rubber' was totally dependent on the previous day's closing price of his rubber shares which moved up and down with great elasticity. All the regulars let casual visitors know that special privileges wouldn't be extended to them by the staff. 'I've been here seven years' was what counted. Two weeks at this hotel, or was it a boarding house, seemed long enough. 'I must have the sea,' said Mum, not pacified by Dad saying that if you were at the centre of the country, as he had been as a boy at Leicester, you could visit many different seasides with equal ease.

Next morning Ruth and I talk more nostalgically walking beside the Avon, an accessible river with the majestic backdrop of Warwick Castle and the town with its churches on higher ground.

The prospect is familiar from more frequent visits in the past, usually with a string of authors and booksellers to call on: authors into organic gardening, show-horse riding, antiques or some other specialist subject about which there was a hungry public wanting to be better informed. And Miss Pinder, the railway bookseller whose life mainly revolved round her cats – remember their names and the order would be bigger – who demanded the most perfect of copies for her 'special customers'. Only one or two packers in the warehouse were up to selecting unblemished copies and packing them so well that the carrier – the railway in those days – didn't damage them with routine carelessness. For years, Miss Pinder operating from the one room in her house out of bounds to the cats, placed the largest initial orders we received for new railway titles.

One day I'm determined to explore Warwick's historical sites thoroughly, and to get to know better the unexciting but inviting countryside to the southeast crossed by the SW to NE Fosse Way, here only a not-very-fast B road. This morning however, since I'm still a boy at heart, back to Leamington Spa and by one of Virgin's short and scruffy locomotive-hauled cross-country trains, single track for the first part of the route, to Birmingham New Street, where a tight connection to Derby works well.

Derby to London with Anxious Passenger and Pre-war Memories

Despite its relatively new city status, and its cathedral with pinnacled tower, today's Derby isn't an exciting place. But for me it has frequently marked the beginning and end of interesting journeys, by car and train, often to or across the Peak District. For many years in the days of rapid growth at D&C, I held an annual author's conference here, and have vivid recollections of the daytime excursions to points of canal, railway and industrial interest and of the formal evening sessions, where quite a few writers first made their public mark or gave their swansong. Naturally, the venue was the railway's own Midland Hotel, beside the vast station and a short distance from the huge locomotive and carriage works.

The Midland Hotel, now Best Western, three-star still with an AA percentage rating of 74, provides a late light lunch while I go into a nostalgic reverie. The hotel was as solid as the Midland Railway which had its headquarters close by. The Midland was a no-nonsense line, offering its passengers superb comfort, and total reliability to the traders who supported its more lucrative mineral and freight services. Even well into my publishing days, thousands of railwaymen were employed at Derby. They had – or so they thought until rudely awakened – a safe job for life. Was not the largest fleet of new diesel cars named after Derby which, with its nearby test track, was as much in the forefront of modernisation as it had been with earlier stages of railway development?

People lived and breathed railways. The bookstall on the station was not supposed to stock books but did a roaring business, reaching a new peak when we published OS Nock's locomotive monograph on the Derby-built *Midland Compounds*. The bookstall's manager said it was more than his job was worth to place an order, but so long as he unofficially asked for the books, yet could say we'd acted on our own initiative and the supply was technically a mistake, his manager would turn a blind eye. Visits resulted in stealthy orders. Several times I both delivered books and secured a new order rapidly enough to rejoin my train on which I'd left my luggage before it continued on its way north, the best part of the journey skirting the Peaks still to look forward to.

Today I know nobody in Derby, and have come for the memories and the journey by Midland to St Pancras. Today's franchise, Midland Mainline, runs a good service, the power of the High Speed Train sets well used, though nowhere is it possible to take full advantage of the 125mph capability. For years BR had stupidly denied that the HST would allow acceleration; but then BR frequently got it wrong.

With periodic glimpses of the River Trent, skirting Long Eaton, we veer south and race through where once was the intriguing Trent Junction. This was laid out so that a train going from A to B could arrive in either direction at the station in the middle of a featureless flat area. Then, still without stop, through Loughborough, alongside the River Soar and the Grand Union Canal, and through Quorn country, where keeping hounds in full cry off the track has always required vigilance. Though there's a lot to see that's pleasant, industry, and its lingering aftermath, is pretty continuous.

The route brings me back through Leicester, with many passengers to exchange with a train from Nottingham beside us. It calls at intermediate stations to London, while we are one of the day's few trains that do the hundred miles non-stop, in 71 minutes. Exhilarating stuff.

Originally Midland trains shared the Great Northern route to King's Cross. Congestion at King's Cross, and bad treatment of Midland excursionists to the 1851 Great Exhibition, forced the building of the independent route to St Pancras. By that time economics prevented the luxury afforded the early railway builders of going straight through obstacles. So curves abound, and the main intermediate stations are in dips requiring speed restrictions at their approach followed by fast acceleration. The HST suits it a treat.

Midland expresses, dispatched from St Pancras in rapid succession, were flyweight, often only four or five carriages plus restaurant car. Less happy was the way that, after the establishment of the London, Midland & Scottish railway, the Midland men, holding sway in locomotive matters, insisted that trains were double-headed (given a second engine) on the former London & North Western out of Euston. They could not admit that the 'Premier Line' had superior machines.

One reason I enjoy the Midland is that much of its individuality survives; another is that for a memorable year, 1938-39, we lived at Harpenden. My portfolio of happy dreams still regularly includes 'takes' of the 4-4-0 Midland Compounds racing past Harpenden Junction soon after the higher semaphore signals had been raised.

St Albans was another place where we stayed at a hotel for several weeks to see if my parents thought it would be good to make our home there. Our hotel rooms overlooked a traffic-clogged crossroads decades before the word motorway had been invented. My parents liked the city and district, and settled at nearby Harpenden – before realising they had made a poor choice and uprooted once more to go west to the sea at Teignmouth. Another dream is walking, with Mum teaching me multiplication tables, along a tranquil path near the cathedral with gently-flowing water on either side. I've always intended to return, yet haven't dared spoil that childhood memory.

Harpenden – 18 Hollybush Lane, Harpenden, Herts, not an easy address for those who couldn't say their Hs – was a green, growing suburb. It was partly chosen for St George's School, where there was a strong emphasis on sport. The admonition that 'Your son could go up one form, possibly two, if only he were better on the football field' turned me into a truant, spending time in 'The Hole', a small, well-hidden area of public land level with the quadrupled main line.

It was a fascinating location. A single-line branch from Hemel Hempstead came in here, but what actually gave Harpenden Junction its name was the double junction allowing trains to and from the fast lines north the choice of the fast or slow lines south to St Pancras. All stopping passenger trains crossed by the junction, a southbound one usually quickly overtaken by an express staying on the main line. North of the junction, the slow lines were for goods only. The up one had 'permissive working', allowing southbound goods to queue behind each other, nose to tail. Most of them were coal trains, some of enormous length hauled by Beyer Garrett articulated locomotives. Every now and then a coal train or two was released to follow a stopping passenger train south, the procession of waiting trains moving up. Meanwhile the signals would be raised for another northbound express overtaking a string of empties returning to their specific collieries (the names and liveries of these private-owner wagons is now the stuff of model railways) to be replenished to feed the capital's hungry boilers. I spent hours both standing on the bridge with its bird's-eye view and beside the track at a point we nicknamed 'The Hole'.

Recently, for the first time since 1939, I revisited Harpenden. The bridge, and nearby track-level 'Hole' are still much the same, but gone are the long coal trains trundling their way to the capital, the semaphore signals, and the old Midland Railway atmosphere. Thanks to suburban electrification and the cross-London link to the south coast, there are more trains than ever, though it is hard to get excited by the passage of an electric multiple unit. Harpenden itself, spaciously set out on garden city lines, is full of interest and individual shops. People know how to look after themselves around here. Though the basic layout is unchanged, none of today's shops rings a bell and I cannot find where I first went to the cinema to see what seemed a frightening Snow White and the Seven Dwarfs.

Today's journey is proving too exhilarating – Railtrack have certainly allowed sections of track to deteriorate, giving a rough ride – for a gentleman opposite, who joined at Leicester when I was feigning sleep. 'Are we safe? It's awfully rough.'

I try to comfort and then ignore him. 'Look at those bushes growing out of the wall. Disgraceful. Haven't they heard of a stitch in time?'

Then he spots growth actually in the slow tracks. 'Just look at it. They don't even bother with the weedkiller train. I hear they've stopped painting the Forth Bridge. What next?'

Next is an attack on what many people criticise, the leaving of old sleepers and equipment by the railside, offering vandals ready tools. 'Ridiculous. Why don't we write letters about it? Will you?'

He's not an easy chap to shut up. Eventually I succeed, perhaps a bit cruelly. 'Yes, but whether we're going to have an accident or not, let's enjoy the journey.' And I close my eyes, ignoring further mutterings.

The motion lulls me and I am barely conscious of braking and accelerating through places like Kettering. I come to life, steadfastly peering out of the window to avoid the attention of the chap opposite, just before Bedford where there is an enjoyable view of the wriggling Great River Ouse, which we will meet in greater detail when we reach the Fens. Gone are the windmills lining it and the brickworks which once employed armies of men. Today's pleasant river gives no hint of its former commercial glory. Though 75 convoluted miles inland, Bedford was once far better known as a successful port than for John Bunyan who spent most of his life around it and must have drawn on the local countryside for some of the images in *Pilgrim's Progress*, written in Bedford Jail.

One of the few journeys we made from Harpenden involved changing at Bedford and catching a local train on the long-closed branch to Northampton, where we were hosted by WJ Bassett-Lowke, who had established his famous model-making business as a young man. Going over the factory, producing track, stations, beautiful locomotives and carriages, and also a huge half-section model of the then new *Queen Mary*, was one of my pre-war highlights. I can still see burly men, with the large hands of manual workers, carefully fitting individual lamps to the tables in the liner's dining rooms.

Bassett-Lowke, dapper with an expensive taste in suits and ties, was the 'father of scale models', in a different league from Hornby. Later on we saw a lot of him, especially in the war years when he visited Teignmouth to photograph Dad's layout while questioning whether the Germans would allow his firm to continue when they took Britain over. When there was an air raid, he was sure they were actually arriving.

He was the first businessman I had met. Were they all as careful, nervous and yet as impatient? Because the taxi he ordered for our return to the station hadn't arrived within ninety seconds, he summoned a second from a different firm – and then a third. Giggle giggle as all three turned up together and there was much shouting and arm waving. The taxi we were bundled into took us to a sleepy terminus with six departures, weekdays only. The railways were already under financial strain and it was about to be closed and the trains diverted to Northampton's main-line station a mile away. The return journey, in darkness, was memorable for the way the sky was lit up by factory furnaces.

Back to this afternoon's journey... Bedford is where London's pull begins to be felt and the frequent electric service starts. A surprising proportion of the journey is now through real countryside, with a brief skirmish with the M1, to Luton, which we were all taught was the hat town as Leicester was hosiery, Nottingham lace and Northampton shoes. I catch sight of three Easyjet planes. There's talk of a new station to serve the airport better. We flash past Harpenden Junction, where again I fail to spot whether 'The Hole' is still there. St George's School *is*. No doubt most of today's as well as yesterday's boys were better prepared for the games field than I was, not having been at school at all during the previous eight months and earlier only at a single-teacher private school. We overtake an electric train in the cutting before St Albans, where at our speed the station is just a blur. We really must come here, at least for a day. St Albans is said to be one of the most appealing and convenient places for walkers near to London and is packed with Roman, early Christian and trading history and relics. Yet would I spoil those childhood memories? I even recall the individuality of several of the ducks of 1938.

The Gothic Glory of St Pancras

Overtaking more electric trains going through and under London to places like Gatwick, we pass the familiar string of inner suburban stations until we dive under Camden and come to rest beneath the great single-span Gothic roof of St Pancras, the train's front only a hundred yards from Marylebone Road. My fellow passenger mutters but I avoid his eyes as he rushes out. If he's going on by road, I wonder if he appreciates he's finished what is still by far the safest part of his journey.

There's only one St Pancras. How proud Derby's Midland men must have been of it, functional – underneath the station a huge storage space was designed in units of Burton-on-Trent beer barrels – but sturdy and daring. At its apex the roof (689 ft long with a 240 ft span) towers 100 ft above the rails. Not everyone likes it, but thousands come to admire it, especially its bold Gothic frontages. An American tourist looking for a place of worship is said to have gone into St Pancras, doffed his hat and, meeting a well-attired individual he took to be a beadle, enquired the time of 'the next service'.

The station wasn't built without a cost, and this afternoon I linger and think of the poor workers who in 1866 had to enclose the Fleet River, really a sewer, in an iron pipe, and those who had to remove successive layers of graves of the old St Pancras Church. At first many human bones were left lying around, and there was uproar. Few however were worried by the 10,000 evicted without compensation from the 4½-acres site needed for the terminus, though their moving into neighbouring areas, creating new disease-prone slums, did cause a headache for the health authorities.

At the time of the station opening in 1868, only the foundations of the adjoining hotel were ready. 'As it took shape, the Midland Grand Hotel became one of the most-talked about buildings in the country, its outward extravagance more than matched by the interior arrangements. The original coffee and dining room was 100ft long, 30ft wide and 24ft high, while the double intertwined grand staircase, decorated with iron scrollwork, ascended to the third floor under a beautiful vaulted ceiling 80ft above the ground,' says Alan Jackson in his *London Termini*, a fun book to publish. There were 400 sitting rooms and bedrooms; and 'everywhere were pointed arches, carved oak doors, marble-faced walls'. Once declared 'the most sumptuous and the best-conducted hotel in the Empire', at the turn of the century it was London's first to be fitted with a revolving door.

From the early 1930s its trade suffered from the lack of central heating and sufficient bathrooms. It closed in 1935, and so has not functioned as an hotel during most of my lifetime. In BR days, headquarters of railway hotels and train catering used to be here: at least they kept the fine wines well, once so well that a huge quantity was forgotten and, when rediscovered, sold at truly bargain prices as a restaurant car special offer. Then fire regulations made it hard to use the building sensibly even as offices. Things deteriorated creating an architectural outrage: for years rain was allowed to pour into the top floors. Though intact, the massive staircase was uncared for. Mega money is being spent on restoring the hotel and, seeing the builders hard at work, I eagerly look forward to a stay as soon as it reopens after nearly eighty years.

St Pancras station itself was once under threat. However, soon the main platforms under the roof will be the preserve of Eurostars taking their new fast route though Kent and, largely underground, around Eastern London. Midland Mainline will then move to new platforms beyond the present ones. Meanwhile St Pancras, serving only Midland Mainline, is the quietest and easiest-to-monitor London terminus.

Before I leave, I think of Dad as a young man alighting to begin his publishing career at Chapman & Hall, and how soon his and everyone else's world fell apart with the start of World War One. And there, running as soon as a train from Nottingham has stopped, a young man dashes into the arms of his waiting sweetheart. Romance has always been special at St Pancras.

· XVII ·

A PROVINCIAL PUBLISHER'S LONDON

Taxi Tour Down Memory Lane

To those who set store by provincial values, London is simply the largest place in Britain. Distinctly not the be-all and end-all that it seems to so many people in the southeast of England. In my career, I despised those who thought that Hadrian's Wall and civilisation ended somewhere near the Watford Gap. This was reinforced by the fact that the books I published didn't do particularly well in London. That was because the London market was still adequately supported by literary genres. We made our mark in provincial Britain, since its booksellers urgently needed the new kind of non-fiction niche publishing which we pioneered. Partly it was about timing; partly about my having a chip on my shoulder. The son of a literary journalist, how could I possibly publish literary books, or indeed any kind of fiction, from the railway station in Newton Abbot?

London was a challenge. While poor sales at its 'establishment' bookshop, Hatchards, might not matter much, it was here that the WH Smith chain controlled their national buying (especially of titles to 'scale out' to branches around the country). It was the obvious place to meet key authors and especially American publishers seeking titles for their lists... not to mention merchant banks, business solicitors, literary agents and the rest. Though my career was dedicated to never having to live in London, there were frequent train trips, starting in the days when that meant at least four hours each way on the rails. It later came down to under three. Most of the trips and overnight stays were by myself and today, before meeting up with Sheila, who won't be returning from her sister in Hampshire till later, I decide to relive some of those lonely times when I would be alternately exhilarated and depressed about what was being achieved.

318

Especially in the early days, there were few places in London where I could relax. These made an odd list, headed by great railway stations, large and impersonal hotels, and parks besides the Thames, especially on the South Bank where I had been much impressed by the 1951 Festival of Britain. Taxi drivers, many of whom were characters, gave me the closest thing to companionship. So, on leaving St Pancras station, it is natural to go 'next door' to the altogether more utilitarian King's Cross, with its twin and less-distinguished train sheds. Yet, I recall, when it opened it was so much admired that the Great Northern's shareholders complained about extravagance. That irritated the company's chairman who retorted that it was 'the cheapest building for what it contains and will contain that can be pointed out in London'.

It cost only £123,000, less than that spent just on the portico and Great Hall at Euston... another of the termini on the Marylebone Road, since railways from the north were not allowed any closer to the centre. The graceful arches of the original frontage of King's Cross have long been obscured by additional building, while in Euston's 1960s modernisation the Doric arch through which one's taxi arrived in style was needlessly destroyed – along with the Great Hall which was perhaps more appropriate for singing carols than waiting for trains. Little of London's modernisation of the 1960s is now respected – but, then, things were just as bad in the country. This was the decade when most provincial cities exchanged taste for modernity, record mileages of hedgerows were ripped up and country houses demolished at a great rate. In many respects, we have come a long way since then.

After briefly queuing with Northern businessmen who have arrived on an express from Edinburgh, I tell the taxi driver that I want to take an unusual kind of tour, explaining that I'm writing a book.

'I'm writing one, too,' he replies. Like many would-be authors, he launches into a long description of his, 'about bloodlines and feuds in Turkey'. He gives up when I cease asking him questions about his plot, which I can't really understand, and subsides into silence, leaving me to my own thoughts and only asking 'Where next?' after each stop. He's a young man, unlikely to be a lifelong cabbie like some of the drivers in the old days who provided me with real experiences... and manuscripts such as the one I was presented with on the spur of the moment and successfully published as *A Taxi Driver's London.*

First stop is Bishopsgate. I look at where Hambro's Bank once proudly stood, spreading into neighbouring buildings as it grew in size and stature. That was in the reign of Jocelyn Hambro who, in 1970, was the last to arrive at a cocktail party ahead of lunch where I was to be vetted as a fit person to be lent money for expansion. Directors arrived at two-minute intervals, each making an outrageously testing remark. Jocelyn's shot was: 'So you come from that part of the country where they have those silly Liberal MPs?' In preliminary discussions at Newton Abbot, it had been established I was a Liberal supporter.

As rush-hour traffic builds up in Bishopsgate, I recall that challenging lunch. I didn't seem to be making much impression in the directors' grand dining room on the top floor of 41 Bishopsgate, to which I'm looking up. The table setting was the most impressive I'd ever seen, but the comments 'What – you don't like crackling?' and 'But carrots help you with night blindness,' 'You sure you won't join us in a second helping?' didn't bode well.

As pedestrians sweep by to catch their trains at Liverpool Street, I recall the precise moment at which the tide turned. Over coffee, an untouched basket of glacé fruits appeared. It would have cost more than a week's salary, and routinely I declined to break into it. 'Do,' persisted Jocelyn. I did. All eyes were on me, but as a television reporter I had learned how to cope with that. Given confidence by a second glacé fruit (pear this time), I enjoyed being questioned, and soon an offer was made and even one condition partially renegotiated before shaking hands and being given a tour of the fantastic offices.

That I hadn't successfully renegotiated the whole instead of part of that one condition led to serious trouble in the economic whirlwind of the mid 1970s. Hambro's were still able to threaten me with total bankruptcy – 'We'll have everything except the clothes you're wearing' – unless I handed over management control. Though eighteen months later, it was won back at another lunch – no glacé fruit that time – relations remained uneasy. The grapevine had it that Hambro's made a habit of quickly falling out with those with whom they made investments. Before getting back into my taxi, I glance up at the top floor of an adjoining office where only watching the traffic kept me sane while they discussed my fate. Hambro's faded away – and *The Economist* still speaks of investment banks' 'remarkable instinct for self-destruction'.

We stop briefly at Liverpool Street. The Great Eastern Hotel, the only one in the city, where John Betjeman had his wedding feast and where we spent our first short London family holiday in the late 1940s, is closed for renovations. The station has been more than renovated. The dark, gloomy interior – in foggy steam days you often couldn't see across it – has given way to a state-of-the-art glass palace.

Then by London Wall and Aldersgate Street, the forest of tall construction cranes telling of the financial sector's prosperity, to short St Martin's Le Grand. I remember the scene at the solicitor's offices here when the completion meeting was held as David & Charles became a public company, albeit a small one. That was when Hambro's Bank had their money to count, and so ceased to worry me. As usual at tense meetings, the most difficult issue was shelved till last. It was two in the morning before I sought a taxi. My cabbie, indeed my staff, couldn't imagine the turmoil a key player has to go through. Even now, memories of it are disturbing, so quickly I'm back in the taxi and we're on our way again.

It is sheer relief to enjoy a brief glimpse of St Paul's Cathedral. Then by Ludgate Hill into Fleet Street, as busy as ever, though now without lorries delivering huge reels of newsprint, vans dashing off with finished newspapers, and journalists rushing in to file their reports. The evening music of throbbing printing presses has long moved elsewhere. Though most journalists have also long departed, it is good to see that St Bride's is still the church of the newspaper industry. I have always loved its tranquil setting in its private court, and Wren's tallest steeple cheekily competing with St Paul's for attention. Amazing to think that Wren built fifty (almost half) of the churches in the City after the Great Fire of 1666, many in the small parishes of lanes, courts and little quiet gardens.

Then the familiar succession of the Strand and Charing Cross Road, and past a busy Foyles. It is still a grand bookshop, but in earlier days was of unique importance to publishers. We had a salesman spending almost half his working week here checking stock. Categorisation could be haphazard, leading to scarcity or over-stocks. It was such a labyrinth of showrooms, corners, corridors and stairs that even some staff had to ask the way to the toilet. Thousands and thousands of young people recall their spell at Foyles. Staff turnover was rapid – to avoid giving employment rights. Yet Christina Foyle was delightful, especially enjoying sharing her interest in gardens. She wasn't always well served by her immediate subordinates. Though of course key people lasted longer than the general staff, many ultimately seemed mysteriously to disappear overnight. And the system! Fine if you knew where the purchase authorisation stamp was kept, and avoided one of the black-out periods when, for cash control, there was a total buying embargo.

Next, Covent Garden, like so much of London now a commercial and tourist attraction, but in its market days offering joy to country eyes and nostrils. Many walks between appointments necessitated taking a short cut through it, weaving between carts and trucks grossly overladen with flowers, fruit or vegetables. What displays the merchants mounted! How much, or realistically how little, of the prices charged were remitted to the poor growers? I regularly read *The Western Morning News*'s market reports, and it seemed that Covent Garden spokesmen were always claiming that supplies were sparse or too plentiful, and complaining of late arrivals or the poor condition of Scilly Isles daffodils, Cornish broccoli or Devon anemones or violets.

Covent Garden, where there is now much less to distract from the appreciation of the fine building, is a powerful reminder that London was a working city where people made things, moved them about and sold them at a margin. Factories, workshops and markets have disappeared, at least from the central area. The docks have gone almost totally, and events like the Motor Show moved elsewhere. The headquarters of WH Smith are now in Swindon, where Reader's Digest and Book Club Associates also conduct most of their business. What does everyone do today? It is a question often asked. We don't manufacture, but support a hugely expanded financial services industry. We import and buy, and we make much use of mobile phones. There are many more hotels and restaurants, the latter largely supported by another greatly expanded brigade, those in public relations. Certainly there are many more people driving taxis, too, which is an improvement when you're in a hurry. Yet it doesn't quite seem to make economic sense.

London has always been evolving. One of my favourite childhood pleasures was turning the pages of a three-volume set of *Wonderful London*, a delightfully enterprising work with superb writing and black-and-white photography, published at the end of the 1920s. Edited by St John Adcock, after whom I was given my middle name, it proclaimed itself: 'The World's Greatest City Described by its Best Writers, and Pictured by its Finest Photographers.' The introduction talks of 'Every new generation, coming in with new customs, new inventions, new ways of living and thinking, extends its borders, and more or less rebuilds or remoulds it'. Familiar though the pages are from boyhood, they portray street scenes, hawkers and traders, social occasions and pastimes that now seem as deeply ensconced in the past as the London of Dickens, yet in the capital's core the great buildings are those we know and love today, for much of non-residential London has not been seriously rebuilt since the coming of the railways. Only the financial district and Dockland have changed dramatically and, for all the wartime hardship, Hitler's bombs left less of a mark than the Great Fire.

Much of London truly is a changeless stage on which the action is perpetually different. At least repairing the streets is less painful, and certainly a lot less labour intensive, than it used to be. *Wonderful London*'s picture of a street being dug up shows a veritable army of manual workers.

Piccadilly is one of London's great streets where the buildings seem timeless and one wonders if in the lifetime of today's youngsters the traffic passing between them will look as odd as that depicted (all buses are open tops) in *Wonderful London*. I've come to take a brief look at Burlington Arcade, remembering how proud the person who taught me most about publishing, John Baker, was when he went independent and set up his office there. While running the Phoenix House imprint for Dents, John published my first books, and his later persuasion resulted in the purchase of Readers Union book clubs which he also ran for Dents. Founded in 1937, Readers Union itself had a loyal following of those happy to receive an unabridged quality (usually non-fiction) work each month for less than the price of taking *The Times*. In those days belonging to a book club was like subscribing to a magazine for a set period. 'An unabridged hardback a month for less than the cost of taking *The Times*,' was a compelling line when many people were prepared to have their reading chosen for them. I am still enjoying some of those reprinted titles.

The book trade had viewed John as a dangerous man and, to ensure they were not bypassed, bookshops handled many of the subscriptions – while titled people expected their books to arrive in plain covers so that it wasn't made obvious to the butler that they were reading on the cheap. The changeover from 'reprint' to 'simultaneous' book clubs happened in my time. The emphasis is now on choice, and few people would be happy to have their books picked for them. Progress, perhaps, but with today's rents and rates, Burlington Arcade would surely be out of bounds to struggling independent publishers. But, then again, today's John Bakers hardly need offices at all. Now you can do almost anything from anywhere in the country, even the Highlands of Scotland.

Soon the taxi tour takes us through Berkeley Square. When I ask the driver to go round again and stop in the corner where Reader's Digest used to have their offices, he suddenly shows interest. 'Reader's Digest,' he grunts. 'Always promising money. Does anyone win their prize draws? Once you're on their list you're on it forever.' I explain that RD bought my company. 'So that's why you can afford this zigzag trip tonight.'

RD courted us twice, with amazing meetings in their plush offices. The first time we withdrew; the second (with a much better deal) we sold. It wasn't a happy result, though, for I was told to keep away and scores of my former staff were rapidly 'let go'. In a few years David & Charles were sold again.

Sheila will soon be at the Italian restaurant near Paddington station where we've arranged to dine. It has been an emotional couple of hours; a very personal journey... With only minutes to go, the driver grovels: 'Sure you wouldn't like to see my manuscript?' I explain that my publishing days are over. 'Living on Reader's Digest's riches, I suppose?' Which I suppose means he hopes for a decent tip.

Paddington Again and the Travelling Post Office

We so frequently travel to and from Paddington that coming here for the evening seems crazy. But we are regulars at the Italian restaurant, are warmly welcomed, and the fare is tasty, appropriate and sensibly priced. The real reason, however, is that once more – and possibly for the last time – I want to post a letter to Devon in the Late Box of Great Western Down Travelling Post Office, which departs at 10.10pm. Not for much longer, though, for the Royal Mail – beg their pardon, Consignia – are said to be planning the withdrawal of all trains on which letters are actually sorted at speed.

In past years, overnight visits usually meant staying at the Great Western Royal Hotel at Paddington with its Brunel marble bathrooms and staircase. It was once the Empire's largest and most modern hotel. My routine before going to bed was to hear my whistle echo down the stairs to the station on my way to post a letter home in the Late Box on the side of the Great Western Travelling Post Office, and see the Royal Mail men on the platform adjourn their conversation with those on the train till the next evening as the train was whistled away, always exactly at 10.10.

The GWR TPO, (at the time of writing still so called) was a marvel. Because it was in Bristol Temple Meads in the small hours at the same time as the Up TPO, and also those from and returning to the north of England and South Wales, any letter bearing an extra halfpenny stamp posted through its Late Boxes was delivered by first post next morning over much of southern and western England and Wales... even London itself. Letters posted in London for London made (and at the time of writing still do) the trip to Bristol and back. At Newton Abbot there was a Late Box outside the station emptied by staff of the Up TPO during its stop. A letter for, say, Penzance would reach its destination far earlier by travelling to Bristol and back than if you had posted it in an ordinary pillar box. Never once did a letter posted on the train at Paddington by 10.10pm fail to be delivered by 6.30 next morning at my Devon farmhouse.

As journalist and broadcaster, I made several trips on the train, watching the three dozen postman at work and enjoying their unique comradeship. Much of the magic holds true today, though only on my first trip were they still exchanging mail at speed, using a mechanical arm extended from the train to engage with lineside equipment both to pick up and set down mail bags. Like slip coaches and engines picking up water from troughs between the rails, such exchanges at speed have gone into history, and so will the scene we witness tonight: sorters opening mail bags and, with amazing dexterity, popping letters into their correct slot on the great racks labelled afresh each night, some more than once. West of Plymouth this Great Western TPO will again sort Penzance's mail into house and street order, ready for the town's postmen to deliver. It is a system that has worked for many generations, but today it's cheaper to send first-class mail by air. Only second class will remain on the rails. That will reduce the usefulness of the Royal Mail's private narrow-gauge railway under London serving most of the important termini – Paddington is the western terminus – and the main sorting office.

[The name Consignia has been ridiculed out of existence, the last TPO has run and the Royal Mail's underground railway closed, adding to congestion on London's streets.]

As mentioned earlier, privatisation of the railway hotels was badly done, and most suffered a major decline. Now the Great Western Royal is closed for major renovation. It is to become a Hilton. I hope they respect Brunel's masterpiece better than did Maggie Thatcher. I'm sorry it is closed, for I'd hoped to show Sheila the exact spot in the foyer where I made the most effective short speech of my life... about which I'm still embarrassed.

We had been what is colloquially termed 'stitched up' in a deal concerning the acquisition of a large book club to join Readers Union. My solicitor, Richard West, who has since become a close friend and who we meet again soon, warned me on our train journey that legally there wasn't much he could do, so to feel free to try whatever approach seemed appropriate. The vendors and their solicitor so gloated over their strength that I stood up and, without thinking, shouted 'I've been raped!' They tried to quieten me, so I shouted it more loudly. Everyone around stopped in amazement. In two minutes flat a six-figure sum was agreed in compensation. Not for all the tea in China would one make such a scene to order, but the ways of business in London can indeed be weird and wonderful.

[Later we visited the hotel re-opened as a Hilton. Full marks. It has been sympathetically done and even encourages rail users with a new access from the station and – by the porters' desk – a screen detailing train departures.]

We go to our hotel by Baker Street, noting the capital's most majestic tube station (loved by John Betjeman) and see where I used to run our bookshop. Every time I pass I think that, but for that timely relief from the meeting at Paddington, we might have gone the way of so many other businesses. Look at the shops today; many of them will be struggling, some certainly afraid the bank will step in any day. It has often been said that there hasn't been a decent business novel since Trollope. The trouble is that in today's world anything like a real business plot would be complicated and technical, and much of what goes on in real life – the back-stabbing, colossal waste caused by the 'not invented here' syndrome, the personal bias in decision making – simply wouldn't seem credible in fiction. Certainly the City was pretty intimidating, at least until you grew a hide and became unbullyable.

'Glad you're out of it,' says Sheila. Not sure about that. But to bed.

Brian MacArthur and the Newspaper Revolution

We are on a bargain out-of-season break at the Connaught Hotel where, for absolutely no discernable reason, our greatly-discounted price has been combined with upgrading to a penthouse suite. We lose ourselves in it, once literally. Guests to breakfast served in the lounge of our suite are embarrassingly impressed. This is distinctly not how we normally live. I've never before stayed here, though admit to fond memories concerning visiting American publishers encouraging me to make fullest use of the dining room – and learning which of their wives might or might not be an ally in clinching a sale. 'It's so cute, you must have it, darling.' Sometimes the oddest of very British things sold brilliantly across the pond; other times, what had seemed a safe bet mysteriously failed. The reason, I discovered, is that, unlike in Britain, where titles are stocked in bookshops without real assessment of their contents (as opposed to subject and author's reputation), in the States librarians and others seriously follow the considered advice of a handful of literary periodicals.

The next few days are for renewing acquaintance with a variety of authors and publishing contacts, revelling in what the capital has to offer (with, for example, my first leisurely visit to St Paul's Cathedral, suffering from a serious drop in visitor numbers and repackaging itself as 'a place of spectacular adventure'), taking in a few theatres... oh, and shopping for Sheila. It has to be admitted that London's shopping has the edge on Nairn's. For the fun of it, we save money on *Financial Times* bargain lunches. The *FT* was the first to introduce a low-cost fixed-price lunch scheme, and theirs is still probably the best; no coupons or vouchers, restaurants carefully selected, readers having a real voice, and substantial sums raised for Save the Children.

First breakfast guest is Brian MacArthur of *The Times*, with whom I have kept closely in touch since, as mentioned earlier, he went to Plymouth to revitalise *The Western Morning News*, where I began my career and he brought me and a number of other old-timers back into the fulfilling fray. Then, too quickly, he was whisked off to London as founder editor of *Today*. What memories of how Eddie Shah's baby suffered from faults in the technology into which he foolishly rushed. Journalists inputting their own copy, computer page make-up and electronic colour have long since become universal. Eddie Shah was not only ahead of his time, but impatient – 'We didn't even run a dummy paper' – and so failed spectacularly in his bid to break the unions' grip on conventional technology. Brian's *Today and the Fleet Street Revolution* was one of those books whose sales suffered from too much newspaper exposure. If readers can enjoy the interesting bits free, why pay for the rest? Two lessons here: avoid being a pioneer but be ready to move fast when the way is proven; and giving away too much information is often not the way to tempt people.

The point about not adopting new methods too quickly is emphasised by Brian. 'Though Murdoch may be seen as a trend setter, he has always moved cautiously. He kept old-fashioned paste-up at his papers for a long time. Of course the revolution was coming and *Today* may have inspired him to come to terms with the unions. Eddie just tried to be too clever. We wallowed in technology.'

Brian always arrives greatly puffing, as though there's a deadline to be met before the starter is served. But he also knows how to relax quickly and wistfully talks of 'my one entrepreneurial idea that missed the boat'. That was for a magazine made up of selections from the week's papers and magazines, essentially what is now *The Week*, the very title he had chosen for his venture. 'We were all ready to sign up with Charterhouse, when the signs of recession couldn't be ignored.' A reminder that one idea is seldom enough to ensure you can develop your own business and so step off the treadmill of working for someone else. Brian, however, thrives on treading away. He is responsible for the Saturday *Times*'s serial and book pages and each Friday contributes Paper Round, something of a bible of the performance of rival papers and how they do or don't make the most of the day's news and comment.

'All circulations are falling, the tabloids dramatically – three million fewer copies than ten years ago.' He says that the most popular of his first seven books has been *Twentieth Century Speeches*. I love his ability to enjoy the journalistic hurly-burly while standing back to write books of considerable perspective. Above all, he's fun, even when you're on the opposite side of an argument.

He thanks me for introducing him to book writing, 'a whole new world, quite different from journalism'. He adds: 'Of course, it was you who first recognised Middle England, with all those books on subjects that wouldn't wash in London. I'll never forget the hundreds who came to your garden party at Bristol and how many books they bought.' That was an indoor garden party, celebrating D&C's 25th birthday, which we gave Brian the pleasure of opening formally, in Brunel's original Temple Meads railway terminus.

A Better National Trust

Then to St Anne's Gate to what is still, but won't be for much longer, the head office of the National Trust. I've no attachment to the place. It is hideously ugly and out of context. When he was Prince of Wales, King George V dismissed it as 'the carbuncle'. However, antipathy goes deeper than the building. Twice the National Trust brought me up from Devon only for a message to be left at reception that our meeting had been postponed until the following week – 400 miles of travel in vain, without apology. And though there had been an initial good spirit behind our co-operation in publishing National Trust titles, when they decided they would like to become their own publisher, they engaged a top solicitor to tell me so. His letter warned that contracts would be unilaterally broken and I'd be foolish if I expected compensation. They were the National Trust's public schoolboys' days, when 'We're the National Trust, you know' excused anything, and if you lived out in the sticks and were more interested in country matters than the finer points of interior decoration or Queen Anne tables, you were nobody.

I tell today's Irish receptionist I've come to see Warren Davis. 'Is he in?' 'Don't think so...' Only when I ask the Irishman where he's from, and share in talking about the joys of Belturbet, does he seriously pursue the elusive Warren... who rather spoils things for him by greeting me as he alights from the lift.

In the days I was having difficulties with the National Trust in London, Warren was in West Country roles, and we shared much fun, especially in organising joint D&C/NT trips from London to St Michael's Mount. Now, shortly before retirement, 'the last public school boy here', he is press and public relations adviser. By the time this is published, the National Trust's HQ will have moved to Swindon. The 'carbuncle' was built before World War One for the Anglo-American Oil Company and looks like it.

'It ruined the ambience of Queen Anne's Gate,' agrees Warren. And the park, with its private entrance, could tell a tale or two: 'It used to be called Birdcage Walk because of the singing birds. It was supposed to be very exclusive, but copies of keys were given to ladies of easy virtue, and their clients who arrived in sedan chairs were protected from onlookers.' Pointing to the pub, The Two Chairmen, he adds that the chairmen (carriers of the chairs) went there for a drink while waiting to take their gents home.

If this is about as irreverent an introduction as I can give the National Trust, fair enough. Once at dinner on an evening train from Devon, with three other men sharing a table, one commented he hadn't seen that credit card before. 'It's the National Trust's,' said the owner. 'You should all get one.'

'I shan't after what they've done to me,' I interjected.

'Oh, do tell me, I'm the new director-general.' I did tell him; he feigned shock and promised to get in touch, but of course never did.

'Yes, we were very elitist,' explains Warren. 'You weren't the only one treated with disdain by those whose only real interest was the great houses, especially their showpiece rooms and contents. They had forgotten that the Trust's fundamental purpose was to preserve the landscape. Now with our new director, Fiona Reynolds, it's quite different. We're seen as the best means of making sure the countryside is not whittled away. The trouble was that in the 1950s and 1960s, because of high taxation, so many houses came our way, homes of the great entrepreneurs of the past. Visiting those that had previously been in private ownership became a great British passion.

'The elite loved these country houses with their great pictures, books and furniture, but at first they concentrated on the main rooms, and kitchens and nurseries had no part to play. Now, we're doing much more to reflect lifestyles through the ages, with woodmen's cottages, gardeners' bothies, a workhouse even – much more vernacular architecture, so we can see what facilities the man at the water mill had in his day, and of course kitchens and kitchen gardens are now an integral part of the big houses. We've really come to grips with the countryside, and see the buildings as just part of the great heritage. After all, what makes Britain so unique is the combination of our farmed landscape, our rugged coasts and great estates.'

I comment on the Lost Gardens of Heligan in Cornwall. 'That's opened everybody's eyes,' he agrees. 'It's not National Trust in any way, but we, too, are restoring kitchen and walled gardens, making them productive again, and beginning to sell produce to our visitors. But it is farmed landscape that's the real key. We're the custodians of so much and it gives us huge responsibility. We're back where we started in 1895 in a sense, the biggest protector of the landscape, but in its totality. And I say thank goodness that in Prince Charles we've had someone interested in the broader picture.'

It is fascinating to note how rapidly attitudes have changed; as recently as the early 1980s, possibly our finest productive gardens, at Chatsworth and Tatton Park, were bulldozed to make space for more commercial activities.

Warren is soon going to settle in William Barnes and Thomas Hardy country just south of Dorchester. He recalls that it was acceptable for Barnes the country poet to live in his thatched cottage, but Hardy had been forced to build a gentleman's house. Barnes wouldn't go with the flow; Hardy was swept along, unhappily. As mentioned at Boscastle in the North Cornwall chapter, at heart Hardy was much more the basic countryman, though against hunting, than those who have romanticised his novels realise. I recall how another D&C author, Desmond Hawkins, who was once head of the BBC West Region, had far more successfully distilled the spirit of Hardy in his radio dramatisations (half an hour at 8.30 on Sunday evenings) than have television adaptations.

'But if it wasn't for television, there wouldn't be the interest in what we're doing in the countryside today,' comments Warren. 'As I finish my long years with the National Trust, there's the satisfaction in seeing a more rounded interest in the countryside by more of the population than ever before. Of course there are problems, like foot-and-mouth and struggling farmers, but think how much more the countryside would have been at risk if the farming crisis had happened earlier. There's now general acceptance that farmers have to be paid as custodians of the landscape, though it still needs working out.'

Sandwiches with a Favourite Agent

Then to a cramped office in a mews off Theobold Road to meet Doreen Montgomery (or Dottie), the literary agent and administrator of the Chantry Trust, providing autistic children with music therapy. Hartley Booth, a Trustee and my cousin, 'has good contacts. He used to be my MP,' says Doreen. I sometimes describe her as my favourite agent; we published more books from her than any other literary agent, for London agents didn't naturally favour provincial publishers and their more Spartan ways.

She joined the firm of Rupert Crew, working for him and his wife as junior in 1945, so it is an understatement to say she has seen many changes in publishing. We happen to admire many of the same gallery of yesteryear's characters, notably the publisher John Baker. He 'was a most civilised person, who respected authors in a way few do today. He was a pioneer, too, and published the first books on many subjects, including music therapy.' And there was that gentleman of agents, David Higham.

Had she chosen, Doreen might have led a quietish life serving a handful of profitable well-known authors: Barbara Cartland, Cecil Beaton, Patience Strong and Godfrey Winn. But she was always pushing the boat out, and the firm's red presentation folders ('Rupert emphasised that our synopses were our shop window') were familiar to my editorial staff.

After more than half a century, she still doesn't wish to give up, and works closely with her daughter Caroline. 'There are still marvellous new authors with original ideas,' she says, 'but I wish I could say that publishing is as good as it used to be. Our authors need us, because so many royalty statements aren't accurate, and the mistakes nearly all seem to be against the author. So many good, middle-of-the-road publishers have disappeared. Now we have what I call the assembly-line publisher. I agree that many authors will have to self-publish to be published at all in future.'

Doreen and Caroline have provided a sandwich lunch with good wine, over which we share many experiences and opinions. And who am I seeing next? Maggie Whitehouse, daughter of Patrick Whitehouse, who provided the pictures and captions for many of my bestselling railway titles. 'Caroline and Maggie sometimes do dog walks together, did you know?' We will meet Doreen again at my Trust's forthcoming prizegiving.

Afternoon Tea at the Savoy

It is afternoon tea at the Savoy with Maggie. I arrive early, and think of the Savoy's timelessness, all those I've met here who have gone, and the afternoon teas they'll go on serving after my days are over. Publishing is a social business, and everyone with whom a meeting was mooted hoped it would be over lunch. If you work in Devon, there aren't many lunches a year to be had in London so, to spread the load, I invited people to breakfast, lunch and afternoon tea: upmarket breakfasts and teas were at the Savoy, less stately ones at the Charing Cross Hotel a few hundred yards along the Strand.

Invitations to the Savoy were eagerly accepted, and most guests were on their best behaviour. I recall many enchanting occasions, such as with the person who ran the book side of the oil company, Shell, whose head office was then only a few doors away in the next courtyard. Launched with quality authors, Shell Books became a powerful force within a number of selected publishers' lists, and we were proud of our titles, mainly on natural history and the coast.

Only one author let the Savoy down. That was at breakfast, at a window table with a Thames view. My guest was trying to demonstrate his powers of persuasion. 'I'll show you,' he trumpeted. 'Waiter.'

'Yes, sir.'

'Half a cup of coffee, please.' A whole cup was poured. 'Waiter, didn't you hear? I asked for half a cup.'

'Sorry, sir,' as a fresh cup was presented and half filled. It was swallowed in a single mouthful before the fellow had moved five feet.

'Waiter, another half cup,' which was meekly poured. 'There you are. That's called control.' I gave it another name.

Today's tea waiter says he's been here 37 years but this is his last week and he's returning to his native Portugal, though will miss the Savoy. 'Can anything be quite like this?' He spots Maggie on her way over before I do.

With rosy cheeks, Maggie, trim and vibrant, says: 'This is lovely,' and enjoys her tea like a schoolgirl. Among other things in a varied journalistic career, she was at the BBC's Birmingham Pebble Mill at One as producer and has also been a radio presenter in the Midlands. At school she had been forced to wear a teeth brace, and 'talked funny', so had low esteem and has had to fight to make her mark. Salvation partly came through closeness to her father. Seven times in eight years they went on a major railway expedition to China when it was still very much a closed world: just seats, no couchette, and a hole in the floor for the toilet. A TV programme and books were by-products. Then, on one filming expedition, the sound recordist proposed. They were soon married. I recall Patrick, Maggie's father, excitedly telling me about the romance. A year and sixteen days later, the young husband was dead.

'It would have been our anniversary tomorrow,' she says. But then she bubbles about what's she's still learning from life, shows me a proposal to raise money for a Midland-based health magazine, and talks about her novel. 'Which cake are you having?' She's already forty, working with computer whiz-kids half her age but probably with much less bubble.

We talk about Patrick. 'I was so pleased he had that love in his life at the end.' That was when he finally left home to live with his new found-partner. And, yes, he could never stop seeing what was in a meeting or any opportunity for himself. Doreen Montgomery had confided to me that, after I had put her to sit next to Patrick at a formal dinner, he asked if she could get better terms than we'd agreed. 'Yes, Dad was like that, insecurity, I suppose, but it didn't stop him working closely with people, and you had a great partnership with so many bestselling books.'

The Portuguese waiter has looked after us as though we were a courting couple. It has been a warm meeting and the farewell is emotional, though it is unlikely our paths will cross again. Like so many meetings arranged on these travels, it has been a one-off, like a goal in injury time.

I leave by the back entrance to walk part of the way back to our hotel along the Thames. While most places used to ignore their river fronts – Glasgow's, for example, was awful – our mother river has always been respected at least in our capital's most important area. Freight movements are largely a thing of the past, but there are plenty of passenger boats today.

The Excesses of London

Next day we enjoy a personal selection of the extraordinary range of interest that London offers, and especially its retail excesses. Where else in the world...? Determined not to be seduced, we walk from the Connaught down Mount Street pretending we're in a TV show having to 'invest' £100,000 in antiques within half an hour. It don't go far! A tallboy that would look perfect in our bedroom – and we've been searching for months – is about the same price as a new Jaguar XJ6. There goes well over a third of our hundred grand, so we're not encouraged to complete the game. Then to Selfridges, where we especially love the Food Hall, and have an *FT* lunch. After that, a long walk through London's streets, enjoying the parks and trees, shop windows and so many familiar buildings and vistas, of course always knowing what to expect round the next corner but enjoying it for its familiarity.

Such a lot of quality small towns and villages rolled into one; that's how I see London. But then in Scotland we are used to going to the dentist in one place, doctor in another, buying our fish miles away from where we get our basic groceries. There's just so much to London, so many fine buildings in addition to its most famous shops, art galleries, museums and more obvious tourist attractions. No wonder it's popular with overseas visitors who come here – often so many of them that parts of the capital lose that essential everyday, matter-of-fact feel, which says 'London's all this but we take it for granted'. Parts of Oxford Street, once such a mecca of quality, now seem especially over-ridden by tourists and cheap 'outlets'.

I realise my understanding of London will always be superficial, certainly when compared with that of Peter Ackroyd, whose 822-page tome *London: The biography* is as compelling in measured doses as it is overwhelming in its totality. He told a newspaper that his passion for London is really a passion for writing: he lives and breathes the capital, and so perhaps, not surprisingly, isn't interested in the countryside: 'It's too noisy and too dangerous.' Too noisy? Yet he tells us that by 1860 London already had 3,000 omnibuses each carrying roughly 300 passengers a day; today's London traffic cacophony is soul destroying. As a matter of fact, yet again I see it is claimed that the traffic is moving more slowly than ever. The speeds are similar to those that encouraged the building of the first underground.

London is timeless in many ways. For example, any new building will always be a minor part of the scene, for what predominates is the heritage of many centuries. But there is a timelessness in change itself: in London it never ceases. A current surprise is that, after decades of decline, the population is increasing. By the time this is published London will again have over eight million people. The last time it was that size was in the 1950s. By 1983, largely as the result of government dispersal policies, the population was down to 6.8 million. The director of the Greater London Group at the London School of Economics was recently quoted as saying that the capital is Europe's only city offering jobs at £1 million a year, 'and where you can turn up in the morning as an illegal immigrant and be in work by the afternoon'. With house building a little more that half that needed for the extra residents, and powered by excessive salaries, the housing boom is as inevitable as it is harmful.

Last night's dinner at the Connaught was marvellous, though to be honest one could eat just as well at many carefully selected restaurants for half the price. It never ceases to amaze me how much of London is still based on snobbery: 'But, my dear, I couldn't possibly go there; suppose someone saw us?' The desirable 'in' restaurants where people want to be seen thus get away with murder – one of London's excesses that are part of its unique character. If you want good food and good value, ask a few cabbies, or go to any eating house outside which there is a combination of taxis and posh cars including Rolls Royces.

One such is the Sea Shell in Lisson Grove, where for a few years in my later publishing days I had a small flat. I once invited the chairman of the International Food & Wine Society to dinner. 'You're close by the Sea Shell, aren't you?' he asked.

'Yes.'

'Would you think me peculiar if I suggest we eat at home and bring in a fish cake from across the road? There's no better taste in London than a Sea Shell fish cake.'

The dinner, that might have cost the sky, was 80p a head. This was of course some years ago; I sold the flat after D&C went and had less need to be in London. We had been publishers to the International Food & Wine Society, since the days of its founder, George Rainbird, a notable publisher himself, pioneering expensive coffee table books for sale in different countries. He taught me much about the appreciation of food and London's extraordinary range of eating places.

Lisson Grove was a marvellous location: handy to Paddington, a great street market starting only yards away, canal walks and Little Venice close by, Marylebone station just round the corner. There is a story about the young cleric who asked his mentor which church or chapel he might recommend for quiet praying. 'My dear man, if you want to pray in London, you don't go to a church but to Marylebone station.'

The station was terminus for the last of the railways to reach London, the Great Central, and was usually quiet, never having done as well as was expected – until, in BR days, there was a plan to sell it. The National Coach Company upset the applecart by putting in a bid to make it a kind of northern Victoria coach station, converting the rail tracks into a private road leading north. Surprise, BR quickly found it was, after all, indispensable, and it has been greatly improved and given a far livelier role. The Chiltern Line – one of the best of the privatised franchises – runs frequent local services and expresses to Birmingham's reopened Snow Hill and beyond to Stourbridge. Across the road is the Landmark Hotel with its amazing central atrium, a deep glassed-over courtyard. It had been one of the earliest railway hotels to close and, in BR days, when the top-heavy management structure was based there aloof from the real world, it was known as The Kremlin.

Merchant Banker and Solicitor Extraordinaire

First visitor next day is Jonathan Davis, for whom I've bags of respect... despite the fact he was a merchant banker when we first got to know each other. Not a typical one, though; he has too much self-doubt and humanity – and also a sense of the ridiculous. He was chief designer of the package that took Hambro's Bank off our backs. Then things really improved, and we moved on to become a small public company, enjoying business and thriving. Hambro's shadow remained heavy, though. At the last moment, Commercial Union withdrew from the D&C share issue, having been cautioned that 'Mr Thomas is someone who doesn't take advice'. Says Jonathan over breakfast: 'That wasn't my experience. But of course it depends on what advice you're given.'

Jonathan was the only merchant banker I trusted to give an honest opinion, not one tainted by self-justification, ego or downright incompetence. He adds: 'It's not surprising the City has been racked by failures and fraud. Accountants have to take a lot of the blame, too. One problem is that they've expanded so much into other things, such as consultancy, that proper policing has taken a lower priority. I'm glad I'm out of it, that's for sure.

'Everyone's under such pressure. Even when people realise there's an overheated bubble, fund managers who don't join it will be criticised if their short-term results lag. And the best intentions can be ruined by greed. I totally disagree with Maggie Thatcher's boast that "greed is good". Greed breeds collective hysteria. We've learned nothing since the South Sea Bubble – and the Tulip Bubble before that. And you have to remember that most City people are frightened for their jobs. They don't have sufficient economic independence to be able to stand back and if need be walk away. It's a very competitive environment.

'My father was an industrialist. He didn't leave me much but just enough, a buffer, that made walking away possible. When I went to Guidehouse, I did so on condition I didn't have to work with clients I couldn't respect. When people are driven into doing what they know is wrong, you're bound to have problems.'

Jonathan – 'I'd rather be remembered for common sense than intellect' – combines that rare touch of sincerity with cynicism, earnestness with a deep laugh. He always looks directly at you. In his merchant banking days, he used to talk of the curious way in which he earned his bread. He smiles and says I had been right in not having him as a non-executive director after the share issue. 'Much easier to talk in a corner, but if you're one of the team that can be divisive.'

His new career is as business mentor, meeting those running their own businesses one-to one, and surely inspiring confidence and common sense. He never wonders what there might be in it for him. 'There you touch it,' he says. 'Things are so competitive that "What's in it for me?" has become bog standard. Business mentors, they say, are born, not trained. You need that balance between self-belief and self-doubt which the successful entrepreneur has to have too. Running your own business is often lonely, and much of it is about decision-making, the catalytic method of change, such as how do you decide the moment has come to stop expanding or to sell.'

We talk about General Electric which, under the renowned stewardship of Sir Arnold Weinstock, was constantly criticised for hoarding its cash instead of doing something 'interesting' for its shareholders. When Sir Arnold retired, he saw the empire he had built up rapidly crumble. No doubt to 'do something interesting', GEC changed its name to Marconi, and at the time of writing (well after the meeting I'm describing) the over-ambitious expansion resulted in a rescue operation with the shareholders left with just half of one per cent of the equity.

'It's the tortoise versus the hare,' says Jonathan, adding, 'You were right to sell both your businesses when you did. It's never an easy decision, but if the job is too tough or you don't enjoy it any more... whatever the reason, knowing when the time has come is important if you want to stay healthy and happy.'

We're both certainly that at this morning's breakfast, and as we were in our complex business dealings. 'Business should only be part of life. Holistic is the word.'

Glancing at his watch, he rises to go to a board meeting where he *is* non-executive director... unfortunately just before this morning's other guest, Richard West, once our Plymouth-based business solicitor, is able to arrive from Cornwall. But they've often shared worrying and joyous occasions together, and will no doubt swap notes again at some stage in the future.

'I miss our train journeys together,' Richard starts over a cup of coffee. 'There was always something special about them and the way the restaurant car stewards treated us. They were good days.' But he adds that he, too, is sure I was right to sell. 'Everything has changed, even the law. Now it's all about how much you have billed your clients. I'm glad to have got out.' There's that phrase again. Then, as Sheila joins us, we talk about families and his veritable zoo of pets great and small, quiet and raucous – like the excitable parrot who interrupts telephone calls.

Richard has become a Trustee of my Charitable Trust, of which Sheila is secretary. After coffee we move upstairs to our bedroom for one of our twice-yearly meetings. With Richard, a stickler for 'doing it properly', it is a formal meeting: agenda, minutes of the last meeting and plenty of questions and answers. 'We need to know what you want so we can interpret your wishes should you not remain with us.'

The Trust was formed out of money from the sale of David & Charles. At first it was money looking for a cause. That never works. Now we have to ration our funds, and that works brilliantly. We run what is probably the largest programme of writing competitions in the English language, sponsor youngsters to do hands-on work in the developing world in their gap year, and help a range of small charities achieving practical results with minimal marketing expenditure. We talk about giving ourselves an additional objective: guiding small charities, perhaps through a newsletter. Most small charities are one-man bands working in isolation, as isolated as are most writers. They might welcome sharing the experience of others.

Before he leaves, I once more tease Richard about his initial wish to study Scottish law. He fell in love with a Cornish girl; madly in love, and is still in love with Joan. He switched to English law in the nick of time. They are a lovely family with three adopted children. That adds poignancy to his observation: 'I don't like the way society is changing, people putting off having children or not having them at all because of careers and perhaps selfishness. But the way pensions are going, maybe there's no alternative.'

The Vendors of Two Businesses

Now to the stylish Italian Zefferinos in Lowndes Street, sw1, for a rather special meeting. I have invited to lunch Kit van Tulleken who sold David & Charles, and Roger Melody, who a decade later I asked to sell my 'retirement' business, *Writers' News*, which had grown formidably and become too large to continue running from home. Kit, who now owns her business, and Roger have not met before, and at first all three of us are slightly nervous.

'You are my mentor,' says Roger to Kit. 'Mine is a very small business, and it's an honour to meet you.'

'But we'll have the same kind of experiences,' says Kit reassuringly. Inevitably we talk about the sales they have made for me. Kit flatteringly calls me the perfect client.

'And I found you easy, too,' says Roger. 'Most of my business is selling small magazines and you were toward the upper limit of what comes my way. There were several advantages. Firstly, you didn't have to sell; too many come to me when bankruptcy stares them in the face. Running a small magazine isn't all it's cracked up to be, but usually a lonely business on a shoestring. Secondly, you'd been through it before. So we could have fun.' (We spoke to each other five evenings a week for several months, and more solicitors were involved. The completion meeting for the sale of *Writers' News* was at Macfarlanes in Norwich Street where we arrived at lunch time as scores of expensively-dressed, confident and no doubt highly paid young men poured out of the front doors of both their buildings opposite each other.)

'Sometimes clients don't even return my calls,' says Roger, obviously from the heart. 'I work harder for them than they are prepared to do for themselves. But the usual trouble is that they haven't sorted out their thoughts.'

'You can say that again,' chimes in Kit. 'Mind you, most of ours are well-known publishers with good management.'

'So Reader's Digest have sold David & Charles again,' I say. This time a management buy-out.

'Shame it didn't work out for them. Neil MacRae [RD's London boss at the time] was so keen.' I describe the last time I had met Neil, at Heathrow, waiting for a plane to New York, parked out on the tarmac, so we had to take one of those wretched buses. I'd sat next to him, expressing concern that there seemed to be trouble. 'We were on plan, and then for some reason it fell apart.' Sad.

'And how are things with the *Yorkshire Post*?' (I had sold *Writers' News* to Regional Independent Media who at the time, also published the *Yorkshire Post*. As mentioned later, there is now another new owner.)

'Difficult at the start, better now,' I reply.

'There are often difficulties,' regrets Roger.

'Afraid so,' adds Kit. 'If you sell, you've got to make a new life for yourself, whatever any agreement might say.'

I ask them how long they are going to run their businesses. Kit replies: 'We are the ultimate niche business. No saleable assets, just personal contacts and trust which you can't transfer.' Changing the subject, she asks: 'How did the capital gains tax work out?'

It didn't seem fair that Britain still taxed profits on the sale of one business without rollover relief when the money was invested in another. But I tell her of the time my accountant came with me to some gigantic office block in South West London. It was badly run down, reminding me of a third-world hospital; the Inland Revenue were about to move out, and the man assessing capital gains tax was on the point of retiring. He and the accountant quickly got into a technical ding-dong. I noticed a photograph of a Great Western engine on the wall. Apropos of nothing, I asked why it was there, adding: 'Do you know where I did my loco spotting?' The accountant looked as though he could toss me out. The inspector and I went into an animated railway discussion (with, after a couple of minutes, the parenthesis 'What's the lowest price you'd accept?' followed by 'OK' to my answer) about the merits of various old steam classes. 'You'll never guess the deal I've pulled off this morning,' I heard the accountant crow to his mates back at base. So not too badly, thank you Kit.

And so for a snooze at the hotel, sandwich supper in our room, and a visit to the theatre. I enjoy my taxi rides and walks through London's streets, but already am thirsty for country air.

·XVIII·

IT COULD ONLY BE ENGLAND

Across the Somerset Levels

Next morning we join the 7.45am train from Paddington, now the only one in the entire day that has a restaurant car to Bath. And, yes, the tables are already laid, welcoming us to a Great British Breakfast, and great it is. Sadly though, the steward tells us that at the end of the week it will be withdrawn for good. Restaurant cars will cease to be based at Paddington. 'I'm applying for one of the new posts of Travelling Chef,' he says. 'Of course, it can't be the same.' So, at Bath, we pick up Little Car for our continuing journey.

Somerset, it is often said, has as rich a range of scenery as any English county. As was noted in the book's first pages, there are dramatic variations even immediately round Bath, and then there are the Mendips, the Quantocks and Exmoor, and Cheddar Gorge and picturesque villages, and Wells Cathedral. Yet Somerset also has one of Britain's largest areas of low-lying land, mainly reclaimed from the sea, 250 square miles of flat landscape supporting unique scenery and way of life. It is a complex area, roughly the shape of a hand with long, gnarled fingers pointing deeply inland.

It is also an area with a fascinating history. As one might expect, monks were to the forefront of drainage and improvement of the land. Sites of great interest range from the glorious remains of Glastonbury Abbey and St Michael's Tower capping Glastonbury Tor to the Isle of Athelney, where King Alfred is reputed to have burnt the cakes, to battlefields, including the one on which lives were lost for the last time in serious fighting on English soil.

Once the only way of moving things in this low-lying land was by water. Boats penetrated far inland to places where today's rivers don't even suggest the possibility of navigation: Wells, Glastonbury, Langport, Chard, Ilchester and beyond.

The coast south from Weston-super-Mare isn't Britain's most attractive, and the M5 from near Weston's southern exit to Bridgewater is the most boring of roads. The rivers it crosses, especially the Huntspill River and King's Sedgemoor Drain, do not make me want to record them on camera. But questions about any detail of the British countryside bring forth interesting and sometimes unexpected answers. Why, I wonder, are the low-lying lands less frequently flooded than in former times – some years hardly flooded at all? I recall a 1939 train from Paddington to Taunton passing through square miles of deep floods in the Langport-Athelney area, and remember huge floods right until the end of the 1950s. One secret is the creation of the Huntspill River as a military priority in the dark days of the war. Using scarce machinery for such a purpose struck some as wasteful; one indignant army unit threatened to commandeer it for more productive use. But it wasn't the resulting land drainage that was a priority but the water that poured down the river. That was needed for the ammunition factory at Puriton, slightly inland from the M5 a few miles north of Bridgewater. The digging out of the Huntspill River had often been planned in detail but always postponed. The plans were instantly available.

It was the new river, plus the deepening of the King's Sedgemoor Drain, steadily supported by more sophisticated pumping engines, that did the trick, completing the drainage task begun back in Roman days, when sea walls were strengthened, and pursued by the Abbots of Glastonbury and the bishops of Bath and Wells and the monks at various other locations who embanked rivers and even changed their courses.

By the seventeenth century, when Cornelius Vermuyden (who we will encounter again in the Fens) had a hand in it, still only a third of the low-lying land had been drained. Then came disruption: the Civil War, the defeat of the Royalists at Langport in 1645 and the finale, the Battle of Sedgemoor in 1685, near Westonzoyland, where the Duke of Monmouth's rebellion was bloodily put down. Incidentally it was at Westonzoyland that in 1830 the first huge steam engine pumping station was built to lift water out of the River Parrett. Seven more were to be added along the same river, their need emphasised by the fact that in 11½ miles the river drops a mere 11ft 6in, or 1 in 5280.

The Parrett, often seen as a miserable ditch at low tide, and higher up always as a very slender affair, has frequently proved a difficult river. The tides in the Bristol Channel are among the world's highest, and great surges come in past Combwich and through Bridgewater, occasionally with such force as to capsize boats. For centuries the tidal water flowed inland uninterrupted, but of course holding back floodwater trying to escape. The worst floods inflicted serious damage – the loss of life and property went into folklore – and caused great isolation. Once the water was said to be eleven to twelve feet deep at the foot of

Glastonbury Tor, where in prehistoric times there was even a water village. Nor is catastrophe all in the deep past; the disastrous 1929 floods can still be described by a few from living memory.

I remind Sheila that even the building of the M5 on such soft, low-lying ground was challenging, needing an extra five feet of foundations. We leave the motorway at Puriton and take lanes leading to Cossington, which I had only previously been through by train. That was when BR was trying to close the Somerset & Dorset's Bridgwater branch but came up against the obstacle (later forgotten) of the Act of Parliament stating that trains had to call there in perpetuity. Then by a Roman road, not exactly a racing track, toward Street with its vast Clarke's Village, Glastonbury Tor dominating the skyline. At Ashcott, we double back heading southwest crossing the King's Sedgemoor Drain to visit Westonzoyland, sometimes regarded as the capital of the low-lying Levels, almost surrounded by the even lower and virtually uninhabited moors.

Most visitors come especially to see the large church with its 100ft tower visible for miles. It is outstanding, with marvellous craftsmanship even in a county famous for its churches. And it played a vital role in the protestant rebellion when Monmouth, the first illegitimate son of Charles II, who had been 'crowned' in Taunton a fortnight earlier, met his end. Family feuds always being the most bitter, James II, who had come to the throne on his brother's death, showed no mercy. The church's register records how about 300 rebels were killed on the spot, some hanged in chains from the church, and 500 prisoners put into it, several dying of their wounds. Judge Jeffrey's Bloody Assizes left a deep mark on the area, where for generations 'transportation', done with such harshness to make hanging seem the better punishment, was whispered as scarcely mentionable. But the church continued about its business, paying the bell-ringers for ringing in thanksgiving for the victory – and also dealing with the bill for frankincense 'after ye prissoners was gon out'.

Travelling over the Weston Level, where we see men at the perpetual task of clearing the ditches, we cross the Parrett, looking very innocent this morning, and pass the great landmark of Burrow Mump. Like Brent Knoll, the Isle of Athelney and Glastonbury Tor, Burrow Mump is a lias remnant not yet worn away. It is only 75ft above its surroundings but, like Glastonbury Tor, crowned with a ruined chapel, dedicated to St Michael. Alfred, King of Wessex 871-899, skilfully made the best of geography to prevent the country falling to the Danes – we see a monument by the roadside – and built a causeway from the Mump to Athelney.

Breakfast on the train now seeming a long time ago, we make our way via Stathe to stop for our sandwich lunch at Oath Lock. Behind us is the sluice that prevents today's tides surging further inland; in front the main line from Paddington to Penzance with its occasional HST thundering past. It is fascinating coming to rest at a spot I have raced past hundreds of times. There is also an interesting notice:

The Levels and Moors of Somerset are the most important area of 'wetland' left in England. The area was once an inlet of the sea and the flood plain of five rivers. Over hundreds of years a wide coastal belt – **'The Levels'** – was built from clays deposited by the sea and this restricted the river flows to the sea. The in-land area – **'The Moors'** – thus became marsh, fen and bog. The river valleys became filled with peat deposits which contain well-preserved remains from past activities from 4000 BC, including prehistoric trackways and lake villages. There are other historical associations with both King Alfred and the Monasteries. This is the landscape which gave Somerset its name... 'the land of summer'... a fertile land providing grazing for animals in summer but largely covered with water and inaccessible in winter.

The area is still not well drained. The 'Levels' are higher than the 'Moors', the rivers have slight gradients to the Bristol Channel and some of the Moors are at or below sea level. The history of the area is of man's struggle to overcome flooding from the rivers and sea. The monastic estates were responsible for many flood containment banks still seen in the area and over the last 800 years a complex arrangement of rhynes (ditches), drains, tidal sluices and pumping has developed.

The nineteenth and twentieth centuries saw the greatest changes when demands for food promoted new initiatives. The enclosure of common land was followed by schemes involving new rhynes, straightened river channels, new main drains such as the King's Sedgemoor and tidal sluices and pumps – at first driven by steam and later diesel. Bigger, heavier machines allowed more ambitious projects culminating in the construction of the Huntspill River. A permanent state of waterlogging has thus been effectively prevented.

The importance of the area for wildlife is associated with 'wetland' habitats. These are among the most threatened habitats and this area is one of the few remaining in the United Kingdom. Breeding and wintering birds, swans, meadow flowers (a typical unimproved field may have 40 or 50 plant species present), mammals, including the otter (this is one of the last places in England where otters survive), amphibious and rare insects including beetles, damselfly, dragonfly and 22 species of butterfly and many other creatures can be found.

After our sandwiches and forty winks, we took to the road as it climbs slightly to pass through Curry Rivel, where we look down on empty West Sedge Moor, and Langport, before dropping down again to Muchelney. Here we take a brief glance at the Abbey remains and the better-preserved priest's house, now National Trust. An enterprising leaflet tells us of the 800 years of Benedictine life 'on the Great Island of Muchelney' which William the Conqueror's surveyors saw amid the floods of 1086, and of all the things you can do at this remote spot today. The locals are certainly very welcoming, not to mention enterprising, pasture and even crops of vegetables benefiting from the high water table. Here and there, fields are still flooded annually for the river's gift of rich silt.

The landscape is unmistakably unique, set off by the pollarded willows lining the rivers and many ditches. It is a tidy land of well-controlled rivers, drains and ditches, neat rows of trees, and everything manmade such as gates and fences in good order. We are still beside the River Parrett, whose Trail from source to mouth, a fifty-mile hike of three or four days, is something Sheila says we will have to do once this book is finished. A 'book' published by the Trail Partners, a wonderful example of co-operation, is in fact a cover enclosing a series of excellent laminated folders you can take out one at a time and can even get wet without trouble.

As we go further south, through Kingsbury Episcopi, still beside the Parrett, we realise we will soon have to say farewell to the Levels and Moors. The sun shines between clouds, making a fast-moving pattern of light and shadow. We can see for many miles. To the north, we count five, and there might be more, Somerset church towers towering (there is no other word for it) above everything else, Langport's and Huish Episcopi's being on the skyline, a reminder that it was the Church that first reclaimed the land.

Margery Fish's Cottage Garden

Then to one of England's most famous small gardens, Margery Fish's at East Lambrook Manor, South Petherton. It is a miracle it has survived in its present form for, when they bought the cottage, the present owners had not heard of Margery Fish. Their first viewing was after dark, so they didn't even see the garden. 'We were wanting to escape city life, and I was heavily pregnant with Number Two. We just bought the place, incredibly naive, and then discovered there were two gardeners, one of whom had been here since Margery Fish's time, the other for nearly thirty years,' so explains Mary Anne Williams. 'It was all a bit fraught. My husband and I had never even visited a garden before, but we went to Hadspen at Castle Cary, and that showed what might be expected of us. We either had to close it for good or open it up properly.'

Quite a challenge. 'They've done really well,' confides Maureen Whitty, one of the gardeners, gently pulling a weed from a clump of tulips. 'The future was very uncertain, and there's a lot to learn. Margery was famous for her free-flowing planting, cottage style, informal, giving the feel of a wild garden, which all gardeners know is much harder than formal planting.'

We wander round, and see it is all in the spirit of Margery Fish but, yes, there's a lot to do to achieve her unique tidy untidiness or, if you like, pristine informality – not that weeds didn't sometimes get out of hand, or what should have been discreet cottage plants didn't occasionally turn out to be uncontrollable monsters.

I knew Margery in her last years, when she was already a legend, but dropped by her former publishers after takeover and confusion. I reprinted four titles, including the famous *We Made a Garden*, and persuaded her to write *Gardening on Clay & Lime*, for we both had experience of that common but unfortunate combination. We spoke with religious fervour of top feeding and avoiding deep digging. I shall always remember how, while I was enjoying afternoon tea at East Lambrook, my own gardener took advantage of my absence to disobey instructions. He buried the lovely top soil of a new bed in double digging 'to let the frost get at it – everyone knows it should be done, maister'. I phoned Margery for solace, and if we didn't actually cry together, it felt like it.

How proud she would be to see her garden maintained, more popular than ever, a third of a century after her death. Of course, it changes, for plants are not static. Many of the ornamental bushes and apple trees have had to be renewed. But the guiding lights are the same. With its gravel paths providing access for the gardeners as well as for the sightseeing public, the area is intensively used, thousands and thousands of bulbs and plants (annuals and perennials) performing each season, with time-honoured and experimental colour combinations and shades of foliage never forgotten. Above all there is great vertical interest, such variety of walls, hedges and trees that it comes as a shock to realise the whole site is less than an acre. God's own intensive acre, in which she lovingly laboured for up to eighteen hours a day well into old age, sometimes hard to spot, gently planting away, towered over by bushes. Yet, she also found time to give advice to innumerable callers and correspondents, and was great fun, passionate but never cautiously 'proper'. She happily discarded any plantsman's edict that didn't give her the effect she desired.

So, back to the new owners, Mrs Williams's husband Robert is soon off on a Royal Horticultural College course 'so he doesn't have to explain he doesn't know about gardening'. They employ an astonishing 28 staff, though not all full-time. We certainly enjoy the very informal tea room, the shop and – upstairs – the art gallery that displays the work of a different artist each fortnight. An informative quarterly newsletter lists specialist study days, and gardening, painting and craft courses.

'We have to work hard to make a success of it.' They are just forming Friends of the Garden, and I question whether the time won't come when costs have to be controlled by an element of voluntary help, à la National Trust.

Oh, and there's a specialist plant nursery. Do visit what describes itself as the Home of the English Cottage Garden, signposted just off the A303 at South Petherton, Even better to approach it by a wander across the Somerset Levels.

So to Martock to spend the night. With so much of greater interest around, it seems a poor choice, though we are given an exceptionally warm welcome by the vicar of Martock, proud of his large church and its famous carved or 'quilted' roof. The last time I was in Martock I was eating strawberries and cream in an engineer's saloon the day after the railway closed.

Our hotel has bedrooms in a large purpose-built block with endless doors in long corridors, not quite in keeping in a village of old stone cottages and houses. Though there are no specific deficiencies, it is a bit of a disappointment. So I spend the evening rereading *Avalon & Sedgemoor* by Desmond Hawkins, who seemed too gentle a man to head the BBC's West Region but superbly adapted Thomas Hardy's novels for radio, as already mentioned, etched so much more deeply in the mind than were the later television ones.

Vicar Unusual

Next morning we enjoy another drive across the Levels and Moors to Somerton. Then, within sight of the railway curving on embankments, through Charlton Mackrell to Charlton Adam, to meet one of today's team vicars, Jim Hill, who was Sheila's tutor for her Christian Foundation Course as part of training to become a Lay Reader. 'I think you'll get on well,' she says as we walk up the path to his modern house; there's a smiling face at the door.

There are five churches in the group including the mother one at Somerton, services and pastoral responsibility shared with one colleague. 'Retired people, teachers, doctors, those who work for Clarks shoes at Street, Westland Helicopters at Yeovil, Yeovilton Royal Navy Air Service base and Haynes the publishers at Sparkford as well as local villagers make up the congregation. A nice mix of people. There are of course still a few farmers, but there've been barn conversions and there are a lot of second homes. Actually, you could say that, with so many professionals and retired professionals, I preach to a particularly bright lot. They take real note of what's said in sermons. It's pretty rewarding.'

One of the fun things is that many people follow the services from church to church. Occasionally there is a service such as evensong for the whole benefice, while Charlton Mackrell, beautifully proportioned in warm stone, and Charlton Adam, a large cruciform church (there used to be a community of priests here in the Middle Ages), are used more or less interchangeably. So though only a few services are held at some churches, the congregations are much bigger than they would have been when each was on its own. 'People were nervous at first, but it has fostered community spirit and the appreciation of the special quality of each church.'

A bachelor with a keen interest in films, theatre and books, interest in other faiths, and seven years spent in a community, Jim is scarcely a conventional village priest, and he is certainly not 'narrow'. I happen to share many of his beliefs. We're both indebted to the work of Canon WH Vanstone, and were especially influenced by his *The Stature of Waiting*, whose challenge is summed up in a short passage in another title, *Fare Well in Christ*:

> I cannot believe, as some Christians do believe, that Jesus, being the Son of God, was endowed with a unique foreknowledge of the future – including the foreknowledge that he would die as he did in Jerusalem and on the third day be raised from death. If he had this foreknowledge his death, though painful, would have been attended by a confidence and comfort denied to mortal men, and his words upon the cross both of forgiveness and of dereliction would be no more than charades.

'Vanstone brings it all to life for me. Christ was a remarkable mystical teacher, a human being rather than someone acting out a script ending with pre-ordained death. It surely makes his divinity, his crucifixion and resurrection all the stronger.' But we agree that, if I dare say this in my book, some people will stop reading it.

'If you depart from the conventional, it is easy to be misunderstood. Some people get angry on sound bites from David Jenkins (former bishop of Durham) without ever really hearing what he's saying, but he takes everything so sensibly with real understanding, caring and compassion.' And Richard Holloway (former bishop of Edinburgh)? 'He's always getting quoted out of context. People find anything different intimidating, and so throw their hands up in horror, though if you listen you'll be nearer to God, and you don't have to agree with every detail to achieve that.'

Heavy stuff? It doesn't feel so at all. We're very ordinary people enjoying an ordinary drink before going out for a good pub lunch. At the pub at Sparkford, which is better for not being a showpiece, many of the other customers are obviously from Haynes, the specialist publishers of car manuals. Though they have not been successful in moving into broader territory, they have the car-manual business tied up, internationally. Their manuals are so much clearer than the manufacturers' own. Haynes begin with the purchase of each new model of car, taking it to bits so that everything is clearly understood. Not a cheap business.

Somerton to Lyme Regis

Refreshed, we return to Somerton, market town of ancient Wessex, with a mixture of touristy and basic shops, all kinds of customers mixing in the bookshop with a tempting selection of local-interest titles and business boosted with mail order. Pevsner describes the market place as 'one of the most happily grouped urban pictures in Somerset'. There's a lot to see here, including the large, unusual church in dark grey stone with brown Ham Hill dressings. The hostelries, notably the elegant Red Lion, speak of former grand days and many individual shops, banks and houses that repay study. Somerton obviously enjoyed long periods of prosperity. That was lost when the town was left out by railways. The Castle Cary-Langport cut-off was opened in 1906, too late to reverse the damage. Expresses thunder through each way almost hourly, but none stops and, even when the station was open, it only had a handful of local Castle Cary-Taunton push-pull trains. Though people explore extensively these days, this is real Somerset, not holiday land. On the way back to the car, we see some interesting hand-turned items of local wood for sale in a cottage window: there never was a sharp distinction between trading and non-trading establishments in such places. We are instantly in the front room, where the carver sits in a wheelchair while his wife sells Sheila knobs in apple, cherry and other woods for the pull chords of our bathroom and toilet lights.

Then, following the Westport canal as closely as we can, through Westport and on to Ilminster with an enjoyable cross-country run through very different landscapes via Chard Junction (still so called, though now no junction or even station) and a spectacular if roundabout route through the deepest hilly countryside and Lambert's Castle and Wootton Fitzpaine to approach Lyme Regis from the east. Steadily the sea gets closer, but when we reach it at the bottom of Lyme Regis there is nowhere to park, so we shoot up the hill west before descending to the Cobb, the intimate little crescent-shaped harbour sheltering small craft. We then saunter back along the promenade to what I have just described as the bottom of Lyme Regis, with time to poke through the antique, rock and fossil and bookshops and catch a cup of tea before returning to collect our car as the tide comes in. The Alexandra Hotel has proved a reliable choice over the years. Portions at dinner are generous, but Mathew, my grandson who lives nearby, relishes his own and what we cannot manage.

He loves Lyme, a mellow little town with interesting shops on the slopes of unstable cliffs. There have been huge cliff falls, attracting geologists and fossil hunters, while the Cobb has been immortalised in the filming of The French Lieutenant's Woman. We leave by the high-level road a mile or so inland along some of Britain's least stable cliffs till we drop into the Axe Valley.

Along the East Devon Coast

We are now back in Devon: a very different Devon, with the county's fastest-growing town, Exmouth, but otherwise remarkably unspoilt. East Devon is a land of more sun and less rain than the rest of the county, of rolling hills retaining their essential character – and a coast of high cliffs and pebble beaches which have deterred popular tourism through the ages, and so have that more genteel touch that for generations has proved especially attractive to the aged and infirm.

Through Axmouth, centuries ago an important port, and we reach Seaton over a wide bridge across the Axe which has replaced Britain's first concrete road bridge. Parking on the bleak promenade, with its new protecting wall to prevent high tides rolling into houses, we walk back to the narrow river's mouth and see there is still considerable boating activity. Sheila and I last came here 45 years ago, when we both lived in Teignmouth and her father was amazed I had taken her (by eight different trains) on an afternoon trip to Seaton, returning well within tolerated time.

Old-fashioned non-corridor compartment carriages were then used on the local line alongside the estuary; I recall a porter telling the guard: 'They'm 'avin a good time in there.'

The railway has long gone, but the track bed is used by one of Devon's more successful tourist attractions, the Seaton & District Electric Tramway, which in season runs a frequent service of narrow-gauge trams of sundry vintages offering close-up views of the estuary and its bird life.

There has never been a proper harbour between Lyme Regis and Exmouth. Commercial fishing survives, mainly from boats launched from pebble beaches straight into the waves. Years ago I got to know some of the local fishermen, colourful chaps who made good copy, and it was at Seaton I first heard the phrase 'cuckoo fishermen' – those who

PLATE I: Nairn. *Top,* home and office at 10.15pm (page 27); *Bottom left,* Gordon Macintyre (page 28); *Bottom right,* Toby MacArthur (page 29)

PLATE 2: Island Characters. *Top,* Colonsay, Kevin Byrne talks with author Barbara Crawford (page 35); *Middle,* Coll, artist Kip Poulson (page 41); *Bottom,* Barra, Mary Hatcher (page 44)

PLATE 3: To the islands. *Top,* at Tobermory (page 61); *Middle,* Gareth St John Thomas waiting for the Glenelg-Kylerhea ferry (page 53); *Bottom,* Lady Claire Macdonald (page 53)

PLATE 4: Authors. *Top,* Sir Patrick Moore (page 96); *Bottom, left* Polly Samson at her writing hideaway (page 85); *right,* Jack Hill (page 93)

PLATE 5: Characters. *Top*, Ron Warwick, Master of the QE2 (page 124); *Bottom*, authors *left* Thomasina Beck (page 664); *right* Anthony Burton (page 132)

PLATE 6: Newton
Abbot. *Top,* The
famous signals
(page 161); *Bottom,*
Ipplepen fruit farm
(page 173)

PLATE 7: David & Charles occasions. *Top*, John Arlott (page 167), the author and Charles Hadfield (page 127) riding on a miniature train; *Middle*, Indoor garden party at Bristol; *Bottom*, 'Pied Piper' followed by three hundred at Topsham (part of a Victorian weekend)

PLATE 8: West Country characters. *Top,* Don Breckon (page 198); *Bottom, left* John Southern driving miniature train (page 196); *right,* Rick Stein (page 250)

PLATE 9: More West Country personalities. *Top,* Crispin Gill makes a point (page 275); *Bottom; left* the long and short of it, Joan Rendell (page 262); *right* Trevor Beer and Bracken (page 366)

PLATE 10: *Top,* Ruth Johns (page 308); *Middle,* the information board at Oath Lock (page 341); *Bottom,* Robert and Mary Anne Williams, owners of Margery Fish's cottage garden (page 343)

PLATE II:
Top, the Sand Pilot of Morecombe Bay leads a large group (page 415); *Middle,* David and Charles of D&C Publishers at Lakeside; *Bottom,* typical scene at Gretna Green (page 570)

PLATE 12 (OPPOSITE):
North West Scotland. *Top,* notice
at Kylesku Bridge (page 442);
Middle, Old School Restaurant
(page 444); *Bottom,* unloading fish
at Kinlochbervie (page 445)

PLATE 13 (THIS PAGE):
Top, left Ron Ransome (page 596);
right Sir Neil Cossons (page 623);
Bottom, abandoned train tunnels
above Clydach Gorge on new
cycleway (page 602)

PLATE 14:
Yorkshire characters.
Top, Geoffrey Smith
(page 536); *bottom,*
David Joy (page 659)

PLATE 15: Clerics. *Top,* Father Tony Clements (page 454); *Bottom, left* Bishop Richard Holloway (page 590); *right* Rev Canon David Adam with new Celtic carpet at Holy Island (page 296)

PLATE 16:
Country bookshops.
Top left, South Molton
(page 364); *Top right,*
Stroud (page 133);
Middle, Dervaig (page
58); *Bottom,* bookshop,
Achins (page 439)

had bought boats with new-fangled engines which meant they could catch more on calm days and so didn't have to go out when it was rough.

Beginning to feel hungry, but always enjoying the coast between Seaton and Sidmouth, we take a mere glance at Beer, with its delightful if short main street and glimpse of beach and sea beyond. The fishing community here has always been tightly knit. No time to be tempted to buy another locomotive for my model railway, and the outdoor narrow-gauge passenger-carrying system is still in its winter sleep; Peco are Beer's largest employers, their main speciality being the manufacture of their own model railway track, though they also publish the most successful model railway magazines.

No time, either, to relax in Branscombe, spread out along the hillside in a particularly delightful way. The village hall, church, daffodils waving in the breeze and hanging baskets give a welcoming message to anyone thinking of retiring here, as many who care about their environment have. The water is deep in the ford leading to the beach restaurant... anyway Sheila has said that for old time's sake she would like to stop at the Bowd Inn, just inland from Sidmouth.

It proves an interesting choice. One woman guest is offering her son for holiday duty. 'I'll see he phones this afternoon.' The pub, it seems, desperately needs help. The new manager, retiring from running a hotel at Perranporth a year ago, was relief manager here for a time. 'The "permanent" replacement didn't like Devon or Devon people, and the list of those who'd applied for work seems to have been thrown into the wastepaper basket. So the brewery asked if I'd rescue the place. Not as a relief, I said, only if I can take it over. So here I am, a challenge to get it right again. Thank goodness it's quiet today.'

Then into Sidmouth, where you shouldn't take much notice if folk tell you things aren't quite what they used to be; they are splendid in this oasis from the rougher world. Where else do you find such a range of top hotels in so small a town? Or quality shops? Or such parks and walks? We especially love the Connaught Gardens at the west end of the promenade, the clock tower on its little restaurant, and the archway leading to Jacob's ladder down which you can descend to another beach, when it is not closed by cliff falls. The recent heavy rains, which made it quite an adventure daring the ford near the town's centre, have resulted in many cliff falls, on both sides of the town.

The road up to the mighty Peak Hill might need another of its periodic moves inland, while to the east, just before the cliffs change from terracotta to pure white, we see that a house I had once fancied for its long garden has now lost it. All the footpaths are closed. Long gone are the cottages and limekiln that used to be under these cliffs. At least the seafront now seems safe. After storms seriously threatened it and much of central Sidmouth, a fortune was spent on building a kind of breakwater a hundred yards or so from the shore. The beach has always been tricky in rough weather; once a paddle steamer, loading passengers stern on, was swung round by a sudden wave and smashed to pieces in minutes.

'If ever we move from Scotland, let's come here,' says Sheila. The yellow spring-flower parade – daffodils, primroses, tulips, forsythia, relieved by multi-coloured magnolias – definitely issues an invitation.

The narrow rollercoaster road past Peak Hill to Budleigh Salterton is covered in deep red mud, and inevitably we have to back several times, which everyone seems to do with great speed and precision today compared with the immediate post-war years when many new drivers first struggled in 'the narrows'. Afternoon tea is with Colin and Liz Elliot, just off Otterton's main street with its famous stream in full spate.

I first knew the Elliots when they ran the Quayside Bookshop in Teignmouth; a good small-town general bookshop with the useful addition of maritime speciality and a touch of publishing. Colin has always been fascinated by sail and commercial fishing, and his own Tops'l imprint included insights into cruel lifestyles, man against the elements, and the fishing 'wars', when West Coast Scottish and Cornish fishermen fought invading East Coasters to prevent fish being landed on their precious Sabbath. Troops were called in. Colin got to know the East Coast men, too, especially those from Lowestoft, and he rescued many of the historic photographs that grace his books and are now displayed in fishing museums. Writing and editing in the bookshop's back office went hand-in-hand with bookselling in the traditional manner.

His fishing list was later absorbed into D&C, for whom he wrote several new titles including a notable *Discovering Armada Britain*. While I'd always enjoyed the bookshop, we had more time to pursue friendship after they retired to Otterton and I spent weekends at a flat in Budleigh Salterton. As always their lounge with its books and pictures is a restful setting for real afternoon tea and talk... about the good old maritime days – he met Liz on a Brixham trawler 'when things were hard but individuals counted' – family topics, changing tastes in books, and Otterton's gossip. On my visit he was still writing and editing, bright and cheerful as ever and, unless you had been told, you wouldn't realise he was fighting cancer. [Sadly he died a few months later.]

The clifftop flat at Budleigh Salterton was my escape from the pressure of running D&C. From it I could watch sun and shadow chasing each other along the beach, the Otter estuary filling and emptying twice daily (water pouring through its narrow channel in the shingle that had once been navigable) and fishing boats being pushed into the sea and winched up the beach on return. Even at the height of the season the shingle beach is never busy. I adore that rhythm of moving shingle and, when waking at night, could instantly tell the state of the tide and weather.

The one drawback was the politics of flat life. Somehow I became chairman of the block's residents' association, while a breezy technical freelance book and magazine editor, Christine Channon, was excellent secretary. The strangest of human happenings, from two stormy residents' unhappy marriage in their nineties, to insistence on the right to flush the toilet when the plumber briefly disconnected the outfall, made TV sitcom seem tame. Several old ladies could (according to their mood) see perfectly or be totally blind. One professed to see the smile of a favoured relative while her less-liked sister standing beside her remained invisible.

'It certainly taught us a few things about human nature,' says Christine during a brief meeting. Since her mother was one of the residents, she laboured on after me, but ultimately there was so much dissention that the block's affairs were sub-contracted to a well-insulated management company. It was good practice, no doubt, for Christine's more serious politicking; she's leader of the County Council's Conservatives hoping to wrest control from the Liberals.

Until you get to know it, Budleigh Salterton might seem a dull little place, but I fell in love with it, warts and all. Tolerance is not an especial virtue here, but then millionaires are thick on the ground – while widows living on their own recall wealthier and more influential days. Conversation in the restaurants and tea rooms, and at the shops where everyone knows one another, often contains distinctly comic elements. I particularly remember a retired admiral, standing safely back himself, giving snappy instructions to those on the front line about how to deal with a wasp. Language was blue as six grown men failed to catch, kill or expel the intruder.

Not that the town has been without real crises; after conversions to flats, it is without any sizeable hotel, and cliff falls are again a worry. A Budleigh speciality is the early hours at which people retire for the evening. 'I don't answer after six,' is commonly said. For a good read about Budleigh's earlier eccentrics, find a copy of *Henrietta's War*, a collection of World War Two magazine pieces by Joyce Dennys.

For the night we move on to Exmouth, these days separated from Budleigh by only a few hundred yards of remaining countryside, but totally different: bigger, brasher, its famous large magnolias showing off as single trees. Exmouth is still a thriving holiday resort with its long sandy beach; today there's sand all over the road along the front. There is quite a good shopping centre (plus huge out-of-town supermarkets) but also the inevitable houses, flats and homes for the retired.

I first came in 1938 and, on the day after the Munich crisis, was asked by my parents to pop into the hotel dining room for their newspaper placed on the table. 'IT IS PEACE' shouted *The Times* in the small editorial space it allowed itself on the front page, normally reserved for all small ads, when there was something epoch-making to report. I was more interested in the fact that the toast was also on the table nearly an hour before breakfast; disgraceful.

The Imperial was one of two Trust Houses at which I stayed that later had fires with serious loss of life. It was rebuilt, making good use of its seafront position and, as group hotels go, was excellent. Now we are told it is always full so we can never make an advance reservation. It seems to be run more as the private affair of a coach company, who pack it with tours... but also allows touring car drivers to enjoy a package deal using several of the company's hotels. I look round somewhat nostalgically – and the receptionist tells me how I 'might' be able to arrange to stay in future. No such problems at the hotel we've booked at instead; no great stay, either, though the view over other hotels to the prom, sea, river mouth and across the shore to the main railway to Plymouth, the flat line of Haldon in the background, takes one's mind off shortcomings in the accommodation.

Less happy is my first visit to the harbour since it was closed to commercial traffic by a property developer. It is now a marina surrounded by new homes and flats as Exmouth's own effort at gentrification. Pity, since it was busy till the end, the only harbour between Weymouth and Teignmouth. Commercial vessels going up the Exe to the Ship Canal, Britain's oldest, are also a thing of the past; not even the boat carrying sewage on its daily trip to dump at sea now passes through the lock gate at Turf.

Librarian and Publisher

Books and bygone days dominate conversation with this evening's two visitors, Alison Shute, former Devon County Librarian, and Simon Butler of Halsgrove, the publishers based near Tiverton.

Alison was Devon's county librarian, who tells of the changes she saw during her career, rising from the ranks. At the start, several towns and even villages were still opting out of the County Library to maintain their own. At Lynton, opening hours were organised around the librarian's television watching; in another town, where 'fantastical autonomy ruled', the librarian sat by the fireplace listening to classical music on his own record player. Many of the librarians of the old school were self-educated, if educated at all; hence a request for something about King Arthur and his Round Table was answered by proffering a copy of *Whitaker's Almanac*.

'When I first visited the library at Laira, Plymouth,' says Alison, 'I found the cleaning lady in charge but persuaded her to make an exception and lend me a book when I was still under age.' She continues: 'It became much more institutional in my day, but we encouraged libraries to be individual, several with splendid local collections.'

It was many years ago that I suggested to her that Newton Abbot's library might develop a railway collection to mark the fact it was a railway town. My railway collection goes there on my death. Meanwhile a splendid specialist resource has been developed, much consulted by historians. 'One doesn't often have the chance to start a practical project of national as well as county importance,' she boasts. Another of her successes has been to make multi-purpose use of libraries, for example, a country town's information point about forthcoming events. The County Council's involvement in publishing was also largely inspired by her.

From its Devon beginning, Halsgrove local-book publishing developed with a staggering total of 28 local authorities. Though the number has now been substantially reduced, it retains the West Country ones including the two National Parks. Halsgrove has generally become more commercial. 'Right now, Devon Books accounts for about ten per cent of our business; other affiliations about double that. Working with councils was important at the start... though actually, it was you who made the whole thing possible, for David & Charles uniquely got West Country people into the book-buying habit because of the kind of book you published.'

Many of today's books are real tomes and profusely illustrated – made viable with new production methods opening up the possibility of short print runs. For example, 817 well-illustrated A4 pages, only 1,000 copies, a published price of £25: an equation which wouldn't have worked in my day even without taking inflation into account. That is for *Fisherman's Friend, A Life of Stephen Reynolds,* to which I will return in a moment.

Much more production work is done in-house these days – 'we never pass proofs around' – and forty per cent of business is by mail order with minimal if any discount. Relations with local retailers are however important... so much so that Halsgrove, unusually, will not sell copies to wholesalers such as Bertrams, anyway not at a normal wholesale discount. 'We're as independent as Dartmoor farmers.'

Job satisfaction is obviously considerable. 'I really feel I belong, and our books satisfy people's deep desire to belong somewhere. We're seldom directly educational, but help people learn about the background of their towns and villages, so we suck in traditional book buyers and those just curious about where they're living.'

Even in the north of Scotland there are many fine Halsgrove titles on my shelves. As an example of how classy local publishing has become, Simon arrives bearing the gift of a delightfully evocative *Down the Deep*

Lanes. With an accessible text by Peter Beacham, it features the deeply nostalgic photographs of James Ravilious. Anyone would be proud to publish such a work. The timing is made poignant by the recent announcement that, because of foot-and-mouth disease, the part of North Devon mainly covered has been virtually closed to tourists.

Of *Fisherman's Friend*, I'm more doubtful. I've duly spent my £25 and at least speed read the entire tome, but it really is a case of not being able to see the wood for the trees, for at the end few essential details really stand out about the life of Stephen Reynolds. Yet he was someone who fascinated me. His *A Poor Man's House*, about living with a working Sidmouth fisherman and his family through troubled as well as good times, has run through several editions over the years but should still be more read as one of the minor classics of Devon (and working class) literature. It tells, usually in simple terms, but with occasional philosophical insights, how fishermen's wives prepared to survive in lean times after plentiful harvests, of the companionship between fishermen, and their deep understanding of the sea – even when well away from land they never missed the turn of the tide – and how usually it was up-country folk who introduced bad language and habits. For example, a price was always accepted as it stood: take it or leave it. Tourists' insistence on a bargain meant that even trips round the bay had to be at artificially inflated prices to allow the discount expected by the better off. Says Reynolds:

> To live with the poor is to feel oneself in contact with a greater continuity of tradition and to share in a greater stability of life. The nerves are more annoyed, the thinking self less ... knowledge is not everything, nor even the main thing. Wisdom is more than knowledge: it is *Knowledge applied to life, the ability to make use of the knowledge well.* In that respect I often have here to eat a slice of humble-pie. For all my elaborate education and painfully gained stock of knowledge, I find myself silenced time after time by the direct wisdom of these so-called ignorant people. They have preserved better, between knowledge and experience, that balance which makes for wisdom.

To Poorer North Devon

After a short visit to Newton Abbot to catch up with old friends we're off to North Devon by a route I have used in all conditions, day and night, for a multitude of business and other reasons: Moretonhampstead, Whiddon Down, North Tawton and Winkleigh. It is mainly a series of narrow lanes, hugging the undulating countryside. Most people travelling between the Torbay area and North Devon have always preferred going to Exeter before turning north, and today's quickest way is further east up the M5 to Tiverton and along the North Devon Link Route. But I love the area's geography and like to respect it, so gladly forego the saving in time offered by modern roads. Even though my route's worst corners have been ironed out, it is a slow affair. It allows ample time to adjust to the huge differences of landscape, culture, social conditions and outlook of the different countrysides through which we pass.

First we twist and turn on Dartmoor's eastern fringes with majestic panoramas under development pressure. Even the former sanatorium (once such a necessary institution) at Hawkmoor is being turned into homes. For those who know, or care to follow a good guide book, there is great historic interest. Wreyland, for example is where Cecil Torr lived; his *Small Talk at Wreyland* is another of Devon's minor classics, rural history at the time when railways were new, journey times were steadily shortened and change was afoot in many ways. He records the setting up of village schools concentrating on the three Rs, and the introduction of new varieties of wheat allowing staggered sowing and harvesting. Torr spells out how those who invested in the local branch line lost most of their capital but received good value in the benefits it bestowed. We read of ill-behaved navvies and the scarcity of agricultural workers while the line was being built. Some of the bridges and viaducts are worthy of high praise, he says, made of granite, and so well proportioned that there would be many paintings of them, 'could they be transferred to Italy and attributed to Roman or Etruscan builders'.

At Moretonhampstead I always note the long and now little-used footpath up from the former terminus station to the village. The station yard out here on Dartmoor seemed a crazy place for a haulage contractor to base his fleet of artics, but the business has obviously flourished. Clouds cast shadows along the road passing Chagford. I have always loved the long beech hedges at the approach to Whiddon Down, where we now dive under the A30, before bumping along to North Tawton. This section, once full of blind corners, was widened as a summer Saturday holiday relief route, but in recent years the peak-season traffic has declined sharply. After passing under the former Southern Railway, the road is joined by another of those long pavements connecting station and town: two miles of it.

Brilliant groups of daffodils in the hedge beside the pavement emphasise how things have changed at North Tawton. Planting them was one of many recent community efforts, bringing new life to the town that had been stopped in its tracks when the railway opened and local enterprise was snuffed out by Exeter's aggressive traders. The streets of Victorian cottages simply stopped when the need to house extra workers ceased: for over a century, no new building, not a hint of semi-detachery let alone bungalows. Shops died, many of them a slow, lingering death. Until relatively recently, taking refreshment here was an earthy rather than gastronomic experience. Exeter, Barnstaple, Newton Abbot: they were beyond the ken of North Tawton's old people, an age-group which dominated as youngsters moved elsewhere and the school roll fell. Now there is new housing, new enterprise, once again real spirit. There is even to be a new book on North Tawton; I've just placed my order with Halsgrove who have invited the support of subscribers, a list of whose names will appear in the work. It's back to the old way of doing things, of course making publication less risky.

[North Tawton was the choice of venue for a drama commissioned by the Southwest Division of the Royal College of Psychiatrists after my Charitable Trust had become founding supporter of its appeal for funds to help people with difficulties in the countryside devastated by foot-and -mouth. John Somers, artistic director of the Exstream Theatre Company, explained that North Tawton was in the right area, was of the right kind of size and, especially, had good local groups involved with amateur theatre. The play, *Living at Hurford*, addressed the problems caused by rapid agricultural change with foot-and-mouth lurking in the background. Heavy audience participation was involved in determining what course of action would be right for the farming family at the centre of the drama.]

Then on to hilltop Winkleigh, which I have often cynically described as the 'centre of civilisation'. Like most villages, it was left out in the cold by the railway, but had a huge military airport in World War Two. A dour industrial estate and caravan parks sprang up around its abandoned runways but now the Winkleigh Cider Company adds a touch of zest.

For centuries, life was poor on the vast undulating plateau north of Dartmoor. The unsympathetic clay soil is poorly drained, too wet most of the time, but drying out rapidly in drought. Farming was mainly at subsistence level. It truly was a different world, penetrated by few visitors with little obvious to attract them. Steadily things have changed: the phone, motor car, electricity and – above all – piped water have ended the gloomy old order. Farms have merged. Attracted by cheap property, incomers have become numerous enough to make their own life and set their own values, for example supporting restaurants which also pull in customers from further afield. Yet, with welcome progress, we have lost that unique feeling of deep slumber one experienced in so many villages in this land of repeated Atlantic rainstorms.

This morning, there's a different feeling of desperation, for we are in the heart of foot-and-mouth country. 'Closed' and 'No Entry' are the standard welcome. Now on the Copplestone to Torrington road, we are regarded suspiciously when calling at a shop. Business is terrible. 'We don't get many visitors and can't make up our minds if we want them.'

Back on the road, we enjoy a big African-style sky but, just beyond Beaford, are brought sharply back to reality with the smell of burning cows: acrid, persistent, North Devon's curse probably imported from Northumberland. You can hear the locals saying there's altogether too much to-ing and fro-ing, 'not like when we were on our own'. With bizarre timing Benny, my daughter-in-law, calls from Sydney. Her honest enquiry as to how things are is answered by an up-to-the-second commentary on the pyres and the smell that burns into the very soul. Down under, of course they've heard of our foot-and-mouth crisis and show real concern.

Down a long hill to cross the river not much above sea level, and then up an equally long one to Torrington, beg its pardon, Great Torrington. A hilltop town, it is different; hardly pretty with its long stone terraces and brick window arches. The chief business used to be glove making, mainly by outworkers whose front doors were never locked. It certainly looks more prosperous these days. We enjoy a quick run round the visitors' centre of Dartington Crystal alongside the factory that is now the town's largest employer.

Down again to the site of Torrington's old station where the single coach off trains from Waterloo terminated and a line came in from the south, serving the mines on its lonely way from Halwill Junction. Offered a day out on the railway's engineering saloon, my selected route included this, where the normal passenger trains were almost always empty. We were hauled by the first-ever diesel locomotive to Torrington, and left it there since it couldn't be restarted after lunch.

We are soon beside the tidal Torridge which I cross by the bridge that started life as an aqueduct of one of those early eccentric West Country canals. Charles Kingsley's Little White Town of Bideford sparkles in the sun, but this morning poor Kingsley's statue is crowned with a traffic cone. Parking is difficult because there are two ships tied up, one unloading dredged sand and the other timber and bark. This is the starting point for most trips to Lundy, that two-mile long narrow granite plateau, home to puffins and many other birds.

I can picture the scene at Westward Ho! with the Atlantic rollers heading in remorselessly up the gentle sands. When visiting one of Devon's principal booksellers based at Westward Ho! I often enjoyed these rollers, and the shipping at Appledore, where sailing ships traded later than in most places, and the view across the combined Taw-Torridge estuary to vast Braunton Burrows. Still ignoring the North Devon Link Road, with its high-level bridge, we use the historic one over the now broad Torridge estuary. Lunch is at Instow, one of those rare quality river resorts of endless vistas and things to watch, especially across at Appledore where the great maritime tradition of building splendid ships is kept alive.

At the next village, Fremington, we take the winding lane to the quay, long-since closed to commercial traffic but for over a century the busiest port in the administrative county of Devon, exporting ball clay and bringing in coal for the Southern's large Barnstaple locomotive fleet. A secret, deserted destination for years, it is on today's walk and cycleway using the railway's track. And this afternoon it's a hive of building activity. I'm not popular with the drivers of several giant earth movers already having problems in sorting themselves out in a tight space. Even Fremington Quay is becoming gentrified with modern flats, though there will also be a new visitors' centre on the walk and cycleway.

What would Henry Williamson have said, even about the path being named the Tarka Way? He was an interesting if cantankerous sort, with a flair for the countryside, and its wildlife – including the maidens – who assumed publishers and others wouldn't recognise his worth. *Tarka The Otter*, the simple life story of an animal was revolutionary, unlike anything written before, to be the model followed by many other natural history writers, none of whom had the advantage of originality. The Tarka Way stretches from the clay land at Meeth, south of Petrockstowe, through Torrington and Bideford to Barnstaple. Including the Exmoor & Dartmoor Two Moors Way, there is a network of 180 miles of path through a remarkable range of landscapes offering the naturalist possibly the richest wildlife in Britain. Attitudes have improved, for when the branch line to Moretonhampstead was closed, local councillors were determined to see the route blocked, keeping walkers away from their farmlands.

The Tarka Way would have been kinder on the eye than the road approach to Barnstaple. Part of the route is new and, even where it isn't, many buildings are postwar, though every now and then familiar survivals from earlier ages come into focus, especially as we cross the long bridge over the Taw estuary. Despite the suffering of traditional industries, North Devon prospers in a way that, as so-called West Country economic expert, I thought was plain impossible. As regional centre, Barnstaple has naturally benefited disproportionately. Local government, hospital, social services have all had to grow with the population. No longer a backwater, North Devon has become an estate agent's dream. The marked inferiority complex of former days has gone.

Barnstaple's pannier market bustles; physically little changed, but what a difference in what is sold and how they go about it: Pannier market Tuesday, Friday and Saturday, antique market Wednesday, craft market Monday and Tuesday. There is only time for a quick run-round, getting lost in today's one-way system, noting the unchanged streets of yellow-brick workers' cottages, just like Newton Abbot's, amid vast new development. Today even Barnstaple needs a Park & Ride! Then by the old road to South Molton, where I lived between the ages of twelve and fourteen. This was the way taken daily by the school bus, fifty minutes in each direction. I hated going to school in Barnstaple. I was bullied, undressed, robbed of my food, sometimes poor horsemeat, at lunch. I was especially teased because I was picked as a safe one to sit with the girls upstairs on the bus. Of course I wouldn't dare challenge the boys who came up to take the girls' blouses off, to which several lasses seemed to offer little discouragement. Such activities ceased when one of the girl's parents complained.

Wartime South Molton

The first village, Landkey, is now part of Barnstaple, whose pull is so strong that at the next village, Swimbridge, I see the shop has closed but plans are being discussed to develop social life. It was just beyond here that the then fearsome hill began. Sometimes on market days, Fridays, we all had to squeeze into a single-decker powered by a gas engine in tow, which meant getting out and walking. A few curves, notably at this hill's top, have been ironed out, and there has been a modicum of widening. Overall, though, the road is surprisingly unchanged from 1942.

As then, the most interesting section is through the parkland of the Fortescue Estate near Filleigh, though the large 'Keep Out' signs because of foot-and-mouth spoil it a bit today. The railway route was also at its best in this area, and has been revived, for the North Devon Link Road follows much of it west from South Molton and utilises a viaduct, skilfully widened from a single railway track to a two-lane main road, using the original piers, enabling one once more to enjoy familiar views.

In the war, we usually passed fewer than a car a mile. Sometimes though, there were long military convoys and occasionally bumper-to-bumper American tanks for the entire dozen miles. I saw one demolish the Landkey's memorial to the previous war.

The impact of the American military on North Devon, and particularly on South Molton, was shattering. An early memory is of a special parade and demonstration in South Molton square. A long convoy of American tanks was brought to a stop. Two GIs in the convoy halted by the Midland Bank, opposite the market, popped up their heads to see a man with a stirrup pump fail to put out a blaze in a bucket on the bank's flat roof. 'Gee, to think we've come across the ocean to see this,' said one of them laconically. It wasn't clear if he realised it was the first of several set pieces to show how fire fighting had become more sophisticated.

Sophistication is not a word you would generally apply to South Molton and surrounding area. People very much kept to the immediate district. Many villagers saw no need even to visit South Molton.

Virtually nobody made a daily journey to work. Many people had never been on a train, few to London. Quite a few villages did not have or even want a bus service, though attitudes differed and there were a few places that had busy market day buses and even popular trips to the coast until they were stopped by the war. It was fascinating to note that the patterns of life in villages with and without a regular bus continued along their different lines for decades, even after the war.

Few people out in the sticks expected running water and electricity. South Molton was more up-to-date and enjoyed a handful of dim street lights even in the blackout, though oil lamps were common. The oil lamp, dampness, especially of musty curtains, and the storage and preparation of home-grown produce were key elements in the smell, different from that of 'civilisation'. Hanging meat and game, animals coming in from the rain to feed by the log fire, and underclothes usually worn for a week, were other ingredients. Even when slightly repugnant, it spoke of human warmth and God's own earth.

Most country people either produced or received, maybe in a barter arrangement, nearly all the food they needed for their simple tastes. Only four imported 'products' had become more or less standard. Tea. A newspaper. Tobacco. And baker's bread, though this more as the result of the flour industry's marketing than out of necessity. As a matter of fact, all over rural Britain 'town bread' killed home baking decades before other things were made 'convenient'. You certainly wouldn't buy jam to put on your bread or the cake to follow it, but baker's bread saved real time and effort, and was generally well liked, even preferred to homemade. Coffee was for a few toffs. Children who could get them of course liked sweets, and like me hated the day we had our last legal ice cream. Pasta was unknown, and dried fruit had scant sales even when freely available. Few had eaten a banana before they disappeared from sale.

It was a land flowing in milk and honey, if not luxuries. Rationing was pretty irrelevant, for there was a thriving Black Market – and inspectors from the Ministry of Food were fools to be teased. Coded messages like 'Mrs Smith forgot to turn her iron on' would send folk scurrying. Surprise, the inspector found nothing amiss. The Beehive Stores in South Molton Square had 6,000 registered customers who deposited their ration books. Apart from tea, few claimed their entitlement – particularly of butter and eggs. It was the same at the butchers. The very term Black Market was too severe: why waste when some people happily paid? At the gentlemen's outfitters, 'Any socks today?' meant any eggs stored under the socks. Butter was shirts. Bacon? Pants, of course.

After spending a few weeks at the George Hotel, in the square, as voluntary evacuees from the 'front line' in Teignmouth, my family settled at 65 South Street, bang opposite the police station. When the milkman delivered banned cream, my father's protest brought the reply that the police – who of course had their own cream – might find it suspicious if we were the odd ones out. Being different was being difficult. You talked of the seasons and crops and Hitler but not of ideas and ideals. The first books I ordered from the newsagent, in the Dent's King's Treasury series, were spoilt by having a reference number scrawled large across them.

True, young men went off to war, some never to return. However, that had happened on a larger scale in 1914-1918. There was much personal grief, yet North Devon's rural heartbeat continued to tick as before, in the way they no doubt thought that God had ordained. In the minds of the rural population, there was no hint of the social and economic revolution that lay around the corner. To return to the American military, however, the great build-up to D-Day was all embracing. Eisenhower regularly visited North Devon. The trial PLUTO, pipeline under the ocean, was across the Bristol Channel. The American sentries guarding a depot in the town were an especial talking point. Flirting girls went right up to them. Soon favoured lasses sported early tights. Boys were given gum.

But then the 'ordinary' Yanks disappeared and in their place came thousands of black soldiers. Seen as decent people, they gained instant support from all South Molton. To the astonishment of their white chiefs, they were waved at, cheered, invited into people's homes, willingly into several girls' beds. Mixed race kids, then still a rarity in the Midlands, were soon common in South Molton. In any dispute, to a man South Molton supported the black soldiers against the whites. When a black soldier who had been moved to a neighbouring district returned 'off bounds' to repay a debt, and was treated roughly by a couple of white Yanks, there was a spontaneous riot. Fighting spread and became ugly until the white Americans were 'contained' by an alliance of South Molton youths and adults and hard-pressed police. We had a ringside view of some of the proceedings in the police square through the arch opposite us. It was the talk of the town for years. 'And him only wanting to repay his debt – they wouldn't let him do it. Disgusting.' Paying a cash debt was as basic as remembering to deliver the swede bartered for a piece of cheese.

It was going to take Attlee and Thatcher to bring about real change. Meanwhile the village characters went about their business. The list has to start with Swearing Johnny, shouting foul language from the church tower while having one of his fits, and about to be despatched once more to Exminster psychiatric hospital, in the 1940s called mental hospital, or more usually loony bin. Then, the spinsters running their father's gents' outfitting business, fearing that the sale of eggs, butter and so on had put them under the thumb of their male manager. The dentist pacing up and down outside his surgery getting up courage to make an extraction. The local Mainwaring and his pompous Home Guard parades. Miss Poole valiantly defending her stationer's shop by raising her fist at lorries looming close and occasionally trying actually to push them away. The retired farmer particularly up in arms that another colleague had been punished for cruelty to his stock: 'For goodness sake, he didn't kill them.' The inevitable ladies of easy virtue making a fortune with Americans. The bus driver mortified when told he swore too much. 'Bloody hell, bugger me, I always speak the bloody King's English.' Even the budgerigar at the George Hotel which attracted ladies with sweet nothings and then launched into really vile language: 'Where did it learn it?'

It Could Only Be England

'What's it like to be back at The George?,' asks Sheila.

Very natural, yet different, for the past sixty years have seen South Molton and indeed much of North Devon change and change again. In 1942, Ilfracombe's heyday as a resort still lay in the future. The single-line railway and the road through South Molton were not at their most stretched until summer Saturdays in the late 1950s. Then queues of cars and coaches waiting to pass through the square stretched back for miles. Today's peak Saturday traffic is however a shadow of its former self, and anyway goes by the Ring Road, not through South Molton. Often criticised in my reports and broadcasts for not looking sufficiently to its future – twice the council called special meetings to protest – Ilfracombe has declined more than most resorts. Last time I visited the harbour in its spectacular setting, the shops around it were more disappointing than elsewhere in the West, with amusement arcades and tourist tat.

We talk about all we have seen since we left Scotland, even since leaving Bath. What contrasts there are throughout Somerset and Devon – differences of people, wealth, ways of life. What on earth can I call the chapter combining the Somerset Levels with something of Dorset, East and also North Devon?

'It's only in England you'd find such differences so close together,' says Sheila.

'Thank you. "It could only be England".'

Then we talk of the common threads that somehow emphasise the differences, like the churches that reflect their area's natural resources and past importances and hopes. We wonder how the Benedictine monks, in whose footsteps we are so often treading, reflected local differences. Though we are bound to comment on changing times, the remarkable thing is that so much persists in its time-honoured way.

Many of the phrases and words commonly used in one part of Somerset or Devon are scarcely understood in another so, if you're an expert, you can tell exactly where people come from. Then, we conclude, even if many people take little direct interest in it, surely to some extent we are all under the spell of our local landscape when it happens to be as distinctive as those we have passed through in this chapter.

· XIX ·

FROM SOUTH
MOLTON TO BATH

Tonight's South Molton

After sixty years, I am again staying at the George Hotel. Our room with its commanding view of the square (or Broad Street to give it the correct name) could be the one my parents had in those worrying days of 1942. The square is surprisingly the same. Still to be enjoyed are the ornate Medical Hall, the archway and tiled steps leading to the church, the Beehive Stores of the 1870s, the 'Post Office' cut deep into its handsome stonework (though it's now the delivery office and the actual Post Office is a franchised business elsewhere), and especially the large market hall with a fine facade continued on arches over the pavement. There isn't much through traffic, for that now uses the Link Road, and it is easy to park.

Look a bit deeper and it is quite different, for most shops are in trades that either didn't exist sixty years ago, or if they did wouldn't have been economically possible here: computer and financial services among the former, art gallery, antiques, bookshop, flower shop the latter. First stop after checking in at the hotel is the bookshop, where I'm greeted by 'I know you,' as if I were a wanted criminal.

'Nobody buys books like you.' A crime to give business?

'Anyway, it won't be long now.' Have I missed something? Apparently yes, for the owner had recognised me as long-time employer of the person he's about to marry.

Congratulations; there's a real surprise. I must have missed him telling me first time, bemused by discovering a copy of the small paperback *Dicky Slader*, about Exmoor's pedlar poet. Years ago it was a D&C local bestseller, much in demand at our old newsagent from which I had bought my first books when it was still the town's only source of new books, albeit tentative.

Until foot-and-mouth hit, business was brisk at this new, largely second-hand and bargain bookshop, though with some new titles.

'We've taken out a five-year lease, a good move, providing things get back to normal soon.'

Over a cup of tea in a café facing down wide East Street, we learn that catering is down forty per cent; a greater worry is that the family cabinet-making business employing twenty is in peril. Because of access restrictions, timber is not available from the usual local source and is being expensively sought elsewhere. The café is in a little block of shops and houses at the end of the square or Broad Street, allowing a single lane of traffic to pass either side. The Post Office is similarly on its own as an island defining the square's other end. The road to Barnstaple used to be further narrowed by another island building including Miss Pool's stationery business. This has long been demolished; few now remember the shabby stuffed Edwardian Father Christmas that used to appear in the window each December.

South Molton dates from Saxon times and was incorporated as a borough as long ago as the twelfth century. Later growth and prosperity were based on successful wool trade, supported by flocks of sheep for miles around including high up on Exmoor. As that trade declined from the end of the eighteenth century, South Molton's role as coaching and servicing centre took over. The painter Turner's grandfather lived here.

Times became hard when the first railway was opened to Barnstaple, along the Taw Valley, and a new market was established at Eggesford. By the time South Molton had its own station, on the later, meanly-built Taunton to Barnstaple route, most of the ancillary trades servicing coaching and the cattle markets had been lost. South Molton continued to have its market day, but the momentum had gone.

Because of this, there was little pressure for redevelopment, and in many ways South Molton embodies the unspoilt character of a really old market and coaching town with fine buildings, including the large church built on the wealth of wool. We enjoy our perambulation today. Several streets have distinctive raised pavements protected with railings. Just beyond North Street, there is a fine view toward Exmoor with the Link Road and the buildings of the old railway station deep in the valley below. For those arriving by train, the walk was a steep one of well over a mile for, like Torrington, South Molton is a hilltop town safe from the risk of floods.

I take Sheila down mainly brick-built South Street and point out No 65, our wartime bolthole, with the police station opposite, Moors Garage still next door. Farmers filling up on market day used to rest their bums on our windowsill and darken our front room while having a gossip. I ring the bell at No 65. There is no reply, but a net curtain is pulled back to reveal a pair of anxious young faces. The bell isn't answered. Will the kids remember their years spent at No 65 as they are so vividly etched into my mind and into my sister's? Can South Molton possibly change as much in the next sixty years as it has in the last? Though physically surprisingly little altered, it has certainly come in from its cold isolation and prospers with keen community spirit.

Everyone talks of it being a happy, tight-knit community, with many societies and events, rich in crafts and culture. There's a lively Film Society, for instance. People who have moved to it seem to stay. Estate agents are happy, and there are certainly many more of them, pleased to talk and 'fill me in' when I explain the purpose of this visit. One describes it as a 'jolly little town' and, though I would never have expected that to be said of South Molton, it is hard to disagree.

The George Hotel is certainly jolly. Even in 1692 it was referred to as 'an old and established Inn', and through its doors have passed the famous and infamous of many days. A roof fire in 1995 revealed many hidden features and spurred the desire to restore it faithfully. It gives a warm welcome to our dinner guests and serves a meal that wouldn't disgrace a sophisticated London dinner party... except that perhaps the portions are more generous. Trevor Beer is North Devon's naturalist, writer and photographer, especially known for his daily offering in *The Western Morning News* and his books.

With a quizzical expression behind his full-blown beard, he looks as though he's been cast in the role of mischievous though benevolent TV granddad. Endymion, his adopted daughter and working partner, is a delightfully bubbly young lady hiding behind rather mask-like make-up, obviously applied with meticulous care, that scarcely seems to belong in rustic North Devon. She knows her natural history almost as well as he. They care passionately about it and about helping others to appreciate and understand it.

Though newspaper, magazine and book work is important to both of them, financial security has so far been based more on taking people on conducted tours including nature weekends. Access restrictions have abruptly stopped that, and we discuss possible new ways of making it easier to pay the bills.

'Since 1968 we have taken in 4,000 animals and birds and nursed them before putting them back into nature,' says Trevor.

'The food bills are huge,' adds Endymion, as anxious to help Trevor's career as she is to see hers take off, albeit along slightly different lines. Periodically she sends me samples and discusses ideas. 'I'd just love to break out of the North Devon market.' Therein lies the difficulty. Trevor's *Wildlife of North Devon*, of which Endymion gives me an autographed copy, is top quality, real expertise in sensible perspective with photography anyone would be proud of. Published under the Devon Books imprint of Halsgrove, it will have a solid but mainly local sale. The truth is that there are too many naturalists looking for a national audience. The book's introduction is by my friend Tony Soper, once a familiar face on natural history TV programmes. Tony's initial book for D&C, *The Bird Table Book*, was the first ever about attracting birds and other wildlife to the garden and, as pacesetter, supported by TV publicity, must have outsold all the later imitators put together. Success in the media is sweet but fickle.

Trevor hopes to break out of regional constraint with *Old Red*, the story of a fox. I am sure it will be excellent, the natural history observation sharper and probably more accurate than Henry Williamson's in *Tarka The Otter*, but it won't sell a hundredth as well because it will be perceived as 'another' such book. Unless published locally with *The story of a Devon fox* as subtitle, it could fail to make its mark even here. 'A local audience is better than none,' he concedes. But with less regional fame behind her and the enthusiasm of youth, Endymion is impatient. If only she could host a TV natural history show. She'd do it brilliantly, but of course there is much more young talent on offer than can be used.

Meanwhile deep satisfaction comes from natural history observation. Says Trevor: 'I've enjoyed seeing a pair of breeding red-backed shrike, especially as the RSPB says they're extinct. We still have red squirrels. Then I spent two days watching an otter look for her cubs. Sadly, she never found them, but sharing tribulation as well as joy is part of nature watching. Nature doesn't all run smoothly.'

Endymion: 'No, but we can do a lot to help, like our safe havens, keeping a bit of natural habitat when there's development.'

Then, back to their careers. They work hard. Trevor has tremendous productivity.

Tempting though a wider audience sounds, their local recognition is significant, 'and there's no other part of the world with such a beautiful range of habitats and species as we have here in North Devon.'

[Shortly after our meeting, Trevor was awarded an OBE for his journalism, and he won £1,000 in the photographic section of a series of 'This Britain' competitions run by my Charitable Trust, while the Safe Haven project quickly topped 6,000 acres in which wildlife is respected beyond man's greedy needs. Endymion keeps me posted! If you would enjoy an in-depth look behind the scenes into North Devon's wildlife, write for details: Trevor Beer, Tawside, 30 Park Avenue, Barnstaple EX31 2ES.]

To Wistlandpound

Before breakfast, we pop into the market hall and see all manner of stalls being set up. Gnomes, jewellery, food, ironmongery, second-hand books, fifth-hand paperbacks, brand new religious books, clothes of all kinds, super-quality and cheap bedding, fourteen kinds of olives. 'Buy here and you'll not get egg on your face,' says a notice at the egg stall offering small, medium and whoppers.

We buy a venison and mushroom pie from a stall run by the Pie Shop in East Street. Its owner, Graham Wright, who came from Essex five years ago, tells me: 'It was like coming to the Stone Age. We got involved with the Chamber of Trade and any suggestion about doing something different was greeted with horror. When I went back to Essex, at first it was like going back home, but not now. How did I cope with the pressure and traffic? I've taken root here; this is home and they're good people.'

After breakfast I return and comment to a stallholder that the till is quiet. ''Tis, but then 'tis understandable... I'm from farming stock and we're all worried stiff.' Chattering ladies seem to smile and joke, but when you study and listen carefully you realise it's the kind of joking you get around the grave at a funeral: muted, the expressions more worried than cheerful, as customers are scarce. Farmers anxious to keep their holdings isolated are certainly not here this morning. 'I might take forty per cent of what I usually do,' says one stallholder. 'It would be worse if all the regular stallholders were here, but several have stayed away.'

There will be more to say about South Molton at the start of our forthcoming stopping-train country journeys, for it was here my love of railways took root, as I was unofficially allowed to man the signalbox. The next station up the line, with which I frequently exchanged signalling codes, was Bishops Nympton & Molland. I knew that station, an important trading point, but have visited neither of the places which it supposedly served. Sheila especially wants to show me Molland church, and how right she is.

We take an intriguing route via sleepy North Molton, once a boisterous mining town. Then down a straight steep narrow lane with high machine-cut beech hedges, little used by visitors, to even sleepier Molland. Here is one of those villages (in reality little more than a hamlet) where time seems to stand still and the only movement might be that of a cat rising to stretch itself before settling into another long snooze. At St Mary's, time has literally stood still. No Victorian damage here; the only change since 1740 has been the removal of the unsafe gallery. The 44 Georgian box pews, and the more imposing pews for the gentry where they could hear but not be seen except by the minister in his triple-deck pulpit, has been untouched for two and a half centuries. In front of the altar, today's worshippers kneel on cushions incorporating the Molland lily, unique to the area and said to have started when local monks visiting Spain brought back seeds in mediaeval times. Such continuity is so rare as to be almost scary. We note the average rainfall on the foothills of Exmoor is nearly sixty inches and that damp has caused problems. The triple-decker pulpit has been declared unsafe so, marvelling at being able to enjoy something so unconsciously unchanged, we make a small contribution toward the cost of its restoration. If you are in this neck of the woods, don't miss St Mary's.

After a few miles, we pass the pub and cluster of industrial buildings where the old station used to be. It is still a few miles further to Bishops Nympton, larger but pretty, again without anyone in sight. There are dozens of these quieter-than-quiet Devon villages between Dartmoor and Exmoor; this one is probably in danger of becoming a fashionable retreat from 'up country' and all the undesirable elements of modern life that Devonians imply in that simple phrase. Then by the main road back to South Molton, again surprised by the long run into the town centre between centuries-old buildings. Yes, once South Molton really was important.

But we are on our way again, now on one of the routes taken by the baker I used to go out with on his rounds while German planes on their way to attack northern cities were droning overhead. One of very few regular callers at remote hamlets and farmhouses, the baker was as important for his gossip as his bread. Many homes we visited were primitive, but the welcome unfailingly warm, generous cups of tea and other refreshments frequently offered. I learnt the hard way that receiving is as vital as giving. It was at a cottage reached through a churchyard where on really dark nights finding the way without tripping over and upsetting the basket of bread was quite tricky.

'Do have some nuts, love,' said a very old lady almost hidden behind her black shawl. Living by herself, she was obviously quite poor, so I declined, to prevent depriving her.

'Oh please,' she said. Stupidly, I stood firm.

Returning through the churchyard, the baker exploded: 'What God-given right do you have to upset a dear old lady by refusing her nuts, you twerp?' It was the last time I rejected a gift. Generosity includes giving the impression of enjoying even pet hates.

We wander beside the Bray in its deep, tree-lined valley, through Brayford and then climb onto the wide, open moor, along the land that now marks the boundary of the Exmoor National Park, by Five Cross Way, Wallover Down and (steeply down and then up) Challacombe Mill at Barton Town. Soon we are at Blackmoor Gate, a wild, open and almost uninhabited place and see the remains of what was once the most important intermediate station on the narrow-gauge Lynton & Barnstaple Railway. This was where the world's first-ever railway bus service, from Ilfracombe, met trains. The brain child of Sir George Newnes, the publisher, a leading local light, it lasted only a short time since, reported the local paper, 'one of these cars was travelling at a little over eight mph on a high road when the police interfered, a prosecution was instituted and a heavy fine inflicted'. The buses were sold to the

Great Western Railway, which used them for its pioneer service from Helston to the Lizard. Blackmoor Gate became an over-large station with little purpose till the line was closed in 1935 after a very short life. Had it survived, today the narrow-gauge line through spectacular landscapes would be one of North Devon's chief tourist attractions. A section is being lovingly restored.

Then it is time to report to the large reservoir, looking like a natural lake tucked into its deep valley, that is Wistlandpound.

When Electricity and Piped Water Were New

'God never intended us to drink Exmoor water, maister,' was typical of comments I received when covering those exciting years from the early 1950s when rural deprivation was supposed to be conquered for all time. It meant endless digging-up of roads and lanes, diversions and lengthy delays at traffic lights – early automatic ones occasionally getting disastrously out of sync so that deadlock ensued. They were heady days for contractors and the manufacturers of pneumatic drills. Long delays and bumpy surfaces inspired cartoonists. One sequence went something along the lines of 'Our road was pretty sporty until the council made it up. But then electricity dug it up, water tore it up and gas ripped it up. And now I'm happy to say once more our road is fairly sporty.'

The closure of numerous village and small-town gas works and, slightly later, the introduction of North Sea gas resulted in thousands more miles of trenching. New sewerage works and a greatly-extended telephone network – until well into the 1950s, you had to book a trunk call and were often restricted to three minutes – added to the chaos. But the main diggers-up were water and electricity. After a few hectic years, mains water and electricity were available almost everywhere.

I closely followed the work of the North Devon Water Board, serving a vast tract of the central Devon plateauland as well as real North Devon itself. It was an ambitious project, injecting vitality into a countryside of frequent summer droughts when the old wells ran dry. It especially helped small farmers with dairy herds. Though the huge majority of the rural population could now have tap water, many older people found it too new fangled and continued their routine of fetching water from the pump, where they had long chats with neighbours. The education authority refused to pay for indoor sanitation at many village schools. 'What was good enough for our parents and grandparents is good enough for ourselves and kids,' was expressed in many ways. Anyway, who could say what happened to water transported through pipes from a 'foreign' part of Devon? ' 'Tisn't natural.'

It was the same with electricity. Often half the householders initially decided against going on the mains, sometimes resulting in a supply also being denied to keen neighbours. As most people (admittedly often of the next generation) eventually wanted water and electricity – and gas and sewerage, too, where available – the initial refusals greatly added to the costs and resulted in later digging-up of lanes and streets.

It took much longer for the telephone to become ubiquitous. Even in the 1980s, you could by no means assume even younger rural people would be connected, and there are still older folk who aren't, partly on cost grounds, partly because 'us 'ave niver had it'. From the 1950s, there was usually the comfort that, in an emergency, the village telephone kiosk could be used to summon help. Little queues of people waiting to make or receive a call were once part of village social life as much as visits to the post office and shop, and gatherings at the bus stop for a trip to the market at the nearest town. One by one, points of social contacts have been reduced. Even mobile shops and touring ice-cream vans less frequently punctuate the rural rhythm. We are all so much more self-sufficient and contained. It is perhaps not surprising that doctors find resistance to the appointment system, since waiting in a crowded surgery with 'open appointments' provides one of the few natural opportunities to mix with others. In many villages, however, loneliness is now decreasing as more incomers support social events and enjoy meeting the remaining indigenous population.

Wistlandpound reservoir. The only time I was previously here was in the mid-1950s when a large workforce and much machinery was milling around deep down in the hollow beneath my vantage point. Today we are greeted by Toni Furse who has come from South West Water to explain how things have changed. For a start, since other reservoirs have been added, Wistlandpound now supplies a smaller area. What I especially like, though, is that while reservoirs were once insulated as though they were danger areas, today they play a major part in sporting activities, sightseeing and tourism.

Says Toni: 'It was South West Water that set the example. There's a series of independent charities or trusts to which the company gives a small fee to cover their essential legal obligations. The rest is financed on a charitable basis. The aim is for the South West Lakes Trust – again the first of its kind – to make the best leisure use of the lakes. They are reservoirs of course, but we call them lakes which sounds more friendly. We've only touched the surface of possibilities yet, but the public are being made welcome at many lakes with parking, toilets, water-sport centres with instructors, fishing and – at several – visitor centres and tea rooms. The lakes are an asset waiting to be used. Each separate scheme is grant-financed.' Wistlandpound is run by the Calvert Trust. It even has a hotel plus self-catering accommodation and offers a huge range of sporting activities and there's support from Friends of the Calvert Trust Exmoor.

This is great. So is Toni, a slim and enthusiastic young graduate from Bude who read public relations and media studies, a charming representative of the new outlook. She would have been a pretty unlikely person to meet in the water industry's past, when 'Keep out' was what we were told if we got too near to a sheet of water. Many of the manmade lakes across the South West, as indeed the rest of Britain, seriously enhance nature and have always appealed to me, though not their conifer-lined banks.

With Toni's Bude background, inevitably we talk of the Tamar Lakes, the first of which was begun by the old Bude Canal. 'Oh,' she says with animation, 'in Bude there's talk of putting a swing bridge back at Falcoln Bridge.' Equally excited, I tell her how long I've wanted to enjoy this day of such positive news and thought, for I'd not previously heard of the South West Lakes Trust. Yet this morning we can't walk around Wistlandpound: foot-and-mouth.

Exmoor

Up the valley and all around upon that easterly side rose the wild heights of Exmoor, upon which in those days reclamation had laid but a tentative hand. Between us and the moor, half a mile away, lay the little village of whitewashed, slate-roofed cottages, with their pleasant reek of peat smoke, strung along the edge of the stream. Above the village the moor rose almost at once into the wild, its lonely summits nearly twice as high as any hills I had ever seen. It made a fine half-circle round our whole eastern orbit, and proclaimed to us by night and day, under moons and suns, and not least in the grey gloom of winter, that we were at the end of all things. For the moor, as I soon came to feel, represented seemingly endless solitudes, stretching far away beyond the bounds to which our fairly adventurous steps ever penetrated. If the long road from Barnstaple to our Rectory and village was little travelled by any but our parish folk, beyond the village, it wandered up and away through many gates over the moor towards Simonsbath, passing, by the way, the big boundary stone which divided Devon and Somerset.

The quote is from one of my favourite parts of A G Bradley's *Exmoor Memories* of 1926, which from age seven or eight, I often took down from my father's shelves. Though later I read *Lorna Doone*, from the start it was the real wilderness that appealed. I feared by the time I first experienced it things would have become much more tame. The supposition was both right and wrong. Even by World War Two, when I first penetrated the real moor in the blackout with the baker, it was a lot less cut off. But little of its character had been eroded. The great threat was forestation, for the key to Exmoor is its openness, the long lines of grass and heather-covered rolling moor. It was in the 1960s that the resorts that depend on people visiting Exmoor forecast they would go bust because its character would be killed by uniform conifers. Now the threat is that housing prices have been pushed up beyond the means of local people by the number of properties that have become little-used second homes. They are discussing a proposal to make it necessary to get planning permission if a house is occupied for less than half the year.

To go back to Bradley. He was writing about being sent as a boy to a parsonage near Simonsbath, at the key crossroads between the main west-east route across the moor and roads from South Molton and Lynmouth. Dozens of times I have climbed from South Molton up through smaller North Molton to pass through Simonsbath. Simonsbath was where the Knight family lived. Buying the central 'Forest of Exmoor', they sought to 'reclaim it'. But 'forest' only meant hunting reserve, and the tenant farmers they introduced made surprisingly little impact on the landscape. Hunting on Exmoor has always included stags, a pursuit generally acknowledged as more barbaric than fox hunting. In recent years, hunts have been seriously disrupted by anti-hunt rallies. You'll, of course, still catch glimpses of deer on the skyline. What Exmoor did undoubtedly perpetrate longer than most areas was the worst of the more worldly-than-thou huntin' parsons.

From Simonsbath my normal route then continues to Exford, where you can start a four-mile gentle walk up to Dunkery Beacon, at 1700ft Exmoor's highest point – especially delightful in the heather season. Then across the A396 from Bampton to Dunster to continue on the top of the world along roads with neat beech hedges to Ralegh's Cross, close to which – and with much of the South Wales coast usually closely in focus – you can see the great inclined plane of the West Somerset Mineral Railway and the remains of the engine house where the great drum was set in motion to wind up the cable pulling trucks up at 1 in 4 for two miles. There were extensive mines on the high ground. Beyond Ralegh's Cross, I then usually drop down sharply, to Williton.

Since we are already so near to Lynton, this morning I've abandoned my favourite route for another great experience, down to Lynmouth and then along the dramatic coast where Exmoor meets the sea. The disadvantage of this way is often heavy traffic, including convoys of underpowered coaches struggling up Countisbury Hill out of Lynmouth but, with foot-and-mouth, traffic should not be a problem today. Far from it, we discover when, with a new clear view of South Wales via Martinhoe Cross, we bypass Lynton to descend by the Valley of the Rocks. There is not a single car in the car park at Watersmeet. At Lynmouth, only two passengers are waiting to be taken up to Lynton by the cliff railway, a gift from Sir George Newnes. The railway advertises itself as 'the South West's most popular working attraction'; the weight of water in the tank of the descending car pulls up the loaded one. Very simple but precise. Under the cliffs, Lynmouth's vast car park is all but empty. Tourism is at its lowest level since the Lynmouth flood disaster of 1952.

'The Most Delightful Place for a Landscape Painter'

The coast is just as much Exmoor as the open moor. There is no cliff scenery that beats this. Gainsborough thought Lynmouth 'the most delightful place for a landscape painter this country can boast'. Many famous people have favoured it over the centuries. Shelley brought his sixteen-year-old bride Harriet here for their long honeymoon during which he wrote *Queen Mab*.

Such dramatic geography comes with a price, most of England's record-breaking cloudbursts have been on Exmoor, especially around its coasts. The 1952 Lynmouth flood disaster was just the worst of them. The heavy loss of life in a holiday village at the season's peak uniquely stirred the public's imagination, resulting in an appeal fund for the first time raising far more money than could be sensibly used.

For decades after the disaster, each season Eric Delderfield, an early D&C director, sold thousands of his commemorative book to souvenir and other village shops whose owners became personal friends. *Lynmouth Flood Story* vividly records how the disaster unfolded, the true extent not instantly appreciated since land lines were cut as darkness fell on that fearful Friday night. No mobiles in those days, even for police. Some people were drowned unawares, while a few tried to save themselves valiantly but in vain. Many more would have been lost but for the inspired efforts of neighbours who, through local knowledge and observation of earlier lesser floods, knew exactly what they could do and what was beyond them. Whole hotels were wrecked, and dozens of cars washed out to sea. The famous Rhenish Tower guarding the harbour's entrance disappeared. As the world's media descended, for this was August, the 'silly season', local officials found themselves instantaneously famous, internationally.

Earlier heavy rainfall meant that Exmoor could absorb no more, and already there was flooding when a cloudburst deposited five inches in one hour. That amount of water cascading off a single roof can cause problems, but there were five inches over the huge catchment area of the two Lyn rivers. The West Lyn changed course to join the East Lyn. Where they met, the water was 20 ft deep. Over 100,000 tons of boulders, some of several tons each were propelled toward the sea. In places they combined with trees and debris to build up dams. Water cascading down when its weight overpowered a 25 ft high dam caused some of the worst damage.

Only the week before, in one of my holiday reports, I had praised Lynmouth for its enterprising hospitality. In those days, the twin villages of Lynmouth and Lynton naturally attracted more adventurous visitors, many of whom arrived by public transport and then bought a car. With less red tape than today, and car rental less developed, a fortnight's ownership of an old banger was common. One vehicle might have a dozen owners each season, the risk being that an expensive repair would suddenly be required.

This morning Lynmouth sparkles in the sun and, as we patronise a few shops with no other customers, we feel as useful as we would giving business to a remote African village. The Rhenish Tower has been rebuilt as a symbol of the new Lynmouth. Only the river's widening, lest there should be another such cloudburst, makes Lynmouth less intimate than it used to be. I still adore it; but oh, its business is suffering today. That there is a future is emphasised by hearing that a new section of the coastal footpath is being built in difficult terrain beyond the Valley of the Rocks to the West: a joint project between the National Park and the Lee Abbey Fellowship (a Christian holiday and conference centre particularly popular with the young) which will take walkers off a dangerous road and offer them fabulous views round the headland of Crockpit.

To Porlock Weir

Then up Countisbury Hill. Not merely do we have it to ourselves but it has been widened and is altogether less challenging. For the first time as driver I can enjoy the view. Once most of us were scared. Would that descending coach be able to stop? Could we start again? I recall a newspaper report praising a coach for having brakes that held when its engine failed as though that were exceptional on a 1 in 4 hill. I also recall reports of how in 1899, when a rudderless ship off Porlock Weir sent distress signals and a northwest gale prevented the launching of the 34 ft long lifeboat at Lynmouth, it was loaded onto a horse-drawn cart and pulled (and pushed by many volunteers) up this hill. Even more difficult was guiding it down the just as steep Porlock Hill. Skids, repeatedly moved in front of the lifeboat, had to be used, but they had thought of the need for them and brought them. A cart carrying tools had been sent on ahead, too, to remove gate posts and other obstacles where the road was too narrow for the wheels of the vehicle carrying the lifeboat. At the approach to Porlock, a cottage wall had to be removed. The old lady living there, who had never seen a lifeboat before, let alone one on wheels, was not amused.

The rescue of the ship, *Forrest Hall*, was eventually successful. The lifeboat men reached safe anchorage at Barry having been without food for 24 hours.

Such dramatic country breeds heroism. Many a tale has been told of the feats of shepherds working in foul weather miles from habitation. But it is time for us to descend. Though Porlock Hill is easier today, I remain loyal to the longer toll road, mainly through woodland but with an occasional glimpse of sea below. It costs £2 which we leave in a box since there's nobody at the tollhouse: not surprising as we haven't passed a single car. No backpackers, either, but red notices warning of a £500 fine if we dare use a footpath. The home-made hairpin bend signs provide a touch of light relief.

The first time I visited Porlock Weir was in the early 1950s in the car of one of the councillors making me welcome as a journalist visiting Minehead to assess local tourism. Yes, in those days people turned out to welcome someone who had only come from South Devon. Our evening trip, which included a walk close to Dunkery Beacon, had a fascinating finale, for Porlock Weir was that very night dying as a commercial port. The last-ever collier from South Wales was offloading its cargo into lorries at low tide. How on earth had it got so far into the dried-up harbour? A parallel row of tree branches must have guided it through the narrow zigzag course. Surely that would be difficult enough even in calm weather for a vessel whose keel cannot have been much above the shingle. But it wasn't that calm. 'It isn't always easy,' the skipper told me. 'Overland will be cheaper and I suppose safer, but 'tis sad to see these little harbours dying. Soon there won't be any call for vessels as small as her. The old ways are goin'.'

And so it was. Yet there is still a parallel line of tree branches to guide today's yachts, now aground at low tide. A boy throwing stones into the channel is told to stop. 'Be private property. What's the point of us digging them out if you's hell bent on fillin' it up?' The boy was well out of ear reach before this monologue finished. We stroll to the Ship Inn, crowded with guests. The owners tell me business had been well down until it was reported on local TV that seaside places, still very much open, were being just as badly hurt as farming areas by universal 'stay away' publicity. Out came crowds to enjoy themselves and give support. However, we cannot purchase the piece of Bristol Blue glass we had promised ourselves, because the shop in a converted warehouse obviously didn't think it would be worth opening. But have faith, there's life yet: 'Trotters Independent Trading Co New York Paris Porlock,' shouts a yellow three-wheeler. It raises money for charity.

With its little pier and lovely buildings including the pubs, Porlock Weir never disappoints. Nor does the road east through Porlock, a pretty village usually with too much traffic. We take the splendid diversion just off the main road to Allerford and Selworthy. Name just one perfect spot in Somerset and it would have to be Selworthy. This afternoon we have it to ourselves: the ancient church with its south aisle's glorious wagon roof dating from the 1530s, and the churchyard with its outlook across to Dunkery Beacon worth dying for. North and south, the hills with steep slopes and high bluffs seem to have been arranged by a skilled artist. The walk from Allerford to Hurlstone Point is one I shall never forget, nor that along the Somerset & North Devon Coast Path, forced well inland because of the steep contours at this point, to the viewpoint Bratton Ball. It is of course closed today.

Brendons and Quantocks

There is so much of interest around Minehead that it does better than many resorts and generally looks after its very varied visitors well. Beyond the seafront station serving Britain's longest steam railway, the West Somerset, Butlins has been upgraded. But why mock supermarket exuberance with those exaggerated gleaming white tent-like spheres topped with twisted spires?

There are excellent cafés in Minehead but on the spur of the moment we go into one where a young waitress has just dropped a tray of cutlery on to the floor in front of the counter. She picks it up and, having handled it, puts it back into the tray's appropriate compartments.

Surprised, I ask: 'Aren't you going to wash it?' And when there's no response: 'Did you hear me?'

'Of course she heard you,' rattles the manager or owner, but still no action.

'So are you going to wash it?' I persist.

'Sorry, dear, some people always make trouble. You'd better wash it.'

So we decide to check into our hotel, the two-star Channel House with a 78 per cent AA rating, where not only is it all spotlessly clean but everything perfect in a charming, matter-of-fact manner not found in most grander establishments. We are not surprised to hear that the ups-and-downs of tourism pass them by since 'we're always full, mainly with repeat business'. It is a very happy choice, at the foot of North Hill at the older or harbour end of the town which boasts a long history even before the Great Western Railway turned it into a popular resort. Once there were seasonal non-stop expresses along what is now the West Somerset Railway, the longest preserved steam line in Britain, whose Minehead terminus is actually on the seafront.

Next morning first stop is the mediaeval village of Dunster, dominated by the curious castle which Victorian restoration made 'into something more like a Rhineland Schloss than a Norman stronghold'. It doesn't appeal to me, but the village certainly does... especially the main street with cobbled pavements on either side, the hexagonal Yarn Market at which farmers converted their wool into cash, and quality shops. There's a small display of Bristol Blue glass in the window of Toward the Light, an unusual gallery close to the Yarn Market. Porlock Weir's loss might be Dunster's gain but, much to our surprise, instead of Bristol Blue we come away with a bronze of a cat, tail up, muscles realistically ripping as with curved body and bent head it is obviously approaching someone. I, of course, imagine it is me.

When I ask the owner about the economics of running a small gallery, he makes the amazing reply that annual turnover of his own art is £350,000. Virtually all the pictures on display are prints of his work. 'A few originals, too,' he adds, 'for those who must have an original, but they often go off with one of my least satisfying pictures, since naturally I only make prints of those I'm really happy with.' They are mainly Exmoor and Somerset scenes, romantic in an individual style that obviously appeals to a wide market. 'It's what I do,' he says, as though he needs to apologise. 'I love it. I do what I want, and won't take commissions that constrain me.' His son runs another gallery with an even more generous display of his work at the other end of the main street.

We could spend a whole morning in the shops (including bookshop) and galleries here; it is a fun place catering for residents as well as the stream of visitors, these days without a sharp summer peak but an almost year-round season. Once the Luttrell Arms was a higher-ranking Trust House/Forte but, like so many others, suffered after ownership change. 'Back in private ownership' boasts a notice outside, which encourages us to try it for an early light lunch. Martin Tarr, one of the new owners, says it is the first time in 500 years it has been privately run and 'yes, thanks, business is promising'. Lunch is excellent.

Then on to Watchet. Here, the harbour was once commercially prosperous, among other things importing esparto grass for the nearby paper mill. Later the subject of a fraud enquiry, it has long been gentrified. In fact it was here I first saw the quality paving blocks and ornate lamp posts that now seem obligatory at ports which have lost their commercial business. This afternoon, however, tourism is being further pursued. A cone-shaped hollow has been sunk in the harbour as prelude to deepening the whole thing. A new wall is being built with two sill locks to provide high water in the outer marina, so yachts will be able to enter and leave except at lowest tide. Suddenly it has become cold, with a stiff north-westerly breeze.

Williton next, where the problems of running a steam railway were brought home when I was temporary 'signalman' for a TV programme. A spark from a passing locomotive set fire to a corner of a barley field, all of which was under threat. 'Where do you keep your wet sacks?' demanded the farmer's angry wife.

When told, there weren't any, she railed: 'You run steam engines and don't have wet sacks!' We went to assist beating out the fire and won. In summer when the full timetable is running, I still enjoy watching two steam-hauled trains 'crossing' in the station loop, exchanging the single-line tokens and taking on water. The West Somerset runs through great countryside, and the signalbox is similar to that I unofficially operated as a boy.

The cold wind heralded driving rain so, after following the railway route of many happy summer Saturday memories to Stogumber, we thread through sodden lanes by pretty Milverton to our chosen hotel, near Wellington. Good hotels come and go. This is a new one of a very welcome kind, though by its very nature not cheap: Bindon Country House Hotel. Even the arrival of its brochure had helped justify our decision to spoil ourselves: 'Nestled amongst seven acres of stunning formal and woodland gardens there is at once a sense of calm... "je trouve bien" (translated 'I find well') is the motto of the house... Enjoy our hotel as we do, take pleasure in your stay.'

The story is slightly unusual. When Lynn and Mark Jaffa sought a suitable hotel, they couldn't find one, so they faxed the owners of what was a private 400-year-old house. Yes, they were prepared to sell. There was a lot of work to do, re-roofing and getting rid of wet and dry rot, as well as all the conversions necessary to turn it into a superior hotel.

Says Lynn: 'From the start we set out to get three red stars and three red rosettes, but you start with nothing, and are of course out of sync with the guide books. We wanted to get into *Pride of Britain*, but they said come back another year. So we did our own marketing. We targeted Newbury with an insert in the local paper, and got in touch with 2,000 companies within two hours travelling time. Doing it ourselves helped build a team spirit with the staff, and the results were quicker than had we gone to a specialist. It worked.'

Then the cruel blow. Foot-and-mouth struck, the nearest case only two miles from the hotel, on a smallholding whose owner is a relief milker at a dozen farms, all contaminated. 'So you'll almost have the hotel to yourselves this evening.'

There is just one other couple at dinner, the (presumably) Dutch husband keeping up a running commentary on the cooking. It is nearly all favourable; our dinner isn't what you'd routinely cook at home, but not too rarefied either.

They will surely do well, for their attitude is spot on. There's a keen core staff with whom everything such as letters from guests is shared. Everyone is expected to muck in, so the receptionist helps serve breakfast. In the summer the staff total swells to about thirty, but they are all treated as individuals. 'Three French in the kitchen, and we try to make waiting more than a job for a gap year. Every year we all go out together. It's been quite an experience. We're even beginning to work with The Castle Hotel at Taunton (where we are going for our next night). [Foot-and-mouth of course ultimately passed, the hotel is now in *Pride of Britain*, and the AA have awarded it three red stars but so far only two red rosettes.]

We wake up on a sparkling spring morning. Wooded countryside is all around, gently rolling with few definite lines before the distant long ridge. Except for the Keep Out notices and the straw with disinfectant at farm gates for those authorised to enter, it is so different from last night's gloom. First stop is Wiveliscombe, where the buildings of three and four storeys, with their overhanging top floors and wooden balconies and dormers, tell of ingenuity and former importance. The library tiled in orange red with a slightly curved frontage on three floors isn't a run-of-the-mill small town building either. Wiveliscombe is remote in the hills, one of which it rests on, at the junction of the new red sandstone to the east and the older red rocks of which Exmoor is mainly formed. Its setting and its ability always to stay ahead of neighbouring places – its market once dominated a large area – give it special interest. Though solid, the core is quickly explored. I'm disappointed to discover the large second-hand bookshop, where the stock suggested a literate population, has closed. On our way up the steep edge of the Brendon Hills we pass the large primary school with red and black diamond-pattern tiles. Deep etching says that once it was only for girls and infants.

Then up and down by Clatworthy to Clatworthy Reservoir and west, again with real hills, to the large newer Wimbleball Lake, once bitterly opposed but now listed as a scenic attraction with its own tearoom. Then steeply down off the Brendons by Elworthy and along the edge of the Exmoor National Park. Sandwiched between Exmoor (of which it is almost part) and the Quantocks, the Brendons have their own character and tradition. They rise far more steeply than Exmoor's central upland, though ironically, while Exmoor is at its most excessive where it meets the sea, the Brendons peter out well short of it. Dramatic but tidily civilised might be one way of describing the Brendons.

Now, back at Williton, in sunshine instead of yesterday afternoon's rain, we take the Bridgwater road, among southern England's most interesting. First of a series of places of special merit comes West Quantoxhead, with another picture-postcard church at the start of an easy walk down to the coast, rocky at this point. Then Holford, where a pleasant road south beside the roaring stream divides in two, one going to the Alfoxton Park Hotel, the other up Holford Combe serving the rural Combe House Hotel.

I love every inch of the roads with their highly distinctive geography and, when staying at one hotel, have made a practice of walking to the other for dinner. The approach to the Alfoxton hotel is especially surprising, though when you get there you discover that the building turns its back on the broad view across the Bristol Channel to Wales, main rooms looking up at a steep hill. They no doubt thought it would be cosier that way. Once, most homes by the sea were built to minimise the wind, not to maximise the outlook. 'This property comes with the benefit that you are close to the sea and can often hear it without seeing it or feeling the wind coming off it,' said an estate agent's proposition of years ago.

I mainly remember the Alfoxton Park Hotel for a conversation between the waiter taking orders and the chef to whom they were shouted down a hatch.

'Well, I suppose I can do that if they really want it,' muttered the chef about one order. The next party wanted the same.

'You're having me on,' exploded the chef, but agreed to take the order. We diners were now beginning to titter quietly among ourselves.

After the next order was shouted down, the chef bellowed: 'They want it how?'

'That's what they've asked for,' replied the waiter, as though used to the chef's tantrums.

Our giggles weren't quite so quiet. Wondering what reaction would be caused, the next diner, a gent on his own, placed his order. 'He expects me to do that just for one?' shouted the chef. 'Look, we've four parties so far, and you've encouraged them all to have something special.'

'No, he hasn't,' we all shouted.

'What are they shouting?' asked the chef. One of the diners then jumped up and bawled down the hatch: 'Look, stop the fuss and get on with it. We've all picked things straight off the menu...'

'No you haven't,' muttered the chef as he rushed upstairs to face us. Only then did the penny drop. There were two quite different menus, both correctly dated, using the same basic ingredients. Maybe the owner's wife overruled her husband? Who knows, somewhere along the lines, someone had decided to do chicken this rather than chicken that. The chef, insisting his menu was the correct one, collected ours, and – subdued – we ate what we were given. It was good.

William and Dorothy Wordsworth once lived at what is now this Alfoxton Park Hotel. Samuel Taylor Coleridge frequently walked over from Nether Stowey, our next place of interest. In 1797, he moved into a damp cottage at Nether Stowey with his wife and baby. He kept traditional writers' hours, at his desk morning and evening, growing vegetables and tending his chickens and pigs in the afternoon, before going over to Alfoxton for the day's end.

The Rime of the Ancient Mariner and much else of his best work was written during a sojourn of just under two years. The collaboration with Wordsworth which produced the start of *The Lyrical Ballads* is said to have inaugurated the Romantic Movement which so changed English poetry.

Coleridge thought nothing of the three miles there and back to Alfoxton, but then he once walked to Bristol for a meeting, and took only two days to cover the ninety miles across Exmoor to Lynton and back. Exercise however didn't keep him healthy, for his opium habit got out of hand. Some critics say his best work came from personal brilliance enhanced by opium. His marriage and also his friendship with Wordsworth came to a sad end, so at Nether Stowey we see him with his early promise never quite fulfilled. Nether Stowey certainly cashes in on his memory and mementoes, but it is also a natural centre for the Quantocks. More manageable than the Brendons, though scarcely tame, and full of good churches and other buildings and interesting people who need somewhere different to call home, the Quantocks are what many people think of as real Somerset.

At Cannington we turn left, on the road which goes on to Hinkley Point atomic power station, but takes us rather less far, to the curious little port of Combwich. This is truly hidden Somerset. The village appears in no guide book, old or new, that I have seen. It does little to cater for visitors – parking is easy – and looks out forlornly on what at most states of tide is a dirty ditch, a tributary of the River Parrett. A few homes also enjoy or try to hide from the Parrett proper. Here that is a ferocious beast, tides ripping in from the mouth, five or so miles to the north, and then on to Bridgwater, via many bends a further ten miles inland.

Though there is little evidence of commercial shipping today, Combwich has the atmosphere of a place dependent on the river, as today's fishermen undoubtedly are. Even Americans would be hard pressed to say that it reminded them of somewhere back home. If it belongs anywhere, it is surely at the start of the Levels proper on the other side of the river, but there's not even a house to wave at across there.

A Destination in Itself: Its Owner and His Book

With a short snooze before dinner in mind, now cross-country to Taunton, and by the bus station (only one wrong turning) to the Castle Hotel. Little Car is kind to us and has many good features, notably that it fits into the very narrow garage at Bath. Poor dear, she does have an inferiority complex which, especially when Rolls Royces and Jaguars are much in evidence, she somehow passes on to us. 'Park me over there, and take your luggage in yourself,' she says, hoping we will avert the attention of the porter on the doorstep.

'Good evening sir, madam,' he greets. 'Let me have that. Which is your car? I'll put it into the garage for you.'

Muttering self-consciously about it being a second car, I hand over the keys. The porter looks down as though he can scarcely see something so insignificant as Little Car. Why should we feel flustered, or is it amused?

'It's not good enough, and that's that,' shouts a woman at reception. 'Why do you need a fire in the first place?'

'I was trying to explain, madam, it's not a fire we wanted. It's one the system thought we had. It was a false alarm.'

'I told you that it's not good enough having a practice when people are taking their snooze before their pre-dinner drink. Practices should be in the morning.'

'They are, madam. This wasn't a practice. It was a false alarm.'

'It woke me up.'

'Well, I'm very sorry madam, but it was meant to. If it had been a real fire...'

'It's not good enough...'

The receptionist, no doubt as pleased to have a distraction as we are to forget the porter's condescension to Little Car, checks us in with aplomb – though not till I've raced up to the gents' which, I am happy to say, still has its famous (or infamous) art gallery. Then it is all plain sailing, as The Castle usually is. Another porter takes our bags up the complicated route to the back of the hotel, where our room has a view over the ruins of the castle where Judge Jeffries was so feared.

Says Murray's *Hand-Book*: 'The historic memories of Taunton Castle have not availed to preserve its buildings from dilapidation, decay, and neglect. The Castle Green is entered by a fine archway, now incorporated within Clarke's Hotel.' Clarke's is now forgotten as the Castle Hotel has brought Taunton into greater prominence than any predecessor. That Taunton has such a highly-regarded hotel is due to Kit Chapman. Kit's life is totally devoted to fighting mediocrity, whether within the hotel or as demonstrated by the town's planners. I've been reading his *An Innkeeper's Diary*.

> The potential for disaster is high in any hotel. This is because hotels, in essence, trade in the foibles and frailties of the human condition. Ultimately, our mission is to introduce a little sunshine, a little interest, a little levity, into the stresses of people's everyday lives. We are in the happiness business and, as such, we are especially susceptible to 'Sod's Law' and the whimsy of the human being.

The lady complaining about the fire alarm wasn't untypical. Hotel guests can be the most unreasonable of people. When the hotel's main electricity cable was cut by a contractor working on an 'enhancement' scheme at seven o'clock one morning, and the electricity company's emergency service couldn't find the hotel listed under its postcode – and why couldn't they find their reference number in the dark? – some guests were simply unable to take in what had happened.

> At 7.20, two suits walked in asking for breakfast. 'We rang yesterday,' said one of them. 'We were told you were quite busy and your girl advised us to come early.'
>
> Andrew peered at them across the gloom of the reception desk.
>
> 'I'm terribly sorry but our power's down and at the moment I simply can't offer you any breakfast. To be honest, I doubt anyone's going to get breakfast this morning.'
>
> 'But we did call yesterday,' insisted the suit. 'And we were told there would be no problem.'
>
> At this point, Andrew was getting a little exasperated. The message was not sinking in.
>
> 'Were we clairvoyant, I am sure my receptionist would not have told you that breakfast was available,' he said.
>
> 'Well, can we just have a coffee?' droned the suit.
>
> 'As I have explained, Sir, none of our equipment is functioning.'
>
> As they left, one muttered to the other: 'Don't understand it. They can't even do a simple breakfast.'
>
> 'And we did call yesterday!' added the other.

Kit is pretty outspoken about awkward customers, and I'm not surprised when he tells me there have been libel problems with the book; and that the paperback misses a few paragraphs in the hardback. 'It was a diary of the moment with all the frustrations and emotions of trying to make a hotel work despite all the difficulties. Though the publishers checked it carefully, it was bound to ruffle a few feathers. But then, sometimes we're reduced to tears: the planners, the contractor who cut off our electricity for three hours at breakfast time, the hotel inspectors like the one who (temporarily) took away our Michelin star, and the guests who are rude to staff. The customer is king, but only one of our kings. "You do know who I am, don't you?" often signals trouble. I'm not very good at recognising people, but have a sophisticated spy system.'

Over the years, I've watched Kit's progress with fascination. Nobody works harder or more enthusiastically; nobody listens better. His standards are high and, for an establishment in which everyone expects to be treated like an individual, it is not small. There are just over a hundred staff. The secret, he says, is in recruiting and retaining good managers... especially, in the kitchen. The Castle always has a superb staff, but chefs especially are known to be a temperamental breed. And Taunton? *The Stockholm Times* called The Castle 'a brave hotel in an

English hole'. There was more of a storm when, in a travel magazine, Jonathan Meades described The Castle as a jewel in a town that 'has always seemed uncouth in a boorish, West Country way... will the three-headed sheep-shaggers come in from the Levels and the Blackdowns'? Asked to comment on the article on radio, Auberon Waugh added fuel to the fire by calling Taunton a dreadful town. I disagree: apart from its traffic, it has much going for it.

In any case, though somewhat uneasily situated beyond the bus station, these days The Castle is an established destination in itself. Dinner was brilliant; our room marvellously comfortable and delightfully furnished; breakfast also great, though I preferred it when served in the dining room. You now go to the Brazz, pleasant but with footsteps irritatingly intrusive on the wooden floorboards.

It was after breakfast that Kit and I met in his office. He began: 'I hear your wife likes breakfast in the Brazz but you don't.' He's nothing if not well informed, very much on top of his demanding job. Whether local people appreciate what they have in their midst will always be questioned. 'Nearly all our complaints come from local postcodes,' he says. 'They are the ones who find dishes praised by everyone else inedible, insist on overcrowded table seating for a function and then get a solicitor to write a letter saying it was too crowded.'

But there's no hint of the hotel wanting to ignore the local market. Its character depends on its unique mix of business.

When we leave we slip out while the porter's attention is elsewhere, but then notice that there are a couple of vehicles he could have been even snootier about than Little Car.

Hestercombe Garden and Back to Bath

It is already mid-morning. Soon we're in lanes heading to Hestercombe Gardens, now run by the County Council since Somerset's fire service has its headquarters in the historic house on this eastern flank of the Quantocks. A Lottery grant has helped convert what used to be the fire engine servicing workshop into a visitor centre. With the Mill Pond as a central feature, the gardens have developed piecemeal over the last century and a third, with a natural (or so it seems) Great Cascade and a whole range of buildings, real and mock: Gothic Alcove, Temple Arbour, Witch House, Mausoleum, Orangery.

There is no shortage of interest on the hour's circuit making the best of the contours, though for many expert gardeners the top appeal is the Formal Garden. Designed by Sir Edward Lutyens and planted by Gertrude Jekyll in 1904-6, it was a collaboration that had an indelible influence on later garden design. Here is what might be called the home of real English gardening, combining contained cosiness with distant views, daring formality with plants which look as though they have always been where they now flourish, and vertical features that tall plants of mainly light-coloured foliage at once emphasise and soften. This isn't a run-of-the-mill garden, and this note does it far from justice. The colour combinations, relative sizes – and always surprising shapes, alluring steps and water – enthral us. Its gardeners, too.

'I've been here six years though an OAP for eleven,' says one of them. 'There are six of us and we don't run out of things to do. We've all been to [college at] Cannington.'

It is slightly chilly eating lunch outside but we can still feel the garden around us. At the next table a couple are explaining they are pleased to have their Labrador as an excuse. 'Honestly, we're delighted we can't go away for Easter. We stay home and do what we want to do. The one place we love coming to is here. It's like an entire country rolled into one endlessly varied landscape and this cafe is good.' The Lab agrees, flapping its tail.

The Somerset Levels beckon us back, for we have been warmly recommended to visit the Willows & Wetlands Visitor Centre, just outside Stoke St Gregory, south of Burrow Mump, and so close to where we were at the start of the chapter before this. To get there, we have to cross the A38, M5, Bridgwater & Taunton Canal, the main railway to Taunton and the South West, and the River Tone. My oh my, I knew that willows and basket work were adaptable but, fancy a duck nesting basket, a grand hooded chair, an invalid carriage – or perhaps a coffin for a green funeral? Here's your opportunity, though the World War One lightweight wicker aeroplane seats aren't for sale. We instantly fall for a trio of plant troughs and a couple of key rings, yes in wicker. Well, they'll stand out.

There's an excellent video presentation, showing how willows are grown, harvested in November (machinery has taken over some of the traditional 'rowing'), processed and used in basketwork. We learn that 'bottom strength' in baskets, chairs and hampers comes from two-year-old canes. Stripping is still by hand. It used to be done in the field as part of harvesting by women and children, but is now a separate task. White-coloured canes are kept in water till May and have their bark removed without stripping; buff are steamed; brown is achieved naturally.

Old notices emphasise the different way of life with its own lingo, regulations and threats to those who didn't pull their weight in the effort to keep rhynes clear.

Chris Coate, who runs the centre, says his is the fifth generation of willow-growers on both sides of his family. 'Not easy today, with unlimited imports, and it is pretty labour intensive. That's why we've diversified into the visitors centre, tourism really, like so many, but at least we still have eighty acres of willows in cultivation and the Centre is a real working industry, which is why it's closed on Sundays when the machines are untended. There are still four or five willow-growing families with around 250 to 300 acres, but it used to be more like 3,000 acres.

'They say we're an independent lot, and I suppose so, but willows are different and there's a lot of working out there on your own. Mind you, the media like us to be twee. At the end of the day we're in business. Though imports are a nightmare, we export to 35 countries, especially charcoal, another of our products, for sketching. And here in the visitors' centre we're about to open a tea-room.' He recommends a pub for lunch.

Stoke St Gregory and the next villages we pass through going north seem prosperous and the route provides a welcome pub lunch. Then again past Burrow Mump and up the A361, before heading north across country through Shapwick, one of a row of villages on slightly elevated ground overlooking the empty moor to the north. On Shapwick Heath we cross the remains of the original main line of the Somerset & Dorset Railway, from Burnham-on-Sea. The 'Bath Extension' came later. The original line across the Levels used to serve the peat industry both here and at Bason Bridge, where Fisons have now closed down. Once peat seemed marvellously organic and green. Expensively, I used to buy a lorry load yearly for my fruit farm. Now, it's 'a diminishing resource' and extraction is frowned on. The National Trust have launched a new peat-free compost, and Shapwick Heath, once intriguingly criss-crossed by narrow-gauge railways taking out the peat, has become a nature reserve. People like me need to be smacked for having done the wrong thing.

Rehabilitation of much of the wetland system of the Brue Valley (the river that runs through Highbridge) is the order of the day, though there is still a small Peat Production Zone. Peat soils are highly organic and the undecomposed remains of plants rapidly break down if there's too much drainage and air is allowed, even briefly, to replace water. Severe cracking through horizontal shrinkage is a nightmare for archaeologists. Plant life does however regenerate even after there's been too much drainage. And enthusiasm seems to generate common sense among the authorities and volunteer organisations working together in a series of partnerships.

We park at the Peat Moors Centre, not as I had first imagined the peat equivalent of the Willows Centre, for they certainly aren't pushing sales of peat, raw or otherwise. It is all about history, extolling ancient trackways including the Sweet Track, discovered close by in 1970 having lain buried for 5,800 years. 'However it is probably the reconstructions of roundhouses from the Glastonbury Lake Village that leave people with a lasting impression.' All this we learn from a leaflet.

The Centre is closed, though the garden centre sharing its car park offers a friendly cup of tea (and the leaflet).

On by Wedmore, one of the next line of villages, facing south over the same no man's land, to Cheddar. It is raining again and cold with it. Never has Cheddar Gorge seemed so grim. There's nobody in sight, nobody buying the cheese still made in the gorge. All the way up the twisting gorge, parking space is blocked with foot-and-mouth signs. Even being held up by a lorry belching out black smoke would be better than this ghostly emptiness. The gloom makes it hard even to rekindle happy holiday memories. It is time to knock off and get to Bath in readiness to return to London.

FROM LONDON
WITH PRIZEGIVING
TO NANTWICH

Sacked General Manager Turned House of Lords Spokesman

First visitor when we are back in London next morning is Bill Bradshaw, almost the last general manager of the Western Region. He would have been last of all but for the fact his boss, BR supremo Sir Robert Reid, fired him, annoyed that a bad back had prevented his attending a management meeting. Bill was as approachable a general manager as he was unusual. Unusual in encouraging the managers under him to stir themselves and do something useful, orthodox or unorthodox. For example, a very Cornish Rusty Eplett at Truro was made manager of the newly-invented Cornish Railways, which gave huge pride to the Royal Duchy and soon resulted in better traffic. 'Rusty was a one-off, always on the radio, never really charging expenses.'

After his sacking, Bill pursued an academic career. What he had to say from his seat of learning made great sense, but few took much notice of a sacked railway manager. However, when the Liberals were given the opportunity to create additional life peers, he became Lord Bradshaw, a singularly appropriate title echoing the name of the old *Bradshaw* timetables that for generations were the essential tool of the travelling public (and much loved by parsons). He combines experience with good judgement, and what he says as Liberal transport spokesman in the Lords at least gets some attention. He says the boss who fired him believed in 'creative tension... for which read quarrelsome with all power transferred to the centre'. Creative tension is a phrase in modern management I hate as much as I love 'creative destruction' as a description of how the coming of the inter-city railway helped bring enlightenment to a Britain it transformed in its first thirty years (1830-1860). That was surely the generation that really changed the country, what's happened since merely being the completion of new trends then set in motion.

Says Bill: 'Management was by fear, a very uneasy relationship. It made it hard to persuade managers to risk doing new and better things. If you explained it to them and gave them confidence, of course some would be adventurous, but there were too many who buried their talents.'

So what about today's railways? The important thing here is that Lord Bradshaw's feelings exactly echo what all the small band of those with experience and common sense have to say. There are only those slight shades of difference between us, if I can be bold enough to include myself, that are natural within any coherent group. Yet there is *not* a coherent group, and Bill questions whether an attempt to create one would be successful, since the chiefs among them, such as Chris Green, general manager of Virgin Trains, have their individual pressures, are scattered and do not meet on a regular basis. Yet, while the opinions of those in charge of making policies seem to vary with the wind and are seldom shared between more than two or three, there is remarkable unanimity in the common sense approach which would give our railways a bright future... if only.

Bill goes on: 'It is a great pity that John Major, who wanted to return to something like the old pre-1923 railways, yielded to the Treasury and management experts who were determined to see the system split into business sectors and isolate the railway from the real world. The separation of track from operators has added a substantial extra administrative burden, people arguing within the industry rather than fighting the real opposition, rival forms of transport.

'Too many traditional railwaymen, both operators and engineers, have been pushed out of the frame in favour of marketing people and business managers who often hold engineers and operators in contempt. Once the operators were the marketing people. The new businessmen came with no railway background, full of fluster but without substance and things costed in such a way that they can prove anything. Experience showed me that any maintenance contractor does as little as possible.

'The BR system was handed over in basic good order. Traditionally, the area permanent-way inspector was there for life. He told his boss what needed doing, and the boss carefully selected the priorities he could afford, though proper training really ended when Sir Robert was chairman. Railtrack let standards slip, sweating their assets as they put it, and without practical engineers able to monitor the outside contractors, until disaster struck at Hatfield and it became clear how bad things had become.

'I think you have to go back to vertical integration, with fairly autonomous general managers as before. We need clear lines of responsibility, with real railwaymen in charge. It's daft seeing two-car trains take valuable peak-hour capacity at Paddington. Too many short trains have created congestion. Pragmatically we want the opposite of competitive running.'

Lord Bradshaw cynically talks of the 'non-safety culture'. He explains: 'Carrying people around at great speed is inevitably risky, and no matter what you do to stop them, there are bound to be occasional accidents. Of course, we should analyse and learn from them, and Hatfield was anyway different; an accident waiting to happen. But what we have is the absurd spending on a commitment to total safety, time-wasting defensive driving (creeping around is also dangerous), while the government is ambivalent toward lorry drivers using mobile phones while careering round corners.

'Trains have always been convenient for those bent on suicide. In the old days someone fetched the stationmaster, they'd go to the scene, kneel down, pull the unfortunate person out, wash their hands, and get on with things. Now traffic can be held up for hours when there's been an accident, even when the cause stares them in the face.'

Morning Coffee with Jeremy Thorpe

Time to take a taxi west, to see Jeremy Thorpe. This morning it is all Liberals. I recall a similar trip to West London to see Lord Jenkins, a superb author who on my visit, however, denied he had promised something I was certain he had; later he phoned to say he had remembered and apologised. Only big people do that. His biographies are written with understanding that only comes with quality.

When Jeremy takes Lloyd George's walking stick out of his hat stand and passes it to me commenting on how short it is, I recall I am wearing the scarf given me by the former Liberal leader in the Lords, Viscount Simon, who became a great friend in his last years, entertaining me with the recitations of his comic poetry. But what sufferings these Liberals have endured: attack for daring not to be Labour or Conservative – defeat, smear, intrigue. They also seem to have remarkable memories. When we talk about North Devon, his old constituency, and the *North Devon Railway Report* he commissioned me to undertake, Jeremy suddenly recalls that at a Barnstaple meeting well over a generation ago, he had quizzed me on one aspect rather toughly. 'You were of course right,' he says this morning. They all know everyone in Liberalism, which invites the response that if once all your MPs could almost squeeze into a single taxi, they would; and Jeremy seems to be able to call up from his memory the vote in dozens of constituencies when he all but engineered a Liberal landslide.

It is my turn to apologise. After Jeremy was forced into the wilderness, when I was the chairman of West Country Liberals, he desperately wanted a role – even one within the local North Devon constituency – to give him a peg from which he could hang occasional comments on the world. Not all the king's horses and all the king's men would persuade the North Devon people to give him a nominal role. Though most judged him innocent of the alleged infamous plot against Norman Scott, he was bad news, and North Devon had to be brought back into the fold without his involvement.

'I'm president now,' he says, confidently. So he should be. Not merely has he done so much for Liberalism, but he knows and loves his North Devon, and uniquely understands what makes it tick to its own special beat.

Because he was a Liberal, not every MP visiting his North Devon constituency extended the customary courtesy of telling him about their visit. As one might expect, Harold Wilson did. Jeremy offered him a lift from Taunton, where the car was left to save the excruciatingly slow journey by stopping train via South Molton. In his autobiography, *In My Own Time*, he describes how they set off, down the old road with its numerous bends:

All went merrily along, until we rounded a corner in remotest Exmoor to find a haywagon fully laden with bales of hay sideways on, blocking the lane. 'I suppose this has been laid on', said Harold jocularly. 'Yes', I said, 'this is an ambush by the North Devon savages.' It became clear that the shaft of the haywagon had broken and the farmer was frantically moving hay bales into the neighbouring field. I became slightly worried and turned to Harold and said: 'It is a point of honour for me to get you to your meeting on time. We must get out and help carry bales of hay, but please leave your pipe behind.' Harold rolled up his sleeves and obliged. The farmer said: 'Good evening, Mr Thorpe, I am sorry to delay you.' He kept looking quizzically at Harold, as if to ask: 'Where did I last meet you?' 'Oh', I said, 'Let me introduce you. This is Mr Harold Wilson who has very kindly come down to help us with the hay harvest!' 'Very kind, I'm sure', said the farmer.

But the point of the story Jeremy especially enjoys is that Harold later confirmed that the small number of people at the meeting was exactly what he had forecast as they had left Taunton. Nobody stirred in North Devon without Jeremy knowing.

I first recall him as a bouncy man who could mimic anyone and who revived that almost evangelical fervour that Liberalism once enjoyed in the deep rural West. He won at the second attempt in 1959, the only new

Liberal of that general election. When he became Liberal leader, times were hard, the party nearly bankrupt. Largely through his persuasion, four million voted Liberal. It didn't show in MPs; 'and ever since we've been haunted by the 1970 election when we received only 18,000 fewer votes but lost seven seats.' The bitter lesson of those days has now led to the Liberal Democrats winning the highest number of seats for generations.

Knowing that he has long suffered from Parkinson's disease, it is delightful to discover his sharp mental agility is unimpaired. He talks of his passionate belief in electoral reform, how with it Britain might have retained Ireland, Mandela was a wonderful man, but Zimbabwe's Mugabe as bad as Uganda's Amin of an earlier era, and how Thatcher had been as bad as Lloyd George with favours granted. 'I've been tempted to write a book on unseating petitions because of corruption through the ages.' He nods enthusiastically when I mention the human dynamo that was Lillian Prowse, the North Devon Liberal Agent.

We also discuss his highly readable autobiography. This cannot avoid the trial on conspiracy to murder, a not very edifying episode in British legal history. This morning he talks of how he felt let down by his Liberal colleague Peter Bessell. 'The case would never have started had one piece of vital evidence that came through later been in place then.' Instead of feeling bitter, he remembers how many had still voted for him when he lost his North Devon seat after he had been forced by the brouhaha to resign as party leader. He correctly assumes I would not have questioned his innocence; it is more than likely that South Africa, still white-controlled, engineered it. 'The trial itself was not fairly reported, he says, 'but then *The Sunday Telegraph* had offered to double its generous payment to Bessell for articles, if the verdict was guilty.'

Prizegiving at the English Speaking Union

On the way to my Charitable Trust's annual prizegiving, I ask the taxi to drop me in Berkeley Square, and walk to the corner where *Reader's Digest* used to be. Lighter memories are of the reaction of taxi drivers when they saw where I was going: 'Tell them to stop mailing me,' and 'Do they ever actually pay out their prizes?' Heavier memories...? No, not today.

Outside Dartmouth House, the English Speaking Union's august headquarters, I run into David Thorp, who was head at 3is in Bristol when they lent us significant money and who, in a break from his career in finance, became the ESU's director-general. For a while he employed me as consultant for building their membership. Recommendations to the governing body of such organisations are usually enthusiastically received... and shelved. Soon David was back to finance, but today he's revisiting the ESU as one of our prizegivers. Walking slowly up the double staircase, where later in the day we will photograph our line-up of winners for this year's picture of the Stairway to Success, he says that publishing is no longer seen as a desirable investment. A husband-and-wife team is also bad news today. The only way for the small publisher to expand is to find a 'Business Angel'. That is someone who invests privately, enjoys tax relief and usually has a management role, often I suspect too interfering, since they will be nervous of their investment while not necessarily understanding the trade.

Richard West arrives as Trustee, and he and David refresh memories of different days. Tension builds as people, including a team from Leeds from where the new owners run *Writers' News*, start arriving for the prizegiving. Most of our competitions are still run with the magazine.

After lunch, the team of prizegivers and the winners, many supported by family, take their places in the Long Drawing Room. There is the inevitable 'Fancy seeing you'. Pam Rhodes, best known as presenter of TV's *Songs of Praise*, greets Luigi Bonomi from Sheil Land, the literary agent, for the second time today; she has only an hour ago popped in to deliver the manuscript of her latest novel. Richard West is surprised to see that the winners include the former Plymouth doctor, Hugh Montgomery, and stunned that he's won an award for self-publishing a children's book in verse.

The top table take their seats, Sheila, as the Trust's secretary, takes the chair, and we're off, with an agenda of 61 items carefully prepared by the former editor of my writing magazines, Richard Bell. We're into the two hours a year when I perhaps have a right to feel a worthwhile citizen. The packed audience looks happy, but the joy of writers collecting their certificates and cheques (and in some cases also silver cups and trophies) and having their photographs taken – and of selected poets being asked to read their winning entries aloud – knows no bounds. So what kind of people would you expect to win? There are about the same number of men and women. Even from the top table we cannot possibly guess who are the poets. In fiction and non-fiction alike, young people in their twenties and thirties are as prominent as oldies. The largest number of entries are always for ghost stories, but many have entered the race to produce the best proposal for a full-length novel. As part of the fun, I briefly interview each of the presenters, the agents (including Doreen Montgomery) being seduced into giving these promising writers a few practical tips.

Our written agenda leaves out the name of three winners who will only be announced this afternoon. The four teams shortlisted for the Writers' Circle Anthology Awards have got to know each other over their buffet lunch, so all are enthusiastic when the overall winner is announced, Strathkelvin Writers' Group who, like us, have come all the way from Scotland. Then the outright winner of the various Self-Publishing categories, who takes the title for the Self-Published Book of the Year, is declared to be Hugh Montgomery. Richard West jumps to his feet to show enthusiasm for Plymouth's achievement. Finally, the Winner of Winners. Young Kim Latham, smiling through her long golden hair, who has already collected £500 for the Summer Ghost short story is now invited back to collect the extra £1,000 as Winner of Winners. She steals the show – and talks of upgrading her word-processor with a laser printer. [Her winning story was only her second to be published, but she soon had stories accepted by three other magazines, a typical and encouraging story.]

The annual prizegiving's one disappointment is that it receives no media interest, famous writers who come to present prizes such as Edwina Currie and (pre-prison) Lord Archer hardly believing that there aren't any journalists present, except perhaps for a few local newspapers pressed into action by prizewinners in their area. [But there is a twist. Sky Television mentioned Hugh Montgomery's success with his profusely-illustrated children's narrative poem, *The Voyage of the Arctic Tern*. Seeing the newsflash, a Plymouth television journalist requested a copy, and this resulted in a rave review, and crowds going for copies to bookshops next day. Waterstone's in Plymouth ordered 200, a tenth of Hugh's print order. A doctor, now partly engaged in research at a London hospital, Hugh and his fiancée delayed their wedding to finance the book; expectations were realistic, and detail well executed. Saturday mornings meant repeated bike journeys taking copies to the Post Office. Because of the success in Plymouth, a well-known commercial publisher, Walker Books, was alerted and paid an advance, clearing the rest of the debt – the young couple were by now married – and published a substantial trade edition the following spring. The story made an excellent lead for the first issue of *Aspire*, the newsletter for the newly-formed Friends of the David St John Thomas Charitable Trust. It shows that even with modest resources, a charity really can make a difference.]

Two Hours Non-stop to Crewe

After the customary glass of wine following the prizegiving, we go to Euston to catch a train to Crewe. There is nothing more relaxing than a non-stop two-hour run – especially when you have reserved a seat in the restaurant car.

Virgin Trains, bless them, burst our bubble of enthusiasm. When we arrive in the restaurant car to take our seats, we are told that all reservations have been 'automatically cancelled'. Please move to the next coach. There we are welcomed by a steward pointing to a brief menu offering FREE refreshments. There is an assumption that if something is free you will automatically ignore anything better. The refreshments are, of course, light snacks, not the kind of thing, naughtily, we had been looking forward to. After questioning two stewards, the penny drops. 'Oh, you want d-i-n-n-e-r. Of course you can have that in the car next door, but you'll have to pay – and move.' So we change back to where we were in the first place, indeed sitting in the precise seats allocated in our automatically-cancelled reservation. One bonus is that the mobile phone brigade clearly plan so much talk that they won't be able to manage more than a snack. Only three others, phoneless, come to the restaurant car. We enjoy a satisfying steak and cheese with the rhythm of the train as sole background sound. The price is reasonable, too. Pity we had to play musical chairs first. [Soon after this Virgin announced the withdrawal of all restaurant cars as 'customers no longer want them'.]

On arrival at Crewe the sight that greets us is of a single-coach train, what railway enthusiasts call a bubble car, tastefully decorated with scenes of Devon & Cornwall. There is a long way to walk through Crewe station, still a sizeable place, though much reduced since the days of steam trains when day or night there were always waiting crowds. Little happens at night now, for people have become fonder of their own beds. First daytime trains leave earlier, for we are better at getting up these days than in most of railway history; and you can certainly leave London much later to arrive in places like Crewe and Manchester in good time for a night's sleep. Once the great junction was agog throughout the small hours. There were endless sleeping-car trains, newspaper trains and all manner of parcel trains and mail trains including the West Coast Travelling Post Office immortalised by WH Auden:

> This is the night mail crossing the Border
> Bringing the cheques and the postal order,
> Letters for the rich, letters for the poor,
> The shop at the corner, the girl next door.

Most of that business now goes by road or even air.

If you are old enough, you may record how changing trains, and especially waiting in the refreshment room for a late one at Crewe was a wartime music hall joke. The BBC's Entertainment Department was evacuated to Bangor in North Wales and, after performances, yesteryear's comedians were brought back to reality having to while away the time for their nocturnal connections, usually late and overcrowded. And in those days people were always singing 'Oh, Mr Porter, what shall I do? I wanted to go to Birmingham but they've taken me on to Crewe'.

Nantwich and Surrounds

Since the timetable suggested we might have to spend the whole night at Crewe, the last train to Nantwich being due to leave simultaneously with our arrival, we pre-ordered a taxi through the Crown Hotel, Nantwich, where we are going to spend the night. Our driver is at the top of the exit stairs holding up our name, and we are soon at the hotel.

It was salt springs that gave Nantwich importance in Roman days. A fire of 1583 resulted in much of it being rebuilt in half-timbered Elizabethan style. It is still attractive. Not surprisingly, our Crown Hotel, mentioned in Doomsday, is a Grade 1 listed sixteenth century coaching inn. Rebuilt in the reign of Elizabeth I, with timber from the nearby Delamere forest, it has plenty of exposed beams, creaking, not to mention uneven, floors, and crooked doors. Our room has more character than convenience; bed to bathroom is a challenging expedition, dangerous to the head and feet and knees. The hotel is in a pedestrianised area, a nice little square, but we discover that Nantwich people don't stop walking about very early and that talking loudly seems a necessary part of being a pedestrian. Until at least half past one, Crewe station would have been quieter.

In daylight the full character rather than the inconvenience of the place comes to the fore. Breakfast is good, and soon our taxi driver is back to take us south to Market Drayton, where Sheila's aunt (her father's sister) now lives, aged 99, and looking forward to receiving her telegram from the Queen. On the way to the excellent old people's home, we pass houses, old and new, delightful properties and the smallest starter homes we have yet seen.

As always, Aunt Mill is anxiously waiting. 'I've been worrying about you,' is her standard greeting. No need to worry about her... ever. She is frail, but her mind and memory are sharp. Like most living in a home, however good, she has inevitably become institutionalised and wants to show us off to her friends, the other residents. And wouldn't we like some coffee? Tea? Biscuits?

Aunt Mill kept up her own home well beyond the time most people thought she was too old and frail to look after herself. She was certainly luckier than another old lady in her nineties we know who, after she had temporarily suffered memory loss, found herself in an old people's home minus virtually all her treasured possessions. An unknown relative or friend had moved her, and claimed the spoils.

As more of us grow older and there are fewer young ones to care, even if they have a mind to, the way we treat the previous generation is going to become much more discussed. The subject rouses passion. For instance, I hate the attitude that an old person has all they will ever need. We live in a consumer society, and new things have become necessities for our well-being, not optional luxuries. 'For goodness' sake, don't buy her any more knick-knacks; dusting is already a nightmare,' and 'We don't go shopping because she doesn't need any more clothes,' said about other old ladies, are statements that bring out my natural rebelliousness. Even if a jumper for a birthday present is a size out, the pleasure it gives is priceless. Always encourage old people to live, and to use their money. Too often one sees scrimping and saving, any 'extravagance' avoided in old age, and money passed to the next generation blown away carelessly. Many old people find it hard to realise that following generations not only know how better to look after themselves but usually enjoy a fuller life style than they have done.

Aunt Mill used to live with a wide view of gently rolling country at Pipe Gate, close to other family, in the open, attractive and civilised border country of Shropshire and Staffordshire, just west of that world apart, the Potteries. There is a family legend about a bus conductor rattling off 'Adeley, Madeley, Kale and Castle,' meaning he was inviting passengers for Audley, Madeley, Keele and Newcastle-under-Lyme. When a teacher asked her class what country the Pyramids were in, a boy shot up his hand and volunteered 'Egg-ipet, Miss.'

'And how do you spell that?'

'Aye, Jay, Way, Pay, Tay.' Perfectly correct if you could understand the Stoke accent.

Even during half my lifetime, the Potteries, and especially Stoke-on-Trent, were frequently under a pall of black smoke. Stoke-on-Trent is much changed yet retains more of its traditional industry than most of those towns associated with a particular industry. It has always been that little bit different. Inevitably one thinks of it as Arnold Bennett country; what a wicked sense of humour he practised. As a boy I was much impressed by the story of the newly-married woman nagging that she needed a particular dress for a special occasion. Eventually her husband 'gave in', while actually planning to teach her a lesson. He secretly had the fancied dress copied and, at the social occasion for which it was so necessary, his wife found herself facing another woman flaunting the duplicate. Bennett, as gritty as his Five Towns, was one of the few novelists to deal with trade and everyday jealousies.

So back north again across the county border, alongside the Shropshire Union Canal. That is now part of the recently revived Four Counties Ring of canals, a major tourist puller, for those who boat, cycle and walk. It is a wonderfully varied route showing off the countryside to full advantage. According to the *Four Counties Ring*, in an enterprising series of user guides written and published by Michael Pearson, 109 miles, 94 lochs and 55 boating hours, splendid sights including great engineering works to enjoy on the way. There is more restoration work nearby, notably that of the massive 125-year-old Anderton boat lift near Northwich. When completed, boats will once more be transferred between the Trent & Mersey Canal and the River Weaver fifty feet below. Exciting.

398

'Help start her up,' begs an attractive leaflet for the Boat Lift appeal supported by the Inland Waterways Association, Friends of Anderton Boat Lift, Anderton Boat Lift Trust, British Waterways and the Waterways Trust – the kind of joint effort that gets things done these days but wasn't encouraged in the first period of nationalisation. The historic boat lift, the world's first and a listed national monument, closed when it became unsafe in 1983. The leaflet must have been around a bit, for by the time this was written it was announced that reopening was imminent.

So, for the second time today, we pass Stapeley and now pay a brief visit to the Stapeley Water Gardens and Palm Tropical Oasis. It was many years ago, when producing *The Stapeley Book of Water Gardens*, that I first appreciated this corner of Britain. The book, I discover, is still around, but the two surviving brothers of the three with whom I negotiated now live in Cyprus. Though they rarely visit their property, the enterprise still carries their flavour. It was one of the earliest sales organisations to turn itself into a major tourist attraction. The gardens have grown yet larger. Today's car parks are enormous. Everything is wheelchair accessible and there is a fleet of wheelchairs at the ready. Today it is cafés in the plural. The outdoor pools and fountains, the flowering bulbs and unusual planting schemes, beckon in the sunshine. This spring day is blustery, and most of the few morning visitors head for the Tropical Oasis.

This, with its impressively tall glass roof, is as good as you will find anywhere. The free sketch map points to the zoo room, the world of frog and special exhibitions, jungle tropics, pythons, a fountain at one end of the main path round the central koi pool, the central palms area at the other, and on the other side Amazon parrots, tunnel of underwater life, sharks, macaws, and stingrays. We enjoy them, especially the humid warmth, the general scale, the waterfalls and the exotic tropical plants growing out of tree trunks.

Then back to our hotel for a sandwich, and a short walk to the station, once starting-point for a Great Western branch to Wellington, connecting with a North Staffordshire Railway branch at Market Drayton, no doubt used by Aunt Mill in her younger days.

Now Nantwich is a typical unstaffed station, though the signalling is old-fashioned semaphores and the signalman still controls the level crossing. He's Railtrack and ignores the public waving for news of their train. Not long before ours is due, the single Scenic Railways of Devon & Cornwall car we saw at Crewe last night passes in the opposite direction. 'They'll still need their ten-minute break at Crewe,' volunteers a waiting passenger, confirmed by others. 'You should just make your connection at Shrewsbury, but this is very much a backwater; trains stop only every two hours. Great place to live, though.' Eventually the scenic car returns and stops in front of us exactly when the locals had forecast.

· X X I ·

STOPPING TRAIN COUNTRY – PART I

The Wondrous Legacy

Stopping trains still reach most parts of Britain. They run beside the sea and atop cliffs opening up vistas not enjoyed from roads. They wind intimately alongside rivers. They cross mighty moors, again often away from roads. They plunge through cities, and get much closer to country towns, villages and hamlets than do motorists unless making diversions specifically to explore them. A large proportion of the routes on which they run have mellowed into becoming an attractive part of the landscape, famous for their verges, though woodland is expanding faster on railway land (routes open and closed) than in any other environment.

Above all, the stopping trains carry real people, going about their daily living, shopping, going to school, visiting hospital, or connecting into main-line trains for a visit to another part of the country. And there are people like me who still enjoy exploring by stopping train, but on nearly all routes in the national network we are in a small minority. The slow trains are an everyday thing, running at a loss, reluctantly made good by the government, without the Lottery and Millennium funding which has made possible such a recent expansion in the canal and cycle networks. These are consciously tourism, supported with the same kind of thinking as are the arts – important, but not matter of fact.

However, in addition to the national railway network, there are now dozens of restored and preserved lines, opening up their own intimate landscapes. Working and travelling on such lines is probably Britain's second most popular outdoor activity, beaten only by fishing, pulling far greater numbers than, for example, football matches. Though the benefit in opening up further tracts of landscape is enormous, the prime attraction of most of these lines is the steam engines which work them. The cult of the steam locomotive knows no bounds.

The steam engine is fascinating in many ways. Historically, it first took man faster than the speed of an animal. For generations, it brought every new piece of equipment, every visitor with new ideas (including the first trade union leaders, and politicians on their first national tours) into the countryside. Day-old chicks and young calves carried in the guard's van of passenger trains helped improve stock on the farm in the same way that making it easier for people to travel to neighbouring towns and villages resulted in better human stock and the extinction of the village idiot.

Then there is the grace and power of the locomotive, awesome with its travelling furnace. Many engines are beautifully designed, deserving the names bestowed on them. They excite youngsters, while we oldies remember when they were still the workhorses of commercial communication and holiday journeys. At least two of the people featured in these pages admitted to playing truant when the first of the latest express class came to their town.

Finally, there is that great relationship between man and machine. 'She' needs understanding, coaxing. Sometimes you can tell the character of the drivers from their locomotive's performance... and, uniquely, the steam engine can for a time give out more power than is being made, for steam is stored as well as made on the journey.

For all this, and much though I enjoy the privilege of footplate rides, the locomotive is to me but a small part of the country railway. It is the landscape it opens up, and the way it changed things – and to some extent still does – socially and economically that fascinates me, and encourages me still to explore by train.

The impact on a valley's community of the arrival of trains can scarcely be overestimated. Where milk could economically be taken to a railhead, it doubled in price. Coal (once as important on the farm as in the factory) halved in price if there were a station within horse-and-cart range. Farm produce fetched higher prices in big cities... so much so that sometimes increases in price resulted in local food riots.

People started attending the funerals of far-off relatives. Those curious people, tourists, began reaching even remote corners. And did you know that the first people to wear uniform in the country were railwaymen? Another first is that the stationmaster (often with a bigger part to play in local life than the minister, doctor or schoolteacher) was the first to be promoted from the ranks. Railway children were automatically expected to learn quickly at school and act responsibly. 'And you a railway child,' was a terrible telling off.

In most cases, the telegraph came with the railway. Even if you never travelled by train, you went to the station for your news and newspapers

– and for companionship and to keep an eye on things at what was nearly always the locality's chief commercial centre.

At school we were all taught that the railways made their profit from goods and that carrying passengers was the icing on the cake. This was even more true on the branch line than on main routes. Deep in the countryside, few local trains were other than spasmodically busy carrying human cargo, but business in the guard's van was consistently brisk. By making friends with the guard, the state of the local economy could be gauged. What kinds of produce were being sent to which markets, which towns and villages attracted what perishable produce such as ice cream, much of which continued to go by train long after basic groceries switched to lorries? The comparative size of mail bags was also interesting. At virtually every station, a couple of daily trains each way were met by a Post Office worker with his red trolley. Parts for broken-down boilers and tractors, letters using the railways' own urgent letter system, to which most journalists trusted their copy, racing pigeons to be released at a set time at stations down the line, empty cages collected on return journey, medical supplies... they were all in the guard's van, often reeking of the smells and echoing the sounds of the countryside.

South Molton and Life on the Branch Line

The closure of branch lines was already well under way in the Thirties. Had it not been for World War Two, the process would have gathered pace. The war put the clock back, fossilising things in a way that enables many of today's older people still to tell of the days when the occasional train chugging up and down undulating branch lines retained unique importance. My own experience, told more fully in *The Country Railway* and *The Great Days of the Country Railway*, was mainly at South Molton in North Devon, to which my family was evacuated for two years, 1942-44.

By keeping a watch on what was arriving by which train, I could not merely tell Mum the time that scarce off-the-ration sausages would be delivered to the Beehive Stores, but also see how rival businesses were faring and especially how farmers were doing. Though only a few dozen passengers arrived off the five daily passenger trains in each direction, they included virtually everyone coming in or leaving the locality, including military personnel with their passes.

After days of being seen just watching, I steadily earned the trust of the station staff, and eventually was allowed to issue tickets, weigh parcels, and signal trains including exchanging the single-line token. That involved setting up the line-side apparatus, to be done at speed by automatic exchanging in the case of one of the three daily goods trains each way, and also the many extra goods and military specials that did not stop.

The Great Western Railway's Barnstaple branch was an intimate, family affair. Everyone knew everyone, though there was natural jealousy between stations, each with its separate passenger and goods staff, signalmen and stationmaster. Neighbouring stations were linked by their own phone circuit, but talking further afield, including with Control in Exeter, had to be on the 'omnibus' circuit, to which each station responded when its own code (ours was long-short-long) was rung out.

Listening to a signalman, worried about what to do in bed on his honeymoon, given advice by the mate at the next-but-one box, taught me the basic facts of life. Listening in to conversations indeed provided a fund of memories I still draw upon in my writing. Many country railwaymen were still nervous of the phone, and spoke as though addressing a somewhat out-of-earshot public meeting, a bit like the butler Hudson in the TV series Upstairs, Downstairs. Often goods and services were exchanged by courtesy of driver or guard... especially cider for stations not fortunate enough to be close to their own pub. It might be paid for in eggs or a rabbit. A newspaper could be read at half a dozen stations, and a romantic novel make its way up and down the branch for years.

Apart from newly-promoted and relief stationmasters, whose authority sometimes went to their head, the railwaymen were the salt of the earth, working long hours for sparse pay (£3.50 for a 48-hour week for my favourite signalman whose collie, Blackie, took me for walks between trains). Being 'one of them' and often working responsibly, since they were often hard pressed, helped make me the man I became.

Evenings were especially fascinating. In season, they started with our rabbit special, the only one in Britain. Horses and carts, and tractors with makeshift trailers and lorries queued up to deposit their wooden crates with the rabbits head down, tail up. When the train arrived, its engine had to be shunted from one end to the other and allowed to take on water before its footplateman adjourned to the signalbox or went to the nearby pub, the Tinto, for a pint, while the crates were loaded. That was a smelly and sometimes bloody job, tempting railwaymen to pull out a large rabbit and replace it with a measly specimen.

Once the special was away, the big question was how late would be the evening train from Taunton, with connections from up country, and therefore where would it pass the day's last up passenger train? We did everything possible to prevent it having to 'cross' at South Molton. Uniquely — because of the heavy parcels traffic we generated — our station was signalled so that, if there was no down train, the up one would come into the down platform, beside the parcels office.

I was fourteen when I misinterpreted a telephone message which suggested that on that particular night the 'cross' between trains would inevitably have to take place at South Molton. The doodlebug raids on London had just started, and there was a wave of new evacuees. The down train was exceptionally crowded but – until my mistake delayed it – surprisingly on time. Always ready pragmatically to make the best of a situation, the signalman explained things to the guard, who sensibly suggested the standing passengers be allowed to alight for ten minutes.

'Is that a coo?' asked a Cockney. 'Would that be a rabbit?' Never were ten minutes more enjoyed or educational. My mother was there. It was the excitement of her watching me man the signal box that probably led to my misunderstanding . Till the end of her life she described it as a privilege to see city people take their first country air – on a lovely summer's evening.

Even in the war, summer Saturdays brought extra traffic, out-of condition locomotives inevitably losing time hauling trains of eight carriages instead of three up the steep gradients. The rule book for this line, built on the cheap rather late in railway history, specifically warned that time was not to be made up running downhill. Yet the permitted 6omph was far faster than anything moved on the roads in wartime. On Saturday evenings, I often answered the phone when the signalman and porter slipped to the Tinto for a quick one. Farmers anxious to know if day-old chicks or a piglet had arrived, called on the 'public telephone', which meant running down the signal box steps and unlocking the parcels office to answer it. If the enquired-after item had arrived, it would soon be fetched. At least a third of callers made their cross in the parcels' ledger because they couldn't read or write.

Useful tips could be earned from visiting horse and cattle dealers on fair and Great Market days, wanting their letters read aloud and answered. 'Show me where she says she loves me,' said a smiling horse dealer. That was worth an extra sixpence, a whole shilling in all when I swore that what I had written back to his loved one was exactly what he had told me to say. Riches indeed. Yet there was great knowledge and interest, naturally derived from earning, and seeing other people earn their livings, from the land. Reporting what a particularly go-ahead farmer was up to was big news. And there was also delight in music, even poetry.

'Here, you take her over,' said the driver of a goods train to his fireman. As we trundled over the switchback to the next station, he demanded silence as he went to his box and brought out a copy of my father's wartime paperback collection of inspirational poems called *The Inner Shrine*, (1s 3d, 'from all bookstalls and booksellers'):

FRIENDS
Last night I mused before the fire, alone;
And, as I dreamed of this thing and of that,
There suddenly rose before me, as I sat,
The faces of all the friends that I have known.
A very motley company, I own!
Yet was there none in which there did not shine
Some small, peculiar hint of the Divine –
One ray at least from the great Lustre thrown.

And, as I thought of all earth's myriad men,
Living and dead and yet to be – each still
Revealing his own glimpse of the one Will,
His own fresh gleam of the one Radiancy –
Oh, all my heart and brain grew dizzy then,
Thinking how infinite Good Itself must be.

The goods station was of course busier than the passenger one. Two full hours were allowed for the day's main shunt, the tender locomotive going to and fro dozens of times, the shunter with his pole running beside trucks to be detached and propelled into the various sidings. About twenty trucks a day arrived and departed. The goods shed was where parcels and large individual items sent at the cheaper goods rates were unloaded, while things like coal and fertilisers went straight from trucks parked on a siding into lorries. Unlike many country stations, we did not have a quarry or local industry producing lucrative outbound traffic, and neither were local conditions conducive to specialised horticulture. But we did need regular cattle specials, which required several hours' preparation with repeated shunting.

The staff told me that until recently a horse-box had been kept on hand lest someone urgently needed to take their animal with them. Horse-box business was especially brisk at the next station, Filleigh, where passengers were scarce but a weekly ticket was issued to Henry Williamson going 'all the way to Bristol to broadcast on the BBC'. Though wartime economies and hardships were obvious, it all seemed as permanent as the name 'permanent way' suggested.

Shocked was I when the signalman told me that soon after the war buses would be sufficient to cater for passengers. Often, even in the war, a three-coach train had much less than a busload of passengers on it. However, on Great Market day more women might arrive than could be accommodated on the small station bus run by the George Hotel and which delivered parcels between trains. As it happened, freight traffic declined fastest after the war, when new-found prosperity increased passenger business, especially on summer Saturdays when the crowds travelling to and from Ilfracombe taxed things to the limit. Ironically, today more South Molton people travel by train than ever. They drive to Taunton for occasional journeys to visit London or other parts of the country.

The Railway Heritage that has been Lost

The railway network is still greater than the ardent explorer is likely to use in their lifetime, but a brief word about what has been lost. I have travelled on around 150 routes now closed. From Darlington through Barnard Castle to Keswick and Workington. Beside the Tay and Dee. Through the Wye Valley at Symonds Yat and past Tintern Abbey. Along the cliffs at Robin Hood's Bay, and across the flat lands on both sides of the Humber where, sharing the driver's view from the front of the first diesel trains allowed you to see endless level crossing gates opened ahead. Up many Welsh valleys where nearly all passengers were miners, pleased to describe their work and especially ready to open up when told that Dad was a poet. What magic. I took a taxi between two stations in Grantown-on-Spey. I saw the telegram a soldier had prepared passed round the refreshment room at Moat Lane Junction to demonstrate how impossible his writing was to decipher. I arrived at Castle Cary via Westbury in the slip coach of an express that didn't even go through Westbury, and then walked to Evercreech Junction for a stopping train to Bath.

Planning itineraries with bookmarks in the timetable involved considerable ingenuity and, especially when I was still with my parents, amused other guests at hotels. Making friends with railwaymen and passengers was rewarding, and led to great experiences. A Welsh comedian on his way to his father's funeral was so enjoying our conversation that, when seeing a crowd on a platform going to market at the next town, he whipped off his socks and hung them in the window. He then snored loudly with his dress dishevelled, his bare feet up on the opposite seat. The few that got as far as opening the door decided it was better to stand elsewhere, and our private fun continued.

The other day I drove through a Welsh village where the chemist shop has long been closed, along with the railway which had a Halt over a bridge up a steep hill. When, back in the 1950s, I explained to a guard that I'd run out of film, he arranged with the driver to wait while I dashed down to the chemist and puffed my way back.

'Don't interrupt, young man,' had me explaining I had a train waiting, and the whole shop full of customers going out to check. When on another empty train on a little-used line in North Devon, I said to the guard that things seemed a bit quiet, he retorted angrily: 'We do have passengers, you know.' Mrs Thompson had gone to visit her family in Bude and would be sure to return soon.

Though many lines that were closed would be doing much better business if open today, as are most of those saved from the closure list or since reopened, undoubtedly there was dead wood in the 1950s. 'Would you prefer to move to first class or go on the engine?' was an occasional invitation when I had a train to myself. As at Tetbury, the crew sometimes delayed departure to allow a longer exploration. Like most people, for decades I have seen most of the countryside by road, but the railway offers a different view as well as an overall experience much to be relished.

Now that canals and cycleways have been so extended, and the Welsh Highland Railway to be rebuilt through the Snowdonia National Park, maybe a few more of the specially-attractive parts of the national network will also be valued as more than a utilitarian means of transport. 'Utilitarian' usually means run as cheaply as possible, which in turn means cramming in seats even against window pillars blocking visibility. A major change in attitude is overdue. 'Health & Safety' will have to be reined into sensible perspective. For example, the cost of building new stations longer than the longest train serving them (many older stations have 'grandfather' rights) deters ingenuity.

Now to our stopping train country journey. It takes us from Whitchurch to Nairn, maybe not throughout the length of the whole country, but still 578 miles by the route we are choosing, with a total of 80 stations including request stops. 'Quite enough to be going on with,' says Sheila.

'Wrong Way' to Chester

'Do you know where you are going?' challenges the conductor.

'Chester.'

'Wrong train. You should be going the other way, via Crewe.'

'But I'm meeting someone in Shrewsbury.'

'You want tickets to Shrewsbury?'

'No, we're running late, there won't be time to rebook there, and I'm not allowed on a train from a station with a booking office without a ticket.'

'That's a problem.'

'Matter of fact, it's two retired railway managers I'm meeting, and we're going to Chester together.'

'OK, tell you what. I can't issue a ticket to Chester till Whitchurch. Be my guest to Whitchurch. Rules and regulations. Hope your friends didn't make them. I'm always having to tell Nantwich people the route to Chester is by Crewe. But at least you know where you're going,' which seems to imply that some don't have a clue.

Thirty-plus people are on our single-coach train, a few joining and leaving at most stations. Some have come off other trains at Crewe, or will make connections at Shrewsbury. In between, for a few, the train provides the only practical country transport. That leaves just a small minority who choose train instead of road transport for a purely local journey. It is today's pretty standard pattern on rural railways.

Now there are no junctions between Crewe and Shrewsbury, the line providing the only link between the Wolverhampton-Shrewsbury and Crewe-Chester routes. Apart from a few goods trains, it is mainly used by expresses from South Wales to the North West, but the two-hourly stopping service obviously meets a continuing need. Even if there may not be many passengers at any one time, over a year there must be many thousands transferring.

As we approach Whitchurch, the conductor returns clutching our tickets, which he trusts us with before taking our money as a few people alight and join. 'Now you're legal.'

In my young timetable browsing days, planning trips in the hope of being able to afford them, an interesting table was headed Whitchurch, Oswestry, Welshpool and Aberystwyth. The Cambrian Railways used to begin here, at Whitchurch, where it accepted most through traffic for mid-Wales and the Cambrian coast. Alas, the whole route to Welshpool and its fascinating offshoots was closed before I had enough money.

Most of the way to Shrewsbury we are in low-lying country, less than a hundred feet above sea level. Our arrival is still ten minutes late. Shrewsbury used to be a great station where, for example, Great Western men who had driven an express all the way from Newton Abbot via the Severn Tunnel marvelled at the quite different type of locomotive the LMS provided for the rest of the journey north. All manner of trains once stopped here, many full-length ones with restaurant cars. Now virtually everything is a short diesel-unit train. Only the enormous signal box, looking so out of date and place that it should be declared a national monument, tells of different days. When the branch lines closed, the district superintendent is said to have drawn the curtains of his office window. Yet now the platform is thronged with passengers – I beg your pardon, in today's parlance, customers.

Among them, we spot Bill Kent; and, as our train comes in, we see Hugh Gould, carefully timing its arrival, comfortably ensconced at a table, where we join him. Bill and Hugh are coming with us for the rest of our Stopping Train Country trip back to Nairn. Both are former railway managers who came in for tough criticism in my railway reporting days, but we have remained friends. For a special birthday years ago, they took me from Newton Abbot on a 'day trip' to Aberdeen and Inverness, using the sleeping car service that then ran between Devon and Edinburgh.

As we head north on the Great Western's former main-line racing ground to Chester, we lament the way that BR steadily pared the network of through trains from London, removing places such as Shrewsbury, Blackpool and Lincoln. Under privatisation, one or two have been restored but, exploiting our railway legacy, much more could be achieved. My friends agree that a single through train on important secondary routes, out of peak hours if need be, could make a big difference. 'There's just not the rolling stock,' says Bill, echoed by Hugh's: 'Electrification has been stopped in its tracks under Railtrack.'

As Sheila is beginning to discover, Bill and Hugh are very different, but both seriously care as well as sharing a store of stories and gossip about yesterday's railways and railwaymen. And if Sheila thinks I am into railway minutiae, she quickly realises that Hugh is a more extreme case. Everywhere he announces how many minutes and seconds we are early or late. One station we leave ninety seconds early. 'Leaving late is bad enough, we used to tell staff, but going early is unforgivable,' declares Bill. They were the visible kind of managers who fired off memos and asked offenders to visit them in their offices – a hands-on style currently out of vogue.

We cross the Vale of Llangollen, sniffing at Wales, and start twisting and turning through Ruabon and Wrexham. Here the land is more hilly, with bubbling streams and ruins ancient and industrial. But the best view is of the Dee and Chester Castle as we approach tonight's resting place. Chester still has a decent hotel by its station and, after checking in, I join another railway friend, Rex Christiansen, for tea in the lounge. Like me, he decided to make use of his interest in railways for a career in newspapers. An enterprising chap, he married the daughter of his first paper's boss, before becoming Chester reporter for the *Liverpool Post* and then the Manchester one for the *News Chronicle*, the death of which we again briefly mourn and say how much more attractive its value system would be now than in those days of hard left and right with little liberal thinking. Rex actually left it two years before it closed, to join the BBC newsroom at Manchester, where for a period he also produced a regular railway programme.

Book writing started with a two-volume history of *The Cambrian Railways* for David & Charles. 'There've been plenty of books since, but everyone copies my original research,' a comment made by many who did original research years ago. 'But the great thing is that there's so much interest. What you published at £4 now commands at least £40 on the second-hand market.'

And the fate of the Cambrian system itself? 'It's been battered to death. I suppose it's something that you can still get to Aberystwyth and Pwllheli, and they're doing some good things, but are desperately short of rolling stock.'

Recently there was a report about a charter group being advised to go by bus as the train couldn't cope. Back to positive points: 'The Chester

City Link bus from the station, free to anyone with a train ticket, is just what's needed; and Wrexham trains now link at Bidston with the Mersey Electrics... and they're great.'

For us there is only time for a fleeting visit to central Chester, which pleased Boswell 'more than any other town I ever saw'. With its Rows (the raised arcades) and two miles of historic walls enclosing much of first-class interest, Chester is a natural attraction for overseas visitors. What I especially like, however, is the feel of the countryside. Chester is a regional centre, seldom inward looking, and much of the country around it (English and Welsh) is also highly individual. Cheshire itself is often underrated. Selling books in Chester, and meeting local authors, was very much of the City and the countryside it serves. Just one problem. While rail connections were fine, parking was even more of a nightmare than in central London. Once, when no doubt I happened to arrive when something special was taking place, I spent two hours patiently queuing and never made it even to within sight of a car park.

'They've both got hearty appetites,' says Sheila after dinner with 'the lads'. Already it is clear that Bill likes the good things of life, while gentle Hugh, someone you couldn't possibly want to hurt, is so neatly dressed in his bachelor way. With his dry humour after telling an anecdote, Bill's laugh is infectious. Hugh, with his Glaswegian humour, is more married to railways, and at breakfast next morning already has a report on the day's performance.

Manchester, the Midlands and Samplers

True to the chapter's title, we catch an all-stations train to Manchester, except that – as Hugh of course reports – we miss one request stop, and there are more suburban Network stations beyond Altrincham than provided on our route. Like Euston, Manchester Piccadilly is a 1960s functional creation, but there have been some imaginative improvements. Finding the left luggage office is an initiative test since signposting is not keeping pace with development. Eventually we win and take a taxi into what always used to be talked about as Britain's second city. Especially with its new trams, it has a real metropolitan feel about it, though competition from other centres (notably Leeds) is now tough. However, the ride from Piccadilly doesn't do the city justice. Improvements here, and along most other routes into the city, are imminent. Manchester will be making the most of the Commonwealth Games and the Queen's Golden Jubilee.

I used to spend much time here, for D&C's non-London style of publishing went down well. There were endless signing parties and special events. One evening's not very successful signing party is fixed in my memory. I had been driven by someone with extreme leftish tendencies. However, even he was upset by the fact that a crowd had gathered round an actor masquerading as the Queen. Impatiently, I took a short cut through the crowd, in front of the performance. At the bookshop, the manager said: 'It will be a bit thin tonight; tough competition with the Queen in Peter Square just round the corner.' Oh dear.

Authors were usually entertained at the Midland Hotel, where in those days trade union leaders were to be found eating in the French restaurant, and a telephone call from your room immediately brought you a newspaper neatly presented by a diminutive page boy. The boy at the head of a short queue jumped into action when the head porter blew his whistle. Manchester was also different in that its seamier side was pushed by many taxi drivers. No sooner had you got in than the driver sought to make a commission on persuading you to spend the evening at a night club with, he assured, girls who knew how to make the best of getting undressed.

We're only in Manchester for a few hours, and most of those will be at what has become an upmarket Holiday Inn, the Crowne Plaza: the same great building physically, AA 74 per cent, but this lunch time overrun by conference delegates in a way that certainly would not have happened in its railway days. Because of the conference, I can only offer my lunch guest a light meal in a lounge, but that proves good with a happy waitress saying 'No bother at all' to a special request.

Brenda Keyes, who writes needlecraft books, especially on cross stitch, tells a typical story of the joys and tribulations of being an author. Joys include networking among like-minded writers and working with a supportive agent and helpful editor. Less easy to cope with are rapidly changing fashions in publishing, and the ever-greater concentration on short-term marketing results.

When she was offered a contract by a publisher for her first book, *Alphabets & Samplers*, another craft author told her to find herself a good agent, which she did in Doreen Montgomery. 'She and Caroline are so supportive; it makes a real difference. D&C became my publishers. They were happy days; I made a lot of friends through D&C.'

But a more recent title, *Traditional Samplers*, was remaindered after only eighteen months. 'Enquiries were just starting when there wasn't any stock left. And though most other needlecraft authors have gone out of their way to be helpful, a woman lifted a lot of my material with not even an acknowledgement.'

Having developed a kits business, she has decided – here's that phrase again – to go back to basics, doing original design, mainly historical, using various techniques including cross stitch. 'Of course, all the shops I used to supply are upset, but that always happens when you give up.

I'm going to do what I want which certainly won't include the needlecraft caricatures now in fashion. The magazines are full of them.'

You feel she could have helped other businesses avoid ghastly mistakes. 'When Marks & Spencer opened their supposedly flagship store, it was obvious they were going off the rails. Even though half of it was sold to Selfridges, it still feels like a half-full office block. We had enough of Sixties-type architecture in the Sixties. There's a specially strong feeling in Manchester that we should have buildings worth looking at. Our individuality is coming back; there's great enthusiasm.

After lunch, back to Piccadilly, collecting our luggage and taking it to the far end of the station and over the bridge to the busy two through platforms. An improvement in recent years is the number of local trains running through cities, in one way, out the other. Plans have just been announced for a much-needed extension of facilities on the through platforms.

· X X I I ·

S T O P P I N G   T R A I N
C O U N T R Y – P A R T 2

Lake-District-on-Sea

We cheat only marginally by catching a through train from Manchester to Grange-over-Sands; it misses a few inner-suburban stations and one on the branch from Carnforth.

Industrial Lancashire has never appealed as much as Yorkshire. It is flatter and its towns run more into each other; and such used to be the volume of traffic that there are railways, open and abandoned, everywhere, while motorways are also pretty intrusive. Even Hugh is confused about the geography of closed lines.

Beyond Bolton man has been less intent on spoiling his surroundings though, coming this way, I never find myself relaxing until we're through Leyland, over the Ribble and beyond Preston. Then it is pleasant countryside, though in close company with the M6 – and still without hint of the great landscapes ahead.

All three railway routes north to Carlisle are magnificently endowed. The main West Coast route seriously flirts with the Lake District hills. The Settle & Carlisle, north of Leeds, was saved from closure by a successful public campaign; nicknamed the Long Drag, it commands the nation's finest main-line scenery, and we will meet it later, albeit by car. The third route is the longest, the coast line, round by Grange-over-Sands, Barrow-in-Furness, Whitehaven and Workington. Of course, we have chosen this way. Sheila scarcely believes it when she looks at the map.

Beyond Lancaster, the West Coast main line offers its unmemorable view of the Irish Sea. Then Carnforth, where platforms now only serve the coast line but there has been much renovation, and a posh restaurant is about to open. Many call in to see where Brief Encounter, starring Trevor Howard, was filmed, and the Friends of Carnforth Station want to ensure visits don't disappoint.

Swinging left off the main line, we are instantly in a different world: extensive saltings with a massive area of sand, since the sea has made one of its twice-daily retreats. Slowly crossing the long, low viaduct beyond Arnside is a joy at high tide, with miles of salt water on either side. Even now, with hungry herons on the sands, it is interesting. I make sure to look back at the National Trust's Arnside Knott from which I have enjoyed the famous view of Morecambe Bay to the south and the Lake District's mountains to the north. Our train is now part of the country, or rather seascape, it serves. The mood on board is distinctly lighter, and not just because there are now fewer passengers. We veer slightly south along a sea wall into Grange-over-Sands, where a taxi waits.

It is good to be back. The last time I was here was with 300 guests for a David & Charles Victorian Weekend. Our twenty-first birthday celebrations included taking everyone across the sands, led by the Sand Pilot of Morecambe Bay, Cedric Robinson. He and his wife Olive are dinner guests tonight. But now it is still sunny and there's time to walk through what might be called Lake District-on-Sea, especially as at most places they have to assure themselves they are on the coast – below half tide the sea is almost out of sight. It is a south-facing, charming resort with an Edwardian flavour.

People, including a party of smartly dressed women having a cup of tea in a café before catching a coach for an evening out, obviously love living here. You can see why. There are delightfully individual shops. Two family butchers still face each other across the street. The South Lakeland Council serves the place well, and it has been taken to heart by the Civic Society. There are plaques full of historical tit-bits, while the extensive gardens, with many kinds of water birds on the large lake, are a cut above those of most seaside towns. There's a sunken Victorian garden, and other separate gardens sponsored by various individuals. Perhaps because it is not the type of place to attract lager louts, Grange is thoroughly welcoming to its visitors. It offers a large choice of hotels and guest houses.

It is an excellent centre, too. The mediaeval village of Cartmel, with its neat square and priory, is within walking distance. Nearby is Ulverston, with its festivals and twice-weekly street market, and Barrow-in-Furness. The latter's publicity boasts that it is: 'a destination of surprises, a Victorian town with a proud heritage of innovation, surrounded by beautiful beaches and inspiring scenery.' The Lakes Peninsula, as they call it, must be one of the least appreciated parts of the English coastline, yet is close to large cities – and from Grange-over-Sands the southern tip of Lake Windermere is only a few miles away. The road from Barrow-in-Furness via Barrow Island to Vickerstown on the Isle of Walney, with nature reserves at the extreme ends, is interesting at any tide or season.

At Grange itself, the railway was allowed to hug the shoreline on condition it provided a promenade for the public's enjoyment. The station, now listed, was built to impress, and is one of the best small ones you will find anywhere. A notice acknowledges all those who have helped in its restoration. It even boasts that rarity, toilets (with generous baby-changing arrangements) of a quality you wouldn't object to in your own house.

Sand Pilot of Morecambe Bay

Enthused, Sheila admits it has been worth coming this way. We walk under the railway and talk of the endless fascination of seeing the tide come in and retreat, exposing many square miles of sand, and read a notice describing the historical importance of the shortcut across the sands, and warning of the hazards of the crossing. Even the OS notes that 'Public Rights of Way across Morecambe Bay can be dangerous'. Going across the sands cuts the 24 miles to Morecambe by half, and was especially popular among those making the peninsula a centre of early Christianity. There are many monastic remains.

Cedric Robinson, appointed in 1966, is only the fourteenth official Sands Guide since they began in the 1300s. They come hardy, and one can see why. Cedric was brought up on fishing – often netting shrimps way out on the edge of the sands, where the tide rushes in quicker than you could possibly walk. Fishing, with a smallholding, has always provided most of the income. The Guide has a house, but has to pay council tax, exceeding his very nominal salary. It is a royal appointment. He is sometimes described as Queen's Guide.

He has conducted the Duke of Edinburgh and many other famous people across the sands, frequently appears on television, and with Olive went to collect his OBE from Buckingham Palace, where he talked with the Queen about what must be one of the realm's most unusual jobs. Yet they are worried about their future. How will they afford a home when the time comes to hand over their official cottage?

'He's raised so very much for charity yet here we are worrying about our old age; but let's enjoy this evening,' says Olive. And they both do justice to dinner at the hospitable, small Netherwood House Hotel.

Our long-ago Victorian Weekend was at the town's largest hotel which chooses to stay aloof from the AA and local hotel guides; I can still picture our reception desk where people picked up their briefing sheets and, hours later, returned to collect their certificates to say they had accomplished the walk across the bay.

At the time of the 21st birthday, D&C had just published *Sand Pilot of Morecambe Bay*. We're all a lot older now. The main changes are that these days Cedric takes thousands more across the sands, and fishing is harder, for example shrimps lacking their former quality. He talks wistfully of rich harvests, when his father and he took out their tractors separately as far as they dare and arranged to meet at a certain spot and time.

'I know every mood of the sands, and watch their daily changes. From the shore they look flat, but they're not. They can vary in height by ten feet, and then there are fogs – that's the real worry, that a fog will come down suddenly – but I always recognise the pattern of the sands and ridges. And the quicksands. They constantly change position and can be ten feet deep. They are suspended sand, very disturbing if you trespass into them, because they offer much more resistance than water. If you struggle, you'll just sink further down. We once had to pull a chap out by ropes we'd managed to get under his arms. The suction of the sands meant he came out stark naked! Having too many people and vehicles can cause the sands to collapse, too. I always go out with my stick to test things the day before a walk.'

Olive chips in: 'He's absolutely mad about the sands. He knows what he's doing, but I don't like it when he goes out by himself and always make him promise to be careful.'

Continues Cedric: 'It can certainly be a harsh environment out there, especially in winter, but there's always so much to see, so much beauty, and birdlife. There's some good samphire, too, what they call the poor man's asparagus. Our walks are of course only in summer, but even then I have to emphasise the dangers and tell people not to wander off. In fact we always have a mobile phone and a tractor and trailer as back-up. But when you emphasise the danger, some people take more notice than others. One little boy told me: "Please, sir, if I don't make it back have my haversack – it's a new one!"

'I don't charge, and many walks are anyway for charity, but people give me all kinds of things. I once had a lovely Lowry print. And we give the walkers a certificate most of them will proudly keep for the rest of their lives. Today most walks aren't across the whole bay, but cross-bay walks from Arnside to Kents Bank. That takes just over three hours, with a rest in the middle. The memorable part is going across the Kent channel. It might mean just a paddle, or if there's a lot of water you could be thigh deep. You dry out quickly, but of course need to be properly dressed.'

As they leave, Olive gives me a copy of his second book. His first D&C title has been reprinted. Did I know that copies have gone up in price fivefold?

Ratty Country

Hugh has left by the time the rest of us descend for breakfast. He is this year's president of the Glasgow branch of the Retired Railway Officers

Association and has gone back to Lancaster to get a direct train to attend today's lunch. Sheila announces she so likes Grange-over-Sands that, rather than break her journey at Ravenglass, she'll take the next train. That just leaves Bill and me.

There is a small knot of passengers on the platform. 'This part of the line is busy,' notes Bill with professional pride. The railway benefits from a shorter route along the coast and is used by many visitors, including those going on walks, who are advised that there is little parking space at Arnside.

We catch a last glimpse of the gardens and lake, and see Sheila waving, waiting for us to clear the level-crossing so she can return by the promenade. Again close to the sea after Cartmel, even from the train we are aware of the speed of the incoming tide. The sun shines on the grass which runs down to the shore as we slow to 15 mph to cross the long Leven Viaduct. A mixture of green grasses, a few sheep, blue water of the river and greys of the sands, look like an ideal subject for a jigsaw puzzle. The view from the viaduct is compelling on both sides.

We veer inland to Ulverston. The National Park is giving priority to restoring the link between here and Haverthwaite, from which steam trains connect with ships at Lakeside. The track was torn up before the private line gained the strength to take over the whole route, making it harder to tour the Lakes by public transport. But one little piece of change has been avoided by all those who have run the Furness Railway since it lost its independence eighty years ago. The old seats with their squirrel-motif cast-iron ends are still on the station platforms. Ulverston was once an iron town. From the placard listing the new industries it has attracted, it is obvious that it has adapted well.

At Dalton-in-Furness, a large party alight for a visit to the popular South Lakes Wild Animal Park. Then the picture-postcard ruins of Furness Abbey, and the start of the roundabout loop serving Barrow-in-Furness. The station tells a sorry tale of industrial rundown and lessening of traffic going further around the coast. We have to transfer to a wretched four-wheeled Pacer. There are only a dozen passengers.

'They've done everything possible to run this section down,' comments the conductor. 'They say that the first seven miles were reduced from double to single track "by accident". I don't know how they got away with it.'

I haven't been all the way round the Lakes' coastal fringe since 1960, when I enjoyed a special train, an engineer's observation saloon. Thanks to pioneering rural transport research being mentioned in Parliament, I had been appointed director of the Lake District Transport Enquiry, the first major independent enquiry into any aspect of Britain's transport.

Then, there were several daily through services from London via Barrow-in-Furness to Workington. One even included a sleeping car to

Whitehaven in which I spent several breakfastless breakfast times; no air conditioning in those days, either. There was also heavy goods and mineral traffic, especially to Millom steel works. Ironically, one of my recommendations was to reduce the then mainly double track to single – however only with the introduction of Centralised Traffic Control, which would have greatly reduced signalling costs and allowed greater flexibility. Even today, the route has had no real modernisation. It is something that it has survived at all.

Morning coffee was served on the 1960s special; even if you had brought your own coffee this morning, you couldn't possibly drink it on the heaving Pacer. It is hard enough to concentrate on the view. That is first class going round the Duddon Sands, with a memorable glimpse – remains of the iron trade in the foreground – of the National Trust's Sandscale Hawes Nature Reserve, a fragile, ever-changing system packed with bird and plant interest. If you can only visit one reserve on the Lake's coast, make it this. It has easy and indeed historical access, first-class wildlife, dunes with stories to tell and fabulous views. I especially like the way you can see the familiar profile of the Lakeland Fells. We enjoy a glimpse of that from our rocking train as we round the estuary and veer SSW. This begins to explain that, while by West Coast main line it is only 64¾ miles from Carnforth to Carlisle, this way it is no less than 114½ miles and, of course, much slower ones. On a day like today it's worth it, but staying on the seat is a bit like riding a boisterous horse. 'They aren't meant for this length of journey,' says Bill. We stop to take on a passenger at Foxfield, now a request stop, but once the junction for Coniston. By 1960 Coniston had already lost its passenger trains, so I travelled on a goods train which, over rusty, grass-covered track, left the last-ever truck at Broughton-in-Furness, where Branwell Brontë was briefly station clerk.

Millom's industrial heyday began with the discovery of haematite near the lighthouse by Hodbarrow Point. The ore extended out under the Duddon estuary, where flooding at high tide was prevented by the 1888 Inner Barrier. After subsidence, an Outer Barrier was added. Mining, by then on a much smaller scale, ceased in 1968 and the associated ironworks, once a notable landmark, closed, leaving despair in the red-brick terraces.

With only nine passengers on board beside ourselves, it is interesting to note from my report that in 1960 the average number of passengers per train (and many more trains then) was almost fifty at Millom. But then, when I undertook the research, only just over a third of the Lake District's rural population owned a car, and the biggest single category of people lived in a household without a car.

At Silecroft we enter the only part of the National Park to reach the coast; there are splendid views of the skyline of Black Combe and the western fells, though the coast, anyway sometimes out of sight, isn't exciting. The coastal National Park section ends just beyond Ravenglass, a curious place with a three-in-one (rivers Irt, Mite and Esk) estuary system protected by sand dunes on either side of the narrow sea entrance. Cottages of the single main street look forlornly out toward mudflats, and it comes as a surprise to learn that the Romans were here in force. That was because Ravenglass is the coast's only natural harbour. So supplies were brought in. There was a fort, which the Furness Railway cut straight through, but a Roman Bath has survived well.

I'm alighting here for a different reason: the Ravenglass & Eskdale Railway. Douglas Ferreira, former general manager, meets me with his car, where I can leave our luggage during a brief visit. It was while I was conducting the Lake District Transport Enquiry that the R&E's previous owners put the line up for auction. Preventing it going for scrap metal was a close-run thing. Eskdale, unusually for this part of the world without a lake, is an especially inviting valley, and there is no better way to enjoy its detailed intimacy than from the train chugging gently along with a dozen, or maybe 100, passengers squeezed into the carriages running on the gauge of only fifteen inches. The railway fits deliciously into the gentle landscape. For decades, the arrival of the railway's quarterly journal has brought a sparkle to my eyes. Staff and passengers, railway and valley: there's perfect harmony. The railway has discreetly modernised itself (originally you sat in roofless trucks even when the western Lakes' weather was wettest) and pioneered railway signalling in a way that brought real railway signalmen along to learn.

As though it is not enough just to be there, I am ushered into the *Eskdale Belle*, an observation saloon, for coffee and shortbread. Then, a walk round the miniature but often crowded station, and to the signal box which controls the whole line by the radio signalling. Another of the railway's stalwarts, Peter van Zeller, drives this unusual diesel car up the valley. It is a lot more comfortable than the real train we have just left. As a bonus, there's a red squirrel in one of the boxes provided near the line.

Douglas tells me he began adult life as a rolling stone – and first knuckled down as salesman for the Bond mini-cars, built in Preston until the factory closed in 1964. His involvement with the railway pre-dates its purchase. 'It's been a great life. We've given so many people enjoyment, and all looks well for the future. There's planning permission to extend the line to Muncaster Castle.' There is already one through platform at Ravenglass leading to a short extension beside BR and it will continue by the Roman Bath.

Douglas ceased being GM in 1994, but you will gather is still very much involved. Peter is still on the payroll: 'I'm engine driver and curator,' he boasts. 'Know anyone else with that title?' Steam is his natural preference. After we reach the two-mile post – as far as there is time to go this morning – and he moves to the driving position at *Eskdale Belle*'s other end, he finds he cannot engage gear. So he has to drive backwards from his original position. Douglas reminds me that it is now over a third of a century since I first published the railway's history. 'I've still got my certified copy of the first edition.'

Bumpily the Wrong Way to Carlisle

Bill has meantime been at the Ratty Arms, the pub with a railway theme but – I suspect – more on account of the range of malts on offer. Our two-car train has come to a standstill before he appears. One of the units is a Sprinter with bogies. Hurrah! But it is locked empty and the conductor forces us into the other vehicle, another four-wheeled affair. Sheila has something of that look when we're in a storm at sea. 'They tried to turn me off. When he saw my ticket as we left Grange-over-Sands, the conductor said "Wrong train". But I told him we were meeting up. "So you're going to go all that way round?" he asked as though I was mad. Sitting in this, I think I am.'

With the four-wheel movement and noise, it requires concentration not to be flung to the floor. We cannot eat and talk. So while we munch our sandwiches, it is mum, but hardly silence. We now run closer to the coast than the section through the National Park. Close we may be, but it is scarcely the sort of seaside that makes me want to give up everything and make it home. It could be called plain boring but actually there is plenty of hidden interest. First comes Seascale, where the ambition of early developers to build a kind of Torquay with terraces along the contours overlooking the sea came to little. For a start, the flat boulder clay wasn't conducive to their dreams; a section of cliff has to be held back by cages filled with stones. You'll look in vain for the promised pier. Then Sellafield, the huge atomic station from which alleged escape of radioactive waste is worrying people across the Irish Sea. This is where most of the sleeping-car passengers used to alight; I never envied them working in such a miserable set of buildings – as out of place as Millom's iron works and industrial housing must have seemed in earlier times. No doubt its day will come to an end, though closing Sellafield will take longer and cost much more than did setting it up.

Later, Bill frowns at a string of what looks like do-it-yourself holiday homes, some in pretty awful condition, served by a deeply rutted lane. Next stop St Bees, where a Benedictine nunnery, later attacked by the Danes, was founded as early as AD650, though archaeologists tell us that there had been human habitation there for several thousand years. What a world apart it must have been. Or was it? As was emphasised to us in Cornwall, the sea was the main way to travel until the railway engineers and Macadam resulted in the main arteries going inland. So, when building Hadrian's Wall, the Romans naturally thought it prudent to defend the coast from St Bees to the Solway Firth with a whole string of forts.

Veering inland, we catch a glimpse of the continuing cliffs, now of deep red sandstone, and are soon running into industrial Whitehaven, with the compensation of what is today a lovely marina, protected by floodgates. Exporting coal (mainly to Ireland) was Whitehaven's staple business; you used to see strings of coal wagons parked on the quays waiting for the next ship. Because of its isolation, Whitehaven is an unusual place, though most of the original architecture of the planned seventeenth-century centre has been lost. I'm sorry there's not time to mingle with the shoppers, though. In fact, very few visitors usually do.

With an influx of passengers, the coach next door is unlocked, but with the crowd it's too late to bother moving. The brown sandstone cliffs now tell of coal. Well above the sea, we slow to fifteen mph round a curve on a section that has recently had to be rebuilt. The ridges of dark rocks stretching out into the sea are not inviting. This section has always seemed grim, and you cannot argue about its choice for a wind farm, on both sides of the track. At Parton we pass the site of one of the Roman forts; I had forgotten how picturesque the little harbour is at Harrington. Nothing picturesque about Workington, where the expanding steel works made the town turn its back on the sea.

'They're working flat out there,' says Bill, pointing to a string of trucks loaded with rails needed urgently by Railtrack to replace those cracking on curves following the Hatfield accident. 'World leader in rail technology,' boasts the factory's notice.

Today there is no junction between Carnforth and Carlisle, but once the district around Workington was thick with railways. The branch to Keswick and Penrith began here. Such was the waste in BR's early days that nobody was surprised when the very last train to call at Workington Bridge delivered a new heater for the waiting room.

With the bonus of a clear view of the Isle of Man and the Galloway hills, we hug the coast until Maryport. In the 1960s, following the closure of the harbour from which coal used to be exported to Ireland, this was the direst place in Cumbria. Now it is back in business with tourism (the sandstone quays are popular with yachtsmen) and commuting. The train is now quite full, and travels faster inland – through the countryside devastated by foot-and-mouth. Suddenly there's that terrible smell of burning cows. One pyre is well alight. Nearby dead cows are placed in a circle around another, while a pair of lorries are bringing in supplies to keep the conflagration going. Foolishly I nudge Sheila; she unhappily looks the other way, but can't avoid the smell.

So into Carlisle station where we often glance out from our sleeper in the wee hours when several platforms are full of resting local trains. As well as the West Coast main line (on which – surprise – all Virgin trains are reported running late this afternoon) four routes converge here, exclusively served by Sprinter-like trains or worse.

By South Western to Glasgow

Most of the local trains, several leaving before their connecting Virgin services have arrived, are obviously well patronised, as is ours heading for Ayr. We are taking the former Glasgow & South Western line, once a fine route, but 'rationalised'. BR's favourite trick was to throttle relegated secondary routes by singling the sections at either end. Traffic, including coal, has held up better than expected, and predictably at the end of the long singled section, a coal train is waiting for us to clear. Everyone agrees that if only funds were available it would be sensible to redouble the singled sections – and that many possibilities would be opened up by even a Saturdays-only 'proper' (ie not Sprinter-type) through train from London via Leeds, over the Settle & Carlisle, and on to Glasgow by the way we are now taking. The deliberate breaking of routes into self-contained sections has hurt. I recall how at Carlisle I put my mother on the then through train to Nottingham and how she enjoyed the Settle & Carlisle's scenery. At her age, she couldn't have managed the change at Leeds.

Conversation seems to change the moment you cross the border. Maybe the Scots are less Scottish even when they are in Carlisle. But then, as more Scottish passengers replace others alighting, we find ourselves reverting to Scottish words and phrases that have people guessing if we accidentally use them in England.

Dumfries to Kilmarnock is a great rural route, especially through Nithsdale. We gently wind and climb beside rivers and over the hills, majestic even with their tops cloud covered. Again that smell; another pyre. At Sanquhar, the station boasts 'Alight for the Southern Upland Way,' but not today, for foot-and-mouth has closed all footpaths. We pass a couple of trains carrying coal imported at Hunterston, the dock of the closed steelworks south of Largs, but at New Cumnock there's a train being loaded with coal, presumably still produced locally. Bill nostalgically points to hills where as a boy he first experienced snow; a bit like remembering where you were when President Kennedy was shot.

Through Kilmarnock, with its very Scottish large industrial buildings, and for the first time I am on a new route to ink in on my old railway map, the short link across to Troon, where we alight for the night. Troon is always enjoyable: a golfing resort with good hotels attracting upmarket Glasgow commuters. There are long sections of promenade either side of the harbour. And there is roaring business with the new ferry to Ireland, threatening Stranraer's traditional role.

I especially enjoy the view to Arran, 'Scotland in miniature'. These trips don't allow time to revisit, but the very sight of the island brings back happy memories. It is the only place about which I published a book that sold three times as many copies as the total population. It was written by Robert McLellan, most of whose work was in Gaelic. He lived in one croft up a hillside without a road, and pushed his way among the sheep to a second used as his office. We admired each other across what seemed a deep rift separating our cultures. Deeply suspicious, he wasn't exactly an easy author, but his *The Isle of Arran* remains one of the finest island books ever written.

Hugh returns from Glasgow in time for dinner, and we all declare the Lochgreen House Hotel the best of this trip. Also at dinner is the owner of the house when it was last a private home. Cochrane Duncan, who lived here for 26 years, imported Persian carpets. The magnificent examples in the drawing room were left by him when the building was sold, and others bought from his business. Tonight they are celebrating his wife's eightieth birthday.

Opened in 1991, the hotel (three AA red stars and rosettes) is lovingly run by Bill Costley, 'a young man from an ordinary background who is now one of the best-known and most successful businessmen in Scotland, started as a chef but dreamed he would one day buy a hotel of his own'. So says the publicity material for *The Costley & Costley Story* on sale at reception. The hotel is one of three now owned by him. As group hotels seem increasingly standardised and tend to economise at the edges, Britain's catering reputation will increasingly depend on such individual flair. The surrounding estate is meanwhile steadily being put back together.

'It's fine running a successful business, but so many fail,' says Hugh thoughtfully. Which is Bill's excuse to say that he nearly lost everything – and indeed did lose his inheritance and pension lump sum – as a Name at Lloyds.

'We had several terrible years. I suppose like everybody else I was greedy, but it all seemed so natural, and everyone told me that Lloyds was as safe as houses. Eventually I acted on advice from the *Daily Mail* and made what seemed a sensible investment'

More Authors than in London

Next morning, Sheila who wants to be home soonest, leaves early. The rest of us have a leisurely breakfast before catching one of the frequent electric trains between Ayr and Glasgow. The track runs close to the sea, separated only by a long golf course. Over a river bridge with a view of the Garnock estuary and its mouth, Arran and Kintyre beyond, then inland alongside the River Garnock, past several lochs, and so into the turmoil of the approaches to Glasgow, across the Clyde and into Central Station.

This is familiar ground. D&C had more authors here in Glasgow than in any other city – not excluding London. Several visits a year were based at the Central Hotel, then a fine railway institution attracting the cream of business and society. The top floor was cheaper. From it you looked down on the station's enormous roof and heard the announcer, lyrical about boat trains to Gourock (among the last to be steam hauled) and the boat connections to Dunoon, Innellan, island destinations and occasionally Tighnabruaich. Announcements ceased at night, for then there were no trains.

How different things were here was brought home by eavesdropping on neighbouring tables, especially between women over afternoon tea in the lounge. Conversations were not about poodles, lawn mowers and social trivia as you might have expected at English tea parties, but about value and money. It didn't seem to matter so much what a new garment looked like as long as it was recognised as an astute purchase. Daughters weren't just leading a good social life but earning well. They nearly all smoked before and after tea. Two prim and proper small old ladies suddenly lit up mini-cigars and complained: 'That person from Perth was perpetually pissed!' In the evening, when men predominated, Glaswegian humour came into its own, and of course drinking was heavy. Some invitations had to be politely turned down, such as: 'I've got to get drunk. I'll give you the money to get drunk with me. I've just won the contract for every motorway sign in Scotland.'

To be sure, the Glasgow of the 1960s and 1970s was pretty grimy, and at weekends a shade unruly by then English standards. After a D&C paddle steamer cruise, I spent an anxious two nights: there was nowhere safe to leave several thousand pounds in cash.

Though Scotland has now been home for well over a decade, there is less need to go to Glasgow these days. My authors and friends have dispersed... and the city isn't quite the same. Actually, it is very much better, famously the city of culture, with some of the finest buildings in the land, cleaned and wonderfully restored. It makes excellent use of its river, once little more than a sewer. People get very enthusiastic about it, but it is not the Glasgow I knew and loved, though our walk through George Square between Central and Queen Street stations is a pleasant tease.

Trains rev up as they start and disappear into the tunnel at Queen Street station's end, for the gradient up Cowlairs to Springburn is steep, originally built for working by rope. Springburn once had four large works building steam locomotives for much of the world. My namesake and close friend, John Thomas, Scotland's renowned railway historian, was a Springburn man. The first book he offered in my early publishing days was indeed *The Springburn Story*, about the locomotive works set against the town's social and economic background. After a quick read, I returned it, accepting it but requesting a few changes. That was the last time I made the mistake of returning a manuscript I was accepting, for John assumed it had been rejected, and – in depression – didn't open it for weeks.

Springburn had a large population but no bookshop. The millinery department of the Co-op agreed to stock John's book and sold hundreds, the first lesson that sales didn't have to be restricted to bookshops. John was so important to D&C that we honoured him by holding a literary lunch in a restaurant car at Springburn. He lived in one of the large tenements that were steadily being replaced with soulless tall-rise flats... till common sense reigned. He was just saved from having to move by a decision to restore the remaining old blocks, starting with his, and that made his remaining life much happier.

Retired Railwaymen in Discussion

Between Glasgow and Stirling, three former railwaymen take a professional interest in our progress and the railway's infrastructure; we have been joined by Jim Summers, now an independent consultant, who was Scotland's chief operating officer under Chris Green – 'one of the few people who knew what he was doing'. In those days, engineers exercised great influence, and the culture was one of safety.

Bill: 'It certainly isn't that now. Of course, some good things have to come from privatisation, but not the separation of track and trains. At heart the structure of BR was simple. A big bureau, yes, but everyone knew where they fitted.'

Hugh: 'Someone walked the track everyday. There were various other checks, even the whitewash car.' (If it jolted over rough track, whitewash was spilt.)

Bill: 'And the engineers on the ground reported upward till the chief mechanical engineer of each region got involved. Deficiencies were quickly remedied, though cash was always short for major works, and priorities had to be set.'

Jim: 'But unfortunately it wasn't always about value for money. "While we're putting in the new signalling, would you like the track through the tunnel and up the incline to Cowlais to be made bi-directional for £25million?" is the kind of sensible question that wasn't asked very often. Many economies were actually false. They costed the saving of an engine to justify taking off the sleeper to Stirling, but there wasn't an engine to be saved. As you'll have seen yesterday, they throttled the Glasgow &

South Western line through Dumfries by singling it at either end and we were robbed of flexibility by closing too many of the links to the coast, so handling the coal traffic from Hunterston is more expensive. The government interfered too much, of course, but privatisation has seen the baby thrown out with the bathwater: too few people who understand the engineering, too little co-operation with operators, endless blaming each other and too much work for cost accountants.'

Hugh: 'If what they spend on solicitors and accountants went into the real railway with tight control from the top, we could still show the French a thing or two.'

Jim: 'The operators and track people don't even play golf with each other now. That might sound a stupid thing to say, but Chris Green used to emphasise how valuable it was to keep in touch with those who one might need to deal with quickly. BR did silly things, but we've gone a step backward.'

Bill: 'Look, there's the last splitting distant signal in Britain.'

Jim: 'BR did a string of signalling schemes, some of them no doubt over the top. But if there's anywhere in Scotland that should have been modernised, it must be Carmuirs Junction.' [The triangle with old-fashioned manual semaphore signalling where many trains are delayed.] Of course, they were beginning to play the political game even before privatisation. Prideaux killed *The Clansman* because he wouldn't pay for the Caledonian main line to Motherwell.' [*The Clansman* was one of two daytime trains between London and Inverness, and Dr Prideaux headed InterCity.]

Hugh: 'The feeling among retired railwaymen at yesterday's lunch was that there's everything to play for, but something is going to have to be changed at the top – and soon. I'm glad I'm out of it.'

Jim: 'That's the trouble. Too many of us who at least knew our way around have retired early or quit. As I say, they've thrown the baby out with the bathwater.'

Hugh talks of the lunch he presided over in Glasgow yesterday. It was addressed by a community officer from British Waterways on the huge Falkirk lift which will complete the reopening of the Forth & Clyde Canal, closed since the 1960s. (See chapter 15.) 'There seems almost more spirit of adventure on the canals than the railways these days,' says Bill.

'Extraordinary,' agrees Hugh. 'And it is that spirit of adventure that comes out so strongly in the oral history collection of retired railwaymen's memories that I'm working on for York Railway Museum. As Bill was saying, railwaymen knew their lot, how they fitted in, but they were often at the cutting edge of new technology and developments and enjoyed a sense of real achievement. We have to get that back.'

Soon we change to a train from Edinburgh taking us through to Nairn. Fine, except for the state of the toilets. Late running had left inadequate time to check things on turnaround in Edinburgh. There often seem to be toilet problems, especially on the otherwise excellent new Turbostars. From Glasgow to Nairn, there's no shortage of passengers. People obviously want the trains, which have faster schedules than ever. But I've found myself taking the car rather than challenge my bladder. Certainly, whenever possible, many of us use the sleeper or the one daytime High Speed Train, *The Highland Chieftain*.

· XXIII ·

NORTH WEST
SCOTLAND

To Gairloch and Ullapool

First stop, well out from Dingwall on the Ullapool road, is at a remote garage where traditionally we top up with fuel and sandwiches freshly made-to-order. This will be the last time for fuel: 'No money in it,' says the proprietor. With many fewer garages, trips into sparsely populated areas require careful monitoring of the fuel gauge. Then Achnasheen, which first developed as half-way point along the 'Skye Railway' from Inverness to Kyle of Lochalsh.

'What a funny place,' says my daughter Alyss who, along with Stephen, is taking this trip with us. Unusual Achnasheen certainly is. When the railway arrived, the local inn hoped to benefit, but the new business was captured by a railway-inspired hotel with its front door on the platform. When Queen Victoria transferred from train to horse-drawn vehicle she noted there was only a small station and two or three little cottages and must have missed the hotel. Recently that burnt down, adding to the challenge of the environmental renewal project around the lake beside the station detailed on a display board.

'They're trying to make something of it, but there's nothing here,' says Alyss. That however ignores the Post Office, nicely rebuilt, and the substantial craft centre and tea room where one tenant is Susan Plowman. Her workshop and retail outlet has sufficient to occupy you while waiting for a really late train, though it might prove an expensive wait. 'We're really Scottish in our designs, not like some shops whose so-called Scottish stuff is partly sourced cheaply elsewhere. We use good silver and 18-carat gold, as in these brooches, and fine enamel is a specialty. Our problem is producing enough.' The workshop's previous owner is helping make the twenty-five silver spoons needed daily to fulfil an order from Liberty in London. She carefully wraps a delicate silver Scottish christening spoon with a rattle for a present – telling us that her two kids are among the nine at the local school. On the margin of civilisation, one family makes a notable impact in the community.

At 11.20 a smart Postbus arrives from Torridon and Kinlochewe with two passengers who have an hour and a half's wait for the next train to Inverness, though today no-one is making use of the tighter connection in the other direction. Publicity is confined to the Post Office's own *Postbus Timetable*, not widely known though fun to study. Local Post Offices stock it from time to time. The Skye Railway isn't what it was when it carried most people and goods going through this remote part. I first came through Achnasheen as the signalman juggled with no fewer than four trains passing or overtaking each other, while also shunting the day's only restaurant car from the back of the westbound to the front of the eastbound train. I still regret I couldn't afford the six-bob (30p) lunch cost for either that journey or on the Far North line where restaurant cars changed trains at The Mound.

In the Skye Railway's early days, when it ran only to Stromeferry, there was rioting as fish was landed for a waiting train on the Sabbath, and a military contingent had to rush in to restore order, putting commerce before local religious beliefs. More extraordinary, in 1880 seventeen passengers took three months to get from Inverness to Portree. They had transferred to the Highland Railway's steamer *Ferret* – hijacked by the crew. Eventually they were dropped off on an uninhabited island in the Canaries and had difficulty in conveying their plight to Spanish fishermen. Three months after their first departure, the railway thought it was generous not charging afresh for the journey from Inverness to Portree. Disguised, the *Ferret* ultimately surfaced in Melbourne, Australia.

Having followed the railway for many empty miles, the Gairloch road now takes its own single-track mountain course, dropping steeply through Glen Docherty. It is Queen Victoria's turn to describe our route. One marvels at her memory for detail when she was usually feverishly busy as Queen of many countries and Empress of India. Her *Journal of Our Life in the Highlands* says that – in 1887 – Loch Maree 'came in view most beautifully' as they descended what she called Glen Dochart. 'Very shortly after this you come upon the loch, which is grand and romantic.' Horses were changed at Kinlochewe, and they set out afresh, her factor Brown (she was sometimes secretly nicknamed Mrs Brown) on the box.

The drive along the lochside, for ten miles to the hotel of Loch Maree, is beautiful in the extreme. The hills to the right, as you go from Kinlochewe, are splendid – very high and serrated, with wood at the base of some of them. The windings of the road are beautiful, and afford charming glimpses of the lake, which is quite locked in by the overlapping mountains. There are trees, above and below it, of all kinds, but chiefly birch, pine, larch, and alder, with quantities of high and most beautiful heather and bracken growing luxuriantly, high rocks surmounting the whole. Here and there a fine Scotch fir, twisted, and with a stem and head like a stone-pine, stands out on a rocky projection into the loch, relieved against the blue hills as in some Italian view. Part of the way the road emerges altogether from the trees, and passes by a mass of huge piled-up and tumbled-about stones, which everywhere here are curiously marked, almost as though they were portions of a building, and have the appearance of having been thrown about by some upheaving of the earth. We had several heavy showers, which produced a most brilliant rainbow, with the reflection of a second, quite perfect. Then it quite cleared up, and the sky was radiant with the setting sun, which gave a crimson hue to all the hills, and lit up Ben Sleach just as I remember having seen it light up Ben Nevis and the surrounding hills at Inverlochy.

The Journal does rather go on and was never a particularly hot seller, though it enabled Disraeli to use his famous 'We authors, Mam'. A sensibly edited selection is entitled *Queen Victoria's Highland Journals*.

Loch Maree is one of those lochs that had a steamboat service with a well-publicised timetable in the Victorian era, but one presumes it is now only possible to sail along it and examine its islands privately. And a queen would scarcely stay at the Loch Maree Hotel today. Beyond the loch, up again, and more single-track road (progress hindered by timid drivers not tucking themselves smartly into passing places) down a beautiful valley and along the sea into Gairloch. In two and half hours, we have reached the west coast.

Alyss and I recall the family holiday we spent in Gairloch in a furnished bungalow in the 1970s: such a different way of life, and scenery with ever-changing skies that seemed to rush in from the Atlantic. There has been much scattered development since then, though there is no real centre, and shops and garage are still sorely taxed at busy times. The bakery I visited daily is closed. Many homes have industrial-size deep freezes and breadmakers, for fresh supplies have always been difficult. Not that freezers help with things like flowers and laundry. That means Inverness. New and innovative, however, is the imaginative Heritage Museum.

Like Iona and Skye, Gairloch is a name that frequently crops up at English cocktail parties. The magnificence of the bay and the fine sand show why. Alas, the large hotel facing Skye is now owned by a coach company, and open for only five days a week, but many properties are let by the week and also offer views to remember. For the best outlook, though, you have to go out on one of the peninsulas sheltering Gairloch and its harbour. All the minor roads that peter out at peninsula ends are fascinating along this coast. What one sees changes with every twist and turn. Feeder roads divide into more minor ones serving isolated settlements where, today, visitors renting a slice of perfection might find that their neighbour in a stylish bungalow is running a profitable business by computer and phone.

We head inland to gentle Poolewe, and then – inevitably – stop at Inverewe Gardens, the Scottish National Trust's northwest showpiece. Totally recovered from the damaging 1989 storm, the gardens warrant their reputation, for what can be grown in the mild climate at the same latitude as Labrador and Siberia is amazing. The situation, perched on the edge of Loch Ewe, is unbeatable. One is struck by the friendliness of staff helping wheel-chaired visitors enjoy it all. Even the loos are award winning, the car park spacious. Yet on busy days such as this, it is too busy and organised for me: a long way from what Osgood Mackenzie must have had in mind when he started bringing in exotic plants from warmer climes in the 1860s.

To get closer to gardening, I strike up a conversation with a young woman carefully tending a newly planted bed. Sue Pomeroy isn't shy. 'My dream came true when I pulled out a *Horticultural Weekly* from a bin and saw this job advertised. You need to be self-motivated, don't you. I studied propagation in East Sussex, but in my time I've had to sell matches on Rotterdam harbour. I'm the propagator here and look after this part of the garden. I'm just recently back from a month in South Africa. Wonderful plant life there, though we could teach them a trick or two. If you go to the walled garden, the gardener there is my partner and at the end of the season he's going to Chile. There's a lot to see and learn in the gardening world.' She's impressed when I say I published the Hilliers' books. 'Oh that bible; I used to work there, too. They've just swapped plants with the Dundonnoll Gardens.'

The gardens are extensive, and the crowds ease off even at the pond garden where the water lilies are throwing up their first leaves of the season. There are few people in Rhododendron Walk where the colourful display makes our own home efforts seem puny. Inverewe's success owes as much to its skilful wind protection as the equable climate. Bambooselem, with its maze of paths, towering eucalyptus and many other plants from the Southern Hemisphere, is particularly sheltered and, even on a busy day, almost deserted. It is named after a bamboo fence that used to hide an outer metal fence protecting against deer. The National Trust has protected the whole 60-acre site against deer but, apart from a single clump of one variety, the bamboos died from a reason we lost all ours: they flowered.

The next part of the journey is always enjoyable, and especially on a fine afternoon such as this; we have long since finished those fresh sandwiches. North along Loch Ewe, across a peninsula and then along the north-facing coast with fairy-tale beaches looking out to Gruinard Island and the low, scattered Summer Isles beyond, through the townships of First Coast, Second Coast and Little Gruinard, and soon along the south shore of Little Loch Broom. At Dundonnell, whose excellent hotel (AA 74 per cent, two red rosettes, nestling between the towering ridge of An Teallach and Little Loch Broom) we happened to stay in recently, I cannot resist a diversion to Eilean Darach to see how the restoration of the Lodge is proceeding. It is still largely in plastic wraps, but a delivery by Inverness Marble & Fireplace (who sell comfort and style to an enormous territory) suggests internal work is preceding apace. The new owners must have been at the hotel when we stayed there, for at breakfast conversation was full of the woe of slow progress. They don't rush things on the west coast. But everyone smiles at you.

Though today one notices new development, thirty years ago the eye was constantly drawn to abandoned crofts and crumbling cottages, for nobody had bothered to tidy up after the Clearances of the previous century, when landowners had realised there was more money in sheep than people and thousands of folk were literally driven away. Most of those evicted emigrated, never to see Scotland again. Many never made it to enjoy a new life; many more perhaps enjoyed material riches they couldn't have imagined when having to eke out a subsistence in the hovels on their crofts. For well over a century, everything in the remoter Highlands seemed inevitably downhill. Those who somehow stayed behind faced an increasing struggle for survival, and maybe got into the habit of smiling and enquiring kindly of neighbours and visitors to keep themselves going. Yet while everyone smiles, nowhere else in Britain will you find greater religious intolerance. The Free Presbyterian church was split by the uproar caused by the Lord Chancellor Lord Mackay attending the funeral of a Roman Catholic colleague. We are told how a local couple have ever since frostily set out for separate churches each Sunday.

As we head southeast to the National Trust's Corrieshalloch Gorge to join the direct road to Ullapool, our passengers have become restive. Who was it who asked if we couldn't have taken the direct route all the way? Today's generation lack Queen Victoria's staying power. The gorge, the most interesting in Scotland, looks attractive even following our U-shaped route around it – as a reminder of the Clearances, there's a local Destitution Road – but we lack time to explore both it and the iron suspension bridge of 1874, designed by Sir John Fowler of Forth Railway Bridge fame. The National Trust's Gorge *Development Plan* says that 'Crossing this bridge provides the visitor with a heart-stopping view into the depths... Experiencing the various emotions of fear, awe, exhilaration it provokes is the primary reason for visiting the property.' The gorge is also a convenient stopping point, especially for coaches. The plan regrets that though it does not own the car park and toilets 'this may not always be realised by visitors who associate the Trust with their poor condition'. The current main concern is preventing seedlings from adjoining commercial woodland taking root on difficult-to-reach damp ledges and ousting the rare natural flora.

We descend the valley and soon head north alongside Loch Broom itself, with a clear run to Ullapool in a beautiful setting and by far the largest place in these parts. It is seething with activity. The afternoon ferry from Stornoway on Lewis, a large roll-on roll-off vessel, is heading in. Lines of cars queue for the return trip, their passengers wandering around killing time. Once the ferry ran from Kyle of Lochalsh and was part of the Skye Railway's raison d'être. Booming traffic on this shorter route has rapidly brought extra prosperity to Ullapool and its numerous catering establishments and gift shops, notably the large workshop and showroom of Highland Stoneware, displaying very collectible pieces with Scottish scenes in vivid colours. It is more than just decorated – it's the basic design.

Though the grid system shows that Ullapool is a planned town, it is a far cry since the British Fisheries Society founded it at the height of a herring boom in 1788. Perhaps because it seems too intent on cashing in, it has never been a personal favourite – and even a visit to the fabled Altnaharrie Hotel, now closed, proved disappointing. We went by ferry (the only way) full of excitement. When booking it was explained that the dinner menu was fixed. Was there anything we didn't like? It never occurred to me that that the main course at one of Scotland's most expensive hotels would be rabbit and was criticised for 'springing' my dislike of it at the last moment. The objection comes from having seen so many bunnies deformed by myxomatosis struggle and collapse around my fruit farm in the 1950s.

James Hawkins Way Out West

We head north out of Ullapool but quickly turn left and descend toward the sea at Rhue. This is home to James Hawkins who *The Scotsman* recently described as 'one of the best contemporary landscape painters in Scotland today'. Sheila first fell in love with James's work when our Inverness accountant Andrew Duncan had several large pictures on approval while choosing that which now adorns his boardroom. Then we found a couple on sale at the Kilmorak Gallery, in a disused church out in the wilds west of Beauly. The rich colours of bold semi-impressionist scenes of lochs and sea and stark mountains is quite different from anything I personally would have bought, but its appeal grows... and now James's pictures are found in the board or reception rooms of many organisations as well as at public art galleries. Sheila has long hoped that the painting we selected at the Kilmorack Gallery might be joined by a partner.

James and his wife Flick are in their kitchen, but immediately give us the kind of welcome one comes to expect in this part of the world. James shows us where he works, and walks us round his gallery where some huge pictures – one in three separate panels – are displayed. Though occasional sales are made to individual callers, the gallery's main function is to assemble work for the major exhibitions, held in Edinburgh and Glasgow, London and overseas.

'Hanging the pictures helps me see my work in perspective,' says James. Perspective is his favourite word, and what most of his conversation is about even when he doesn't actually use it. His enthusiasm is driven by seeing things in a slightly different way. The eye is drawn to the vivid (sometimes almost raucous) colours of say the vegetation along the shore of an otherwise bleak loch, or perhaps to the evening radiance of a range of mountain tops beyond a solemn sea, or everything looks different seen through the natural trellising of close-up bushes and branches. Some paintings are more impressionistic than others, but all are unmistakably of the Western Highlands and Islands.

How did his unique style develop? 'To begin with I suppose it just happened, but once you've got something distinctive of course you work at it and try to reach perfection. And we're living here within easy reach of such provoking images.'

He clearly cares passionately about his environment. But this is not a struggling artist. He's become his own highly commercial fashion. Totting up the aggregate asking price for the score of pictures (some in several panels) in a recent exhibition, there isn't much change from £100,000. The exhibition, held at Dover Street Art Gallery in the West End, was appropriately called Way Out West. His introduction to the catalogue says:

I have often thought of the mind's eye as a camera on a long telescopic boom. If one can think in this way it is possible to picture the same scene from different viewpoints, a little to the left maybe, looking up from below or down from above. After climbing Ben Mor Coigach in the ice and snow with my son Sam in early January, I moved from considering a small enclosed space with glimpses of beyond to exploring large panoramas from a great height. The day was short but clear and we sat at two thousand feet watching the sun set behind the islands to the south, the light flooded across the sky and glinted on the water; sometimes clouds and small squalls moved between us and the islands. The sense of infinite space was tremendous and as a result I have made a series of paintings that explore many locations on both sides of the Minch. These too have multi-, not single vanishing-point perspective implicit in their construction as the eye finds distance in first one and then another part of the horizon or sky.

To live way out west in this part of Scotland is to live with a constantly changing sense of the land and the sea, to see in each calm beauty and furious wrath; it is to live both on the edge and at the centre, in the heart of nature.

James's commercial success owes much to Flick. She was joint organiser of an exhibition of many West Highland artists and sculptors called Living the Land. Its catalogue enterprisingly described not only them and their work but that of farmer, fisherman, architectural student and others with close associations with their unique environment. Always man co-operating with, or more usually battling against, the elements.

James enjoys our observations and is eager to explain detail. It is relaxing without a hint of pressure to buy – though he is delighted at Sheila's choice. The only obvious commerciality is that even at this remote spot delivery arrangements are readily on tap.

Summer Isles and Hydroponicum

Returning to the main road north, we are now in the country of serious mountains with occasional noble peaks. Soon we turn left again to take the first part of the coastal diversion that over the years has given me the deepest pleasure. More of that anon, for this evening we only follow it for forty-five minutes along two long freshwater lochs between hefty mountains, before taking the dead-end road that brings us to the Summer Isles Hotel at Achiltibuie.

'There is a marvellous amount of nothing to do in Achiltibuie,' reads the brochure, and dozens of English intent on doing it in the bar. Nothing to do? The famous Hydroponicum, where we are expected tomorrow, is bang opposite, and there is plenty of daylight, sunlight indeed, for an after-dinner walk along the road passing scattered bungalows, crofts and bleating sheep. We are back at the hotel ready to turn in before the sky reddens up over the curiously shaped Summer Isles, as the sun takes leave for the short May night.

What secrets do those assorted islands and the rugged mainland around them hold? As throughout the Highlands, the combination of beauty and harshness must have inspired unsung Hans Christian Andersens. Though the coast is rich in folklore, many tales told even into the twentieth century have been lost for the lack of being written down. There would certainly have been a local monster à la Loch Ness, which is really just the best known of dozens in local folklore. *Selected Highland Folktales*, now in the House of Lochar's list (chapter I) contains part of R Macdonald Robertson's work in recording what he could find out in the 1940s and 1950s, but much is irretrievably lost.

Though we can see an inviting harbour on the largest of them, Tanera Mor, where there are cottages to rent, most of the Summer Isles are uninhabited. Summer Isles Cruises ferry sheep for their summer grazing as well as passengers to Tanera Mor, and run fishing and wildlife trips.

Next day, we don't feel like going anywhere, other than on foot to the distinctively shaped Hydroponicum. Established in the mid-1980s, its original purpose was to supply fresh produce to the hotel in a remote area where there are often storms even in the short growing season, and where anyway the soil is too thin for regular market gardening. Now a private venture, it is a nice mixture of productive and teaching unit, tourist attraction, retail outlet and eatery. I became interested in hydroponics when I bought rights to the first book published on the subject from a South African company, and sold editions to Australia and the USA as well as having it on the D&C list. It did well, though I am sure there have been many books since. Growing salad and other crops the hydroponic way has become especially popular in dry areas. Plants need to develop much smaller root systems, and can be at least 70 per cent efficient in the use of water, while in soil usually less than ten per cent of available moisture is taken up. Intrigued, once I planned a whole hydroponic greenhouse, but lost my nerve at the last moment.

In season there are conducted tours of an hour on each hour, but the manager, Nick Clooney, meets us and whisks us around the tourist parts and behind the scenes. First impressions are stunning: all kinds of vegetables and fruits, even bananas in the appropriately heated zone, are flourishing weedfree without the need for pesticides. No soil, so no soil-born pests. No blackfly either, though there is a touch of biological control and anyway bumblebees help pollinate. Fancy 35lbs of tomatoes from a single plant? Potatoes to harvest after six weeks, and more from the same plants for weeks thereafter? Delicious-tasting raspberries such as Glen Ample, eating and cooking cherries ripening with clockwork regularity? Strawberries that can be picked without stooping and are unaffected by the weather outside?

Trees naturally need deeper root systems in the growing medium, Hydroponicum Gold, a sterile mixture of perlite and vermiculite enriched with an initial supply of nutrients developed and manufactured here. This inert growing medium buffers the roots against temporary irregularities in the flow of water. A slightly different balance of nutrients is added to the water flowing round the separate circuits serving vegetables and fruit. There are also individual plants in specially-designed pyramid pots with a tapered removable top. The pyramid reduces the growing medium's top surface area to reduce evaporation. Each pot is fitted with a capillary matting wick to take up the water with nutrients to the growing medium. A plant-lover's delight: go on holiday and plants will not run dry – or be over-watered by well-meaning neighbours.

We pass two parties of eager visitors on their guided tours. Children seem enthusiastic, too: they have their own fun trail, seeking out gnomes in the cottage garden, butterflies in the South of France and lizards and frogs in the Canary Island zones. We hear several visitors say that they will try out the system themselves, 'A few will buy a pot or two, and one or two take a catalogue and think about ordering the equipment for a circuit,' says Nick.

Our tour ends at the central Lily Pond Cafe where the menu is supplemented according to what is harvested each day. It seems perfect. What are the snags?

'Making it pay,' says Nick. 'Everyone has seven jobs to cobble our income together.' As manager he is jack of all trades, helping the one and a half staff responsible for the horticultural side as well as looking after the overall business. He came to Achiltibuie after running a small landscape business and garden centre in Derbyshire. The family flat is upstairs and a second child is on the way.

'About half our visitors are Scots, who aren't renowned for being great gardeners. Less than ten per cent are from overseas. We need the admission charges – about 8,000 take a tour each year – the sale of equipment, the money from the crops we sell, and of course this café to make it work. You can see we believe in what we're doing, but it's remote here and the level of outside interest is low. We're rarely mentioned on TV or radio, for example, and if we do it tends to be quirky. It's a bit of a struggle in the winter when we're closed to visitors but still producing crops. Sometimes I think we're seen as freaks. We're different, yes. There's nowhere like this in Britain, though tomatoes are raised hydroponically in the Central Belt. As water becomes scarcer the world over, this is the future.'

Yes, we will buy a circuit, though concerned about leaks at weekends when there's nobody around. 'You'll be all right,' he says.

Back at the hotel I discover a new side to my daughter. She demolishes a huge pile of langoustines at lunch, and lingers in her deliberation over dessert. Stephen smuggles a bottle of champagne to their room before dinner. Though she is a good cook, especially for large parties, I used to think she would never be really interested in food and wine as an art form. But she's still not quite sure where she stands. She's absent when the owner tells us about tonight's fixed meal. She has told us several times that she doesn't eat red meat, so I arrange an alternative to the starter of carpaccio. When I tell her, she's annoyed: it is a special favourite, would you believe. For our part, the afternoon allows a satisfying nap, waking up to enjoy the panorama of the Summer Isles afresh, and then a stiff walk toward the end of the dead end road before another culinary treat, starting with smoked salmon instead of raw beef. We could stay here a week.

Britain's Most Scenic Minor Road

If I had to suggest which is Britain's most enjoyable minor road, it would be the huge winding loop from Drumrunie, north of Ullapool on the A835, to near Unapool and the Kylesku bridge on the A894. Nearly 60 miles long – but allow at least three hours – the loop offers non-stop drama and breathtaking scenery. Lochinver, in its middle, can be reached by an A road, but that lacks the wonderful sense of adventure as the minor road plunges and rises, twists and turns, through many types of terrain with sparse population. I wanted to call it Britain's best coastal road, for at times it offers great intimacy with salt water, and at others unbeatable distant views of sea, cliffs and islands, but the proportion of time the sea is in view is not sufficient to justify it.

At that point I must slip in that after our quiet day at the Summer Isles Hotel we returned home for a few days with Alyss and Stephen, and it is a couple of weeks later that we are back at the beginning of the loop with my cousin Anne, the retired doctor missionary we met at Peterborough in chapter 16. It is a lovely morning and after a quick early drive from Nairn we have again headed north from Ullapool to Drumrunie, raring to enjoy what the loop offers to the full. In her eighties, Anne travels widely and loves good landscape and the story of the people living in it.

Never will I forget the impression this route first made on me, back in the 1960s. There are several reasons why it felt more adventurous then. In common with most my age, I had not travelled beyond the British Isles and become blasé about the wonders of the world. I had indeed never seen such wondrous mountains as those topped with memorable peaks we raise our heads to take in on our right. Much of the route was then a rough, bumpy track. There was almost no traffic. One was truly at the edge of what we call civilisation.

The drive is scarcely tame today. The first part, to Lochinver, is known as the Motor Trail. As on the way to Achiltibuie, we pass the two long freshwater lochs but then turn north and climb through wild terrain. The only sign of life is sheep and their lambs. It is the time of year when care is needed not to hit a lamb feigning independence but in desperate need of its mum when danger appears in the form of a four-wheel drive.

Much of the way the narrow road seems to be lit up by the gorse glittering in the sun. Suddenly, on rougher surface, we are in a wood in a sheltered valley, and descend steeply with an unforgettable view of the intricacies of freshwater Loch Sionascaig – not a familiar name even to most Scots who profess to know the West Highlands. Running alongside other lochs, we then wind through more woodland, emerging for a brief run beside the sea before climbing steeply over another spur. So far we have passed a Post Office van and one car. Down another wooded valley and I pull off the road to park outside Britain's most romantically situated bookshop, Achins at Inverkirkaig.

'You must be joking,' says Anne when I say that over the years thousands of D&C books found their ultimate buyer here. Once inside, she's won over. 'Wonderful selection.'

Though reached by a drive urgently in need of attention, and in what looks more like a military hut brought from Salisbury Plain after the war than a shop, Achins is a serious bookshop well known to publishers and book buyers alike. Its ridiculous remoteness ensures that no bookish person anywhere in the area misses it. Over a period, more of the trade's personalities probably call here at least once than at any other bookshop, certainly outside London. 'True,' says Alec Dickson who is notching up nearly a twenty-year stint as its second owner. 'And they all expect me to recognise them, even in their jerseys or anoraks.'

Founded by Bangor Jones, a civil engineer, and his Gaelic-speaking wife from Lochinver, Achins was a timely gamble that paid off because of its quality and size. At noon, customers are pouring in. While some are leafing through books and a few already holding titles they are going to buy, others are seeing how they might look in an island jersey or other garment, buying cards or souvenirs, and others again ordering toasties which Alec goes off to prepare. I follow so we can talk. Recently we bought a pile of books and enjoyed a tasty toastie in relative solitude; today I want to know more about Achins and what it is like running it.

'We wouldn't be profitable without all the things we do. Indeed I opened the food side. But we don't have to be apologetic about our book stock. Many tell us we've a better selection than they see in the cities. That's because we help keep good backlist titles alive and don't make such a big thing of the latest releases.'

He has no regrets about 'having' Achins. Even when you buy it for cash, in this part of the world you don't own a property but 'have it' for your tenure. He is ready to hand it on to the next couple who ever that might be. 'Achins needs an injection of new enthusiasm. We've lost our edge a bit. We've no money to repair the drive.'

Back to the latest releases: 'Who can blame people for buying the new Delia Smith elsewhere for £9 when I'm charging £15? Like all small shops we lose out on the bestsellers, but that was never what Achins was really about. People come for the broad selection, and the experience. There's only one other bookshop between us and Thurso.'

So, though Christmas remains busy, the shop is not open much in winter. 'But it really is very hard work in high season,' he says producing toasties at a rate seldom seen in kitchens with hired staff. Forty to fifty people are milling round the shop and cafe, and there is only one assistant – obviously part-time. Usually among Achins's customers are serious walkers and climbers, for here is the starting point for the hike to Inverkirkaig Falls at the base of the sandstone dome of Suliven, sometimes described as Scotland's most distinctive mountain. No hikers today, though, for all paths are still closed because of foot-and-mouth.

Toasting more slices of bread, Alec talks about the relative merits of wholesalers and says that supply has become much easier. Elsie Bertram of Bertrams, who we will meet in chapter 25, has been a regular visitor over the years.

'What a lovely shop,' says Anne, who has chosen herself a jumper and a card or two for friends. I tell her about an earlier occasion I hoped to have lunch here. Staying in Lochinver, I thought it would make a nice walk to Achins. The three and a bit miles are, indeed, the West Highlands in miniature: a little development and village school on the outskirts of Lochinver, a steep double bend, a couple of freshwater lochs, a drive leading to a hotel, a touch of woodland, two wee settlements, great hills and finally a heavenly crescent-shaped beach. A delightful walk. On the way out we passed a hearse and cars with mourners. 'Closed for funeral,' said a notice when we arrived at Achins. Hungrily we had to walk back, again passing the mourners now returning after the funeral. We were just in time for lunch at the Culag Hotel where many other mourners were celebrating the life of a youth cut off in his prime. Once the showpiece of the Vestey family, the Culag Hotel ceased to be upmarket when a large fish market was built on land reclaimed from the sea opposite it.

Vestey's new Inver Lodge, above the village is in the AA's top 200 and is where we have lunch today. Only one other nearby table is occupied. Two women are discussing the merits of the local artist. 'You need an element of mystique, but then there's that fine line if you're going to create distance between you and your subject. He's good at listening and can bring out those special features that are unique but he depends on local inspiration for his integrity.' We'll return for a stay here after this book is finished, and for lunch maybe take a pie from the special pie shop back to our room, presuming it will not be clement enough to munch it in the open. Lochinver offers much including a good community spirit, but you can't compare its climate to the Costa del Sol's – but then, would you want to?

Back in the car, we take the main road out of Lochinver. Even it, passing alongside seven-mile Loch Assynt, has its attractions, especially for fishermen, offering good salmon, trout, Arctic charr and large cannibal ferox. Assynt is the name for a big district and famous for the fact that the Assynt Crofters' Trust organised the first community buyout of a Scottish estate. Though that was only in 1993, others have followed rapidly, giving dignity and economic hope to many crofters.

We are barely on the A road a mile when we turn north onto the second part of my favourite loop. Unlike the first section, this is awarded a number, the B869, and there is certainly more traffic. A fast road it definitely is not: almost at once we climb, only to descend down the first of the marked steep gradients to Achadhantuir, idyllically situated in woodland between lochs. There are walks in all directions. We take the winding minor road to Achmelvich, overtaking cyclists obviously bound for the large youth hostel. Even in May, it is quite busy here. The white sands and turquoise water might attract people anywhere, one thinks, before realising that not a soul can be seen on the nearby gorgeous sandy beaches. Back on the B869 and up and down another steep hill. The route is nicknamed the Breakdown Zone as visitors roar uphill in cars that have spent years on easy roads. The few overworked garages joke that, the less experienced the drivers, the faster they rev.

We briefly explore the peninsula just off to the northwest of our route, which excels with contours, dramatic cliffs, caves and a natural arch, sandy beaches, lochs, and isolated settlements reached by an extensive system of narrow roads and tracks beyond the tarmac. One track leads to the Point of Stoer at the peninsula's tip, and (slightly to the east) a view of the fabulous offshore rock pillar known as the Old Man of Stoer, where hundreds of seabirds nest and somehow teach their offspring to fly without falling into the abyss. I remember it on a wild day when wind currents suddenly lifted birds fifty feet or more skywards.

The lighthouse at Raffin is one of many built by the Stevenson brothers, one of whom was Robert Louis Stevenson's father. Louis, whose novels of course draw on experiences on remote islands, wrote: 'When the lights come out at sundown along the shores of Scotland, I am proud to think they burn more brightly for the genius of my father.' We still benefit from that genius, whose memory is refreshed even when listening to the shipping forecast. *The Lighthouse Stevensons*, by Bella Bathurst, tells a remarkable story of invention and stolid determination, often on sea-swept rocks.

Back on the B869, we take a zigzag route east, occasionally giving hands-on views of the sea and the rugged coast to the north, sometimes glimpses of the uninhabited land of highly irregular hills sheltering innumerable lochs to the south. A hint that we might be returning to more civilised country is given at the attractive little fishing-based settlement of Drumbeg. We briefly pop into Drumbeg Designs. Beside saltwater Loch Nedd there is even a rare patch of woodland. But the most testing part of the Breakdown Zone still lies ahead: a twisting switchback with repeated steep inclines. Famous climbing country is now to the south. Enjoyable though this long way round has been, Anne sighs with relief as we join the A894 and head north. At Unapool, I cannot resist dropping down the old road to the abandoned ferry terminal where, though at a dead end, the Kylesku Hotel is renowned for its seafood. From here you can catch a boat to view Britain's highest waterfall, 650ft Eas-Coul-Aulin, enjoying seals and perhaps dolphins on the way. My memories are of long waits for a small but free ferry in pre-bridge days.

The long, narrow and gracefully-curved Kylesku Bridge high above the meeting point of three major sea lochs is a delight. In a populated area this would be a point of pilgrimage, but there are only two other cars in the view point car park. Here is possibly the best information board we come across anywhere on these journeys. Not as mobile as she used to be but hating to miss out, Anne asks me to drive to the board so that she can see it from the car. It includes a map, a touch of history and suggestions of things to do on the journey south or north. She reads out the northern suggestions: 'You might consider a short loop out to Handa Island nature reserve, and you may also like to visit Kinlochbervie, where boat trips and the busy fishing market provide interesting diversions, before continuing your journey northwards to Keoldale and Durness.'

Kinlochbervie: Harbour to the Western Fishery

To keep an appointment, we have to travel express to Kinlochbervie. The first part of the road is encouragingly improved, but many narrow sections remain, not to mention steep hills. Every mile is fascinating: one moment across a machair plain colourful with spring flowers, then beside rough rocks sticking up above the world. We pass beside small freshwater lochs where white and pink water lilies will pleasantly surprise many summer visitors. At the scattered crofting-cum-catering community of Scourie, we catch a brief glimpse of another great sandy bay, and of Torridon red sandstone Handa Island, once inhabited but now a bird sanctuary. Years ago Scourie proved an excellent centre for an active weekend; boat trips allow one to land on Handa Island.

Laxford Bridge, from where there is a direct road to Lairg and the south, and then along the tip of two long sea lochs, until at the mountain rescue centre at Rhiconich we take what might be called a much unimproved road into Kinlochbervie. We stop at the Kinlochbervie Hotel, welcoming but distinctly old fashioned; 'dated', says the AA. [Next year it disappeared from the *Hotel Guide*.] Times are lean. Commercial fishing does not bring the business visitors it once did, while the local rivers are closed because of salmon disease and walkers kept away by foot-and-mouth. We are the only people staying. 'So I've prepared a dinner menu especially for you,' says the manager, who continues smiling when we hesitatingly say we'd prefer to eat at the Old School Restaurant; she even offers to make a reservation. Our huge bedroom has motley bedspreads and curtains; the bathroom is period-piece dark.

Kinlochbervie's centrepiece is the modern deep-water harbour and adjoining fish market.

Finding the harbour master, James McIntosh, means negotiating a complicated route through largely empty upstairs offices, but there is an informally warm welcome in a large room with a commanding view of the harbour and its entrance. At first he prefers to talk about his own boat and the nearly two hours it recently took to stand off Cape Wrath, the mainland's northwest tip. When eventually he talks about the harbour, I learn that the first white fish was not landed at Kinlochbervie until well after World War Two.

'That was at the old harbour, only accessible for half the tide. Here the water depth is no problem; they blasted it to 9 feet and then again to 4.3 meters. Yes, in its early years this harbour was a great boon. It helped the population climb from what they said was as low as 200 to about 600. The late 1970s into the 1980s, they were the boom years, forty boats working from here; now only twelve. They used to stack the boxes in the market seven deep. Now it isn't more than just a single layer, so you can see the lot without having to lift anything. Skippers have had to sweep the oceans to pay the bills. Nothing is as busy as it was: less diesel, salt, fewer lorries collecting the fish... and stressed skippers desperate to make a living.

'The last thing they want when they come in dejected is a harbour master shouting at them. The West Coast men play fair but go on about the French and Spaniards over-fishing, and about the regulations that result in fish having to be thrown back in. It's a nightmare all round the coast, with too much harbour capacity, too many fish markets, many of them relatively new like this, as well as too many boats. It takes hours to put the diesel on the big ones, 45,000 litres, £7,000 to £8,000 would you believe... size has gone to its limit. But they say the future will be only a handful of big boats and only a handful of buyers, too. The good times won't return. I've just happy memories of how busy it was out there.' In a reverie, he holds his arms outstretched toward the water. In happier mood, he then tells me about a £1million research project, creating a large artificial reef off Oban, which might help point to solutions for the industry's woes. I also pick up a leaflet describing the work of the Atlantic Salmon Trust, another of the growing efforts to improve fishing's long-term future.

I remember those busy days, too. When at a fishing port I have always bought the *Fishing Times,* whose pages were then joyous. Now Kinlochbervie seems cast in gloom, and I am pleased to collect the ladies and drive a few miles to the Old School Restaurant in the hamlet of Inshegra. I once had a quick snack here, noticing the blackboard and the old maps of the world of North America and the provinces of New Zealand's South Island that must have held special significance for the children of remaining families when most of the population emigrated. The maps are still there and on the tables are notebooks used by the kids. An elderly local couple, here to celebrate his 81st birthday, says that children's pets were welcome in school to help heat the classroom. 'It was always a struggle to get warm.'

The restaurant is chock-full, a far cry from eating on our own in an otherwise empty hotel dining room. Some of the guests are staying at the restaurant's own B&B; others are locals or like us have made a point of returning for a special meal. Half the guests are from overseas, mainly European, though a noisy American lady is quoting Bob Hope saying that Scotland is the only country where you experience spring, summer, autumn and winter in one day, and reading out a familiar note about how most things we take for granted today were invented by the Scots.

'This is the best school dinner I've ever had,' says Anne. Plaice with mimosa in a savoury filling with egg, cheese, parsley and breadcrumbs. Hard to resist a tempting pud; Anne and Sheila certainly can't and order different ones so they can swap. The five-year-old Bordeaux superieur costs just £10. Then off to another meeting.

We arrive back at our hotel as the local postman, George Mackay, turns up to talk about his job – 41½ hours plus ten hours overtime last week. He revels in being a vital cog in a far-stretched machine, and loves the long walks (an hour and a half to one settlement). 'No two days are ever the same. I like sorting when the mail comes in off the various Post Buses, too, but it is hard to keep my desk clear. There are three extra pressures: increasing population with more houses, mostly scattered here and there; the increasing weight of business post; but above all reorganisation. The Post Office means well, and the ideas behind each alteration are usually attractive, but there's too much change. We can't keep pace. And things they do in Glasgow or Birmingham don't automatically work out here. I start soon after seven and try and finish by 6.20 in the evening.'

As well as unwelcome red tape, he's miffed that a press statement about his long walks to outlying places appeared in the papers without his being consulted... and about non-action by his controlling office in Lairg: He adds: 'The Post Office's real problem is the unhappiness between staff and managers in the big offices. That's what has led to many firms abandoning us. Out here everyone loves us. We still deliver for Parcel Force, including mail-order clothing. OK, there's only one daily delivery and collection, and most people can't reply the day they get something, but without a unified Post Office across the country life here would be unthinkable. At least my customers are pleased to see me and thank me. That makes it worth while after a long, slippery walk when it's really nasty. It's a good life, healthy they say. The Post Office wants us to do more by van, but that's not as simple as it sounds.'

At breakfast at the hotel next morning, the manageress goes off to cook our porridge and make fresh toast. Serving the porridge, she says: 'The nearest bank is at Lairg, part-time, though there is a travelling bank – £10 a transaction unless you belong. You have to plan what you're going to need out here. They say it's a bit like living on an oil rig.'

Soon I am back at the harbour. The fishery officer laments that trade can only deteriorate. He repeats what the harbourmaster said: the local West Coast boys give little trouble, but visiting fishermen, even from the East Coast, have to be watched. 'We might have 1,000 to 1,200 boxes today,' he adds. 'Don't often get four boats in together now, but when there were forty boats working out of here six or eight were common. The auction will be at 4pm and then lorries will take the fish away through the night. Much of it will be auctioned again at Grimsby.'

The *Coronata*, spending four months working from here though normally based at Fraserburgh, is unloading fish, a couple of boxes packed with ice at a time. I ask the skipper, John Alexander, if there is any chance of buying a fresh fish. He takes me over to the huge fish market, where he tells a boy laying out the single layer of boxes in one corner to make a straight line. 'What kind of fish would you like?'

'A nice fat flatfish?'

'They don't come that thick these days. Not like they used to be before the sea had been hoovered out.' There's that phrase again.

I am appalled by the small size of the different fishes sorted on board into their separate boxes. Naively, I had thought that the best fish were whisked off south leaving the thin things for the local market. John digs deep into several boxes and discovers a good-sized turbot which that evening we eat with pleasure, well before the English-bound fish will even go on sale. We also take a few plaice. Along with most other kinds

445

of fish, they are minute. Catching fish of that size is like eating seed potatoes. When I take out my wallet, John insists: 'My pleasure. Good meeting you.'

The Far North

Back on the main road, we are on the last leg of the northbound journey. The A838 is now down to a narrow single track with passing places. The scenery is yet more surreal, and occasional swirling mist helps give the impression we might be reaching the end of the world rather than just that of mainland Britain. Between two sets of mountains, there is scarcely a sign of habitation. Finally downhill and we run beside the sheltered end of the great Sound of Durness, and make the familiar detour down to the waterside hotel opposite which the ferry starts to the desolate peninsula ending at Cape Wrath. In summer this usually makes connection with a mini-bus running on the isolated rough road up to Cape Wrath. Because of foot-and-mouth the peninsula is out of bounds except to the military. Their presence, along with frequent fogs which close the mini-bus service even in normal times, adds to the queer feeling. Previously I'd only seen Cape Wrath and the nearby highest cliffs in Britain from the sea.

Durness, where we reach the northern coast, has an unequalled setting round sandy coves, with grassy low cliff tops in between. Like most settlements in these parts, however, its population is widely scattered, as though people are afraid of each other's company. 'They choose the sites for their homes as though it were permanently sunny,' says Anne. One begins to long for the comfort of an English village centre.

An artist we are intent on meeting, Lotte Glob, works in the Craft Village, still looking a bit like the military base it used to be, a series of separate rectangular buildings with flat roofs. 'The village began well, but support has fallen away,' she says. 'It seems to happen, doesn't it? I'm pulling out, because I'm moving to Laid on the north coast to create the ultimate rock garden with many sculptures, something quite different to look at for those who take the trouble to go round the north of Scotland.

'You want to know about my creative processes? Well, they include an intense relationship with the landscape and the wilderness. From my hikes into the mountains, I bring back rocks, sediments and other materials. When I combine them with different clays, I can create sculptural forms – my response to the physical nature and their geological origins.'

We select a large, heavy plate combining a myriad of greys, fawns and blues. 'I'd have done that in white heat, 1300 degrees centigrade,' she says, adding: 'Metamorphosis. I love taking risks at high heat not knowing what will happen to some of the natural materials. You know it's different living up here. Though I'm Danish, I've been here thirty-two years. My apprenticeship in pottery was thirty-six years ago. I have to live as an individual, and never get tired of the elements in this unique landscape and interpreting them my own way.'

Her work was in the Living the Land exhibition, along with that of James Hawkins mentioned earlier in this chapter, and we had previously bought two of her plates at the Kilmorack Gallery near Beauly. In the catalogue she is described as ceramicist and mixed-media artist. And that is what is confirmed at Laid where, hopefully sheltered one day by the 3,000 newly-planted trees on an exposed site on the western side of Loch Eriboll, overlooking an island and the eastern shore, she has already displayed scores of pieces of her work ranging from the sublime to the (to our eyes) ridiculous, but unified through their unique creativity. Indeed, a celebration of life in the landscape.

If you're not already an individualist, the elements must surely make you one when spending decades up here. This is a very different Scotland. Because of the time it takes, few visitors take the circuit that includes the north coast. 'I can see why,' says a hungry Sheila, horrified at how far it still is to Tongue, where I've promised lunch. We have just passed Laid and Lotte Glob's new garden when she takes out the map and realises we have some miles yet to reach the bottom of Loch Eriboll, and it is then a long drive up its eastern shore before making progress east. Surrounded by limestone mountains, the loch was nicknamed Loch Orrible by those stationed nearby to monitor progress of the wartime convoys bound for Russia. I tell her to be grateful one no longer has to make another long detour around the Kyle of Tongue, and how much worse the road was when I first drove it in the early 1950s. The single track sections were narrower with fewer and smaller passing places. Miles and miles of supposedly main roads were unsealed.

Sealing them was a disruptive business. One was frequently waved on by roadmen to drive over bare stones. At one point, the chap in the car in front jumped out and came back to invite me to join in a protest and then, without better result, tried to coerce the drivers behind into staging a demonstration. 'Just get on, man,' was the universal response. He shouted at the roadmen. 'You should be ashamed of yourselves. It wouldn't happen in England.' Instant giggles; another crazy Sassenach.

Sparse traffic on the curved bridge over the Kyle of Tongue makes it possible to stop to take in the fine view of ebbing tide and sunlit cliffs. No sign of mist now. How I would like once more to drive all the contorted way along the north coast past invariably deserted sandy beaches and the Dounreay atomic plant, to the very individual metropolis (comparatively that is) of Thurso. The view toward Thurso includes the Orkneys, which would surely look inviting in this midday sun. Why not also visit them, a world in miniature with great scenic variation but always a friendly entrepreneurial approach to life? We could again enjoy the World Heritage Sites (plural) and, for example, explore Europe's first 'housing estate', which had been covered up by sand since prehistoric times before a storm exposed it. When we took a short holiday in Orkney, I recall saying with total sincerity that if one had to take all of life's holidays here it would be hard to exhaust the interest and things to do and see. Each island is different and, as in the Shetlands further north, there are around 600 roll-on roll-off internal ferries between the islands each week.

But after lunch at Tongue's Ben Loyal Hotel under the shadow of Ben Hope (3040ft) and Ben Loyal (2509ft), we have to set off home. There is a long way to go, so I drive hard. Anne, who finds it easier getting in and out of the front passenger seat, quickly falls asleep, and I hope Sheila will drop off too... only to learn when I stop for a moment later she says she is feeling very car sick. It is single track with frequent need to use passing places all the way to Lairg and somewhat beyond. At Lairg we meet the railway, deliberately diverted inland so that it (obviously the only one that could be afforded) served the interior as well as the coast. All the roads radiating to the west and north – the postal address of dozens of settlements is BY LAIRG – are more fun to drive than be driven. Each of them crosses a wilderness watershed before descending into friendlier terrain.

Anne wakes up just in time to see Carbisdale, more like a huge German castle standing guard over the Rhine than the youth hostel it now is, while Sheila is at last asleep. She wakes up to instruct 'Not over the Struie', a hideously curvy short cut with a great view of the Dornoch Firth, and then with amazing brightness suggests that going by the Cromarty ferry wouldn't take much longer. Of course it does, but the crossing by the minute two-car ferry is refreshing. A few weeks ago it was me who suggested coming this way. I parked where instructed for the ferry, heard a vessel out in the Firth and said 'It's coming'. Ten minutes later Sheila said: 'Coming my foot; the ferry's still closed for winter.'

Coming off the ferry today, we still have thirty miles to go. Almost simultaneously we all three mention tea. 'There's so much of Scotland,' says Anne in one of the tearooms. Yes, well 40 per cent of Britain, which taking industrialisation into account, must mean that over half of unspoilt scenery is north of the border. 'I feel as though I've seen it all these two days,' says Sheila, pouring Anne another cup. But immediately around us are the lanes and vennels and tourist attractions of the port village of Cromarty, perched at the end of the fascinating peninsula called the Black Isle.

AROUND THE WASH

Fens Furiously

We have come again by *The Highland Chieftain* from Inverness to Peterborough. It has been a good journey, mainly in mellow autumnal sunshine, crops harvested, trees beginning to turn. As ever, the highlight was the Northumberland coast past Holy Island. But as evening approaches, it rains and Peterborough is scarcely welcoming.

Peterborough is a city with much to offer, and has attractive places such as Oundle and Stamford clustered around it. If you are coming from the north or west, it also the obvious gateway to eastern England. But the journey east has never been great, by rail (though things are looking up on the surviving line) or road. Remarking that even today Peterborough brick looks more at home here than in many of the distant places to which it was transported by rail, as one of the earliest products to enjoy something like national distribution, we are immediately into impatient rush-hour traffic, stopping and starting with little more than the brake lights of the crawling vehicles ahead to enliven the scene between the successive roundabouts which have been plonked along the A47.

Gradually we become aware of the more positive attributes of the Fens. The mud on the road has been coming through gates of obviously prospering farms, and there are tractors working with powered gadgets fore and rear. We pick out a wetland sanctuary and a gravel pit, and then a rose nursery. The signposts for the village of Thorney, where the Benedictine monks, who always chose wisely, built a great abbey, are among the most enticing we have seen. It is hard for those who come through the mountains of Scotland and along the coast of Northumberland instantly to adjust to the Fens, but Sheila boosts already rising spirits by suggesting we take a side road.

So in the gloaming we arrive at Outwell (near Wisbech) via Friday Bridge and a winding road with little traffic through the village of Upwell, on the banks of what looks like a branch of the river Nene's old course before the main one was developed miles to the north in a much straighter line. Boats are tied up at the landing-stage of the hotel where today's journey ends. Inside we are fascinated by an imaginative display of historical photographs, including many of rivers and abandoned railways. Apparently this part of the navigation had once been blocked off and became foul, but today quite a few visitors arrive by boat, though the Wisbech Canal, which used to come this way, was filled in decades ago.

The Crown Lodge is a curious establishment. A notice at reception says that drinks must be ordered from the bar, but reception is the bar. To get a drink, you just have to make sure you are on the right side of the mini-partition jutting out into a snooker lounge. Soon Sheila's niece and family arrive and we all, especially the two boys, tuck into an excellent meal while we catch up with news of domestic life.

The proprietor used to run a garage here. The hotel seems to have been a change of mind. 'A five-year project which took twenty-five,' he says. He runs it with natural style and it is obviously doing well. We picked it out from the AA *Hotel Guide* for its high percentage score and red rosette. 'The fish is from the person who supplies the Queen at Sandringham. At first we didn't get many local customers. It's a poor area this, but many have moved in because property is cheap and we are benefiting.'

At bedtime I couldn't resist opening up the local Ordnance Survey maps, seeing what we had missed, and reviving memories of former Fen forays. It is not my favourite part of Britain, but I can well understand why it has many adherents. The people are marvellously individual, and ensuring that there isn't surplus water remains an obsession.

On this visit, there won't, alas, be time to explore the Old Bedford River or the equally straight New Bedford River or Hundred Foot Drain, or to hear how things are going in the half-mile wetland reserve of the Hundred Foot Washes between the two. The Ouse Washes are on quite a scale: nineteen miles long, with 65 miles of ditches acting as stock boundaries and holding rare water plant communities. There are 300 individual fields, with nearly as many different owners. Co-ordination is shared by the RSPB and the single Wildlife Trust for the four local counties. Birds such as whooper and Bewick swans, and ducks such as wigeon, gadwall, pintail, shoveller and teal, are here in internationally important populations, wigeon alone having a five-year average count of nearly 28,000.

We are especially disappointed not to have another opportunity to re-explore the complicated junction of rivers and drains that can just be glimpsed from the train to King's Lynn south of Downham Market. The key river at this junction is the Great River Ouse, and I recall the excitement when first reading the manuscript of the pioneer *The Great Ouse: The history of a river navigation*, published in 1973. Then it had national importance; today's equivalent would probably be a self-published work, selling well in its locality but not much beyond. The Great Ouse itself has much more than local importance, for it was key to the commercial prosperity of a vast territory through King's Lynn and as far inland as Bedford. For the record, both the Old Bedford River and the New Bedford River or Hundred Foot Drain are manmade short cuts, the river itself wandering off to encompass the Isle of Ely.

Two things come to mind at this point. Firstly, the Fens were seldom in the forefront of English history. It was a land of acquiescence and refuge rather than rebellion. When the Isle of Ely was hastily fortified and provided with ample food stocks, it was for defensive purposes because occasional intruders could inflict considerable damage on local farms, not as a base from which to launch major counter-attacks. Invaders on any scale were deterred by the sodden trails and precarious watercourses. So for the most part the Fens were on their own, apart from the mainstream of English history.

Secondly, there's tremendous interest in the story of the Bedford Level Corporation: shareholders' conflicting interests, opposition from those with rights and customs going back to before Doomsday, intrigue, and trial by fire as well as water, since all the records were destroyed at the London office (which it was easier for most to reach than another part of the Fens at the time of the Great Fire). It would make excellent study for anyone doing a doctorate in business. Practices, established 'time out of memory', regulated the management of the Fenland streams, and better drainage naturally hurt many people's lifestyles, especially when fish, including eels, came up fewer streams. And all that is before we bring in the engineering problems. Many familiar names crop up, not least Cornelius Vermuyden, one of many who brought their experience from Holland's hard-won land reclamation. Tenuous foundations on soft ground limited the weight of banks, which had to be consolidated slowly:

> Even within the limits imposed, the weight of the increasing heights of the flood banks caused the soft, unstable clay beneath them to spread, and the banks to sink still further, creating a vicious circle with remedial work causing even greater instability. And since the peat wasted more quickly on the dry side of the embankments than it did on the river side, the banks settled unevenly, inclining towards the Fen, until their outer slopes became dangerously steep. There were other problems. In a peat zone the almost total absence of easily accessible, stiff clay added yet another phantom to the nightmare, as this inevitably resulted in the construction of the majority of the banks from too light a soil. The consequences were obvious and inescapable. The intense

pressure to which these 'hollow counterfeit banks, made of so light a composition it will both burn and swim' were subjected at high water, made breaches unavoidable. Colonel Dodson underlined this danger in his address to the Bedford Level Corporation: 'Thus the floods increase in our rivers between the banks, and riseth, and lieth on them at a great height, and as I have said, these moory banks will deceive all that trust in them: it is confessed that the moor earth is tuff so long as it lies wet, but is good no longer then till it is rotten, and that it will be if it lie dry four or five summers, and then it sinks, and becomes a light black mould; and if it chance that a flood lie upon it but three or four days, it soaks in the water and becomes sobbed, and is neither earth nor water, and then it leaves you when you have most need of it, and drowns the fens more, than if there were no banks at all.'

The quote is from *The Great Level: A history of the drainage and land reclamation in the Fens*, which Dorothy Summers was persuaded to write after the success of her *The Great Ouse*. Later we published her *The East Coast Floods*. My earlier explorations were partly to become familiar with what these books so vividly portrayed.

Over a cup of tea in bed, next morning there's time to reread a piece by David Bellamy, helpfully putting things in broader perspective. 'Here you can see "great clouds along Pacific skies" with Lowryesque spires and steeples into the furthest distances. There is hardly a tree to get in the way of each breathtaking view.'

The Fens began taking shape at the end of the last Ice Age, when the rivers flowing out to the Wash silted and huge areas became waterlogged. Lack of oxygen killed the vegetation, which rotted to form the rich layer of peat that even the first settlers realised could produce excellent crops – if only it could be drained. Though communication was only possible by water, the Fens began providing a self-sustained, highly individual rich living with its 'boatbuilders, fishermen, eel-babbers, wildfowlers, thatchers, basket weavers, potters, wattlers, and daubers.'

Though bold drainage attempts began with the Romans, the serious business of straightening rivers, digging new channels, and cultivation on a grand scale took roughly two centuries to achieve, beginning around 1630 when the Earl of Bedford brought in Vermuyden. Each new development upset vested interests: there were even riots. Had he been around, David Bellamy would have been outraged... and rightly so, for virtually all the Fens have lost their natural character in the race to produce bigger crops. Even the very small proportion of fields which retain some peat are now well below sea level. Nowhere else has such permanent damage been inflicted, yet we produce too much food.

Mostly around its rivers and drains, the Fens have seen many fascinating engineering problems and solutions. One that comes to mind is at Crowland, north of Peterborough, where the problem was caused by an eighteenth-century diversion of the river away from a bridge thought to have been built by the monks of Crowland Abbey in 1360. Without water, the sub-soil became steadily drier, compacted and sunk, until cracks showed in the curious Trinity bridge, under which you can walk, or over which you can cross by a Venetian-like combination of steps and arches. The solution is what is called the Uretek Deep-Injection Method. High-density supportive material is injected in liquid form into the dried-out ground through small boreholes just before setting. No need to disturb the ancient structure, now curiously crossing nothing, except to fill in the cracks.

We get up bright and early, crossing the road to examine the waterway and the boats tied up opposite the hotel before breakfast, and over it recall some of the epic stories of man's fight against water on the vast area that used to be part of the Wash, and which now produces much of the food we eat and the bulbs we enjoy in spring. Not my favourite part of the country? Maybe not, but I'm finding it increasingly interesting – we pass briefly through Wisbech, catching site of The Brinks, one of the least-spoilt Georgian streets, built on the town's wealth as port and trading centre following the drainage of the Fens, and I become positively irritated that, because there is so much else of Britain to visit, they can't be properly included in these journeys. What stories each mile of waterway, navigable or not, can tell, and what riches are in the history of earlier times when there were only isolated islands of civilisation. As Hilaire Belloc skilfully put it, of all natural obstacles to communication, 'marsh, neither land nor water, is the only one wholly untraversable by unaided man'. I tell Sheila that the Fen's fabulous churches are nearly all on the sites chosen by hermits for their cells, centuries before drains, cuts and sluices became the way of life.

Terrington St Clement

We see one of them at the village we are heading for, Terrington St Clement, a large, ugly village, a few miles from the Wash of which one is always conscious but rarely sees. So far as the Wash is concerned, who knows where water meets land or where the boundary used to be or will be next. The Wash comes instantly to the mind of anyone drawing an outline map of England, yet it is the most elusive part of our coastline, a shallow, declining area of sea which some would like to place a barrage across, and others are prepared to defend to the end. Locals used to guide travellers on their way from Lincoln to Norfolk, not always without a problem. In 1205 the rising tide caught King John who lost his jewels and baggage train in quicksands near Terrington St Clement.

We don't feel we miss much as we pass through quickly to go to see what in recent times it has been best known for: the African Violet Centre. The man who developed it, Tony, or Father, Clements, meets us in the tea room. The last time we met was well over a generation ago in the boardroom at D&C. Not merely did he write the standard book *African Violets*, but the Centre purchased large quantities of the volume, and is still actively selling it.

Sometimes known as the cathedral of the marshes, Terrington St Clement's church has a vastness emphasised by its solidness, imported stone being used, since the marshes did not even yield flint, and for the detachment of its great tower. When the sea occasionally flooded here in bygone days, the tower gave the villagers a refuge and the kind folk of King's Lynn ferried in food. Sunsets over this flat, damp land are brilliant at all times seen from the road or field. What a wondrous perspective the tower must have offered in the days before planes – and presumably still does, though we haven't time even to enter the church, let alone see if one can mount the tower. We simply note the scale and fifteenth-century perpendicular appearance, for the original building, started in 1342, was eventually perpendicular-encased.

In those days Tony was an Anglican priest. Why African Violets, sometimes described as the poor man's orchid or the idiot's houseplant? After reading theology and becoming a full-time priest, he decided to earn his living independently. Working under pressure as a priest on a large housing estate, he had sought relief in growing and hybridising African Violets. So the centre was bought in 1973, and soon concentrated on retail rather than wholesale selling. He had no horticultural training, but natural affinity. The rest, as they say, is history.

The centre prospered, giving many thousands pleasure with the ever-increasing range of styles and colours that are possible with this uniquely user-friendly plant, that seems to thrive on neglect. Not that the business of creating stunning new hybridisations lacks skill, as the eleven gold medals awarded at Chelsea testify. People flock to Terrington St Clement to choose their plants from the tremendous range on offer, and thousands more are bought by mail. Though the display of African Violets, showing them in various stages of growth as well as in sheer variety, continued to be the centre's raison d'être, steadily it became a major garden centre, with an even larger mail-order plant fulfilment business meeting the postal requirements of all kinds of seed companies, newspapers and others making plant offerings to their customers.

Over our coffee, Tony points out that the teashop is a former mobile classroom. 'It was delivered in two pieces... the kind of thing we did as we grew. It was always fun.' Then he takes us round the centre, which he sold several years ago, the mail-order plant operation being sold separately for a large sum. He is greeted warmly both by the centre's new owner and former staff who still work here, obviously enthusiastically.

Glad to renew our acquaintance, we share a common value system concerning the role and purpose of business... but are on more shaky ground when we turn to theology. He was finding the Anglican church too liberal even before the ordination of women. 'That was just the last straw.' He found himself unable to go along even with Rome, so he joined the British Orthodox Church, apparently one of two rival Orthodox churches in this country, with its English bishop and ten English priests. We are to follow him to his chapel.

He is a rapid driver. King's Lynn, sometimes claimed to be England's most romantic city, now has a most effective bypass and must have improved as a result. A city of fine mediaeval merchants' buildings built to last, it was once single-minded in its devotion to trade and still exudes a feeling of Old England, though today it serves more as a regional commercial and cultural centre. Gone are the days when everyone would have been interested in the latest arrivals from the Baltic or Newfoundland. It is hard to remember that once King's Lynn and its arch-rival Boston to the north shared half the trade of England, including the sheep and wool of the East Midlands. Navigable itself to Bedford via Ely, St Ives, Huntingdon and St Neots, the Great River Ouse had tributaries also bringing in the trade of Cambridge, Thetford and Bury St Edmunds. The history of the Great Ouse is almost that of the fabric of the wealthiest part of England.

We skirt around King's Lynn, straightforwardly enough for me to take a final glance at the area on the OS map which we pass out of almost immediately: no time to see where the South Holland main drain enters the Nene, or to cross the Delph Bank and through the bulb fields of South Holland to Spalding, or for that matter again to experience the architectural richness of Boston, once Britain's second port, in a challenging situation up a river.

While Sheila follows Tony round roundabouts, I wonder if I shouldn't have started this project earlier in life... but then as a publisher I produced dozens and dozens of regional titles. Another publisher to do so was Collins, whose excellent Companion series includes a fine East Anglian volume by John Seymour. Oh dear, what have we missed: Seymour's index ingeniously starts with a list of subjects 'of specialist interest for the enthusiast', including fen lighters, fisheries, mills, tidal water and wind, wherries, wildfowling, all of special Fen significance. Then I take the official guide to Lincolnshire from the glove compartment. The first paragraph I light upon says that the independent-minded people are not easily swayed by the latest fashion and still mainly support family businesses, so there are few chain shops in the high streets which have largely retained their character. The Fens remain remarkably different, and there is good reason to believe they will continue to do so. Many agencies are working together not only to enhance the existing reserves but, helped by increasing co-operation from farmers, to rehabilitate many other areas.

Oh, why hadn't we planned to stay here longer?

King's Lynn to Seahenge

Beyond King's Lynn, thoughts naturally turn to what we more usually think of as East Anglia, Norfolk and Suffolk. I am dumbstruck to discover that my copy of John Seymour's Companion guide is of 1974 vintage. It is certainly something that today's HarperCollins wouldn't publish.

Sir William (Billie) Collins was an astute Scot out to make his company's fortune in London, with top fiction and the like, and so incidentally opening the way for Devon-based D&C to enjoy a period as the principal Scottish publisher. But he was of the old school, also building series such as the unique New Naturalist and these Companion regional volumes, which sold more slowly. He became as excited about a manuscript of solid quality as he was about a dead-cert success. He cared for the countryside, and would occasionally telephone or invite me to his London office for a discussion or piece of advice on a countryside project which, as he put it, 'would wash its face' in due course. How much more fun it would have been to explore together the different Britains that we both genuinely believed beat jetset travel; twice we followed each other around the world on trips representing our respective houses' international lists, but not expecting to find much overseas market for books about our own country.

Now, over my new-found enthusiasm for the Fens, I quickly re-read Seymour's initial description of East Anglia:

> In spite of being so near to London, East Anglia is still very much a country place. This fact has often been put down to the dreadful service of the old LNER and the utter inadequacy of the A12, but I would say that it is more probably because East Anglia is not a *pretty* place. Surrey, Sussex, Kent and Hampshire have wooded hills and valleys and picturesque little villages (the latter almost entirely inhabited by people who are either retired from – or commute to – London). And further, in the winter time, over East Anglia a cold wind blows: some people say it comes straight from Siberia. True, we have rather more sun than anywhere else in England, and our summers are lovely. And our villages are not yet inhabited by commuters, but, for the most part, by true East

Anglian country people. We have our weekenders, and we have our retired people, and they are accepted and welcomed into the community; but they do not overwhelm it as they tend to do south of London. East Anglia is a large lump of England, and our culture is very distinctive and very strong: until the Fens were drained, and the Essex forests cut down and made passable, East Anglia was very much cut off from the rest of England.

How true that was, and is still largely so, especially in Norfolk beyond Norwich, and Suffolk beyond Ipswich. Essex, by the way, though eastern England, is definitely not East Anglia, which is generally assumed to be Suffolk, Norfolk and the eastern part of Cambridgeshire. Flat for the most part, yes, but seldom dull. It is a richly varied land, with distinctive if shallow valleys, delicate folds of hills, scattered woods and trees, villages and small towns that have so obviously grown out of the countryside they serve, fabulous churches, great halls, and an intensive network of B-class roads and winding narrow lanes. Even today, the pull of London is largely expended by the time you are a dozen miles north west of Norwich and, in much of this delightfully-private world, signposts seem designed as much to confuse as encourage visitors. In North Norfolk, the pull of the sea, which forms half of the country's boundary, is probably greater than that of Norwich.

We drive only a few miles along the King's Lynn-Hunstanton road, just inland from the Wash's eastern shore, before Father Clements (as it now seems appropriate to call him) signals he is turning left, at the crossroads at Babingley. We park beside the curious St Felix Chapel. Erected in 1894-5 under the direction of Edward Prince of Wales (Edward VII), it is built of corrugated iron, lined with American pine. The roof is thatch, or you might call it mock rural, hardly fitting in with the prefab architecture. The overall impression, though definitely not indigenous, is not unpleasing. On the Queen's Sandringham country estate, it had become redundant, with wild flowers growing out of such deteriorating thatch which had not yet fallen off, when the lease was offered as a gift to the British Orthodox Church in return for a guarantee of restoration and maintenance of the churchyard.

It is cosier inside than out. The evidence of Orthodoxy is obvious. And there are no pews, just a few seats against the wall. The congregation – now fourteen – stand throughout the two-hour weekly service, participating actively. 'The time just goes so quickly,' says Father Clements. 'You don't find standing at all tedious.' I am fascinated by, rather than comprehend, many of the details he explains about the theological and historical background and the icons. Though much is beyond my experience and understanding, it is clear that Father Clements and his congregation share real joy.

St Felix, incidentally, came from what is today Burgundy. Born at the end of the sixth century, as a monk he befriended the exiled Prince Sigebert of East Anglia, who he converted to Christianity. When Sigebert was recalled to East Anglia and became King, he sent for Felix to preach to his heathen subjects. Calling first at Canterbury to receive its blessing, Felix arrived via the Wash and the Babingley River, landing only half a mile from today's chapel. That was in about AD630. Bishop Felix, as he became, established his first episcopal See at Dunwich, where his cathedral was lost to the waves along with most of that once-large place. Today he is perhaps best known for having the port of Felixstowe named after him.

Now on the road to Hunstanton, we recall that the strip between the eastern shore of the Wash and the gently undulating Norfolk hills has long been favoured: there are numerous ancient relics, mediaeval buildings, good restaurants and of course Royal Sandringham – as ugly as country houses come but with fine gardens. It was at Sandringham that King George VI died half a century ago. Each of the villages between King's Lynn and Hunstanton is characterful. It was not only St Felix who came up the small Babingley River, for it once looked as though Rising or Castle Rising would be a focal point for trade, and you could happily spend a whole day exploring 'one of the most interesting places in England for lovers of that strange and foreign race, the Normans'. The castle itself is massive. Rising's importance was curtailed when the retreating Wash left it miles inland. Again, in the Wash, where does land end and sea begin? As someone once said, God made the land, the sea and the Wash.

I never came to Hunstanton by train, but when I first visited it, the town was obviously struggling, with abandoned hotels missing the business the railway used to bring. A town facing the sea in two directions, today it is enticing, with busy Saturday morning shops, on a manageable scale with individuality.

Things change when, north of Hunstanton, the A149 turns abruptly east and the coast is north facing. This is better yet, though not so much for its villages. They tend to be narrow and as drawn-out as their settings near or on the more complex systems of tidal water. It is the rivers themselves, many protected by high dunes, and the salt marshes with their unpolluted open skies which attract many, including artists. The first of the villages, Holme-next-the-Sea, is actually off the road, far more basic than Victorian Hunstanton with its resort amenities, and is still largely inhabited by real North Norfolk people. It is said they used to enjoy the grandeur of marshes and sky meeting the sea more in a winter storm than in summer, when a few visitors were about. Yet it must once have had spiritual or other importance since two ancient routes, the Peddars Way and the Roman Icknield Way, end here. Was there once a ferry to Lincolnshire? The Romans would certainly not have liked crossing the Fens.

Then, only a few years ago, hordes of the curious came to catch a glimpse of what was media-nicknamed Seahenge, a 4000-year-old circle of 55 timbers set vertically around a great central upturned oak, submerged at high tide and in a bed of peat at low tide. By any standards, it is a remarkable discovery. The people of Holme-next-the-Sea had their peace shattered; for many, even discreet visitors going to the Norfolk Wildlife Trust's Holmes Dunes Nature Reserve were a nuisance. For their part, the ornithologists were horrified that such a publicity-creating discovery should be made bang in the middle of the reserve. A television programme, including making a replica timber circle, fanned the flames of attention and dispute.

While we are in Norfolk, the dispute rumbles on: the Druids and spiritualists angry that such a ceremonial monument should be tampered with at all; archaeologists anxious to excavate, learn and educate; and nature lovers wanting people to keep away. Tempers are not helped by English Heritage determining the monument should be reburied and then, changing sides, co-operating with the excavation. At the time of writing, no decision has been taken on the ultimate fate of the ancient timbers, currently preserved in a tank.

Little is known about Seahenge except that it must have had a deep meaning of some kind in this extreme northeastern corner of Norfolk, which has always seemed to have had a special if, again, not really understood significance. The use of the name Henge to parallel Stonehenge is understandable but not scientifically accurate. What we do know – interestingly enough – is that the Iceni tribe, under Queen Boudicca, had a bloody revolt against Roman occupation of their land, where they had a series of hill forts among the shallow valleys, and buried gold and silver neck rings (or torcs) for their gods, and that never before has man been so interested in its past as he is today.

NORFOLK

The Magic Coastline

The northwest coastal strip of Norfolk is strong in its own type of beauty, churches even grander than the highly impressive standard generally found in East Anglia, and a value system more akin to that found in Celtic Britain than, say, at busy Thetford. Yet, unlike Celtic Britain, this remote corner was fully conquered by the Romans. And that gives one the essential clue, for its character owes much to man's subservience to the elements, especially the sea. Many Roman remains have indeed been gobbled up by it. A thought: had the Romans built effective coastal defences, there would be considerably more of East Anglia today. But for the improved defences of modern times, yet more would have disappeared. We will find much evidence of the sea's greed as we work our way round the great arc of where East Anglia ends.

The rain is on, as they say in Scotland. It comes on repeatedly with increasingly heavy showers: their arrival from the North Sea we easily foretell at each glimpse of the coast from the road on toward Blakeney. They are long but marvellous miles. Brancaster, then Brancaster Staithe, a yachtsman's dream on one of the larger estuary systems also serving Overy Staithe: every village exudes maritime tradition. Most have notices offering mussels and fish for sale, and boat trips to see seals. The pubs have nautical names, including Nelson, Trafalgar and Victory. Commemorating Britain's most popular winner of battles is quite an industry in the land where he grew up and first experienced the waves. He was born at Burnham Thorpe.

Collectively the Burnhams once formed a major port, but here the sea has added to rather than taken away a piece of Norfolk. It placed them several miles inland as it dumped huge quantities of Yorkshire sand and shingle on this stretch of coast. The delights of the Burnhams – showpiece Burnham Overy and once important-Burnham Market – benefit from not being quite in the front line of tourism. Mind you, tourism here is the ultimate in discretion, heavily based on sailing, bird-watching, walking, exploring the large churches and making the most of history. Overy Staithe, which was developed to replace the Burnhams as a port, is charming with its windmill and warehouses from the days of trading vessels, and pubs and boats for today's 'mariners' who have ample estuary to explore if not wishing to go to sea.

So to Wells-next-the-Sea, unlike Holme next the Sea, hyphenated by Ordnance Survey whose maps are perhaps used as intensively here as anywhere else on Britain's seaboard. Wells has always been a personal favourite, thought about daily at home, since my grandfather clock was built here in 1701. How surprised those clockmakers (working two centuries before the motor car became a practical proposition) would be to see and hear their creations telling us it is time to turn on the telly and put supper in the microwave!

Few small coastal towns used to so consciously deny their uniqueness as Wells, which resulted in a period of indiscriminate development and loss of many flint buildings. The voice of preservationists may have made the town more self-conscious, but at least it remains unique. Sheila pipes up that we must return to explore in greater depth. Though the coast is very special, again never underrate the attraction of Norfolk-beyond-Norwich's villages, unfailingly characterful in their layouts and individual buildings in as unassuming, non-touristy a manner as you will find anywhere in England. But even as this was being written, *The Economist* reported that North Norfolk has become the latest area to be swept by the property boom, an estate agent from Holt saying three quarters of enquiries for houses come from outside the area and that larger cottages have shot up to £300,000. House prices have been increasing throughout East Anglia faster than anywhere else; having been a poor place with an oversized-cathedral, Ely is now said to be the centre of the fastest-growing area of population outside the City of London. At least North Norfolk is too far from London (in terms of time anyway) for there to be hordes of daily commuters. (A map of travel times from London shows the whole of North Norfolk further away than it is geographically, Cromer taking as long to reach as Manchester.)

Though Wells-next-the-Sea has much to offer, including boat trips and a steam narrow-gauge ride to Walsingham, personal choice of base for local exploration has always been Blakeney, which comes next on our journey. We pay to park our car on the mud left by the receding tide and go to the dining room of the Blakeney Hotel to enjoy a crab salad with the familiar view of dried-out watercourses, today's boats waiting for the tide to return and yesteryear's gently rotting on the salt marshes stretching almost to the horizon. Above the marshes, the eye catches a thin line of the bank which (usually) protects Blakeney from the sea, above which the sea is just discernable, there being no sky to be seen today.

I have always enjoyed seeing people board the pleasure boat while it is still high and dry in an empty channel next the quay that will take a circuitous route to Blakeney when the tide arrives, hesitatingly at first, and then in a rush. The boat floats rapidly and within a few minutes the water's depth is sufficient to start motoring seaward. Blakeney is a place where memories come easily: memories of invigorating walks toward the roaring sea, of the whole river system beautifully lit up at high tide by a full moon, and of buying second-hand books and quality prints and souvenirs on a special birthday.

Since then, several shops have closed to become holiday cottage booking agencies. It happens when places become too popular and the more modest demands of locals are relegated. But if Blakeney itself is now short on retail therapy, that flourishes at nearby Holt, a delightful country town with an old-fashioned grocer (whose stock must rival that of London's Fortnum & Mason) and many other excellent individual emporiums. There is also a wondrous café and delicatessen, Byford's, in what is said to be the town's oldest building, painstakingly restored. If I had to eat here every day for a year, the menu and dishes would never bore. There are plans to open Byford's Posh B&B above the café, which will require additional staff 'with the right attitude. We love our industry and would be interested in any likeminded people.' We arrange to give a newly-wed couple a night here to celebrate the first anniversary of their marriage.

The Blakeney Hotel, which can't resist boasting that it is built upon the site of a smugglers' inn, combines the best of old and new with its timeless outlook. The distinguished gents is sensibly unmodernised, but the general décor much improved from the cream and brown glowingly described in old notices, when six guineas (£6.30) bought accommodation with four meals daily plus 'Attendance and Baths', but guests were requested to 'state definitely' how long they wished to stay when booking. On our way back to the car, hours before the sea would cover it, we spot a notice and realise that as late as 1958 the flood topped my six-foot-plus height, though that was nothing compared with the Great Flood of 1953.

East again, to Cley next the Sea, another favourite, with a great windmill and much other evidence of its former port status on the River Glaven and, unusually along this coast, a road out to the sea and the old lifeboat station. It occurs to me that visitors to these villages, and also the new residents attracted by the wild sea, marshes and winding estuaries, must have bought as many D&C books as those in any other part of Britain. Years ago when staying here, I routinely saw people buying and carrying our books, including those of the Readers Union's Book Clubs' country, natural history, sailing and photography ranges. Funded I suppose by the profits those customers gave us, we relish being here again.

So alongside the North Norfolk preserved steam railway to Sheringham. 'A fossilised flint-built fishing village inside the growing brick shell of a railway-age seaside resort' was a view of a generation ago. Then to Cromer. Every boy who had the good fortune to be brought here remembers the breezy pleasure for the rest of life. Cromer was once special, with its long Victorian pier (still surviving with people heading out to sea against the wind at angles up to 45 degrees), cliffs, steep steps, cosy streets unknown in suburbia, and superior cafés where they knew how to charge for the mandatory but delicious crab sandwiches on brown bread.

Generally style was in the air... sorry, wind. I disgraced myself when, for the first time ever given the controls of a motorised object, I drove head on into another boat on the smart lake, giving my mother's leg a knock she complained about for the rest of her life. Much of the best of Cromer, including the pier, can still be enjoyed. If one ingredient is missing to render today's mixture less memorable, it is the style. Like so many seaside resorts, Cromer is yesterday's place. The only hotel listed by the AA as having more than a dozen rooms scores a miserable percentage rating. Cromer is another place where the fascination is in its past, and there is plenty of that to admire.

For sad nostalgia, however, the next two 'resorts' take some beating. Beyond Cromer's extensive windswept golf links, Overstrand's architectural ambitions, fuelled by Sir Edward Lutyens love of the place where he took on three projects, disappeared with bungalows and roads ending on unstable clay cliffs. Mundesley was once even more ambitious, seriously hoping to rival Cromer as upmarket resort, but the cliffs here are higher and fell more spectacularly. What hopes and fears, and arguments over insurance claims, there must have been. On which note, without time to go a few miles further to see the recent devastation at Happisburgh – 60 miles of land were lost in the three years following the erosion of sea defences in 1998 – we have hastily to retrace our tracks through the rain. We are warned that climatic change is speeding cliff erosion and that, as at Happisburgh, will see more cases of half a century of loss in a few years – especially along the ten per cent of our coastline made up of soft cliffs.

At breakfast I was reading that erosion isn't confined to cliffs. Because of heavier rainfall, especially more frequent exceptional downpours, many river and other banks which have stood the test of centuries are now deteriorating, while the stability of several privately owned dams is being challenged.

Steam at Thursford

We go back inland through Holt, oozing community pride, to keep an appointment at Thursford's famous steam museum.

Famous today, and for many years past, perhaps; but, when I first visited, it had barely become a tourist attraction. The planning authority had been gobsmacked to discover what was really a 400-seater theatre on a farm, while the owner was equally amazed to be told he needed planning permission. The whole thing just happened, told in *Steam at Thursford* which (like African Violets this morning) is still very much on sale.

George Cushing drove one of the district council's traction engines when the responsibility for road upkeep was transferred to county councils. Despite a spirited attempt to prevent him getting above his station, the local council accepted his offer for the redundant machine. He began working for himself, in harsh times. Carting stone at three old pence a ton from the nearest station paid; cut to tuppence halfpenny, 'there wasn't much in it'. But more lucrative work improving the roads followed, needing more engines and men. Then came the 1934 Road Traffic Act, taxing heavy engines prohibitively and hastening conversion to motors. George saved his own and then bought others for a song. Steam organs and great fairground rides followed, all purchased cheaply as showmen ceased touring and the fairs, which had drawn the largest crowds ever seen at East Anglia's market towns, declined.

All were placed in a huge shed on the family farm. Naturally it became a mecca for enthusiasts, always welcome but steadily encouraged and catered for. Performances were attracting the capacity 400 when the planners cottoned on.

There is now proper theatre-style seating, and for decades it has been possible to see and hear the great steam organs, together with an enormous Wurlitzer, brought from the Paramount at Leeds. This is a point of pilgrimage for those whose knees knock at the sound of names like Burrell, Aveling & Porter, Ruston & Proctor on the traction-engine side, and Gavioli, Marenghi, Carl Frei and Wellerhaus among organ builders.

An important personal date was 21 May 1978 when the famous organist, Reginal Dixon, gave a performance on what he described as the finest preserved Wurlitzer in Britain. I came from Aldeburgh in Suffolk by the two-car ferry over the Yare at Reedham, with Gerry Fiennes; a distinguished railwayman (of whom more anon), he somewhat spoilt my front-row enjoyment by obviously finding it hell.

There are many other memories – George Cushing for example emphasising how tough things were for the country people before World War Two, but which, as in so many other rural areas, proved the great social turning point. Though East Anglia has always avoided the worst of recessions, for most living was very basic. Apart from the church and the railway station, and possibly an annual horse-drawn expedition to the sea at Wells-next-the-Sea seven miles away, when

George was young most men had to find their pleasure in their work. A Sunday afternoon walk might be to see how straight those employed on neighbouring farms had managed to plough their furrows. Few had money for the pub, and cottages lacked most creature comforts but, with engines as individual as horses, and occasions such as harvest and threshing involving the whole village, work was full of fascination and challenge and provided most of the social life. 'If you watched, there was always something more to learn,' says George.

Steam at Thursford, first published in 1982, was the story of man's relationship with yesteryear's engines, of survival and then expansion as the roads were steadily improved (helped by the old lengthmen ensuring drainage on their patch really worked, the first tarmac laid often lasted decades) and of how the old engines, organs and fairground rides were assembled 'in the hut'.

It is a nasty afternoon. The car park is nearly empty. But passing several new 'period' shops with their tempting window displays and friendly staff, a particularly tantalising home-made ice cream shop, and then a substantial new block of toilets, on our way to the entrance, it is clear that the Thursford Collection is thriving. Geraldine Rye takes us to a plush tearoom in an old barn. She works for George's son, John, who leads the Trust which took over George's private collection. Visitor numbers, she says, have remained static at about 150,000. As at most British tourist attractions, the drop in summer tourism has been offset by special events. The Thursford Spectacular is Britain's largest Christmas show, yielding an astonishing £2 million in ticket sales.

This afternoon Blackpool's youngest-ever organist, Robert Wolfe, is at the Wurlitzer, playing requests from an audience of about seventy, scattered in the theatre-style seating; with ample standing room, up to 1,300 attend concerts. Lighting and effects have become more professional, perhaps even over the top, since the earlier informal days when George told me to help myself to the Wurlitzer. The sound remains out of this world, though other organs and fairground rides are more visually compelling. Here is an attraction that can genuinely be called unique, evolving from one man's love of old things he couldn't bear seeing going to the junk yard.

Since, now well into his nineties, George is not feeling too lively today, I pop across to his home where his wife Minnie is as always anxious to please. She's never quite got to grips with the fact that her young man from the village turned out to be the one attracting the crowds. George's memory is as sharp as ever. He recalls travelling to Devon soon after *Steam at Thursford* came out: 'I've never got over the fact they made a special display on the bookstall at both Liverpool Street and Paddington.' Then he's back to his favourite theme: 'Nobody who wasn't one of them could possibly know how poor we were in the countryside. We didn't know what a treat was, yet somehow we were happy. It was natural to take pride in your job. So many of the skills we picked up as we went have now been lost.'

When I talk about traction engines, the familiar wry smile crosses his face. He's proud of what he has achieved, though privacy must be at a premium. [George died in 2003, aged 98. Minnie predeceased him, dying soon after my visit.]

Steam and agriculture have always been closely allied in East Anglia. Much of what we see here at Thursford was built in the region, a notable example being the traction engine from the famous Garrett works at Leiston, near Aldeburgh, while another D&C author was Alan Bloom, whose interests in plant production and steam railways have long been neatly combined to make Norfolk's own Bressingham into a famous nursery business and tourist attraction. The landscaped gardens and the commercial fields can be enjoyed from narrow-gauge steam-hauled trains running in large loops, one train occasionally having to wait for another to clear.

That there should be this close link between steam and growing isn't surprising, for the region has always been the most intensively farmed in Britain. The steam plough (engines on either side of a field activating wires to pull the plough) and steam threshing were greatly used, attracting large village crowds. It is also interesting to recall that in the 1920s and 1930s, increased agricultural business from East Anglia (including the developing sugar-beet traffic; until in World War Two we didn't need to import any cane sugar at all) offset industrial business that was already in sharp decline elsewhere in eastern Britain. Even in the 1920s there were complaints of the British liking for Danish beer, putting people at home out of work.

It might be added that during the war the LNER carried a brand new traffic into the East Anglican countryside: materials for the rapidly-built airstrips and supplies for our own and American bombers and fighters using them. Most were abandoned long ago, though you can still see plenty of evidence of the invasion that temporarily revolutionised much of East Anglian rural life. Remember the story about the American airman and the daughter at the village post office? Like many another, their romance halted when he said he had to return home, 'to his wife'. Decades later, he visited the post office, which she was then running, her mum long dead. 'And how is your wife?' she innocently asked. 'Wife? I've never been married.'

On our way to Norwich we pass through Melton Constable, once the headquarters of the Midland & Great Northern Joint Railway which, like the Somerset & Dorset, retained its unique cross-country independence until well after nationalisation, but was then almost totally closed. Today's guide book refers not to that but to one of the great halls of North Norfolk, built on the wealth of sheep and wool. Everywhere we see great houses, great churches, and pass vehicles carrying one of the county's present sources of wealth – turkeys.

Norwich: The Genuine Old English Town

Norwich's tentacles stretch far these days, and I note our passage in reverse of chronological order through the various stages of urban growth, starting with modern estates, the fifties' and then the thirties' and twenties' housing, until after a short Edwardian district we are in streets of up-marketed Victorian villas. Making the layers surrounding a city as interesting as are those of rock strata was something taught me by an old friend, Richard Joby. We travel through Hellesdon, once an isolated village, now a suburb, on which he has self-published an excellent book, recording a long and colourful history. This is the very first lively work I have seen on a suburb, as opposed to a still-independent village, yet many more people live in suburbs and are not automatically uninterested in how things developed.

Back in D&C days, Richard was a super author of railway books; and he always brought in the human touch. His *Railwaymen*, owing much to his father, was an especial triumph. We've kept in touch over the years, and over dinner he presents me with a collection of his latest Norfolk writings.

A weekend at Wells-next-the-Sea started Richard's love affair with Norfolk. He came to Norwich as a geography master at the grammar school. With a later degree in economics, he opened new horizons in all kinds of ways... in his teaching, including adult education lectures he's still giving, and in numerous books. He's another who, when the new owners of D&C gave up interest in railways and such like, used the experience he had gained to start self-publishing. Pointing to the station's great frontage that can be clearly seen across the river from our hotel window table, he talks of the pride and problems of the Eastern Counties and later Great Eastern. The first volume of his system's full history has sold 2000 copies: 'profitable, not bad for an amateur?'

Where does our itinerary take us? Did I know that Hunstanton was a planned resort? It was meant to be, but never was, like Essex's Frinton. But then, twenty years earlier, Lowestoft was originally developed in layers of quality by Sir Samuel Morton Peto, who had many railway and hotel interests. Expensive villas were next to the prom, then high-class boarding houses, cheaper ones further inland. Once Lowestoft had two daily non-stop Pullman expresses from Liverpool Street. 'It has always been good at adapting, and when quality tourism declined won port business and industry that might naturally have gone to Yarmouth, where they found it harder to keep up with the times. The two ports were always too close for comfort.'

Back to the Bath-stone-clad station with its zinc-covered dome across the river: 'In 1940 a bomb did a lot of damage, but they had the place reopened within an hour. Compare that with how long the Transport Police insist on stopping traffic today.' Then we discuss East Anglian and railway characters we have both known.

It is as though he is trying to compress as much conversation over tonight's dinner as we might have enjoyed had we dined together monthly should my career have brought me this way... a reminder that, about the time he came to Norwich, I was seriously in the running for a BBC post here. Panicking that perhaps I would really only blossom in the West Country, I deliberately threw away my chance by interrupting a test interview to ask my subject to remind me of his name.

No wonder our wives are having their own gentler conversation. Though it is perhaps easy to tease Richard for bubbling like a teenager, there are especially happy memories of how satisfying an author he was to work with. His more academic recent outpourings are also totally without pomp, and there's always humanity behind the geography, history and engineering. He really appreciates his East Anglia.

It seems an age since we came from Berwick-upon-Tweed yesterday; we are truly immersed in East Anglia. Just one shock before bedtime. Taking a short walk over the river, we pass a veritable array of East Anglia's female vulgarity on its way to late pub or club. The general state of exposure, not to mention conversation and lack of consideration for older walkers shown by groups of four or five intent on securing their sex's priority, beats anything I've seen even in Blackpool or Manchester. These are not young ladies we are likely to see rows of in Norwich Cathedral tomorrow.

Sunday starts slowly, with a leisurely walk along the river, much pleasanter than when I was first here in the 1950s. Everywhere in the city the river is more respected. There is even a city public boat service, as well as longer trips. But today's emphasis is totally on leisure. Though the Yare has recently been dredged, it seems there is no industry remaining to be served by cargo boats.

We turn toward the close, and converge with other streams of people heading toward and pouring into the cathedral. Though we cannot begin to do it justice, we at least briefly revel in the long history and great traditions – and testimony to the fact that this part of the world could afford such riches. Founded as a Benedictine Priory in 1096, it is said to be our country's finest complete Romanesque buildings... but is more than just that with its tall tower, art collection and much more, not to mention a full Sunday morning congregation and resounding music. There are a thousand paintings of Bible scenes on the great ceiling though, on the way out, we more easily study the detail of the cathedral's newest carving, of Mother Julian, the great inventor of sayings in her meditations, and author of the first book in the English language.

Then the short journey to the village of Barnham Broom for a family lunch. Hartley Booth, a cousin, and his family live in one of those ubiquitous old East Anglian halls. Empty for four years before they bought it, its restoration has called for as much ingenuity as funds. Going back to Saxon times, it certainly has a long history. Each room bears evidence of past owners and tenants, a Tudor Rose and Lily of France carved in 1519 at the front door, a fine Jacobean ceiling, and a dog gate of about 1620 on the staircase to prevent the deerhounds from going upstairs. Comfortable? Depends on whether you're used to being warm or not. Remember the days when the half of the population who had not yet had central heating installed professed to an almost religious dislike of it? The Booths keep up that tradition, though in fairness installing it would not merely be costly but probably damage the fabric, and the upstairs 'state room' is very cosy when the galloping fire consumes several tree trunks at a go... as at the eightieth birthday party of Hartley's half-sister Anne, who we met on two previous occasions on these journeys.

Real food and people give us a welcome break from hotel living. Then Hartley and Adrienne, a doctor, proudly show us the land they have reunited with the hall, whose last period of decline was when it served no agricultural purpose, but incomers were still not ready to move into a countryside of poor amenities and communications. They have just given their drive its third route, so the approach has more impact. One day it will be through a thriving wood, though currently the tubes protecting the hundreds of newly-planted trees make it temporarily look more like a military cemetery. Hartley and Adrienne perhaps typify the new East Anglia.

While standardisation afflicts many things (village shops close and locals cannot afford houses), newcomers respect historical features and delight in their surroundings. The countryside is far more loved and walked through by those who commute by car than natives.

For Hartley, the paradox was that he felt he had less power as a junior minister serving under Mrs Thatcher than when, before he became an MP, he was in her policy unit or 'think tank'.

'Then, if you made a recommendation and it came back ticked, things really happened.' Though he still frets about issues – '£1 per head spent by the Government in England means £6 a head in Wales, £18 in Scotland, and £48 in Northern Ireland –' he's 'done' his 'political thing'. He now makes things happen in business and charity, in the latter case working closely with Doreen Montgomery, the literary agent we met in chapter 17. But mainly we talk about family, inevitably referring to the coincidence that as young men our fathers were billeted with each other's grandparents.

Then a quick visit to Anne's house, half a mile away in the village. Wherever she's lived there have always been birds; they abound in her neat garden and give her obvious pleasure. She's past the time of life to indulge in another love, a cat, and so is free of the conflict of what a feline does to birds when it turns from cuddly pet to savage beast.

'See you soon,' we say, Scottish style, hoping she'll indeed come back to Scotland between her Italian and Irish trip. [Alas, not to be, since she died of a heart attack in the early summer, before we met again, though there were cheeky letters and giggly phones calls.]

We have to leave, enjoying the rolling countryside, though for the last few miles to Norwich it is a bit overwhelmed by new roads, to keep an appointment... come to think about it with one of Doreen Montgomery's authors, Patrick Goldring.

Meet *Good Housekeeping's* one-time resident sex expert, Uncle Ben of *Reynolds News*, the Chief Wagoner of the *Farmer & Stockbreeder*, and staff member of the *Daily Worker* till he walked out at the 1956 Hungarian uprising, when it became clear that telling the truth wouldn't be tolerated. Starting while he was still at school, he compiled the skeletal crossword for the *Sunday Express* (as he did the cryptic one in the *Daily Mail*) for forty years. Aged sixteen, he joined a Fleet Street agency (who among other things supplied crosswords and children's features), but has spent most of his life making a good living as freelance journalist. And that's before mentioning his many books.

A down-to-earth sort of chap with wide interests, Patrick Goldring has never been short of work or comments on life and ideas. Why does he live at Loddon, half way between Norwich and Lowestoft?

'Marvellous country, marvellous people. One of East Anglia's great strengths is that it is not on the way to anywhere. You can stroll through the many small towns with their wool churches and even enjoy the cities without being overwhelmed by visitors or other outside influences.'

We talk of the pre-railway days when Norwich was a thriving port, and you could get to the Continent more easily than to the next city. Norwich might be cosmopolitan, he admits, 'but it's always its own place. The best English city... nowhere else like it.' As true as when George Borrow described it as 'the most curious specimen at present extant of the genuine old English town'.

He asks if I remember his first book for me, agented by Doreen Montgomery. When I don't, he passes me *Friends of the Family*, looking all its thirty-year age. Subtitled, *The work of the Family Service Units*, it was about the organisation founded by Sir John Wolfenden in World War Two 'to help some of the most defenceless members of our community'. He adds: 'We're getting old I suppose. Who now talks of that, or remembers *Reynolds News*, a quite different Sunday paper?' He adds thoughtfully: 'Newspapers were more a way of life, less driven in those days.'

One of the people I am especially looking forward to meeting in Norwich is Elsie Bertram, whose achievements include revolutionising the book trade by making it easier for booksellers to order wholesale than direct from the publisher. Bertram Books, about as large and enterprising as they come, could almost be said to have kept many small bookshops alive, cutting out the delays, costs and frustrations of having numerous small accounts with individual publishers. Following the postwar collapse of Simpkin Marshall, the only wholesaler willing to take single-copy orders, there were decades in which individual customer's special orders (invariably for single copies) were a nightmare to all concerned.

Are you old enough to remember how you had to wait up to a month for your local bookseller to supply a book you needed in a hurry? In those days, publishers refused to deal with individuals directly. Bertram's aren't today's only large wholesaler, but they did more to change the scene than any other. Because they started small, there was never doubt about attention to detail and service to customers.

A couple of years ago Elsie sold up, and has been like a fish out of water since, fretting that she's missing the chance to fine-tune things, though she's had time to be a better correspondent. Tonight's proposed dinner together was planned months before... but only days ago she fell in the dark on the way to the loo in the middle of the night. Injured and shaken, she wasn't found till hours later. She's now in a wing of a hospital so private that even the taxi-driver has difficulty in finding it, the ride emphasising that, while East Anglia as a whole may be flat, Norwich is a city of hills.

Looking even smaller than her normal diminutive self, and very frail, she nonetheless has immaculately tidy white hair, and after a merry greeting tells me my first job is to open the sherry she's waving about. Talk about spirit! She's in her ninetieth year, 'bored to tears' because she no longer controls the business, but is still writing letters on behalf of Norfolk's diabetics... over £1million raised to date. The Bertram Diabetes Eye Unit was opened recently by the Prince of Wales, who she excitedly tells me brought a basket of the purple Brussels sprouts she had admired during a visit to Highgrove.

'You know the story? It began when my son Kip took a holiday job selling Pan books into the holiday camps. When he went off for a full-time job, I thought I'd take it on. Customers asked for hardbacks, so I added the Hamlyn list. Paul Hamlyn – he was an inspiration – supplied a van. I kept the stock in my chicken hut. It was hard work, 25 calls a day in the little van, but great fun. Even the traffic wardens became my friends. "But you should know I'm always here at ten on a Thursday," I'd say when they told me I shouldn't be on a double yellow line. It would end by them saying: "All right, I'll make sure there's nobody in your way in future".'

Soon Kip joined her full time, and steadily the empire developed, respected equally by suppliers (publishers) and customers (bookshops of all kinds). But Kip nearly died of diabetes, from which his brother also suffered. So the charitable work got underway, with a large initial donation from the already prospering firm.

'I didn't take a penny when I sold the business, but how I regret there isn't more to do.' Until the accident – 'How could I have been so stupid?' – at least she sat at her old desk once a week, though it isn't clear if there was anything for her actually to do.

'My charity work and my friends – I still do 600 Christmas cards – keep me going. But it was fun building up that book business... such nice people to deal with. I just hope I'll be all right for my ninetieth and they'll all come to a great party. You *will* come, won't you?'

Next morning, after an early breakfast, I take a taxi to St John Maddermarket. 'Who are you seeing there?' asks the curious driver. 'Well, not sure I should tell you, but a voluntary organisation that arranges lifts for the old and disabled who need a bit of help.' He asks for more details. 'Sounds OK to me,' he says, remaining friendly. 'I often help old dears who can't get their shopping indoors, but *some* drivers!'

Many of us have an idea that's not quite practical. Seeing how many old people rapidly go downhill when there's no driver left in the family, I've long idealised about a national organisation that would encourage people to get out and about by publicising those taxi firms or individual drivers undertaking to meet certain standards, above all showing patience, for a small extra fee. In my dreams it would be backed by taxi tokens, a bit like book tokens, that could be given as presents. It has always been the case that, while owning a car is an essential and the cost has to be borne without question, most people still regard calling a taxi as an unwarranted extravagance. Argue as you will about how many taxis you can afford just out of the saving of car tax and insurance, it is in the English (though curiously not so much the Scottish) psyche that, at least for old people, taxis are expensive, a luxury to be used sparingly, if at all.

Then I came across Norwich's CarLink, which was featured in the first issue of *Aspire*, the newsletter serving the newly formed Friends of my charitable trust. Though I haven't visited before, CarLink inspired us to offer an annual prize to help the best such service operating anywhere in Britain, though whether there will be adequate takers remains to be seen. That there is a need for such help is demonstrated by CarLink's outstanding success. Run within Norwich & Norfolk Voluntary Services, it is masterminded by Don Johnstone.

'It is very much software driven, and I found it really worthwhile developing the program, because it *works*, and we're helping a lot of people who might otherwise stay at home. Our drivers are considerate, never in a rush, and actually the drivers, all volunteers, find it as worthwhile as the passengers. They get 32 pence a mile and, especially newly retired people with plenty of time, enjoy driving and meeting people.'

Early on a Monday morning, the phones ring constantly. Since the two operators are working on messages left over the weekend, all fresh calls are recorded. 'We've got 270 drivers throughout Norfolk, and after three years are getting up toward 2,000 journeys a month – 64 are organised for today,' says Don. 'But we're not a taxi service – their bag is moving people about in a hurry. Our drivers will wait, though if it is for more than an hour, they have the option of treating it as two separate journeys.'

He proudly demonstrates the flexibility of his software system, Could it be adapted for other places?

'Yes and, since you put that to me over the phone, I've worked out that it would cost £5651, but I don't have the authority to go ahead without consultation. We might get some funding to help. Who might be interested?'

There's the rub. As in the world of small charities generally, how do you locate the few people who might be waiting for such an opportunity to knock on the door? And one rapidly discovers that there's more practical get-up-and-go here than in most parts of rural Britain, especially those many areas where the locals tend to sit back and leave it to the incomers, whose 'interference' is then somewhat resented. All one can do is spread the message, as I'm doing here in the hope that one or two interested people might respond.

'Yes, most passengers are over sixty. Many had not previously taken a taxi, though the service is limited by having to book well ahead and I've heard of those who haven't used taxis before now feeling free to do so if we can't help. It's partly an attitude of mind. But we are uniquely suitable for older folk.'

What restriction might there be on future growth? 'Not the number of drivers, or those wanting lifts, or the software. It would be the telephone.' Since the bells are still ringing incessantly, I can believe that. CarLink may turn out to be a mould-setter or just remain as a successful local scheme, but has certainly proven there was a need.

Don sits on Norfolk's successful Rural Transport Partnership. In recent years I've noticed the enthusiastic common sense behind its efforts to get better co-ordination between the parties involved. For example, much is done to attract traffic to the remaining branch lines, even down to an imaginative programme of organised walks, out to one station and back from another.

To Great Yarmouth

It is already time to move on from Norwich. Sheila demands how soon we can come back, 'for we haven't begun to touch it'. At this rate we'll be spending much of our remaining lives in East Anglia! There are certainly worse places... it just doesn't happen to be our home, though I wonder what might have happened had I secured that BBC job. We have, I have to admit, only walked through a couple of Norwich's famous narrow streets this time. Knowing there is no way I can do justice to the city, I've hardly tried.

Each of my taxi drivers presumed I had far greater knowledge of the city than I do, and were genuinely surprised that anyone would come from Scotland or for that matter London without wanting to spend longer here. 'It's not a bad place, you know,' summed up my last driver, taking me back from CarLink to our hotel. Though commercially successful throughout most of its long history, and avoiding the depths of recessions, Norwich remains amazingly individual.

Usually I've gone east from Norwich by train. There are still two routes to Yarmouth, each coming intimately to grips with the low-lying countryside and its waterways. The more interesting is the southern route, close to the Yare as far as Reedham, and then in an almost straight line northeast across the lonely marshes through Berney Arms, the remotest and most romantically situated station in England. But it is the Lowestoft line, which leaves the southern route at Reedham and proceeds by swing bridge over the Yare before running parallel to the River Waveney's New Cut, that is specially splendid. When the Broads are alive with boating activity, you positively look up to the craft floating above you, the top of the sails of larger vessels seeming to touch the sky.

Today we go by car. There is no road equivalent to the southern rail route, but at Acle we leave the main road for a hasty look at Reedham which surely has one of the best river frontages in all Britain – never to be forgotten if you first saw it from a steamer making its way up to Norwich. The whole village is a river place. There's great history, too. East Anglian kings are said to have ruled from here; it would have been an excellent choice in the days that only water transport was really effective, though the river also brought up the Danes. The Reedham ferry, East Anglia's only one for cars, is a mile or so upstream and still provides a useful link, for there is no bridge between Yarmouth and Norwich. It is a chain ferry. The chains had to be lifted for the passage of boats of substantial draught when they came this way.

I'd also hoped to go straight across the main road at Acle to renew acquaintance with Burgh St Margaret (Fleggburgh), close to three of the larger Broads, but time is scarce. We talk Broads, once thought to be naturally created but now known to have been abandoned mediaeval peat workings. Norwich Cathedral alone consumed 400,000 tonnes of peat a year. The workings steadily flooded, the shallower ones silting up. Once there were nearly 3,000 acres of open water, but today's Broads, protected by Britain's newest National Park, cover little more than half of that. We regret that we've never had a holiday messing about in boats here for, though traffic jams on the water are common at the most popular spots, there are many places you can quietly commune with nature. Indeed more places than formerly, for the number of boats to hire on the Broads has more than halved in the last quarter of a century; today's visitors are mainly lovers of the Broads, as opposed to holidaymakers just seeking something to do.

The main Yarmouth road runs beside the northern railway toYarmouth, both dead straight across the marshes. Travelling fast, we almost miss the River Bure to the north as it meanders on its way to join the Yare at Yarmouth, distracted by looking south at the great muddy expanse of Brevdon Water, a narrow central channel still flowing.

Two ruined windmills and a much dilapidated train station seem to set the tone at Yarmouth. Once coming here must have been a real adventure. Dickens makes that clear in *David Copperfield*, with its dramatic description of an East Coast gale. Later, Yarmouth was in the vanguard of popular tourism, beating Skegness in scale and probably being just as bracing as that resort's famous railway poster boasted. Families with youngsters came for fun. They still do, but on such a reduced scale that gives the whole place, especially the long promenade with its attractions competing in sheer hideous inappropriateness, a rundown feeling. The ugly piers, rollercoasters, water chutes, tall tower – and much, much more, for the 'attractions' go on endlessly – look depressing, or at least in need of rejuvenation, even on the rare occasions that they are still under pressure, but out of season one longs for the North Sea to exert its hunger and gobble them up.

'Boys under fourteen must be accompanied by an adult' is the warning outside the gents. None of the three taps I tried would work. Nobody else expected them to.

'Yarmouth is even worse than I remember it,' says Sheila. 'I never want to come back here again.' That's a relief, then. I would however quite like to see Britain's first commercial offshore wind farm, planned a mile and a half from the coast here: sixty metres above sea level, the 38 proposed turbines can only enhance the present scene.

The back streets with garages and hoardings are easier on the eye as we return, though the most interesting thing to catch our attention is the big ship being repaired on the river.

What of the hotels? Sheila, who is driving, tells me to consult the AA Hotel Guide. 'YARMOUTH, See Wight, Isle of' is all it says. Surely there must be at least one reasonable hotel left? Silly me. We're not in Yarmouth but Great Yarmouth, I beg its pardon. There are no fewer than ten hotels listed, though by far the highest rated is in Gorlestone-on-Sea, on the other side of the river, where the better residential areas are. There are few 'attractions' along Gorleston's promenade, but a feeling of things being more up-together, even in the old streets, showing that this was also once an important port in its own right.

It is from Gorleston that there's the best view of the Yare's mouth, two miles south of Yarmouth. It looks really forbidding today, and for centuries has been a well-known hazard, with many a captain failing to get his ship correctly angled. But how romantic! What trade has perilously passed through.

Fishermen went far in pursuit of their living, though fish-wise Yarmouth once especially meant pilchards, which in time disappeared as mysteriously from this coast as from around Cornwall. More colliers (bringing coal south for East Anglia's own consumption) were registered in Yarmouth than anywhere else, not excluding London. All goods for Norwich, once second only to London, came in from the sea here. Though large ships once regularly reached Norwich, much inland cargo was transferred in Yarmouth to the famous Norfolk wherries, 58feet long but only four-foot draught, wonderfully manoeuvrable if you had the knack, carrying up to forty tons. Scottish sheep were imported for fattening: 'So delicious for taste,' said Daniel Defoe, 'that the inhabitants prefer 'em to the English cattle.' Come to think about it, the *Hebridean Princess*, on which we took the first of these journeys, will be back at the end of season for her usual short winter lay-up and steady enhancement in Yarmouth.

Have we been unfair to Great Yarmouth? To the promenade, surely not. And the town is definitely not of a piece. Many old buildings not destroyed during the war have been bulldozed since. But Yarmouth does have its adherents. It is still of the sea, and is a useful base for those exploring the extensive Broads and their linking waterways. It also offers visitors great value, especially with early and late breaks for coach parties. But it is not a place to which we'll return soon, if ever.

Just south of Gorleston, at Hopton on Sea (the majority of British places 'on Sea', with or without OS hyphenation, seem to be along this coast) we say farewell to Norfolk to continue our travels down the Suffolk part of the arc of East Anglia's coast.

THE HUNGRY SEA

How Suffolk Became Smaller

It would be hard to say which section of Britain's endlessly varied coastline is the most beautiful, or even most photogenic. Without pausing to think, parts of Yorkshire, northwest Scotland, North Devon and the Cornwall seaboard immediately present themselves. When, however, it comes to singling out one section uniquely fascinating, and making you want to read more about it, Suffolk's Heritage Coast has no contender. Every mile between the Norfolk and Essex borders is full of dramatic history, with its own variation on the everlasting theme of nature versus man, and of man's striving for prosperity – or simply wanting to survive in peace with his livelihood.

This coast has its own brand of beauty: shingle beaches are lapped or pounded by waves of varying force, with extra power in gales striking at an angle. Beyond are great open skies. The estuaries have infinite variety, with magical sailing opportunities at high tide, great birdlife at low, and views of huge churches built of the wealth that came from the wool which sailors bravely took across the sea to foreign lands... and villages prospering, decaying or disappeared leaving only a few traces.

Since we are now considerably nearer to London than in North Norfolk, it is not surprising that the coast has proved attractive to visitors and retirees, especially those seeking the quality of life that goes with shingle beaches and the trappings of culture of a well-heeled immediate hinterland. For many years I have been a regular visitor to Aldeburgh. This time, my curiosity aroused more than previously, I found myself wondering how much those attending the concerts of the Aldeburgh Festival at Snape Maltings know or indeed care about the continually changing natural stage on which so many human hopes have flourished or perished.

Like many another visitor, I had regarded Aldeburgh as a neat little resort with colourful people who liked good standards. Part of its charm is based on the very plainness of its seafront overlooking the great expanse of the North Sea, incidentally known as the German Sea until we went to war in 1914. Yes, there is still a lifeboat station with, in fact, two lifeboats, whose crews have sometimes performed heroic deeds. And from the southern end of the seafront, beyond the last hotel, there is a marvellous view of a huge estuary system, which the map shows flowing up to the Snape Maltings, its mouth not entering the sea for many miles to the south, by which time the River Alde has changed its name to the River Ore. How little did I know! Not even that the reason for the river's two names was that, in olden days, those living along each part had so little to do with each other that a common name was not needed.

One evening, always conscious of the eerie presence of Sizewell atomic station to the north, while walking on the seafront, watching old ladies with white hair struggle to park their cars, I took a more detailed look at the Moot House with its overhanging timber roof. It is only just off the shingle beach, which until now I had presumed had always been the case. However, a notice says that it was built in the sixteenth century as a meeting place for the people of Aldeburgh, 'and still is today' (along with its museum and town clerk's office open on weekday mornings) – on the third street inland. In a great storm, the sea gobbled up the two outermost streets.

It was at Aldeburgh Bookshop I discovered that a former D&C author, Robert Simper, had written a series of books about the East Anglian coast and its estuaries. His Suffolk books frequently refer to the loss of land to the sea, estuaries changing their shape, river mouths being blocked – and rivers cheekily decapitating each other and stealing the water so that an independent one becomes a tributary. Indeed, most East Anglian rivers were once tributaries of the Thames. They are drowned river valleys invaded by the sea. We think of geological history being so long as to be incomprehensible by all but experts, but the last time East Anglia was covered with ice was barely more than five times longer ago than the birth of Christ.

My curiosity stirred, I discovered that at the southern tip of Aldeburgh there was once a thriving separate little port of Slaughden, on a narrow strip of land between sea and estuary. So far and yet so near, for periodically the sea broke over Slaughden. Then it took most of it away too. But not only here, for at those famous times of great East Coast surges, the sea gobbled the salt water of the estuary. Like others, this estuary's shape has changed many times, the mouth periodically being blocked by shingle. But the great bulk of water here compared to that of lesser estuaries has meant that it has always flushed itself out. I discovered, too, that many more ships were wrecked, many of them trying to get in or out of the estuary, than I had realised. So hazardous was this coast that several rival 'beach companies', belonging to and manned by local nautical people, set themselves up as salvagers with tall lookout towers where the horizon could be studied for ships in trouble. And there, on today's seafront, are the 'Up towners' and the 'Down towners' towers in perfect order, though possibly eyed by the jealous sea for devouring in time to come, by way of punishment for depriving it of destroying the many ships that the beach companies saved.

The details continue. The fishermen once operated from the river, with a convenient quay at Slaughden. When that became too dangerous, and catches were declining, they switched to the beach, having to push their boats straight into the waves, when conditions allow. They make up for the smaller catch by selling it retail from huts on the seafront. Though there are now fewer of them, these fishermen's huts are a feature of today's Aldeburgh scene. We will meet some of the fishermen later.

That the sea has sometimes fed its mighty appetite along the Suffolk Coast is best known from the famous decline of Dunwich, but I had never realised how persistently so much of the coastline has been chiselled away, losses in many parts being a mile or more wide, within recorded history. And what efforts have had to be made to keep entrances to ports and estuaries navigable, especially at Southwold. A major interest along the coast undoubtedly lies in the very mixed fortunes of its ports and towns and villages, from the total disappearance of the substantial port and town of Dunwich, to the unique commercial success of Felixstowe as Britain's chief container port.

There are places of national if not international importance, such as the bird reserve at Minsmere and prehistoric Sutton Hoo, where the excavation of a tumulus yielded the extraordinary ship burial of a Saxon chieftain with gold, silver and enamel treasures. The history of this coast is as rich as it is long. Almost throughout, its inhabitants have been enterprising and prosperous. Today the charm of many of the small towns and villages is helped by the fact that they are better maintained than those of many coastal areas. Yet everyone knows that, for all the money invested in flood prevention, the time will come again when the hungry sea makes new claims. Surging at an angle to the shingle and cliffs, the sea can suddenly become more powerful than for decades or even centuries before. Lifeboat men will tell you of individual storms outstandingly more violent than anything they have previously encountered. There's a high quality of life along this coast, but it really is life on the edge.

So let us continue our journey southward from the Norfolk border.

Lowestoft and Southwold

Almost at once we are in the first of two great ports at opposite ends of the Suffolk coast, very different from each other and giving no clue about the magic that lies between them.

Even in my time, Lowestoft has displayed many changes. When I first came, the quays were agog, though numerous trawlers spent months at a time fishing in distant parts, their catches being ferried home. Then once, on a dank winter's day with a long gap between 'connecting' trains, it all seemed to have disintegrated. There was hardly a boat at the substantial quays.

The great days of fishing are certainly over, but this morning we are impressed by Lowestoft's apparent prosperity. The town is smarter than Great Yarmouth; at least some new industry is thriving, and the esplanade is certainly better kept. And tourism makes the most of Oulton Broad at its back door. Oulton Broad, magic at quiet times and noisily congested when busy, is where George Borrow did most of his writing, and one can understand his opposing the railway, though it was the trains' early arrival that laid the foundation for Lowestoft's prosperity. It is unfortunate, perhaps, that two places as large as Great Yarmouth and Lowestoft are close together, but they certainly make an interesting comparison.

The sun comes out as we leave Lowestoft. Each of the minor roads down to the sea offers exciting glimpses of wetland and remote farms. Hunger forces our pace to Southwold, surely among the top half-dozen gems on the British coast. Almost everything about it is good. The small town (actually a large village, but it feels solid enough to be a town) is virtually on an island, the boundaries of which have constantly changed.

It was the sea that gave Southwold its harbour, by breaking through north of Dunwich, where men were hated for jealously blocking up the new channel. Over many centuries thereafter, the harbour was persistently blocked and had to be dug out afresh. 'It is pitiable the trouble and damage (the fishermen) do daily sustain by their naughty harbour,' was written in 1609, when no doubt another shingle blockage had appeared.

When I first saw the great church, I made the common mistake of assuming it was another of Suffolk's fine wool-financed examples. Not so. Until tourists began to favour Southwold, maritime business was everything. The harbour might have been challenging, but fishing of many types (this was the mediaeval base of the Icelandic fleet), the export of cheese (for which there was special licence), boatbuilding, wreck rescuing and so on are what made Southwold prosperous and individual.

The story of the problems with the harbour entrance could fill the entire chapter. Things seldom went smoothly. At the beginning of modern times, when the present harbour entrance was built, the sea's swell rushed in with such force that, at least temporarily, the ferry over to Walberswick, a smaller port on the opposite side, had to be abandoned.

Today, people drive right round the Blythe estuary to reach the other side. More recent schemes have stirred controversy too, but somehow the harbour battles on, and there is still fishing, and again boatbuilding. Over the generations, keeping the lifeboat in a ready state has been distinctly challenging.

The story of the narrow-gauge Southwold Railway is also full of the unusual. Apocryphal it probably is, but I especially like the part which begins about how we, the British, first forced a railway on the unwilling Chinese. Once we had extracted payment, the Chinese said something like: 'So it's ours'; and when this was confirmed: 'So we can do anything we like with it?' Whereupon they promptly dismantled it as a devilish device and, second-hand, it was shipped to Suffolk and used to put Southwold on the railway map, though pretty ineffectively. The gloomy, rattling narrow-gauge carriages had their passengers sitting on two long benches facing each other. Though there is now talk of re-opening a section of the line as a museum piece, the only practical legacy is its bridge a mile or so up the estuary which pedestrians find useful.

Those who know Southwold will not be surprised we make for the Swan Hotel, a truly old-fashioned coaching inn where the floors creak and I have to mind my head. We go to the bar for a snack, and are greatly entertained by a group of the town's other publicans enjoying beer and a pub lunch. They chatter non-stop, swopping experiences and hints with mild maliciousness. I like the revealing titbits about their wives, some of whom seem to be better at easing the landlord's lot than others.

Not to put them off, but unashamedly eavesdropping, I pretend to be absorbed in a generous brochure on Adnam's various hotels, which include the Swan in Southwold, and its famous brewery. It is the largest employer in the town, and possibly the most successful independent brewery in all Britain, and is certainly vital to the Southwold character: 'Wonderfully distinctive beers for discerning drinkers in East Anglia and beyond.'

A publican talks of his beer and food and how they're regulated by the landlord, meaning the brewery who leases the premises. 'Our barrelage of course they know, though we drain a barrel down to the last drop, but the amount of food you serve is harder to find out about... but then they don't know about the problems of employing staff to serve it.' The Swan gives the impression it has always been above that kind of thinking, and I enjoy an old notice saying that it has received such extensions and improvements 'to accommodate Visitors, for any period, with comfortable Beds and Sitting-Rooms commanding extensive and pleasant views of the sea, and the adjacent country'.

It is not only the other publicans who come to the Swan for special occasions. When we last had lunch here, I was tempted to spend money on (or should I say invest in) two great railway posters. Leslie Sherlock, who normally sells by post, is a regular summer visitor, gently unrolling the posters by commercial artists, some household names in the art world, extolling yesteryear's services and resort attractions. Though eager to do trade, Leslie almost sheds a tear when he has to part with a couple of his treasures. 'Do let me know if you ever want to sell them. Finding them is harder than selling them, you know. They are romantic with historical interest because the railways created the seaside resort. There's keen appreciation for their bold lines and vivid colours. Of course, in their day the railway companies employed the very best artists, like Tom Purvus and Jack Merriott, and paid them substantial fees.' Posters are a useful sideline, for Leslie is mainly an antiquarian bookseller. He loves visiting Southwold: 'People who come here cover the whole spectrum of my customers.'

The Swan is precisely the kind of place you'd expect to come to buy posters of Devon and Cornwall, and Southwold exactly where you'd expect to find eccentrics. We see them on the streets: a couple of bent old ladies talking away, neither taking the least notice of what the other is saying; and an octogenarian, if not nonagenarian, with beard matching flowing hair, not paying the least attention to what his wife is prattling on about either. Shop windows are fascinating, revealing much about Southwold's idiosyncrasy. There's an excellent dress shop, says Sheila, and the bookshop shows that at least some people read today's bestsellers as well as period pieces and books about the area. This coast has a literature as generous as North Cornwall's.

'There'll only be 243 beach huts this year,' announces a customer as though it's just been flashed on television. 'The two demolished last year won't be replaced.' From what we hear of the sea's cruelty hereabouts, the loss of only two in a season seems very modest.

Not that the sea conquers quite all. The Victorian pier, an important part of Southwold's personality, not merely withstood the elements but the Army found it tougher than expected when it tried to blow up one section in the early days of World War Two. A drifting mine caused surprisingly little damage, too. It was repaired in 1948, but the pre-war prosperity and paddle steamers didn't return and steadily the pier deteriorated, till even the large landward pavilion boasted little better than the cheapest beer in town.

Then a local man grew in confidence, or what most people initially thought was sheer madness. Chris Iredale wanted to buy the pier and restore it, something that has not been so fully achieved anywhere else in half a century. He's done it! He is on holiday today so cannot meet us, but says we're welcome to walk out to the very end of the pier where, treading carefully, we can talk with workmen laying the final boards of the decking. They are all local builders and craftsmen, proud to be involved and expecting their work to be admired for decades if not generations to come.

We read in the new pier's guide: 'With only a minor proportion of the funds coming from a European grant, Chris has himself, with the backing of his bank, funded the remaining costs, in the region of £1million. This... is the burning ambition of a man who has been captivated by piers ever since he was taken to Southend at the tender age of ten.'

When I spoke to him on the phone earlier, Chris told me: 'I looked at the pier one day and thought what a shame it was, seeing it deteriorate under our eyes. So I bought it. That was fourteen years ago. Planning wasn't much of a problem, but getting the engineering right has been important – and the money. Quite a struggle you might say. We've just got to add the fendering piles and we'll be ready for a ship to call. My ambition is to bring the paddle steamer *Waverley* here, but we'll probably have to make do with the motor vessel *Balmoral* to start with.'

Having chartered the *Waverley* from the restored pier at Clevedon in Somerset, I share the joy of restoring the pier's transport role. Lamented by John Betjeman, it once looked as though Clevedon pier was also doomed, but it is now a regular calling point for the *Waverley*. However, the achievement at Southwold has been altogether more challenging. But what about the insurance and weather risk?

'I managed to get cover through Lloyds. It is said they'll cover anything. But there's a £10,000 excess, and one day of course there will be a great storm: it might be a once in 100- or once in 200-year storm. It will probably damage it but I hope it doesn't happen in my time. By the way, did you know that there is an active National Piers Society? They have been very helpful.'

Southwold pier reaches 623ft into the North Sea with a T-end and sufficient water depth for any ship likely to call. The ability to accept ships and their passengers gives the pier soul, but of course there is more to it than that. Apart from offering a great walk with fine views of sea and town, there are all kinds of interesting points, a huge variety within a display pavilion part way along:

Pier Entertainment
At the more desperate end of the live entertainment scale were the many self-styled 'Professors' who could be found at many resorts and specialised in performing high diving feats off the pier. Sometimes they would leap into the sea blindfolded or in flames but always their assistant would approach the admiring crowds with the exhortation 'don't forget the diver' as the collecting boxes went round.

The catch line 'don't forget the diver' in the famous Tommy Handley *ITMA* radio show came from the piers, of course closed in the dark days of the war. We look at the grim pictures of pier disasters, especially fires, which led to rapid demise such as at Cleethorpes, and then come across an enterprising display of bits and pieces on books and magazines. Did you know that the first edition of the comic *Beano* is so rare that a collector recently paid £6,200 for a single copy? And this self-publishing, or at least subsidised, gem: 'Lewis Carroll estimated that if he sold the entire 2,000 first print of *Alice in Wonderland* he would lose £200. By selling another 2,000 he would make £200. If more a bigger gain. "That I can hardly hope for." Before his death six years later, 180,000 copies had been sold.' The young at heart enjoy another small pavilion full of period-piece slot machines. Old pennies can be purchased to set them going.

One pier activity that doesn't seem to change is fishing. Though the end is not yet completed, already there are sea anglers with their relaxed look (or is it just resignation?) dangling lines into the sea. If you're interested in a good beer, the pier no longer sells the cheapest in town, but quality Adnams. Of course.

To the City under the Sea

It now is time to walk back up the cliff path and take a final glance at the harbour mouth before following the estuary's northern shore to Blythburgh.

This is evidently a much decayed place, small but with ruins telling of better days. Tidal water flows right up to it, but there's little indication that once it was a major port. Then I recall that its church is famous as 'Cathedral of the Marshes', and in the nick of time ask Sheila to turn off the busy road into the correct lane.

Holy Trinity at Blythburgh, on a slight hill, is more than a landmark for many miles around. It positively forces itself on the attention. Its size is as impressive inside as out, yet the architecture is memorable mainly for the tranquil way in which it speaks through the ages. Large, but not overwhelming, the church sums up so many fears and hopes, in that order. The angels in the splendid roof vaulting, the playful pew ends, though most of the huge space is simply floor (much of it brick), and the bright atmosphere with dazzling shafts of light cast by the sun, already low in the sky, are just a few of the details that I will remember forever. As we leave, from a distance we can see the sun's declining rays through the windows high in the nave walls.

I have never been against sensible rationalisation, including closing a few oversized churches where the costs of basic maintenance aren't socially justified, but you'd have to be hot on economics and dull on humanity to include Blythburgh's Holy Trinity in any money-saving scheme, even though the village's surviving population could be accommodated ten- or twentyfold. That money was at one time spent cautiously is shown by the oddity of one side of the long building being much grander in scale and carvings than the other. Money must have been tight indeed when the nearby priory was closed at the Dissolution of the Monasteries, leaving the church to struggle alone through the Reformation and Secularisation. At least it was not attacked by Modernists.

Taking a final glance at the large expanse of the Blythe estuary, which opens out several miles in from the sea, we drive through Dunwich Forest to what I always think of as one of the quietest yet saddest places in all England. This afternoon the waves are lapping so gently that we might be on an inland sea. There is only one other visitor's car in sight. Sheila, never claiming historical genius, admits she has never even heard of Dunwich, and in Scotland and the West Country, not one in ten I question has either. Yet this is Britain's only major city, once fourth largest in the land, to be lost to the waves. Many of those who have heard of it did so through their love of Turner encouraging them to discover the background to his picture of the ruined All Saints then perched perilously close to the crumbling cliffs, while other buildings still slightly further from the edge are portrayed as already abandoned ahead of inevitable catastrophe.

While some losses to the sea (such as Ravensrodd on the Humber, and Old Winchelsea in East Sussex) could perhaps have been foretold and prepared for, one can hardly criticise Bishop Felix for his choice of site for his episcopal see for the conversion of East Anglia to Christianity. That was back in 630. Dunwich was on high ground, well inland. It flourished for centuries, with formidable wealth recorded in the Domesday Book. The three churches then steadily increased to nine plus three chapels. In the thirteenth century, Dunwich owned eighty great ships. It had an important market, and was the coast's chief port. It was famous for its high tolls and grasping merchants, till it lost much business to the new port of Blythburgh, with which relations were far from neighbourly.

Sitting in our car close to the beach in one of the most peaceable scenes imaginable, looking north toward Sole Bay beyond Southwold, I take out a book bought at the Southwold Bookshop and read about the hostility between Dunwich on the one side and Blythburgh and Southwold on the other. *Southwold: Portraits of an English Town* is published by Phillimore of Chichester, whose local-interest titles are legendary, and has excellent coverage because chapters are contributed by different people, with the overall work editorially well co-ordinated. We are told that Edward III complained of almost daily 'assemblies of men at arms, burnings, homicides, robberies, &c.'

Proud Dunwich couldn't face up to Southwold being a competitor. For their part, the Blythburgh men attacked Dunwich's hated tollhouse and killed the bailiff. Human greed unevenly interrupted by nature has always been a potent blend. Hostilities continued for many decades: 100 years after they were told to leave Southwold's newer market alone,

Dunwich men still attacked it in force, demanding fancy tolls from ships using the estuary that the sea had made independent of their own haven.

Of course, coastlines have never been fixed features, but looking out where houses, churches and the market once stood, on high ground whose 'loam and sand of loose texture' crumbled like dry cake each time gale-driven waves struck it obtusely at very high tides, I ask Sheila if she has ever wondered how our personal collection of treasured coastal spots around Britain will ultimately meet their fate. Every year someone's favourite place, if not home, goes under the waves. For example, at the village of Hallsands in Devon, despite the fishermen's correct forecast as to what would happen, the beach was systematically robbed of its shingle foreshore for the development of Devonport Dockyard. Nearly all houses were lost. Much more recently, what had been Scarborough's best hotel steadily disappeared.

But Dunwich is Britain's most significant single loss to date. The great storm that blocked its harbour was as early as 1328. Later I looked up what Adrian Robinson and Roy Milward had to say in their *The Shell Book of the British Coast* that we published:

> The continual losses taking place from mediaeval times can be seen in the history of its churches with St Michael's being destroyed by 1331, St Leonard's sometime after 1350, and those dedicated to St Martin and St Nicholas during the fourteenth century. The church of St John the Baptist in the Market Place was demolished in 1540, to be followed by the chapels of St Anthony, St Francis and St Catherine before 1600. Later centuries have also taken their toll for St Peter's was dismantled in 1702 while the last victim, All Saints, gradually came closer to the cliff edge in the nineteenth century until finally, in 1912, it went over the top. Huge pieces of flintwork were occasionally seen on the beach until quite recent times.

Everything on earth is transitory, but that doesn't prevent one making the most of it, or even taking the long-term view. Without that, there'd be no rebuilt Southwold Pier or many greater improvements that will last for centuries, or 'forever' as interpreted by the human mind. I revel in today's quiet scene, marvelling at what was once here. How long will our own little part of the coast last and how will it ultimately disappear?

Aldeburgh

As the crow (or more likely gull or duck) flies, it is only a few miles from Dunwich to Aldeburgh, but along those miles we find as much variety as you could anywhere. First, on a hill, still within Dunwich, come the remains of the Friary, the city's last relic. The road passes the abandoned walls. Then Minsmere cliffs, above which is the National Trust's Dunwich Heath, a draughty spot. The most famous of the RSPB reserves, Minsmere, follows on. It attracts bird lovers from near and far throughout the year. The Minsmere Level in which the reserve is set has a fascinating history. Its drainage was completed in the early year of the nineteenth century by William Smith, the father of British geology, who we first met in the Introduction. As an anti-invasion measure in World War Two, it was reflooded.

The RSPB has done splendidly, the reserve including cliffs and numerous islets, offering a range of natural habitats for many species. They say that, if you are lucky, you might see fifty different species in a single summer's day. The birds thrive in safe confidence while humans enjoy them to the full from the imaginative path system. Full marks for the mixture of hides available to all visitors and those exclusive to members. Mind you, some of the twitchers laden with equipment are more of a sight than anything in the bird world.

Next comes one of the worst human aberrations, Sizewell atomic power station, as already mentioned, an eerie presence on the Aldeburgh scene. Naturally you cannot keep to the coast there, the road forcing us inland to Leiston with its streets of workers' houses, built for Garratt's great labour force. Garratt, with its huge and for its age sophisticated factory, made this one of Suffolk's most prosperous industrial spots. There is a lively Garratt museum to keep the memory alive. We of course saw one of the famous Garratt traction engines at Thursford in the last chapter; they were once at work all over rural Britain.

We get back to the coast at Thorpness, one of those seaside curiosities whose heyday has long passed yet is still of interest. Only the threatening presence of Sizewell has lessened my pleasure in walking the two miles above the deserted shingle beach from Aldeburgh to Thorpness on several past occasions.

It was the very emptiness of this part of Suffolk that attracted Stuart Olgilvy to conceive a new kind of resort. Thorpness was an integrated toffs' affair with clubhouse, wide range of housing, mainly in mock-Tudor with black weatherboarding. The founding company never really flourished, World War One obviously hurting seriously since building had only got underway in 1910. Reports of the meetings, and how each immediate post-war season was or was not shaping up well, give fascinating insight into upper-crust holiday and business habits of the day. Rationing of water by the water-carrier, on his daily round in droughts when the water butts of individual properties ran dry, deterred repeat visits.

Though the portable dhoolie bathing machines and Vittesse (a Daimler with open seating pulling a double-decker bus) that met trains have long gone, don't miss the famous House in the Clouds, in reality a disguised water tower, the mock-Tudor that still survives, and the man-made mere. Boating on the shallow mere is a welcome activity for family visitors to Aldeburgh, while I find fun in comparing the unsuitable designs of chalet-style homes and seeing how their owners have best prolonged their lives in an exposed position, especially right in front of the shingle. Thorpness is horribly out of context, but on a scale that creates its own peculiar charm, towered over by the greater inappropriateness of Sizewell.

At first glance after this, Aldeburgh might seem conventional, but it has curiosities enough, geographical and its slightly upper crust character. Its clientele of retired people and visitors relish the shingle since the lack of sandy beaches 'discourages' young couples with children. The sea isn't cosy, even when not downright angry. As early as 1590, the locals were warned not to remove any stones from the beach under threat of the then enormous sum of three shillings and fourpence for each offence, because 'the sea daily wynnethe of the land against this Towne'. As already said, the Moot House, now within feet of the shingle, was once in the third street inland. The cottage where Aldeburgh's famous poet, George Crabbe, was born was to the shore side, while his father was Saltmaster (collector of salt tax) based at the then busy port of Slaughden, most of it also now washed away. Crabbe wrote of its trading days:

Here samphire banks and saltwort bound the flood,
There stakes and sea-weeds withering on the mud;
And higher up a ridge of all things base,
Which some strong tide has roll'd upon the place...
Yon is our quay! those smaller hoys from town,
Its various wares for country use bring down.

It was a coast where working men struggled and samphire made a tasty addition to the diet, and where the temptation of smuggling was often present; a coast where man challenged but seldom kept pace with the elements, and shipwrecks were frequent. Also a coast of simplicity and bleakness attractive to those who didn't like being surrounded by too much sophistication. Many of those who settled here were of artistic temperament, their own people with independent outlook. But they supported a surprisingly sophisticated range of shops to support the lifestyles to which they had been accustomed – a bit like going into the wilds for a back-to-nature picnic with an elaborate picnic box, chilled sauvignon blanc and smoked salmon and cucumber sandwiches with delicate chocolate cake to follow.

The most famous of Aldeburgh's artistic folk was Benjamin Britten. Born in Lowestoft, he was living in the States when by chance he read

Crabbe. That was powerful enough to persuade him to return to Suffolk, and it was Crabbe and the Aldeburgh setting that inspired the opera Peter Grimes.

People settling here have always selected Aldeburgh with care. Gerry Fiennes, and his widow Jean, with whom we have dinner tonight, were typical. They studied every small seaside place from beyond Southampton to Southwold, looking for quality of life within less than two hours' train journey from London. Gerry was a great sailor, which is one of the reasons why Aldeburgh won, for the estuary system is enormous.

I knew Gerry when he was general manager of BR's Western Region, occupying Brunel's office looking across the transcept of 'Paddington Cathedral'. There was one famous journalistic encounter. Gerry deliberately leaked to me that the region's Plymouth Division was to be abolished. The staff met in the car park until Gerry or I made 'a further statement'. When the political going generally became too hot, my editor suggested I go along with the demand that we retracted our report. I refused. Immediately Gerry became a friend for the rest of his life. He was writing his second railway book in bed until a couple of days before his death. His first, *I Tried to Run a Railway*, had him sacked for being too outspoken about his colleagues.

By then he was general manager of the Eastern Region, based in York. When passing through York the other day I recalled with amusement the story told me by another of my railway authors, Derek Barrie, then second in command of the Eastern. On the Monday Gerry was to start at York, the top brass put on their best suits. No sign or news of the new boss in the morning; nor during the afternoon. 'Instead of going home at the usual time, we felt we had to stay at our desks,' Barrie told me. 'Then came a report from Barton-upon-Humber. He was making his mark inspecting the ultimate in railway backwaters.' Gerry wasn't conventional. A signalman told him he couldn't be who he said he was because 'general managers don't walk'. He upset an inspector at Reading by insisting he blew the whistle to hurry up the waddling commuters from Newbury. He could be deliberately indiscreet in front of his public relations man, but he was a much-loved achiever, especially of sensible speed increases won at modest engineering cost. Many a pre-dinner drink was enjoyed at their old house overlooking the lifeboat station. Jean now lives by herself still surrounded by railway memorabilia, and wistfully talks of earlier days, 'though I never liked the yachting... couldn't see the point'. She serves local Dover sole, and she's made some of the arrangements for me to meet people in the next few days. It is only recently she has given up her daily dip, after she'd been 'badly mauled' by a strong wave.

Over coffee, I pick up a copy of the East Suffolk Travellers' Association *Member's Bulletin*. First Gerry and, after his death for a long time, Jean, was president of this ginger group keeping the management of the East Suffolk (Ipswich to Lowestoft) line up to scratch with adequate publicity, consultation over timetable changes, and sensible connections. Throughout Britain, such groups of train users have made a real difference. Several sensible things have been done, like using a travel agent based at Saxmundham station (where there is a seat in memory of Gerry) to issue tickets. Signalling is now controlled by radio.

In the morning once more we walk around Aldeburgh. If none individually is of great architectural merit, seafront homes are an interesting collection. The High Street is full of shoppers, who mainly manage to park close by, but it is only when you go into detail that you realise the choice of ordinary shops, grocers, butchers, greengrocers and bakers, has been drastically reduced over recent years, their place taken by boutiques, galleries and cafés dependent on the visitor. And when we walk along the seafront after dark, we see few lights on, for many are second homes, only used for short periods, though a few no doubt bought ahead for intended retirement. Flowers and plants in the windows of all-the-year homes make a statement. Despite the reduction in food shops, however, Aldeburgh is still pretty self sufficient, certainly in comparison with other places of its size.

It is a real outpost of culture, with numerous local active societies, some making good use of the hotels and restaurants – and the cinema. Once upon a time there were the normal weekend queues outside for the 'one and thrupennies'. Then, as television killed most cinemas, the question was how long it would be before it closed its doors. But it didn't, and is an honoured member of today's small band of thriving private picture houses. Litty Gifford was the initial driving force behind its rescue. From the early Seventies until 1994, she economised, raised money, bought new equipment and gave it sense of purpose.

'Litty was marvellous but couldn't go on forever, but when I said I'd take over she stayed on for nine months to guide me,' says today's manager Felicity Ann Sieghart. 'Taking it on was one of those impulse things. I like good films and could see how valuable the cinema was to Aldeburgh, but it's been hard work. Though we are proud of the original Art Deco lighting, actually we have one of the best up-to-date sets of equipment in East Anglia. There's endless updating. We have broadened the market, with things like the annual weekend documentary festival, and there's the cinema club of 1100 supporters who pay a £15 annual sub but get reduced prices on tickets – and we organise occasional trips to the theatre in Ipswich and Norwich. But we only seat 280, enough for a cinema but not to make live shows economic.'

There's a buzz at the cinema this morning, for one of the monthly mailings is about to go out, the CD shop which leases space is full of customers, and everywhere there are people attending one of the small conferences regularly held here. I have to ask permission to take a glimpse inside the well-raked, narrow cinema itself, certainly no fleapit. 'We promote a friendly ambiance,' says Felicity. That is obvious from a casual visit.

Opposite is the Aldeburgh Bookshop, a well-known institution making the most of the many authors who live here. Its owners, John and Mary James, newcomers to bookselling, noticed the shop was up for sale when John was bored with his career in commercial property. They gambled on the town being able to support one good bookshop but there not being sufficient business to attract competition. A literary festival with a string of famous writers is one way of expanding business. A 'rover ticket' covering all ten planned talks costs £65 without accommodation; two-night packages including hotel accommodation are also available.

The Festival

Nearby is the town office of the internationally-famous Aldeburgh Festival which holds its concerts a few miles up the estuary at Snape Maltings. Here there's been a particularly imaginative transformation from industry to art, helped by there being virtually no other development in the vicinity. Benjamin Britten was responsible for putting the Festival on the map. He relished the way that industry and music flourished side by side, and that commercial shipping was revived for a time. Now it's all tourism and arts – not to decry that. Many of Britten's compositions were given their first performance here, with what has been described as spontaneous combustion.

The story of how Snape Maltings developed is fascinating. Though it is twenty circuitous miles to the river's mouth, sailing barges took away huge quantities of locally-grown barley for use at Scottish distilleries. It was Newson Garrett, youngest son of the founder of the famous Garrett works at Leiston, who realised that a fortune could be made by processing the barley and despatching malt instead. Some of the earliest buildings have a tie rod inscribed 'Newson Garrett, Freehold 1846,' cast by what were then his brother's works at Leiston, while his own brickworks made the mellow red bricks. The last of the buildings, a silo to store the grain until it could be processed (only possible in winter, when temperatures could be more easily controlled) was not added until 1952, but blends well with the rest, including the central archway bearing the date 1859. Other buildings bear the dates 1874, 1884, 1885, 1890 and 1895.

They must have been heady days. In its various branches, the Garrett family were amazingly entrepreneurial. Newson Garrett's daughter Elizabeth was Britain's first woman doctor, who founded the Elizabeth Garrett Anderson Hospital for women in London, and at Aldeburgh became the first woman mayor. A suffragette, she worked closely with Emmeline Pankhurst.

Today's visitors are often surprised by seeing the masts of a sailing ship at the quay; in earlier times people would have been amazed had there not been several ships there. At some high tides, short processions of them left, some carrying several hundred tons of malt. A freight-only branch line later competed for the traffic, and from the outbreak of World War Two, when much coastal shipping was curtailed, held a near monopoly – until diesel lorries began to make inroads. The last of the maltings closed in 1965 because the low-lying damp site prevented installation of modern machinery. The great complex has been treated with respect as the private owner has developed various activities – the Festival rents its own car park – including unusual shopping and eating, but it is the music that attracts most of the half million annual visitors.

The Aldeburgh Festival was first run from, but rapidly outgrew, the Jubilee Hall and the churches at Aldeburgh, Blythburgh and Orford. Benjamin Britten was much involved in the creation of a concert hall in one of the maltings. It had an auditorium and stage large enough for opera without spoiling the building's character. Because of flood risk in the pit at spring high tides, members of the orchestra were advised to bring Wellington boots. The hall was opened by the Queen at the start of the 1967 Festival. Three years later she was back to open its successor, since fire destroyed the original on the first night of the 1969 Festival. Confidence had risen, and the replacement concert hall is one of the world's finest and best known.

For the first time in years, I stop at the Maltings. Sheila goes exploring and shopping (she buys an exceptionally worthwhile paperback, *Port on the Alde, Snape and the Maltings*) while I find my way to the busy Festival office to meet today's head of external relations, Regis Cochefert. Effectively supremo of everything except the artistic side, and among the most coherently fluent bosses I've ever met, he surprises me by telling me he is French. He answers questions with bubbling enthusiasm, and has stunning command of detail. He'd have made David & Charles a super managing director.

He speaks reverently of Britten and admires the mixture of well-known and experimental works now performed. He too uses that phrase 'spontaneous combustion'. He then tells me that just thirty-eight per cent of expenditure is funded by ticket sales. Public organisations contribute only another fourteen per cent. The rest is funded by the operation's own commercial trust and investments, and by private individuals. £2.3 million expenditure this year; 28 full-time staff, eighty volunteers including four ushers for each concert. The Aldeburgh Festival of Music & the Arts in June is in fact only one of four major annual events. Chief of the others is Snape Proms in August, and the longest concert series in the country outside London. With other activities, the postgraduate music school, the education department which involves every Suffolk school, and letting the hall for conferences and weddings, things happen on nearly two-thirds of days year round. Of just under 80,000 concert tickets sold, sixty per cent goes to people living within a two-hour drive, though for the Proms it changes to sixty per cent being bought by visitors from further afield.

Back to the music itself. He also speaks reverently of today's artistic chief, Thomas Adès, just thirty at the time of my visit: 'today's bestselling British composer as well as conductor and pianist. We're back to the same principles as when Britten began it. Since the new team has been here, box office receipts are a record. Britten and Peter Pears [the tenor with whom he was to form a lifelong artistic partnership] would be pleased.'

As I prepare to leave, he tells me to spend sufficient time looking round the remarkable complex and says I should come back on a sunny evening to see one of the sunsets over the Alde. 'I can't imagine anywhere nicer to work'; not even in his native France.

Rejoining Sheila, first it is a walk to the quay, then to the complex once covered with railway lines where horses pulled trucks round sharp curves and it was occasionally necessary to resort to turntables. Finally, we linger in the retail area and enjoy a leisurely cup of tea, over which I tell Sheila of a concert here years ago when thunder roared. The conductor was so skilful with his baton that it always seemed as though he was bringing the thunder into the music and under his control. Afterwards, we saw the lightning flashing brilliantly over the broad water at full tide.

FROM ALDEBURGH
TO HEATHROW

Fish and Fraud

Next day it is fish, leisure rudely interrupted, and then again fish. It begins well enough, with visits to half a dozen of the fishermen in their huts on the shingle. There are fewer of them now than when I first came, yet we would be happy to have just one in Nairn. The variety of fish on offer is impressive. From makeshift, with minimal hygiene, to spotlessly clean mini-shops, the style of the huts varies as much as their occupants. Though some are suspicious at first, the fishermen open up when I show I'm genuinely interested in their trade and know at least a little about it and its current difficulties. Their moods are very different, from the everlastingly pessimistic to 'not as easy as we'd like, but still a great way to earn a living'.

They are mainly selling last night's catches. Tesco might be cheaper, but quality and freshness are unrivalled. Sole, bass, dabs, skate, rock eel, herrings, dressed crab, lobster; but it's not quite a case of you naming it, for there are no Dover soles or plaice today. The plaice have gone. 'I used to catch them fifteen to twenty miles out; last spring I had to go thirty to forty miles. It's not just the fact that there's been over-fishing, but the seasons are changing. We're getting ready to change over from sole to cod, much earlier than used to be the case.'

In common with inshore fishermen all around our coasts, they complain bitterly about the big trawlers hoovering everything up. 'Regulations make them throw back fish that are too small, but they're dead. They analysed a recent catch. Twenty-one per cent of the haddock caught were juvenile – over 100 tons of haddock that should be breeding simply taken out of the sea for nothing!' They say the Danes are the chief culprits but animation increases when the conversation switches to current rules and regulations: universally, the opinion is that they make their own lives unnecessarily hard without achieving the desired results.

One fisherman's lot is not a happy one. 'Do you know, this boat cost £50,000, I spend £10,000 a year on gear that wears out and gets smashed up; even a rope to haul the boat up the beach is £200, and I need two of those a year. Three people have to scrape a living from her. [Even working boats are of course female.] Sometimes it's £35 each for a week.' But he proudly shows me a 2lb 9oz cod caught last night; that will fetch £10. And our parents thought cod too dull to bother with! 'Farmed salmon is cheaper than cod these days,' says another fisherman.

'It's a different way of earning a living,' adds a third. 'For a start, when there's a northwest gale off the Humber, we've to get through very choppy water till we're 100 yards offshore.' I have often wondered how exactly they calculate what waves should be braved as they push off from the shingle, and even more how they know it will be safe to come ashore at the trip's end.

'I've another job, house painting, when it's too rough to go out,' says another. 'It's not too bad fishing through summer. It's not a piece of cake either but if you understand the sea and the fish, you're more in charge of what you get than some people admit. I don't want to change.'

Customers interrupt some of these conversations. A few 'specials' have been put aside for expected regulars. One or two ponder and deliberate. For them, buying a piece of fresh fish seems as challenging as deciding on the pattern of wallpaper for the living room. Even small orders come to a significant number of pounds. In some cases, fillet steak would be cheaper, weight for weight. These retail sales are obviously important, but some bulk goes to market.

Then it's morning coffee, our own conversation halted by listening to that of the locals with obsessive interest in each other. We were going to debate whether we would have fish for lunch as well as supper but, attracted by a window display, we go into a shop that had better be nameless. We make a purchase of rather more than £100, first checking that they accept Visa, because stupidly I've failed to bring sufficient cash for our trip to Madeira the day after tomorrow. Problem. The card is rejected. A painfully slow call to Visa tells the shop to tear it up. 'This doesn't happen every day,' says the owner. The silence is deafening as other customers watch. I talk to Visa, who tell me to call the issuing bank, where no human being is on hand.

I explain my predicament, and show my guarantee card. 'Only covers £100,' says the owner unsympathetically,' though by this time a local resident has recognised me in a way that suggests I am not a crook. 'We don't make the rules,' says the owner. 'I'll willingly cancel the transaction, but if you want it you'll have to pay the balance in cash. I can't make any exception.' Grudgingly, I see my already inadequate cash shrink. Maybe the Madeira hotel, which is sure to take American Express, might come to the rescue. Maybe not, says Sheila.

So relaxation is off the menu, and we retreat to our hotel with a sandwich, and I spend the next hour and a half on the phone... the hotel's phone at that, for mobiles are out of range. Eventually I'm given a lengthy number, which turns out to be in Maryland, USA, and an equally long reference code puts me in touch with a friendly but lethargic American. He finds it harder to understand my 'special accent' than I do his Southern drawl, but eventually he recites the hotel number accurately, and soon he calls back at Visa's expense.

By the time he has understood my mother's maiden name and goodness knows what else for my 'protection', he offers to have an emergency card couriered anywhere in the world in 48 hours. But his system won't work without the street address of Madeira's most famous hotel; remarkably Sheila finds it. 'It's been a pleasure talking to you, sir; anything else I can do for you?' [The card was duly waiting on top of a pile of brochures in our hotel room. Later, the bank admitted they might have warned me they were blocking my card. Three months before I'd questioned an item on my statement which, without telling me, they had concluded was fraud.]

It was mid-afternoon by the time I ate my sandwich, and then I fell asleep. By the time I wake it is too late for our planned trip – and the heavens have again opened. So, over a cup of tea, I re-read *Smoked Salmon & Oysters; a feast of Suffolk memories*, by Richard Pinney, who I first met many years ago at his Butley Oysterage restaurant at Orford. Decades ago, I came across the restaurant in Orford's neat square at lunchtime on my first visit to these parts and have enjoyed delicious fish on every return visit. Tonight we're continuing the tradition of taking Jean Fiennes there. The book offers the best mixture I know of tales of boats and fishing exploits, recipes and mouth-watering photographs, and personal reminiscence highlighting changing times. It is a self-published masterpiece, selling briskly in the shop over many years. It concludes without coyness:

Now, at last, I can put up my pen (along with my filleting knife, and oyster knife, put away some little while ago) and bid you all farewell. Perhaps we shall meet sometime in our 'sampling kitchen', our little Orford restaurant. The Butley-Orford Oysterage, with these four corner-stones – oyster-growing, salmon-smoking, catering and now extensive fishing, should be able to keep up-to-date, one department after another coming up every fourth year for examination and, possibly, new investment. We *should* be able to stay in business. I hope so. But much will depend on the acumen of future generations.

Richard died in the early 1990s, so I have arranged to talk to his son William ahead of our dinner. We're quickly into detail. He's been using the fyke net, a set of three funnels, to catch eels, three feet long, three to five pounds. 'But my remit is to grow oysters and catch fish.' The latter is done with no fewer than four family boats. 25ft *Lady Joyce* and 30ft *Raxone*, day boats with a crew of two, are based here in Orford, while the fast long-lining trawler *Nicola Dawn* is at Harwich, and the sein netter 52ft *Kesteven* is based at Lowestoft and stays at sea for three weeks, even a month. Quite an operation.

'It doesn't get any easier, but isn't as bad as it's painted. Cod have been scarce, but two years ago we had the best cod fishing ever. Generally it could be a lot worse. Plaice aren't handy to Aldeburgh, but there are plenty in the North Sea, 25 miles out.

'What makes it a nightmare is all the bureaucratic rules and regulations. If people are sensible, things should be OK. Even those tales about the oceans being vacuum cleaned of fish are exaggerated, ...' At which point he launches into an attack on overseas rivals, this time the Spanish and French with 'their tradition of landing small fish, sexually immature, useless. No farmer would send their piglets to market, but that's what they're doing with haddock.'

Jean, who we picked up on our way on a particularly stormy night, and Sheila have meanwhile had their own conversation, which also seems to have been fish-led. As I join them at the table, they point to a notice saying that it was in 1950 that Richard experimentally started smoking sea trout he had caught off Orford Ness. The same principles are used for much of what is currently on offer: 'first salted or brined and then hung in the smokehouse, flavoured and preserved by gently smouldering whole oak logs in the specially designed smokehouse.' Trout, mackerel, sprats, eels and cod roe are hung for a few hours before being hot smoked. Salmon, the bestseller of what is sold across the counter, is cured and smoked for 48 hours over an open fire. The same notice advises that sole, bass, mullet, lobsters and crabs are plentiful from spring to autumn, cod and skate most of the year, sprats and herring winter specialities. We are like schoolchildren making our choice, sticking to the familiar: smoked eel, smoked cod's roe, sole, sea bass and salmon. 'This is wonderful,' says Jean, the excitement more the equivalent of hearing a favourite CD once more than in experimentation.

Bringing chairs close to the table is always a noisy business on the bare floor, and don't expect soft-furnishings or designer tablecloths. The plain walls are decorated with posters lining up many varieties of fish in neat formation. But even on a wet night like this, and well out of season, tables steadily fill up until a couple have to wait for us to finish. One comes here for real fish. Patrons are divided between those once more enjoying a favourite dish and those pushing out the boundaries of experience.

Bury St Edmunds: The Gem of Suffolk

Next morning, we take the familiar road up past the church and Aldeburgh brickyard. The long history of making bricks from the local brick earth isn't over, though no longer of course loaded at the private quay at the works' back door into their own boat for London. Left, past Snape Maltings, and then we bump along the winding road, splashing through the same puddles as last night, back to Orford. Again it is raining hard. But I'm determined to walk from the square, where we parked for the restaurant last night, down to the quay. This is on a kind of raised causeway, lined with neat brick cottages. Before it was silted up, the original quay may have been alongside, where there's still a sunken area.

Orford is an interesting little place, once a busy port on the sea, now well inland. If you think the church large, it was in fact built as daughter church to that of Sudbourne in which parish the planned town of Orford took shape. Across what was the market place are the castle ruins dating from Henry II. Built on a mound to a new design with three projecting square turrets above a circular central core, it became a familiar landmark to sailors. An 1805 plan to pull it down was stopped to prevent putting mariners at risk. A few years later, Orford joined many other little ports in being disenfranchised in the great Reform Act. One of our democracy's great moments comes to life when visiting the rotten boroughs.

Though it bustles with pleasure boating in summer, this morning we have the large quay to ourselves. In front lies a huge expanse of water; behind a feeling for history. But there's also history enough across the water at Orford Ness, though today that's hardly visible. We'll see it more clearly, albeit from further away, when in a later chapter we're back in Suffolk, at the mouth of the river deflected for many miles by the shingle banks of centuries.

The weather is getting even worse, but before we leave the area, I want to take a glimpse – and that's all I get – of the Butley River, once its own affair, a busy commercial lifeline, but turned by the lengthening of those shingle banks into a tributary stream of the Alde or Ore. Now, Sheila navigates us across the soaking Suffolk countryside to Bury St Edmunds, somewhere I've never yet visited and have been told that when I do I will modify my general lack of interest in the county's interior.

We take an enterprising route through narrow roads to Ipswich, taking longer to get through it than to reach it. Several really rural diversions beyond, too, but I stick to my point: high Suffolk is not cosy countryside – not that anywhere would feel inviting in today's rain. With poor visibility, the approaches to Bury St Edmunds seem pretty ordinary, too – as they did when seen from railway and the main road on previous occasions, never encouraging stopping off even briefly. After we are well off the main road, there still seems little point. I've almost written off Bury St Edmunds as being no better than an inland Ipswich when, suddenly, we land in a charming square with our hotel almost opposite the cathedral entrance.

Driving through an arch into the hotel's yard, we unload and are given an old-fashioned welcome. In fact the whole experience, the square, the hotel, the welcome, the other guests (few of them today's office workers that dominate most bars), reminds me of arriving with Mr England at the end of one of our 1930s trips to a new place for my parents to 'try out' to see if they liked it enough to move there. Such feelings are real, though hard to analyse, let alone set down, but details of the England of over sixty years ago – even what the cars and the steam engines and lorries and signposting were like – come flooding into my mind. How fortunate I was to have experienced that age, currently more forgotten than Victorian times. The Angel is certainly a market square period piece, with ancient timbers, low beams and creaky floors, but there's more than that to ambience. Respect for the heritage?

The rain stops long enough for us to take a quick walk around what Cobbett described as 'the nicest town in the world' and another writer speaks of as a pearl in a bad oyster, a delightful centre – 'as it was Cobbett's, it is now' – surrounded by London overspill. Ipswich people had told Cobbett that Suffolk's second town was much to be preferred to their own. Bury St Edmunds is a historic but much-alive centre, the gem of Suffolk. The secret of Bury St Edmunds, I discover, is that its heyday was a long time ago. Prospering in the eighteenth century was good for a town; in the Victorian days, usually bad, since 'improvements' were often without respect or good taste. Bury St Edmunds is an absolute treasure, its small but definite core not in the least brushed by Ipswich's tar of later commercialism.

Though I am pleased to have sampled even this much, there is only time for a rapid survey of the cathedral and the large gardens beyond, and a few of the quality narrow streets, the slope up Abbeygate Street with its county-type shops being specially attractive. They say that the legacy of monks pervades the town and certainly they made their mark, but Bury St Edmunds has a particular historic claim. It was in the time of King John the greedy (immortalised by the tales of Robin Hood) that English freedom with constitutional government could be said to have been won here. After John's French defeat in July 1214, 25 barons gathered at the high altar of St Edmund to meet the Archbishop of Canterbury. Their resolve to curtail the King's demands led to the signing of Magna Carta at Runnymede, near Windsor, soon after. And while the surrounding countryside may not be my favourite, there are many great gardens around Bury St Edmunds, appropriate since the 'father' of landscape gardening, Sir Humphrey Repton (1752–1818) was born here. So much to see, so little time.

Of Buses and Trains

I've arranged to meet and spend the evening with an old friend, spoken with in distance radio debates on transport several times since we last saw each other in the flesh. John Hibbs is, yes, another author. His first book was the definitive history of *British Bus Services*; other works include evocative studies of *The Country Bus* and *The Country Chapel*. But there's much real-life experience, too. He has managed and owned country bus services, gone bust running one, been railway manager, and transport historian. A decade or more beyond the time when most academics retire, he is now Emeritus Professor of Transport Management at Birmingham's University of Central England, frequently presenting papers about today's transport dilemma. He often pops up on radio and television. As though that's not enough, his weekends are busy as Congregational preacher.

Though for many years we have only exchanged a Christmas card, he is one of those people you can access instantly; he combines common sense with a delight in the ridiculous. Good fun. Our talk ranges widely, from our first meeting giving evidence at the Jack Committee on Rural Bus Services through bus timetables and religion to marital relations and back to railway economics. We start by having tea in a busy part of the hotel where we occasionally comment on the appearance of more exotic guests. We agree that much television is infinitely less compelling than observing what passes in front of us. Not quite what you would have seen in the 1930s, but definite similarities. It is obviously a privilege to be here... and to be seen. 'Oh, darling. Fancy seeing you,' is answered by: 'But I always come on such-and-such a day'.

John talks of the good old days of developing bus services, when drivers were respected and thanked at the end of journeys. Those who later had to work in factories felt they had half died. And of the problems of excessive and often downright evil legislation. He recalls that on a Wednesday market day in 1931, the owner of a country bus parked at his usual spot in a nearby secondary square. A prohibition notice was slapped on the bus, too wide for new regulations. 'He simply abandoned the bus, and asked another operator to take his passengers home at the day's end. That was one effect of the 1930 Road Traffic Act.'

Another was that railways were forced to give up their bus services and prohibited from running them again – though encouraged to remain part owners. Co-operation between rail and road virtually ceased, yet outright competition was also impossible. This ridiculous state of affairs persisted until well after most branch lines had been closed in the 1960s. We agree that had the railways been allowed to run their own replacement buses, specifically to maintain connections with main-line trains, carrying heavy luggage and with through tickets and proper publicity, the Beeching closures would have caused far less hardship – to the railways themselves as well as to rural life. When branch lines closed, and in most cases only existing bus services could be used, the railway traffic simply evaporated. Another evil of the 1930 Act was that it encouraged monopolistic territorial bus companies, which often unreasonably harassed surviving independents, and hardly ever co-operated by including details of their services in local timetables.

We enjoy that rarity of today's sights: across the square a goodly queue of shoppers and workers returning to their country homes has formed for a private bus. Rare indeed, yet the private operator knows his business far better than can a large, centrally-controlled one naturally giving priority to their main money-earning routes. Usually private operators are based at the far end of the route, avoiding dead mileage, and can run a local weekly or daily service dove-tailed with charter and school work. In many cases money could have been saved and services improved by territorial companies sub-contracting lightly-used rural routes to private operators. Alas, while political thinking changes radically, such common-sense detail is never the flavour of the moment.

Thus the nation argues about whether the Post Office should retain a monopoly or not, but never considers sub-contracting the monopoly service even in the remotest islands. It has to be red Royal Mail vans – or nothing. But then, when the Post Office yielded control of telephone services, soon nearly all telephone kiosks placed beside village post offices were expensively removed. A Telecom spokesman was upset when I described this as wasteful. 'It's not waste at all,' he said. 'We just don't want to have anything to do with the Post Office.'

'Ridiculous,' says John, a word we use repeatedly as we alternate in relating shocking experiences of monopolistic power, such as private operators not being allowed to pick up passengers on the last miles into town, or forced to charge more if they do. How much better it could all have been – and still could be with understanding and practical, pragmatic rather than theory-ridden governance.

John gives me a pile of his recent papers; one about bus services is subtitled *A tragedy in three acts*. John has never been orthodox. When working for the Eastern Region, wanting to electrify the non-electrified pocket of the Lee Valley route, he put forward quite spurious reasons to persuade the government to come to the right decision. Joining the Common Market, he said, would immediately render all those greenhouses so uneconomic that the land would quickly be sold for housing, causing a surge in traffic that could only be handled by electrification. Do politicians get other matters so persistently wrong as they do transport?

Motorway to Heathrow

Next morning Sheila is up early and moves the car from the hotel car park, where she is just able to manoeuvre out with the help of the night porter, to the square. Carrying our luggage down the hotel's steep steps to the car park again reminds me of the days before World War Two. The journey east and south distinctly does not. Dual carriageway even all the way, around Newmarket to the M11. We have been much cheered by the announcement of a ten-year plan to encourage rare plants to flourish undisturbed beside sectors of motorways. Railways have long had their colourful embankments and wetland nature reserves between adjoining routes; and now the motorway people recognise that since they own this unusual linear estate it is appropriate to manage it for biodiversity.

With the challenge of the M25 ahead, I resist stopping at the one place I should have loved to revisit: Saffron Walden. There are vivid memories of changing trains at Audley End and crossing by a slippery snow-covered bridge for the short trip to Saffron Walden for Christmas 1938, and of the extraordinary ancient roof lines of the Rose & Crown. Mother said our room was a fire trap; it was over Christmas, decades later, that visitors' lives were lost in a fire at this then Forte hotel.

I've never been back to Saffron Walden, still I am sure a little oasis of pleasantness just off the M11. Another memory is of Christmas Day itself, seeing a postman walk through the snow past a gate where an old woman waited. Would anyone remember her? The postman passed by just shaking his head; not even a 'Happy Christmas'.

As it happened, there would have been ample time for the diversion, for today the M25 works perfectly, and we arrive at Heathrow ridiculously early. Terminal Two, the oldest, is the least well-endowed with shopping and other diversions in that vast town of scarcely-connected villages that is the airport. Yet for all its inconvenience and ugliness, Heathrow as a whole I find fascinating. It grows on me the better I understand how it fits together and works. There is an amazing range of architectural variety and quality, while around the periphery one unexpectedly sees traces of what things had been like when flying from London meant going to Croydon. With seasonal, weekly, daily patterns, Heathrow changes through many moods. I feel more at home here than at smaller and no doubt more convenient but less well-understood airports. And, if things are dull, there are many memories of journeys starting and finishing here to draw upon.

It is a fertile place for the fiction writer simply to wonder and observe. Heathrow is pivotal in the crystallisation of so many hopes and fears. Concrete jungle where construction work never ceases? Maybe, but also very human, with many civilised enclaves, and never losing its capacity to surprise. At five in the morning, after a rough flight from the Far East, in the days when even Brits had to show their passports, presenting mine brought the response: 'I've just read your *Country Railway* twice.'

BAA Heathrow publish some enterprising booklets, one of which points out that the first sustained international service started on Hounslow Heath as far back as 1919. Pilots followed landmarks, particularly railway stations, many with their names painted on the roof. Croydon then took over, the tin shacks were burned down and the heath once again became a place for walking the dog, though by then suburban sprawl had taken over most of the market gardens that once flourished on the well-drained soil.

Surrounding residents have a precedent for being suspicious, for Heathrow came back to life as a level site for a long runway for experimental flights. 'Only a few a day,' they were assured; no need to worry. It was using war-time emergency powers that what we know as today's Heathrow was established, absorbing the 'Great West Aerodrome' and given a triangle of wide runways. Such was the area of concrete, that excess water had to be channelled into the River Crane, with 'balancing reservoirs' on either side of the A312 to hold the overflow. The system is still in use, part of the Causeway Nature Reserve, the area dedicated to the conservation of wildlife around Heathrow which you see immediately on take-off to the west, before Windsor Castle comes into view.

Civil control of the airport began in 1946. Another precedent was established: flying and construction would take place simultaneously. Official opening was on 31 May 1946. Official completion will surely never be achieved, but Heathrow is truly wondrous especially in the sheer volume of traffic it handles. BAA claims the airport gives, directly or indirectly, employment to 83,000 people locally. It has its own life just as much as any place with so large a workforce; it could indeed be described as the pulse of the nation.

The main problem is that the heart beats loudly, so planes can be heard even when listening to the Queen broadcasting from Windsor Castle. Planes for Inverness pass at a low level close to our home, but there are so few of them that we enjoy them – as, in Devon days, I did the sonic bang of approaching Concordes several times daily. It is not merely the volume of noise but its near-continuity that reduces the quality of life for so many in the Thames Basin. BAA do their best. New aeroplanes become steadily quieter but, even when all the really noisy ones have been replaced, nothing could induce me to swap the calm of the Moray Firth for the admittedly delightful small towns and villages of the Thames Valley.

·XXVIII·

DAY TRIP TO
SUFFOLK

Breakfast from Liverpool Street

'Lovely day; not a cloud in the sky,' our cabbie greets us. He adds: 'Hope you're going to do something nice for yourselves a day like this.'

Indeed we are. We are back refreshed from our week in Madeira spending two more nights in London, at a cheaper hotel! And now we are into the wonderfully transformed glass cathedral that is today's Liverpool Street, even hurrying passengers look relaxed, no queue to speak of at the ticket office, the only discordant note being that the train from Norwich which forms ours to Ipswich is running late... and later, as it crawls into platform eight, defensively driven in the way deprecated by many who care about safety. It finally halts only eleven minutes before we are due out. A crowd of over 400 alight, and the train has to be cleaned and seat reservations applied, before we are allowed on. Three minutes before departure time we are warmly welcomed into the restaurant car. 'Late in, so a bit of a rush, but we won't be long,' says the woman stewardess, while the plumper lady chef busies away clearing up the breakfast just served to 24. Miraculously, we leave only a minute late. The next two trains from Norwich have already arrived. Our porridge arrives as soon as we are on the move.

The glass cathedral stretches only so far. Soon we are in that Stygian gloom of the approach to Liverpool Street I recall from before World War Two: the continually-curving six tracks, archways on either side, and sometimes between pairs of tracks. I clearly remember the surviving platform of the first station out from Liverpool Street that my father told me in 1938 had even then long succumbed to tram competition.

Who, we wonder, would choose to live in Tower Hamlets, over there to the south. On our return, the taxi driver taking us back to the hotel told us that, having been brought up and lived there all his life, he'd recently moved to Bexhill 'to give my family a better standard of life. Tower Hamlets used to be a good place to live, but the crime rate is right over the top.' But, then, we're not sure about Canary Wharf towering in the distance, though enjoy seeing the natty little Docklands' trains as we approach through the horrific junction complex of Stratford.

It is then familiar childhood territory through Manor Park, Ilford where there was a favourite aunt, Seven Kings, Romford where I was born, and Gidea Park where I spent my first years. That was then where London really stopped. Much of Gidea Park itself was built in the late 1930s: hundreds of what were advertised as quality but seemed small houses, some of eccentric if not vulgar design. All the menfolk moving in walked to the station for their steam suburban trains to Liverpool Street, their briefcases including the standard spare collar for midday change. And there, to the south just beyond the station, is the raised path on which I walked beside my dad, begging him to lend me a few coins, always carefully counted on their return, so I too could enjoy the sound of jingling in my pocket. We loved looking at the Continental boat trains, and the goods trucks which ran on to the train ferries operating out of Harwich, and named trains such as *The Fenman*.

Even in those days I disliked seeing good fields being built on, and hated the Great Arterial Road to Southend-on-Sea, eating up land, taking people off the safe trains and killing them. Hideous billboards announced how many lives had been claimed in the last few months and how many more people had been injured. If you are in a gloomy mood thinking of things that have deteriorated, remember that, despite vastly increased traffic, only half as many people are killed on the roads today as in the 1920s and 1930s. As we pass the junction for Southend-on-Sea and make light of Brentwood Bank, we comment how much more road-conscious dogs and even cats have become in the last half century: natural selection, we suppose.

Our train, by the way, is not anything as modern as an HST, but has old-fashioned coaches with a separate engine, now pushing us. The service is good, every half an hour to Norwich, but the congested first fifty miles out of Liverpool Street have always been the operator's nightmare, and periodically we are checked by adverse signals, making it easier to drink our tea.

Ingatestone I recall as an unspoilt village. The demand for housing seems endless today. Then Chelmsford, our first stop, a great sprawling jungle of houses, roads and supermarkets. Free of signal delays, we are now a real express. There is still pleasant countryside before Colchester: especially around Kelvedon, at one time junction for an idiosyncratic Light Railway down to Tollesbury and a pier on the Blackwater that once carried much of Wilkinson's Tiptree jams. The rough shunting even of mixed passenger-and-goods trains must have broken a fair few jars. Through Marks Tey, still the junction for Sudbury, where I remember visiting eccentric authors living in odd places like Mersea Island.

If there is a single part of Britain where one feels that, against the odds, geography has helped retain individualism, it must be the Thames marshes. Though at the end of a B road, on a quiet day in a fast car, Mersea Island is only an hour away from much of central London. Over fifteen million people have it comfortably in reach of a day trip. Many who live on Mersea Island go to work daily in London, and of course suffer from the high house prices in what is today almost the inner, certainly the middle, ring of London's commuting territory. Yet Mersea Island, edged by smooth or choppy salt water at high tide, plenty of mud and dried-out creeks at low, is almost as much its own place as in bygone days. Yes, fewer people earn their livelihood on the water, but enough retain ancient skills. Some skills that were lost have, however, been recovered. Partly because of poison in the paint then applied to the underside of boats, oysters were once declared unfit to eat from around here. Since that paint has been banned, the oyster beds have become productive again. And enjoying life on the water, though mainly as a hobby, are far more people than ever before. You see them in all manner of craft, including many Thames sailing barges, once the working monarchs of the local scene. They look especially majestic when seen from a low angle riding smoothly above the reeds and dried-out creeks, their sails protruding into those great open skies of the soft, low-lying coastline.

Mersea Island with its excellent fish restaurants isn't the only treasure along this coast. Even Southend-on-Sea has marvellous estuary life on its doorstep, and rivers like the Crouch, the great Blackwater which reaches the sea just south of West Mersea, and the Colne up to Colchester are much loved by locals who tell you enthusiastically that 'there's something worth hanging on to'.

Not everyone would be happy to live in the Essex marshes; since people are much more mobile these days, geography now plays a greater role in attracting those who like its particular manifestations. That happily results in a substantial core of incomers working closely with the admittedly declining population of locals enthusiastic about their setting. They mix especially well in things maritime, upholding long traditions and practising techniques built on centuries of experience. So, despite initial fears, there is ready acceptance of selective efforts to put the clock back, such as deliberately breaching a sea wall to allow a contained area of farmland to revert to salt marsh, and increase the tidal flow. Yes, there are conflicts: 'This is a fishing area. That's our field. You can't play football and cricket on the same field. But most people agree there's something worth hanging on to.' There's that phrase again. Increasingly they talk of the joys of their soft landscape. Mountains and cliffs aren't everything to everyone.

Mind you, there are also eccentrics in many of Essex's inland villages. One was Mary Whitehouse, whose obituary I have just read. She seemed to be much gentler in the flesh and more useful in her campaigning for decent standards than the media generally allowed. Her promised book was never finished.

Though it is sad to hear it has just died as a port, Colchester, our next stop, I've always found to be a welcoming place. Just beyond, we note the junction with the Clacton line, which later throws off a branch to Frinton (so exclusive that they don't know what a bucket and spade is and there's been a powerful lobby to prevent a fish-and-chip shop opening) and curious Walton-on-the-Naze on another very individual section of Essex's amazingly unspoilt coast.

Then Manningtree, its large car park full of commuters' vehicles left there at the daily price of what would buy a reasonable pub lunch. That is my difficulty in this part of England. Without taking back a word about the character of this coast, you are never away from the pull of London, and that goes for everywhere we will visit on today's trip. It is not my provincial Britain. No reason not to enjoy it, though, any more than not enjoying interesting places overseas where I would actually want to live less than the Essex Marshes.

A highlight of the journey is the viaduct across the River Stour offering a wonderful view of the estuary at low tide, Manningtree's own waterfront and that at Mistley, where they used to build boats, now devoted to luxury housing. One of my better-known editors, James MacGibbon, who looked after our maritime list, ended his days enjoying a commanding view from his Manningtree flat. Always with an appreciative eye for a shapely female, he once defected from his wife but was soon snatched back and for the rest of his life obediently conformed in every detail of life at home.

Eastern Britain's first deep-water quay, Parkeston Quay, where many Continental holidays begin, is seen in the distance from the viaduct, on which we are presented with our surprisingly modest bill for a Great British breakfast perfectly served; much more colourful Harwich itself being tucked around a bay out of sight. Charming Dovercourt is round the corner facing the sea, though from it you can see every ship for Parkeston Quay, the Ipswich complex and Felixstowe. The Stour, which comes up to Manningtree, and the Orwell, which reaches Ipswich, of course share a common estuary system. The entrance, described by the OS as Harwich Harbour, sees enormous passenger and freight movement, yet both estuaries have their peaceful stretches, some tree-lined, and of great appeal to yachtsmen.

Before the days that jumping on a cross-channel ship was routine, many well-heeled people used to spend a night at Harwich or

Dovercourt, giving them a quality feel. The Great Eastern Railway claimed its 250-room Felix Hotel was 'the finest on the East Coast', though it always seemed to need a lot of marketing to keep it busy. For three-quarters of the year 1922, four guineas (three for children) bought a first-class train ticket from Liverpool Street plus full board from Friday dinner to Monday breakfast. Then came the depression, hotels closed and there was real hardship as things almost literally fell apart. Now they are well up again and, though there's no grand hotel today, it is a pleasant place to stay. Not that many people come to Felixstowe for holidays of any kind today. An old man portrayed by Eric Sykes in a comedy we saw at a small London theatre last night indeed invoked laughs by the very thought of taking his holiday here.

Incidentally, for a century and a quarter, paddle steamers ran on the Orwell: a big, mainly railway-controlled business. The river's saltings are the winter feeding ground for wildfowl from the Arctic. The Suffolk Wildlife Trust's Trimley Marshes Reserve was financed by Felixstowe Docks as part of a controversial trade-off.

Ipswich, where we alight, is strategic gateway to eastern England but not an endearing place. It has a fascinating history, for its geographical importance is undeniable, but its position and sheer size don't make up for its lack of heart. To this day, there's no real centre, no feeling of warmth. The railway, which enters it by a short tunnel, sweeps north, and it is only in relatively recent times that the road to Felixstowe has crossed the mighty Orwell by a high bridge south of the town. We have to change at the over-used station where I've seen more confused passengers than anywhere else on Britain's railways. A station inspector once said he was not talking to the 'general public' in protest at losing his assistant and an engine driver sitting on a seat refused to answer a simple question too.

Over the bridge to our distinctly down-at-heel single-coach train called *John Constable*. He wouldn't be flattered. 'Call this a train?' grimaces Sheila. But it is, with around sixty seats, luggage and bicycle space and even a toilet, still much better than a bus, and providing many useful connections.

For the first few miles, sweeping round Ipswich's northern part, the East Suffolk line accommodates the busier Felixstowe passenger and freight traffic. Handling more containers than all other British ports put together, Felixstowe is a real success story. As a new venture, not merely was it staffed mainly by former agricultural workers and not included in the notorious Dock Labour Scheme, but at those ports that were included, the dockers, true to Luddite tradition, refused to touch containers at all. Felixstowe, though always itself unionised, made the most of its chance. A long container train comes off the branch as we pass the junction: diesel hauled, for even for this priority business, most of which is for electrified routes, nobody will pay for the wires to be extended to Felixstowe.

To Shingle Street

Today we alight at the East Suffolk line's second station, Woodbridge, where the railway took the town's best view as well as cutting off access to the commercial dock (the Suffolk word for a quay) and so stealing much of the trade. Out of a score or so of passengers on the single carriage, half a dozen get off before us, an alert Robert Simper (the author of books about East Coast sailing and ports and estuaries mentioned in chapter 26) keeping an eye out for us with his wife Pearl. We clamber into their four-wheel drive for a wonderfully down-to-sea-and-earth experience.

We take a short tour of Woodbridge, with its antique shops, moored yachts, and the tidemill of 1796 vintage, the last to be worked in England, till 1956. Water was trapped in a pound at high tide and, as it ran out the current drove the machinery. At the head of Deben estuary, of which more anon, Woodbridge has always been a desirable place to live. Tudor buildings were erected by shipowners and shipbuilders and others enjoying maritime prosperity. Woodbridge was indeed once a top-ranking port. Boats joined those from other Suffolk ports in the Icelandic fishing trade, generations before the cod wars of the twentieth century. Shipbuilding, drawing on the abundant supply of oak in High Suffolk to the north, peaked in the seventeenth century, by which time the town had already attracted a small intellectual contingent. Hard times came after the arrival of the railway and today's prosperous tone is set by incomers, including many who go daily to London, who love the position and the 'country life'.

Then we go off south east across the Sandlings peninsular, over Sutton Common, open land in the eighteenth century, abandoned in the nineteenth and ploughed up in the twentieth. We see where atomic bombs used to be kept at Woodbridge airfield... till the whole place closed down, along with a second base nearby. Relations had not been happy between the locals and the Yanks in this 'Little America', where the servicemen kept to themselves, but visitors could visit the cinema. They might pay in sterling, though prices and change were in dollars.

Across the common, with pheasants bred and released for shooting everywhere, and through Hollesley to the point where the River Ore (River Alde in its higher reaches) currently reaches the sea. It is over twenty miles by roundabout waterway to Snape Maltings, where barley used to be carried in a 250-ton barge when traffic was revived well after World War Two and lasted until 1978. In the distance we can see Orford church tower and lighthouse, yet it is strangely difficult to connect this with our recent visit to Aldeburgh, Snape and Orford.

It is not a cosy spot. Shingle Street, the nearby village is positively peculiar: no street at all, just a string of houses, many looking rather temporary affairs, on the shingle. Shingle is everywhere, great ridges marking points reached by various tides. Currently the sea is a respectable distance from the houses, but a single storm can so toss the shingle about that it changes the whole geography. The shingle moves relentlessly on a bed of London clay that appears about twice a year at very low tides.

'I think it's a downright dangerous place,' says Robert. 'I've been here when the breaking waves have gone right up to the houses, with much of their white water seeping out from the porous foundations on the inland side. When it floods, they are totally cut off here. We're in the parish of Bawdsey, but the sea's taken the road. It must take a special kind of courage to live here, but those who do love it. It's remote all right, yet in summer there are non-stop trippers coming to take a look.'

It is also an eerie place. In addition to the atomic bombs already mentioned, atomic research, the first-ever parachute jump and a pioneer Cold War Early Warning station are among the claims to fame of Orford Ness, up there to the north. The Ness has often been incorrectly called an island to discourage visitors. And as though the sea wasn't sufficient threat to Shingle Street, in the early days of the war, when most local people were evacuated, the Lifeboat Inn was destroyed in a practice run of the famous bouncing bomb, developed by Barnes Wallis for the dambusters. Dropped on the beach, it bounced into the erstwhile pub, much to the delight of the inventor who was close by on the shingle and threw up his hands with delight when he saw how effective his device had been. Added to all that, tucked just inside the estuary at Hollesley Bay is a large open prison, formerly a borstal. The grey North Sea and shingle dominate the scene, the present river mouth disappointingly insignificant at low tide. Nobody who didn't know could possibly guess at the length and scope of the estuary.

A notice for visitors tells us that 'Shingle Street is a very special but vulnerable place where people, rare plants and other creatures live. It is part of the Suffolk Coast and Heaths area of Outstanding Natural Beauty, and is a site of special scientific interest.' Pictures show what we can look for: skylarks, little terns that fly in from Africa to nest, sea peas and yellow horned poppies. Why any plant should choose to live on vulnerable, swept shingle isn't explained, but we delight in seeing clumps of both the sea pea and the yellow-horned poppy.

'The estuary extended southward over the years and captured the Butley River and Hollesley Haven so preventing them making their way to the sea,' says Robert. 'A year or two ago, the river went further south, but it's been retreating a bit recently.' We see a huge pit, a bit like an excavated building site, the site of its previous exit. Yes, some yachts and occasional fishing boats still come in and out, but most people who sail in the Aldeburgh area are content with their own inland waterway system, and it takes a considerable time to reach the sea anyway.

Who, we wonder, would want to live here. I'm half for knocking at a few doors and asking, but not today. 'They pay a lot for the houses,' chips in Robert. Recently a Martello Tower, hardly an ideal home, one would think, changed hands for £200,000. Martello Towers are another oddity. Those who built and manned them, and generations later Early Warning System, must have thought they had been sent to the edge of the world, especially when they heard about how much of Suffolk the sea had already gobbled up. 'After Dunwich, there seemed to be an attitude that all this would go one day,' says Robert. Our restaurant-car breakfast seems light years away, yet we reached here in two hours from Liverpool Street.

The Deben and Maritime Books

Glancing at the map, I realise that once, many years ago, on my first-ever visit to these parts, making my way north, I drove through Bawdsey (which we won't have time to do today) and beyond to the point where a pedestrian ferry crossed the River Deben near its narrow mouth to Felixstowe Ferry. That wasn't exactly a cosy experience, either. The ferry notice, where the road bleakly ended, gave details of when the last-ever ferry would run; that was already the previous Saturday. Between 1894 and 1931 there had been a chain ferry for vehicles, known as the Bridges. If any member of the Quilter family who occupied Bawdsey Manor, turned up to be taken across, the ferry had to come to pick them up immediately, even if it were almost completing a journey toward Felixstowe Ferry. In 1935, the Manor was bought by the government and used to develop radar. None of the joyous warmth of a cosy English village there.

I'm curious about the Deben, whose name I probably knew all those years ago but had long forgotten. It is hardly the best-known of English estuaries. I called it Deben to rhyme with Devon but am told it should sound 'Deeben'; but then every place, such as Hollesley, which apparently should be pronounced 'Ho'ly', I pronounce wrongly, an habitual problem for those who use maps and railway timetables to explore new lands. 'Funny thing is that incomers do that so frequently that in some cases their mispronunciation seems to be becoming the norm,' says Robert.

I ask him about the Deben. 'Its mouth is pretty restless too.' Then I recall he's written one of his books about it, *The Deben River, An enchanted waterway*:

On a very low tide in the sea, off the Dip at Old Felixstowe, a few rocks can be seen which are marked on the old maps as Walton Castle. This is one of the few reminders that coastal Suffolk was once part of the Roman Empire and that the area had small Romano-British farms. The Romans had considerable trouble with Saxon pirates from northern Germany who came over and raided the coastal settlements of south east England. To combat this they built a chain of forts at strategic places which they backed up with a fleet of galleys which went out when pirates were known to be on the coast.

One of these forts, Portus Adurni, was built at the mouth of the Deben River to guard the Sandlings coast. That seems to have been rather an odd choice because Harwich Harbour has a much better deep water entrance and all major shipping activities in modern times have been centred here. Obviously Harwich Harbour has been greatly improved by dredging, but the Deben must have had some great advantage which has been lost, because all the early people were attracted to it. The answer was probably Goseford, which was then a sheltered creek behind Felixstowe. In bad weather the small oar and sail craft of the past would have found little shelter in the open Stour or Orwell, and in their search for a safe anchorage near the open sea Goseford would have been the best bet.

After the Roman army had left and returned to the European mainland the Angles and Saxons came across the North Sea and settled along all the rivers of Suffolk and Norfolk. These new Anglo-Saxon people soon began to war amongst themselves for control over the land they had occupied. Again control of the Deben seems to have been critical and holding it allowed one group of war lords, the Wuffings, to push out and create the new Kingdom of East Anglia. Although the Anglo-Saxons continued to use the abandoned Roman settlement on the Felixstowe Cliffs near the fort, this was too open to attack from the sea so the Wuffings made their headquarters inland at Rendlesham.

While the estuary is navigable to small craft at all tides there's as little as four feet depth at the mouth. One of the book's maps shows how it used to fill about twice its present area at high tide. From 1200 to the early 1600s, they were continually narrowing it by walling up banks to create new grazing, while several side creeks have ceased to be tidal at all. So there is much less water to scour the channel when the tide's going out.

We head back through Hollesley and then west to the Ramsholt Arms, further up the Deben, in an isolated position on its bank. There used to be a barge dock here, but it's all pretty desolate today, and I'm not surprised to be told there's a crashed bomber submerged there. A broadish river in a basically flat landscape, it lacks the scenic splendour of most in western Britain. But it is low tide, no doubt as unimpressive as it ever looks. The easterly wind is blowing gentle waves inland.

'Do some visitors come by boat in summer?' I innocently ask the landlord.

'You must be joking. There are 200 moorings out there. In summer we become a village pub.' And soon I spot a notice giving details of a boat offering pleasure trips.

Now that we are out of the wind that had been bending our ears, there's time for gentler talk over an early lunch. The Sandling Peninsular used to be all farms and farm workers, an area that kept itself to itself, but where the farm workers used to live there are now accountants, airline pilots and, in gamekeepers' cottages, computer programmers, all of course with fast cars. 'They live here, but they're not of here.'

I glance across at Robert's wife, Pearl. 'Oh, I'm not exactly from here either. I'm from the other side of the river, but a Suffolk girl all right, brought up in farming. We met at Young Farmers.' We'll hear more about farming when we go for coffee at their home, or hall. But, why, when they were busy raising children, not to mention farming 1,600 acres, did he suddenly start writing maritime books?

'Always been fascinated,' says Robert.

'It's been an obsession,' chips in Pearl, 'and you led him on.' We recall his books for D&C, and some of our other maritime authors. Notably Harvey Benham, who I am sorry to hear has died. I always thought he'd make an interesting character in a novel. He was one of the Colchester newspaper family, but those running the business clearly thought he was a bit odd taking such an interest in sailing ships. In my novel, he would have come out on top, and in a sense he has, for books such as *Down Tops'l* will be appreciated for decades to come when yesterday's newspaper margins and profits will be utterly irrelevant.

'Your timetable for *Maritime Britain* was pretty impossible,' says Pearl, apropos of nothing.

'First I was told I had what was quite a tight schedule, and then you cut it back by three months,' complains Robert. 'The portable typewriter went with us everywhere, and there were index strips all over the kitchen. However, we made it.'

'Just didn't clean the house,' says Pearl adding: 'Then you gave up.' What she means is that, after I had sold D&C, they no longer wanted his books.

'But then I realised I'd learned enough to feel I could carry on by myself,' says Robert.

Now his tightly-focused list has about fifteen titles, books I've read with great pleasure, telling the story of the various extraordinary estuaries and ports of eastern England, their craft, and a few about individual voyages. This is self-publishing at its best. Sensible use made of outside advisers, but responsibility for sales remaining where it should, with the author. They deliver where they can, personal contact leading to extra sales but, when they couldn't sleep the other night, instead of sheep they counted up to 22 book outlets, if not all fully fledged bookshops, which used to display their titles and have been closed since Waterstone's opened in Ipswich. As with other self-publishers, mail order has become increasingly important. 'One book helps sell another, but advertising... forget it. Mail-order customers pay upfront, so Pearl doesn't have to chase them for payment, which she has to do hard with some bookshops. Such a timewaster. You call, and "I've left the cheque book at home", or "it's already in the post" when they know you know it darn well isn't. But Pearl wins them all in the end.'

I ask Robert why there were so many different kinds of craft in this part of the world: the Fen Barges and lighters, Norfolk wherries, Woodbridge smacks of shallow draught, Thames barges and more. 'One thing you can forget is Dutch influence. Nothing was modelled on anything; every area was so independent that it developed its own craft, best suited to local conditions. They all kept to their own areas. Each craft had its little tricks. The Norfolk wherries were a very difficult boat; you needed to do a lot of punting to keep it going. But in its own area, they swore by it. Only two Norfolk wherries have been preserved, but there are 28 Thames Barges left. People will say they were a copy of the Dutch barge but, for goodness sake, Holland was the enemy, and the Thames ones were like the others developed locally. Majestic they were too.

'These Thames or Spritsail Barges were the sailing wagons of the East Coast. Their flat bottoms and spritsail rig controlled by winches made them versatile and they loaded freight in lonely creeks at windswept farm wharves but sometimes went on long voyages equally happily. Because they were cheap to run, they went on long after all the other sailing cargo vessels gave up.'

Then back to the car, and past the Anglo-Saxon church now standing on its own, but where the village used to be, and very briefly to Ramsholt Hall. In truth, it is really a farmhouse, and is so marked on the OS, but I don't enquire about the name change. Robert is so busy telling us about the fields he's bought and sold, and what grows and what doesn't on the poor sandy soil, and what crops they're experimenting with to stay in business, that there isn't much opportunity to do so anyway.

Now writing his 28th book, one wonders how Robert finds time to farm at all. 'I only farm just over 400 acres now,' he replies as though that were nothing. We had 1,600 acres, mostly arable, at the peak, but if you're arable that's not really enough today. On the poor sandy soil of the Sandlings, they say you need 5,000 acres to spread the cost of the machinery you need. Agricultural workers are largely a thing of the past.'

However, the last sale of a few hundred acres was to raise capital for intensive mushroom production, now his son's project. 'At our peak we had 36 men. We're back up again because of the mushrooms. We need fifteen for the mushrooms, now the main venture.' Asparagus has also been introduced.

How easy is it to find workers? 'Very difficult. We've two from Hollesley prison. It's not what people want to do today.'

I hear of the problems of balancing supply and demand, reminding me of my strawberry-growing days. London doesn't offer much hope right now because 'the Dutch have dumped their surplus there'. Liverpool and Birmingham are full of cheap Irish mushrooms, dumped to keep up the price at home. So, as with my strawberries, it is the local market that matters. The mushroom production cost about half a million pounds to set up. Other new crops like the fields and fields of asparagus, are expensive, too. 'The last few years have been very difficult.'

Not that agricultural depression is anything new. It was much tougher in the last thirty years of Victoria's reign than most people realise. Then, when someone who had made his fortune in industry thought he would turn to orthodox farming and asked about an estate, the agent replied by asking him what kind of estate he wanted. A hunting, fishing or shooting one? It was assumed not an ordinary farming one. It was Victorian ingenuity that helped keep the countryside populated by introducing sporting ventures like pheasant breeding for shooting. The Victorian agricultural depression changed much. It started the drift of Scottish farmers coming south in search of easier land. That hurt local customs, such as the standard Suffolk practice of sealing a deal with the merest nod. (Local people had always disliked the insistence of Midland dealers shaking hands.)

Then the first tractors came and mechanisation and reduction in the labour force went on remorselessly – though there were profitable breaks in both World Wars and farmers were happy enough in the Attlee years after World War Two. Attlee's determination to save foreign currency yet take food off rationing meant high prices and subsidies for everything, including taking hedgerows down. The land has proved so uncertain over the years that no wonder better-paid jobs as dockers at Felixstowe seemed attractive. In a sense it was the region saving itself, for the local farm workers were perfect for providing labour for the rapidly expanding container port. But it is a far cry from the days when the Baptist version of a plain life being rewarded in heaven was shared by a large proportion of the rural East Anglian community.

Robert's *Family Fields: Eight generations living in the countryside* tells of continual ups and downs over the centuries. Even in their own time, Robert and Pearl must frequently have wondered what hit them. Innovations, such as growing early potatoes under black polythene, only helped for one season since competitors quickly cottoned on. All the houses now have mains services, but not everyone would choose to live quite so far off the beaten track. They leave an outside light on to cheer them up on their way home from social occasions; it can be seen from the main road well before the car plunges into the sunken and deeply-rutted lanes leading to the farm. It is a lived-in rather than grand house, and not built to make the most of the view of the Deben estuary. You have to walk across the back lawn to enjoy that. But Robert breathes salt water as much as he does farming. While authors come in all shapes and sizes, I've never known so enthusiastic a writer, let alone self-publisher, whose roots are on the land. Seldom do real (as opposed to hobby) farming and intellectual pursuits seem to go together.

It is time to make our way back to Town. Belle, the shy labrador, insists in jumping into the back luggage space. We take a different road to Woodbridge than that used this morning, and so pass one of the archaeological wonders of our age, Sutton Hoo, the ancient ship excavated sixty years ago – one of the most exciting finds ever dug from British soil – but only now being fully exploited by the National Trust. Robert is on the committee organising the building of a full-size replica, whose building can be watched from a new visitors' centre to be opened shortly after our visit. He writes:

In 1939 a great warrior leader was discovered buried in his longship, with all his treasure and personal effects, at Sutton Hoo. This was England's equivalent of Tutankhamen but, although it is known without doubt the young Egyptian king's name, no one can be certain exactly who was buried in the Sutton Hoo mound. The most likely candidate is Raedwald, the most powerful of the Kings of East Anglia, who died in about 625 and had his palace at nearby Rendlesham. The Sutton Hoo longship was around 89ft long, but all that was actually found of her was a dark stain in the soil and the iron rivets used to fastened the clinker planking. In 1939 'experts' claimed that this ship, because it did not have a keel, was not a sea going vessel, but just a royal river barge. However ten years ago Edwin Gifford built a half scale replica of this craft and she has proved to be fast at sailing and will, if slowly, beat against the wind.

What was called Mound One, when opened, contained the remains of a long open clinker built boat, in which the pagan Anglians had placed all the necessities they believed their chieftain would require in the next world. The most notable of these was an iron standard with the old northern emblem of royalty, the stag or hart, on a ring at the top. Another object identified with kingship was a carved ceremonial whetstone. To show the dead chief was a warrior, there were the remains of a fine shield and helmet. The most precious find was the great gold buckle of elaborate design and beautiful craftsmanship. For the chief's more immediate needs there were silver bowls, spoons, some more practical pottery and small Merovingian gold coins. But nowhere was there any sign of the body of the dead king.

The National Trust have taken over the Sutton Hoo Estate and the Anglo-Saxon burial site and are opening the new impressive visitor centre, as with Cornwall's Eden Project literally just after our visit. Another place to which we will have to return. 'Since no one knows exactly how the original ship was built, some power tools will be used in building the replica. However it should be capable of sailing at twelve knots,' says Robert.

With the thought that the Deben really was a Royal River, we return to Woodbridge. The days of trading ships may be long over, but the number of boats bobbing about on the water shows that the estuary retains commercial importance of a kind.

Liverpool Street and the Tower of London

Back by another grubby single-coach train to Ipswich, and by proper train to Liverpool Street. Until I was seven we lived at Gidea Park, so Liverpool Street was our gateway to London on rare but memorable visits. I recall one journey in a train of four-wheeled coaches, just like goods trucks. Even by then, Liverpool Street's traffic, though enormous, was slightly in decline. Traffic had peaked just before the 1926 General Strike, though for a long time the Jazz (so called because of the yellow and blue stripes under the roofs that donated the class of accommodation) suburban service remained a wonder of the world: 40,000 passengers an hour, up to 1,000 people apiece on fifty trains arriving in a single hour. All were hauled by what one D&C author described as 'diminutive but vociferously pugnacious tank engines'. Well I remember the soot they belched into the station's enclosure, the steady pumping action of brake, and the violent roar as air was released when the fireman disconnected the incoming engine, which ten minutes later followed the departing train out ready to back on to its next load. With electrification, by the early 1970s, much of this, including the thick internal smog, was a memory. But it was still pretty traditional gloom and grime, and nobody could have dreamt of the bright glass cathedral of today's Liverpool Street.

I recall our family holiday at the Great Eastern Hotel just beyond the buffers and how, when I returned from my inevitable visits to the station, Mum always complained my collar was even dirtier – and how my younger sister had ventured out with us into the morning rush hour and stood in amazement asking: 'Where do all these people think they are rushing to?'

The Great Eastern Hotel was a marvel. Its food was far better than the Great Western's Paddington. Select English fare was served in the dining room under the supervision of Stokes, the stooped head waiter who might have stepped straight out of Dickens. At lunch the restaurant was full of City people, the serious eaters choosing the joint of the day, carved on a handsome trolley dexterously wheeled between secluded tables that were the haunt of the regulars generously tipping Stokes and the joint carver, if not the more humble waiters.

This afternoon, we climb the steps at the platform's end to see if we can gain access to the Great Eastern Hotel. The hotel fell on bad times when Maggie Thatcher decreed that Transport Hotels should be sold off. The hoped-for permission to allow it to be redeveloped for offices happily didn't materialise, and millions have been spent on refurbishing it. However, today's direct entrance is only for staff – like the Russian airline that demands its passengers remain seated at their destination so that the staff can alight first. Unlike that of the restored Great Western at Paddington, perhaps today's management doesn't like it to be thought of as a hotel for travellers? So we walk round into Liverpool Street itself, the station named after it being far better known than the street.

Wow. The hotel is different. Overwhelmingly so. Very contemporary. Yes, a great hotel again, though we wonder whether we oldies would feel at ease in it. Everyone illustrated in the extravagant brochure describing the transition into something contemporary seems to be less than a third of our age. 'This brochure tries to give a sense of the amazing diversity you will find behind our doors. Every one of our 267-bedrooms and suites is different, whilst our four restaurants and three bars offer an extraordinary range of food and drink, whatever your criteria. Here is a splendid Victorian hotel that has been beautifully restored, but at the same time a radical spirit of modernity has been injected.' Much of it is good of its kind, though will surely date faster than the very traditional businessmen's institution it used to be.

Soon we are expected at the Tower of London. We are announced as 'the Gaoler's guests'. Hitherto I've known John Keohane as a leading light on the South Devon Railway. Indeed, as its Postmaster, he seems to use the Internet to keep us up-to-date by the hour rather than day.

After years as a Beefeater and Yeoman Guard (occasionally using his ceremonial dress to greet trains at Buckfastleigh) he has been promoted to Yeoman Gaoler. Since the South Devon Railway is going ahead with its share issue to buy our freehold from the rival Torbay & Dartmouth Railway, I make a note quickly to promise support lest we get incarcerated, as later visitors from Devon ceremoniously were. Gaoler sounds pretty forbidding.

He certainly looks handsome in his dark purple and red. Back in the sixteenth century, the Gaoler was the one who accompanied prisoners to and from their trials, holding the blade of the hefty axe turned away from them. If found guilty – beheading was usual – the blade was turned towards them. No axe today, and he's not quite finished work, and there's time to look around, as had been planned.

The sheer extent is greater than I'd imagined. With its many separate historic buildings, towers and entrances, road system, street lighting, staff housing and even its own chapel, the Tower of London is like a large village, with a gracious village green in the shape of Tower Green. The village atmosphere is emphasised by the staff walking round toward the end of their day, greeting each other and exchanging snippets of news. The Beefeaters are the main guides, enabling visitors to reach many parts that can't be explored on one's own. There is so much to see, and to cogitate about even if it's gone or decayed, like Henry VIII's fantastic wardrobe which needed a whole building, only a masonry stump of which survives. Fancy what in mediaeval days was probably the country's largest manufactory being here; with up to forty furnaces to melt the metal and dozens of workers striking coins into their moulds, it must have been hard to make yourself heard – and all this wealth and the Crown Jewels cheek by jowl with prisoners spending days in a degree of luxury according to their rank, whatever the alleged crime.

From the top of the south wall, which takes quite a bit of climbing, the Thames and Tower Bridge make a splendid sight as darkness falls on a crisp autumn evening. The Thames through central London has always been the one piece of river in the city properly respected and lined with fine buildings, in a way never seriously copied by any provincial city. Because even in early times London was difficult to get around, the Thames has acted as its chief highway. It was not just for ceremonial reasons that craft plied to and fro and anchored at the Tower, or that the dreaded Traitor's Gate could only be approached by water.

There's obviously a defect in my character since, while I seek out the unusual around Britain and beyond, I've always resisted the obvious tourist traps, especially those on our doorstep. Many of London's greatest attractions, such as Madam Tussaud's, I've only visited for signing parties and other business events. This evening, I feel genuinely ashamed. How could I have been so stupid as not to visit the Tower of London in my three score years and ten? It is impossible not to agree with *The Rough Guide to England*: 'Despite all the hype and heritage claptrap, it remains one of London's most remarkable buildings, site of some of the goriest events in the nation's history and somewhere all visitors and Londoners should visit at least once.' Well, I've made it.

The sense of history is overpowering, yet it doesn't seem strange being here so quickly after visiting Shingle Street. That is probably because the day has been without discernible weather, and at the end of the Tower's visiting hours we have it almost totally to ourselves. Not an American in sight to compare it to somewhere back home. Beefeaters and other staff are more numerous than the few English visitors walking round; out of season, the last hour is obviously an excellent time to come. We are good tourists, though, buying the excellent official guidebook, which gives us sense of direction and soon stretches our imagination.

So, there are a couple of the famous Ravens with their clipped wings so they can't fly away, the Chapel Royal (which is already closed to further visitors today), the great White Tower in the middle, and the rest of the buildings so familiar in literature and from TV. And such a long and varied history for, as well as being used for containing prisoners, it has also been armoury, mint, observatory and royal residence. Yes, we should have come many years earlier when our memories would have been sharper, but we are as impressed as we feel privileged to be here as guests with hardly anyone around. Our luck is emphasised when we bypass the arrangements for queuing to view the Crown Jewels, in the castellated Waterloo Barracks, just north of the White Tower.

Yes, the jewels are every bit as remarkable as our expectation is built up to find them by an enterprising series of preliminary displays and notices. What money has been spent here! No wonder they need careful keeping (the reason behind much of the Tower's security) and are so popular that everyone has to see them. The moving walkway past them is obviously necessary at busy times, but is nuisance for us today with no other visitors in sight. Without delay, we slip round several times.

It never ceases to fascinate what memories one takes away. For us, it is the tradition emphasised by such details as the Coronation spoons of the seventeenth and twentieth centuries being remarkably similar to that of the twelfth, while there seems to be only slight differences in the various monarchs' coats of arms over their seats. The over-elaboration of everyday items, even if made to hold and dispense what were then expensive ingredients, also speaks through history. If we were given it, we couldn't accommodate the eighteen-inch high gold salt cellar plastered with emeralds for the most ceremonial of our occasions!

Changing times are marked in all kinds of ways; we particularly note the model of Tower Wharf in 1676 sent to Virginia as part of the bonding process between homeland and colony. And nothing makes the village feeling come more to life than the black cat purposefully walking between buildings, tail up when it thinks it has caught our attention.

Fifty families, totalling 120 people, live within the Tower walls. We go to the early eighteenth-century Old Hospital Block to meet John the Gaoler and his wife, Ruth. He tells me that as a boy soldier he had to engage in a hobby as part of training to become sergeant, and that is when his passion in railways began. All Beefeaters and Yeoman Guards are recruited from retiring servicemen. 'I wrote off for details when I was in Northern Ireland in 1989, and next year there was a long warts-and-all kind of interview, followed by a selection board interview. A hundred applicants were whittled down to three from five. Wives were then taken into account.

'I enjoy the job and feel very privileged. It's long hours, mind. I'm involved seven days out of nine, and only once a month get three days off together to go to the railway at Buckfastleigh. But the days are so different here with all the ceremonial roles and corporate events, and you can't avoid being proud to be part of the utter continuity of it all. Britain has a lot going for it: through our background of knowledge and traditions, we put on displays and pageantry that other people can only play at. I'm also involved in the chapel and trade union.'

Their house is surprisingly small and down-to-earth domestic, a far cry from the pageantry sometimes taking place only yards away. For us, an ordinary kind of meal, and easy-chair conversation with coffee afterward, makes the perfect ending to an unusual day. John of course talks about the South Devon Railway's share issue, while Ruth tells of the community spirit among those living in the 'village'.

PROUD YORKSHIRE

Scarborough: 'The Most Improved Resort'?

After another scintillating journey by *The Highland Chieftain* with fine food and spectacular scenery from Inverness to York, we connect into a local train for a quick visit to what claims to be Britain's oldest resort. Scarborough once seriously called itself the Queen of Watering Places. Recently it won another accolade: The Most Improved Resort.

The delightful part of the 42-mile train journey from York is where the line is forced to bend and turn as the wooded hills close in on the Derwent, just before Malton. Otherwise it is full throttle mainly through an empty, flat countryside. Soon we decamp at Scarborough's station, already much reduced but probably still unnecessarily large. Nostalgically, I recall busy weekend and Bank Holiday evenings when a score or more of excursion trains, stored a short distance up the old line to Whitby, were hurtled back into the station, the local shunting engine drivers always knowing exactly where to stop to pick up the return loads of returning trippers. The economy of making the long-distance drivers bring in their own trains didn't work because they were too cautious – and at peak times ten trains an hour had to be despatched from Scarborough. In total there were often over 100 trains a day. The carriages of summer extras had long passed their sell-by date but, especially before 1939, the best services used to be classy.

That has always been Scarborough: quality and mass business, two seaside cultures thriving cheek by jowl. George Hudson, the Railway King, was anxious to build a pioneer line. A local pamphleteer saw what the consequences might be: there would be a 'greater influx of vagrants, and those who have no money to spend'. But the resort flourished, unusually making money out of the well-to-do and the working masses.

Taking their first-ever real holiday, between the wars the families of many workers coming for a week committed the best part of their personal attire to a case sent Passenger Luggage in Advance. Prodigious mounds of PLA built up on Friday evenings. Imagine the consternation when one Saturday a complete trainload of the stuff went missing. On Monday, hundreds of holidaymakers without basic gear kicked up such a shindig that the stationmaster was forced to advance cash for nightdresses, shaving kit and the like. The train was eventually found in a siding at a York marshalling yard. That reminds me of the time I bought a train of three carriages and they clean disappeared. 'Not our responsibility,' said BR. 'Delivery is at purchaser's risk.' It was left for us to track down the carriages. A York enthusiast found them in the same marshalling yard in which that missing train of PLA had accidentally been left decades before. But my train was carefully hidden between rows of box cars. 'You can't take it,' said the yard foreman. 'There'll be a strike.' Workers at the yard had long complained about the lack of mess facilities and had helped themselves to my train. There was much argument before the train I had paid for was delivered.

Every time I come to Scarborough I'm impressed afresh by its great geography. Unlike resorts with a straight line between land and sea, here you are forever looking across water to something interesting beyond. The town occupies a wedge-shaped piece of land with a great headland beyond the narrow end. The main resort area is neatly tucked into a bay, with picturesque inner harbour fronted by black-and-white houses. The headland, shown off by its castle, with remains of a Roman signalling station close by, is marvellous – whether you are looking up to or down from it. Its high cliff, or scar, as in the town's name, is however just one of several highlights along the coastal Cleveland Way. The cliffs continue only a short distance to the south, but northwards almost continuously into Scotland.

Most Improved Resort? Whether Scarborough justifies the description is another matter. Yes, there's some of the best seaside architecture, good beaches, municipal this and that, and undoubtedly good entertainment and sporting facilities, museums and generous shelters from the elements. A lot of money has been spent by a council keen to keep Scarborough firmly on the tourist map. The extensive gardens have probably never been better. There's some prosperity, too. This afternoon's crowds may not be on the gargantuan pre-overseas package holiday scale but are still considerable. There are boarding houses galore, many pleasingly up together. Some of them must look after visitors who seek a touch of old-fashioned gentility and still regularly favour Scarborough.

A gastronomical judgement doesn't flatter. Fish is caught and you can buy seafood treats from stalls to eat on the trot; but there's no tradition of good fish restaurants. Currently only one hotel is shown with an AA red rosette and it scores a lower percentage mark than any of the five so blessed in the diminutive Isles of Scilly whose entry happens to come next. A newspaper recently said that one of the huge hotels wouldn't look out of place in downtown Bucharest. 'It is a holiday camp parcelled up in a wrecked seaside chateau.' I've stayed at both the over-sized hotels, eyeing one another like jousters ready for battle.

The big hotels are said to alternate between turning people away and being half empty. It depends what conferences are in town. Conference arrangements are outstanding, but I wonder how many delegates are sufficiently impressed to bring their family for a weekend or longer. Yet much of the year weekend business is actually quite good. Convoys of coaches bring in the elderly on special spring and autumn breaks. There are good bargains to be had in high summer, too, but few families settle for a week or fortnight nowadays. Most of those roaming through the Old Town, taking snaps around the harbour, bathing, paddling, eating mussels and cockles, entertaining or just sunning themselves this afternoon – there's a sizeable throng up around the Castle – are daytrippers. One way or another, the tills still ring, and that pays the builders' and decorators' bills – and enables those who work during the long season to enjoy sunning themselves overseas in the autumn and winter.

If you're within convenient driving distance, Scarborough seductively lures. We enjoy our few hours, not least seeing happy faces, young and old. Because of the shortness of our visit, having walked around Old Town and the harbour area, again surprised by the sheer range and scale of entertainment and especially the scope of the huge Spa complex, we take a taxi up to the Castle and briefly around the headland and along Scarborough's other (north-facing) coastline. The driver is not communicative. Twice when I comment he simply says 'That's Scarborough', implying it is a place you take as it is. Scarborough the one and only. Why try to learn tricks from other resorts, such as the hotels of the Scilly Isles?

Yet, given its size and fame, it is surprising there are not more really good hotels. The number of hotel bedrooms declines remorselessly along with Scarborough's population. Can any council do more than delay the decline?

What was one of the best hotels, where we once enjoyed a summer evening, didn't so much close as disappear. Soon after our visit, each night national TV showed how the large garden was steadily being swallowed by the sea, which then burrowed through soft ground to take the entire building. We saw the bedrooms and bars disappear at drunken angles. Later, dozens of QE2 passengers interrupted their lunch on a cruise down the coast to view the great penetrating hole the sea unpredictably grabbed.

I love the coast to the south – and even more to the north. A most memorable experience was the train journey from Scarborough to Whitby, on a line long closed and which must have been tremendously expensive to run. The train had to reverse at both ends, and the engineering works and gradients were considerable. Emerging from the tunnel at Ravenscar, there was an unforgettable view of the North Sea, great cliffs and rocky foreshore, with Robin Hood's Bay way down below. In the reverse direction, on a train from Whitby, one might catch a glance of Ravenscar, high up and only three miles away... but five miles and fifteen minutes of hard slog by train. When a sea mist rolled in and the rails became damp and greasy, many a train – once just a locomotive with no load – slipped to a standstill. Sometimes Ravenscar station was only yards away, but couldn't be reached.

The most dramatic of all coastal railways, this is the only one of the three main routes to Whitby to have been completely closed and demolished. A large part of the one from Malton is now the highly-successful North Yorkshire Moors Railway, offering a different kind of drama through Newton Dale and past the grimly-sited original Early Warning System. Remember how we used to discuss what we might do in our last four minutes? This route was pushed forward even before the Scarborough line, which left it at Malton, no doubt because Hudson the Railway King invested heavily in Whitby's tourist development. At the time of writing, the third route, from Middlesborough, is still part of the basic national network but the subject of an interesting plan for a mini-franchise. That, as hinted earlier, is something long overdue: giving a handful of rural lines to local people to manage in greater detail, making the most of the scenery and looking after the interests of isolated communities. A number of organisations are working together to create what they hope might be a model mini-franchise that could be adopted elsewhere. Don't count on it, but could there be an outbreak of common sense?

These thoughts about routes to Whitby make me want to go there again. That's the trouble with my Britain. When I'm only in Scarborough for a few hours, my mind wanders further. And anyway is it right to describe Whitby as a remote place? Only in terms of its very roundabout remaining rail link. On fine days, probably more people arrive at the harbour by boat, let alone the weekend hordes by road. When I was last there, and the sea mist was thick, with the abbey ruins on the headland visible only spasmodically, a pleasure boat took a load of those who had been foolhardy enough to join a trip round the bay. It returned ten minutes later. So rough was it that just about everyone lost their lunch in those minutes that must have seemed an eternity. We wondered whether they were in a state to care about getting their fares back.

On better days Whitby is a lovable place of cobbled streets and busy fishing vessels whose catches are partly sold at the popular take-away stalls. Here you can also find fish decently cooked in proper restaurants. Compare notes with a connoisseur if you can and be sure to seek out your chosen eating place early at busy times. While Scarborough declines, Whitby thrives. Of manageable size, it perhaps makes you feel more of an individual. The river, harbour, sea, headland with abbey all seem to be there just for us. Yet there's plenty of fun, with good sport and entertainment. Somehow it is more in tune with today's tourist demand. But choose a day when it isn't both foggy and rough.

Unhappy at Leeds

We have a fast through train to Leeds, where the massive task of extending the station to provide more platforms is all but complete. Business is booming, with more trains and passengers supporting a wide range of routes leading to this born-again, vibrant city.

Though things began working well with a new team appointed within six months of my selling *Writers' News*, the initial treatment by RIM, owners of the *Yorkshire Post*, left one of the deepest hurts of my life. I shudder as the taxi taking us to our hotel passes the *Yorkshire Post* building. It was there that, during negotiations, I was assured they would want to continue working with me and my Trust; soon afterwards the story was that things 'never work with previous owners'. When I met Sheila after a particularly difficult meeting, she was full of enthusiasm for Leeds, especially wanting to share the 'brilliant' City Market with me. But I was so desperate to leave Leeds that I suggested we bought a sandwich to eat on a train... and then foolishly stepped on the first to Sheffield, a diabolical four-wheeled 'Pacer' which rocked and rolled violently.

But today we'll make the best of Leeds, and really are looking forward to my Trust's prizegiving tomorrow. It will be organised by the new team running *Writers' News*.

The Malmaison, AA 75 per cent, on Sovereign Quay, typifies today's stylish hotels of a kind you wouldn't have found in Leeds even in the 1970s. Along the waterfront is a little oasis of calm, but it feels somewhat artificial. Few people are making real use of the waterfront. In the evening, though the restaurants are busy, it is mainly with businessmen and women, going straight to eat there and, afterwards, purposefully moving off again. We have come here because we were advised that another hotel we first thought about might be noisy. Such is the pace of change in central areas that pneumatic drills beaver away well into the night. This hotel is fine, and the nearby Italian restaurant deserves its popularity. Though only April, it is a balmy evening and we enjoy our stroll along the waterfront, seeing how the satanic mills and warehouses have been given new life.

The ability skilfully to extend the central area owes much to the resurrection of the Leeds & Liverpool Canal, which leaves the broad

River Aire south of the station. That has to be welcome. Of course, something had to be done with the huge area of waterside grain mills and warehouses, and converting them into trendy apartment blocks, expensive hotels and restaurants cannot in theory be a bad thing. Nor bringing life to the dark areas under arches of railway bridges in the form of trendy craft shops and the like. Many of Leeds's own mills have survived for other use, but it is on the Aire at Saltaire, beyond Shipley, that Titus Salt's mill and model village for the workers has been declared a Unesco World Heritage site. The mill had been the only one in Britain weaving alpaca wool. Monopoly and philanthropy; factory system and social concern.

That wasn't usually the case in Leeds itself. Leeds was indeed one of the last northern cities with real slums and long terraces of back-to-back houses (you used to see them from curved railway embankments and bridges). One cannot fail to be impressed by what has been achieved on the housing front here, too. One way and another Leeds is well on its way to become a more powerful centre than Manchester or Edinburgh. With the grime, the soul has surely gone. It has become a harsh place and, judging by today's younger females buying their designer clothes at silly prices in Harvey Nichols, it will steadily become harsher. If I were a young man on the look out for a good wife, Leeds wouldn't be the place to come! 'Whatever anyone says, I'm going to enjoy myself,' says an over-painted lass. 'That means I'll not think of anyone else. Just me.'

As we settle down for the night I reflect that happiness cannot have increased with material comfort. There must be much anxiety and suffering in today's brash money-making, furious-living Leeds.

In the morning Sheila is persuaded to have her hair done at Harvey Nichols whose branch has been a trendsetting success in excess. She says she couldn't possibly think of, never mind justify, buying the expensive designer clothes. £400 for a flimsy blouse. And one could say what's a boob if not seductively shaped by a £130 bra? With extortionate house prices, an average lengthy journey to work, there must be outrageous debt. And once Yorkshire people were so cautious.

I recall how, in publishing days, I used to walk miles here to save bus fares, once all the way to Hunslet as we were preparing to publish LTC Rolt's *A Hunslet Hundred*, celebrating the centenary of the Hunslet Locomotive Company that made shunting engines for the world's marshalling yards. 'Time is the thief of money,' was the motto of the managing director, urging quick production.

Banging out metal and converting cloth into cheap garments was what Leeds excelled at in the days when the handsome elliptical-domed Corn Exchange was what it said it was. Leeds was also where shrewd Yorkshire farmers came to turn their corn, wool, cattle and other crops into cash. On my first visit, arriving by fast train from St Pancras on the day Russia had sent up its first sputnik (my first book-writing commission was confirmed during my couple of hours in London), I found Leeds wondrously down-to-earth, gritty in more senses than one, totally different from other northern industrial cities such as Sheffield which I already knew. Fools weren't suffered. Even at the hotel (a minor one in the outskirts), and the station booking office, you needed to state your business with a precision that in Devon would have been regarded as indecent haste. When I visited the hellhole of the second station, Leeds City, now long closed, it made even London's sooty Liverpool Street seem hygienic.

Leeds is the place to which Marks & Spencer traces back its ancestry and Leeds still trades with gusto. Perhaps nowhere else outside London can such rich ranges of goods be found at all price levels. Those selling cheap jewellery, CDs and clothes in today's Corn Market are, after all, trading and earning a living. Yet the big money seems to come from paper-pushing, property and pugnacious take-overs. I remember the time when the bookshops sold a particularly unsophisticated selection, which was fine for me with my interest in gritty subjects. Some of the elite chose to go elsewhere for their belles-lettres. Now Leeds is a shopping mecca for all including those seeking literature.

'So do you want to go back to the station?' asks Sheila. Why should only young people spend money? I hail a taxi for Harrogate, glad to shake the dust (now metaphorical it has to be admitted) of Leeds off my boots. But one day Leeds will call for a special celebration. You too? If you are into shopping and eating, come for the jolliest (if not cheapest) of weekends. Choose your hotel and restaurant carefully for not quite all are yet of our times.

'North of England's Chief Watering Place'

An undoubted advantage of Leeds, and indeed many northern cities, is the proximity to fine countryside and characterful smaller towns. Harrogate stands out as especially convenient and attractive. Soon we are between the Stray, a large open common, and one of the fine terraces in which I once rented a holiday flat.

While Leeds's success has depended on change, Harrogate thrives on continuity, especially at the visual, surface level.

This section's subtitle comes from a 1950 guide. You would hardly call Harrogate a watering place in today's parlance yet, despite the resurrection Buxton has so far achieved, there is no other inland resort or holiday place in the north that can touch it. In 1950 it was still possible for the guide to say: 'The chalybeate, sulphurous, and saline springs to which Harrogate owes its reputation are eighty eight in number, and are used both internally and externally. The baths and other equipment are quite equal to those of the leading Continental spas, and the variety of treatment is quite as great.' You can still take a Turkish Bath, but quickly the spa element became an exotic sideline; today's guide says that the Spa Heritage begins with the Royal Baths Assembly Rooms and, just round the corner, the Royal Pump Room. You can still taste the infamous water, of course, but most visitors enjoy cuppas and dwell on the past, such as the stories of Russian royalty. The well-maintained buildings themselves however fit well into today's Harrogate. What of their future? Recently the English Tourism Council said that Spa tourism is more lively than generally appreciated and should be expanded to create 20,000 extra jobs.

Though there are still grand houses with colourful gardens in individual ownership, and discreet old ladies staying at the better hotels for a pick-me-up, large numbers of today's inhabitants have at least one family member working in Leeds. The huge hotels are mainly kept going by the burgeoning conference trade. However, the continuity runs rather deeper than one might expect. Afternoon tea, for example, is still something greatly to be savoured here, not least at Bettys famous tearoom, while many visit the town for its gardens including the huge Valley Gardens where the famous spring show is held, and Harlow Carr (of which more in a moment). Entertainment, especially good music, continues to thrive, and antique shops and art galleries draw business from all parts of Britain and beyond. Harrogate, though somewhat divided in two, is also considerably larger than one might expect. Locals complain of the invasion by high-street chains, but there are still quality individual shops.

Passing the hotel from which Agatha Christie organised her own much-publicised disappearance, and noting where Byron once stayed, we start our visit with a short tour of art and antique galleries. First call is the Walker Gallery, where we meet Ian; his brother David runs the Walker Gallery in Honiton, Devon, mentioned in chapter 36. If we had to make do with a single picture for the rest of our lives, here are at least three strong contenders. This gallery (there are two other Walker Galleries in the town) deals in the best of traditional and British European painting – at prices that make it the stuff of public art galleries so far as we are concerned. Real genius, beautiful with fine detail, but beyond our pocket. Since 9/11, as the destruction of the twin towers of New York's Trade Centre, is now universally referred to, the usual flow of American customers has become a faint trickle. But, we hear, trading with Americans is still strong. Mail-order marketing and illustrated e-mail have come to the rescue. 'It is a two-way business, too,' says Ian. 'Our reputation for paying fair prices for good quality pictures means successful reverse marketing. Many pictures come back to us this way.'

Antique shops tell the same story. There are, incidentally, three dozen of them in Harrogate itself. It is easier to sell good antiques than acquire them, and today some of the best pieces come from overseas including North America. 'It is as though we loan older people a piece for fifteen or so years before they have to give up their homes, when we are privileged to sell it again,' says one dealer, adding that his stock is insured for a million pounds. He explains: 'Trade is good because there are quite a few of us here. Harrogate has come up in the antiques world while Edinburgh seems finished, Bath is dying, London colossally expensive. Even the Cotswolds and Brighton don't really rival us.'

Most purchasers are, however, outside the local area. 'Country people go to auctions and put their hands up, often beating us, but if they come in here they try and knock us down,' says one dealer.

Unlike the booksellers in Hay-on-Wye, the dealers speak well of one another, and make the point that, because good pieces are expensive, they expect customers to take time considering before deciding. No pressure salesmanship. Good quality, sensibly sized chests of drawers especially seem to cost a ridiculous sum.

We spend longer at Derbyshire Antiques, fascinated by the range of old pieces and pictures of various eras including modern. Robert Derbyshire relishes explaining that he has been the subject of a tax investigation. 'They wanted to know how I could afford to be unlike other dealers. When the investigation was over, they promised I would never be subject to another.'

The reason they are different is that they took over a large consignment of antiques on its way from Devon to Melbourne, Australia, when the consignee inconveniently died. Prices in this gallery are certainly competitive. Mr Derbyshire is communicative, telling us about the sad loss of his wife and the goings-on in the antique trade, as well as about specific pieces that catch our attention. We drool over a small walnut chair c1695, and then a lovely summer landscape by Michael James Smith, about whom we are given an encouraging biographical note. 'He rivals even the most celebrated exponents of this genre, such as Constable, Gainsborough and Stubbs... with rich colours of the countryside on canvas often featuring a lowland stream, its glossy reflections an indication of Smith's unique ability for intense observation.' We'd love to make a purchase, but there is one special thing I've set my heart on finding on this visit to Harrogate. Mr Derbyshire obligingly points me to the appropriate dealer: Lumbs.

Over thirty years ago, from a long-closed Harrogate shop, I bought a historic mahogany wine cooler. The Booksellers Association's conference was here, and so was my car. For years I loved that wine cooler in which I displayed a plant or two, but somehow lost it. No shop I have visited in Bath, Brighton or elsewhere has had one. Lumbs has exactly what I'm looking for in the window. Like a nervous young reporter, I rehearse what to say, to find out the price without seeming too keen. It is lovely. We are given details: 'A George III Chippendale period oval brass-bound mahogany wine cooler with two brass bands and cast brass oval top carrying handles; on its original stand supported by four square legs with brackets and inner chamfer. Circa 1770. Warranted genuine.'

How long can you seriously examine something you hope to live with for always? We inevitably fall into the trap of spending longer examining things we don't want, couldn't accommodate or afford, but enjoy transiently as we would in, say, a Venice art gallery.

When we leave, Sheila asks me what was wrong with the wine cooler. Only the price. Divide it by the number of words in the description and the writer was on to a good earner: my crude journalistic way of looking at it. By any yardstick it is a serious purchase precluding even considering any other.

We go back to say we'll have it. The owner isn't the least surprised. We ask who will be tomorrow's customers. 'Not the nouveau riche, that's for sure. They'll be ordinary people like yourselves who have no doubt quietly succeeded at something. People who really appreciate a few nice things around them.' Well there. Later we are happy to see our four-wheel drive that seldom leaves Scotland brought down by a member of staff for tomorrow's prizegiving. The wine cooler will go on our tour of the Lakes and South West Scotland before seeing Nairn.

Meanwhile we go to Bettys for afternoon tea. How wonderful, a reminder of childhood shopping, is the coffee-based aroma. And the gentle ambience but also hive of activity in the gracefully traditional shop through which entrance is gained. Like a schoolboy, I have to spend my pocket money immediately: cheese straws, dark chocolate-covered marzipan, fudge and cherries with stalks seductively sticking out of them. Then, to serve to a special friend back home, a small quantity of rare St Helena coffee. One also comes to Bettys for a good read. With the coffee comes a delightful leaflet in which chairman Jonathon Wild introduces coffee buyer Mike Riley, who explains his like of organic-grown beans, and how we should support small coffee-growing communities where people are doing their best to help themselves. The section headed 'Feeling good about coffee' assumes that taste buds and social conscience are linked.

There is the inevitable short queue for tea, upstairs and down, but interesting reading matter on the walls. An old notice headed IMPORTANT ANNOUNCEMENT states: 'In view of the considerable number of patrons not taking cream with tea, we have DECIDED TO REDUCE THE CHARGE FOR AFTERNOON TEA to 6d per person. Our inimitable service obeisance and quality will not be reduced.' When we are seated, the best reading of all is the long menu. It starts with a potted history, 'Where the Dales meet the Alps,' explaining how a talented young Swiss confectioner came to England to make his fortune and took root 'where the air seemed as sweet as in his native Alps'. Then pages and pages of tempting dishes and treats. After careful discussion, we plump for hot buttered pikelets, or Yorkshire crumpets.

Incredibly, it is a year since my Charitable Trust's last prizegiving in London (chapter 20). This year it is at the Majestic Hotel, a grand Victorian hotel very well maintained for today's needs. The programme, perfectly staged by *Writers' News*, is too similar to last year's to warrant comment, but much laughter greeted Phil Powley's winning entry in the Malapropism competition:

MISGUIDED TOUR Good afternoon, ladies and gentlemen, and welcome to Sheridan Abbey.

The earliest indications that we have of the Carpathian Order occupying this site lie buried under our feet. Unfortunately little of hysterical interest survives.

Now, would you please follow me. The refractory which you see before you is where the brothers took their meals. Silence was compulsive, though Bibulous reading would accompany each sitting.

The brothers enjoyed a wholesale diet of fish, meat and vegetation, washed down by six pints of weak beer each day. Many lived to a ripe old age: centurions were not unknown.

Now we come to the Abbey Church, a fine example of mediaeval constriction with its soaring archives and flying cutlasses. Building began here in 1125 and the church was constipated by Bishop Anslem in 1150

Finally, we come to the Cloisters where the Brothers could permanganate at their leisure in tranquillised surroundings. On the way out you will notice...

Professor of Land and Leisure

Though relatively few readers may have heard of him, many will have been affected by the advice he has given, and especially by the decisions of committees on which he has sat. I refer to one of the two prizegiving presenters we are spending time with this evening, who I've nicknamed him Professor of Land and Leisure. It would not be a bad description, even if it didn't happen to be the title of the first book he wrote for me, *Land and Leisure*. Ahead of its time in 1970, it exercised considerable influence among geographers and planners. It also gave birth to a particularly worthwhile series: Problems in Modern Geography.

Professor Allan Patmore has kept cropping up in my life: as geographer working closely with other authors, notably at Liverpool and Hull Universities (for a busy period he was vice-chancellor at Hull), member of the North Yorkshire National Park and of the 1991 National Park Review Panel, railway enthusiast, co-editor of my Regional Railway History series, chairman of the Friends of York Railway Museum, friend with whom to have dinner (such as when he was at Stirling, where the Motorail departed at night for Newton Abbot) and much more. For years he was an active member of the Sports Council and now helps determine how the National Lottery allocates part of its charitable spending. Also, because of commitments as magistrate and local preacher, it is often hard to find him with a free date even when not overseas, particularly in New Zealand for which we share deep affection. It was his first trip to the United States, touring national parks, in the early 1960s that gave birth to his interest in interpreting landscape for visitors. Soon after that he was given a British Academy award for research for *Land and Leisure*. It came from a fund established by the donations of Jewish wartime refugees as a thank offering to Britain.

This section could also appropriately be headed THE FOURTH WAVE, as is Allan's own first chapter divider in *Land and Leisure*. That chapter opens with a quote from a Civic Trust paper by Michael Dower, another opinion former ahead of his time:

> Three great waves have broken across the face of Britain since 1800. First, the sudden growth of dark industrial towns. Second, the thrusting movement along far-flung railways. Third, the sprawl of car-based suburbs. Now we see, under the guise of a modest word, the surge of a fourth wave which could be more powerful than all the others. The modest word is leisure.

Much of our time together we discuss how this Fourth Wave has been handled. One thing is certain: the visual effect has been as great as the earlier waves, even the industrial revolution, though in more subtle ways. More unblemished, natural countryside has been lost, if only by making it too accessible. At times Allan verges on the despondent.

'The countryside is being gentrified. It is especially bad in the national parks. Many areas are being positively sanitised. You can't go anywhere unless there's a paved footpath. I was horrified on a visit to the North Yorkshire National Park last year. Of course we must remember the disabled, but does everywhere have to be accessible to wheelchairs? Both of the national parks in Yorkshire are bad. I've loved the Dales since my teens, but there are few places left totally natural today. It is hard on walkers, perhaps those following in the steps of Wainwright.

'My favourite view of the central Pennines is of Buckden Pike, over 2,000ft up, as approached from the village of Buckden. Last time I could only enjoy it by trespassing. They want to sanitise the North Yorkshire Moors so that it's like walking down your garden. They are spending too much money. It might be better if budgets were tighter. Of course it is hard to protect without tarnishing, and the moors are there for people to enjoy, but there's real danger of making the whole thing a showplace, nothing left naturally.'

Yet Allan is as enthusiastic as I am about the reopening of canals, and the rebuilding of the Welsh Highland railway through Snowdonia. 'They are things that fit into the landscape and enable more people to enjoy it without doing real damage,' he says. 'It is general over-development, the official's tidy mind coupled with spare money to spend at the end of the financial year that's the real problem. Of course I'm not against people restricted to wheelchairs enjoying the countryside, but create masses of wide, paved paths for them and how can it look natural?'

At the prizegiving Allan appropriately presented the awards to winners in the various categories of my Trust's 'This Britain' writing and photographic competitions. He has strong Harrogate roots, one of his first books being about the town. We talk about High Harrogate being fossilised, the value of the Stray, Low Harrogate's purely medical start in life, and how the railway drew everything together. Allan lives in Hull for which he has fond regard, though regretting that most shipping has deserted the port. 'Each dock had its separate character, and of course Hull was totally different from other ports. Waterside gentrification brings too much standardisation.'

At which point we get nostalgic about the way one crossed the Humber before the building of its great bridge: having refreshments on an old-fashioned steamboat connecting with trains at the strange outpost of New Holland. And about the frequent trains for trippers that once ran from Hull across the level-crossing riddled wolds to the small resorts of Hornsea and Withernsea, and south of that the changing shape of Spurn Head.

Back to Allan: 'Dad ran four shoe shops in Leeds. I hated every hour in a shop, but Dad was very supportive of what I wanted to do. There's no academic tradition in the family.' And about growing older: 'Sadly at seventy you have to give up as magistrate. Just when you think your judgement is best.' And, of course, about other books, by pioneers such as Dudley Stamp, whose *Structure and Scenery in Great Britain*, is still worth reading, WG Hoskins who pioneered more detailed understanding of the landscape, as well as D&C titles such as *The North Yorkshire Moors* in the Landscape Heritage series which Allan edited. He surprises me by saying that he has had the greatest fun writing and editing railway history. Inevitably we list the idiosyncrasies of some of the authors of various series, including *Railway History in Pictures*. Some were brilliant. Some thought they were brilliant when they were not. Others realised they needed help. The obvious choices for their subject fell into all three categories, so achieving presentable uniformity meant much burning of the midnight oil.

We toy with the idea of spending a few days getting under the skin of parts of Yorkshire, but with the pressure on both of us, that is what it will probably remain: just a dream.

As he leaves, I wonder if Allan has been fair in his judgement on the national parks. He is, of course, right about wide paved pathways destroying naturalness. Everywhere there's too much development. I've often thought that from south to north, Teignmouth to Nairn, officials cannot leave alone empty grassland near the beach. It depends what you want. For the energetic purist, used to enjoying lone mountain-top views, the Fourth Wave must spell disaster. From my standpoint, occasionally wanting to drink in different landscapes, the national parks, if not perfect, haven't done badly. The battle will go on being fought and I'm glad that people like Allan and those with even more purist views maintain close watch.

Yorkshire Nationalist

Geoffrey Smith, who went home after the prizegiving to collect his wife Marjorie, arrives for dinner. He recalls that the last time we dined together was at the Midland Hotel in Manchester at the end of its great railway hotel days. He was writing *A Passion for Flowers*. I was charging round Britain for a piece describing a day in the life of BR. Having been here and there, I dashed up by the old *Manchester Pullman*, returning by a summer Friday-night Newquay-bound train full of cheerful holidaymakers who applauded the driver when he walked through wishing everyone good weather. 'I felt the least I could do was come across from Harrogate,' says Geoffrey.

Our meeting before that, he says, was for lunch at Clumber Park, near Sherwood Forest. I recall Geoffrey enthusiastically explaining details of what remains of the home of the Dukes of Newcastle: a Gothic-revival chapel, stable block, greenhouse and some gardens overlooking Clumber Lake. The house was dismantled in 1983. A decade or so ahead of the revolution started by the Lost Gardens of Heligan, over our National Trust lunch we had discussed how disappointing it was that more attention wasn't being paid to looking after and restoring the working parts of the gardens of great estates. As few can do better, he rapidly brought alive the days when the chief gardener would have commanded a small army and planned their day with military precision – and when relations were usually taut with the 'customer' for much of the produce and blooms: the kitchen.

At that time many instantly recognised Geoffrey as TV gardening personality. But few people have less supported the cult of the personality. Though he enjoyed sharing his love of plants, and especially how they were discovered and introduced into Britain, Geoffrey is one of that rare band who gave up TV long before it would have given him up. He is one of the gentlest, most modest people I've ever met... and also one of the most opinionated: biased about Yorkshire! He doesn't believe that anywhere else can touch its grandeur and variety.

He goes on so much about the county's brilliance, its sheer size and scope, the many ways in which it knocks London but also Devon into a cocked hat, that I wonder how I (or anyone else) ever persuaded him to go beyond its borders. Or is he winding me up a little?

Mind you, he's not far off the mark when he says: 'There's everything you could wish for in Yorkshire. Two great national parks, unsurpassed natural beauty in high sea cliffs, holiday resorts and fishing ports, great mediaeval towns and lots of abbeys, priories and other fine buildings and ruins, some of the most outstanding gardens in the world... look what we've here just around Harrogate. There's so much of Yorkshire that no one can fully know it all. And the people,' and away he goes again eulogising characteristics – including directness – that not everyone in Southern England would like. The clincher is: 'Yorkshire is more important than the whole of many smaller independent countries.' True. However, despite my cheeky section heading, he doesn't advocate a unilateral declaration of independence.

I teasingly state that were Yorkshire independent there'd be an awful lot of internal squabbling over what part of government should be seated where. He squints not so much in disapproval as perhaps suggesting that as an outsider I'm not really qualified to comment. He does however allow that I do understand part of the magic of Yorkshire's complicated ingredients, but abhors the gaps in my experience and suggests which should be filled in first.

Then we had talk about individual dales. His favourite is Teesdale, not as much under pressure as most southern dales but with top scenery. His second favourite Swaledale, where he loves getting off the beaten track down green lanes. That is still possible in side valleys off the rocky central part, even though many motorists on long-distance journeys relieve their frustration of the A1 by taking a breath of fresh air up this great byway. Geoffrey makes me positively angry with myself for not having been back for years. Reeth was once one of my favourite villages.

The perspective suddenly changes when he reveals that for some years he had a cottage on the edge of the Broads at Hickling, near the small village of Potter Heigham, in Norfolk. How disloyal to Yorkshire.

I gather it was in a lovely spot, but made him even more appreciative of the value of his own county's more vertical landscape. Quickly we are back to discussing individual dales and their history and culture. 'There's history everywhere. Take the lead mines. They have a fascinating tale. A great culture was built up among the miners. They often recited poetry and explored value systems. The men went underground and the women ran the farms.'

Then I lead the conversation to Harlow Carr (the Northern Horticultural Society's showpiece), where Geoffrey really made his gardening mark. It was a bare field on the western outskirts of Harrogate when it was decided to create a distinctive northern garden. 'When I saw it, I thought I'm going to learn plantsmanship here as nobody else has done.' When he was offered the job as director, and responded 'If I can have a free hand for eighteen months', he was accused of 'the arrogance of ignorance'. But he got the job as he wanted it. 'Harlow Carr was the marvellous creative thing in my life.'

Nobody would dispute that the creativity was indeed marvellous. Harlow Carr showed off not merely what could be achieved in northern conditions but how wonderful it is to make a garden look natural, growing out of the ground rather than a series of pieces imported from elsewhere.

His period at Harlow Carr was long and fruitful, but ended sadly when he resigned on a policy point. Harlow Carr, with its peaceful arboretum, streamside garden, and gently undulating summer carpets of colour, is his creation but sooner or later committee people had to get involved. Now, he says, the place is spoilt by having the offices and plant sales at the top rather than the bottom where the pub (originally hotel) is. And now you go in through a side entrance instead of the great sweeping gates.

Inevitably the Lost Gardens of Heligan are mentioned. Geoffrey welcomes increasing respect for the productive side of yesteryear's great country gardens: 'an important part of our heritage'. He recalls how head gardeners vied with one another to grow the juiciest variety of grapes, have the earliest strawberries and richest range of home-grown citrus fruit ready for table. The evening ends with fond memories of walled gardens, huge lean-to greenhouses in sheltered positions and ancient coal-hungry fuel systems and large bare pipework with hefty control taps.

'Gardening generates an extraordinary amount of good will,' is his parting shot. 'And a lot of hard work and correspondence,' adds a smiling Marjorie.

Saved by the South Sea Bubble

Though only four miles from Harrogate, Knaresborough is a different world. I love its old narrow streets clustered on the northern bank of the

River Nidd, which here runs in a deep gorge. By road or rail, the journey from Harrogate to York is mainly flat and dull, but the daring railway bridge over the gorge challenges many photographers. It looks more spectacular when you're not on a train. The town is anyway best explored by foot. Cross by the high-level bridge; come back by the low-level one looking up at the wooded hillside to the rocks above, topped by a ruined castle. If you're into cathedrals, minsters, ruined abbeys and castles, names around here just drop off the tongue: for starters York Minster, Ripon Cathedral, Bolton, Jervaulx and Fountains Abbeys. And there hardly seems a hillock that isn't capped with a ruin.

After a lazy day going no further than Knaresborough, next morning we leave Harrogate, making our first call at Fountains Abbey. The short journey is Yorkshire in miniature. Ripley is as Yorkshire as villages come: unified mellow grey stone around the square with stocks in front of a cross, the castle entrance at the far end. It only takes a moment to go beyond that entrance to catch a glimpse of the lake that makes Ripley Park so attractive. Returning to the main road, we soon fork right into an off-the-tourist-track land of narrow lanes, tractors with large trailers and a well-cultivated undulating country. It is just one of thousands of such tracts that fed wealth into the fine mediaeval towns, churches and abbeys. Soon we see one of the hillocks that seem to abound west of the great Vale of York: How Hill, and sure enough it's capped by a ruin. Boarded up, it appears to be partly built into the hillside. Being British and with greater ruins to study, we aren't even curious about its date and history.

Americans can never understand why we get excited about some ruins and don't seem to care at all about others. Their difficulty is that they always have to relate things to their own experience. There just aren't ancient ruins in the United States. 'When things pass their sell-by date, we knock 'em down and build fresh,' has deprived America of much of what architectural heritage it might now enjoy. I recall that in York several years ago, a local guide was explaining the size and importance of Yorkshire when an American interjected: 'You mean a kind of mini-Texas.' Well, not exactly. And his explanation of what he thought were poor hotel standards was scarcely accurate either: 'If your major tourist attractions are ruins, I suppose we shouldn't be surprised that the hotels are rundown.'

But at Fountains Abbey, which we approach by the back entrance, we are still taken aback when the volunteer selling tickets tells us that yesterday an American demanded: 'When are you guys going to get round to putting the roof back on?' The volunteer explains: 'Some of them just can't get the hang of ruins. I heard a kid complain: "Mom, it's all falling down." It isn't just that they don't have anything like it back home but can't let go of the values they've been brought up with.

Yet when it comes to dates and kings and battles, some of them know more about our history than we do. It's like they and we are on different planets.' He'd earlier been much concerned that, when I found I'd left my National Trust life membership card behind, he had to charge admission. Since that life membership cost me £25, an investment made in the late 1960s when I feared I might go bankrupt and lose everything that was transferable, paying up at Fountains Abbey seems only just.

I've only been here once before and it left such a deep impression that I've been reluctant to return. That first visit was on a fine summer evening in the 1950s, before I'd even started the business that nearly made me bankrupt, and decades before the National Trust's involvement. There weren't many visitors then, and no organised tours like those we see this glittering spring morning that have attracted dozens of people. I recall the natural beauty of the setting, the clever use the monks made of it to enhance their view, how the river supplied them with fish and fresh water and washed away garbage... and of course the sheer scale.

This visit, Sheila's first, doesn't disappoint. If there is one ruined abbey one should see beyond all others, it must be Fountains. In the first place, it was – and remains – the largest in all Europe. It is colossal, Yorkshire (even maybe Texas) in size. Yet peace pervades. The grounds, set off by the Skell, in places a natural river, in others formally canalised, in others again running through lake or pond, are in a class of their own. Of course one cannot knock other great ruins such as Tintern, but this really is unique. From every angle the great roofless mass of Fountains presents the perfect picture. Much more has survived than of most monasteries, which were generally regarded as a source of building stone in the centuries after the Dissolution. Though much is roofless, most walls are intact.

There is a very Yorkshire explanation for why so much remains standing: the South Sea Bubble of 1720!

At the end of the previous century, John Aislabie, already Tory MP for Ripon, inherited the adjoining Studley Royal estate. An ambitious chap who made a timely change of allegiance, he became Whig Chancellor of the Exchequer. That was in 1718. Having apparently decided to run down the estate, but with his fortune now riding high, he began making a park in the wooded Skell Valley.

His resources were mainly committed to the South Sea Company, whose Parliamentary Bill he personally promoted. The South Sea Company was, of course, an early example of something being too good to be true. When the Bubble burst, in 1720, Aislabie went bankrupt, and was not merely expelled from Parliament but disqualified from ever again holding public office.

He turned inward, devoting all his energy to making his garden. His son William completed the work after purchasing the abbey ruins for a relative song. The grounds of Fountains Abbey and Studley Royal were now a single unit, and the memorable approach to the east front was designed for maximum impact. And while John had designed things formally, William quickly took to the new romantic style. Though the main Abbey roof had of course collapsed by now, and some building stone taken, Fountains – just far enough away from growing towns – was still much as it was when the last monks had been forced to leave. John's delight in showing off the ruins was as good as a latter-day preservation order. One form of Yorkshire excess had saved another.

So it is that this morning we can marvel at Fountains Abbey recalling Pevsner's statement that: 'There is no other place in the country in which the mind can so readily evoke the picture of thirteenth-century monastic life.' The morning's last well-attended tour has now moved off to the water garden, so we share the great complex of buildings with perhaps three other visitors. The thrill of walking around is the greater because the National Trust has avoided labelling the different parts. With a simple plan, we look and imagine. The only sound is of an odd plane passing overhead. What peace the monks must have experienced.

This was a Cistercian monastery, itself founded upon dispute. Northern monasteries were among the first to be re-established after the disruption of the Norman Conquest. Among them was the Benedictine St Mary's in York. Feeling that life there had become too soft, in 1132 a group of dissidents pleaded for a return to the older, more spartan ways: they had been impressed by a group of monks of the French new Cistercian Order 'rejoicing in their poverty' as they passed through York. Trouble increased until there was a riot. Then Thurston, Archbishop of York, took thirteen of the reformers into his protection. Two days after spending Christmas at his Ripon palace, they moved three miles up the Skell to a bleak parcel of land he gave them. After three years – three very hard years – Fountains was thought to be secure enough to be admitted to the austere French order, the circumstances of whose own founding had not been dissimilar.

So we picture the monks, the 'White Monks' in their regulation habit of undyed sheep's wool, 'poor as the poor of Christ', going about their daily worship and business. Individual poverty has never meant lack of architectural appreciation. Fountains was severely practical in its first creation. Though from the start sheer size must have made impact, it was steadily extended over generations. And what was lacking in decoration was compensated for by the wondrous setting and equally practical arrangements of the almost square block.

As we look at the pattern of shadows cast by the spring sunshine down the long nave, between the great matching east and west windows, we think of the lay brothers who shared the church but were cut off by a screen from the full (or 'choir') monks. Such is the scale that it is clear that Fountains, supported by its great estates, couldn't have been made to operate without these lay workhorses. Illiterate, they were better fed, slept longer and of course attended fewer services. They must have been much more crowded in their infirmary than were the monks in theirs. We go to see the remains of both structures, at opposite ends of the complex. Both were built across the river. We are fascinated by a chute down which a container could be lowered to bring up fresh water, and by an early kind of waste-disposal unit, a mesh through which discarded food and other waste could be dropped into the water to be flushed away. Presumably one of the channels into which the river was separated flowing past the abbey kept some water fresh for the lay brothers downstream. We have to remind ourselves that an infirmary was where monks retired and spent healthy years as well as where they were treated when ill.

Though the rows of rounded arches seem to go on endlessly, and it is impossible not to be impressed by the network of curved stone supports holding up the still-intact roof of the magnificent west range, it is in the domestic details that the reality of the monks' life vividly comes to us across the centuries. For example, beside the steep day stair, rising from the cloister's south side to their dormitory, is a recessed arch. There used to be a cupboard in it where towels were kept in readiness for the monks to dry their hands after washing before meals in the refectory. I wonder if they sometimes ran out of clean ones?

The story of Fountains is as complex as the buildings are large. We come across just one plan, interestingly colour-coded by age. Unfortunately there isn't a version of that plan we can carry round. But we came more to be awed, to feel part of a great history, than to analyse and understand. You can in fact both imagine and understand here uniquely well, but you need quiet, gentle time to gaze and simply wonder to touch the meaning of life.

It is hard to tell whether the distant view of the ruins or Fountains internal detailed arrangements made the greater impact on us, but the unity of the two is all powerful. It is good to know that since my only previous visit Fountains Abbey and Studley Royal are again in common ownership, and that today's National Trust is not intent on the standardisation of presentation that afflicted it in earlier times.

Do visit Fountains, enjoy what are arguably the best water gardens in England, explore a richer range of monuments from past ages than you'll find anywhere else, and above all experience the peace. As we walk back to the car, we reflect that much of human history is written in greed. Though the Dissolution of the Monasteries began by tackling real abuse, and was genuinely not at first intended to be all-reaching, and though the Cistercians were almost certainly above the selfish practice that ran through many (especially smaller) religious houses, in the end Henry VIII, needing the cash, suppressed the lot. Built without thought of defence, once Fountains was seen as so permanent as to be chosen as storage for Royal Treasure. Its dissolution was in 1539. Thank goodness for the South Sea Bubble, say we; without it there would be a lot less to see in a less dramatic setting.

We take one final glance. Fountains: mellow, peaceful, romantic... and key to so many of our yesterdays.

Out of Yorkshire

I've one last item on the shopping list of this brief visit: Nidderdale. I just happen to have become especially familiar with it, and that has bred love. Because of industry and especially reservoirs, it isn't even in the Dales National Park and, perhaps because of that, is not put so much under the microscope. But it's not inferior.

We start out on the B625 which, if we stay on it, could interestingly take us back to Grassington. But at Pateley Bridge we turn north into Nidderdale. Gouthwaite Reservoir may be an aberration to purists, but over many decades I have enjoyed occasional drives beside it and the earthworks of the long-abandoned railway. Time is now becoming of the essence so, after a hasty snack at the Lofthouse, where the hills really begin to close in, we turn round. Back through Pateley Bridge, alongside the fast-flowing Nidd for a time, and then steeply up through Dacre we head for the more mundane A59. Next time, I promise Nidderdale, we'll give it more time. But now we must get to the Lake District.

The A59 is busy as always, but this part of Northern England has too much geography for any road to lack interest. At Blubberhouses we touch the northern tip of another great reservoir. Hazlewood Moor looks positively inviting lit up by the afternoon sunshine. At Bolton Bridge, tantalisingly we only have time for a quick glance at Bolton Abbey: another ruin in a great setting, if not quite in Fountains league. So, bypassing Skipton, we head northwest, once again beside our old friend the Settle & Carlisle Railway wrestling with the hills and occasional valleys.

Then more fine limestone country through Clapham, home of *The Dalesman*, to Ingleton and out of Yorkshire. When I think of the conversation of only a few days ago with Geoffrey Smith, I feel a bit of a cheat. Even though we'll soon be back in the Dales (chapter 34) when we hope to have dinner with David Joy, one-time editor of *The*

Dalesman, we will miss more of Yorkshire than we've seen. As we head past Kirkby Lonsdale, we laugh about Yorkshire humour and recall one of David's shorter anecdotes. A patronising newcomer phoned the coal merchant: 'My man, half a ton, si vous plaît.' It took ten measured seconds for: 'Certainly, Madam. Would you like it à la cart or cul de sac?'

· X X X ·

THE LAKE DISTRICT

Our Best-Loved Landscape

So many poets and non-fiction writers have expressed tribute to the Lakes – 'the loveliest spot that man has ever found,' said Wordsworth – that it seems scarcely sensible to attempt another. There are, of course, technical explanations for the extraordinary range and depth of the Lakes' majesty; to begin with, virtually every kind of rock is found in Britain's busiest geological melting pot. What energy was released in creating England's favourite landscape!

There is much individual perfection; no part of the area is scenically dull, and we are all undoubtedly influenced by the culture, especially by the Lake Poets, spreading the message that nobody with an enquiring mind should miss this part of our heritage. Even most of those southern Englanders who lamentably never cross the border into Scotland feel that they have to experience the Lakes.

It is not surprising that this is the only area in Britain where railways were not eagerly greeted. From the eighteenth century, people wanted to protect the natural beauty. Yet no rural area is richer in man-made artefacts, from arts-and-crafts cottages to stately homes, clusters of little buildings that add the finishing touch to many a village scene, and stone hedges that villages and farms grew out of the landscape, literally in many cases with hand-collected surface stone, totally different between each geological zone. Gardens are renowned for their beauty and setting. Lush low-level vegetation features in many of the best Lakeland views. Even historic craft on several lakes add their distinctive touch.

There is a saying about Alaska that if you go there, you'll never come the whole way back. It is even truer of the Lakes. Visiting after a long absence, one instantly feels at home again. The magic of the landscape draws one to it. 'The variety thereof smileth upon the beholders and giveth contentment to all that travaile it,' said William Camden in the first topographical book ever in the English language (in its second translated edition of 1695). I had the pleasure of reprinting it for a new generation of readers.

The Lakes are bold without being harsh. Often in the Highlands one feels on the very edge of civilisation, sometimes beyond it. In the Lakes there is civilisation. The Lakes themselves add to perfection of shape, proportion and the everlasting play of light and shade. Who, knowing the area well, has not been especially thrilled by one of those morning mists constantly changing what it chooses to hide and to reveal? There you go; I can't resist attempting my own appreciation.

Once I took a pre-breakfast trip on a boat on Derwent Water. It was autumn, and soon we were lost in a great descending fog. Panic. Would the hotel have stopped serving breakfast by the time we returned? Might we miss our train? Then sheer thrill as a mountain top tentatively appeared, and valleys played hide-and-seek, and the boatman began to recognise our position. A watery sun shone through as we made for the shore. By the time we walked away from the boat, only part of the skyline was shrouded in mist, and there were perfect mirror images of much of the wooded shore and lower fells beyond.

I love being awed by terrific Highland and indeed Swiss scenery, but the Lakes I drink in and in. Though there are of course great drives to be enjoyed, this is not a region for just passing through, but in which to be. With so many caring people to cater for, the Lake District abounds in good hotels and restaurants, and nowhere is there a richer variety of tourist attractions to be found in so compact an area.

Yet the wild grandeur that especially captivates the fellwalkers who come in ever greater numbers must not be played down. They come, not so much for exercise or to achieve, as to learn, look and take in the awesome mountain tops, the Lake District's roof, especially around Skiddaw in the north, where we find the oldest, most-friable slate rocks eroded into many dramatic, often weird shapes. That was a mere 10,000 or so years ago, yesterday in geological time, in the last Ice Age which cut its way ruthlessly through the rocks, obliterating evidence of previous ice ages. Go to Spitzbergen today to see what the Lakes would have been like at that time, around 8000BCE. It is hard not to feel humbled by the energy that went into the Lake District's creation – energy still clearly visible in the detail of many rock formations and audible in the rushing of countless streams, some with waterfalls where one has to raise one's voice to be heard. The lakes themselves are more peaceful, at perfect peace when the last boats have been tied up for the night and maybe a red sunset heralds another day to refresh the spirit.

Shipping Magnate's Mansion

We start our visit at Bowness on Windermere, around which are found six of the AA's selection of the 'Top 200' British hotels, boasting twelve red rosettes between them. At Storrs Hall, a Georgian mansion in wooded grounds and with its own private jetty south of Bowness, we are shown to the very room which Sir John Leggard, a Liverpool shipping merchant whose fortune was partly based on the famous triangular slave trade, designed as his bedroom. It commands a stunning southerly view down the lake. Leggard wasn't one to share things. To achieve his selfish perfection, every last piece of human habitation was removed from the view. Uncannily, close to the most crowded centre of the most pressurised of our national parks, there is not a stationary light to be seen after dark. Leggard couldn't however stop the passage of craft up and down England's largest and best-known lake. The first thing that catches our eyes is the progress of one of the larger tourist vessels of the fleet once operated by nationalised Sealink – but now privately owned. We walk around the grounds, especially by the lake, and then admire a score of vintage Rolls Royces belonging to drivers who have come for a special Owners' Club dinner.

As private house and then hotel, for centuries Storrs Hall has welcomed the great and wealthy. Visitors have included Beatrix Potter, Robert Southey, George Canning and Sir Walter Scott. The latter two arrived together in 1825: 'Fifty barges sailed up Windermere' to celebrate their arrival, Wordsworth and other Lake Poets leading cheers. We are, indeed, in hallowed company. Wordsworth wrote: 'The lower part of this Lake is rarely visited, but has many interesting points of view, especially at Storrs Hall and at Feel-foot, where the Coniston Mountains peer nobly over the western barrier.' Even then the 'mischief' of conifers was being corrected by planting native trees.

First call next morning is at the Windermere Steamboat Centre and Motorboat Collection, at Bowness. A delightful place, attracting 25,000 visitors a year, it houses many historic vessels, bobbing gently at the rows of jetties. Dolly, for example, is the world's oldest mechanically-powered boat. SS Raven was built by the Furness Railway in 1851 and, after rescue from the lake's bottom, steamed again on her one-hundreth birthday. A cargo boat, and in winter ice-breaker for the steamer service, her name was inspired by the story of Elijah being fed by ravens. The railway directors saw the analogy of feeding remote lakeside settlements with coal and food. The 65ft *TSSY Esperance* inspired Captain Flint's houseboat in Arthur Ransome's *Swallows and Amazons*: 'She was a long narrow craft with a high raised cabin roof, and a row of glass windows along her side. Her bows were like the bows of an old-time clipper. Her stern was like that of a steamship.'

Those were the days when the great Furness industrialists liked to live in fashionable Bowness. *Esperance* was built for HW Schneider who left home each morning accompanied by his butler carrying breakfast on a silver tray as they walked down to the private pier. The meal was served in a panelled saloon on the voyage to Lakeside, where a special train for Barrow-in-Furness waited. Now the oldest boat on Lloyd's Yacht Register, and the first-ever twin-screw steam yacht, she was actually built on the Clyde, and the cost of delivering her to Lake Windermere included singling the double-track railway to provide clearance. Nothing was too expensive for the personal comfort of Schneider and his kind, whose luxuries were paid for by the mean treatment of their workers. Barrow-in-Furness witnessed some particularly nasty labour disputes.

When I was last here, and the museum's founder, GH Pattison, was alive and active, he took me for a spin on his personal boat. *SL Branksome*: 50ft long, 9ft beam, hull of carved teak, side-fired boiler, with a Sissons compound engine, and speed of 14mph. 'Like a cup of tea?' he enquired, effecting nonchalance when we were under way. He proceeded to make a pot with water from the 'kettle'. It takes ten seconds to make a gallon. It works by boiler steam being condensed passing through coiled pipes inside the urn. *Branksome* typifies Victorian elegance. Many boats had similar kettles, and silver tea services engraved with their names.

Pattison was a cheerful guy with contagious enthusiasm which one can still enjoy in his hardback *The Great Age of Steam on Windermere*. He describes how rivalry between well-heeled owners led to 'the finest variety range of inland craft ever seen together'. That enthusiasm is echoed in today's friendly museum. It pleases both the mechanically-minded, who enjoy the technical explanations in the notices and conversations with the custodians, and children who just enjoy something different and pick up fragments of information about 'the olden days'. Long may it flourish.

Around Ambleside

After coffee at the Steam Boat Museum, buying the latest issue of *The Funnel*, the magazine of the Steam Boat Association of Great Britain, and a last glance at the graciously shaped steamboats, we walk around Ambleside, look at the shops up the busy main road toward Windermere town, and rest on a bench near the piers. Watching boats load and unload, and people enjoying snacks and ice creams, is fun. Two ladies who have bought a packet of flaked maize are feeding ducks. Seagulls here must be so well fed that they don't spoil the party as usually happens elsewhere. The swans of course don't miss a trick.

This waterside is probably the busiest point in all Lakeland. In 1960, when I was conducting the Lake District Enquiry (see chapter 22), my team and I spent several days here interviewing visitors and locals about their transport habits and expectations. That was in high summer, when it was far busier than this crisp spring morning. Aged thirty, I had landed the post of directing the Transport Enquiry before, curious though it may sound to today's generation, I had not even heard of the existence of smoked salmon. No doubt as part of a campaign to be seen in a favourable light in the enquiry's report, the Ribble Bus Company's top brass who invited me to lunch at The Old England Hotel persuaded me to join them in having some as a starter. They had driven up from Preston; travelling by bus, and the humble diet that no doubt most bus passengers then ate wasn't for them. They were, I discovered, an inflexible bunch, not at all interested in buses connecting with trains. The nature of the real battle to come, public transport as a whole versus the private car, hadn't yet become clear, at least not to them.

Over the years I frequently returned to The Old England, for short breaks and occasional meals, savouring the dining room's lake view and the best of Trust House Forte fare. Some readers may recall the days when a selection of plain chocolates from Terry's top-of-the-market 1767 range was handed round at coffee after dinner. The Old England's offering was especially generous. For nostalgia, I'm back for lunch at The Old England.

As at many other former Forte hotels, there's now a sorry state of affairs. There are only bar snacks for lunch; I see that the lift isn't working; the gents doesn't seem to have been redecorated since Forte days (some taps lack tops). It takes full forty minutes for drinks to be served. Everyone is complaining. Eventually our main dish comes; one portion of plaice instead of the two ordered. When a second arrives, it is still ice-cold in the middle. I call the waitress:

'Yes, the gentleman over there was complaining too.'

'This used to be a wonderful hotel.'

'So people keep telling me.'

She returns to say she's only going to charge me for one portion.

'That was really horrible,' says Sheila. She's taken a box of matches provided by the ashtray as a memento. It feels light; it's empty.

Then we meet Victor TC Middleton, who I first came across one evening in a sleeper train's lounge car from Inverness, where he told me that years ago something about the Lakes' landscape had lit a fuse in him and determined the course of his career. A consultant specialising in landscape and tourism, he quickly makes some interesting points. 'Farmers are the de facto managers of the landscape. The National Trust began here – Ruskin took the founder, Octavia Hill, under his wings – and now owns ninety tenanted farms.'

Victor undertook work for the National Trust report *Valuing Our Environment*, emphasising the economic benefits of maintaining the integrity of the 'cultural landscape'. He likes the intention to stop fast boating on Windermere – formal notice has been given – but says that the discussion about the long-term future of road traffic in the National Park has to start afresh. *Motor Transport Strategy*, trying to lay down which roads were used for what traffic, was an 'absurd document'. One thing should be started forthwith, however: 'Persuading the road authority that they don't have to apply urban standards to country roads. Concrete kerbs, an abundance of 'Go slow' and 'Caution' signs and repeated warnings of the speed restriction are quite unnecessarily intrusive.' Another thing: 'Big coaches should be used to bring people to the Lakes, not take them round. Local services would be much better for that.' He talks of the success of the Mountain Goat bus initiative.

A wiry, energetic sort who spends much of his life travelling, having arrived from chairing a conference on visitor attractions he's now off in haste to another appointment before returning to his home near Ulverston. He is the first of a string of people we meet whose passion for the landscape has led to a dedicated career of seeking the right balance between giving visitors what they want, while preventing them spoiling what they come for. He perhaps sees himself as a latter-day supporter of John Ruskin, the great Victorian watercolourist who first made a reputation through publication of *Modern Painters*, a defence of Turner and other landscape painters. The Ruskin Museum at Coniston is possibly Lakeland's best. Coniston Water is a gorgeous lake, *Swallows and Amazons* country, which often I've enjoyed on the steam yacht *Gondola* making its timetabled journeys.

On our way back to Storrs Hall, we pass a huge building where speedboats and jet skis are stored and wonder what the future holds for that business, since in a year or two speeding is to be prohibited on Windermere. A full ferry sets out on its short crossing, no doubt with some vehicles on board for Coniston via Hawkshead – a splendid run, and a long one, combining elements of almost every type of Lakeland scenery if you head to the west coast at Ravenglass. Already a couple of cars are waiting for the next sailing of what remains an essential service, saving time and congestion along the winding road around the lake.

Waiting at the hotel is Jo Dadley, one of Cumbria's fifty licensed Blue Badge Guides, a lively former British Airways stewardess who loves driving her big car with seats high enough for her guests to see over the stone walls. Unlike many of the guides, she doesn't do fell walks, but enjoys conducting guided walks round towns, gives commentaries on private cruises, visits hotels for evening lectures... and loves the idiosyncrasies of those she has time to get to know when out driving. Her guests, mainly from overseas, are obviously not a typical cross-section of those 'doing' the Lakes. 'They are amazingly well informed, and really study my itineraries, which take a long time to write before each individual tour. The English who sometimes come with overseas people think they know more than they do. They've read *Daffodils*, spend twenty minutes at Dove Cottage and think they are experts on Wordsworth.'

For a special occasion, she recently dressed up as Peter Rabbit for a 'Tale of Beatrix Potter' walk from Windermere Ferry to near Sawrey on Esthwaite Water on the road to Hawkshead and Coniston. 'The Japanese simply love Beatrix Potter,' whose work was largely inspired by the Lakes. Beatrix Potter was a regular visitor before buying her first property, near Hawkshead – a farm paid for by her royalties. In its first two years, *The Tale of Peter Rabbit* sold 50,000 copies.

'Wordsworth visited this house as a guest for the 1825 regatta,' says Jo referring to our hotel. 'He was the pillar of society, an establishment figure, author of the bestselling guide book of its day. The first visitors to the Lakes were those who admired people like Wordsworth, Ruskin and Coleridge (looked after by Southey when separated from his wife). The literary associations once attracted people to the Lakes. He may have a museum named after him, but not many would come because of John Ruskin today, would they? Yet he was famous as social visionary as well as artist and writer, and many well-known people came to see him. Popular tourism began a lot later, but the foundations were built on luxury hotels and great houses, some of which like this are now hotels.'

Rising to leave, she recalls the seamier side of the history of this building. Apparently the profits of the three-way slave trade helped the owner keep a black mistress in the Caribbean. Under the hotel are dark tunnels; I hear of a child who died, and how the prophecy 'no male heir will inherit' had been proved true.

That seems to cast a spell over tonight. Last night's dinner was excellent, but served very slowly, blamed on the Rolls Royce party. Now the trouble is that there's only one other couple in the hotel. Nobody seems to want to take our order. Eventually we stress we'd like to eat as soon as possible. The under-employed staff insist on doing things their way: slowly. Despite pleas to the waiter – and my twice going to reception to ask if they can stir action – three courses take three hours from the time we arrive to order. The menu is the same as last night; we learn it only changes occasionally, and we don't want to eat from the same short, though good menu for four nights. A supplementary menu headed with our names is thoughtfully provided next evening but, again, despite jumping up to ask reception to intervene, the waiter hides and then blames the chef. The same thing happens on our final night, so we rehearse a complaint letter. [The manager replied that our disappointment was a pity because, if we had so requested, dinner could certainly have been speeded up!] But the position is fabulous. During the day there's almost ceaseless activity on the water, many boats purposefully progressing up and down the lake as though it were a major highway. At dusk peace descends.

By Lake to Lakeside

Next morning we lie in bed as the mist rises and the wooded shores and mountains are perfectly reflected in the still water, mirror images. No boat or yacht has yet made passage. It doesn't seem to matter that there is so much buzz during the day when there's emptiness in the long evenings, and early starts to the fresh day. It is, of course, usually at dusk and early morning that the Lake's ripples are minimal. There is usually a breeze when people are actually out on the water.

There's much to learn about Windermere. Who, for example, isn't surprised to know that, though netting was banned in 1924, sufficient Arctic charr are caught to support a small commercial fishery? This is as far south as the species, which needs good-quality deep, cold water, is found in England. When sewerage seriously threatened the lake – things are better now – its survival owed much to the oddity that the fish in this particular lake are split between autumn and spring spawners. There are also perch, pike, Atlantic salmon and trout, and eels. A thousand ducks, geese and swans stay year round, supplemented by many winter guests.

Since I was last here, the sailing season has been extended; in fact there are some timetabled services on the lake every day except Christmas Day. We take the 10.30 from Bowness to Lakeside. About thirty of us make light demand on one of the three large vessels inherited from Sealink. Views from the water continually change but, now that a breeze has whipped up wavelets, nothing quite equals what we saw from our bed. Coffee on the move is civilised, though, with Wordsworth's *The Solitary Reaper* on the sugar packets. The commentary tells us that water from Windermere can be piped to anywhere in northern England, that the County Council runs the essential cross-lake ferry, and that we can see every species of native tree growing by the shore. As we dock at Lakeside, we pass the oldest member of the big-boat trio, the graceful *Tern*, which began life as a steamship.

Lakeside I have always loved. It was once the main gateway to Windermere, where people transferred from train to boat. The Furness Railway built a handsome range of buildings for the terminus of its branch from Ulverston. The Victorian-style train-boat link is maintained by today's independent steam Lakeside & Haverthwaite Railway, but it hasn't yet started its shorter season, and destroying the line between Ulverston and Haverthwaite has inevitably relegated Lakeside's importance. The brick-built station complex has a good shop, café, and the freshwater Aquarium of the Lakes. We marvel at the amazing diving ducks which we see both above water and foraging for food under it, while fish take no notice and go about their business. We don't like the pike (they've a real behavioural problem) but, now in a glass passageway and underwater ourselves, love the mischievous otters. There's also a saltwater section with sharks and rays. It is a small aquarium, but size isn't everything. A much larger aquarium we paid expensively to visit in America recently wasn't half as much fun.

This is the life! In holiday mood, having bought sandwiches to eat on our return boat, I suggest a pre-lunch drink at the Lakeside Hotel opposite. It is served in a conservatory overlooking the point where Windermere narrows into the River Leven. When joined by the Crake flowing out of Coniston Water, the river soon reaches the sea at Cartmel Sands. Though there isn't a trace of seaside atmosphere at Lakeside, we are only a few miles from several resorts, including Grange-over-Sands (chapter 22). We say we must make the Lakeside Hotel a base for a later trip to the southern Lakes and Cumbrian Coast. Privately owned, everything about it seems good.

Then to our return boat, going all the way to Ambleside before alighting at Bowness. Our journeys on the Lake stretch further than the shortest crossing of the English Channel. We're delayed by a ferry, pass another large busy boat and dozens and dozens of smaller ones, see extravagantly designed boathouses, including a castellated example with the boatman's accommodation over it, a reminder of old coach houses with the coachman's room above, the thriving youth hostel at Ambleside, and lush woodlands topped by mountain ridges designed in heaven.

Modern Business with Old-Fashioned Values

In the 1970s, when I pioneered publication of books about microwave cookery, sales were suddenly swelled by massive orders from a new firm in Lakeland called Lakeland Plastics (now Lakeland Limited). A free book was sent with every microwave sold. Such big orders from new customers tend to involve the risk of late or non-payment. However, driven by keen brothers, Lakeland didn't seem a firm whose solvency could be questioned with impunity. The brothers clearly knew what they were doing. I needn't have worried, for Lakeland has steadily expanded to become a household name. Its catalogues are full of creative kitchen gadgetry, utensils, storage ideas and solid value.

We have come to the HQ offices and shop beside Windermere train station to meet Michelle Kershaw, customer director. 'The business was started in a garage in 1962 by the brothers,' she says. 'Now we've 1000 staff, half of them in the Lake District. The state-of-the-art warehouse is in Kendal. Getting planning permission took seven years. We're proud of what we've done for the Lakes, a big boost to local business, and lots of good publicity too, but there's no real unemployment in Kendal and we have to take care to restrict our catalogue mailings to orders local people can handle, many on a part-time basis.'

Values are traditional. Catalogues are prepared with old-fashioned paste-up; it gives them 'a better feel'. And it is more important for me to meet the oldest member of staff, Eileen Barnes – 'You've been a busy little bee for 37 years, haven't you?' – than be dazzled by science.

'We are as good at thinking up gadgets for kitchens as we are at designing catalogues,' is her main boast, and one thoroughly justified judging from the esteem in which we and several friends hold Lakeland. The catalogues are very individual, Michelle being the company's public face. The business is run in just the way I'd like to achieve were I owner. Customers are king, treated personally on the phone, invited to comment and suggest new ideas. There's a great fan club. But, as we return to the car, I muse that it is exactly the kind of business that could run off the rails were it taken over by a larger concern. There's a younger member of the family in it, and hopefully it will remain a private enterprise, though everything is against such continuity today. Meanwhile it's a great modern business with old-fashioned values.

Just as we're about to get into the car, a well-filled train arrives at the terminus and a few passengers transfer into buses. The connections, of course, aren't advertised, at least not outside the Lake District. Cumbria County Council publishes a timetable with details of all train, bus and boat services, even listing voluntary car-lift schemes, and with fascinating snippets encouraging one to visit interesting places by public transport or on foot or by bicycle. It is a model other counties could well follow. But Windermere is now the only station in the National Park's heart: the junction on the West Coast main line advertises itself as Oxenholme Lake District.

Guardian of a Unique Heritage

Every now and then one meets someone who not only seems the perfect match for their job but spent years preparing for the appointment. Enter Paul Tiplady, National Park Officer; or rather, hearing he's ready to see me, I go to his office. He's a thoroughly believable kind of chap, energetically caring for the great landscape, the guardianship of which is his special concern. 'I always knew this was the job I wanted,' he says; ever since as a youth he took deprived kids round the Lake District. It is as though his training as geographer and accountant, the eleven years with Essex County Council, and working with protected landscapes in the South Downs, his master's degree in environmental planning, and much more, were a well-rehearsed route to success. When he first hoped to be appointed, it was indicated he still wasn't sufficiently qualified, so a master's degree in landscape archaeology followed. Dedication.

Interesting points pour off his tongue. Current priorities are to reduce the speed limit on Windermere to ten mph; to improve access; to encourage public transport; and, always in the background, to prevent uniformity.

'Because of their special heritage, the Lakes attract an enormous number of visitors. But it is worse than that because, today, few come here for their main holiday, they take three and four-day breaks. It gives us a year-round season, but the constant comings and goings add to the pressure. Yes, there's a big traffic problem we've not yet cracked. One has to recognise the art of the possible. Many people won't leave their cars. Coaches have increased in size because of national regulations. Everyone says that the survival of the village shop is vital, but we don't control the size of the delivery lorries which have become bigger and bigger.

'But there is much we can do. A lot has been put behind public transport initiatives, such as the integrated Windermere Lake cruise, Mountain Goat bus and Coniston launch service. The new cycleway network is important, too. There are bike racks on ferries and buses for those who want to cycle one way. We need the railways again to play a greater role. Top priority is to install one or two passing loops on the line from Oxenholme to Windermere, currently just a single straight track. One day we hope that Lakeland station on Windermere will be linked with the main line around the coast, and certainly we'd like to see freight back on that, especially at Workington.'

Fighting standardisation is something about which he feels deeply. 'We can't control the nationally-adopted traffic signs, so we have to put up with those irritating speed restriction repeater signs. We have a good say in local signage, but what happens if a Continental coach can't cross a packhorse bridge? We can't yet make people transfer to smaller vehicles to get to their destination, but maybe that time will come. There's growing support for sensible policies.

'People come for spiritual refreshment and tranquillity. They expect the Lakes to be different. One way in which they are different is in the use of local stone. Colour, texture and style are important; traditionally, only very local stone has been used, and certainly we don't allow building in one valley with stone of a different kind from another. That's one of the great things about this Park: because of the geological complexity, the differences in style and colour are often very local. The historical pattern is still clear even in honeypot areas. So Bowness is still a fishing village with a few fishermen earning a living. That's important.'

Smiling in a moment's pause he adds: 'It is not a question of asking who has the greater influence, Beatrix Potter or Wordsworth, but of respecting individuality, the relation between the stone walls, the farms, the hamlets. Of course, there's a limit to what we can achieve by force. In the end there are few tools beside persuasion.'

Judging by the string of publications produced by the National Park, education is also important, or is that part of persuasion? Do I need planning permission: *A householder's guide to extensions, alterations and additions; Rights of way; Coach driver's handbook* – all full of useful information, contacts and maps as well as the message not to interfere with local life. *The enforcement of planning control; Outdoor advertisements and signs; The care and protection of trees*, and many more. *Welcome to the National Park* says it is 'a very special place. Its spectacular landscapes, rugged fells, tranquil lakes and tarns, wildlife and cultural heritage are an inspiration to many. Over 12 million people visit the Lake District every year to enjoy the splendour of the mountains and lakes and to experience its special qualities.' It describes the interactive visitor centre at Brockhole and lists the National Park's dozen information centres. 'To help you enjoy Coniston Water... call the Head Boatman.' Another publication lists the 800 annual events held within the Park. There's also a series of local newsletters. The one for Lake Windermere says that there are to be no exemptions from the ten mph speed limit so that from 2005 events like the classic motorboat rally will no longer be possible.

Looking at racks of literature, it is also clear that relations with the National Trust, County Council, Nature Conservancy and other bodies is happier here than in some national parks. But then spending is higher, too. Including fifty or so employed seasonally, 200 people work for the National Park, Britain's largest. The biggest spend is on visitor information, but the National Park's planning authority, the busiest in Cumbria, receives 1,200 applications a year. 'That requires a huge commitment in time,' says Paul. 'I hope that every application will lead to enhancement... that someone has cared about it. We don't even want to think about fossilising the Lakes. There are many lively communities who of course need change to keep pace with modern standards. And there's still an element of independence which should be encouraged. It is interesting that the old county boundary stones are still there.' To celebrate the National Park's own first half century, new boundary stones mounted on plinths have been erected at major entry points. A different kind of rock is used at each entrance.

We talk of land erosion, the problems of total access but how walkers and climbers keep to the recognised rights of way: 'You only have to look and see where the paths are at Skiddaw, Scafell Pike, the Old Man of Coniston and Helvellyn. But what happens when 2,000 people in the Three Peaks Challenge on their way between Wales and Scotland descend on small hamlets with no loos? Sometimes we have to preach that there are wrong ways to raise money.' Then he makes the point that, while windfarms will undoubtedly be kept out of The Lakes with their small sky, there is a danger that ultimately there could be a ring of them just outside the National Park.

Finally, we talk about how the National Park used to be administered, almost as a sideline of the old Westmorland County Council, long-since abolished. Its clerk was my boss when I conducted the Lake District Transport Enquiry. 'That's a long time ago, but I dare say many of the problems you met then are those of today. But perhaps the Park's first fifty years haven't been too bad in protecting "The Lakes as a thing of beauty for ever". A modest enough claim. Further evidence of co-operation: before I leave the HQ, he suggests I call on the Friends of the Lake District.

Supporters' Club

Though it was Wordsworth in his bestselling *Guide Through the District of the Lakes* who first spoke of the area as 'a sort of national property', and the National Trust who first took practical steps to protect parts of it, the Friends of the Lake District have played an especially important role. Founded in 1934, their first task was to lobby for the creation of a special legal status to prevent undesirable development. Just over half a century ago, when the National Park was created, their objective was changed to work alongside it in protecting and preserving the landscape. It also plays a useful educational and practical advisory role. For example, among its many publications is a leaflet on environmental improvement grants. It offers student research grants, even supports specific bus services as well as working with the County Council to ensure that money available for public transport is used sensibly. Its remit covers all Cumbria, not just the Park. Currently it is undertaking another study on traffic and local roads.

Jan Darrell, policy officer, emphasises that often it is the detail that matters: 'We are very conscious of the accumulation of incremental change. You don't just have to do big things to make a real difference after, say, five years.'

In recent years they have conducted studies into the effect of drought, and how the economy might best be brought back to life after the foot-and-mouth outbreak, and are keen to encourage agri-environmental schemes enabling farmers to continue their traditional role of maintaining the landscape. What strikes me, especially in contrast with, say, Dartmoor, is that confrontation is rare. Recently, only the support for the introduction of the speed limit on Lake Windermere seems seriously to have raised hackles. The emphasis on co-operation is partly because nearly everyone actively wishes to see the local economy thrive. Co-operation and common sense are reflected in the fact that, uniquely, the Friends act as the local branch of the Council for the Preservation of Rural England. Nowhere else have I so repeatedly wished to clap my hands to support common sense. The comparison with Dartmoor is of course not wholly fair; for example, there would have been national outrage had the military proposed using part of the Lakes for firing practice.

Says Jan: 'Ultimately it only works because of people's passion for the Lakes, and that goes well beyond development issues, though had those deep quarries that have already bitten seriously into several areas been allowed to spread, the results would have been disastrous. But the starting point is love of the Lakes.'

This they celebrate by encouraging new members – currently there are 7,000 Friends – who enjoy two issues of a report and newsletter and also two of a well-presented magazine each year and, at the time of writing, on joining are sent a copy of *The Lake District: A special place*. This is beautifully (and factually) written by John Wyatt, who makes the point that many of the world's national parks are wildernesses, which we don't have in England:

> However, here are landscapes completely unspoiled, even after very many generations of human occupation, which retain substantial areas of wildness, if not wilderness, and need special legislative protection. There are our fells. Not so high as mountains world-wide, only a handful require a climb of over three thousand feet. But they still have the exciting stamp of greater ones, and uniquely they are crowded so closely that the eye is deceived into believing that height and distance are greater than they really are. Then each valley has a character of its own. The buildings we see and the field boundaries, the dry stone walls, are made of the rock on which they stand, grubbed out of the soil, levered off the crags. If the farms look as if they have grown out of the land it is because, in a way, they have. So to the farmers we owe the colour, texture and the intricate field patterns of the lower fells. Those lanes, the winding ways, the warp and weft of walls; they are organic and have developed naturally over the ages. The beauty of the Lake District valleys has all to do with a thousand years of human adaptation to uncompromising landforms: a reconciliation of natural and human elements.

So for a quick walk through the hilly streets of Kendal and the many narrow courtyards leading off them – built, so it's said, to help defence against marauding Scots. Kendal is very much an agricultural town, with delightful old shops and ways. We pop into the Friends Meeting

House overlooking the River Kent to see the 77-panelled Quaker Tapestry, the work of 4,000 people from fifteen countries celebrating 350 years of Quakerism and social life.

Then back to Windermere town, which has never been a favourite place. It sits uneasily between down-to-earth Kendal and tourist-committed Bowness. Parking isn't easy either, except at the station. That makes me reflect how even in problem industries, such as the railways, attitudes are actually vastly better than a couple of decades ago. I was filming in front of the buffer stop here as a train arrived. Three of the alighting passengers, heavy-built railwaymen, walked straight in front of the camera, destroying our 'take'. Had we paid for a 'facility fee'? Yes, actually we had. 'Just checking. The trouble with people like you is that you see us just as railwaymen. We're not. We're good businessmen today, and our time's too precious to waste while you finish your talk whatever it's about.' If the trio are still working at all, they will now be in a different industry and hopefully one that recognises the value of courtesy.

On to Keswick

Most journeys between Windermere and Keswick have been on business and so in a hurry. In the sharp peak season of the early 1960s, when many people came to the Lake District for their main holiday, there were often inordinate delays. Though there are still convoys led by a slow-moving lorry or caravan, today's road is infinitely more user-friendly, but at the cost of being more dominant in the landscape. Why do national standards need to be so strictly enforced? With imagination and care, most of the benefit could have been achieved for less than half the damage inflicted.

Today, as we finally leave Storrs Hall, we have time on our side, so make our first stop at Ambleside, and go to look at, but only from the outside, the home of another wealthy man who chose to live in the Lakes, a Liverpool merchant whose Regency-style Rothay Manor is now also a hotel. Twenty years ago, when I was testing the meal at various establishments for *The Breakfast Book*, and had intended taking breakfasts at two different hotels, the Sunday traffic caused serious delay. A phone call to Rothay Manor had the proprietor laughing that, of course, she'd be delighted to serve breakfast when the dining room opened for lunch. It was a lovely day, with time for a leisurely stroll round the wooded gardens and down to the shore of Lake Windermere, before a great Taste of England breakfast.

In the kitchen, the proprietor, Mrs Bronwen Nixon, bubbled with enthusiasm; she had recently won a top prize for afternoon tea and was consulting menu cards for the evening's dinner. I can still see her. Soon afterwards, she was murdered by a former employee, who the police arrested as he left the train at Euston. I discover that her sons still run the hotel. 'Personally managed by the Nixon family for over thirty years' sound such innocent words! But continuity is happy, and just looking at the hotel has laid a ghost to rest for me. One day I'll return for an orthodox breakfast after a night's sleep in that spot of usually exquisite peace.

For the first time since that visit, then by Skelwith Bridge, enchanted by the waterfall, and Elterwater to the showpiece, gracefully curved Langdale. Here's a vivid reminder of Cumbria's diversity. Ahead are the commanding twin Langdale Pikes, at 2,403ft not especially high even by Lakeland standards, yet so positioned atop the slope rising dramatically from the valley's bottom as to seem challenging if not threatening.

Walkers and climbers, and their facilities including a mountain rescue centre, show what is the main activity round here. Something must be lacking in me since I've no desire to climb; is it only lesser mortals who are satisfied looking up? The OS shows there are many more mountainous miles than my mental map of the Lakes accommodates. With their own creed, climbers are often seen as a race apart: a very decent, indeed good book-buying race I discovered in publishing days. But to them the Lake District doesn't mean peaceful reflections in water, but dangerous fissures and precipices that will never be visited by those of weaker disposition. Perhaps unfairly, I find myself wondering if many of them would be interested in knowing that, once, sufficient explosive was made in Elterwater to blow up a large city. It was used to extend the quarries yielding precious grey-green slate, of which the village itself is prettily built. But then, how many of the quarrymen realised they worked in (and later, it was generally felt, seriously damaged) one of the loveliest of places? Next I reflect that I enjoy the craggy skyline when miles away from the Langdale Pikes, far more than closely under their shadow. The quiet tarns which one can reach by walking across lower ground are altogether more appealing. Good job – certainly for the book trade – we're not all alike.

And now Grasmere, and Wordsworth's Dove Cottage, or Town End as it was called locally, a delightful place. We greatly enjoy our visit, marvelling at Wordsworth's acumen in instantly realising how right the cottage – a real cottage with low, beamed ceilings in a sylvan setting – would be for his muse when coming across it. That was on his famous visit back to his childhood haunts, when he was showing off to Coleridge with whom he and Dorothy had become friendly while in Dorset and Somerset. It is hard not to be moved when confronted with the desk at which much of the work of the world's finest landscape poet was committed to paper.

Less constructive thoughts come to my mind as an American addresses her husband in a long drawl across the room: 'Darling, *my* friends would simply love *you* to take *me* sitting in the bard's writing chair.' He points to the protective cord. Ignoring him she turns to an obviously enthusiastic English lady: 'Doesn't it make you want to recite *Intimations of Immortality?*' The transAtlantic putdown takes some beating: 'I'm in the middle of saying it to myself *silently.*' There's excess even in Wordsworthism.

The museum one cannot fault. It is gentle and informative in the way it celebrates and honours. The staff are informal and friendly. Tours take small groups through every half hour but there's no regimentation. Individual questions are answered with care. The Wordsworth Trust, by the way, was formed as long ago as 1891, and Dove Cottage acquired 'on eternal possession... for those who love English poetry the world over'. The museum also calls itself the Centre for British Romanticism.

We admire a 200-year-old quilt, scales for measuring out opium, a picture of the border terrier Pepper given by Sir Walter Scott, who was an amateur breeder, and doggie presents. The lavatory, 'The Necessary,' was round the back, the main coach route passed immediately by the cottage.

The tearoom is equally welcoming. Over elevenses I recall how happy the Wordsworths were here. They often explored together and he was definitely not on his own when inspired to write one of the world's most famous lines, 'I wandered lonely as a cloud'. But he generally practised what he preached: 'Poetry is the spontaneous overflow of powerful feelings: it takes its origin from emotion recollected in tranquillity.' While he wrote, Dorothy tended the garden whose crops, a pleasure to grow, also helped ease financial constraint. I remember how emancipated Wordsworth was when, during his time here, he came into sufficient money to end financial anxiety, but how the muse slowed and eventually almost stopped as he became seriously wealthy, a revered man of the world. His radicalism was extinguished, too.

On again, and past Thirlmere. In earlier times its very name made Lake lovers snarl. The water industry had done its worst: three miles of alien conifers along the main artery to the northern Lakes. KEEP OUT. Gradually hardwood trees have been introduced and, when we take the road up the western shore, there is a sight I never thought I'd see: two yachts on Thirlmere. Who says things can't get better? We pause at the car park under Cockrigg Crags for the best view: across the reservoir, now generally called lake, to sixteenth-century Dalehead Hall, another luxury hotel.

Deciding to press on to Keswick for lunch, we make straight for our hotel. Originally just called The Keswick and opened in the 1860s when the railway was new, I've chosen it for nostalgic reasons... but am amazed to discover that not only has it extended itself to part of the old station, but (by pure fluke) we have been allocated the very room which was my headquarters when conducting the Lake District Transport Enquiry. It was actually the stationmaster's office. Scarcely surprising, that functionary wasn't best pleased that someone in higher authority had told him to turn out. What memories: especially of the ice melting as we became good friends, relaxing together in train talk. Skilfully converted, the office makes a stunning bedroom.

I cannot help thinking of how things were in 1960. Briefly, the branch line through Keswick was run with unbelievable waste. Engines and crew whiled away the hours. Only semi-sensible use was being made of the new diesel units and, though little more than a passing loop on a single line, the layout was controlled by two fully manned signal boxes. There were long periods without any movement, but in summer The Lakes Express was still steam hauled and, on Saturdays, lengthened at and given a second engine here. Summer Sundays brought the week's only buffet car, on a twelve-coach train from the East Coast headed by two Pacific locomotives which spent over an hour running forwards and backwards till they had both visited the turntable, taken on water, and the whole ensemble was ready for its evening return.

Every time we visit our bedroom, we unlock the station entrance, passing by a still-active letter box, notices and LMS red paint, which help give the illusion that trains still call. A plaque erected 25 years after the last train ran says that the buildings constructed by the Cockermouth, Keswick & Penrith Railway in the 1860s are 'a fine example of Victorian railway architecture. They are particularly notable in the fact that being constructed of Lakeland Green Stone they are one of only two examples of railway architecture using this medium. Of great importance is the magnificent glass canopy extending some 240ft along the rear of the main station building above the old platform one.'

Standing under the canopy outside the stationmaster's office, I recall the occasional crowds but more usually little-patronised trains of 1960. I look west along the first section to be abandoned when Keswick temporarily became the terminus, to where a refuge siding used to be. It is here where we parked for lunch, when my request for a trip by engineer's saloon better to see the route's infrastructure was granted. The hot lunch, prepared in the saloon's mini-kitchen, was just being served when suddenly the steam engine dashed away at speed to the furthest end of the siding. 'Why's the engine left us?' I enquired. 'So you can enjoy lunch in quiet, sir.'

Dear Derwent Water

Until the end of the eighteenth century, few people appreciated the beauty of the fells, only the sheep they supported and the wool the sheep provided. We can but guess what the natives and invading Romans thought of the landscape; before the days of easy communication, life was perhaps too harsh for anyone to point out a special view. What we do know is that when it first became fashionable to comment on the scenery, it was nearly always done as nature's explanation for art.

Dr John Brown, who might be called the father of Lakeland tourism, pronounced in 1752: 'The full perfection of Keswick consists of three circumstances, Beauty, Horror and Immensity united.' He went on to analyse Derwent Water in terms of the Italian painters, and established set 'stations' where this could best be achieved. It was not sufficient for the early Picturesque writers simply to extol beauty. Nature required to be compared to art. Even after the Lake poets were well established, some of them living in Keswick and all of them familiar with it, Wordsworth's Guide was still proclaiming: 'Sublimity is the result of Nature's first great dealings with the superficies of the earth; but the general tendency of her subsequent operations is toward the production of beauty; by a multiplicity of symmetrical parts uniting in a consistent whole.' A bit like saying don't just allow a great poem to enter your soul: parse and analyse.

That's not what I'm in a mood to do when, after an early dinner, we walk through Keswick's familiar streets, past where the hotel at which I was based for many weeks in 1960 and early 1961 used to be, to the shores of Derwent Water. If there's a single place where landscape most readily conquers my soul, this is it. Derwent Water offers uncompromised beauty and of course great continuity. It is as though the lake were a stage to show off the ring of woodland and fells rising to the mountain tops around it. Islets are part of the stage scenery. Many great politicians, poets, painters and others have fallen under its spell.

For me it also means personal continuity, for here I've enjoyed great companionship, suffered deep loneliness, experienced elation and fear, acceptance and rejection. It is the easiest of places to commune, discover oneself. Dear ever-changing yet perpetual Derwent Water. Tonight it is in one of its most colourful moods: the mauves, pinks and azures of the sunset are surreal. Though not at its more ordinary evening gentleness that I had expected, it is full of stunning promise of a fine morrow.

On numerous occasions when in Keswick, I've always walked along the shore, usually approached by the main landing stages nearest the town where activity is perpetual by the day but dies totally at sundown. The Keswick Launch service, half-hourly around the lake in each direction, calling at seven stages for most of the year, has always employed stylishly proportioned craft which add an interesting foreground touch to many photographs. While the National Trust looks after much of the lake's shoreline with impeccable reserve, I dislike the shop. Do we really need another retail outlet so prominently here? A low-profile café would be more appropriate. Apart from that minor criticism, the final approach to the lake has been well protected, and one cannot complain of the improved route from the town, the enlarged car park or the Theatre of the Lake. Relatively new, the theatre seems successfully to serve many different interests. We're just too late for the run of a homemade production claiming to bring the lake to the theatre: *Neville's Island*, described as a comedy in thick fog.

We're back early next morning, delighted by mirror-like reflections of the sublime wooded shores and fells rising to what seem the dizzy heights of Skiddaw and other mountain tops. I can't resist the boat trip, and cricking my neck gazing at the ever-changing skyline, Skiddaw of course coming into view at the lake's south end.

Apart from an increase in popular tourist shops, central Keswick and its gardens are little changed. At the first junction out of town, however, the road people have wrought their worst: huge forty mph signs, on each of three routes, would look ugly even in London suburbia. We set off on one of the roads which makes Keswick such a superb centre: down the eastern side of Derwent Water on our way to Borrowdale and then by the Honister Pass to Cockermouth. Lunch first, though, at the Mary Mount Hotel. With a landing stage served by the Keswick Launch, it is one of many small, quality establishments attracting those who return year after year and are committed to the immediate area almost as a way of life. 'We *always* come to the Northern Lakes,' is among the phrases I pick up in the dining room. 'Windermere is just too popular.' That reminds us of a recent advertisement for the Lake District: 'Each year half a million people come here to enjoy the solitude.'

The Northern Lakes are certainly different. Having much of the top scenery, walking and climbing, they are increasingly popular yet still much less commercialised. Keswick, by the way, has marvellous bus links. We hear a woman tucking into her quiche say: 'When I arrive I park the car and don't touch it except for storage until its time to go home. It's good discipline.' More of us should emulate her for, despite the good bus links, traffic has spoilt much of Keswick's immediate surrounds. I'm dying to ask her what book she has at her elbow, but we aren't resident and so not in the inner circle.

Then, it occurs to me, many who dedicate their holidays to Ullswater wouldn't be seen dead staying around Keswick. Wordsworth said that Ullswater has 'the happiest combination of beauty and grandeur of any of the lakes'. This trip doesn't give us time to renew acquaintance with that lovely, unspoilt stretch of water where even the passage of an occasional launch is seen by the purists as somewhat vulgar, and bus services are minimal.

There's certainly great diversity in the lakes themselves, the villages and mountains around them, the geology and the people exploring, walking, sailing and climbing. And, of course, in what people read and think. Keswick, once famous for its pencil making, has always catered for a niche market. A trip round Derwent Water or a six-hour climb up to Skiddaw wouldn't exactly thrill the sunbathing, beer drinking crowds that fill the Costa del Sol. But serving growing minorities has always been good business... too good by half for the traffic system. If I had to make an investment in a Lakeland hotel, I'd pick one of the most isolated.

Borrowdale and Bassenthwaite

So we set off on what must be one of the most dramatically varied drives of its length anywhere. A mile or so beyond the end of the lake, we run beside the River Derwent and are soon in precious, gentle Borrowdale. Curved, green and gentle at its bottom that is; there was great geological fun in the creation of the steep land on either side, of course given its final shape by the 'recent' last Ice Age. Climbers, and their buses, bikes and cars, and staging posts to rescue those who get into trouble, make the lover of lower land feel a freak. It is, however, a pleasure driving up the Honister Pass, grand if scarcely beautiful. There's demonstration of how ugly slate quarries can be. We recall the feeling of relief we used to have when we topped the summit, carefully watching the temperature gauge, in our first-ever underpowered third-hand vehicles.

No risk going downhill either, today. Even the driver can drink in Buttermere far down below like a little hole the plasterer forgot to fill in.

At Buttermere village, I'm tempted to head into the Derwent Fells and return to Keswick by intriguingly-named Little Town, but we continue our descent through the Lorton Vale to Cockermouth. Though it does its best to welcome visitors and has many specific attractions including another Wordsworth home, I've always regarded Cockermouth as a rather plain little agricultural town. From mid-19th to mid-twentieth century, its focus was mainly to the west, for it was on the edge of the great industrial belt centred on Workington. Later today, however, I'm sorry not to have got our hands dirty reliving letterpress days at The Printing House, where visitors are encouraged to handle the old machines, wood blocks and linotype slugs.

As we head back to Keswick, there is a particularly disappointing run beside Bassenthwaite Lake. The highlight of the train journey from Workington to Keswick – for me often an early-morning journey after a sleeping-car night – used to be along the intimate, curving single track hugging the lake. There was even a little station called Bassenthwaite Lake where on the platform a solitary mum with an old-fashioned perambulator might be waiting. But this fast, partly-dual carriageway road is anything but intimate. No doubt it is good that it's hidden from sight for those out enjoying the lake, but trees growing along the old railway obstruct much of our view. How wonderful, I recall, a steam train looked puffing its way alongside the lake when one was out on a boat. Many a section of motorway is more interesting than this road.

The water that tumbles down through Borrowdale and finds temporary peace in Derwent Water then flows across the flat piece of land north of Keswick to take a longer pause in Bassenthwaite Lake before going on to the sea. One river; many environments.

After dinner back at our hotel, we walk again to the shores of Derwent Water. As the last rowing boat is tied up, waves gently lash the landing stages. No sunset tonight. No sun, or bright light at all. A storm is coming in from the Atlantic. We are likely to have a windy if not wet journey tomorrow into the only area of Scotland still totally new to me.

DUMFRIES AND GALLOWAY

Another Great Land

Dismiss any area of Britain as relatively dull, spend a few days exploring it, and then almost certainly conclude that it is a place of special interest. That at least is my experience. Scotland, two-fifths of Britain, has more than its share of relatively little-discovered areas. Over the years I've been just about everywhere of importance, including many minor as well as the more obvious islands. One gap only is left: the land north of the Solway Firth between the west coast and the main traffic arteries to Glasgow.

We promised ourselves that after leaving the Lake District, or at least after Gretna Green, we would secretly explore what wouldn't, we felt, make good copy. How wrong! A fulfilling lifetime could be spent in this great uncrowded land. It is impossible to keep the notebook tucked away.

First, however, we have to leave Keswick. The horizontal rain on our final morning lessens the pain of lacking time for even a fleeting visit to Derwent Water. We have scarcely finished breakfast when our guests arrive so we ask for coffee to be served in the conservatory that used to lead out on to the station platform. 'It will again,' says Cedric Martindale confidently. He is leading a brave – some might say foolish – attempt to restore the standard-gauge railway from Penrith. That is a hilly route of over eighteen miles which was always expensive to maintain and operate.

'It can be done,' he says.

'And he's going to do it,' chips in his wife, Margaret.

Railway promoters were ever optimistic yet, though a doubting Thomas, I find myself steadily swayed by their single-minded enthusiasm. 'We've done our market research, costed the engineering works, have the backing of the main-line railway operators.' A businessman, he certainly knows his way around. 'We've even identified a builder-partner.'

For years I have been on the mailing list for his press releases and bond prospectuses. 'Return to Keswick on a modern train from your station,' is the message. If only...

There are problems, he admits. Bridges have to be built to cross the modernised road. New development has somehow to be penetrated in the final approach to the main line. And there's no public money available for exploratory work. 'We have to provide our own seed corn and get on with it ourselves. Last year's bond issue raised £155,000. That paid for the initial plans and costing. Now we've a year's environmental work to do. We put construction at £25million. Of course it will take time; we have to build confidence as we go.'

Might not a light-construction, perhaps a narrow-gauge line like that going through the Snowdonia National Park, be more practical? 'No,' says his wife. 'It has to be a proper railway.'

To which he adds: 'Keswick has to be reconnected to the nation's railways. There's the demand for it; it can be done.'

More unlikely things have certainly been achieved by those driven by such conviction. I begin to feel ashamed I have not supported the bond issue for, having fought hard for the retention of the line in *The Lake District Transport Report*, nobody would be more pleased than I to see trains running once again. And he is right in two respects: the original line was never properly exploited, and today's demand would be considerably stronger and spread over a longer season. Optimism swells and I almost reach for the cheque book when I bring myself down to earth recalling that while we have been travelling around Britain, Railtrack has gone from crisis to oblivion, the government creating a new Network Rail and a Strategic Rail Authority. Even improvement plans already agreed are in jeopardy as everything is reassessed against the background of higher costs and shortage of money. They are not good times for railway expansion. Some official has said that it would be cheaper to build a brand new dual carriageway from Blaenau Ffestiniog to Llandudno than upgrade the railway between them to carry slate waste.

We thank Cedric and Margaret for coming so early this Saturday morning and give them our good wishes. If anyone can achieve the impossible...

To Gretna Green

As we leave the hotel, a graceful 'Cumbria Classic Car', an old-fashioned coach, pulls up outside the station just like connecting buses might to collect those who have arrived by train. And, there's an animated conversation going on about the recovery from foot-and-mouth: 'If there's any good come from it, it might be that more people are buying locally produced meat. Customers used not to care where it came from; price and appearance was all that mattered. Now they're prepared to pay a bit more for something they can trust.' He might be in the butchery business, perhaps talking to a farmer who replies: 'We need a bit more money, I can tell you.' Then, it being Saturday, they follow the nation escaping into talk of the day's sporting programme.

The weather has been kind for our stay in the Lakes, but today is nasty, with wild wet squalls. The road paralleling the railway we've just been talking about used to be slow and painful. As so many other routes in northern England, it has been greatly improved and, even in this weather, in no time at all we have missed the opportunity to visit Rheged, the 'village in the hills', combining various Lakeland experiences and shopping in Europe's largest covered building, near Penrith. The National Mountaineering Exhibition has just been added there.

On to the M6, we head rapidly north. Early in the day and in the season, the motorway is almost deserted. As the windscreen wipers collect streams of water, we're grateful for the absence of splashing lorries and forget all about what we might usually enjoy looking at along this stretch. We skirt Carlisle, and are still on a fast road all the way into Scotland.

First over the River Esk and across a flood plain. Until it was agreed that the River Sark marked the border, part of this flat area used to be known as the Debatable Land, the haunt of lawless freebooters. Just beyond the wandering Sark, Gretna offers us the first break in the sky.

Gretna seems dull... until one recalls that it didn't exist at all until 1916, when the world's largest munitions factory was built here. Officially it didn't exist even then. Along with the sister creation of Eastriggs, it was codenamed Moorside. Miracle Towns was the more flattering description given it and its sister by Conan Doyle when he happened to be shown around in 1918. Though thrown up in a hurry, they were designed on garden city lines by top architects of the day. It was also Conan Doyle who invented the name Devil's Porridge for the explosive dried paste (nitro-glycerine and nitro-cotton) that was hand-shaped into cordite for shells and bullets. At the peak 30,000 workers produced ammunition. They were unusually sober for Scotland; the government took over and rigorously regulated the pubs.

An exhibition tells how the huge factory produced more arms than all other British ones put together. Long since demolished, it had its own power station, bakery, laundry and private 125-mile railway system with 34 locomotives. The site was chosen partly because it was out of reach of spying German planes, and partly for its strategic position on the railway map... a reminder that in 1915 Britain's worst railway accident happened at Quintinshill, near Gretna. Of a total 227 passengers killed, 214 were of a Royal Scots battalion who had set out from Larbet en route to Gallipoli. The signalman forgot he had left a Welsh coal train on the track The wreckage caught fire when a northbound gas-lit Euston-Glasgow night train ran into it. Many were burned to death, but in those grim times most would almost certainly have faced death had they reached Gallipoli.

This is perhaps a peculiar moment to say that we are on our way to a wedding in neighbouring Gretna Green... not a particular wedding, just any one for the experience. Never having been here, or even read about it in any depth, we discover we are ignorant. Just where is the famous Old Blacksmith's Shop, and what do you find when you get there? Signposting seems confusing, referring to several wedding locations. Foolishly, we stop to ask a local.

'Depends on where you're going. Where's your wedding being held? Got an invitation have you?' No doubt seen as a moron from south of the border, I apologetically explain we have just come to have a look. The Scot retorts: 'There are a lot who do that, but they usually know what they're looking for.'

Suddenly we are surrounded by those who have already been married having their photographs taken, shivering in the drizzle, while others sit in their cars waiting their turn. This however isn't the traditional venue. When we find that, it is a huge complex with hundreds of people milling around. There are several wedding groups. The turnover, in and out, reminds one of the pressure on a big crematorium after Christmas when there's been a cold snap. Apart from their dress, and the ribbon on their car, some of those about to be married might indeed be mourners. But, as we will soon discover, appearances can be deceptive.

After the service, they stop to have their pictures taken. Because of the pressure, that has to be outside, and it is really no weather to linger in smart but flimsy clothing. If only the sun would shine.

As soon as their photographer releases them, the newlyweds, relatives and friends, dash into the restaurant at the centre of the complex. As we approach the door, we're held up by a minister who would have become an instant star had she made a guest appearance in The Vicar of Dibley. She is in a hurry since her watch suggests she's taken too long a break warming herself up between weddings. The first surprise is to see ministers here at all; we are then amazed to learn that at the time of our visit all weddings at the famous Old Blacksmith's Shop are conducted by ministers of religion. Now we need to warm ourselves over a cuppa.

On the wall is a large, gruesome cartoon-type painting depicting grotesque dads chasing errant daughters. After England's marriage laws were changed in 1754, Gretna Green was the place to go for couples under 21 whose parental consent was withheld. For centuries marriages were performed 'over the anvil' by blacksmiths, ferrymen or anyone else ready to oblige for a fee. Only two witnesses – and they could be hired – were necessary. Churches saw it as wicked, but it was not until 1940 that hurried Gretna Green weddings became illegal. Even then, however, there remained a two-year age difference for marriage between England and Scotland, and the Registry Office was available.

The popularity of today's Gretna Green is purely romantic, but then, cleverly exploited, nothing is more commercially successful than romanticism. Around 5,000 marriages a year now take place here, nearly one in five of all in Scotland. Most are religious, though the council manages up to 21 daily weddings at their expanded registry office. Altogether it is big business. There are many places to stay or eat, while hairdressers, kilt-hirers, florists, photographers and firms providing an enormous range of old and romantic (as well as cheaper) wedding cars, and even horses and carriages, obviously thrive. It is no mean business for the ministers and official registrars, either.

Some of the ministers are retired, we learn. We have been joined by Lynda Denton, who is marketing manager. 'The ministers spread the work out between them; there's a limit to the number of weddings any one person can conduct in a day. It's all pretty informal, even between the denominations. Mind you, it is crucial to the local economy. Gretna Green attracts three quarters of a million visitors: surreal, you could say. The Old Blacksmith's Shop, the original famous wedding venue, is probably the most photographed building in Scotland. There's a lot to see and do even if you're not getting married, or renewing your vows which is becoming popular. There are many quality shopping opportunities.' There is also a fine display of early road carriages. The one thing missing, perhaps, is an adequate supply of indoor studios for after-wedding photographs, especially when it's cold and damp as it was when we arrived.

The best surprise is the last. We are taken to witness an actual wedding. Whatever we might have imagined it would be like, it is far better. There's not an iota of tackiness, but great respect and sincerity as a minister of the Church of Scotland leads Rebecca Wood and Richard Banks into marriage. The distinctive tone of the anvil rings out at the crucial moment. It may happen many times a day, but is still very individual, caring, everyone anxious to make it a special occasion.

Later I speak to the new bride, who comes from The Wirral, while the groom, who is in the Navy, is Scottish. 'We just happened to stop at a service station displaying what Gretna Green offers; intrigued, we sent for an information pack. It seemed very romantic, so we paid for the wedding ourselves. There are just 22 of us including relatives and friends: small, intimate, perfectly lovely.'

Our perception is totally changed. The sun *is* out when we emerge from the Old Blacksmith's Shop and there's now a smile on people's faces.

The Solway Firth

Heading west, after three miles we pass Eastriggs, the other of the pair of 'garden city' towns built for munition workers. Two miles further on, just before Annan, we find our way south to the shore of the Solway Firth at a settlement called Seafield. I want to see the remains of what is perhaps the most extraordinary railway in Britain: the Solway Junction, which linked England and Scotland with a viaduct over a mile long, on 193 cast-iron piers deeply sunk into the shifting sands in an area where the weather strongly influences the rapid tides. From 1870 the line was busy with passenger trains as well as heavy freights. The latter mainly carried West Cumberland hematite to Lanarkshire steel works. Though only single track was laid, the viaduct was wide enough to accommodate double, and for a few years it seemed that this might be necessary.

The engineer guarded against scouring tides by protecting the piers with timber buttresses. He did not, however, find a way to prevent ice forming inside the cast-iron columns. These began cracking in the severe winter of 1875-6. A few years later, in 1881, ice floes demolished 45 of the piers. This afternoon we see where the embankment suddenly ends, but there's no trace of the bridge, and we can only guess at what the outlook must have been like as the piers were steadily rebuilt. Traffic resumed. Soon, however, there were other interruptions. When the Lanarkshire mills began buying cheaper Spanish hematite, expensive repairs were hard to justify. The route, including the bridge, was closed.

After World War One, with renewed optimism, traffic resumed. But only for a short time, for receipts were now meagre and, due to neglect during the war years, maintenance high. In 1921 the viaduct was condemned as unsafe. For the next decade the only 'traffic' was occasional pedestrians, especially Scots popping across to England for a Sabbath drink.

Then followed the most extraordinary episode. Demolishing the bridge and removing all the foundations, as insisted upon by the Admiralty, took several difficult years in the early 1930s. Pulling out the piers proved much harder than building them. Work was restricted to a mere hour or so during daylight low tide.

Looking across the misty water, I can mark out only the smallest evidence of the railway's landing the other side. While we have been gazing at what is a new firth for us, the tide has been sweeping in and we can no longer pick out the channel of the River Eden, the senior partner of those feeding the upper firth. There used to be a considerable trade up it to Carlisle.

Formerly a thriving port and industrial town, neat Annan still treats its river with respect. Not merely are the rivers new to us, but I've hardly even heard of most of them. By taking a minor road, we keep close to the mysterious Solway Firth, now dotted with islands and, according to newspaper reports, soon to be planted with wind farms actually in the water. That will surely present engineers with another challenge. We cross Lochar Water and, inevitably past a ruined castle, are forced north by the Nith, then travel along its banks most of the way to Dumfries. This was already rich agricultural country when the Solway Firth, now largely deserted by shipping, was a major highway with many active branches, the estuary up to Dumfries being especially busy with passenger as well as cargo vessels. The waterfront remains the most attractive part of Dumfries, but, wanting to get back to the Solway Firth, we are in no mood to delve into the torrid history of battles between Scots and English, or – to me – the even more torrid sanctification of Robert Burns who died here aged 37. From previous visits, I recall his mausoleum as in hideous taste. Nothing makes me feel more English than the exaggerated reverence in which Scotland's national poet is held. A genius, yes, but too often a misguided wench-hungry one who scarcely warrants the hyperbole gushed out at Burns Night suppers.

Beyond Dumfries everything is totally unfamiliar; we glance at the map as we might do exploring a Southern Hemisphere coastline. This is obviously great countryside, many people spend their lives revelling in its depth and history but, to feel at home, I'd have to spend a lot more time here.

Heading down the Nith's western side, the first surprise – at the head of a dried-out little tributary estuary – is the magnificent ruin of red sandstone Cistercian Sweetheart Abbey. We have to consult the guide to learn that it is so called because its founder, Devorguilla Balliol, was buried here, having carried her husband's heart around with her for sixteen years. Their son was King John Balliol (rival of Bruce), but she is perhaps best remembered as founder of the Oxford college named after her. Again, wealth came from these farmlands, especially during the seemingly rare occasions the Scots were neither fighting the English nor themselves.

On the landward side the road skirts the mass of Criffel, easily climbed and gentler than most Scottish mountains in the same way that the countryside is lusher and more mellow. From various vantage points, we catch sight of the deserted, steadily widening Solway Firth, only running alongside it briefly before another river, today's last, again drives us north: the Urr Water which reaches the Solway by its own Rough Firth. This is glorious, wooded countryside, National Trust on the eastern side. We follow the winding Urr Water, skirting Dalbeattie Forest almost into grey, granite Dalbeattie town. Granite quarrying was once the business here; huge quantities went down the river for London's Embankment; each shipment had to be small, since the narrow river only accommodated ships of a few hundred tons.

Across the river, we turn sharp left on to the peninsula on which we stay tonight. At pretty Auchencairn, by an especially colourful garden, we take the road alongside wooded Auchencairn Bay, past Balcary fishery. Jutting out into the firth, this is what looks like a decaying network of oak timbers supporting dozens of funnel traps, each one on a three-legged base. Soon we are at the Balcary Bay Hotel and shown to a room with a view reminiscent of Ireland's southwest coast, across a great stretch of dried-out sand to the three gentle mainland headlands, and a steeper island with a lighthouse atop. Hestan Island's only other feature named by the OS is Daft Ann's Steps at its southern tip.

Naughtily we order crab sandwiches – are they good! – for afternoon tea, and then have to walk them off past some holiday cottages where new arrivals are unloading groceries from their cars, past a mysterious tower to Balcary Point where in romantic evening light something of the sheer size of the Solway Firth can be gauged. The tide is well and truly out, yet there are many miles of deep water. We absorb it wondering who Daft Ann might have been, why she was on the island and if indeed she successfully negotiated her 'steps'. Home in Nairn is several hundred miles away. We feel we might as well be on a different continent.

By Creetown to Newton Stewart

The sun shining, we are away early next morning to continue our zig-zag journey. England is now out of sight across the wide firth. Our first village is Dundrennan, partly built of stone from the picturesque ruined Cistercian Abbey where Mary Queen of Scots is said to have passed her last night before being ferried across the Solway to England.

The Dee is the first river to force us north today. Totally different from its better-known namesake, it rises as several tributaries in a remote mountain area before becoming the Water of Ken and flowing through several lochs including long Loch Ken in Glenken. Only as it leaves Loch Ken does it change its name to the Dee, a substantial river running into a broad estuary. We reach the estuary or bay opposite wooded St Mary's Isle, in fact a peninsula. Its southernmost tip, Paul Jones's Point, is named after a pirate who hoped to make off with the Earl of Selkirk but that gent not being at home, contented himself with the plate and a silver teapot. The teapot was returned 'on the remonstrance of Benjamin Franklin'. Just one piece of the turbulent history around here involving saints (Kirkcudbright is the 'Kirk of Cuthbert' because the saint's bones were housed there for a time) and villains, not to mention bloody battles in the everlasting struggle for power. Another detail: when Catholics ruled here, the Spanish Armada was offered sheltered anchorage, but of course never appeared.

This morning Kirkcudbright looks innocently peaceful: a charming little town with interesting buildings and a splendid waterfront. We have to steel ourselves to keep going – along minor roads around another fascinating peninsula with spectacular cliff scenery, before it is the turn of the Water of Fleet to force us north, through Gatehouse of Fleet. Just before that small town, we are tempted by a woodland road past a lake to the Cally Palace Hotel, an eighteenth-century granite extravaganza with such fine pillars and other splendour outside and immediately inside that I wonder whether a request for mere morning coffee might be looked down on.

Not so. A waiter accompanies us to a huge lounge and enquires our itinerary. When we say where we intend spending tonight, he smiles. Our choice is 'another of the five great hotels run by the McMillan family. Five different styles, all the best of their kind.' Real loyalty of the sort more frequently met in Scotland than England. We conjecture what it must cost to maintain the 150-acre grounds, and heat this imposing range of buildings. It is not just large but very civilised. Guests have exclusive use of the 18-hole golf course, par seventy, 5,802 long yards around the lake. It can only be Scotland.

After Gatehouse of Fleet the main road obligingly hugs the coast in another semi-circle. We are toward its end, heading almost due north up the east side of the River Cree passing through grey Creetown. The rain is on again. Suddenly I recall I've read something about this dull-looking town of 750 people, and backtrack down the deserted street to the Creetown Exhibition Centre or museum. Sunday is one of the days it is open in late spring (daily in summer) and we're warmly greeted and told that it began a few years ago, more or less by spontaneous combustion. Andrew Ward explains that several people in a pub discussed the need for a new idea for Gala Week. A collection of 200 old local photographs proved unexpectedly popular. 'The people who loaned them let us put on another exhibition. Then we copied them, returning the originals, which encouraged more people to lend us their treasures. Then we thought we might as well put on a permanent display. Do you like the Exhibition Centre?'

It is magic, especially in the way its home-spun ordinariness touches the lives of real people. We listen to a tape about World War One which ends with a son writing to his mum saying how he saw his brother fall on Flanders fields. You can't get more poignant than that. There is much about the granite quarries, whose labour force was once greater than today's total population. The quarries were developed when the cost of small shipments out of Dalbeattie was too great for the engineers of Liverpool's great docks. The quarries being on church land, Creetown became the richest parish in Scotland. The old railway line, nicknamed the Paddy Road since it carried much Irish traffic, including trainloads of cattle, is also brought to life. No route had a more colourful existence or has been more seriously missed than that between Dumfries and Stranraer. It is immortalised in David Smith's *Tales of the Glasgow & South Western Railway*. The Exhibition Centre has also turned publisher and bookseller, so we can learn more about Creetown's curious past.

Enterprising Creetown has more. The Gem Rock Museum is of international quality. With birthdays coming up, the shop, offering a huge range of stones and gems, costs us dearly. Lunch in its café is a real bargain and gives us time to study an excellent interpretive guide with colour photographs and drawings and a compelling text ending with a quote from John Ruskin: 'Let a man once understand this crystal and the polish of this plane surface given to it by its own pure growth, and the word crystal will become a miracle to him and a treasure in his heart for ever more.'

Back to Andrew Ward: 'A few of us in Creetown realised that as fishing has almost disappeared, farming and forestry are struggling, the outside world won't rescue us. We've got to do things for ourselves. Our Country Weekend, the third weekend in September, is the biggest in Scotland. The first year we attracted a few thousand. In our eighth year 72,000, a hundred times our population. With mock frontages for buildings, the whole place is transformed. People come for the music, the displays, the atmosphere: it's a great occasion.'

All travellers have to be selective and we have undoubtedly missed much along this extraordinary route from Carlisle; yet those who race through Creetown miss a very special small place. There's great pride and friendliness. Fascinated by the fishing stations we have passed during the last two days, and remarking that Creetown has its own, I'm directed to John Dalrymple. Yes, he says, he normally rents it, but for the last two seasons it has been closed, like fields being 'set aside'.

'Our best season was as recently as the mid-1980s, but the salmon collapsed in 1989. Once I'd get perhaps thirty fish a day for a few weeks in season. We just hope the salmon will come back. But don't be confused by the fact that the fishing stations look battered at the end of the winter. These oak stake nets and their funnel traps take a beating in bad weather, but if we get the go-ahead they can easily be repaired.'

Galloway the One-off

Then on to Newton Stewart, a typically unassuming southwest Scotland small town serving a massive but thinly-populated hinterland. It makes a convenient centre for the enormous Galloway Forest Park and other places along the coast to the west. That leaves just a mile to what we rapidly conclude is the best hotel find we've yet happened upon: Kirroughtree House. With three AA red stars and two rosettes and winner of all kinds of other awards, it could be over the top, or dangerously basking in its own success. We found unassuming perfection with imaginative attention to detail and a pleasure in pleasing. Why, one has to ask, does such a hotel seem a miracle when so many establishments, including most expensive group ones, fail in some way or other?

A handsome mansion with four tiers of bay windows, Kirroughtree House was built in 1719 by Patrick Heron, an industrial architect, as a symbol of his family's wealth and status. A note for today's guests tells of the family's great days and of the estate being divided after a quarrel. Sadly, 'over the years both estates dwindled in size due to heavy debts and mismanagement,' while 'there are many gaps in the history, mainly due to the fact that sons were repeatedly named Andrew or Patrick and most of them did little'. In the heyday, visitors included Robert Burns who frequently recited his poetry sitting at the foot of the main staircase. It is a 'Modesty' staircase, with small panels to stop anyone in the lounge seeing the ankles of ladies going up and down. Such minutiae always fascinates. However, unlike many hotels in historic buildings, Kirroughtree is strong on convenience for today's guests. We have never felt more at home in a hotel. It markets itself well, too, even across the water in Ireland.

Never having read about this area before, after dinner we do some homework. I start by looking at the blurb of *Wild Men and Holy Places: St Ninian, Whithorn and the Medieval Realm of Galloway*. It makes startling reading:

This is the first and only history of Galloway, vividly depicting the events and personalities of that ancient realm. This mysterious region of south-west Scotland has for centuries attracted pilgrims to its holy places, especially Whithorn, the site of Scotland's earliest church, founded by St Ninian. Yet the inhabitants were notorious for being savage, lecherous and irreligious, and men thought little of exchanging their wives for cattle.

Galloway played a pivotal role in the Celtic commonwealth throughout the Dark Ages and the Medieval period, yet incursions by Romans, Picts, Vikings and Anglo-Normans did little to dispel the unique character and distinct loyalties of its people, and their eventual assimilation into the Kingdom of Scotland was a gradual and stubborn process. The region witnessed fierce conflicts during the War of Independence, and was of great importance in Robert the Bruce's ultimate victory.

577

Then I read about the special claims of Newton Stewart's museum, inspired when the wealthy area suffered heavily from the closure and demolition of many of the numerous fine country houses built on agricultural wealth, but impossible to maintain with high death duties in the years after World War Two. Many artefacts that would otherwise have been destroyed found their way to the museum. Kirroughtree House and the Cally Palace are two great houses to have been saved by tourism, but that didn't help as much here as in most of Britain. Until relatively recent times, the whole of the huge region west of Dumfries, with its rivers in deep valleys running south from the even remoter mountainous interior down to the Solway Firth, was a low priority on the visitor map. The further west one went, the fewer strangers one would meet. The early closure of the entire railway network between Dumfries and the west coast at Stranraer didn't help. Except for the Ulster ferry from Stranraer, whose traffic is dwindling, Galloway is on the way to nowhere; and a glance at the map shows how lengthy most road journeys are. No wonder the military favoured it as an area where they could do things little noticed even by friends and unseen by the Germans. There were airports, and later we will visit the place where the famous floating Mulbery Harbour was tried out and perfected.

'I didn't know what to expect,' says Sheila. 'Galloway is certainly very different, a one-off.' Then she asks if I know that 'The Royal and Ancient Burgh of Wigtown, set deep in the glorious countryside of Galloway, is Scotland's National Book Town'? The leaflet she has picked up says that it became the Scottish book town in 1998 and lists 25 book-related businesses. She reads another quote: 'Few towns in Scotland occupy a more delightful situation than Wigtown. It is a "city set on a hill", and commands a beautiful prospect of the estuary, which bears its name, and of its picturesque shores. There is a peculiar, quiet air of antiquity about the town.' That is from William McIlwraith's *Guide to Wigtown* of 1875.

Wigtown is also a place where grisly things happened. My old Murray's *Hand-Book* tells me that in the royal burgh of 1469 there is an obelisk commemorating the Wigtownshire Convenanters, including an old woman and a girl of eighteen who were tied to a stake and drowned by the rising tide. 'Drowning was an old mode of punishment in Scotland, and especially in Galloway, where the right of pit and gallows... inflicting death by drowning of women or hanging of men subsisted longer than in other counties.' Yes, Galloway has always been different.

Scottish Book Town

While in this remote corner we are anxious to see what attracts most of those visitors who come specially to look at evidence of the first days of

Scottish Christianity and to take an opportunity to retrace the steps of St Ninian. But, it being closer, Wigtown is first stop next morning. We are greeted by a spacious square flanked by shops with old-fashioned signs, terminating in a grand county building (from the days when Wigtownshire was a county) or town hall. At least it will be grand again when it's unwrapped at the end of its £1.9 million restoration. Parking no problem. The space in the middle of the broad street is where people kept their stock when the town was under attack or threat of it.

Books are much in evidence. So is the rivalry between booksellers of the kind we met in Hay-on-Wye. 'Everyone claims to have set up first,' points out John Carter, making his own case and saying he rents out cheap space in another building so that newcomers can put their toe in the water without major commitment. 'Four tenants so far. Yes, books have woken the place up. Before we became a book town, the Bank of Scotland didn't even have a cash machine. One requirement of the selectors was that the chosen town had to have a stock of empty shops so that the book side could expand rapidly. It's worked.'

Not all plain sailing, though. He photocopies a spread from *The Bookdealer* containing a letter from two of the official selectors condemning what the third member of the team had previously written. The odd one out is none other than Richard Booth, book leader of Hay-on-Wye, miffed because he didn't get his way in persuading the others to pick Dalmellington as book town. Though Richard Booth set the whole international book town thing in motion, that he follow an unconventional line is born out by his ad above the letter: 'Peerages for sale for only £50 at Hay Castle.' The 'king' of Hay is graciously setting up a Hay House of Lords for those prepared to pay.

'Mind you,' chips in John Carter, 'there's a keen second-hand demand for the D&C book on Dalmellington, its engines and men, and now *The Industrial Archaeology of Galloway* goes for £32.50 – if you can find a copy to sell.'

Reverting to Wigtown's being chosen, he adds: 'There were about twenty places in the running, but we won hands down. We had adequate buildings, good access and parking, a colourful history which has attracted historians and archaeological specialists. It was all done officially, with a full-time project manager included in a grant for the three-year launch. Business is still building, and – despite boasting – we all actually help each other, for there's no such thing as competition in second-hand bookselling.' His own specialised stock is tempting, but he's especially pleased when I buy *Apples in Scotland*, one of six new titles he has so far published. He learned an expensive lesson, though, in printing too many copies of the work of a local poet.

It is good to see bookselling revive such a town, but we wish it wasn't hundreds of miles from Nairn. Several other booksellers make the point that today many order electronically and a high proportion of those who come to this remote corner are serious book buyers. Curious, perhaps, but that makes it feels upmarket of Hay-on-Wye.

What first gave Wigtown importance was its harbour, near the mouth of the River Bladnoch, now a forlorn site where a grassy mound marks where there used to be a castle, built primarily to help incoming ships find their way, but no trace remains of Devorguilla Balliol's Dominican priory. This bonny morning we have the harbour all to ourselves. A notice tells of noisier days: the castle was captured by the English, and destroyed when the Scots retook it to prevent the English claiming it again. The Martyrs' Stake (upstaged by the later obelisk above the town) tells of the drowning of that pair of ladies; there is such a long period without water that there would have been time to spare to tie up those whose lives were to be extinguished by the incoming tide and still leave them with hours to live. What, I wonder, was that eighteen-year-old girl's last thoughts? Ahead lies the huge Wigtown Bay nature reserve where 'traditional activities such as wildfowling and fishing are managed to ensure economic benefits to the local community and the long-term future of the Bay's wildlife'.

Without bookselling and allied services such as bookbinding and repair, Wigtown would struggle hard in today's world. Yet these small places don't accept defeat easily. There's an enterprising *Wigtown Trade Directory* which lists local shops and services and tells us that Scotland's most southerly distillery, Bladnoch, is back in production. It offers guided tours, a visitor centre, a function room which can be hired, camping site and even trout fishing.

Whithorn: Place of Pilgrimage

Heading south along the main inland road, we think of a saint who never came to these parts but for hundreds of years has provided the main (if questionable) evidence of how Christianity was brought to Whithorn in the century before St Columba arrived in Iona. The Venerable Bede, sometimes described as Britain's first historian, perhaps deserves a place earlier in these pages. His *The Church History of the English People* is a marvellous work, albeit more often read in short quotes about other saints than in its entirety. We recall that it was nearly three hundred years after his death at Jarrow in 735 that his bones were stolen so that they could be added to the growing collection of the relics of ancient saints (including those of St Cuthbert from Lindisfarne) already at Durham Cathedral.

What especially interests us this morning is that recent archaeological digging at Whithorn largely confirms what Bede says. St Ninian was a local Whithorn man who went on pilgrimage to Rome and studied there. After he returned, about 397, St Ninian introduced Christianity to what were then known as the British Kingdoms of a very divided Scotland. Until the Scottish Reformation snuffed it out 400 years ago, Whithorn attracted a steady stream of pilgrims by sea and land. There were constant comings and goings by sea. Strategically placed, Whithorn was an important maritime crossroads. Scotland's Stewart kings, James I to V, nevertheless took a long land route, incorporating other holy places, for their slow pilgrimages. James IV is said to have prevented boredom by bringing along a retinue of minstrels and other entertainers.

In modern times, a few have always made a special point of coming here, but only recently – fired by the archaeological revelations – has pilgrimage taken off again on a serious scale. Today I suppose one could call it thematic tourism. Though we are sincerely interested, in truth, like most visitors, we are more curious than committed to pilgrimage. We enjoy learning about Whithorn and why it is unique, for that it certainly is. St Ninian, 'the light that shineth in the darkness', a 'most revered and holy man of the British race' established the first Christian community in all northern Europe half a century before St Columba arrived in Iona.

An ancient little burgh it might be, but without what St Ninian established, there would be little to detain one. Like so many of the small towns of southwest Scotland, it has a solid historic core, a carefully planned wide main street of substantial buildings with easy parking, but little development of later vintage. The clouds are threatening so, hoping to beat the rain, we drive straight through to the Isle of Whithorn which is, in fact, a peninsula.

Though still used by fishermen, it is centuries since it played a pivotal role. After what would often have been a long, rough voyage in a small craft, pilgrims carried their sparse possessions to St Ninian's Chapel, or Kirk as the OS has it. Primarily for the hospitality of pilgrims, it was built around 1300 on the foundations of an earlier building. The peninsula is bleak with low featureless cliffs. A strong blustery wind takes our enjoyment out of walking back from the ruins of the chapel and blunts our imagination while sharpening our appetite.

It is tougher yet trying to reach St Ninian's cave, past Devil's Bridge and round Burrow Head to the west. This was St Ninian's 'dysart' or desert place, where he is said to have retired from the responsibility of being bishop, teacher and missionary. In the exhibition centre we later see a couple of the carved slabs that used to be in the cave, now partly collapsed but with historic crosses still to be seen carved on its walls. Once again pilgrims come to revere the spot. Be better prepared than we are for the elements. In a violent wet squall, and facing a steep, uneven descent, we give up without actually seeing the cave's entrance, let alone catching a glimpse of the crosses on the walls.

Whithorn's main street now seems truly inviting, and soon we are in Historic Scotland's Discovery Centre-cum-Pilgrims Tearoom, where a bowl of homemade soup never tasted better or more warmed the cockles of our hearts. We readily agree with our waitress: 'A bit wild out there.' The welcome, both personal and on the menu, is Scotland at its warmest: 'We wish to make your stay in Whithorn as pleasant as possible. Should you have any other requests or requirements please ask a member of staff ie baby food warming, colouring sheets for children, information about the area.'

Since there is only one other couple eating, it is assumed we all want to talk to each other, and we enjoy the enthusiasm of the staff for the entire centre. After soup we go for the Pilgrim Platter: 'Mature Galloway cheese and Castle McLellan pâté served with oatcakes and pickles, garnished with salad.' In other words, a feast.

The assuaging of hunger happening to coincide with a shaft of sunlight, the two personable waitresses suggest it would make more sense if we went to the other sites before returning to see the exhibition. This isn't yet open for the season, they explain but, since we've eaten here and the way to the toilet takes you through the exhibition, 'It's all right for you to go round it'. So, surprised by how much more welcoming the street, with some really old-fashioned shops, looks lit up by the sun, we turn up a side road to see the site of current archaeological research, the Northumbrian monastery, Whithorn Priory and more.

The monastery site is now restored after recent excavations: the foundations of the large timber church, the church enclosure wall, the burial chapel and all the paths, roads and minor buildings have been replaced where the dig discovered them, adding credence to Bede's work.

The mediaeval Cathedral, which played an important role in early Scottish Christianity, is mainly ruins. That Whithorn is less well known than Iona is perhaps because it was more inward looking, less of a conduit for Christianity's spread. In the Dark Ages the Christian teaching here was strongly influenced by the Jewish tradition. It caught hold firmly and spread locally, but wasn't the powerful intellectual flame that fanned the new religion from Iona. Interest stems from the very early date, the close links with distant Northumbria and the great changes that took place over the centuries. It is impossible not to be moved, especially by the cathedral's surviving crypt (a small part of the cathedral walls can also be seen) – and also by the gravestones, in what is still the parish churchyard, with their commemoration of eighteenth- and nineteenth-century local farmers and traders. In the nineteenth century, I recall, trade was important enough to justify a long branch line from the 'Paddy Road' at Newton Stewart.

The sheer length and variety of history being fascinating, I then look up a map of places where archaeological evidence shows there must have been contact (trading or Christian) with Whithorn. Nearly all of them were on the coasts. It is suggested that one seventh-century trading vessel carrying pottery from Gaul first struck land in the British Isles in southwest Wales, and went on to northwest Wales and the east coast of Ireland before reaching Whithorn, finally serving the area of today's Londonderry. When Lindisfarne (Holy Island) was raided, some monks sought shelter at Whithorn, though its own rhythm of climatic and trading cycles was not immune from the greater stress of local raids.

Archaeology has revealed that in the middle of the ninth century a major disruption (probably a raid, for the Danes were by then firmly established in Dublin) resulted in a dramatic reduction in the standard of living in Galloway's Christian community. Says Daphne Brooke's *Wild Men and Holy Places* already quoted: 'The internal furnishings of the church were dismantled and the former chancel was used as a winnowing floor, while level ground a few yards away outside the church was ploughed up. Northumbrian coins date the change of use fairly narrowly around the year 844.' By then the community, which had come under Northumbrian control, was regularly in touch with the intellectuals of Europe.

Suddenly there's another squall and we hasten back to the Exhibition Centre reflecting that literature as well as understanding of Celtic Christianity in Galloway is building rapidly. A special role is played by the Friends of the Whithorn Trust. The centre brings many strands together and, when mature, will prove a wonderful experience, a single ticket giving entry to the other sites as well as the various rooms here. A leaflet published jointly by the Whithorn Trust and Historic Scotland calls it 'the oldest as well as one of the newest attractions'; and so it is.

It will demand considerable time to do it justice. Workmen are hard at it adding the final touches. We're just too early, but revel in several of the exhibitions already mounted with their descriptions – especially the early rounded crosses with deep-etched inscriptions, some discovered here and also those brought from other Galloway sites. Inspiring, rather than demanding to be understood, they speak of faith across the ages harried but not conquered by fear. We are not at all sure we command even an elementary understanding of the chronology, but one doesn't experience the full 'wow' if dates are more important than feelings.

Back to Kirroughtree House

The clouds again having dispersed, we take the coastal road north. First we pass Cairn Head, and then are soon beside the harbour at Garlieston: the two places chosen for trying out and perfecting the famed Mulberry

Harbour that gave safe landing to tanks and equipment shortly after a D-day beachhead was secured in Normandy. 'Don't argue the matter,' Churchill instructed those committed to the project. 'The difficulties will argue for themselves.' And so they did – in an area well beyond enemy eyes where conditions, including tides, are similar to those of Normandy.

A Harbour Goes to War, produced by the South Machars Historical Society and another nice piece of local enterprise, explains how coping with tide and wave movement was solved by having a telescopic piece in each section of roadway, the length of which had to be increased when the normal straight route became twisted under stress of wind and wave. Men and equipment, including completed pontoons, arrived from many parts of Britain, the roadway itself in sections like Swiss rolls which could easily be laid out. Though many locals were aware of the immense activity – and what a sight the bay must have presented – the area was basically sealed off, and secrecy perfectly maintained. When a security officer visited a local pub to put things to the test, he found the regulars were happy enough to have a pint bought for them but their lips only opened to imbibe it. The project's success was by no means instant; one initial section laid out from Cairn Head was destroyed in a gale.

Where once commercial vessels had to wait their turn alongside, followed later by furious military activity, the harbour is now all but deserted, the imposing four-storey warehouse revealing evidence of failed attempts to turn it to other uses. Will it, I wonder, eventually be demolished or converted into flats, for in this unusually mellow corner of Scotland here is a perfect harbour waiting for exploitation by property developers. Silly idea? Possibly not, if you consider that back in 1760 Lord Garlies tried to develop a seaside village with a regimented street pattern. In the nineteenth century, prosperity depended on shipbuilding and the making of rope and sailcloth rather than tourism. Now, it seems, little thrives. The sleepiness of the pleasant small village is emphasised by the time-warp of the message on a broken-down van dumped outside the school: 'Save Green Shield stamps.' And though the gardens of Galloway House are open to the public, and we put our coins in the honesty box, there's not a soul in sight. Taking advantage of the mild climate, over the years many different species (along with features such as hahas or sunken fences) have been introduced into this woodland, but we describe bringing the enormous walled garden back to life as the most hopeless task we've ever imagined. Apart from a few trees and raspberries, it is empty, the lean-to greenhouses with thick piping and old-fashioned fittings in what an estate agent would euphemistically describe as 'needing attention'.

In the surrounding area are ruined castles and other evidence that man has long enjoyed the maritime access and equitable climate, though not of course the incursions from across the Solway.

Soon we are in Wigtown again, and then pass through the almost stately mile-long main street of Newton Stewart. Back at our hotel, there is time for a walk through the grounds before dinner.

The Rhinns of Galloway

Sunshine next morning persuades us to take the long way round to Stranraer; with such diversions, we will have more than doubled the direct mileage from Carlisle.

Bypassing Wigtown, it is eight miles southwest across the peninsula called the Machars to Port William, which might possibly be the most unassuming seaside place in all Britain. An early trading port, it began with some irregular streets, but later development followed the orderly planning favoured by most of Galloway's villages. Only fishing and pleasure craft now tie up at the deep-water quay, a picturesque spot without another visitor in sight... and there aren't many locals stirring this morning either.

Murray's *Hand-Book* cites only a twice-weekly coach along the 'not very interesting' road which mainly hugs the unspectacular coast to the west, though the OS picks out no fewer than four places whose names end in Port as having special interest. During the rest of the day we find ourselves passing many early Christian sites, some developed very soon after the religion took root at Whithorn.

Forced north, we join the main road at Glenluce, but leave visiting the ruins of Glenluce Abbey (the valued Chapter House of 1470 is intact) for a later time: Sheila is looking for excuses to return to Kirroughtree House Hotel! Now the road runs parallel with the railway from Glasgow into Stranraer.

Though the largest place for many miles around, and undisputed capital of the large, sparsely-peopled area known as the Rhinns of Galloway, Stranraer lacks the bustle of former days and is urgently in need of a new mission. It still claims to be one of Scotland's few real holiday resorts, but is hardly today's obvious choice. Once-important local military employment has almost ceased. Even the traditional short ferry crossing to Larne may not be secure. Air competition and sea routes closer to the motorway system have both hurt. To add to this morning's gloom, shoppers are muttering about a new rumour that the ferry will be abandoned. Heads shake as people gossip outside a shop: 'Who will care about us?' is answered by 'And the ferry is faster and more comfortable than ever'.

With a large arm or peninsula both south and north, the Rhinns have an unusual geography. Those who have not studied the map are often surprised to see the sea on the 'wrong side of the road'. We head down the south peninsula, calling briefly at Ardwell House Gardens to take in

585

an abundance of colour: rhododendrons, azaleas and glades of daffodils, everything much more advanced than in England. Then we drive as far as one can drive before walking up to the lighthouse at the Mull of Galloway. Many people mistakenly call the whole peninsula the Mull, as the whole of Kintyre falsely becomes the Mull of Kintyre. We Thomases know the problem for we are constantly greeted as Tomson or Thompson as though we can't possibly know our own name. The actual Mull, a bold headland with 200ft cliffs, offers a fabulous view of land and sea. Seven tides are said to meet here. We are now almost 300 miles from home in Nairn, and incidentally well south of Newcastle-upon-Tyne, for there is much more of west than east Scotland.

We rejoin the car not far from where the Picts had their last line of defence against the Scots pressing down from the north. Looking up the details, suddenly I find myself angry even with good old Murray, for his *Hand-Book* calls the entire south and north peninsulas promontories. Surely the *Oxford Dictionary*'s definition of promontory as 'a point of high land which juts out into the sea' isn't new? Anyway, much of this lengthy peninsula isn't at all high. Promontory indeed! Logan Botanic Gardens, at which we pause next, seem positively lowland. One of the offshoots of Edinburgh's Royal Botanic Garden, it specialises in sub-tropical trees and plants, species thriving in a way that wouldn't be possible anywhere on the mainland in England. The average temperature is similar to that of resorts such as Bournemouth but, while it isn't as hot in summer, winters are milder.

It seems to take ages along the minor road near the west coast to reach Portpatrick, but this pretty little harbour town basking in spring sunshine gives visual delight – and the fish at a fish restaurant is super fresh. If Portpatrick appeals today, it is because it has reluctantly accepted modest status. Early holiday guides talk of it being ugly and decaying. It took generations to get over the loss of the Irish ferry business to Stranraer which happened as steamships were introduced only six years after the harbour had been expensively rebuilt. A huge hotel became a white elephant, the railway a backwater. Yet steadily Portpatrick improved itself and became this welcoming, well-run little resort.

We read that in the days of sailing craft, in an onshore wind the ferry had to be pulled out by a rope toward the pier heads, while passengers on an arriving ship had to flounder ashore when it went aground in a swell within the (unimproved) harbour. Among them was Liszt, the composer – not a happy man, for he had to wait till low tide next morning for his carriage to be unloaded, and was then stranded by a rare blizzard in Stranraer. It has always been a difficult coastline, subject to violent gales, some of the more notorious wrecks being in relatively recent times. The whole region especially mourned the Stranraer-Larne ferry *Princess Victoria* with the loss of 133 people in 1953.

The tale of that disaster has many ugly details, which Sheila isn't keen to hear over pudding.

Now it is time to explore the northern arm or peninsula, more hilly and with interesting passes, lakes and castles on the roads over the top from west to east. Nearly at the far north, Corsewall Point on a signpost rings a bell. 'Tea in a lighthouse,' I shout. The lighthouse has become an unusual luxury hotel. A pity, perhaps, that tea is served in a conservatory on the ground floor, but up the circular stairs we're shown a room with a marvellous view of Ireland, Kintyre, Arran, Ailsa Craig and the Firth of Forth. Moreover, the lighthouse still works, guiding ships across the Irish Sea and those into Loch Ryan on their way to Stranraer. Close by are cliff walks and even an Iron Age fort.

While paying our bill we gather that all is not well. The hotel is on the market and a sale needed soon. It must be hugely costly to maintain, or is there some other problem? [The hotel flourishes under new ownership, '70 per cent full all-year-round'.]

We now drive almost all the way round Loch Ryan with Stranraer at its southern tip. Heading north on the east bank we pass the site of abandoned Cairnryan Military Port, built in a hurry early in World War Two when many southern ports were vulnerable. It was soon a busy place, with constant shunting on an extensive railway system consisting of rows of sidings and lines stretching out on two deep-water quays. After the war, it specialised in ship-breaking, aircraft carriers, including the *Ark Royal*, as well as German U-boats meeting their end here. Now, again, no work.

The way home is long and varied. First comes a somewhat disappointing coastline; the railway to Girvan goes inland through more spectacular, hilly country and offers a great descent into old Girvan, with a splendid glimpse of that large island rock, Ailsa Craig. We pause to photograph it from the pleasant little harbour.

After a welcome night's break at Turnberry, next morning we enjoy another visit to the Ayrshire coast's showpiece, Culzean Castle clinging to the cliffs facing Arran and Kintyre. Then inland to join the motorway system, which takes us through the heart of Glasgow. After Stirling the traffic tails off, though north of Perth, on the single-carriageway A9 winding through the hills, it only needs a single slow-moving vehicle to build up a convoy. Getting to and from the Highlands demands patience, but perhaps one needs the time to adjust to a very different land and way of life.

· XXXII ·

AN UNEXPECTED
SCOTTISH AFFAIR

Hastily to Aberdeen

While I was in hospital in Inverness with a nosebleed, a nurse noticed a large lump on my arm... all the way round it, so that viewed from any one angle it wasn't obvious. Certainly I hadn't spotted it, and there had been no pain. Alarm bells are ringing. I am rushed into Woodend Hospital at Aberdeen for a fairly complicated biopsy.

Enough of boring medical details. What emerges is the terrific kindness of the staff and everyone else in Aberdeen. A grey, granite city it might sometimes appear, and certainly people are not noted for their financial generosity. In every other way, however, folk cannot do enough for you. Moreover, you are expected to be an individual. If you want two mugs of tea, just say so. 'No bother' and 'You're all right' punctuate sentences.

The whole population gives the impression that it has been skilfully trained in the art of television interviewing. In no time, you find yourself explaining why, how and what about yourself. Refreshingly different from how things are in southern England, Aberdonians appear more interested in you than themselves. Often dismissing their own lives as pretty humdrum, they bask in your experiences.

Woodend Hospital is a grim building (it was a workhouse) in an area where it is said to be dangerous to walk alone after dark. It is of course people, not buildings, that make hospitals what they are. It helps, though, that this small orthopaedic facility is an outlier and not just a department of the huge general hospital.

To get to her hotel, Sheila has to take a taxi. The drivers are particularly skilled at prising out her personal details in a sympathetic way. It is of course seen as a bonus that we have chosen to live in Scotland. Several have happy childhood memories of summer visits to

Nairn and talk about our balmy climate, so different from Aberdeen's, as though we were in the South Pacific.

When I'm given a pass to spend the final night with Sheila at her hotel, its entire staff tell me how concerned they have been for her as she worried about me. Aberdeen leaves a glow in the heart.

Quick Visit to Edinburgh

A few days later, the day we are due to set off on our next travels, mainly through Wales, stopping for a night in Edinburgh for two special meetings. While waiting for the biopsy result, and digesting the possible prognosis of what is euphemistically called limb sacrifice, we decide to keep the Edinburgh arrangement, asking Dave the Taxi to take us down one day and return with us the next. It gives him a chance to visit his mum in Glasgow who, though perfectly fit, finds visiting Inverness too challenging, even if driven by her son. There are many Scots who take it for granted that others enjoy things beyond their ken. So the hairdresser gets a kick out of hearing where her clients are going for their holidays. She herself will just 'stay around', for there are things to do in the house and it will be good to have a rest.

Dave deposits us at The Balmoral at the end of Princes Street. A huge pile towering above the central Edinburgh skyline, for generations it was a luxury railway hotel known as the North British. Its fine location was enhanced by having a subterranean entrance from the station. Here is another former railway hotel hating to admit its original purpose. Of course, for the convenience of their guests, the back entrance is blocked off. It is specially 'convenient' for those arriving at Waverley station by train who have a choice between breathlessly lugging their belongings up killer Waverley Steps or joining the taxi queue for a ridiculously short journey.

Starved of investment in the last days of railway ownership, the hotel deteriorated. So there was excitement when Rocco Forte acquired it as the first of his personal hotels following the loss of the Forte empire by hostile takeover. The renamed Balmoral is plush. There is a kilted doorman, and welcoming fire just inside. Despite its five stars, however, it has consistently scored a poor AA percentage rating. In some ways it is distinctly irritating. Apparently so many guests dispute their bills when checking out that one is forced to sign acceptance of the rate as part of the reception process. And should one, as the Scots put it, 'wish' afternoon tea, an expensive traditional one is still served – but not in the time-honoured style in a comfy lounge where until recently there was often a queue of people anticipating the pleasure. You now sit at a side table in the bar with carpetless floor. OK, it is the same room; but it doesn't feel like it.

Out of curiosity, we walk part way across North Bridge, connecting the New Town with Princes Street, and the Old Town famous for the Royal Mile, to The Scotsman. Formerly the base of *The Scotsman* newspaper, it is now Edinburgh's most expensive and stylish hotel, the AA Scottish Hotel of the Year. We don't get far beyond the door when we're asked to account for ourselves, so have to be content with the view from the bridge. The Old Town is lit up by a glowing sunset, occasional fleecy white clouds blowing across a marbled azure and pale blue backdrop. The whole valley beneath us is filled by Waverley station. The dignitaries of the time were so anxious to welcome the railway that they were prepared to sacrifice the valley overlooked by the Castle.

Later, we cross Princes Street and, after all these years of visiting Edinburgh, for the first time discover the Café Royal or Oyster Bar, a large Victorian pub with decor that elsewhere might seem horribly over the top but fits here. There is a wonderful display of interesting old photographs. The clientele is very Edinburgh, what strikes me as confidently semi-sophisticated. Life is for living, says the attitude both of suited business people propping up the large central bar, many drinking champagne (more is said to be consumed here than in London) and diners ordering carefully from the à la carte menu. Life is indeed for enjoying, even with the possible threat of losing an arm. We thought we'd have a cheap meal. We didn't, but the wonderful Dover sole was worth every penny. And we much enjoyed the interesting display of pictures and photographs of bygone Edinburgh.

Controversial Bishop

Our guest at a very Scottish breakfast at the Balmoral's coffee shop next morning is a fertile author and controversial cleric: Richard Holloway, former Episcopal Bishop of Edinburgh and Primus. Even admitting one has met him, let alone invited him to breakfast, would seriously upset some church people. Yet a warmer, more caring individual you would not find in all Edinburgh, or for that matter Bath or Canterbury.

'I'm the kind of person I used to be furious about in my younger days,' he admits. 'But I can only be sincere. It is not so much that I don't believe in many of the things that most Christians regard as important but that I don't see them as fundamental. Over the years we have turned away thousands of caring, thinking people because they couldn't actively subscribe to some particular belief.' I am currently reading his *Doubts and Loves: What is left of Christianity*. 'Do you regard the Bible as good poetry or bad history?' is the theme.

He explains: 'The Gospels were written decades after the events they described by people who recorded what was handed down orally. And not only were they influenced by their time and the Jewish tradition, but may anyway sometimes have been speaking figuratively. I don't want to strip anyone's beliefs from them. It is just that by demanding universal acceptance of this, that and the other we make Christianity irrelevant to so many.'

He has obviously been hurt by misunderstanding, especially by the fact that an organisation he would have liked to address has said he is not welcome.

'But sometimes you ask for trouble,' I inject cheekily, citing how in his recent television series, in trying to get close to a young audience, he foolishly mentioned rolling a joint.

'It was utterly stupid. I sometimes find myself driven to such stupidities.' Which to my mind makes him a very human person, imperfect like the rest of us, but as sincere and caring as they are made... or in this case has evolved against the tide. We would love to have spent longer with him. He is a great writer reaching a real audience yet, thanks largely to the media making the most of any faux pas, and exploiting controversy without explaining context, he has been sidelined out of the mainstream. I shall always remember this breakfast and his very real concern not only for my health but Sheila's welfare if the result of the biopsy is malignant. A gentle giant.

Writers' News Again

The company that purchased my writing magazines, Regional Independent Media, also owners of the *Yorkshire Post*, has been acquired by Johnston Publishing Limited, quoted on the stock exchange. Their business development manager, Henry Faure Walker, based in Edinburgh, has invited me to lunch at the Balmoral's Number One restaurant.

An eager younger man, he has his finger on the pulse. 'The magazine hasn't been doing so well since you sold it. It needs to grow to be worth our keeping as something of a one-off. What do you think we need to do to make it successful?'

The thought of another change of owner being disturbing, I speak positively and sincerely about the new team in charge. It is a fascinating conversation, for I'm surprised he is so well informed, yet feel he may be holding something back. Staff at Leeds have heard about the meeting and can't wait for me to report what happened. Henry has convinced me that Johnston's will give *Writers' News* at least a controlled expansionist whirl, though the staff at Leeds are not convinced. [Their suspicion was right, for later the owner of a rival writing magazine phoned to say he had been in negotiations around the time of my meeting, and then we were told that the business had been sold to Warners Group

Publications. That has achieved the best of both worlds since they specialise in niche magazines and are full of enthusiasm while leaving the present management in place in Leeds. Everyone is happy. Every magazine needs to be loved to succeed and we all look forward to seeing *Writers' News* and the associated *Writing Magazine* expand once more. They are certainly valued by their readers.]

Jim Douglas

Waiting to meet us before we set off for home are Jim and Heather Douglas. They are both Scots who settled in Canada many years ago. Until recently they had a Scottish base for the summer: a hotel in Cullen, a stylish bed-and-breakfast in St Andrews, and finally a comfortable flat in Edinburgh's fashionable Morningside. Now when returning to their homeland they stay in many different places.

It was as a cleaner pushed a noisy vacuum between us in a New York hotel that I first met Jim. Soon after, in the early 1970s, we set up a joint company in Vancouver: Douglas, David & Charles. Over the years we have met at book functions and socially at dozens of locations in several countries.

Jim is a remarkable bookman. So was his father, devouring volumes on every conceivable subject while living in a typical Edinburgh tenement. When Jim returned from long war service, it was only a matter of minutes before Dad opted out of the conversation and buried himself in his book of the moment. This happened to be *Arcaris, the Biologist's Story of Life*. 'More amusing than upsetting,' says Jim. In those days public libraries issued one ticket per person. Dad claimed the entire family's. When he became ill, it fell to Jim to take back the case of books already read and pick up the next week's. 'It didn't seem to matter much what he read; he just had to keep at it. Then one day Mother came in looking very distressed. Dad had told her: "I've finished reading. Just bring back the library tickets." What an epitaph to a bookman. He died that night.'

Anxious to make something of life, and not knowing how to raise capital to start his own business, after military service Jim hoped to go to university. 'I wasn't allowed to because I couldn't prove I would have done so if there hadn't been a war. That left a deep mark on me. I decided Scotland held no future and emigrated to Canada, arriving in a heavy snowstorm with no job. Very exciting especially as, when they realised I was a Scot, people were anxious to help. I'd had a pretty mundane job with Menzies but inherited my father's love of books so, though I started as a communications engineer I soon turned to books. Doors opened in a way unimaginable back home. Even today nearly all Canadian publishing is controlled by Scots. And in Canada it is not your family background and education but what you achieve that counts.

'Edinburgh still has too much of the "where you came from" for my liking. When we had our Morningside flat I was often asked where I was educated. You should have seen faces drop when I mentioned the state schools, but actually they gave me a good education. And my lack of a degree hasn't made the slightest difference with Simon Fraser University in British Columbia. Canadian Scots are good at adapting while retaining their core traditions. I love Scotland and need to spend lots of time here, but Canada fulfilled all the promise of a new country. You make your own way.'

Jim's way has been extraordinary. He has taken a turn at running many of the major Canadian publishing houses, his own publishing businesses, and profitable consultancy services for other publishers. He has written and taught university courses, received various awards and been president of the main trade associations. It has not always been plain sailing, for the Canadian market faces ferocious competition from British and American books as well as a full local publishing programme, much of which would not be possible without government grants. Our joint publishing venture was a failure. We both feel bad about that, but it has made no difference to continuing friendship.

A member of the D&C Newton Abbot management team didn't help. Says Jim: 'I remember telling him how bad it was that Scotland still had a feudal system and that two couples who had given everything up to buy a hotel in Cullen – all the legal formalities completed – were ready to move in when the superior landlord, the manager of the local estate, announced they were going to exercise pre-emptive buying rights. In another case a liquor licence was agreed to but held up by the police because the estate demanded £500.'

'We had to pay something like that for the right to run *Writers' News* from home in Scotland,' I interject.

'Ridiculous feudalism. Your man dismissed me as some kind of communist, not someone he cared to work with.'

Next he tells me about how the archive of his own publishing company is revered and will carefully be retained for posterity. 'What about the D&C archive?'

'There isn't any.'

'You don't mean it. Why ever not?'

'Nobody was interested locally, and new owners certainly didn't care. Their history begins the day they took over.'

'That's disgraceful. What about the letters from famous authors, the file copies of all those Readers Union books going back to the thirties?'

'All gone.'

'You should have emigrated too.'

'I did think about it and realised there would have been greater openness, but I love Britain.'

'And I am waiting to read your travel book.'

Petite Heather, who in the last few minutes has been turning her gaze left and right as though watching tennis, closes the match: 'Come on you two. You can't have the best of both worlds. We've not done badly, but the journeys take their toll and when we're in Vancouver we miss out on what's happening here, and vice versa.'

We then talk about something common to the UK and Canada: rapid changes in the book trade. 'Whoever would have thought James Thin, the pillar of the Edinburgh book world would go bust?'

I told them that I had recently spoken with Ainslie Thin, the fourth head of the family firm who I always regarded as one of the gentlemen of the book trade. The original James Thin had set up shop in 1848, in the days that individual publishers appointed specific shops as their agents. But, said Ainslie: 'Most of the expansion was during the last period. At our peak we had 37 shops, 650 staff and a million pounds profit. Then the chains came on the scene – backed by huge corporate money and a need to push hard for quick results. We retrenched and were eventually wiped out. Virtually all the famous individual bookshops, yesterday's household names, have gone, though honestly I can't say the public are any the worse for it.'

'That was honest,' says Jim. 'But chains aren't quite the same thing. Every shop used to have its individual character.'

Turning back to ourselves, he adds: 'There are happy memories enough, but a few regrets, especially that I didn't keep copies of your Scottish books.' He then passes me one of my railway books to autograph for a friend back home.

Home and Away

An interesting day, but it may be as far as our long-planned trip to Wales takes us. Dave picks us up for the journey back north. We are heading along Princes Street when a police car stops us. 'You're not allowed,' begins the constable.

'But it says buses and taxis and I'm a taxi.'

'Not an Edinburgh taxi.'

'Where does it say that?'

'Everyone knows what that means.'

'Not me,' says Dave. We're waved off, no clearer in our mind whether a taxi from outside the city can claim to be a taxi or not, or indeed whether a visiting bus is a bus at all.

'Anyway, let me tell you about this extraordinary lady I had in the car... ' starts Dave. It helps pass the time.

Four days later there's a phone call from Aberdeen bringing good news and relief... just in time to keep our Welsh arrangements providing our car can be driven to Bath by our gardener. After furious phoning to trace his wife, he's away with her and most of our luggage within the hour. Later Dave picks us up to join the sleeper.

· X X X I I I ·

TO THE LAND OF
MY FATHERS

The Forest of Dean

Even with a name like David Thomas, I couldn't live in Wales; but few prospects are as exciting as making an extensive journey through it. The reason is, of course, the same: Wales, the land of green valleys where once men toiled in grime, of male voice choirs and festivals, high cliffs and reservoirs set like gems in wild mountains, is different. Different in language, history, culture, value system. Many of my best and worst meals and travel experiences have been here. I've both experienced extreme generosity and been cheated on more than a few occasions. I know I'm going to enjoy the next fortnight or so, though part of it will be spent in Monmouthshire, which used to be Wales but isn't today, and on the English side of the rich border country further north. It's the middle of summer. It feels as if we are going on holiday.

From Bath, where we have spent a couple of days, we start by the M4, taking the higher of today's pair of Severn Bridges, the older one. It is high tide and, though the view is scarcely memorable, there is a huge area of salt water where the Wye joins the Severn. Through Chepstow, the Wye already confined in a narrow channel, and along the busy Gloucester road, we make our first stop near Alvington, just short of Lydney. We are already in Forest of Dean country. It feels as though it should belong to Monmouthshire, but the Forest has of course always been English.

An often-asked question is how publishers find their authors. Not usually in the way that Ron Ransome came to me. We were in a Midland radio studio, waiting our turn to be interviewed about new books, when Ron introduced himself saying: 'I don't think much of my publisher; what's yours like?' That resulted in my taking eleven of his books. Most were practical art books. In the way he wrote and illustrated them, they were assured bestsellers in the USA as well as Britain. One title I knew wouldn't be a great success, but if you value an author, you need to take some rough with the smooth. It was called *Second Time Around*, about having fun in the later part of your life, especially if you have the 'good fortune' to be made redundant as was Ron. He'd started life as a Rolls Royce apprentice in Derby, where he quickly switched to writing workshop manuals. That led to advertising in which he flourished until his employment suddenly ended in a recession. What an opportunity!

He had dabbled in painting, entering a wartime poster competition, and wondering if he might ever make his mark. To develop his skill, he once gave himself two weeks to paint pictures to decorate an entire room – and a clairvoyant told him he was going to write a bestselling book. Quite a number of people get that far. With the need to earn money – fast – he taught himself perspective and how to produce rapid results with watercolours. He quickly found himself teaching others, perfecting his own technique at the same time. Next he taught himself to paint in oils, while instructing classes of twenty or thirty. Painting courses at home led to painting holidays overseas. A mailing list was built and students and other supporters began receiving the *Ransome Recorder* with an order form for further courses... and his books and videos. 'Second time around' was far more enjoyable, not to mention profitable, than his first career. He never ceases to be grateful for being sacked.

'Mind you, it was tough at first,' he tells me at his fantastic country house with a superb drawing room, tall and airy, with the largest single pane of glass we have ever seen letting in the north light loved by artists. At one end there's a large copper chimney for the stove within the fireplace, where the alcove is big enough to display a couple of his paintings; at the other a minstrel's gallery. 'People who seem to fall on their feet have to work for it,' he pontificates. 'I was only fifty and had no prospects, no marketable skill.' And when he had achieved a new life and purpose, there were personal problems. He really loved his wife and loyally supported her when she suffered Alzheimer's disease, and became accident-prone and wandered off aimlessly round the lanes. Eventually she had to move into care. The time came when she didn't even recognise him on his frequent visits. He was good at listening to his publisher, so one day I told him he'd ruin his own health for no purpose, and cease to be able to give pleasure to others, unless he recreated some life for himself.

Soon afterwards he was living with an American, of whom I retain a vivid vision, when we invited them to dinner in a Devon pub. A few days after that he was due to give a painting demonstration in a Liverpool shop as part of a promotion campaign for his latest book. Because of fog, the American lady tried to persuade him not to go, but he said he couldn't let his publisher down. So she went, too, to keep him company and 'safe'. They ran into crashed vehicles scattered over a section of motorway where the fog was especially thick. He told me at the time: 'We said thank goodness we're safe, when a lorry ran into us.' She was killed outright.

Not a man to be without a woman, he quickly found American number two. Risky? Not actually. Darlis (her mother had read a book with someone so called in it) is a perfect match: well groomed and self-assured, sharing Ron's bonhomie, love of painting, gardening and much more. When their vehicle was stolen with many personal possessions, never recovered, on an American trip, they decided it should only be seen as a minor irritant.

He's now been teaching painting for over a quarter of a century, and he and Darlis have been together for nearly ten years. There's a lot of spontaneous fun, and no doubt a good back-up system. It is a pretty sophisticated operation. There are workshops at a beautifully equipped Clanna Gardens. The drawing room is designed for the evening relaxation of an entire class. Demonstrations and workshops are held in the USA, too, as well as painting holidays around the English-speaking world and sometimes the Mediterranean. The books still in print are offered along with supporting videos. After many years of great sales, the book side is winding down; though Ron still writes for artists' magazines. Even with Darlis's support, he can't do everything, and at times, is obviously hard pushed.

Lunch served in a comfortable conservatory shows the American influence with a stylishly presented tasty salad combining shellfish and meat. We are all very relaxed. Though Ron and I used to be in touch several times a week – no agent was involved – inevitably people drift apart when the reason for their contact has gone. But I frequently take down one of his books, such as the lavish *Edward Seago* about the Queen Mother's favourite artist, as well as those illustrated by his own work, and think about happy times. He's put enthusiasm into people's lives. The diary must be consulted in many homes rapidly when the annual *Ransome Recorder* – now a joint Ron and Darlis production announcing the year's programme – pops through the letterbox.

It is only a short distance to Lydney, which seems to turn its back on the Severn, but has a lock-entered harbour still in use. Once the long, narrow basin handled the despatch of 250,000 tons of coal a year, mainly to small West Country ports, the largest consignment for Bridgwater, the smallest for the island of Flat Holm where the lighthouse needed coal. Lydney also had a large tinplate plant. We turn inland, running beside what is now a steam railway, but was once an artery of the highly complex Forest of Dean system of railways and tramways mainly devoted to the carriage of coal and iron. We are heading for Coleford, which is where we think the Speech House in which we are staying will be found. Carelessly we have left the details buried in a case in the back, and lazily leave them there, so find out the hard way that it isn't Coleford we want, but a minor road running deep through the forest between it and Cinderford. Egged on by the delight of passing through woodland with occasional grass rides, we shoot past the Speech House and are soon at the edge of Cinderford. At the turn on to the Gloucester-Cinderford Road near Stockwell Green, there is just the kind of view of the Severn we had dreamed about but were unable to find on the opposite bank some months ago.

The whole of the Vale of Gloucester is laid out before our eyes: Berkeley power station to our right, the Severn's great horseshoe bend in the middle and, beyond, the continuing river disappearing into the evening mist, while Gloucester and its cathedral and dozens of villages with their churches stand out clearly. The docks at Sharpness and the point where the Gloucester & Sharpness Canal leaves the Severn deserve special study. We could stand here for hours, counting the M5's bridges and the roads and railways, the motorway alone excepted, all irresistibly heading for Gloucester. Eventually we can even trace the Severn skirting the city, but the light has gone too far to pick out the docks with the Waterways Museum we explored recently. Even after so many hedgerows have been taken out to aid mechanisation, there's still a huge jigsaw of fields. With the sturdy farms and cosy villages, the bendy lanes between trees and hedges of the centuries, this landscape is obviously largely manmade. It could only be England. It is a very different, yet still the same kind of view of a great patchwork of manmade country, that made Churchill buy and adore Chartwell in Kent.

We return through the gently undulating forest to the Speech House and check in. There's the wedding of the granddaughter of Sheila's closest friends here tomorrow, and immediately we arrange dinner with some of the family. It is a great wedding venue. Meals, taken in the room where the foresters' parliament meets, are fun if service is a touch disorganised. The building dates from the seventeenth century and was originally a hunting lodge. Like so many hotels famous for their history and location, today it doesn't score highly in stars or AA points, but I'm glad at last to have stayed here. Forest lore and tradition ooze out of the creaking woodwork.

Up early next morning, we again enjoy the woods and grass rides. Though it is only 35 square miles, this is the second largest of the British royal forests, the term implying hunting reserve rather than a mass of trees. In fact there are many more trees than in Roman days. The Forest, as in trees, came into its own after a 1668 Act preserving it as a storehouse for the Royal Navy. Today oak accounts for about a quarter

– but the most seen – acreage, other broadleaf another quarter, and conifers just over half.

First stop is at the Dean Heritage Centre, where our approach to a gentle walk beside the pond beyond the waterwheel is interrupted by someone shouting: 'Is that a bat?'

Sure enough, in bright sunshine it is, skimming the water no doubt for flies but, actually getting wet once or twice, and taking no notice of the ducks nearby. 'I've never seen that before. What a thing. I couldn't believe it.' It transpires that he is a sculptor working on a Green Man to go on the Brecon road out of Hereford. The bat caught his eye out of the studio window.

This centre is a cut above most. We're given a super mini map-cum-drawing to guide us round. We see how charcoal is burned, and stoop going into a forester's cottage with sparse period furnishing. In the main galleries we learn about the intricacies of shallow coal mines, the iron trade, and enjoy the engine display. One exhibition is devoted to Listers, who specialised in small agricultural engines that transformed life on the land not only in Britain but especially in the Middle East and India. Once it employed 1,000 people in Cinderford. The display panels are good, too.

The Forest is now numerous got of late
Since married men come here to speculate
(Kitty Drew, forest poetess)

We learn that coal is still mined at just one drift mine and, when we go to the first-floor café, discover that butty butteries, naughtily substantial, are named after the mining system in which the top man looked after his mate, or butty, at work.

Visiting the shop on the way out proves an expensive business, for we come away with hands full of books of local interest. *Work in the Woods*, on Dean's industrial heritage, is a pictorial title showing just how industrial the area once was, and how picturesque are the best of the remains of old tramways marked by the stone blocks to which the rails were directly fastened, as well as surviving elements of factories, harbours and viaducts. You have to look for these, since as you pass through, it nearly all seems virgin forest. For reading back home is Winifred Foley's *A Child in the Forest*, a minor classic about growing up in a poor miner's family as eyes were opened to the free beauty of plants and birds around her. Later, visits to distant places (including London where she was placed 'in service') revealed how spartan life had been at home. But there was irrepressible family love. It is a delightfully artless tale. For example, one day when she was nine, puzzling how to write a letter to Father Christmas to make a bargain – 'Don't bother with anything else but a doll' – her own father came in.

'I be a-feared 'tis no good thee exing Feyther Christmas for that sart o' doll, my wench. 'Im do only take that sart to the rich people's young uns,' Dad warned me kindly.

'You do want to tell the silly old bugger off then. Tell 'im they rich people can afford to buy dolls for their children. It's the likes o' we lot 'im do want to bring the best toys to. Why ever 'aven't 'im got more sense than that?'

Father, who usually had an explanation for everything under the sun, scratched his head and admitted himself 'proper flummoxed'.

On Christmas day, a doll duly turned up: the ugliest apology for one, 'for all the world like an old, darned, black woollen stocking, lumpily stuffed, with a bit of old ribbon tied tightly round the foot to form its head'. Not acceptable; family agony, till her mother brought out clothes from a baby she had lost to dress it up. Real poverty, great family life.

The cushion usually kept on our large car's driving seat having been left in Scotland, Sheila suggests we return via Cinderford to buy a substitute, so once again enjoy the fabulous view of the Vale of Gloucester. Now the tide is out exposing long mud banks. With its tiered cottages and their colourful gardens, at first sight Cinderford seems welcoming, but the centre, with ugly displays of house agents' boards, is pretty awful. Except for the Westgate Department Store, curiously run by the Anglia Regional Co-operative Society. An unexpected oasis of civilised commerce, it displays everything from furniture and kitchen sinks to clothing and, yes, cushions, and even has a restaurant. 'We don't get fat here; there's so much walking to do,' says an assistant we chase from department to department.

Via the Wye to the Head of the Clydach Gorge

On our way back to the Speech House, I spot directions to the Cyril Hart Arboretum. When I knew him, and there were several launch parties at the Speech House I had to miss, Cyril Hart was the senior verderer, with an overlapping love of plants and local history. He introduced and annotated a reprint of *Nicholls's Forest of Dean*, a pioneer work of the 1850s which has pointed the way for all historians since, and then wrote two new titles: *The Verderers and Forest Laws*, with notes on the Speech House, and a massive *The Industrial History of Dean*.

Up early again the next morning, Sunday, we realise how deftly the Forest is placed in the V between Severn and Wye. Going cross country via St Briavels, where Ron Ransome lived in the days we worked together, we are quickly beside the wandering Wye, my favourite English river, and once more take in that prospect of it passing Tintern Abbey, the ruins of which stand as a testament to past ecclesiastical grandeur that has moved so many people to tears – or poetry. We can afford this diversion because at this hour there's little traffic, and soon we're heading back north beside the river. I regret that for decades past one hasn't been able to enjoy it even more from a train running on its banks, though the section from Monmouth to Ross-on-Wye, closely following the Wye through the gorge at Symonds Yat, was even better.

Once more I pay brief respect to Redbrook, which always used to be called Redbrook-on-Wye, where my father's grandfather and great grandfather lived. As a youth, my great, great grandfather was often cited as a threat. Was I not in danger of also being too lazy and too ambitious? This deadly combination apparently led to his being involuntarily exported to Australia, though what was his exact crime remained a mystery Dad never revealed, if he knew. Today people pass through on the Offa's Dyke path, admiring the landscape of steep contours, wood and river. The village is regarded as picturesque in a way unimaginable in its hard-working industrial days. Salmon used to be caught on the ebb tide of the narrow channel by securing a boat across the river, whose red stones (rather than industrial waste) gave Redbrook its name. The fish were netted one at a time.

Sorry we are not continuing alongside the narrower but most attractive upper Wye to Ross-on Wye, we turn left to join the inferior world of the A40 (T) where Sunday drivers seem to care less about speed limits than on safer motorways. Beyond Abergavenny, then on to the A565 (T). This is the Heads of the Valleys route.

We are going to see a cycleway bridge in the process of being built at a point where the course of the railway it mainly follows has to be temporarily abandoned. Though the exact spot high above the Clydach Gorge to the south is marked on the map, so tightly packed are the OS map's contours that it is hard to know when exactly to leave the queue of Sunday drivers. We do so too soon, incurring the steepest and narrowest of rural rides to the village of Daren-felen. Once strictly the home of quarry, railway and similar workers, today it welcomes tourists and has a campsite.

With industry gone, and provided you are not worried about being cut off by snow and ice, this is indeed great country. Even though we are so near to our destination that we can hear part of the new bridge being hammered into position, there's still difficulty in finding the access. So beyond a former level crossing, we climb to much higher ground. Walkers are everywhere, but they can't direct us to the elusive bridge, and the remote cottages (upmarketed into holiday homes) are empty. Eventually a local, driving a tractor, tells us, though now our problem is comprehending his meaning, for his accent is strong. To begin with, I think he's talking Welsh and nearly put my foot in it by asking if he has the English. We have to return, he tells us, to the former level crossing, park the car and walk along the long-abandoned railway. He's surprisingly impressed when I tell him I travelled on one of the infrequent, dirty stopping trains sandwiched in between mineral trains on this long forgotten corner of the LMS. He didn't think I could be old enough. He's amazed when I add that occasionally on summer Saturdays there was a through train bringing miners and their families home from Blackpool.

New Cycleway Bridge and World Heritage at Blaenavon

As we leave the car, sandwich in hand, a couple of the Sustrans volunteers come the other way to collect their sandwiches from the hut that acts as base. William Webber is an earnest fellow, an electro-magnetic engineer from South London taking a holiday and doing his bit for society – 'this cycle network is a great idea' – while keen, wiry young Martin Pulpan from Halifax is doing a stint he hopes will look good on his CV. The bridge, we are told, is nearly finished; at the start there were fifteen volunteers.

'Can we follow you?'

'Not in those shoes. What sizes do you take?'

William hunts through a pile of old boots. My large feet are easy enough to fit; there's no size 5 for Sheila, so she manages with a size 7 on her left foot and size 8 on the right.

'And you'd better finish your lunch first. You won't want to take anything to eat through that mud.'

William says he'll have finished his sandwich before he reaches the mud while Martin stays behind to help us. The first part of the walk, though surprisingly steep for a railway, is on old ballast, and easy enough. After passing the large abandoned quarry on the other side of the level crossing, apparently some freights used to pick up a banking engine here for the stiffer climb through the tunnel ahead. When the line was closed, they blocked up the mouths of the twin tunnels to prevent people falling in the dark. But water built up till the boarding gave way and a miniature flood carried away part of the formation. John Grimshaw doesn't fancy having his National Cycle Network go through the tunnel, either, so the bridge is being built over a deep gully along the course of the 1822 4ft 4in gauge Baileys Tramroad.

'I cleaned the stone,' says Martin proudly, pointing to a railway building that is being retained as part of the scene, as he offers us a cookie from his packed lunch.

Negotiating the deep soaking mud left by the water escaping from the tunnel is tricky. In turn we each need Martin's hand to steady us. Then it is easier going to the bridge, a narrow wooden affair, nothing great, just a practical way of linking up the route. The other workers are lost in what they are doing, not talking even among themselves.

Martin helps us back across the mud, and then we're on our own to enjoy the fantastic view of natural and man-made terracing. Two local walkers with Golden Retrievers point out that this section was carried on a ledge cut out of solid rock. Unlike most abandoned lines, this is too high and rocky to be covered by trees. There is indeed scarcely a tree in sight, but it is railway land all right with wild flowers, including stunted harebells bravely growing out of the ballast, to prove it. Then a local cyclist pauses to tell us what things used to be like.

'I was down the pit at Blaenavon. The pit, the village, the railway, it's all gone. Wouldn't have thought it possible when I were young. Now it's a World Heritage Site, whatever that means... a museum piece, they say, and I suppose it is OK for tourists. But it can't capture the sounds and smells and the dirt and the community spirit when real people did real work. There weren't tourists then, that's for sure.'

I recall Blaenavon as a poor yet proud town of steep streets, and of chapels where all the services were in English, for nearly every worker had moved here from elsewhere. Once the Blaenavon Company operated sixteen collieries and vast ironworks. That what is left has become a World Heritage Site is due to a novel, Alexander Cordell's *Rape of the Fair Country*. In fact it was the sale of the film rights, in 1960, that proved the turning point. The town council decided that the crumbling ruins shouldn't be bulldozed but kept for a film set. The film was never made, but the decision to retain what was left, including the multi-blast furnace complex, the best preserved of its period in the world, was undoubtedly right. Yet I don't want to spoil my memories of well over half a century ago by returning. I do, however, enjoy *Exploring Blaenavon: Industrial landscape, World Heritage Site*, by Chris Barber, who explains:

> This area at the 'Heads of the Valleys' of South-east Wales was to become the most important iron-making region in Britain and people seeking work came in their thousands from the rural areas of Wales, England and Ireland, attracted by the possibility of employment or higher wages .... Coal, fireclay and iron nodules were found together in the coal measures of the Afon Lwyd valley and the mountain top while fluxing stone was quarried in the limestone which lay a few kilometres to the north overlooking the Usk Valley.
>
> The industrial landscape provides a unique outdoor classroom for visiting educational parties, who study the complete story of ironmaking... including the extraction of raw materials, furnace and forge technology, the development of early transport systems

and the social history of the people who provided the workforce over a period of two hundred years.

Astonishing to publishers who struggled with such titles years ago is the fact that several local authorities, the Brecon Beacons National Park, and tourist board, made publication financially possible. Blaenavon is by no means the only piece of preserved industry in today's Wales. I'm so glad to have known the land when everything worked.

By the Rhondda to Cardiff Bay

So, not even tempted by a steam train at work today, we regain the main road and go west, most of the way being north of the valley ends, and therefore of industry. At one spot, where the landscape ceases to be ex-industrial, virgin ground has been used for an Asda. Cheaper building there, no doubt. Just beyond Hiawaun, we take the last of the Cardiff Valleys, the Rhondda. There's great scenery round steep, horseshoe bends till industry, or largely ex-industry, starts with the flourishing railway line at Treherbert. Then mile-after-mile of near continuous housing through what was once perhaps the heart of Welsh mining. Many people also associate it with the best in male voice choirs. What a difference from when I first came this way by train sitting between miners going home at their shift end. Today most homes are well kept – the double-glazing salesmen have done well – and as Sunday teatime approaches there's already a steady trickle of people taking carry-outs back home. It's not just fish and chips these days, but all kinds of Oriental.

The dual carriageway is met at lively Pontypridd with its famous bridge. Then a fast journey almost into Cardiff. We're heading for the five-star St David's Hotel at Cardiff Bay. Though we can see it as clearly as we could hear the cycleway bridge being built, it is almost as elusive. Don't arrive by public transport unless you're absolutely sure of your way. Not that many will. The state-of-the-art St David's is a world-class hotel Cardiff has long needed; right over the top with its height and flash interior design – and its tariff, you might say. It overlooks the Bay, turned by a barrage into permanent high tide. I've always thought it a good idea at just one or two places, and certainly this bay was largely mud at low tide. But having seen it, I'm not so sure. Despite best endeavours, including boating and massive oxygenating machines whirling the water, somehow it is stagnant, though not in the smelly sense. It has certainly encouraged the breeding of midges, dead ones thickly covering the balcony screen windows. A pair of starlings gorge themselves on our balcony.

On a short walk, we see lots of attractions we could visit, and many people are doing so, but we are content watching the passage of an occasional boat across the Bay to Penarth, with its long terrace of middle-class houses in the middle, large ones for the bosses to the west. In the foreground a swan suddenly wakes up her cygnets and leads them into the water. What is there to complain about except it not feeling quite right? Over a top-class dinner we enjoy looking out to the white Norwegian church that is now an arts centre. Perhaps that's it. Everything is consciously done for tourists. Though we would have liked time to go out to the barrage and see the lock gates, how refreshing the sound of waves would be.

Maybe it has always been badly signposted, but I've seldom driven round Cardiff without getting lost. On leaving, we mistakenly pass along the shopping street, where the city's principal bookshop used to be. For fifteen or so years I attended its annual railway evening on the last Thursday of November. The retired railway folk who formed most of the purchasing audience were as friendly as people come, each giving me – the outsider from across the water – a quick resumé of his last twelve months and enquiring how life had treated me. Such warmth. One night, I recall, I couldn't find anywhere to park and, because of the traffic, was anyway late for my speech. I stopped beside a police car. Two constables immediately came to my window and I explained my predicament. 'As you know, it's the Wales versus England game tonight. If you'll wish for a good result, we'll move and let you in. But no cheating, mind.' I told them my name was David Thomas and they were content.

We get lost twice, too, trying to find Llandaff Cathedral, way out in a residential area, but with a very pleasant Close. Standing on one of the oldest Christian sites in Britain, it has an unusual as well as long history. For example, it was in ruins in much of the Middle Ages. In 1734, our friend John Wood, the Bath builder, started restoration, or rather the creation of a church within a church, in the Italianate Temple style then in vogue, leaving the near-ruins of the original walls and pillars standing. But Wood didn't finish it, and a hundred years were to pass before the cathedral took on something like its present shape. Then there was extensive damage in World War Two. Sheila is especially pleased to show me Sir Jacob Epstein's extraordinary sixteen-foot high unpolished aluminium statue of Christ in Majesty. You can't miss it, fixed to the concrete organ casing atop the great arch dividing the nave from the choir, though by no means preventing the view from one end of the building to the other.

Ebbw Vale to Empty Mid-Wales

Then to the Ebbw Vale, past the junction between the separate worlds of the Sirhowy and Ebbw Vales with high woodland between them; there's a seven-mile tourist Cwmcarn Forest drive with views of the old mining towns. The valleys themselves are so hemmed in as to feel romantic if not exactly picturesque. Falling in love with a girl in another valley across the mountain must have been a hazardous affair.

Once these Eastern or Newport Valleys appeared poorer than the Western or Cardiff ones, but these days keeping up with the Joneses has become a fine art. Despite the closure of the Ebbw Vale steelworks and high unemployment and much ill-health, houses are neat and bright. Again everyone seems to have double glazing, and vertical blinds at downstairs windows, though net curtains linger upstairs. It is clean and surprisingly green.

Surveyors are out in force, along the road and railway. The Eastern Valleys lost their passenger trains back in steam days, but the present popularity of rail in the western valleys fuels hope of reopening, possibly delayed by an announcement that a missing signalbox cannot be replaced till general modernisation of the area's signalling seven years hence. The centre of Ebbw Vale itself doesn't seem too down-at-heel. But what does everybody do these days?

Layers of the Brecon Beacons loom ahead. I know no part of Britain less well or in which I am so impressed by the sheer scale and physical beauty. One would need to spend a great deal of time here to do it justice, so we enjoy it very much as outsiders. In pure grandeur, it makes nearly all English national parks seem tame. It is on the kind of scale we're used to in the Highlands, but totally different: grand but less wild, of course much greener. What always surprises me in the Brecon Beacons is the skylines: the patchwork of fields rising further than one might expect and, higher still, often a mixture of great rounded tops, smooth spongy hills of grass, and dramatic peaks that can be seen for many miles, cut by deep valleys with bubbling brooks and glass-like lakes. As a youngster, I used to think that unique among mountains, these actually spoke (or grunted) in their majesty. Yet for all the walkers, cyclists, pony trekkers and campers they attract, the Brecon Beacons are the least popular of the three Welsh national parks. The joy lies in the lack of specific crowd-drawing attractions.

We use the A465(T) for barely a mile before striking almost due north along an unfenced road in an empty landscape. Then right, along a narrower, steeper lane not seeing another vehicle until we pass through the small village of Llangattock, with a string of red notices saying 'No' to some proposed development. Ahead now are the Black Mountains. Alongside the River Usk, in one of Britain's most mountainous parts, wanders the Brecon Canal, somehow managing a 25-mile stretch between locks, the country's longest. The old LMS railway, whose abandoned track we walked on to the new cycleway bridge, was just one of the lines that robbed it of business. As the crow flies, we are close to the Clydach Gorge.

So over the Usk and into Crickhowell. We park and head to the three-storey Bear Hotel, the green foothills of the Sugar Loaf Mountain seeming to rise from its roof. At first Crickhowell may seem an unlikely place for a hotel given two red rosettes and rated at 72 per cent by the AA, but the small market town is a perfect oasis of civilisation, with all kinds of shops selling quality merchandise. 'I could stay here,' says Sheila; who couldn't?

Our Welsh rarebit, served on fingers of toasted special bread, is far and away the best ever. The bar is really welcoming, and the conversation going on around us compels eavesdropping.

'The trouble with skilled people coming here because they like the things they find, is that they immediately want to change them,' says one portly regular.

'Yes, they want to take over.'

'At least this place [the Bear] doesn't change.'

'You can't beat it.'

'That's because you have a permanent seat.'

'Well, why not? But I tell you, I'd not be here if they ever put a manager in. This is still the real thing.' They drink to that.

There's a pile of leaflets about the hotel: 'The most popular and best-loved locally, very much the hub of the community. It is also an hotel which accepts well-behaved dogs much to the dismay of the resident dogs.' Hanging in a corner is an 1852 timetable of coach departures, showing that Crickhowell was then a vital crossroads. It must have suffered when much of the business was lost to the railways taking different routes.

We pop into the market (one stall: 'Just Origami') and read the notices of the clubs and societies active here. There's even an archive centre. Many buildings warrant a close look. We leave our mark on the tills of two or three shops, but our most expensive purchase is diesel on our way out.

'Let's go cross-country,' I suggest. We are quickly in a narrow lane without consistent signposting. Once we have gone too far to make it sensible to return, there's a diversion. As often, the authorities are better at starting you off on it than telling you what to do at successive later complicated junctions. We're hopelessly lost in a valley through the Black Mountains. Which valley? There's nobody, nothing, to help. When we don't know where we are, consulting the OS, hardly at its most legible in this land of close contours, adds irritation to confusion. We agree simply to enjoy the rural journey, wherever we're heading.

'Just where I thought we were,' announces Sheila. 'Llanfihangel Crucorney.' Of course! Anyone would have known that. We then follow the Abergavenny to Shrewsbury railway, where it is relatively simple to find our way (though not always knowing if we are in England or Wales) via the lush Golden Valley to the book town, Hay-on-Wye, only just in Wales. The border accounts for a long chain of castles, many now scanty ruins after their valuable stone was nibbled away for later buildings.

Hay-on-Wye: Book Town

Every time I come to Hay, I'm taken aback by just how bookish it is. 'Not a book in sight' boasts one shop to emphasise the point. It isn't just that there are about three dozen bookshops, but the whole ambience of the place. When we take an after-dinner walk, many bookshop windows have other visitors peering into them mentioning the titles displayed – or reading aloud some of the more amusing notices that dot the place. They talk about books on their constitutionals and even in bars. If you're in Hay, it must be because of books, or related things like puzzles and old prints. My eyes fall on a first edition (1866) print of WP Firth's famous portrayal of *The Railway Station*, with harried passengers every which way, in a carved gold frame and heavy glass of the same date. [Months later it surfaced in Scotland as a birthday present to add to my transport gallery.] Locals who are not actually involved in the trade look bemused, especially when relegated to a corner of their regular bar while the literati demonstrate their sophistication and skill at discovering a bargain. 'At least it pays the rates,' mutters one non-bookish Welshman.

Next morning we're back, talking to some of the booksellers, some busy pricing new purchases. Stock turns over here. Curious lot, the booksellers. 'I don't want to say anything against him, but...' is the warning of several about certain competitors. 'Watch you get the copy you pay for.' And a sharp disagreement on prospects. While one, specialising in uniform sets, bemoans the fact that his customers are getting older and younger people only care about what they read, not what it looks like, another insists that the demand for quality titles and sets is stronger than ever. And 'condition matters more and more'. Says another: 'We've been here thirty years and it still makes an excellent day out from Birmingham, Bristol or Oxford,' adding that Hay is a candle in rural gloom. 'You'd be surprised how many books come from local sources. Collect books on, say, the circus over the years, put them nicely together and sell them to relieve rural poverty. Quite a recipe.'

Another bookseller thanks me for keeping him going. The shop is stuffed with David & Charles titles. 'Probably make more money out of them than you ever did.' True; and more evidence here that what sold best on publication is seldom what's in demand today. As at several other shops, the growing importance of the Internet is emphasised. 'Without loss of turnover, I've been able to save two and a half salaries,' says one.

If you're into books, this is the place to come, but real time is needed to overcome initial confusion and make a sensible search. Choosing the right shop to sell your own surplus books isn't easy, either. One bookseller says that the first-ever, 1944, Giles cartoon book, sells for £400 to £500, but what you would be offered would vary sharply between shops. One of the biggest book selections is in the old cinema. Any building will do. Hay-on-Wye is the ultimate in retail specialisation. Without books, the compact town of narrow streets would struggle as it did for several generations when it was rather too large for its declining rural role. Books give purpose and activity and keep Hay in good order.

It all started with Richard Booth, a colourful and always controversial figure who we find working behind the scenes at one of his shops. When I tell him I'm writing a book, he's scarcely polite. No doubt being interviewed by TV crews is more fun, but when I say I'll take a copy of his *My Kingdom of Books*, the bookseller in him tweaks and he comes across to pocket my £14.95.

'I sold you the first-ever D&C book, *The Hay Railway*, in 1960,' I say. He's not interested in those days. He warms up when I thumb through his own book and notice some of his run-ins with official bodies. 'They go in for what they call horizontal promotion these days, so the fact that we're a book town is used to boost a Hay Festival. Everything done by it will be useless in ten years. Instead of just encouraging us to be a book town, they want to turn Hay into a graveyard.'

Why Hay? It was just where he happened to be when the Castle that overlooks the town came up for sale. He says in the book: 'My decisions when buying books, property or dating girls were always very opportunistic. Behind its magnificent Norman walls I could shelter from my parents' objections to nocturnal female visitors and store as many books as I could buy.' A few pages on he writes:

Travelling around Wales laid the foundations of my radical beliefs. It is a poor country and I saw its cultural traditions – literary societies, historical societies, theological colleges and country-house libraries – being sacrificed at the altar of centralised education. Numerous academics complained about 'the rape of Wales' but never considered their own responsibility for the destruction of the magnificent Welsh libraries I saw eroding before my very eyes. The massacre was quick and thorough. It stretched from Bala in North Wales to the Royal Institution in Swansea and through hundreds of fine libraries in between. A small percentage of the books went to the new Welsh universities but many more were sold to overseas universities with greater buying power.

Opportunistically, as he made good sales from the 1969 break up of the Bala College Library, he added more bookshops, then went bankrupt, had marital troubles, had to sell the cinema bookshop and lost key staff. On one April Fool's Day he gave a dinner at the Castle to celebrate Hay's unilateral decision to leave the UK & EU. He was declared King. Yet between sentences such as 'The history of my relationship with women is largely one of immoral curiosity', and attacks on how public money has been wasted by 'the non-accountable government agencies', there's much to interest book lovers and traders. 'Nobody reads books in Hay-on-Wye,' a quotation on the title page, became as untrue as in my different way I brought books into people's homes in Newton Abbot. Inevitably I empathise with his problems and frustrations. He started the whole thing off and, whatever their criticism, there's grudging respect from other booksellers.

Weobley and the Young Writer

On our way north, past another castle, we have to find a coin at Whitney to pay the toll at a bridge which warns that it is in dangerous condition. 'What's it like just taking people's money?' I ask the owner. 'Better than being stuck in an office.'

This is Herefordshire, land of rich farmland, half-timbered houses and villages of character that would long ago have been swamped by commuters were communications better. It is surely still the least spoilt English county, and very English it seems after Wales.

Do you know that, well technically, it is still legal to stand on Hereford city wall and shoot a Welshman with an arrow – though you cannot park your tractor in Broad Street as people did thirty years ago? There's still no university or motorway, and new shopfronts are now taboo so that more timber framing will be left exposed. However, we're not going as far as the city, but to the village of Weobley (pronounced Webley) that epitomises all that's good in Herefordshire: fine old houses, rich history, books, a love of literature, lively social life. Seldom have we seen more colourful gardens. Some people think it is the finest example of a black-and-white village in England. It is on the black-and-white village trail; those colours are reflected in the title of the lively village newsletter, *The Magpie*. Only the church, established by the Norman de Lacy family, is a bit of a problem, for the local pink sandstone is badly worn, the flying buttresses have suffered and most of the gargoyles have gone. English Heritage have stepped in to restore it.

Passing the old brick workhouse and then making a sharp right turn at the Red Lion – it was at the rival Crown that King Charles stayed a night after the battle of Naseby – and we're in the main street, Broad

Street which, until a fire in 1943, used to have a row of other buildings down its middle. Everywhere there are signs of prosperity, though once Weobley was larger, with flourishing glove- and ale-making. Then we drive through a welcoming gateway to the private house where *Young Writer* is published. Though I've often spoken to her, I've not met the publisher, Kate Jones, who has been seriously ill. She's been better and today's meeting has long been planned; but a sudden crisis has landed her in a Dorset hospital. So we talk in the garden with 'the staff', Lorraine and ex-primary teacher, Julian. Our first discovery is that Kate's husband, Alan, made his mark with the Pink Panther films... possibly the best slapstick ever put on celluloid.

Unlike commercial *Writers' News*, *Young Writer* is purely a labour of love, about to be taken over by a Trust. Published once a term, at the time of our visit it is up to issue 23. Each issue has 60 contributors, almost all youngsters, limited to 750 words of prose or 40 lines of poetry. With a print run of 7,000, of which 3,000 go to subscribers and 1,200 to a trade distributor (the rest directly to schools), it is obviously a struggle, but encouraging the discipline of expression is of fundamental importance in the development of many of tomorrow's leaders. My Trust finances some of the competitions.

Kate had planned lunch carefully with a couple of 'characters' in a super little restaurant high in individuality. Julian leads the way, past the Weobley Bookshop, whose window is full of local goodies. Already sitting at our table is Michael Sharp, secretary of the Kilvert Society which – with magazines, lectures and special events – celebrates the life and writings of the famous priest and diarist.

Explains an animated Michael sipping a glass of wine: 'Not all the diaries have survived – we know his wife destroyed some of them – but we calculate he might have written three-quarters of a million words. It isn't the amount but the quality, of course, that makes them so extraordinary – the comments by a genius on everyday things and people. The diaries were written after he came to Clyro in 1872. That's on the river a mile north of Hay-on-Wye. We have a unique portrait of local life, what happened in the church, what was in the mind of a thinking man, at a time of rapid change in what people did and what they thought.' He did a lot of travel, too, but died while still in his thirties.

Kilvert loved Clyro, saying 'every part is classical and sacred and has its story,' and never tired of singing the praises of Radnorshire. Its hills, rolling more gently than across the border in Wales, were to him what Lakeland was to Wordsworth. And to this day Radnorshire people are, shall we say, more accessible than the Welsh; they speak English, not with an accent but in their own dialect with words you don't hear elsewhere.

The diaries certainly include some fine writing. In September 1874:

Left Hay by the 10.16 train. I never had a lovelier journey up the lovely valley of the Wye. A tender beautiful haze veiled the distant hills and woods with a gauze of blue and silver and pearl. It was a dream of intoxicating beauty. I saw all the old familiar sights, the broad river reach at Boughrood flashing round the great curve in the sunlight over its hundred steps and rock ledges, the luxuriant woods which fringe the gleaming river lit up here and there by the golden flame of a solitary ash, the castled rock-towers and battlements and bastions of the Rocks of Aberedw which made me feel as if I were passing again beneath the Under-cliff of the Isle of Wight, the famous rocky wooded gorge through the depths of which the narrow mountain stream of the Edw rushed foaming to its Aber to meet the Wye.

The other guest lined up by Kate has meanwhile arrived: Mrs Sandra Children (a Kentish name) who instantly decides what she wants to eat and drink so she can launch into an enthusiastic eulogy for another local village priest, the seventeenth-century Thomas Traherne. He is perhaps best known for his *Centuries*, still much read. It began as letters from London to a Herefordshire friend. The letters were numbered, so the first 100 formed the first Century. It has been suggested that 'The Way to Felicity' might have been a better title.

As with Kilvert, there is an active Association, of which Sandra is trustee. She tells us about their newsletter, the Traherne Press, and a special Traherne festival held in his parish of Credenhill, a few miles from Weobley. The son of a Hereford shoemaker, it is said that at Oxford he found tutors in every subject except that he most needed: happiness. His writings were unknown till manuscripts began to be discovered, the first not identified as his work until 1900. Manuscripts are still being found – a substantial one on a burning rubbish tip near Wigan in 1967 – so it is still too early to put him in final perspective. But CS Lewis's view that he shirked the problem of evil is no longer respected, we learn.

Many details of Traherne's life are hazy but, while the personality is important in the work of Kilvert, it is not so in the realms of mystical letters and poetry. Traherne's meditations stand above (or rather go down deeply beneath) the geographical setting and life's trivialities.

'*Centuries* is on my shelves,' says Sheila.

Sandra has done the pictures for a range of illustrated cards of the best of his poetry. 'You'll find them at the bookshop,' she says, telling us that Traherne's writings and insight are of a young man, since he only lived to 39.

'I've learned so much just sitting here and listening,' is Julian's comment. Though we have discussed how soon Kate will be fit to return, the one thing we haven't felt like talking about in her absence is her baby, *Young Writer*.

Then we're off to one of the Hereford villages (Eaton Bishop) where Sheila lived as a child and where her love of the countryside began. Even this far up, there are few bridges over the Wye, none, according to the OS, at Cannon Bridge. To avoid the Hereford bypass, we work our way through Bridge Sollers. Then roundabout, using a short section of Roman road to Eaton Bishop. Only four miles from Hereford and once a weekend resort, it is, today's *A Guide to Hereford* says 'well and truly lost among the lanes'. It is, in fact, a somewhat nondescript place, with very mixed housing on either side of one long road. We drive to and fro, back and forth, but Sheila has only the vaguest memory. She describes a house standing high above a crossroads overlooking a valley of delight with a brook threading through it. The first people we ask – and there are not many to ask – are recent arrivals and look blank. One last try is successful. 'Sounds as though what you want is down there, right and then right again. There's a stream there.' Even then Sheila doesn't immediately recognise it, but – yes – though the hedge has grown high and the old front gate is buried in vegetation, that's it. 'Goodness, we used to walk a long way,' she says. Apart from the hedge, everything looks smaller. It always does. But gradually memories come into focus, confirming what is said in *A Guide to Hereford*, a bulky but very readable village-by-village work by Michael Raven:

> Downhill, south-east of the church, is Ruckhall Mill, a charming group of white painted buildings in the wooded valley of the Cage Brook. All the buildings are now dwellings. The stream is crossed by a stone bridge. A limestone track leads through the woods to Tuck Mill, also now a residence and also painted white. A big, black goat glares at strangers. Just beyond the end of the track the Cage Brook joins the Wye. What a desirable location this is. On the heights of the steep northern side of the valley is an Iron-Age fort. It covers a triangular promontory, with a single rampart on the western boundary.

'That's more than I ever realised about it at the time,' says Sheila.

We have almost as much trouble extricating ourselves as we did in finding Eaton Bishop. Though we are so close to Hereford, this is deeper countryside than you'll find today in, say, South Devon. It is like going back in time... till I realise that one thing missing from much of the county is the once-familiar hop fields. Hops are still grown, but most have been grubbed up because of disease; EU regulations, or so I'm told.

The World of Victorian Spas

For the second time today, we fetch out a coin for the toll bridge at Whitney (it has been quite a circular tour) and head north through Kingston and a gap in Offa's Dyke out of what used to be Radnorshire and back into Wales. Immediately everything is on a grander scale, and different in lots of subtle ways. I'm less enthralled but more at home.

Tonight's hotel, I tell Sheila, might be the worst of the bunch, but I want to go back there for nostalgia's sake. It is the Metropole at Llandrindrod Wells, a sizeable spa town with a setting as inappropriate as Strathpeffer's north of Inverness, but which is obviously doing all right in the world.

'It's enormous,' says Sheila of the hotel. It looks even bigger when we are directed from the front door to the car park and through to the back entrance, noting a line of parked coaches. But it is very welcoming. Our freshly decorated bedroom is positively spacious, with sitting area and the wardrobe in a turret.

'Must have changed hands,' I mutter. The porter hears, and says not so. He reassures me it's been in the same family since I last stayed here in the 1950s, when only a third of the 150 bedrooms were in use as there was obviously deep crisis.

'They've had to work hard, but they're always ploughing back the profits. Hope you'll be comfortable.' Indeed we are. There's a long corridor to negotiate to the hotel's front, a nice touch being historic photographs and notices with interesting captions, while at reception they cheerfully photocopy a booklet, *The Story of the Metropole*, describing exciting early days followed by grim ones, use by the military, reopening in desperate conditions, survival and once again success. We hear of what is planned next for the huge building, the central part of which rises five storeys. With sixteen function rooms and suites, the hotel has become a popular conference centre in the middle of Wales and able to attract custom from north and south.

It is not the only tall, large building in Llandrindod Wells. Most have been cleaned and restored and many boast ornate cast-iron verandas. The Victorians came here en masse for cure and rest. When we walk down to the reVictorianised (they've coined a new word) railway station, there's an interesting notice about how visitors unable to find accommodation used to sleep on the platform. The town isn't that busy today, but does well enough with good publicity for a wide range of activities, the Victorian Festival (200 events in nine days) at the end of each August being especially lively. The station's signalbox is preserved in working order as a museum. There are some interesting private shops, a bicycle museum, good gardens and an abundance of colourful hanging baskets – and a fourteen-acre lake with fishing. As with the rest of the town, that was made in confident Victorian days when Llandrindod Wells was one of *the* places. Something of that confidence is echoed in today's fight for rather more than survival. You can't help liking it.

Next morning we walk round the lake, watching squirrels and ducks, then have coffee on the balcony of the refreshment room, where many customers arrive in wheelchairs. Outside the DYNION or gents', I'm amused by the pictogram of a man sitting as well as standing to show the facilities offered.

Llandrindod Wells, by the way, still has a spa of sorts, with complementary health centre, tearooms and heritage centre. The original spa building was burned down. Its six attendants in white coats used to serve 1,000 glasses daily of the curative water that had been forced up through fissures, having filtered down for a millennium. A notice outside today's Rock Park Spa quotes a doctor as saying of the waters: 'Their good effects are so conspicuous that they give the place a name in Europe... as yet I have not met with any of the same kind that surpasses those at Llandrindod.' It also tells us that a typical day would see people drinking saline at the spa after breakfast, chalybeate with meals and sulphur in the afternoon, with baths taken at suitable times in between, while 'for many conditions the application of heat, light, electric currents or massage was administered'. Tough people, those Victorians. I like the tale in the hotel's brochure of how, when a lion escaped from a circus and made toward a gentleman suffering from chronic rheumatism sitting alone outside, the chap made a miraculous dive for shelter. On leaving the town, he congratulated it for curing his problem, though he didn't think it was because of the waters.

> Let England boast Bath's crowded springs
> Llandrindod happier Cambria sings
> A greater, though more modern name
> By merit rising into fame

Llandrindod Wells is an excellent centre, too. The first place of interest within easy reach to come to mind is the great complex, set in the mountains, of the Elan reservoirs feeding Birmingham, seventy miles away, by gravity. Once visitors weren't exactly welcome. Now the Elan Valley Ranger Service runs programmes of walks, wildlife-watching, crafts and other events, some specially for children. Also handy are attractions such as the red kite country, long stretches of the Wye,

Thomas the museum shop and tearoom at Penybont, and lesser spas that have long intrigued me.

After coffee at the lake, we set out to visit three more Wells. First is workaday agricultural Builth Wells, from where we take an extremely narrow, wandering road to the south of the Ifron to Llangammarch Wells. Lloyd George was among the distinguished visitors who came for a cure, but any pretence of being taken seriously in the spa stakes must long have been abandoned. So, now on the north of the river alongside the Central Wales railway, to the larger Llanwrtyd-Wells, unlike the others hyphenated by the OS.

First stop is the railway station, beautifully restored and cared for with an abundance of flowers. But, once more, what nonsense. There's huge enthusiasm supporting the retention of this little-used route from Llanelli to Shrewsbury, the nearest you can get to going from south to north Wales without being forced into England. Because the train service is part of a standard franchise, it cannot be given extra support. So just four single-car trains a day use it. With so few over a long line, it is hard to provide them when most needed, so rail isn't a practical option for us today. Canals and cycleways, and even restored railway stations, can be for pleasure. But trains are for transport, and ne'er the twain shall mix. At least the line is now economically run. In earlier BR days there was dithering incompetence.

Llanwrtyd-Wells is small but has much to offer, including a choice of eating places. We opt for Welsh rarebit in an old-fashioned tearoom where everyone talks to everyone and we read and hear about some of the attractions. This place obviously had serious intentions in the Spa stakes, tall terraces telling of the number of visitors that must once have arrived. Studying a guide (in fact a small guide stuffed in one pocket of a cellophane folder, a short history in the other, with loose maps of walk routes and so on) we learn that there used to be *three* spas here. The oldest was the Dolecoed Wells, established when an eighteenth-century vicar discovered a well in his garden. A sufferer of scurvy, having seen a frog alive and well, he tried the water, and hey presto. The then Pont-rhyd-y-Fferau rapidly became the fashionable Llanwrtyd-Wells. It claims to be the smallest town in Britain.

After lunch we go to the visitor centre-cum-lively shop. There's an excellent video of the life of the red kite, the flagship attraction, coupled with all kinds of activities from cycle rides to participation in a festival of real ale to keep visitors active. And where else would the world bog snorkelling championships be messily fought? There's an astounding range of other wildlife and geological interest in surrounding mountains. It almost brings tears to my eyes seeing so small a place make the best of itself. I'll never think of this part of Wales again without regretting I didn't get to know Llanwrtyd-Wells sooner.

Neither England Nor Wales

We return to our hotel at Llandrindod Wells by the main road and then, it seems repeatedly going up and down, by the B4358 directly across the mountains to Newbridge-on-Wye. Next morning we head on northeast, for a short stay in Much Wenlock in Shropshire. Just one further treat on the way: Presteign. 'Neither in Wales nor in England but simply in Radnorshire,' said George Borrow. It is now just in Wales but certainly isn't at all Welsh or English in character. It thrives on a large catchment area ignoring the border. Like Borrow, in 1867, I was enchanted on my first visit years ago. It is historic with long, narrow streets, but more purposeful than quaint, the solid centre surprisingly large, and surrounds include a river walk. The locals, however, complain there are too many incomers, especially Midlanders escaping the rat race.

The main visitor draw is an award-winning Judge's Lodging, a painstakingly restored Victorian gas-lit town house with courtroom, cells and servants' quarters, and what was described as 'the most commodious and elegant apartments for a judge in all England and Wales'. Thanks to an audiopack round our necks, we go from room to room eavesdropping on Mary, the hardworking maid and other servants and the chairman of the magistrates. We conclude that circuit judges must have looked forward to coming here. We sit in their chair, in the courtroom, learn what is served for dinner tonight in the grand dining room, pump water in the kitchen and put ourselves in the dungeon. We can't fault the way it's done: the combination of period decorations and furnishings, the re-enactment of justice, and the constant window on life in the surrounding countryside. Yes, there is something special about what used to be Radnorshire. Bernard Shaw once said: 'No man ought to be in government of this land who does not spend three months of every year in country such as this.'

· X X X I V ·

S H R O P S H I R E   A N D
N O R T H   W A L E S

A Rip Van Winkle of a Town

It always surprises me how far east the Welsh border lies. For a variety of reasons, such as shopping, or to go by train from, say, Cardiff to Llandudno, people are forced into England. However, the Welsh border country is among Britain's loveliest, and there is no hardship in exploring a corner before returning to the Principality.

As I said earlier, passionately though I love Wales, I couldn't live in it. Though I'd surely miss the sea, I could happily settle in Hereford or Shropshire. There is unspoilt beauty that is rare today, and many of the people hold tight to their independent way of thinking. But Shropshire's geological diversity – there's hardly a typical piece of it – is totally different from Hereford's gentler variation on a unifying theme that reminds one of Elgar's Enigma Variations. In a pub I once heard two men, one from each side, heatedly discussing the rival merits. The fellow from Hereford was drinking cider; the Shropshire man beer. The verbal battle raged, each giving the impression he'd rather be dead than move across the border. Hereford was quieter, soothing, civilised with lots of culture, said the chap from there.

'Anyone would think we're cannibals in Shropshire,' replied the other. 'You only have to take the train through both of them to see which God made.'

As we approach Ludlow, a place I've often fancied for a long retreat, I see the Shropshire man's point of view. Though the whole train journey through the countryside bordering Wales offers a visual feast, the pièce de resistance is undoubtedly in Shropshire. Admiring Ludlow's magic setting and ancient roof lines, I recall great journeys on the West of England to Manchester and Liverpool expresses that used to come this way. They commanded the longest stretch of top-class views of any main line in England, certainly any that didn't climb into the mountains.

The morning express north was especially delightful, since at the front was a Newton Abbot-based engine, in steam days a Castle, driven by Newton men all the way to Shrewsbury. My gardener, an engine driver until made redundant along with other fine fellows who lived and breathed their work, often told me about the challenge of the run to the most distant point worked from his shed. Having been brought up to believe that nothing was as good as Devon, the Newton men were amazed by the scenery at Ludlow and especially around Church Stretton, with Wenlock Edge on one side and the climb up to The Long Mynd on the other. One can still enjoy the scenery by train, especially dramatic through Church Stretton with escarpments on either side.

This morning at Craven Arms we turn right into what is now a railwayless land, with views up the steep, partly wooded hillside to Wenlock Edge, to reach a place new to me: Much Wenlock. The Raven Hotel's brochure sounds good: a fine coaching inn combined with ancient almshouses and a mediaeval hall, privately owned, only fifteen rooms finished to a high standard, a restaurant awarded two AA rosettes overlooking an inner courtyard. Though it doesn't look much from the outside, not at least in comparison with surrounding black-and-white buildings, here is a real find. If there's a disappointment, it is that all the other staying guests (though not those coming for meals) are business people, for it is convenient for Telford, an artificial conglomeration of industry and housing I try to avoid. Perhaps the best things to come from it are Agas. That they are more a way of life than mere cookers in Shropshire speaks more for the county's character than the convenience of supply.

Yet it is much better to have concentrated development in a new town than spoil Much Dewchurch and other small country centres. If it is preserved artificially, then blest be good planning. Much Dewchurch remains a jewel, flourishing on the continuity of having its feet in the soil.

To experience Shropshire fully, one must indeed revel in its earthiness, including that of its literature. AE Housman's elegiac poetry in *A Shropshire Lad* and Mary Webb's novels, especially *Precious Bane* and *Gone to Earth*, reek of the soil and what it means to man. It is not just the deeply rural settings, but the relationship between the land and the human body's short, often harsh and prematurely terminated existence, that question elemental values and makes these works so compelling. Like most who first discovered it when young, I found *Precious Bane* lovely yet deeply disturbing, while the later *Gone to Earth*, probably with more skill, 'explores the suffering which comes with adult sexuality, as individuals who have found their own tenuous unity with the patterns and rhythms of a nature larger than themselves'. The quote is from Erika Duncan's moving introduction in Virago Modern Classics.

I feel compelled to seek a bookshop for local colour and find it a walk of only a few feet from the hotel. Wenlock Books is a treasure trove of books and cards. There's even the video of the restored and digitally re-mastered Powell & Presburger's *Gone to Earth*. Like all today's commercial videos, it contains dire copyright warnings, yet – sadly – the very existence of Mary Webb isn't acknowledged. Every word on the packaging is about the producers and actors of what is indeed a beautiful film in technicolour. How can they ignore the author?

Much Wenlock seems to have many claims to fame. The Olympic Games were invented here. 'A Rip Van Winkle of a place that has remained asleep since the Middle Ages', is one description. While the sun shines we set out along Wilmore Street, going through the Guildhall's pavement arches, which means we have to cross the road to take a better look at the sixteenth-century building in which the town council still meets. Another guide describes it as 'sitting pretty on sturdy oak columns in the middle of the Butter Market'.

That has us backtracking to the nineteenth century Market Hall with its museum and information bureau. 'Mind you keep your eyes open,' says a friendly assistant. 'Datestones, gas lamp standards, cowhouses and pig sties as well as the obvious.' There is a large parish church, and the tall ruins, including the virtually intact end wall, with five tiers of windows, of the priory built in the twelfth and thirteenth centuries over Milburga's Abbey, in a sylvan setting in a slight hollow.

Certainly we enjoy the mixture of Jacobean, Tudor and other buildings. But the liveliness of the shops and social life prevent Much Wenlock from becoming just a period piece. Only a few of those on the crowded afternoon pavements are tourists, though how many come from Telford, to buy the things we see on sale here that can't be found everywhere, it is hard to say. The pubs are busy, too, in the case of the large timber-framed Talbot Inn, no doubt non-stop for centuries. Opposite there's another large, timber-framed Raynald's Mansion, where the guide book has us looking out for the post and bar between doors used as a porter's rest to help lift loads on to his back, and the telltale hooks and bars over the windows and doors that show a butcher once traded here. So one could go on. Much Wenlock is much agreeable, as is a snooze and read of some of this afternoon's purchases before our pre-dinner drink. Then, at bedtime, we read aloud one of Housman's best-known poems:

On Wenlock Edge the wood's in trouble;
His forest fleece the Wrekin heaves;
The gale, it plies the saplings double,
And thick on Severn snow the leaves.

'Twould blow like this through holt and hanger
When Uricon the city stood:
'Tis the old wind in the old anger,
But then it threshed another wood.

Then, 'twas before my time, the Roman
At yonder heaving hill would stare:
The blood that warms as English Yeoman,
The thoughts that hurt him, they were there.

There, like the wind through woods in riot,
Through him the gale of life blew high;
The tree of man was never quiet:
Then 'twas the Roman, now 'tis I.

The gale, it plies the saplings double,
It blows so hard, 'twill soon be gone:
Today the Roman and his trouble
Are ashes under Uricon.

Wenlock Edge and the Long Mynd

Ridge walks have special attraction, and the one along the crest of the high ground of Wenlock Edge is well signposted and quickly leads into a nearby forgotten world. Alone on Wenlock's top couldn't be more pleasurable. Where else do you find so many unspoilt copses or hidden gems of black-and-white houses, or hear such silence? It is actually the lyrical blowing of the trees that edits out the sound of most distant traffic, just as the sea does at home. For us it is only a tease of a walk for, as always on these trips, time presses. And the one thing that we don't discover on foot is a view down the Edge's limestone escarpment, which runs SW to NE for the best part of twenty miles. High we may feel, but we're not above the tree line, and there's an almost continuous wood running along a lower strip of the Edge. Wenlock Edge feels quite different when one is on it than viewing it from the northwest. For really open heights we would be better on The Long Mynd, unchanged for centuries, above the tree line with the turf stretched over the pre-Cambrian Rock, except where the naked crags break through to add drama.

Just after the Pedlar's Rest, we descend through the wooded Stretton Batch into Hope Dale, pass through that woodland at the Edge's bottom and, crossing the closed railway that romantically brought the Victorian tourists up the Edge on their way to Much Wenlock, come out into open country. In the V running NNE from Craven Arms, we pause roughly equidistant from Wenlock Edge and The Long Mynd. Having spent so much time beyond Hadrian's Wall and in the unconquered far West Country, it surprises me to realise the Romans were here in force. But the beauty of this landscape is that, while there are superb black-and-white houses and literary associations galore, and the National Trust is a major landowner, there are no crowd-drawing tourist attractions. In August we have the lanes almost to ourselves.

By a minor lane we emerge at the village of Rushbury, in the dale at the foot of Wenlock Edge which protects it from the east winds. There is ample of evidence of earlier man, including what are thought to be the remains of a Roman fort. Near the mainly Norman church is what is left of a more ancient mound. The name Rushbury implies a fortified place in the marsh. We pause by one of those delectable Shropshire black-and-white manor houses, but our destination is the Old Rectory, 1840s mock-Gothic, and part of a perfect set-piece together with the church and school.

Preserver and Restorer Extraordinaire

Sir Neil Cossons comes out to meet us. My memories of him are mainly as a young man, for example swotting, away from children, in his garage for his MA. He wrote books for me jointly with a number of other authors leading the industrial archaeological movement of the 1960s, anxious to ensure that sufficient of our great industrial heritage would be saved as well as understood. Then he was commissioned to produce the *BP Book of Industrial Archaeology*. By that time his career was well into its stride, and my regular phone calls grumbling about late completion must have been irritating. The delay was worthwhile, for what emerged was the best single-volume survey and gazetteer still in regular use. Many years later, Neil took me round Iron Bridge when he was curator at that famous gorge museum. Even more time has elapsed since our paths last crossed. Old friendship easily revived, we carry our coffee from the kitchen to the lounge, then go out to the garden fully to enjoy the views. It's quite a garden, too. Work has just finished on restoring the mediaeval pond which, in monastic style, supplied fresh fish to the Manor House.

After a succession of jobs many would die for, Neil is now chairman of English Heritage and the Waterways Trust. How did it all start? At Beeston station, the first out of Nottingham on the Derby line. For six consecutive summers he worked as a junior porter, writing in black crayon the depot number by which parcels were to be routed, and loading local ones into what in those days the railways called 'road motors'.

'Starting at the bottom was great experience, £3 18s 6d a week. A great eye-opener being on the station platform wondering about attitudes, why things were done the way they were, and seeing them begin to change. It still gives me many of my folk memories about people.'

His career as preserver and restorer extraordinaire took its first practical step when, at university as a geography student, he participated in a day-long tour of Glasgow's tramway system just before its closure. The students hired car No 1055, which had been transferred from Liverpool. Not content with that, they raised £50 to purchase the vehicle which now runs on the Criche Tramway Museum's line in Derbyshire.

His first full-time job was with the original Great Western Museum at Swindon, but he reminds me it wasn't until he became curator of technology at Bristol Museum in 1964 that we first met. After a period as deputy director of Liverpool Museum, he took charge at Iron Bridge Gorge in 1971. 'There was a great kick in that, taking it almost from the start to a world-class museum.' In fact it is a whole series of museums and displays, within a complex embracing several miles of the Severn, with the humped Iron Bridge – now a symbol of Britain's industrial achievement – as centrepiece.

Following another regular author, Neil then became director of the National Maritime Museum at Greenwich. In 1986, he started what turned out to be the longest period that anyone has directed the Science Museum, opening the new west wing just before retiring. Now he is two years into a five-year stint as chairman of English Heritage. Though sometimes controversial, especially about the antics of railway enthusiasts, it has always seemed to me that he is driven by common sense. The raison d'être for museums is always in the centre of his perspective. And life is not too office-bound. He goes to New Zealand every year, and he and his wife Veronica love their home. 'We kept this house after my years at Iron Bridge, though it means a lot of travelling. In summer when I come home on the Welsh Border line, I think how lucky I am.'

Yes, he realises, English Heritage hasn't always had a good reputation. Politics were once larger than life. 'It's a lot more regular and open now, but don't underestimate the achievements there have always been on the ground.' Turning to canals, he says that remarks about his time on the Waterways Board would 'be unprintable'. But: 'look on the bright side, canals are being restored at a faster rate than they were ever built. We're even building the first new canal for the best part of two centuries, the Ribble Link which makes it possible to boat across the country from the Trent & Mersey. Under the Waterways Trust, there's incredible activity. The chief executive, Robin Evans, who used to head the Landmark Trust, is often on the phone. There are good relations all round. In five years things have been transformed.'

624

Neil lives and breathes the industrial revolution, talks about the practical uses of history and the role of museums. He is thrilled that so many British historic industrial centres are already recognised as World Heritage Sites: Blaenavon; New Lanark of Robert Owen fame on the Clyde; the Arkwright Mills in Derbyshire's Derwent Valley; Saltaire, the model textile factory and its housing at Bradford in Yorkshire; and Iron Bridge Gorge in Coalbrookdale, where it all began with Abraham Darby's furnace. There might be one more industrial World Heritage Site yet. On the list there's Pont-d Cysyllte Aquaduct on the Llangollen Canal, the Forth Railway Bridge, and the Great Western main line from Paddington to Bristol. Though he doesn't say so, methinks the latter might be his choice. Come to think about it, he was also on the committee under the chairmanship of Sir Arthur Elton (mentioned in chapter 6) that used to discuss the future of Brunel's Temple Meads terminus at Bristol. 'It just shows you how attitudes have changed. Nobody would contemplate knocking down something like that now. Today, of course, the train shed houses the Museum of British Empire.'

Time runs out, so he comes with us to The Raven for lunch. Veronica is with her sister in Leicester helping with the opening of their garden to the public. Two Japanese men come into the conservatory for lunch. Are they here to do business in Telford, or to study the history of the industrial revolution? These days what was achieved at Coalbrookdale is probably better taught to students in Japan than Britain.

A Stroll through Gardening History

Shropshire is renowned for its gardens, formal and less so, famous and specialist. There's much excitement in today's newspaper about the unfolding detail of the discovery of the only fourteenth-century garden yet found: beside the dramatic castle ruins and moat of what was once a massive fortress, three miles from Oswestry. For our own glimpse back in gardening time, we drive most of the way to Bridgnorth to keep an appointment with Dr Katherine Swift, one of the most unusually gifted gardening writers of our day.

Over introductory tea, in company with three cats, she talks about human frailty and transience, suggesting we should go along with, rather than fight, our garden. 'Perfection in a garden is bought at a price,' she says, adding that on a recent visit by her landlord, the National Trust, they laughed at her garden. 'They couldn't understand my colour scheme. As though that's everything!'

What Katherine has done is create an historic garden, or rather series of small gardens reflecting the flavour of different periods. If it's untidy in places, so is much human endeavour. We are at the Dower House Garden of Morville Hall, where a Benedictine monastery once stood, though there seem to have been earlier homes and gardens on the site.

'I came to Shropshire to make a garden because of my father. He and my mother ran away to Shropshire on holiday together in one of those last summers before the war, having known one another for only three weeks. They spent their time walking on Wenlock Edge and reading poetry. Pa's view of Shropshire was highly coloured by Housman. Then, going south, he moved from place to place, job to job, and my childhood was tinged with tales from Housman and his longing for those remembered hills, the land of his lost content. It was sixty years before he came back, over eighty, and soon to become ill. I'm glad he had a little time to celebrate being here. In childhood, I remember how he was always planting trees, never staying long enough in one place to see them mature, always the romantic, taking walks in the spirit of Coleridge.' Remember the Greek saying? 'A society grows great when old men plant trees whose shade they know they shall never sit in.'

Her father is obviously still a powerful influence. In the literary gardening quarterly *Hortus*, her 'Morville Hours' are strangely moving. She writes of a time spent on the Fens:

> On Saturdays Pa worked in Lincoln, twenty-odd miles away, following the raised causeway of Roman Ermine Street along the high scarp of the Lincoln Edge, the rich black soil of the fens lapping like an inland sea at its foot. For my brother and I, this was often an excuse for an outing, showing visitors around Castle or Cathedral ('See the Lincoln Imp up there? There!') for sixpence, quickly spent in the second-hand bookshops of Steep Hill; climbing the towers of village churches (which never seemed then to be locked) on the way back; scrambling up the grassy ramparts of Iron Age forts or looking for fossils in the sandy north-Lincolnshire soil; and often Pa would dig a promising-looking sapling out of the hedgerow and take it home. Ash, elm, oak, gradually the little front gardens would fill with trees. The next tenant almost invariably cut them all down. They weren't sensible gardens, gardens grounded in the here and now: they were I think a dream of what a garden should be if only one had a little more room, a memory perhaps of woods and moors, a lost Eden.

Now she writes a weekly piece for *The Times*, is involved in books, and says that her husband Ken, an antiquarian bookseller in Ludlow, holds D&C in high regard and would love to meet me. In academic life in Oxford and then Dublin, she herself became an expert on the antiquarian book trade at the end of the 17th and start of the eighteenth century. One of her papers is on Huguenot book auctions in London.

'Garden while ye may,' seems to be her motto. Explaining she has no help beyond grass cutting and edging, she leads the way out. We know our place and follow behind Grace, the apricot and pale grey cat, who of course doesn't admit she's intrigued with visitors, but frequently overtakes us, tail erect.

'The garden is an academic exercise,' she says. 'I've written about the geology of Orkney. With its old red sandstone this part of Shropshire is a bit similar. The yew hedges aren't part of the history, but just separate the different gardens. There's a thousand feet of them. We sell the yew clippings to help make ends meet.' Then, after we begin to realise how much hard work has gone into this garden in the last dozen years, the stunner: 'You know, we only have a lease here for another five years. But if it all gets ploughed up, that's the nature of gardening. Nothing on earth is forever.'

Meanwhile we trace the footsteps of ancient man through the turf maze, see how an Elizabethan gentleman would have made his knot garden, stroll through the narrow canal garden with box-edged plantes-bandes recalling the time of William and Mary, and take in the old-fashioned scents of roses and peonies in the Victorian rose garden.

'All done from seeds and cuttings, a lot self-sown. I don't do weeding. See that? That's Old Blush which came from China in the 1780s, the first repeat flowering rose in Europe.'

I'm especially interested in the ornamental and the fruit and vegetable gardens with old varieties and curious survivals. There's an incredible amount squeezed into just one and a half acres and well worth exploring when on certain days it opens to visitors in summer. Could the National Trust possibly be so crass as to plough it up? Yesterday, probably; with new enlightenment, hopefully not today.

To the Cambrian Coast

Especially on journeys between the Severn estuary and the Cambrian Coast and Snowdonia, over the years I've criss-crossed Wales by innumerable routes. Most have involved sections of main roads, between the treat of minor roads through sparsely populated, often mountainous country. I recall great glimpses of the route ahead, seeming to fall off one mountain, then running through lush though still pretty empty farming country, before winding its tortuous way up the next steep hill... and not another car in sight. The map begs to be used creatively in Mid and North Wales. Such journeys are relaxing fun. Beyond seeing the occasional billboard, waving at an odd tractor driver or farmer driving his sheep along the road, and at bedtime reading up about the places passed through, maybe one doesn't experience much of local life, but nothing beats the sheer joy of landscape.

The map suggests conflicting ideas for today. We'll decide on the hoof. First we have to skirt around Shrewsbury, entertaining ourselves with our different memories of that ancient town of steep streets as we negotiate the roundabouts of the dual carriageway section of the A5. By casting vote, that is to say one of us feeling more strongly than the other, we stick to the A5, heading NW toward that colourful piece of Wales within England, Oswestry. Before we reach it, I say 'enough of main roads,' and dive into a little-known land of twisty lanes, green fields in the valleys, woods on mountain foothills and unpronounceable village names nearly all beginning with Ll. At Penybontfawr, the exception, we turn SW and climb a deserted mountain before dropping down through woods to Llanwddyn and running along the northern shore of Lake Vyrnwy.

If farmers are struggling for survival, you wouldn't know it from this very mixed journey. Land and homes are well kept. Carefully placed hardwood trees grace many a close-up scene, though the mass, climbing further away, are conifers. Tourism might have helped a little, for some cottages have been tarted up as holiday homes. Yet pride and caring must have the greatest influence on the landscape. Will the farmers who are its custodians always be able to follow that? Yes, suggests a local I buttonhole outside a well-kept public convenience. He doesn't need encouragement to air his mind. 'It's like this. Many people are playing at farming. They wouldn't know how to survive if their life depended on it. They're townspeople whose bank accounts are fat enough to keep up the appearances. How they earn their real money, well that I wouldn't know... computing or something, property perhaps. Anyway, they can afford to bribe the view where they live. That's what's happening.'

His final words say it all: 'They mean well.'

The lake is actually one of those reservoirs I described earlier as set like a gem. It's rather a big, one might say vulgar, gem, seven kilometres long, a full kilometre wide, with a showpiece miniature mock-French chateau. That's actually a straining tower as in filtering, reached only by officials across a causeway. When new in 1892, this was the largest reservoir in Europe, needing up to 1,000 men to build it. A village was drowned. Nearly all the banks are wooded; in a generous car park, where there's a very tame chaffinch looking for a take-away lunch, is a seat carved out of an oak. Though not when the reservoir was opened back in the 1880s to supply Liverpool, today the public is warmly welcome... by the Severn Trust in partnership with the Severn Trent water company.

It isn't only the chaffinch who is hungry. We follow directions to the Lakeview Tearoom. Its outside isn't appealing, and later we watch several cars turn back when their occupants aren't impressed. Inside, though with a curious semi-temporary extension, the building's core is fine, the welcome warm... providing you're a genuine customer. 'No sightseers, no eating in your car, no exceptions,' warns a notice in the car park. By the toilet are dire threats to any non-customer fancying free use. The long menu caters for all tastes and, once our bona fide status is confirmed, there's nice flexibility. When we say we'll share a soup and baguette, we receive separate mini-portions of each. The evening meals sound inviting; there's obviously a captive market among campers and those in holiday cottages.

The sun shines on the lake as we brave a stiff breeze to rejoin the car. Going around the tail of the lake, we take a narrow, unfenced road climbing steeply up to higher ground into really wild Wales. Not having spotted the view symbol on the OS map, we're totally unprepared for the grandeur, the majesty and sheer complexity of the panorama at the first road junction. Ten arrows on the map show the steepness of the road descending to the left. We turn right, the direction of the view symbol, quickly pausing to take in the spectacle of the many-tiered mountains, whose greenness after a wet early summer is emphasised by an overall grey-greeny mist. The mountains seem to rise in everlasting perpetuity, lost in the distant haze. And down there is a shimmering Bala Lake. How well I remember my first journey alongside that, my feet on a newspaper on the opposite seat of the otherwise empty front compartment, the window open on a hot day with occasional smoke from the rhythmic engine adding to the enjoyment. The old railway line from Ruabon to Barmouth has long been closed, but another spur-of-the-moment decision: having come off the high ground, I dash into the car park at Llanuwchllyn railway station, HQ of a new narrow-gauge Bala Lake Railway. Today's journey is very different: there are no fewer than six kids in the front carriage making their first-ever train trip. Bala Lake, though, is unchanged.

Sheila waits with the car at the Bala end, and off we go once more, through pretty Bala town and around a smaller lake. Our immediate direction is now indicated by the tall bulk of Trawsfynydd atomic power station. How they crop up at otherwise remote spots. Then into the Vale of Ffestiniog, till at Minffordd the traffic is near-stationary and we presume there's been an accident. After half an hour, the cause of the hold up is clear. The toll of a few coppers is being collected by a not very fast keeper unable to resist exchanging occasional remarks with his mate taxing traffic in the other direction. A gift of say twenty pounds properly applied would have cleared up the whole mess! Across the embankment or cobb built by Madocks that gave Portmadock its original English spelling, we see the new cycleway bridge that John Grimshaw in Bristol spoke about. Then with a glimpse of the famous Ffestiniog Harbour railway station, through Porthmadog's inferior high street, where nearly all the locals speak Welsh, past Criccieth's coastal castle and the Lloyd George Museum, and we are in Pwllheli. This little place grows on me, its pretty harbour and shops in its narrow streets harmoniously serving both visitor and local needs.

But when, a few miles further on, we reach our hotel, Plas Bodegroes, on the Nefyn road, we're warned that most of the pubs in Pwllheli are dives. Built as a house in 1780 on the low-lying plain that a few centuries earlier had been sea, this hotel (opened 1986) sets entirely new standards for a district not renowned for quality hospitality. Our room and service are of the highest order; a pub – dive or otherwise – in Pwllheli, would jar with this. Dinner is a perfect end to a day that will be well remembered. We wish we had time to test the hotel's claim that the Lleyn Peninsula is 'one of Britain's loveliest places', with a Heritage coastline, great beaches and historic churches dating from the days of pilgrims to Bardsey Island 'of twenty thousand Welsh saints'.

Living Monument to the Success of Edward I

Next morning, a showery Sunday, we cross what I had always thought was an entirely flat Lleyn Peninsula to the coast north of Nefyn, and take the road to Caernarfon. So much for assumptions: the coast road forces us inland with a major hill, if not mountain, Yr Eifl, between us and the sea. The road itself has to ascend and descend a steep hill. That is what I like most about Wales: it is seldom predictable, and nor are its people. During today, we meet those who are most friendly, and those who respond to a query by talking to someone else in Welsh.

Bilingual signposting doesn't help navigation, and I wonder how much political correctness actually deters tourism. The dual headings and text boxes of guide books quickly become irritating. There are German and French editions of publicity leaflets, but English is presumed to mean a mixture of English and Welsh. I'm all in favour of encouraging the retention of local languages but, if separate leaflets were printed in Welsh, nobody would read them, and so expose artificiality. The Welsh nearly all prefer their reading in English, as in their daily paper. Welsh is a language of speech – and singing.

There's a delightful stretch beside a calm sea, patches lit up by sunshine before Caernarfon, where a chatty attendant at the car park under the mighty castle wants to know our personal history and views on Wales. He's an incomer with his own opinions: 'Nice people if you aren't targeted by them.' A car-boot sale is being set up on part of the park, while successive groups board small cruisers for a trip along the Menai Strait separating Anglesey from the mainland. The scene becomes even more animated when the whistle of an old locomotive announces the arrival of a train at the car park's extremity and people hasten to the temporary station.

Of our rail journey, more in a moment. When back from it, we drive over the eastern of the pair of road bridges on to the island of even more impossible place names than the rest of North Wales. Sheila says she'd like to return by Llanfairpwllgwyngyll where, years ago, she bought a commemorative lengthy platform ticket ending in gogogoch.

Anglesey has many unspoilt villages, headlands and harbours, but I'm about to get another surprise. Sheila has arranged to meet a distant relative at a hotel at Beaumaris. The drive, partly through woods but also with interesting buildings, along the Menai Strait's north shore opposite the university town of Bangor, is beautiful, but Beaumaris seems like a piece of county-style England planted here. The antique shops, hotels and restaurants are full of smartly-dressed people with posh accents. The place is so busy that we have to complete a circle along the seafront, with its fine Georgian terrace designed by Hansom of the Hansom cab, and back through the main street, several times before finding a parking space on the grass. Hundred and hundreds of people are out enjoying what has turned into a lovely day. Then I read that Beaumaris (pronounced Biwmares) is an artificial creation, a living monument to the success of Edward I, who hoped to attract English settlers when he cleared out the original inhabitants to make way for his new castle. The reverse of ethnic cleansing. Now there are plenty of Welsh-born enjoying good business and employment here. There's more to see and do than in all the rest of the island; and more good catering establishments, too.

In mid-afternoon the Bulkeley Arms Hotel is heaving. Battalions of waiters dashing about serving both English and Welsh county types finishing their lunches in the restaurant, coffee shop, bar and assorted alcoves. Cakes for afternoon tea are laid out by the main entrance where you might expect to find reception. You make your choice, pay at reception which is further into the hotel, and tea is brought when the waitress susses where you are in which lounge. It is as though this was some special one-off day of celebration, but it is just an ordinary Sunday. Having had a small sandwich for lunch on our train trip, we enjoy afternoon tea, especially with the sunny view across the Strait. There is sand in front of the mainland shore, the mountains of Snowdonia rising beyond. Looking north, we can see Llandudno, and the Great Orme Head. Occasional boats are plying between the piers of Beaumaris and Llandudno. Many more are on the water for purely local sails.

Beaumaris is somewhere you either know or you don't. Many obviously come on day trips from parts of North Wales. It must be especially pleasant for those staying overnight when the trippers have gone home.

Then past a delightful cluster of historic pubs at the village named after the Menai Bridge, around the roundabout at the approach to the original bridge with its familiar twin towers supporting gently-curved suspension cables, and back to the mainland by the new bridge incorporated into the railway one. Stephenson's ugly tube bridge deprives train passengers of a view of the Strait. Years ago the tube's tar-base internal lining was accidentally set on fire by boys looking for bats. Holyhead, the port for Wales, was temporarily without trains.

On our way back to Caernarfon, we take a diversion to Portdinorwic, where half a century ago I recall seeing the quays, cut deeply inland, busy with the transhipment of slate. Now gentrification with luxury flats is in full swing.

The Little Trains of Wales

The narrow-gauge railways of North West Wales are a legend, mechanically fascinating and, in several eras, a great commercial success. Few tourist labels have drawn warmer response than the Little Trains of Wales. As a boy, I read about the wartime demise of several of them, and among the first railway books that gripped me was a classic *Narrow-Gauge Railways in North Wales*, by Charles E Lee, whose foreword explained:

> The great slate district of North Wales developed the narrow-gauge railway to meet the needs of its heavy concentrated loads, but this was merely adopting what had been done for centuries in Central European mines. It chanced, however, that a family of engineering genius [the Spooners] became involved in the work, and the result was a movement which affected most parts of the world.

Steam on 2ft-gauge that could be laid economically, even in the toughest of territory, was, to cite the name of one locomotive, *Little Wonder*. It wasn't lightweight engineering, but perfection of track and rolling stock in miniature. To begin with, few people thought it could be achieved; George Stephenson said it was impossible. Practical experiment and ingenuity, largely provided by the Spooner family, proved otherwise.

There were once many slate lines, winding down from the high quarries to the nearest port. Some had the same 2ft-gauge; others a unique gauge of their own. Each was very much a self-governing affair. Workmen were carried to quarries, where in some cases they camped for the working week. A few also encouraged general passengers and tourists. The busiest were also among the least known. Penrhyn Railway, developed and owned by Lord Penrhyn, carried prodigious quantities of slate from the quarries high above Bethesda to Port Penrhyn near Bangor where long quays were developed. The Padarn

Railway, running from the Dinorwic slate quarries at Llanberis to Portdinorwic, had a unique 4ft-gauge, but at the quarries the standard Welsh narrow-gauge of 2ft was used. Two lines of 2ft-gauge tracks were carried on the 4ft ones down to the port.

All but one of the narrow-gauge lines, from Aberystwyth to Devil's Bridge, which became part of British Railways, eventually closed. But still the books about them came pouring out, for heavy engineering in miniature stirs tremendous interest. Added to that the individualistic lines ran through great scenery.

Then the voluntary railway movement was born, led by LTC Rolt on the Talyllyn running down to Tywyn. His *Railway Adventure* is the classic tale of resurrection by amateurs, a movement which spread steadily to other routes. Mother of all restoration schemes was that of the Ffestiniog, on which *Little Wonder* had run. The tale of how trains once more fought their way up the mountainside is itself a colourful piece of history. The core happening was the winning of big compensation from the Central Electric Generating Board, which had drowned the route where it ran through a tunnel. A famous group called the Deviationists conceived and built a higher line reached by a spiral but also needing a new tunnel. Other lines have been rescued or are still in the act of being brought back to life. And there are newcomers.

Nothing is more extraordinary that the resurrection of the Welsh Highland Railway, with which the Ffestiniog used to link at Porthmadog. Partly built on earlier slate tramways, it ended up as a tourist line – from Porthmadog to Dinas, where it met the standard-gauge. It collapsed in the mid-1930s. For two-and-a-half generations enthusiasts have been driving alongside part of the old route in the Aberglaslyn Pass, where trains used to dive into tunnels through the rocks, regretting that too much was demolished to make restoration ever possible.

The impossible is happening. Soon there will be trains again, serving today's vastly greater market of explorers and walkers. Having at first rejected the idea, and after major battles, Snowdonia National Park backs the scheme as a means of encouraging people to come into the Park's core without their cars. Once more the narrow railway will be an attractive feature of the landscape. There have been all kinds of fundraising, and will be for some years yet. The turning point was Millennium funding kicking in with a few million pounds.

So here we are at the edge of the car park under Caernarfon Castle to catch a train on what in practice is a brand-new railway, a 2ft-gauge route which, with when joined to the Ffestiniog, will stretch all the way to Blaenau Ffestiniog: a three-and-a-half hour journey through world-class scenery.

A small crowd gathers at the temporary station, since Caernarfon hasn't yet decided on permanent arrangements. We set out on the trackbed of the long-closed standard-gauge line from Bangor, turning sharply inland at Dinas Junction, on to the Welsh Highland's old route. Sharp curves mean that now and then we can see the front and back of the long train, carrying several hundred people. Most passengers are just taking the journey for pleasure, though some are planning walks or cycling when they alight. Refreshments are brought to our seat: this is the life. Most remarkable on the 2ft-gauge is the size of the engine: South African No 143. Wheel arrangement 2.6.2+2.6.2T, if that means anything to you. It is vast, the central unit fed by large tanks at either end, the whole thing articulated so it can negotiate the sharp curves. Clearances are tight, so drivers cannot swing their seat outside, from where it used to be driven in South Africa. When I go to admire it at today's terminus of Waunfawr, the driver complains he 'can't see what lies ahead'. That apart, things are going brilliantly, and the once-suspicious people of Waunfawr have thoroughly accepted the 'little' train. Local businesses have benefited, and there are cheap resident tickets for shopping trips.

Passengers disperse and then re-gather for the return trip. At Dinas Junction, where the scale of activities emphasises that this is Britain's greatest railway restoration, we cross a Vintage Train of historic carriages.

Later, on our way by car to Porthmadog, we stop to watch the railhead actually being extended on the section beyond Waunfawr. Though the trackbed (treated against Japanese knotweed) is prepared by contractors, fitting the track is done by volunteers. You can tell from the cameras hanging round their necks that they are a pretty dedicated set. Chris Gorring, for example, has come all the way from Sydney. 'A world-class achievement, great common sense,' he says before helping push another rail on a slung truck along a temporary piece of track.

The road and railway route run more or less together for most of the rest of the way to Beddgelert. I wonder if they will have a lady stationmaster in Welsh dress there as they did until the line closed in the 1930s? Through the Pass of Aberglasyn, with the route to be restored running through the tunnels of mainly unlined rock, I can't count the days before it is possible to make the journey I dreamed about to keep sane in an air raid in the cellar in 1941.

To Porthmadog Harbour station next morning for coffee in the Spooner Café with Tim Davies, corporate and public affairs manager of both the Ffestiniog and Welsh Highland. 'We market them together and separately,' he says. 'There's a lot of engineering co-operation, and eventually rolling stock will be joint, but because of the Ffestiniog's narrow clearances, locomotives won't be able to run from end to end of the combined system.' He talks about the tight controls imposed by the National Park. There are already signs that the Welsh Highland will play a fuller part in local life than does the Ffestiniog.

Attracting an annual half-million visitors, the Ffestiniog has long been a major employer, now of 75 staff, 50 full time. 'But Porthmadog doesn't want to have anything to do with us.' There's been a long history of uneasy relationships. In the 1920s there was near-mutiny at Boston Lodge, the historic loco and carriage sheds and engineering centre just across the embankment or cobb on which the railway runs at a much higher level than the road. The line was then controlled by a distant and peppery Col Stephenson, who ran an empire of down-and-out railways and extolled the virtues of riding on British steel behind engines powered by British coal. And now again there's trouble, in the Boardroom, with resignations.

Time to join Sheila on the curved platform. We walk to the front to wait for our Vintage Train of mainly Victorian coaches. In it we sit looking out to the west while others clamber over the central division to sit back to back with us. This train terminates at my favourite of all stations, Tan-y-Bwlch, set in the trees with a long island platform, again curved, where the route makes a sharp U-turn. There's just time for a walk down to the lake and back before joining a sizeable crowd on the platform. The whistles of the engines of trains approaching in either direction echo through the hills, while the engine of the Vintage Train simmers in the siding. Double Fairlies, a central driving cab between two separate engines, bring their long rakes of well-loaded carriages to a gentle stand. Cameras click. The guards unlock the doors to allow passengers in and out; keeping them locked in transit, because there is so little space in the cuttings and tunnel, is a Ffestiniog tradition. So, especially on the return trip, is looking down from the railway's high vantage point, a ledge cut out of rock, to the widening estuary of Afon Dwyryd.

Blaenau Ffestiniog and the Slate Industry

Next day we return at Tan-y-Bwlch to travel up the rest of the line to Blaenau Ffestiniog. Though full of railway interest, including the spiral to gain height and the run through the new tunnel above Tanygrisiau reservoir, this is the bleaker part of the journey. Cottages are on offer at Blaenau Ffestiniog for £15K. Though a nice lump of slate ceremoniously records the town's debt to the stuff, with its closed shops and down-and-out cottages, Blaenau is not a happy place. Depression is made worse by a cold wind and the fact that the real railway with which the Ffestiniog connects here is on strike. But no doubt those going off to the slate mine will enjoy their underground trip and commemorative photograph. We recall it as a fascinating experience, well done.

It is curious to think this former industrial town is in the Snowdonia National Park, the largest and most visited in Wales. What would have happened had the National Park been in existence in the nineteenth century... or would happen if another rich mineral were found in it today? Though slate was being worked even in Roman days, it was the volume of housing in the new industrial towns that led to its full exploitation: half a million tons annually, from Snowdonia. Slate was as much North Wales as coal was South, with similar industrial disputes, often long and bitter. Britain's longest industrial dispute was at Lord Penrhyn's Bethesda quarries. The miners struck for three years before some were glad to be re-employed at an even lower wage for longer hours, adding to the wealth that exudes at Penrhyn Castle, now National Trust.

As we found at Delabole in Cornwall, some slate is still produced, mainly for high-class flooring, fittings and gifts. Wales and Cornwall still argue about which produces the best quality, but for total output with pretty consistent quality North Wales was unequalled in the world. When I first came to Blaenau, the Ffestiniog Railway hadn't been reawakened by volunteers, but trucks still came down several of the inclines from the waste heaps and ran around extensive sidings. Think of all the fine slates that were extracted to leave those giant waste heaps! Much of the slate from here came from well underground. Calculating how much slate to leave in supporting pillars was a fine art. The quarry that gave the Talyllyn Railway its raison d'être closed when its great gallery came crashing down.

On a previous visit I went to Llanberis and gazed up to the terraces, served by incline planes climbing 2,000 ft up the mountainside, and visited the complex of the slate museum, whose ancient foundry is kept in working order and still turns out occasional pieces for museums. Beside it runs the new Llanberis Lake Railway for a couple of miles along the route of the Padarn Railway beside Lake Padarn. Many more people go to Llanberis for access to Snowdon itself, some by the Snowdon Mountain Railway, others on foot for the challenge of the climb and objecting to the presence of the dirty steam engines. It is a Swiss-type operation, fiendishly expensive with its old-fashioned engines. There is much to do in the Llanberis area these days including the Electric Mountain, where there is a hands-on museum – pedal furiously to make your own electricity – alongside the hydro-electric station within Europe's largest man made cavern in the mountain.

Back at Blaenau, there's an intense conversation between the boy serving in the station's outdoor refreshment kiosk and a young man about the merits of different locomotives. We don't like to interrupt. Anyway, just for the sake of tradition, mind you, we order pre-lunch sherry from the train's own refreshment car for the return journey. No matter that it is served in a plastic tumbler. Lunch is outside on Tan-y-Bwlch station where it is noticeably warmer. Between trains, a buzzard takes off with a wriggling grass snake in its beak. The station was born as a passing place for freight trains as long ago as 1836. At the start the empty trunks had to be hauled back by horses. Even when empty ones were attached to ascending passenger trains, strings of trucks loaded with slate came down by gravity under the control of a brakesman who sounded a horn to warn of its near-silent approach. That is still occasionally re-enacted today. It needed precision engineering to ensure a steady, unbroken downward gradient.

'Like to drive one of those Fairlie engines?' asks Sheila, passing me a leaflet explaining why the FR driving package is unique. Only costs £750! No thanks, but I hope it won't be long before we're back at Tan-y-Bwlch. It's perfect – even the white fencing.

Portmeirion in a Time Warp

All the ingredients seem right, but the cake doesn't. Is it perhaps overcooked? Too popular for its own good? Whatever, the one disappointment of our trip to Wales is the place we had selected to settle for four nights with unrushed time, even a day to lie low.

We are on our last day at Portmeirion, on the estuary near Porthmadog. We are in an expensive room within the main hotel, with a stunning view, wishing we were almost anywhere else and eagerly looking forward to moving on to Llandudno tomorrow.

It isn't like us not to enjoy such a setting and famous location, but we are seriously irritated. And it isn't that we didn't know what to expect, for we've read copiously about Portmeirion, have one of the best rooms with double-aspect windows, and a perfect window table for dinner each night. Several years ago, moreover, I came to the village as a day guest.

The position, at the end of a peninsula jutting south into the Traeth Bach, is great. There is real satisfaction in seeing the tide come in with swirling rapidity and the huge areas of sand drying out more slowly. Even in summer, though, it is clearly a treacherous estuary system.

Out on the front lawn along with other guests taking a pre-dinner drink, we watch the progress of a mum and her children wading through the water trying to cross from the far side to ours. Tension rises as the mum almost stumbles with the youngest child on her back trying to ford the deepest channel fairly close to us. We shout and wave furiously, though whether she hears or sees us, or decides for herself that it is too risky, we cannot know. Someone has gone off to call the coastguard. The tide has started coming in, so it will be harder getting back over a channel she found challenging enough at the start of her attempted crossing.

The coastguard crew arrives with an inflatable boat on a trailer, muttering that the same thing happened yesterday. They take a look and decide to drive to another point. The woman beats them to it and disappears, presumably hoping not to have been recognised. 'It's always happening; we try to take no notice,' says a waitress who comes to tell us that our table is ready.

I could happily just sit and watch for ever and a day: the tides, the birds and occasional fish, the neat vegetation along the opposite side through which occasional trains on the Cambrian coast line to Pwllheli play hide and seek, the green foothills and the rugged mass of Snowdonia rising beyond. So just what is wrong?

Probably the fact that Portmeirion is an artificial creation just plonked here. It doesn't integrate. When it was experimental and new, and authors were among the famous who came to look it over (Noel Coward wrote *Blithe Spirit* in a neighbouring room), there would at least have been excitement to compensate for the fact that Portmeirion does the opposite of growing out of the landscape. Now it neither fits nor is avant-garde. The comment by the waitress about the coastguard said it all: We don't get involved. The surroundings are nothing to do with us. We're Portmeirion!

Unfair cynicism? Possibly. It would certainly be wrong to say that the hotel's service was grudging, but it was thoroughly institutionalised. Most rooms, we found, were occupied by visiting Americans, despatched promptly by coach after an early breakfast so as not to disturb the rest of the guests, who no doubt pay more. The Welsh hoi polloi come for special lunches, but day visitors to the village are carefully kept away from the hotel's attractive grounds. But there's no really nice beach for any of us, for the wet sand is unstable and sinks when you walk on it.

The hotel is reached by a complicated route. It involves going through security, for only resident guests are allowed to drive through the village, where the day visitors aren't anxious to make way for cars. There are so many of them crowded together that it is sometimes hard for them to do so. Exactly what satisfaction they gain from their visit (admission is expensive) it is hard to tell. There are plenty of shops and it is a good place for seconds of Portmeirion's well-known, heavily-patterned floral ware. The café we found positively awful, messy, but then by the time we went for afternoon tea it had been mobbed.

As for the rest of the hillside village with its incongruous mixture of styles, towers, domes, statues and other features, it depends on your taste. There are undoubtedly fine gardens and water features, the cottages of mixed style dotted around as an adjunct to the hotel are well kept, and I like the tall conifers adding to the vertical interest. But for me it is somehow caught in a time warp and has lost its meaning, being different just for its own sake. However, it is hard not to be enthusiastic about the original vision of Clough Williams-Ellis, a tireless campaigner for the environment who created the village to show that development could add rather than detract from nature. 'Cherish the past, adorn the present, construct for the future' he said. When it was at the cutting edge of new thinking, in the mode of the Elmhirst's Dartington Hall in Devon, and attracted writers and other opinion-formers rather than trippers en masse, it must indeed have been the place not to miss in this part of the world.

'So what would you do with it?' challenges Roger Jones, the chairman of the Welsh Development Agency. We happen to sit at the table next to him and his wife for our final dinner at Portmeirion's other and newer hotel, Castell Deudraeth, where the food is good but the ambience for early diners among the echoing noise of children's supper leaves much to be desired. It is a fair question. I'd try and make it a bit more matter of fact, with less arty-crafty emphasis. The layout, especially the typesetting, of the guide book would be a good place to start. I'd like to feel I'm welcome, not just an onlooker of curiosities. Something more to do, especially for younger people, would help. In some ways it is bound to be a museum piece, but places like the Waterways Museum at Gloucester suggest the way to go. It was only later that I realised that Portmeirion had won Gwobr dylunio dwyiethog, the Welsh Language Board's bilingual design award for publicity material. Then, I always tried to avoid award-winning designers. Like design-winning architects, they don't know when to stop being different.

I'm not sure if Roger is convinced or not. He sold his pharmaceutical business because his kids didn't want it. He clearly knows about business and Wales, including its railways. We inevitably mention the missing signalbox delaying the restoration of passenger trains between Newport and Ebbw Vale. He lives near what used to be the first station on the long-closed Neath to Brecon line and is amused to hear I used it. There were plans to give Queen Victoria a Welsh home there; but she preferred Scotland and the Isle of Wight, and never visited.

Roger was recently at one of those all-Wales conferences conveniently situated in the country's middle at Llandrindod Wells and agrees that's a town deserving to do well. Brought up in Bala, he of course speaks Welsh, no doubt very necessary for someone in his position. Discreetly, he doesn't comment when I point out how off-putting Welsh can be to English visitors, both in its perpetual use in tourist literature and in that annoying 'you're not one of us' way, such as when one goes into a pub where the locals, clearly speaking English, switch to Welsh. He's a governor of BBC Wales, and few would begrudge the prominence given to Welsh on the air, though it sometimes prevents us being able to hear the programmes we'd enjoy.

What of the future? One idea is to turn the two-mile long site of the steel works beside the main railway at Llanwern near Newport into an airport. 'Five per cent less fuel if planes from New York land there than at Heathrow,' he says. 'And excellent communications.' Certainly a thought. Talking of transport, our mini-van has arrived to take us back to the hotel. The driver, one of two still on duty, eagerly explains how the efficient internal transport system works. While guests can take cars to the hotel, coaches aren't allowed, so tonight's Americans will be picked up at eight tomorrow morning to be transferred to their coach in the higher car park. There's much that is right at Portmeirion, but it needs a new conductor with an updated mission.

In the morning, though, we take an almost nostalgic look at the state of the tide from our room's main window, and then through the side window at the early sun lighting up the extraordinary village. We agree we're unlikely to be back. Sad, really.

To Llandudno

Our route takes us back through Blaenau Ffestiniog, which I always find hauntingly compelling if scarcely attractive. The desire to stop and patronise shops urgently in need of customers is resistible since delightful countryside lies ahead, down the Conwy Valley. Betws-y-Coed is first stop. Its riverside situation, forest hills, falls and considerable range of superior hotels and shops seem to give it a touch of continental atmosphere: a perfect place to stay. So think many others. As in my youth, often more people arrive in late afternoon and early evening than can be accommodated and so have to move on to other less obvious and certainly less publicised places. We enjoy our short break... until the peace is broken by the arrival of a squadron of bikers who give a final burst to the accelerator before switching off. Then the noise of one of their radios is somehow more incongruously shattering. However, it doesn't deter their machine-worshipping seance – and soon they are again foot-watching as they rev up in chorus. For all its physical attraction, Betws-y-Coed isn't actually a specially good centre, certainly not for serious walking and climbing. But the memory of long-ago summer evenings is of elegant, sunny perfection.

One of the alternative places to which latecomers are often directed is Capel Curig. How it is possible to make such a mistake we won't discuss but, instead of descending down the valley, accidentally we climb up a steep hill on the A5. Soon we land ourselves in this enticing if scattered village dedicated to catering for the needs of climbers and sportsmen. It is hard not to go on further, at least to visit one of the glacial lakes but, retracing our tracks, we enjoy a glimpse of Snowdon itself.

Now concentrating, we take a short cut toward Llanrwst and, because it is new to us, go down the road to the west of the Conwy. This is disappointing, for we miss the best valley views and a glimpse of the National Trust's colourful Bodnant Gardens. While these are always worth looking at in themselves, what I remember is the view from the terrace with lake in the foreground and, beyond the garden's tall trees, the line of bare hills rising above the green foothills. Our compensation is a brief pop in to the Trefriw woollen mills, where traditional weaving produces richly coloured rugs and bedspreads. Then a different view of the broadening estuary: coming down the west bank also means we go through the village of Conwy which couldn't be confused with anywhere else in the world. Passing by the mighty castle before crossing the estuary at its narrows, one of Edward I's 'iron ring' of fortresses to contain the Welsh, we drink in the details of railway and road bridges old and new. Then left for the run into Llandudno.

NORTH WALES TO PEAK DISTRICT AND DALES

Perfection at Llandudno

Perfection. The British Seaside at its stunning best. I'm in a delightful hotel room drinking tea brought by the porter who tells me he admires the way I am pushing the boat out, using room service when there are tea-making facilities at the ready. The truth is more mundane. Still recovering from the operation on my arm, I can't lift the case blocking the tea-making apparatus, and Sheila has gone out in a boat to view the Great Orme from the sea. But the enthusiastic porter is right in other details: this is a fine hotel overlooking an animated scene redolent of happy childhood memories when the sun always shone on a bright blue sea.

The broad crescent-shaped promenade, stretching from the limestone lumps of the Great Orme to the left to the Little Orme to the right, is agog with activity. Children and dogs are dashing around between the hordes of pedestrians gossiping away. Above the general chatter can be heard the shouts of boatmen offering trips round the bay, and the raucous laughter of children alternately thrilled and scared in the time-hallowed way by a Punch and Judy show. Business thrives. Hundreds have paid for deckchairs, while the queue for boat trips is perpetually replenished by the touts, as a speedboat offering short trips and a graceful larger vessel take turns in changing their loads. There are even people with ice creams, though there's no ice-cream stand in sight. They are still not allowed on Llandudno seafront.

Dozens are bathing and paddling, but at high tide, seen from my hotel room, the beach looks negligible, and my eyes focus mainly on the sea of a hue more usually seen in posters than real life. Even in the gently bobbing smaller private vessels, people are colourfully garbed in summer dresses and shorts. This is no doubt an exceptionally warm afternoon, but Llandudno and its visitors unite in demonstrating they expect such splendour. It is hard not to share the porter's enthusiasm. 'Aren't they happy out there? Llandudno's still a great place.'

Earlier memories of Llandudno are of what seemed remorselessly fading splendour. I recall catching an ancient tramcar outside the Grand Theatre well past its grandness, and hotels with lumpy beds, unimaginative food and fading decorations. I didn't think I'd ever again see the place so lively – and giving so many people so much pleasure – let alone in the twenty-first century. And few indeed are the resorts that can boast a seafront hotel equalling this: two red stars and three red rosettes. The whole set-up is, as I say, perfection... and it doesn't disappoint when I take a stroll to the cable-car station where people with ice cream and candyfloss are queuing for an aerial trip up to the Great Orme, while others are making their way to the Great Orme Tramway's lower terminus. The pier and the grand hotel beside it perhaps no longer quite reflect Llandudno's former affluence, but they are still of this world, attracting large crowds. Piers seem particularly prone to catch fire, and this was extensively damaged in 1994, so I'm grateful to take my turn walking out on the neat replacement decking to look back on the beach and up to the Great Orme.

Back on the promenade, there are fascinating notices about the resort's past. 'The finest seaside in Western Europe' is one quote. And a warning that unsociable behaviour towards council staff is taboo. The line of seafront hotels tells of present-day business as well as past glories. The likes of Bismarck, Disraeli and Gladstone don't stay here these days but, beyond the conservatories, the dining rooms and bedrooms of varied quality nearly all offer outstanding value. In real terms, it has never been cheaper to enjoy Llandudno.

The town centre, too, is lively with shoppers actually shopping rather than killing time just looking, as happens on wet days at the seaside. Gently curved Mostyn Street may no longer have some of the finest shops outside London, but there is quality along with tack and, while the passing of the decades has not been kind to all, some of the glass verandas above the wrought ironwork are still first class. An exuberance of quality wrought ironwork was what the Victorians chose to show off Llandudno's affluence. It was especially appropriate, since the majority of visitors came from the Midlands and North West.

Then there are the special attractions, including the museum (which emphasises that the Romans were quite recent in the chronology of civilisation) and the Great Orme Bronze Age Copper Mines. 'Stonehenge is certainly a world-class site but now it is joined by the Bronze Age mines at Llandudno,' says a note from *Current Archaeology*. The oldest, open-cast part of the mine was worked out 4,000 years ago.

We are encouraged to explore the 3,500-year old passage leading to the main prehistoric cavern. It was, incidentally, when the latest part of the mine was about to be worked out in Victorian times that the local landlord and MP, Edward Mostyn, had a dream of creating a holiday resort on the strip of low-lying land between the Great and Little Ormes. Work started as late as 1854, but success was instant. Steadily larger crowds arrived by regular and special trains.

Hard work and vision are obviously behind the achievement of keeping Llandudno prominently on the tourist map. That is said despite the fact that, even with weeks of advance notice, the council insisted there was nobody who could talk to me about today's tourism.

One of the secrets of success must have been discouraging conversion of hotels and boarding houses into old people's homes; another in retaining critical bulk and something of a year-round season, especially valuable in holding on to key staff. The north-facing promenade is undeniably bracing in mid-winter, but there are always things to do and see. The Alice in Wonderland Centre, for instance, is among attractions always open. Lewis Carroll based his Alice on Alice Liddell, whose family lived on the West Shore – a reminder that Llandudno is a resort of two coasts. It is an enjoyable flat walk across the isthmus between the two. And within easy reach are many places of interest, notably Conwy and its castle, the rich Vale of Conwy, Bangor and places on either side of the Menai Strait.

So that we can talk to someone local, we approach a taxi driver and ask him to take us the four miles around the Great Orme's Marine Drive and then up to the 680ft summit, where the outlook is said to be better than from the top of Snowdon. It is a view that takes time to absorb: the long North Wales coastline stretching east and west, the mainly flat land of Anglesey which at this distance and height seems to be separated from the mainland by a mere moat crossed by model bridges, and to the north, across the Irish Sea, the Lake District hills, Isle of Man, Solway Firth and the Scottish mountains, not to mention the complicated geography around the Dee and Mersey. It is easy to ignore the hideousness of the summit complex itself.

Our driver tells us about the copper mines, and about St Tudno who landed on the Great Orme bringing Christianity from Ireland. 'There's a hotel named after him,' he says. 'One of 77 on the seafront, but there used to be 400 in the area.' Sheila says that that's where we're staying. 'Cor, one of the top hotels in Britain, they say. Won an award for the best hotel loos,' he comments.

Then we go the other way past the Little Orme, lit up and shaped rather like an elephant trunk, into what is more typical seaside territory today. Colwyn Bay, once a classy adjunct to Llandudno, seems half empty. The pier is closed. 'It's a drug dump, Colwyn Bay,' says our driver. 'Full of retirement homes, but they're afraid to go out at night. Mind you, wait till you get to Rhyl. Anywhere's better than that. Half the seafront is downright derelict.'

On our way back to Llandudno, we stop at Rhôs-on-Sea and visit a little chapel. 'All reverence is due to this sacred spot. This ancient chapel is built over the holy well of St Trillo, a Celtic saint of the sixth century. Pilgrims turn in and offer a prayer.' We comment that the Welsh have always had their own approach to Christianity and recall how Welsh bibles were introduced in the late sixteenth century, powering an interest in bible reading that became stronger than if local people had always been able to study it in their native tongue. The Welsh Bible actually codified a standard Welsh language. Without it, Welsh might have divided into several dialects, each of which could readily have died out.

Of Rhôs itself there is little to say. The many flats include new ones built on the site of the huge former Rhôs Hotel. Only through the losses on the periphery has Llandudno concentrated sufficient tourism in its golden core.

Though keen to point them out, our driver is not surprised when we say we'll not be patronising one of the resort's two nightclubs. Dropping us back at our hotel, he says: 'Mind you enjoy every minute of it. At that price it's a sin not to.' At our temporary home, I ask Janette Bland, who with her husband Martin owns the hotel, how they came to be here.

Her answer tells all: 'We just happened across it when we were looking for a house in 1972. It had been empty for two years after being a convalescent home for 46 years. There wasn't a table left in it. In a cloud of dreams, we opened it after six weeks. Very rudimentary. It took four weeks even to get the phone in. But so exciting, especially when visitors began telling us they'd come back. We were in tears of happiness: such an honour to be able to please people.' It's not surprising she plays a major role in the town's tourism. She is probably the person I should have sought out in the first place.

'Why do we succeed? Because we care and nothing is too much trouble and many of our staff have been here for years.' We see her beavering away behind the scenes, always conscious of who is doing what. Quite reasonably they wouldn't take an advance booking for a seaview room for a short stay but, when we arrived, pointed out that our superior room with view was available if we were prepared to pay a touch extra. It is worth it, and my impression of Llandudno has changed for all time. I write glowingly about it on view cards to friends who might be persuaded to give it a try. Our meals more than live up to their three red rosette status. Though they are beautifully prepared and tasty, the chef hasn't made the common mistake of being inventive just to be different. Whereas a series of consecutive meals at some famous restaurants can be a gastronomic nightmare, here we could happily eat for weeks ,with attentive, unobtrusive service. It can be done! There are incidentally only 18 rooms, yet at its busiest the hotel employs up to 30 staff including part-timers. In high season the pressure must tell, but the Blands have a recipe for sanity. They bought the house next door as a bolt hole. A novel touch is that details of our room and its price are included in a 28-page booklet which includes advertisements of selected high-class cafés, galleries and boutiques, demonstrating there is quality among the retail dross.

The hotel even has a swimming pool, a seafront rarity. Only one problem: parking is distinctly tight. Our friendly porter waved us back into the garage apparently not noticing a projecting obstacle. 'Come on, back, you're all right.' Crunch. Ouch. A deep scratch on our rear wing. We almost mentioned it, but it seemed wholly inappropriate. Be positive and look at the scratch as a reminder of a great experience, we say.

On our final walk, I come across a notice telling the local transport story in chronological form, always easy to absorb:

Early nineteenth century, shipping services from Liverpool start.
1827, semaphore telegraph station at Great Orme.
1858, Llandudno branch railway opens.
1876-7, Pier opens by private company.
1878, Marine Drive opens by public subscription.
1891, Liverpool & North Wales Steamship Company starts.
1902-3, Great Orme Tramway opens in two stages (cable hauled).
1907, electric tramway opens, West Shore to Rhôs.
1908, extended to Colwyn Bay.
1915, extended again to Old Colwyn.
1901-20, charabancs replace horse-drawn drays.
1928, Marine Drive toastrack buses start.
1930, Crossville Motors take over most private buses.
1956, electric trams abandoned.
1963, Liverpool & North Wales Steamship services cease.
1969, Great Orme cable car opens.

Breakfast in Llandudno, Lunch at Criche Tram Museum

Once an express train journey on a busy summer's day along the North Wales coast was an exhilarating experience. The *Irish Mail* and all manner of holiday trains and local services came this way. Indeed, from the railway's goods as well as passenger traffic, you could tell the state of the economy in much of Ireland as well as locally. Few of today's trains offer quality service and views, while urban sprawl has spoilt much of the route, especially toward the east. Albeit at the end of a short branch,

Llandudno station was once a proud place; its forlorn appearance today must make the few arriving by train feel second-class citizens.

Llandudno Junction, which we pass joining the main road east, is little better. Running alongside a crowded diesel unit, many people sitting beside window pillars, makes us pleased we are driving. Not that the road is wonderful, for traffic is slow and, where the coast is best, we are forced inland.

Where we can, we stay close to the sea, and soon a glimpse of the famous tower shows we are approaching Rhyl. Though forewarned, we are not quite prepared for the appalling state of the two-mile long promenade. Much of the western half is boarded up. That much we were told to expect. The shock is that the tarted-up eastern half is visually worse, with peeling paint, gaudy notices, flashing lights, and virtually nothing a self-respecting architect wouldn't condemn. The sounds and the smells contribute to achieving the miracle of making Great Yarmouth's promenade seem positively classy. Yet, we recall that, in bygone years, this is where many older relatives and friends came for their honeymoon and summer breaks, sending postcards extolling the gardens, hotels and beaches. Just one hotel makes it into today's AA *Guide*. There is also only one at the next assault on our eyes, Prestatyn. It rates a dizzy 67 per cent as opposed to the sixty per cent of the Rhyl hotel.

Today's Rhyl is cheap and (at least superficially) cheerful. There are real bargains in accommodation, beer and take-away food for youngsters who come to push the boat out in their tightly budgeted way, often with a new partner. There's certainly nothing prudish about twenty-first-century Rhyl. For families, both Rhyl and Prestatyn have an abundance of sand and wet-weather attractions. There's also a great hinterland full of architectural and other fascination through the fertile Vale of Clwyd, to Denbigh and Ruthin, a little-visited corner of Wales.

So, sticking to the coast, at Prestatyn, we look at the vast seaside holiday camps and consider pausing at the hotel on the beach. However, we press on to Point of Ayr, where the Dee or Dyfrdwy estuary finally meets the sea. From the air it can be hard to distinguish the Dee from the Mersey. Flights from Inverness to London come this way but, even when it is bright on the ground, there is usually a layer of high cloud as Atlantic air meets land. A reminder that at our early breakfast I happened to read that someone who lived on Cadair Idris in Snowdonia for three years enjoyed cloudless sea views on only nine occasions.

The Point of Ayr is an interesting spot with a broad view of the Wirral. It is the demarcation not only between estuary and sea, but between industry and holiday land. The last of North Wales's coal mines to close is just to the east. While we munch a stale cake that has been in the car for days, a series of mums arrive and patiently unload their kids eager to get to the huge beach. There's no danger of the sands becoming crowded here. And the naughty five-year-old lad who clings hard to the car seat saying he never ever wants to go to a beach again can yell at full throttle without disturbing more than his harassed mum and sister. I rather sympathise with him for, much though I love the sea, sand and the human body have never struck me as a match made in heaven.

With the railway between us and the Dee estuary, the best thing that can be said for the next part of the journey is that it is better than going through the land more disfigured by industry further south. Places like Flint and Connah's Quay (where we say farewell to salt water) have undoubtedly seen better and busier days. So has a sizeable passenger ship we pass moored at a most unlikely spot. 'It's going to rot until it becomes so historic that enthusiasts will restore it,' I comment cynically. This is a journey that encourages cynicism, but the Dee estuary is a Mecca for one great brand of enthusiasts: bird lovers, who delight in the rich variety of visiting waders.

Out of Wales, across the base of the Wirral, and we are on to the motorway system, starting with the M56 running parallel with the Manchester Ship Canal just south of the inland tip of the Mersey estuary with views of planes landing and taking off at Liverpool's Speke Airport. Now we eat up the miles, soon travelling south on the M6 by a roundabout but quick route to the Peak District where, in a fit of geographical madness, we have arranged to stay tonight. To Sheila's surprise and delight, our route takes us through Stoke-on-Trent.

In the suburb of Basford, we quickly find the house where she was born. It still looks in good condition two-thirds of a century later. Tracking down an oatcake of the local Newcastle-upon-Lyme variety – a large oaten English-style pancake, eight inches across, to eat with savoury rather than sweet things – takes rather longer, with constant turning and pulling away from shops who say they don't stock them or have sold out. That quest successfully completed, we skirt the Peak District's southern edges by Ashbourne, still an isolated one-off town with great limestone scenery immediately to the north, and Belper, where the East Midlands textile country begins. The landscape starts becoming dramatic as we head north to Ambergate beside the trunk Sheffield-Bristol railway, as close as it gets to the Peaks. Then the Derwent Valley narrows, and we play hide-and-seek with branch railway and recently-restored Huddersfield Canal. At Criche there's an inevitable stop at the delightfully-situated National Tramway Museum.

Joy, on this crisp dry day we can eat our sandwiches outdoors to the melody of tramcars accelerating, straining round curves and squeakily stopping. As a boy I used to hum the sound in the bath, with the taps as control handles. I'm not the only crazy person: crowds are out, and the museum relies heavily on voluntary labour. Too late, perhaps, to volunteer as driver.

Nostalgic though she can be about many things including Newcastle-under-Lyme oatcakes, one of which she has eaten part of with our sandwiches, Sheila doesn't totally subscribe to the lure of the bouncing tramcar or its noisy motor pumping up the brakes. Not even the ding-ding, please stop, or the louder warning gong, redolent of mechanical music, make her knees knock. Grudgingly, she acknowledges that the Glasgow car mentioned during the meeting with Sir Neil Cossons in chapter 34, looks less uncomfortable than the rest.

With its extensive operating layout and shed packed with old trams, the museum accurately as well as picturesquely portrays a colourful episode in transport history... a period, as said earlier, that once seemed to have gone forever but which, with the opening of a whole new batch of tramways running through city streets, can now be classified as ahead of its time. 'They were so old,' says a woman from Sheffield, herself no chicken. 'I usually waited till a more modern bus came along.' That was the tram's virtue and downfall: the electric cars on rails lasted too long, often three times as long as the buses that replaced them. Their hard seating and other fittings inevitably became outmoded, and after 1945 it was unfashionable to put new wine in old bottles.

Britain's First National Park

I sometimes wonder why I'm drawn to the Peak District. There are many (for me) more accessible areas of higher, grander moors and cliffs less under pressure from human beings. That the Peak District became our first National Park and the Pennine Way our first long-distance path was perhaps more due to the pressure than the landscape; fifteen million live less than an hour or so away from the Park. Encouraging people to enjoy the landscape without destroying it demands hard work and ingenuity. Yet the Peak District *is* unique. Many people experience a longing to take another draught of it. Certainly I'm delighted once more to drive through its heart. At its border we notice one of the commemorative millstones. There's not much demand for millstones today, but they are of that tough grit of which the higher peaks with their sharp edges consist. With their heather-covered flat tops between valleys, they attract the keenest walkers.

What grips me, personally, are the green limestone hills laboriously divided over the years by hedges built up of surface and shallow stones – and the narrow, eroded, wooded valleys between steep limestone cliffs producing some of our finest intimate scenery, such as at Matlock Bath, through which we now head. In the middle of the nineteenth century, Nathaniel Hawthorne said he had never elsewhere seen 'such exquisite scenery as that which surrounds the village'. I used to visit my parents when they stayed at a clifftop hotel overlooking the valley, so there is nostalgia as well as scenic excitement. Local industry has its interest, too, though one cannot see today's National Park allowing such unsightly intrusion.

For me this afternoon, the greater intrusion is motorcycles, and you don't need planning permission to ride them. They are everywhere, going back and forth like disturbed ants, occupying large parking areas, blocking easy access to cafés and shops. Individually, motorcyclists no doubt enjoy the scenery as much as anyone; as a cult, they threaten Matlock's very soul at busy weekends. This sunny afternoon, activity is increased by people trying to keep up with a raft race. Occasional shouts from the river above the roar of motorbikes attract more onlookers.

Continuing up the valley, we soon reach High Peak Junction, where today's High Peak Trail starts along the course of the abandoned Cromford & High Peak Railway, which climbed into the clouds with precarious rope-worked inclines. Watching operations attracted generations of enthusiasts. For my part, I especially recall standing high above the valley and looking down through the trees to one of the last full-length expresses popping in and out of tunnels on its way by the Midland's much-celebrated route to Manchester. Today's line terminates at Matlock and walkers, who enjoy many former railway routes through the Park, are up in arms at the plan to reopen the rest of it, including through beloved Darley Dale.

Matlock itself often seeming an anticlimax after Matlock Bath, we turn up the narrow, wooded Grange Valley, and again reach the land of green fields and limestone hedges. Despite the plethora of abandoned railways and quarries and even Roman Roads (yes, they discovered the hot springs at Buxton), there is space to think up here. Just passing through refreshes some peculiar battery that powers me.

Passing almost as many cyclists and walkers as cars, we bounce along the open road to Buxton. There are also two well-laden Peak Buses of the National Park transport initiative. I well know these miles between Buxton and Matlock Bath, since I sometimes arrived at Buxton by train and the only way of going forward was by taxi. Anxious eyes alternated between the scenery and meter. Buxton still enjoys an excellent train service from Manchester, though the Midland station next door has long been closed. From it a branch once descended steeply to the now-abandoned main line at Miller's Dale.

How things have changed! In August 1948 I was staying with a family in Sheffield when on a Sunday we decided to visit a dentist with a model railway in Buxton. Our route was by the longest land tunnel in Britain to Chinley, with its twin curved viaducts. We changed there and again at Miller's Dale, from which we climbed in a filthy non-corridor train. An old man in the compartment was one of those habitual spitters who helped fill the sanatoriums then dotted round clean-air parts of the countryside. It fell to me to pull the strap to let down the window to discourage him from spitting on the floor, and to raise it hastily as we entered smoke-filled tunnels. In vain. The chap needed to expectorate inside a tunnel, and I failed to pull the strap in time.

Buxton hugely surprised me on that first visit. The dentist, who met us at the station and took us on a brief tour, lived in the grand late eighteenth-century crescent modelled on Bath and overlooking a park. A guide book of the day described it – the highest town of such size in Britain – as 'one of the most frequented and fashionable watering-places in England', still with a winter as well as a summer season. Soon after that, ceasing to be fashionable, its only real role seemed to be welcoming Manchester's wealthier commuters.

This afternoon Buxton again pleasantly surprises. There is restoration and a general liveliness that would make it a perfect place for an extended break, with many attractions such as Chatsworth and other famous houses. The Crescent, built in 1780-1790 by John Carr, 'the Architect of the North' for the Fifth Duke of Devonshire, is fabulous but a bit of a one-off. Overall Buxton is not quite Bath, but is definitely alive and kicking. Especially so the Edwardian opera house, 'the theatre in the hills,' which among its year-round programme hosts the Buxton Opera Festival and the International Gilbert & Sullivan Festival. The theatre's frontage, and the different entrances for stalls, upper and dress circles and private boxes, compels attention, but we have just missed a tour of the building. So we go next door to the Pavilion where the indoor and outdoor gardens and a large municipal-run restaurant, cafeteria and coffee shop, a miniature train running up and down the gardens, the car park and everything else is at maximum popularity. The band in the park has attracted many listeners. Every notice we see mentions places or institutions with High or Peak in their names. Then we run around by car, enjoying the famous crescent, and other individual buildings. With skilful stewardship, and of course financial injection, yet more of the grandeur will be restored. Clearly the demand is there.

The corridor from Manchester to Buxton is excluded from the National Park. The quarrying activity shows us why as we head down through Chapel-en-le-Frith before doubling back into the Park to Eyam, the plague village. This is new to me, though we're all familiar with the tale of how in 1665 a village tailor received damp cloth from London and plague-carrying fleas were released when it was left out to dry. The disease rapidly spread. It claimed 260 lives out of a population of around 800 and, to prevent it spreading to neighbouring parts the rector persuaded the whole place to put itself in quarantine. We see one of the stone bowls in which coins for the payment of food brought by neighbouring villagers were left dipped in vinegar on the outskirts.

It is a moving tale, well told by a 20p miniature history published by the Eyam Village Society. I also enjoy John Clifford's longer *Eyam Plague*, a very human story. Many of the details are brought to life in the church and museum. What especially fascinates me this afternoon is eavesdropping on the visitors, young and old. Young kids mainly think it natural that people should make sacrifices to save those in neighbouring villages. Several teenagers aren't so sure. One lad mutters, 'Suppose your girlfriend lived elsewhere?' to which his friend responds, 'They wouldn't have kept me in.' In real life they might of course have responded responsibly. It's macho to suggest damning the system. What comes across is that the experience did wonders for community spirit. There's much more to Eyam than there might have been without the plague. Lead mining and cotton, silk and shoes may all be in the past, but enterprise thrives, especially in the welcome given visitors. A tall, dark-haired young waitress at a busy café goes out of her way to fit us in for a cup of tea before the final stage of our long day's travel.

Reservoir Country to Holme Castle

Though it is not that part of the Peak District I personally love so much, the rest of our drive is through fabulous scenery. Soon we turn north and are in the Hope Valley, briefly beside the railway with trains from Sheffield to Manchester and Stockport/Manchester Airport. At Bamford we strike north again into the reservoir country of dramatic contours. The highlight is perhaps crossing a causeway between two huge reservoirs. Then the forbidding mass of high tops, with Shining Clough Moss, Bleaklow Ridgeway Moor and Shelf Moor, force us to the west, north of High Peak – under which the railway we recently crossed dives deep on its way west.

Under Gathering Hill we see Crooked Clough, below which the Pennine Way briefly follows Devil's Dike. Then we're on Snake Road on Coldharbour Moor. No fiction writer could better conjure up the names of places at which one would be mightily unhappy to be stuck on a cold, dark night. This evening the outlook is enhanced by fluffy clouds streaking in from the west across an otherwise clear sky. The last time I came this way there was a passionate sunset of rippled reds and mauves, but it feels softer now and there'll be no red sky tonight. At Glossop we turn sharply east, beside the railway which I first travelled on when it was newly electrified by the LNER just after the war. Later it was closed: the Woodhead Tunnel line to Penistone and Sheffield. Part of the railway is now a cycleway, but during the week the road carries non-stop lorries whose loads everyone you meet says should be on rails.

To our south are some of the most famous edges such as Long Gutter, Lawrence and Deer Knowl Edges, and immediately to the north (though we soon cross between two of them) a long line of reservoirs. The thought may be unpopular among lovers of this neck of the woods: the reservoirs do not fit into the Peak landscape as well as do, say, the Mid-Wales or even Lake District ones. Yachts on some of them emphasise their incongruity. Perhaps I'm beginning to long for a natural Scottish loch.

From Woodhead, north of the reservoir by the same name, we strike more drama and, as we top Holme Moss, have to pause to absorb an absolutely fantastic view featuring smaller and more natural-looking reservoirs. The clouds streaking in from the west are now darker: we enjoy the patterns of light and shade on the hills and water as they chase each other like playful kittens. It will surely rain tonight. Then it is only a short if winding descent to Holme.

Years ago my son Gareth made friends with Jill Hayfield and John and has often stayed at their Holme Castle guest house, promising that one day I would come and share the experience. Here we are... more than warmly welcomed, shown a delightful room, and then quickly into conversation over a pre-dinner drink. It started, we're told, when Jill's former husband's business went under and a B&B sign was put out to help pay the bills. When her husband moved out, life was a bit of a struggle. John, 'the boy next door' was helpful, and eventually she suggested he move in. Now they are hosts exceptional, running a small, friendly operation with the smallest licensed bar in Yorkshire. There's organic food and a communal table. They're just getting over the damage done by foot-and-mouth. Their children, Rowan and Emily, thirteen and nine, were traumatised by it, says John.

It is Jill's turn: 'And of course, since 11 September, no Americans. We used to have a lot of them. John's family have been in the village since the 1700s. We're nearly 1000 feet up, with little topsoil and small fields, so only sheep do well. But there's keen community spirit – people club together to buy heating oil in bulk. And every hour a bus struggles up the hill from Holmfirth so that here is a country spot where you don't have to rely on a car. It is a lovely, safe place, great community. Two things have helped us. People who come to Holmfirth because of Last of the Summer Wine and like the sound of us, and my felt business.'

She then goes off to the kitchen leaving John talking about things local, the reservoir country, the reopening of the Huddersfield Canal with its highest and longest tunnel, three and a half miles, through which you can travel on an electric boat. He also shows us the remnants of the house's old pulley system from its wool-making days, when the storage and processing of fleeces began at the top, progressing steadily down through the building.

Now it is John's turn to go to the kitchen, and Jill tells us that accommodating ten visitors is comfortable. During the week many are business people, so her special Fleece to Felt programmes are one-day Felt Fridays and two-day weekend workshops. Those attending are encouraged to stay overnight and buy supplies and finished felts, the large display of which also inspires creativity.

'Felt is a passion I found by accident. The craft is older than weaving. We're in the middle of sheep country. I get my fleeces from local farmers. They're washed and combed so that the fibres all lie in the same direction. I place them in three layers. Friction, soap, heat – and eureka.'

We especially admire a geometrically patterned wall-hanging in black, white and red with thin metallic strips, and ask to have it added to our bill. There is an infinite variety of shapes and colours in the felts displayed on the walls. Soon each member of a party of ten will pay £18 for a talk and demonstration Jill is leading on the 'FUNdamentals of FELTmaking', followed by a more expensive weekend course limited to eight students called 'Pull the other One' on felted cords, ropes, dreads and tassels. Then comes 'Colours of the Rainbow' on blending techniques in felt. It is obviously good fun, and profitable. 'Yes Sir, Yes Sir, 3 Bags full' shows eight students each paying £55 for a two-day course on how to make very individual bags.

A Fleece to Felt programme explains: 'We created a studio in the area where wool was spun and woven in the early 1800s... a large second-floor open-beamed room with a wood-burning fire, commanding dramatic views on two sides, north towards the Pennine Way and south over the garden to open moorland grazed by sheep. I work on my felts here on a regular basis and host the informal workshop weekends which are proving very successful and enjoyable.'

Over the informal evening meal with real food, we drink to Gareth and wonder when he'll next be here from New Zealand. He's obviously made his mark with the children, Rowan and Emily, who he has known since they were tiny. They, too, help with the catering. It is very much a family affair, though they need John's earnings as computer-aided designer in Huddersfield and what Jill makes from teaching felt and allied crafts at college. In so exposed a position, the large house is expensive to heat and keep in good trim.

Last of the Summer Wine Country

Often places opportunistically cash in on accidental fame, such as having had a bestselling author live in them for a period. At Holmfirth, on the other hand, one would be seriously upset if there were not a major celebration of the long-running TV comedy, The Last of the Summer Wine. So much depends on the location. For decades

Holmfirth has become used to being a film set and has shared in the characters' successes, illnesses and deaths such as that of Compo, always wanting to kiss and cuddle the formidable Nora Batty in her wrinkled stockings. That reminds me that one of my favourite characters of years ago was Wally, her hen-pecked husband never able to take her out in his motorcycle's sidecar without being abused.

Holmfirth and the surrounding country were designed to be shown off, and we are just a couple among many spending part of a showery Monday relishing seeing where Nora Batty and others live. We peer into the window of Sid and Ivy's café, out of which the old men whose antics form the comedy's backbone are often furiously chased by angry Ivy of little patience with customers. Sid, the huge but always frightened husband of the café partnership, is another example of a character I fondly remember many years after his actor's death.

Yes, in part, the success of the series is due to pure geography. There's another factor, though: scriptwriting has been of the highest order. In television, more than most things, success breeds success, big audiences justifying higher budgets which in turn lead to better quality. That virtuous circle is unfortunately rapidly disappearing as, with American-style TV, audiences are splintered between more and more channels. The greater the choice, the less worth watching. It is a bit like the longer the distance you fly, the cheaper the fare.

We celebrate the longest-running and most expensive comedy of all time by seeing how closely Clegg and Compo were neighbours, and recognising shops and other buildings that have occasionally been part of the action. Along with other visitors, determined to keep spirits up on a damp Monday morning, we crowd into the Wrinkled Stocking Tearoom, which of course exists on the series' back rather than featuring in it. A mini-tour bus shaped like a delivery van is doing brisk business taking people to see sights such as Aunty Wainwright's infamous emporium.

Though the series has no doubt done much for the area, it quickly becomes clear that many visitors are here as much for the famous scenery around Holmfirth as for the characters. Holmfirth is a fascinating place of ancient narrow streets, steep hills, distant vistas. An enormous sky seem to grow as the rain ceases. As is so often the case in Yorkshire but not Lancashire, industrial relics fit nicely into their surroundings. We pause on the bridge over the stream into which Compo so often plunged, to admire an historic milepost halfway across. There are other tearooms, a second-hand as well as new bookshop. Tills ring. Then at the impressive postcard museum, we see how saucy seaside humour has changed since John Bamford began his postcard business in 1870. The museum is surprisingly bright with natural light. Large mullioned windows are a characteristic of Holmfirth. Weavers, who worked at home, needed all the light they could get.

I've been long familiar with John Bamford's postcards, pictorial as well as saucy. What I didn't know until purchasing a copy of Discovery Publishing's lively little *Summer Wine Country*, is that Bamford was also an early film pioneer:

As an artist, he utilised Holme Valley vistas as painted backdrops to live models of local people, who became the early screen 'stars' of thousands of lantern slides put together in sequence. From 1899, short silent movies, in the style of later Hollywood Max Sennet films, enthralled local audiences in depicting popular songs and stories of the day. Films began to be shot in realistic local settings. Holme Valley businesses lent their support, with banks opening their doors for fake bank raids, the railway company providing special trains, and the Holmfirth Council allowing use of the park. From these early comedies developed adventure, romance, and crime films. Demand escalated and offices were opened in London and New York. Then, an order for 100 films made for Russia was abruptly halted with the outbreak of war in 1914. This was the end of Holmfirth's journey towards international film stardom. After the war, it was decided that further development was impracticable because of the lack of sunlight in the area.

Besides, the war had opened up new opportunities for Bamforths. As men left to fight in foreign fields, a large demand was rekindled for heart-breaking sentimental greetings-cards... Pretty local girls, previously in films, were now transferred to postcards depicting lovers saying 'Goodbye', and illustrating verses of such sentimental songs as 'Goodbye Dolly Gray'.

From Peak to Dales

After lunch up precarious steps in a creaky building, we return for another night, heralded by red sky, at Holme Castle. Next morning, back to Holmfirth. It is crisper and bright again, so we make time for a short drive around the surrounding countryside, periodically seeing outlying buildings, gates and vistas familiar from the comedy. But it takes more than a popular TV series to prevent this superb countryside playing first fiddle in its own right. Then on crowded roads through Huddersfield, catching a glimpse of Halifax's Victorian theatre and stylish centre, and seeing busy shops mainly run by Asians. Surprisingly, there is a flower and antique shop way out on the outskirts.

We comment on the many mills, all enormous, some like towns in miniature, where indeed the boss reigned as sovereign over hundreds, if not thousands, of workers. Even when built close together – they were particularly densely packed at Huddersfield – most had at least a touch of grace and grandeur. Some were beautiful. The latest building and decorating techniques were often used, and they housed the very latest technology. Some have disappeared. Many of the best have been resurrected for a variety of purposes including expensive flats. Others that would have been worth redeveloping years ago now perhaps inevitably await the demolition gang. They all fascinate me, as these proud northern towns themselves always have. But they are not really my Britain.

At Keighley we see the beginning of the steam railway to Haworth and reflect on the Brontës' genius. At quiet times one can still imagine what life must have been like in what was then a remote but busy village with its steep streets and distant views. Today we press on, making our first stop at Grassington, very much my Britain.

I used to love coming to Grassington to visit Arthur Raistrick, the doyen of Yorkshire historians who, for instance, brought several eras to life in *Old Yorkshire Dales* which, while enjoying morning coffee round his fireside, I persuaded him to write. We see second-hand copies priced at ten to fifteen times the new 1967 price, yet no national publisher could afford to produce such a work today. At the Yorkshire Dales National Park Centre on the village's outskirts, I review the much greater range of local titles that are available now. They are nearly all picture-led rather than word-led books, mainly published locally. A few walking and climbing titles warrant national distribution, though Penguin have announced that even Wainwright's individualistic walking guides have ceased to be worth retaining in their list. The demand is too slow. The publisher of this book has taken them over and will surely treasure them.

The Centre itself is first class, if expensive – well, inevitably, if you fall for tomes such as *Yorkshire Textile Mills 1770-1930*. Surprisingly, this is published by Her Majesty's Stationery Office. We buy cheaper titles on the old hand-knitters of the Dales (to earn precious pennies, women knitted as they took their children to school, drove the cattle and visited the market) and Dales's *Tea Shop Walks*, along with pamphlets on lead mining, geology and places we must revisit in future such as Malham and Malham Tarn. The Tarn itself justifies that over-used word unique. No man made building beats the awesome splendour of the great limestone amphitheatre carved by thousands of years of ice and water.

Grassington has that unusual flavour of an industrial village theatrically set in mind-boggling beauty. Living here must have suited Arthur Raistrick especially well, for he loved commercial enterprise, especially with Quaker values, as dearly as the landscape.

The Dales are another of those areas I find a need occasionally to drink in, re-emphasising their beauty and individuality and reawakening memories of many former visits, in mist as well as sunshine. Have you heard the one about the Americans who devoted three whole days to an 'in-depth' study of the Dales? They were shown round by friendly experts, stayed at the best hotels and, despite inclement weather, seemed thoroughly happy. The damp squib was their parting comment: 'We never realised the Dales were so flat.'

We have lovely sunshine for our continuing journey north, starting up Wharfedale. Joyously, we want to take in every height and crag. The giant overhanging rock formation at Kilnsey certainly cannot be lightly passed while, now in starker Littondale, we seem to go into a veritable valley of walls to Arncliffe with its diminutive school and church with lychgate. A few shrubs have forced their way through gaps in the limestone that looks as though it paves an entire field, with great stone terraces above. Littondale offers little protection for trees, though, in a twist in the valley, a few stunted ones huddle by the river. Roadworks on the very narrow moorland road call for ingenious manoeuvring by several over-size vehicles, but out here the roadmen seem pleased enough to see anyone, nuisance or not.

On lower ground again, at Stainforth we turn north and run beside the Settle & Carlisle railway. The Midland's Long Drag to Scotland was a brute to build and, especially in steam days, difficult to operate. British Rail did their best to close it, but it soldiers on happily, busier with freight and passengers than for years. At Horton in Ribblesdale we walk up to the station, where the waiting room is going to be opened as an exhibition centre. There is talk, too, of one of the quarries becoming rail linked again. Hilary Gray, who will be a dinner guest tonight, lives with her husband Bryan (an expert on quarrying) in an interesting house on the station approach at which we have stayed in the past. Right now, having made a very early start on the day's first train, she will be working in Leeds on my former magazine, *Writers' News*.

Soon we come within sight of the great railway viaduct at Ribbleshead, where I recall having to abandon TV filming because the wind, furiously trying to fell the tall piers, drowned anything one said. It was anyway hard to stand upright. Then to lunch at the popular creamery catering for all tastes in that oasis of civilisation, Hawes, an excellent touring centre. Among the variety of patrons are walkers who have come off our old friend the Pennine Way; some no doubt have their own views on the difference between the Peak and Dales sections.

Going west, at Garsdale Head we see two diesels heading a long rake of British Gypsum wagons south. Then we descend Garsdale through Sedburgh, and ourselves head south, partly along a Roman Road, almost as far north as they were built. Soon we are at the Pheasant Inn in the centre of Casterton, near Kirkby Lonsdale. With a broad country view outside our comfortably warm room, we try to catch up with reading but fall asleep, waking just in time to go down to meet our visitors.

What haven't we seen in the last few days? I reflect that there are two things I especially love about the Dales: the pristine brooks babbling round graceful curves; and, even more, the way in which the hillsides begin at a gentle angle and climb at a steadily greater one. A square mile here must accommodate much more land than in lowland England! Some of the stone walls seem to reach heavenward. The Dales' stone walls are Britain's finest: higher, made of larger stones, and probably better maintained than those of the Peak. There is so much to pick out in the best (upright) photographs of the fellsides. The tops of ranges don't mean so much to me here as in some other parts, and personally I'm not fazed by a great wind farm on the Park's perimeter. I am, however, surprised by the sheer size of today's wind blades and turbines, and understand people welcoming the thought of clean electricity providing it is not on their patch. The noise is also considerable. Defenders say it is a pleasant sound. So it might be, but there are still those who cherish silence.

David & Hilary

Though in many ways they could scarcely look or be more different, our dinner guests are two of a kind: outstanding workaday writers and editors. By workaday, I mean that without pretentiousness they get on with their varied portfolios of tasks in an eminently practical manner, giving satisfaction to sizeable audiences. Though they each have a wide circle of both friends and admirers, they will never be famous and don't claim literary genius. But if only there were more like them. They both have a powerful storehouse of experience, and love and know the Dales, from which they draw strength and repay with voluntary work.

In the footsteps of his father, who had been agricultural correspondent, David Joy began life at the *Yorkshire Post*. I first knew him as railway historian and contributor of two of the best volumes in the Regional Railway History series. By that time he was working for *The Dalesman*, in charge of the magazine's considerable list of local interest paperbacks.

Founded by Harry Scott, *The Dalesman* was a remarkable institution, reaching a peak circulation in the 1970s of 70,000, the highest ever achieved by an English regional magazine. Distinctly not socialite, it was perhaps a touch folksy, but that is what Yorkshire folk at home and in exile enjoyed. A critic once dismissed it as run by amateurs for amateurs. Knowing his market, Harry Scott took that as a compliment. Respecting David's strengths, I wasn't surprised when he took over as co-owner and editor, carefully maintaining Scott's traditions. Moving into the top position he however needed a 'right hand man'... the kind of position that fell vacant at *The Dalesman* about once in a generation.

On cue, Hilary popped into the office on what she thought was a pretty hopeless search for journalistic work in a remote area. Most of her career had so far been for the magazine and newspaper company DC Thomson of Dundee. She had just moved to Horton in Ribblesdale to be with her partner Bryan. Now, anyone trained and given responsibility by DC Thomson (she edited teenage magazines amongst others and 'did all and everything' across the board) tends to be seen as a down-to-earth treasure. It took all of a few minutes for David to snap her up.

Their partnership at *The Dalesman* was fruitful. Each has told me a lot about the other. They could indeed write books about each other. Foibles, yes, but always mutual respect and trust. Though it was a time when all regional magazine circulations were falling, Dalesman books did better than ever.

Like me at David & Charles, David wondered about the future of his business, and occasionally discussed it. When he sold, he pursued railway publishing, and – visiting a distant base in Cornwall every few weeks – took over my personal railway titles. He's been a real railway nut, going off to experience steam wherever it remains in service in the world's underdeveloped exotic spots. Three trains at a time can run round the 1-gauge garden railway at the farm that has been in the family for over a century: 800ft up with eighty inches of rain a year, challenging in winter but a suntrap in summer. Then his wife Judith is busy with a substantial self-service holiday rental business, complementing (and I suspect on occasions underwriting) publishing and authorship.

A couple of years after the sale of *The Dalesman*, Hilary went freelance, writing books and articles, editing, and doing public relations work. Though, on first meeting she might seem to be in a permanent state of exuberant fluster, her ability to get down to things and do them thoroughly and quickly, is pretty unusual. She edited another country magazine I took over from David, and also my *Country Origins*, which began well but, with the writing magazines, proved too much to handle with our limited facilities at Nairn. Then she became deputy editor of these writing magazines, still on a freelance basis, for their new owners in Leeds. She goes there three long days a week and does her own writing the rest of the week. She has had a hand in getting this book shipshape.

So here we are in the cosy, busy restaurant of the Pheasant Inn, renowned for its good cooking and generous helpings. Before sitting down, towering well above anyone else in sight, to our amusement David announces he has 'officially retired'. He still edits the railway magazine *Narrow Gauge World*, has just produced a huge Yorkshire title in association with the *Yorkshire Post* and is full of other ideas. Retired! He has, it is true, just returned from a railway holiday in Salvador, but at his busiest he kept himself sane by draughts of steam nostalgia around the world. Once he is seated, winding his legs round the chair, I tell him I've bought his new Dales title – and Hilary that I picked up her *Dales People at Work* from the visitors' centre at Grassington, the latter alas at a knocked-down price.

That sets David off: 'I'm glad I'm out of publishing... especially railway books. Nobody reads today. Pictures and captions are all they want.'

Hilary: 'That's why celebrity magazines have become so important.'

David: 'The other difficulty is that there aren't enough good writers.'

We're getting a bit negative, even when moving to television. 'Remakes are never as good as the original,' says Hilary.

Apropos of nothing, David says that selling *The Dalesman* was painful.

Hilary: 'He'd been there man and boy.'

David: 'It was a way of life, certainly.'

Hilary: 'You trailblazed. But things have moved on. Look on the bright side. There wasn't even Tipp-Ex in those days. We forget how recently technology came to our rescue. It was only in the last couple of years at The *Dalesman* that we had a word-processor. Before that, cutting and pasting meant exactly that – scissors, glue and Tipp-ex.'

David: 'When you couldn't alter things easily, it was good discipline. You had to get them right first go.'

Hilary: 'Yes, but I couldn't possibly get through what I do today.'

David: 'True, and it is because of the lower cost-base that local publishing is still vibrant. The trouble is that people rush into print, publishing themselves, with inadequate editing.'

I agree, but make the point that among self-published books there is a growing proportion of well-produced, sensibly-edited titles, adding that looking through the books on sale at Grassington had been exceptionally pleasurable.

Then, as our main courses arrive, we heartily accept that we should be grateful that rural Britain remains so diverse and protected and that people explore it, write and read about it, in ever greater numbers.

Hilary: 'All those fears that television would kill local dialect and characters certainly didn't prove true. Actually TV has encouraged new interest in the Dales.'

TV and Yorkshire produce inevitable reference to James Herriot.

David teases me: 'And you turned down *All Creatures Great and Small*.'

Yes, but so did nearly every other publisher. I enjoyed reading it lying on bed one evening but wondered who would actually buy it. When a

UK publisher did take it up, it wasn't really successful. Only later, when the publicity of American success was reflected back to England, did Herriot start to become well known.

We spend most of the rest of the evening discussing the book trade's wrinkles and specific places in the Dales where we've earlier met together or especially love: Bolton Abbey, Grassington and Hebden in particular.

Sheila joins us in drinking to the Dales before David and Hilary make their separate ways to their homes in very different but both hilly settings where man has for centuries been inspired, pitting his wits against the landscape.

Next morning we set off early for Nairn through scenery few in Britain's most populous areas experience except on holiday. Though friends in the south often worry about us in our northern fastness, we feel we are privileged.

· X X X V I ·

BACK TO NEWTON
ABBOT AND
TEIGNMOUTH

A Different Route West

We have to go to Devon once more, for an unexpected reason. After a dozen years of assuming I would never return, I have been warmly invited to visit my old company, now in its third ownership since I sold. It now belongs to F&W, an American publishing company, like David & Charles itself based outside usual publishing territory, in Cincinnati, Ohio. Head man, spending a week-a-month at Newton Abbot, is Budge Wallis, who I have known and respected for years. We used to do good two-way business. He has invited me to visit. Arriving straight off an express from Paddington might be too emotional, so we have decided to take a different route and spend a few days on the way.

Our first night is to be in Andover, with Sheila's sister, Barbara, who will drive us the rest of the way. So we travel to Waterloo, busy in rush hour, most trains making much shorter journeys than ours which is Exeter bound.

Once this would have been a proper train with restaurant car. But the Western Region murdered the former Southern line when it was transferred to them. Most of the beautifully engineered route through great scenery beyond Salisbury was singled. Long non-stop runs were abolished. The top brass at the Western had been furious when, its much-publicised diesel programme completed, the Southern's *Atlantic Coast Express* steamed into Exeter in a considerably shorter time than that taken by their supposedly unbeatable *Cornish Riviera Express*. The knives were out.

The rival railways and then regions under BR spent much energy being nasty to each other – in practice, even when it was not official policy. Indeed once, when a Western man asked his assistants to co-operate with the Southern people they were going to meet, the reply was along the lines 'Of course we'll back you in giving them a good hiding!' But management was behind relegating what had been a fine route to the West into a secondary line with long single-track sections. We still pay the price, though it helps us personally that Andover is one of the places where all trains now stop.

Next morning we make an early start by car, so early that I hardly notice the first miles and only begin taking an interest at Wilton beyond Salisbury. Here the A30 seems little changed from the pioneer days of motoring; it is a narrow road, winding and climbing intimately through country of considerable contours – for those not in a hurry, altogether more enjoyable that the busier A303 across Salisbury Plain to the north.

The Embroiderer's Garden

Few homes visited on these journeys are more delectably situated than that of Thomasina Beck at Donhead St Andrews, just off the main road. Sheila and her sister opt for a country walk. Before announcing myself, I take in the stunning view from the doorway. A line of black cows is stretched out on an undulating ridge, the morning sun shining through the still-bare branches of trees looking as though they have been carefully positioned by a great landscape artist. Then her partner Christopher Thatcher shows me into a very comfortable lounge. Both, I discover, are authors, helping each other with their books.

The Embroiderer's Garden, Thomasina's first book, was one of D&C's minor triumphs. She resisted the usual publisher's desire to include a 'how to' element by saying there were already too many practical books on most aspects of needlecraft. She recalls: 'I'd always been fascinated by making things, and loved embroidery, so I'd been to the Victoria & Albert to find what they had to offer and attended a class by Joan Edwards that set needlework in the context of the decorative arts. Like the ripples in the pool, it inspired me to take a diploma in the history of arts so I could understand the historical background, and a machine embroidery class to give an up-to-date view. It gave me a great desire to take embroidery out of the glass cases, to bring it all alive. Who did the embroidery in the past, how, when and of course why? Another pointer was Jo Verso's *The Embroiderer's Story*: not academic, but a joy to read. Most textile books are too broad; they need a tighter focus.'

She spent four years helping English Heritage index gardens, and in the 1970s, 80s and well into the 90s was day lecturer at the V&A – 'a wonderful place'. Saying she loves holding an audience, she mentions various occasions, such as a National Trust conference in Bath, where she had the opportunity to open the eyes of a new audience. Men as well as women learned to study the use of flower themes in decoration. She's so enthusiastic it is as though she is making a presentation of her first book all over again. That, incidentally, was later re-issued as *Gardening With Silk & Gold: A History of Gardens in Embroidery*. Other books followed.

Christopher, who I had not previously met, tells me he has published sixteen titles, including *The History of Gardens*, a standard work in several languages. Their enthusiasm seems to rub off each other and they are enjoying making a vertical garden on a small cliff face.

So back to our country A30, every car ahead of us seeming to turn off into a gateway or lane. This is more like the road journeys of my youth, being part of the community around you, rather than insulated from towns and villages by widened and straightened highways bypassing human life.

But soon we turn off: to Shaftsbury perched on a lump of a hill commanding great views, its small centre delightfully unspoilt because, though the town had great importance in the coaching era, the railway deliberately ignored it. The Salisbury & Yeovil Railway was indeed the best of investments since, unlike most, it was determined to be just part of a trunk route. It routinely ignored the fate of places it bypassed, refusing to connect them by branch line. The disaster that was Railtrack shows that the illusion persists that high profit and public service can be combined.

Almost due south down the A350, we are now in the heart of Dorset, where even the place names add special flavour. Past Melbury Hill with its ancient earthworks, through Compton Abbas with another great hill to our left, then on to Iwerne Minster and Stourpaine and Blandford Forum, one of Hardy's market towns (Shottsford Forum). In one of England's 'most harmonious and complete Georgian townscapes', farmers and growers still turn produce into cash. Earlier buildings were destroyed by the last of a succession of great fires.

With less dramatic hills, now southwest through Winterborne Whitechurch, Milborne St Andrew (no time to make a detour this morning to the rural idyll of Milton Abbas, six miles to the north in the middle of the least-spoilt tract of Dorset), Puddletown and over wooded Fellowham Hill to Dorchester (Casterbridge). The *Mayor of Casterbridge* has always struck me as the most realistic of Hardy's novels. While it is no doubt good for business, I'm not specially interested in how Dorchester now celebrates its famous son, preferring to allow the novels and their characters in the landscape speak for themselves. Certainly few other novelists have ever caught so clearly the spirit of any part of the British countryside as a place where people live and work, and struggle with hopes, fears, jealousies, and obsessions occasionally turning into madness. We miss Dorchester this morning, lamenting that the bypass is one of those dangerous new fast roads with only a two-lane single carriageway.

We soon leave the Roman road to the west to go through the pretty village of Martinstown, a stream on one side of the street of cottages, handsomely set off by ridges of sweeping hills above the general rolling countryside with the gentle hillocks known as Dorset knobs. From the Hardy monument, not to Thomas but to 'Kiss me Hardy', Nelson's flag captain at the Battle of Trafalgar, we enjoy the breathtaking view of the sea, and the great lump of Portland and the Dorset countryside. What a row there would be if they wanted to erect such a monument in so prominent a position today.

So into the little treasure of Abbotsbury, where the long stretch of water, The Fleet, that separates the pebble Chesil Beach from the causeway between Weymouth and the Isle of Portland, finally comes to an end. Besides its delightful situation, semi-tropical gardens and swannery (which we visit briefly but cautiously in the birds' aggressive breeding season), Abbotsbury has everything: red ironstone cottages thatched with dormer windows, raised pavements, chapel on a hill, fifteenth-century Tithe Barn (all that remains of the Benedictine abbey), tranquillity despite the crowds going to the swannery and a children's farm.

As we drive west there is a fine view of the beach under the great cliffs ahead to West Bay. I've always regarded this, with its artificial harbour, as a rather tawdry affair, not even over-popular with Bridport people as their window on the sea. It certainly never took off as hoped for, and the extension of the railway down from Bridport was an early casualty. Yet this morning the scene is so animated and happy as to make me change my mind. There's a rough deep blue sea with white horses coming in, sensible development round the harbour, hotels including busy AA two- and three-star ones, an Abbeyfield retirement home in prime position, even track with a train on it in the disused station.

The cliffs force us inland to brick-built Bridport with its wide streets, a legacy of its rope-making days. Locally-grown hemp and flax were stretched in the ropes twisted between houses on either side. Then along the A35, a route often taken for broadcasts and catching the *QE2* in Southampton. This section is a switchback reflecting the alternating valleys and high ground ending in spectacular cliffs, of which we continue to enjoy glimpses. This, I recall, is as far as a D&C charter of the paddle steamer *Waverley* brought us. We were supposed to go from Torquay to Weymouth, and Brixham coastguard 'confirmed' the vessel was rounding Berry Head on time. However, because of a storm from the north it was half a day late. The cruise had to be shortened, though with the bonus that the cliffs were in unusually sharp profile, every

666

detail standing out, with a bright sun shining from the south into the north wind.

Cottage Bakery and the Making of Dorset Knobs

Chideok we first see nestling in a valley, and are able to overtake a long line of fumy lorries struggling up the crawler lane as we climb the other side. Then we are at Morcombelake. A habit for many years coming this way has been calling at Moores Bakery at Morcombelake, a few miles short of Lyme Regis. For nearly half a century, whenever passing in opening hours, I have dashed in as much for the smell of fresh baking, and the matter-of-fact quaint country atmosphere, as for the bargain broken biscuits usually on offer. Today I have arranged to unveil the secret of this institution.

I have always loved their crunchy Dorset Knobs, rounded biscuity hillocks like those of the local landscape. They are great with cheese – provided you have a plate large enough to catch the crumbs. But apart from the fact they are only sold in a limited area of Devon and Dorset, you can't buy them at all for most of the year. 'That's because they are not profitable,' says Keith Moores. 'We only make them when we're quiet in autumn and winter.' Though unintentional, this has proved a marvellous marketing ploy, adding mystery to scarcity. They have already stopped making them for this year, but there's a good stock for us to carry back to Scotland: bulky but light.

Moores Biscuits have their origin well back in history deep in the Dorset countryside. Flour was milled from the locally grown wheat used for bread, and at the end of the day butter and sugar were added to the dough, rolled into small buns by hand and baked in the faggot heat of the dying oven. We don't know who had the bright idea of calling them Dorset Knobs, though that name had also been used for a type of Dorset button. At one time four bakers in the family made them; they had well-defined delivery areas but socialised where the rounds met. One of the brothers was established at Morecombelake by 1860. A century later, after the business found its feet again following a difficult recovery from World War Two, Keith took sole charge, and new lines such as Dorset Gingers and Walnut Crunch were introduced. It is these more expensive items we see being produced, in a traditional, cramped building, modern machinery coming as quite a shock in the rustic setting. Indeed, about the only thing not mechanised is the manoeuvring of boxes, since they are so short of space there's not room for logical flows. 'It gives me grey hairs,' says Keith, who describes himself as odd-job man since his son-in-law took control; but the busy staff clearly take note of what he says, and his judging of how things are going is obviously a habit of a lifetime. He might be a gentle boss but you couldn't fool him.

'It is inevitable that we've gone a bit touristy,' he says, 'but the good thing is that we're selling in London again and have broken into overseas markets, including Hong Kong. A gallery for the paintings of his wife Gillian (whose artwork adorns the packaging, and there's a splendid mural) helps draw passing visitors, some of whom make a ritual of calling.

We are invited into their house for coffee, a private world overlooking a range of knobs, as in hills. They are great gardeners, loving watching and attracting the birds, though admit that the number of species they can see from their window has declined sharply, indeed halved since 1972. They're buying another two acres for woodland garden as their contribution to saving the day.

Bookseller and Gallery at Honiton

Then through Devon's less complicated, more pronounced hills, to Honiton. Before the bypass a town of notorious traffic jams – 'it took us four hours from Monkton to Torquay on Saturday' – it now supports an interesting range of specialist shops dealing in antiques, books, art and craft. First stop is the Walker Gallery, from which I've recently bought two pictures in pastels by Lionel Aggett, who has come across from his home in Crediton to say hello. The first picture, Devon Red, a close-up of ploughed red fields with the Exe estuary tantalisingly in the background, was chosen from an exhibition when we were last here.

The second was on the cover of their latest catalogue and had only just arrived in Scotland when we set off on this trip. I had to have it, for it combines many things personally special to me. Horticulture in the shape of rows and rows of daffodils, contrasting white and yellow and green. People finding employment in picking them, no doubt to be sent 'up country' to give early-season pleasure. And, a small part of the composition but significant enough if you have long sight, or caveman's eyes, a distant view of Mount's Bay with St Michael's Mount. My favourite Penzance is tucked just out of sight.

How long do such pictures take? 'Three or four days, or a bit longer for something as detailed as all those daffodils,' says Lionel. 'When I have an idea, I make a rough sketch and tend to take them so far, then come back to them. Somehow living with a picture for a bit, even if you've several on the go, gets you more involved. Pastel is an excellent medium, quicker than oil, especially when you're working outside. Pastel is superb for sketching as well as the finished picture. The pigments I use are very pure and intense, though there isn't a jet black.'

How many of his pictures are of West Country subjects? He answers that by handing me an autographed copy of a new book he's written for David & Charles. *Capturing the Light in Pastel* shows an extraordinary variety and depth of work; French, Italian and British subjects shown in moonlight, sun shining on snow, cloud, rain, near-darkness and tungsten light indoors. It is really a 'how to' book, for the budding artist helpfully showing work at various stages of progress. Painting is beyond me, but the step-by-step sequences help even my appreciation of the finished work. What a gift he has, and what joy he's given me. 'Glad you like my work,' he says. Then, slightly less modestly, he boasts that Robertson the greeting card people are publishing him. My daffodil painting is the subject of a large card; I negotiate to buy a gross.

'It's lovely when artist and purchaser appreciate each other,' says the gallery's sparkling manager, Joanna. It is a small gallery but already well supported. Two brothers direct the galleries. Ian is at the well-established Harrogate premises. This venture in Honiton is more recent with about eight annual exhibitions, some solo; others include jewellery and bronzes.

There is more yet, for as part of the marketing those purchasing a painting from the catalogue are offered cream tea for two – a reminder that for D&C's 21st birthday I adapted our slogan 'Good books come from Devon' to 'Good books and cream come from Devon' and sent customers a celebratory quarter pound of the real McCoy. We take our two tickets down the street to Honeybees Wholefood Restaurant, and pile cream and super strawberry jam (Sheila perversely reverses the order) on a brown date scone. 'Live life to the full – this is not a rehearsal' says one of the homely notices on the walls. How about some honeycomb ice cream with clotted cream? Or, suggests our waitress, honey and meringue is scrumptious.

Then to the quaint little village of Gittisham, where we are intrigued by the window display at Gourmet Foods of Gittisham – cream teas are being served in the cottage next door – and can't resist buying a few exotic treats to take back to Bath. Sheila also buys some stamps, for the shop includes the village Post Office.

It is then only a few yards to the beginning of the long drive up to Combe House Hotel, where the new owners, Ken and Ruth Hunt, have taken on the is-it-possible? slowly, slowly task 'of restoring everything to its original'. It used to serve good food in positively gaudy surroundings with over-the-top peacock and floral decorations and bloody sporting pictures. Our bedroom is great.

'Yes, it is slowly, slowly, but we've done the bedrooms and we're getting the old Georgian kitchen back to its original state and will have cookery courses and wine tasting there. We're going to make our own bread and market our own brand of preserves. We've got to have a first-class product and market it well. Some people say it's a dangerous thing to do. Eventually we'll restore the old walled garden which has become an aberration. We've already cleared out large amounts of laurel. The

Combe Estate goes back to Domesday and hardly ever sells any property, but have handed on "this family home" so we can make a real go of it.' I'm delighted to find a 'What the butler saw' is still in the gents and is staying there even though valued at £17,000.

Dinner guest is Roger Collicott of the Honiton Old Bookshop, one of Devon's major sources of antiquarian books, which publishes regular catalogues listing titles of local interest among their specialities. Starting as an apprentice in his dad's letterpress printing business in Ipswich, he realised the litho revolution was about to happen and so became a collector – of handmade leather goods 'at the hippier end of arts and crafts'. That was in St Ives, where 'things got tackier and tackier', so he moved to Devon 'and books steadily took over'. He started the Honiton Old Bookshop in 1980, but went to Ashburton for four years before returning.

He does the round of book fairs, and is always pursuing likely purchases. 'Selling is the easy part. There's tremendous satisfaction in finding something a customer is looking for', but he doesn't do book searches in the usual way and tells me *The Clique*, a trade journal listing 'wants', has ceased. He adds: 'Books are very personal things. I get my kicks when they go to people who will treasure and value them. It's for that reason that I'm fussy over condition'; he recommends a book binder at Wellington, Somerset, for repair work. 'I'm not a salesman pushing just anything.' He's a collector himself, interested in the English Civil War and British topographical works with original illustrations.

I have dealt with Roger for twenty years and always enjoy the arrival of his catalogue. For fairness, he despatches all catalogues together but many titles have already been bagged by keen collectors by the time mine arrives in Scotland. After a catalogue has gone out, there are tense moments on the phone – when you can get through – hearing whether items are still available or been sold. Much of my own collection will eventually find its way to new appreciative owners via Roger when I have to cut down. Indeed, I started selling, but when *Writers' News* was sold more bookshelf space became available. So again I'm a buyer.

It is good to hear that imprint (or the publisher's name) counts in value. Faber & Faber books, 'with their simplicity of style,' go well, Thames & Hudson art titles are always in demand, and 'most David & Charles books have a £20 touch' even if they're not scarce titles. We discuss some of the leading Devon antiquarian booksellers of former times. 'It is a definite way of life, needing patience and detailed understanding. It suits me perfectly.'

So does his vegetarian special, while my sea bream, landed by a day boat at Beer, is so fresh that you feel you could take it off the skin with a gentle blow. The delicate taste is hard to beat. When he gets up to go, Roger wishes me well for my return to D&C tomorrow. It is good that he directs scarce second-hand copies to keen customers. As you might expect, titles especially in demand today are not those that sold best (or were even profitable) when new. *The Roman West Country* was the least successful of a dozen titles published on one last Thursday of the month in 1976. It lost a horrible amount of money. Today it fetches by far the highest price of the batch, for there is a small but definite band of those who don't feel their libraries are complete without it.

Return to David & Charles

Maybe I've built the return to D&C up too much in my own and other people's minds. Time to be calm this morning, with a stroll through the ancient river port of Topsham, which sprung to life with the famous woollen trade with Holland after the shore's owner, the Countess of Devon, put a weir across the Exe and so stopped ships reaching Exeter, killing it as a port... until Britain's first canal was built to bypass the obstruction. Several houses along the riverfront have Dutch gables, while small Dutch bricks are still traded for repair work. Though there are many reminders of trading days, such as the Steam Packet Inn and The Lighter, today's emphasis is on antiques, eating houses and property. A firm of surveyors has even taken over the signal box by the level crossing, used by two trains an hour each way on the run beside the Exe. There is only one wealthy riverside Topsham, yet today it is so much part of Exeter that its independent shops are rapidly disappearing. I'm horrified to see that its last old-fashioned grocer has gone; the owner repeatedly descended to the cellar steps to get what was wanted.

The sun shining, we buy a sandwich and go down by the church steps to find a cosy seat feet away from the incoming tide. Birdlife, including a pair of swans hoping to share our lunch, yachts starting to move as soon as there's enough water, and the trains roaring down the opposite side of the estuary, make a soothing cocktail. We can just glimpse waves breaking beyond the river's mouth, so understand why there have been problems maintaining Brunel's Great Way West. We see the first crossing of this tide by the pedestrian ferry to Exminster as the water has risen sufficiently to restore proceedings.

When I walked out of the front door as the company closed for Christmas in 1990, I thought it unlikely I would ever return to D&C. Directors and staff had been told in future to use the back door. Rebelliously, my last exit was in style! I had already come to fear the worst. When I had handed over to Reader's Digest at my final staff meeting, they launched into a long song of praise about themselves without a hint that our staff might have valuable experience to offer. It was made clear I'd not be welcome at any event for retired staff. No doubt they thought I might be psychologically disturbing, as British Rail once said steam locomotives were to their staff.

Selling your way of life for a pot of money, and saying farewell to your friends and support system doesn't bring the joy many people suppose. Anyway, I cared too much. While in truth I would only have been totally happy had the company stayed in a state of suspended animation, neither doing greatly better nor excessively worse than I had, the tales of woe that soon percolated to Nairn were worrying, and occasional visits to see my portfolio of old ladies in Newton Abbot became unbearable. I'd be talking to a market stallholder when someone would slide up and say: 'You can't guess what they've done now.' Many of those not 'let go' eased themselves out. The Reader's Digest own experts brought in from London also disappeared. A whirlwind of staff reductions created great anxiety. 'You've no idea how bad it is' made me feel awful, yet only one or two resented the fact that I had walked off with the money.

Poor Neil MacRae must have been distressed himself. While his own approach might not always have been imaginative, and his local lieutenants didn't serve him well, his sincerity was never questioned. I had been aware of the fact that Reader's Digest (or Disgust as it was nicknamed) had a history of acquisitions and disposals, but could never have forecast the muddle that was now David & Charles. After a few years, RD sold to two of the managers of my day, who then fell out. Crisis was again in the air when F&W of Cincinnati stepped in.

So here I am this afternoon, founder and principal shareholder for thirty years, while in little more than a decade the third new owner is 'getting things together'. Will I be recognised at reception? Yes, and I see curious eyes peeping out of various offices. One of Alison Shute's former managers at Devon County Library service who I had known for many years steps forward from the sales area where he's interested in stock-clearance bargains. The ice is broken. 'Things are already getting better,' I'm told. At long last they're beginning to change the carpet that was already pretty worn when I left. The offices, and the sound of passing trains, haven't changed, but there's one huge difference. Compared with my day, the offices are like a miniature ghost town. So many fewer people.

Budge Wallis hasn't changed, and greets me with his creative assistant who I also met in Cincinnati and who commutes monthly with Budge across the Atlantic. It is unavoidably emotional, but made easier by the clear demonstration of common sense: new carpet, but not grandiose enhancement schemes; back to the kind of gardening books that inspire and people want to use rather than just look nice; railway books returning to the list which once had more of them than any other in the world; and when I say that the railway signals would be missed by many,

Budge immediately agrees they will stay. Previous managements had wanted to be rid of them; not invented here. Of course the big gantry began as my thing and in a sense is ridiculous, but it has become part of the local heritage. 'I just wish the trains were better,' says Budge, whose commuting from Ohio has coincided with the route to the West Country being especially badly hit by Railtrack's troubles.

The good news is that they have decided to reprint seven of my railway titles. Then, 'I see you still do a lot for the writing magazines,' says Budge. 'We'd have loved to have them now that we've a base here. But why on earth have the new owners [not the present ones] given up the book club?'

After an hour or so, Budge has to go to a meeting, but arranges for me to be shown round – 'though actually he could show us round'. Those tiny details of things that happened here and there many years ago flash before my eyes as happens when a mind is disturbed... overloaded, anyway. I'm shown 'the facility' of the Butler Building, an extra structure we had to buy in a hurry since we were bursting at the seams, but now has well-spaced easy chairs for staff breaks.

The mere dozen staff who have survived since my day are obviously on the lookout. They're a friendly group and are pleased that I, too, think that F&W will be good stewards. Bless them, all those from my days come to see me off at reception. I thought I might never come back; I've already been invited again, though the message is conveyed as nicely as possible that I'd be better looking elsewhere to publish new work. Perhaps old owners are inevitably psychologically disturbing? While waiting for Barbara (who has gone into the town with Sheila) to pick me up, for the first time in eleven years I actually stand under the signal gantry. How much more old fashioned it looks now than it did when it arrived on a low-loader. A reminder that if we keep things we have thrown into our attic long enough, they will become collector's pieces.

Farewell – And Hullo?

We go to the Ness House Hotel at Shaldon for our last night with Barbara, and the last of these journeys. I wonder if Neil Macrae, ex-Reader's Digest, is at his holiday home at Shaldon, where I gather he now spends more time. He didn't respond to telephone messages recently; can't say I blame him, but renewing acquaintance would have been fun.

The view from the Ness is wonderfully evocative: the narrow mouth of the Teign with its fast current in the foreground, ships in Teignmouth harbour, the town with its very different West and East churches, the beach and pier, housing climbing further and further up the hillsides, and – stretching in the distance – the red sandstone cliffs with Brunel's railway built on a ledge under them till it dives into the first of the tunnels toward Dawlish. Every now and then, a High Speed Train dashes past the harbour and emerges on the Sea Wall, travelling much faster than in our youth. It is now well over half a century since Sheila and I first walked together between the sea and railway – and had a snap taken by a schoolboy train-spotting friend. That only picture of us together in the sweet innocence of youth has survived and has an honoured place at home.

We used to cross the river to walk up the Ness by a council black-and-white open ferry just like the one going to and fro today. The Ness is that triangular-shaped great red sandstone headland, pointing upward till its sudden end, standing sentinel at the river's mouth. The trees on it were planted to commemorate Queen Victoria's Jubilee. Since World War Two, it has been floodlit on summer evenings adding a special touch to an already interesting scene. Before dinner we walk on the headland, and then through it by the tunnel. The council claimed it was a smuggler's tunnel and wasn't happy when I revealed that it was actually built by Lord Clifford so he could reach the beach hidden around the corner from the Ness – a popular spot these days. Councils everywhere think there's money in perpetuating smuggling folklore, whether or not based on fact.

One of the delights of Teignmouth as a holiday town is that it is also a busy working port, and just how busy is revealed over dinner. Three ships sail out on the tide: the Russian *Shuya*, 2,889 tons gross, carrying rapeseed which came from Sète on the French coast and is going to Rotterdam; the Danish *Karina Dancia*, 1,325 tons gross, which came in empty earlier today from La Coruna and has left partly loaded with clay to call for the rest of her cargo at Fowey, before going on to Port Nogaro in Italy; and the German-owned *Sea Clyde*, flying the Antigua flag, 1843 tons gross, which also came in empty, from Lisbon, and has also left partly loaded to pick up more clay from Fowey before dropping it at two Italian ports, Gaeta and Civitavecchia. And so it is most days, with timber, fertiliser and crops including potatoes and even cider apples, adding to variety. A cargo not yet mentioned is coal. That used to be the biggest import, and we kept an active watch so we knew when to chase up the coal merchant. But coal, once so vital, is now largely yesterday's commodity.

A ship of 1000 tons gross was once beyond Teignmouth's capacity; much dredging and channelling has been done to cope with larger vessels. Without it, Teignmouth would have died as a port. Even so, the larger ships are a tight fit, and ever-moving sandbanks don't help. Nearly all movements are just before high water, so a grounding might be short lived. There are actually fewer incidents than with the smaller ships of our youth. The pilots have always been the port's elite. Two are involved this evening, one making two return trips on the pilot boat whose movements add to the action.

I think of some of Teignmouth's pasts. How, for example, the wives of the fishermen who went for months at a time to work on the Grand Banks would congregate and peer at the horizon wondering if there might be an extra mouth to feed that evening. Of the time the Danes attacked the West or Round Church over there close to the harbour. And, centuries later, of the last war when much of the area between church and harbour, as well a lot more of Teignmouth, was flattened. Both the long drawn-out night air raids, and the it's-all-over-in-a-flash daytime 'tip-and-run' ones, were frightening. After night bombing, one never knew what one would see on the way to school or what child might have been killed or injured. I recall seeing a German plane shot down over the cliffs toward Dawlish.

It is all in the view: the hotel where my family spent the first night at Teignmouth, our old home with its former billiard room Dad used for his O-gauge railway, the pier recently given a new lease of life, the large grass area fondly known as The Den, the classical columns of the Riviera Cinema (formerly Teignmouth's gentleman's club), a luxury block of flats where Morgan Giles once built ships of distinction, another train briefly out of sight between Sea Wall and harbour, the full tide which carried tonight's ships out, fishermen's huts, another black-and-white ferry bringing a handful of people to Shaldon. Magic, though it has to be added that most hotels have become holiday flats and seasons are nothing like they were in the 1950s and 1960s.

Scotland serves us well. Though we will never really belong north of the border, we love it. But then, when D&C were in less friendly hands and my staff suffering, I felt I had to keep away. This scene still has that special feel of where we belong, where Sheila and I first walked out together.

POSTSCRIPT

Two days later the joys of sunny Nairn are enhanced by a fantastic display by the Moray Firth's bottle-nosed dolphins whose rhythmic cavorting suggests they also find real pleasure in life. An English couple in our holiday cottage are amazed by the local quality of life and our micro-climate and the crops it encourages. 'Do we really want to leave this?' we start asking, reminding ourselves how much better it is to have the choice of belonging in very different places than not to be able to put roots down anywhere.

The depth of these roots is brought home by my morning walk along the promenade. 'Nice to have you back,' is a sentiment expressed half a dozen times. Alas, sometimes followed by 'Do you know what the council's up to now? The paddling pool may not be open next year.' Health and Safety. First it had to be fenced to keep dogs out. Then supervised when open. Now, though fenced off, it has to be covered when not in use. 'Look, it's all of ten yards from the sea,' says one local walking his dog. 'It will be interesting to see how they propose to cover that.' The other controversial topic is a plan to build a large windfarm on the opposite side of the Firth. Between talking (or blethering) with regular promenade walkers, I reflect just how much has happened in the three and a bit years during which we have made these journeys and the book has taken shape. It was a blow when David & Charles rapidly rejected it, though more recently they came back asking to see it... by which time arrangements had been firmed with the enthusiastic publisher whose imprint it carries. Meanwhile foot-and-mouth has come and gone, inflicting great temporary hardship but encouraging greater common sense and understanding... including the acknowledgement that farmers alone cannot be expected to carry the burden of protecting most of our landscape. Not only has the National Trust has become far more enlightened, but much more woodland come under the protection of the Woodland Trust, and thanks to a change in the tax laws, fewer conifers been planted commercially.

A disaster from which there has been no rapid, or even steady, recovery is the Hatfield railway accident. It is already it is clear that Railtrack's successor, Network Rail, lacks the cash and vision needed, and that much of what is being spent is wasted by poor judgement or change of plan. Thus a route closed to put in new pointwork is soon closed again for the pointwork to be reassembled and, shortly after expensive renovation, Rugby station is to be razed to the ground. A great personal disappointment is that we are even further from seeing sensible co-operation between the national network and the rapidly-expanding private railway movement. Even a link between the Swanage Railway and the main line already formally agreed will not now happen on the grounds that all such schemes are taboo. While canals are being restored at a faster rate than they were originally built, that is for leisure. But try making part of the national network, or for that matter a working industry, attractive to tourists, and the official line will be that it will be easier to close down and reopen purely as a showpiece.

Happily the state of Britain generally is much better than that of her railways, though despite occasional industrial bright spots (such as ships again being built at Tyneside) most improvements are leisure-based. After a long interval, one can again bathe in Bath's hot spring; the restored Thermal Bath is a design masterpiece. Spas generally have a brighter future, as do reservoirs for boating and fishing. Beaches have become cleaner, fish swim up cleaner rivers... but the plight of commercial fishing is unimaginable.

I end this morning's walk at Nairn's bookshop, which I recently formally reopened. Like many in small towns without multiple competition, it will flourish and enhance local life. The same applies to good local hotels. Helped by a new generation of discerning guides, top-quality private hotels are doing much better than mediocre chain ones. Many are busy because Britain's heritage has never been better understood or protected. The biggest single reason for rejoicing must be the far greater numbers exploring our amazing countryside on foot, cycle or horse. The new National Cycle Network we have seen taking shape across the land is a truly great achievement.

Have faith! First radio then television were seen as likely to standardise our rich range of dialects out of existence; then it was felt that foreign holidays would destroy tourism in our own country. Not so. The excitement of peak-season crushes might be in the past, but a long season encourages higher standards. And, much though we might decry the messy appearance of today's teenagers lighting up fags and using uncalled for language on their way home from urban schools, many will surely later join the mountain-climbing, canalboating and country-house visiting brigades.

People power is especially strong in the countryside. Those intent on preserving it and its wildlife have a voice that cannot be ignored. Maybe this is partly due to the ever greater contrast between dirty cities and the fresher countryside with its myriad attractions. Some of it might be what I have too disparagingly called as Theme Park Britain, but I love our country in all its diversity, and relish the fact that its survival is more assured than at any other time in living memory.

BOOKS QUOTED AND MENTIONED

Acknowledgements with thanks are given to authors and/or publishers of the following titles from which there are brief indented quotations.

Betjeman's Cornwall. John Betjeman. 1984. Page 253

Charming Place, A: Bath in the life and novels of Jane Austen. Maggie Lane. 1988. Bath. 123

Child in the Forest, A. Winifred Foley.1974. Coleford. 600-1

Companion Guide to East Anglia, The. John Seymour. 1970. Glasgow. 456-7

Cornwall. Claude Berry, 1949. 250

Deben River, The: An enchanted waterway. Robert Simper. 1992. Suffolk. 513

Double Headed: Two generations of railway enthusiasm. Gilbert Thomas and David St John Thomas. 1963. Newton Abbot. 304-5

Eden Project, The Guide. Tim Smit. 2001. 216

Edge of Glory, The: Prayers in the Celtic tradition. David Adam.1985. 297

Exmoor Memories. AG Bradley. 1926. 372

Exploring Blaenavon: Industrial landscape,World Heritage Site. Chris Barber. 2002. Torfaen. 604-5

Faber book of Landscape Poetry, The. Kenneth Baker. 2000. 20

Fare Well in Christ. WH Vanstone. 1997. 346

Flame in my Heart: St Aiden for today. David Adam. 1997. 296

Great Level, The: A history of drainage and land reclamation in the Fens. Dorothy Summers. 1976. Newton Abbot. 451-2

Guide to Hereford, A. Michael Raven. 1996. Market Drayton. 614

Hand-Book for Devon and Cornwall. William White. 1859. 239, 260, 282

Holy Island. M Scott Weightman. 1983. Seahouses. 294

Hound of the Baskervilles. Arthur Conan Doyle. 1902. 194

In My Own Time. Jeremy Thorpe. 1999. 392

In Search of England. H V Morton.1927. 100-1

Inner Shrine, The. Gilbert Thomas. 1943. 404

Innkeeper's Diary, An. Kit Chapman. 1999. 383-4

Kilvert's Diaries 1870-79. Francis Kilvert. Edited by William Plomer, Three volumes, Illustrated edition 1976. 613

Lad of Evesham Vale, A. Fred Archer. 1972. 139

Lake District, The: A special place. John Wyatt. 2001. Kendal. 558

Land and Leisure in England and Wales. J Allan Patmore. 1970 Newton Abbot. 533-4

Lost Gardens of Heligan, The. Tim Smit. 1998. 214-15

Morte D'Arthur. Tennyson. 1912. 220

My Kingdom of Books. Richard Booth. 1999. Ceredigion. 610

Narrow-gauge Railways in North Wales. Charles E Lee. 1945. 632

Night Mail, The. WH Auden. 1938. 396

Our Own Country. 18

Pilgrim in Celtic Scotland, A. John J O Riordain. 1997. Dublin. 43

Poor Man's House, A. Stephen Reynolds.1908. 354

Queen Victoria's Highland Journals. David Duff. 1983. Exeter. 429-30

Severn Bore, The. Fred Rowbotham. 1964. Newton Abbot. 144

Shell Book of British Coasts, The. Adrian Robinson and Roy Millward. 1983.
  Newton Abbot. 486

Shropshire Lad, A. A E Housman. 1987. Ludlow. 621-2

Smoked Salmon and Oysters. Richard Pinney. 1984. Orford. 496

Southwold Pier. Lowestoft. 483

Summer Wine Country. John Watson. Middleton-in-Teesdale. 656

Tintagel Castle. C A Ralegh Radford. 1939. **255**

Way Out West. Catalogue for art exhibition. 434-5

West of Hayle River. Gerald and Sylvia Priestland. 1980. 226

Wild Men and Holy Places. Daphne Brooke. 1994. Edinburgh. 577

Woodbridge A Pictorial History. Robert Simper. 1995. Chichester. 517

The following titles are also mentioned. Authors are cited where mentioned
by name.

84 Charing Cross Road. Helen Hanff. 201

Acaris, the Biologist's Story of Life. 592

African Violets. Tony Clements. 454

Alice in Wonderland. Lewis Carroll. 484

All Creatures Great and Small. James Herriot. 661

All Drawn by Horses. James Arnold. 136

All Made by Hand. James Arnold. 93

Alphabets and Samplers. Brenda Keyes. 411

An Island Camera. John Arlott. 228

Apples in Scotland. John Butterworth. 579

Art of Writing, The. Arthur Quiller-Couch. 201

Astonishing History of Troy Town, The. Arthur Quiller-Couch. 201

Avalon and Sedgemoor. Desmond Hawkins. 345

Bird Table Book. Tony Soper. 185, 367

Blithe Spirit. Noel Coward. 638

BP Book of Industrial Archaeology. Neil Cossons 623

Branch Lines to Midhurst. Vic Mitchell. 91-2

Breakfast Book, The. David St John Thomas 179, 559

Brighton Rock. Graham Greene. 89

British Bus Service. John Hibbs. 500

Bude Canal, The. Helen Harris. 261

Cambrian Railways, The. Rex Christiansen. 409

Canals of South West England, The. Charles Hadfield. 261

Capturing the Light in Pastel. Lionel Aggett. 668

Centuries. Thomas Traherne. 613

Charles Hadfield: Canal man and more. Joseph Boughey. 129

INDEX